Business Studies in action

HSC course 3rd edition

Ji-Hyun Kim 12W

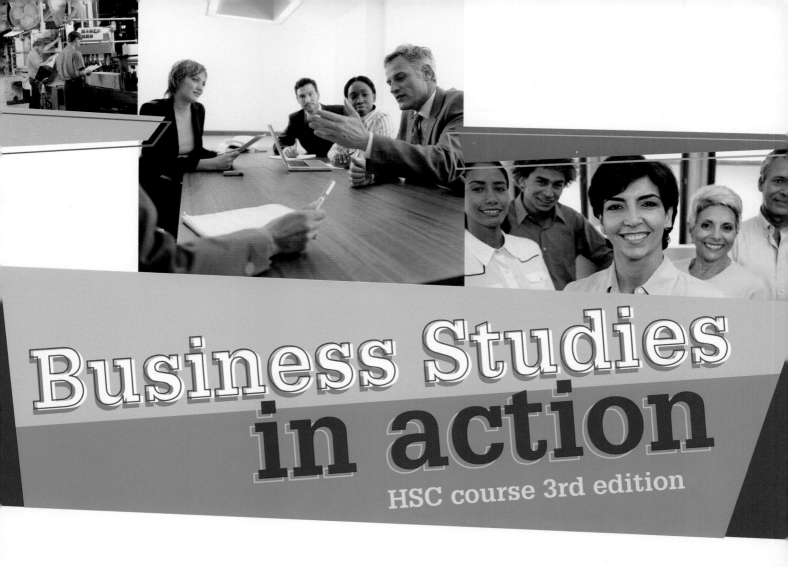

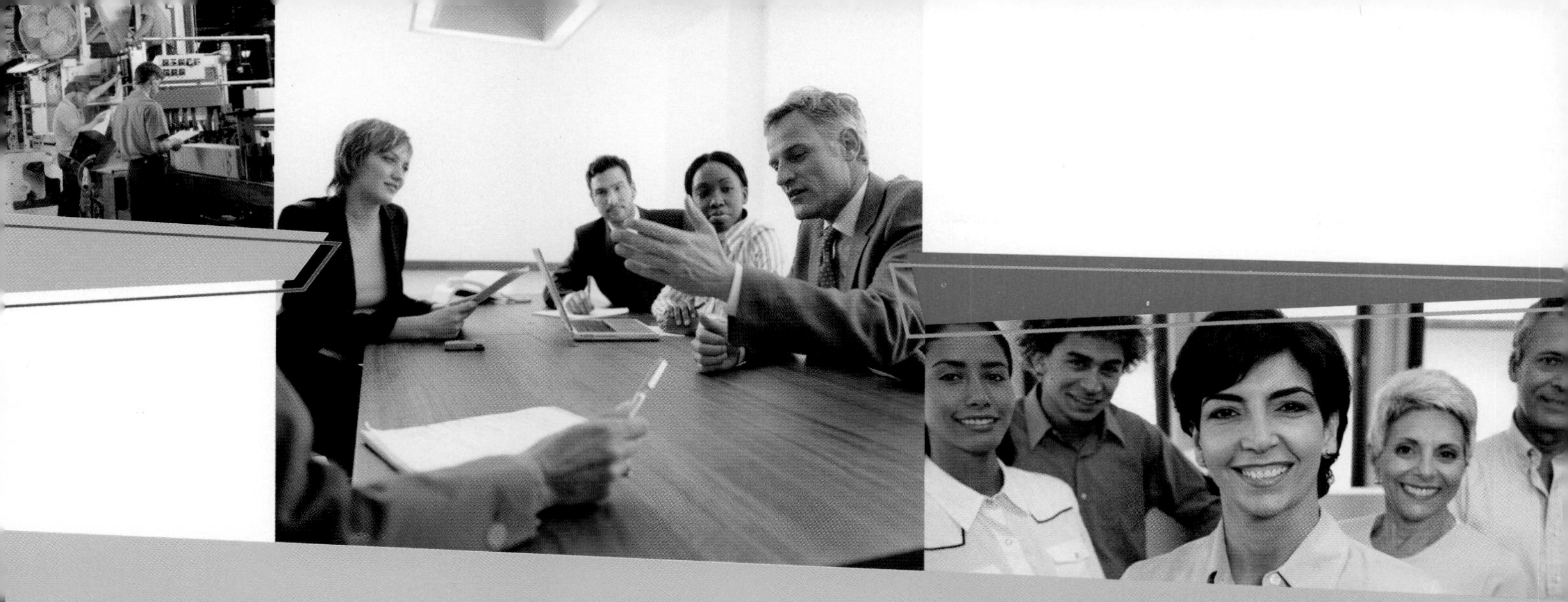

Business Studies in action

HSC course 3rd edition

Stephen **Chapman**

Cassy **Norris**

Natalie **Devenish**

Llian **Merritt**

jacaranda
jaconline.com.au

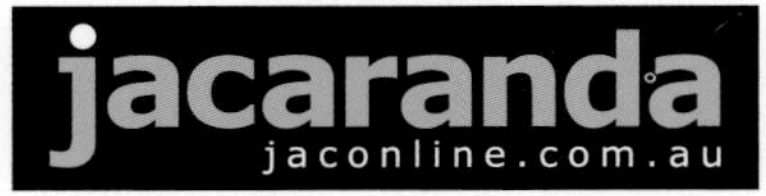

Third edition published 2005 by
John Wiley & Sons Australia, Ltd
42 McDougall Street, Milton, Qld 4064

Offices also in Sydney and Melbourne
First edition published 1998

Typeset in 11/14 pt Times

National Library of Australia
Cataloguing-in-Publication data

Business studies in action: HSC course.

3rd ed.
Includes index.
For senior secondary school students.

ISBN-13 978 0 7314 0311 0.
ISBN-10 0 7314 0311 8.

1. Business. 2. Business — Problems, excercises, etc.
I. Chapman, Stephen (Stephen John).

650

Illustrated by Steve Hunter, Simeon Walker,
Terry St Ledger and the Wiley Art Studio

Printed in Singapore by
Craft Print International Ltd

10 9 8 7 6 5 4 3 2

Contents

Preface ix

Acknowledgements x

Introduction 1

TOPIC 1: Business management and change 2

Chapter 1 The nature of management 4

1.1 Introduction 4
1.2 The importance of effective management 7
1.3 Management roles 9
1.4 Skills of management 15
1.5 Responsibilities of management to stakeholders 24

Chapter 2 Understanding business organisations with reference to management theories 31

2.1 Introduction 31
2.2 Classical and scientific management theories 33
2.3 Behavioural management theories 42
2.4 Political management theories 52
2.5 Strengths and weaknesses of the classical, behavioural and political approaches 57
2.6 Systems and contingency theories of management 59
2.7 Summary and comparison of management theories 62

Chapter 3 Managing change 65

3.1 Introduction 65
3.2 Nature and sources of change in business 66
3.3 Reasons for resistance to change 81
3.4 Managing change effectively 87
3.5 Change and social responsibility 91

TOPIC 2: Financial planning and management 98

Chapter 4 The role of financial planning 100

4.1 Strategic role of financial management 100
4.2 Objectives of financial management 102
4.3 The planning cycle 105

Chapter 5 Financial markets relevant to the financial needs of business 117

5.1 Introduction to financial markets 117
5.2 Major participants in financial markets 119
5.3 Australian Stock Exchange 125
5.4 Influences on financial markets: implications for business 127
5.5 Trends in financial markets 131

Chapter 6 Management of funds 133

6.1 Sources of funds 133
6.2 Financial considerations — matching source with purpose 141
6.3 Comparing debt and equity financing 143

Chapter 7 Using financial information 149
7.1 The accounting framework 149
7.2 Types of financial ratio 157
7.3 Comparative ratio analysis 168
7.4 Limitations of financial reports 169

Chapter 8 Effective financial management 174
8.1 Working capital (liquidity) management 174
8.2 Effective financial planning 183
8.3 Ethical and legal aspects of financial management 193

TOPIC 3: Marketing 198

Chapter 9 Nature and role of markets and marketing 200
9.1 Introduction 200
9.2 What is marketing? 201
9.3 The role of marketing in the business and in society 201
9.4 Types of market 203
9.5 Production, selling and market orientation — approaches to marketing 206
9.6 The marketing concept 208
9.7 Marketing planning process 211

Chapter 10 Elements of a marketing plan 215
10.1 Introduction 215
10.2 Situational analysis — SWOT analysis and product life cycle 215
10.3 Establishing marketing objectives 217
10.4 Identifying target markets 222
10.5 Developing marketing strategies 223
10.6 Implementing the marketing plan 225
10.7 Monitoring and controlling 226
10.8 Elements of the marketing plan — an overview 230

Chapter 11 Market research and customer and buyer behaviour 240
11.1 Introduction 240
11.2 Determining information needs 241
11.3 Data collection (primary and secondary) 241
11.4 Data analysis and interpretation 245
11.5 Customer and buyer behaviour 247
11.6 Types of customer 247
11.7 The buying process 251
11.8 Factors influencing customer choice 252

Chapter 12 Developing marketing strategies 258
12.1 Introduction 258
12.2 Market segmentation and differentiation of products and services 259
12.3 Products and services 262
12.4 Price and pricing methods 266
12.5 Promotion 268
12.6 Place (distribution) 273

12.7 Environmental effects on distribution 275
12.8 Marketing techniques of the Coca-Cola company — an overview 276

Chapter 13 Ethical and legal aspects of marketing 279
13.1 Introduction 279
13.2 Environmentally responsible products 281
13.3 Other marketing ethical and legal issues 283
13.4 Role of consumer laws 284
13.5 Consumer laws and specific marketing practices 285

TOPIC 4: Employment relations 290

Chapter 14 Employment relations: its nature and key influences 292
14.1 The nature of employment relations 292
14.2 Stakeholders in the employment relations process 293
14.3 Managing the employment relations function 306
14.4 Key influences on employment relations 308

Chapter 15 Effective employment relations 318
15.1 The role of employment relations 318
15.2 Importance of communications systems 323
15.3 Rewards 326
15.4 Training and development 328
15.5 Flexible working conditions 332
15.6 Measures of effectiveness 337

Chapter 16 Legal framework of employment 344
16.1 The employment contract 344
16.2 Types of employment contract 366

Chapter 17 Industrial conflict 370
17.1 Definition and causes of industrial conflict 370
17.2 Perspectives on conflict 373
17.3 Types of industrial action 375
17.4 Roles of stakeholders in resolving disputes 382
17.5 Dispute resolution procedures 383
17.6 Benefits and costs of industrial conflict 391

Chapter 18 Ethical and legal aspects of employment relations issues 395
18.1 Ethical and responsible behaviour 395
18.2 Working conditions 397
18.3 Occupational health and safety (OH&S) 398
18.4 Workers' compensation 402
18.5 Anti-discrimination 406
18.6 Equal employment opportunities 407
18.7 Unfair dismissal 410

TOPIC 5: Global business 416

Chapter 19 Globalisation 418
19.1 Introduction to the global economy 418
19.2 Nature and trends of globalisation 419

19.3 Growth of the global economy 420
19.4 Changes in markets 421
19.5 Trends in global trade since World War II 423
19.6 Drivers of globalisation 425
19.7 Interaction between global business and Australian domestic business 430

Chapter 20 Global business strategy 433
20.1 Introduction 433
20.2 Methods of international expansion 433
20.3 Reasons for expansion 440

Chapter 21 Specific influences on global business 445
21.1 Introduction 445
21.2 Financial influences 447
21.3 Political influences 450
21.4 Legal influences 456
21.5 Social and cultural influences 458

Chapter 22 Managing global business 463
22.1 Introduction 463
22.2 Financial management 464
22.3 Marketing 471
22.4 Operations 473
22.5 Employment relations 475
22.6 Evaluation — strategies with reference to a particular global market 479
22.7 Modification of strategies according to changes in global markets 481

Chapter 23 Management responsibility in a global environment 484
23.1 Introduction 484
23.2 Ethically responsible corporate strategy 484

Chapter 24 Integrated case study — Lend Lease 493
Lend Lease: overview 493
Topic 1: business management and change 494
Topic 2: financial planning and management 498
Topic 3: marketing 500
Topic 4: employment relations 507
Topic 5: global business 510

HSC practice questions
Topic 1 Business management and change 513
Topic 2 Financial planning and management 515
Topic 3 Marketing 517
Topic 4 Employment relations 519
Topic 5 Global business 521
Appendix 1 Associated terms used in Business Studies tasks and examinations 524
Appendix 2 Answering HSC examination questions 526
Glossary 528
Index 539

Preface

The content of this new edition of *Business Studies in action: HSC course* is thoroughly revised and updated to meet the requirements of the Stage 6 HSC Business Studies syllabus for New South Wales. The text provides students with a detailed analysis of all five compulsory topic areas.

The rapid pace of change within the business world makes business studies a stimulating area to study, but can also pose challenges for students and teachers accessing contemporary resources. Therefore, in line with the format of the Year 11 text *Business Studies in action: preliminary course*, all topics in this HSC text are supplemented with a wide variety of snapshots — current business issues and the people they involve. This feature enhances understanding and provides a model for students' own research. Internet research is actively encouraged throughout the text via frequent reference to the diversity of weblinks posted on the website for this textbook (www.jaconline.com.au/businessstudies3e).

As teachers and examiners with a diverse range of experiences, we have written this text with the needs of our own students in mind. The language level is accessible to all students. Concepts are explained in straightforward terms and activities appropriate to a range of ability levels occur at regular stages. The HSC practice questions for each topic allow students to gain valuable experience in answering the various types of exam questions with which they need to become familiar.

The main features of *Business Studies in action: HSC course, 3rd edition* are as follows:

- Topics are introduced with a 'story' as a stimulus, followed by the syllabus focus area and outcome statements for teacher and student reference.
- A mind map appears at the start of each chapter, detailing the specific aspects examined for student and teacher reference.
- Biz Words are in bold type in the text and defined in the margin for easy reference.
- Biz Facts contain additional interesting information and examples to supplement the text.
- Full colour diagrams, illustrations and photographs capture interest while illustrating and clarifying concepts and ideas.
- Snapshots from business and the media bring to life current business issues and the people they involve.
- Revision questions can be used to check students' understanding at regular stages.
- Sample HSC practice questions are supplied for each topic, comprising multiple choice, short response and extended response questions.
- Appendixes provide information on course terminology, guidance on answering HSC exam questions and some sample business report questions.
- A comprehensive glossary defines the most important business terms.
- Chapter summaries online at www.jaconline.com.au/businessstudies3e where 'Top business stories' will be frequently posted.
- An **integrated case study** covering the five topics.

Acknowledgements

The authors would like to thank the many people whose assistance and encouragement have made this book possible. Their families and friends were always patient and supportive. Stephen Chapman wishes to acknowledge his parents, Jack and Lorna, who have encouraged him as a student, educator and writer for many years; Shelsie, Max and Wendy who were always patient and understanding, especially when deadlines were imminent; and Claire Polosak, Russell McCulloch, Rae and Thello. Natalie Devenish wishes to acknowledge Mark, James, Georgia and William and dedicates her writing to her late father Graham Kennedy. Cassy Norris wishes to acknowledge her family and Shirley Martin of Lend Lease, whose assistance was greatly appreciated.

The world-class production team at John Wiley & Sons Australia, Ltd are also deserving of the highest praise. Linden George, project editor, for her attention to detail, guidance and technical expertise; Vanessa Tadijan, permissions assistant, for her persistence and creative ideas; the production team for their expertise and professionalism; and Sharon Ottery, publishing editor, for her patience, dedication and excellent project coordination.

The authors and publisher would like to thank the following copyright holders, organisations and individuals for their permission to reproduce copyright material in this book.

Cover:

▪ © PhotoDisc Inc.

Internal Design:

▪ ©Photo Disc © Digital Vision (dollar signs)

Images:

▪ AAP Image: pages 27/Lisa Davies; 277/AP via AAP/Czarek Sokolowski; 391/Julian Smith; 392/AP via AAP/Rick Rycroft; 420/AP via AAP/Paul Kitagaki Jr.; 52/Mick Tsikas; 455/AFP/AAP/Antonio Sampaio; 481/AP via AAP/Yousef Allan ▪ Adidem Group, page 282/used in Australia with permission of The Adidem Group ▪ Alan Moir: pages 374/*The Sydney Morning Herald;* 448 (bottom) ▪ American Express Australia, page 136 ▪ Dr Annabelle Duncan, page 47 (bottom) ▪ AMWU, page 298/Dave Oliver ▪ Audi Australia Pty Ltd, page 253 ▪ Auspac Media: pages 47 (top), 209, 247, 267, 286 (bottom)/ © United Features Syndicate Inc. ▪ Auspic, page 302 ▪ © Austrade, page 463 ▪ Austral International, page 488/© Austral International Press Agency Pty Ltd. ▪ Australian Broadcasting Corporation, page 210 (top) The ABC Shop Loyalty Reward Card is reproduced by permission of the Australian Broadcasting Corporation © 2005 ABC. All rights reserved ▪ Australian Bureau of Statistics, page 364 (bottom), (top) ▪ Australian Picture Library: pages 34 (top left)/Corbis/Bettmann; 124, 386/John & Lorraine Carnemolla; 205 (top)/Heritage Image Partnership Limited; 218; 412/David Butow; 429/Corbis/ James Leynse; 438/Corbis/Michael S. Yamashita; 471/Corbis/Steve Raymer; 472/Corbis/Keren Su; 505 ▪ Australian Securities & Investments Commission, page 71 ▪ Australian Services Union, page 377/Australian Services Union, www.asuvic.asn.au ▪ © Australian Stock Exchange Limited ABN 98 008 624 691 (ASX) 2000, page 126. All rights reserved. This material is reproduced with the permission of ASX. This material should not be reproduced, stored in a retrieval system or transmitted in any form whether in whole or in part without the prior written permission of ASX ▪ © Banana Stock, page 340 ▪ Billabong International Limited, page 485 ▪ © Brand X Pictures, page 357 ▪ Cadbury Schweppes, page 265 ▪ Cathy Wilcox, page 330 (bottom)/*The Sydney Morning Herald* ▪ © Commonwealth Bank: pages 264 (top right), 422 ▪ Commonwealth Copyright Admin, page 361 (bottom)/Department of Workplace Relations, Office of Employment Advocate, © Commonwealth of Australia, reproduced by permission ▪ © Comstock Images page 99 ▪ Coo-ee Picture Library, page 376 ▪ © Corbis Corporation: pages 40, 199, 248, 260 (left), 354 (top right), 400, 417 ▪ Curtis Brown UK, page 15/Illustration by E.H. Shepard, copyright under the Berne Convention ▪ Dairy Australia, page 269 (top right) ▪ Digital Stock: pages 460, 466/ © Digital Stock/Corbis Corporation ▪ © Digital Vision, pages 85, 210 (bottom), 222, 274 ▪ Drizabone Pty Ltd, page 458 ▪ © Elders Rural Bank, page 119 ▪ © EyeWire Images: pages 3, 13, 51, 220, 260 (right), 285, 330 (top), 354 (bottom right) ▪ Fairfax Photo Library: pages 175 (top)/Robert Pearce; 385/Andrew Taylor; 388/Dean Sewell; 435/Eamon Gallagher; 493/John Donegan; 507/Brendan Esposito ▪ Ferrero Australia, page 263 ▪ © Freedom Foods, page 261 ▪ © Geoff Pryor, page 389 ▪ Getty Images: pages 34 (bottom left)/Hulton Archive/Keystone Features; 45/AFP/ Emmanuel Dunand; 200 (left)/Hulton Archive/Picture Post; 296/The Image Bank/Jon Love; 319/Stone/ Walter Hodges; 441/Cancun Chu ▪ © Hewlett Packard Australia, page 458 ▪ GM Holden Ltd, pages 264 (bottom left), 426, 442 ▪ © Image Disk Photography: pages 181, 186, 347 ▪ © Image Source, page 269 (bottom left) ▪ Image 100 Ltd: pages 7, 326 ▪ © John Wiley & Sons Australia Ltd: pages 80/ Peter Van Noorden; 208/Kari-Ann Tapp; 275 ▪ © Katie Lahey, page 300/Business Council of Australia ▪ The Kobal Collection, page 280 (bottom)/Danjaq/ Eon/ UA ▪ Lisa Hogben, page 430 ▪ © National Australia Bank Limited, page 137 ▪ Newspix: pages 77, 119/Brett Faulkner; 200 (right)/William West; 205 (bottom)/Maec McCormack; 299/David Geraghty; 315/Gary Graham; 321/David Crosling; 363/ Brent McGilvary; 370/Marc McCormack; 372/Simon Schluter; 375/Matty Bouwmeester; 396/Mooy Sam; 401/Brett Faulkner; 451/AFP Photo/Paul J. Richards; 504/AFP ▪ Paul Hartigan, page 59 ▪ Phil Somerville, page 418 ▪ © PhotoDisc, Inc.: pages 5, 6, 19, 21, 34, 36, 39, 43, 65, 72, 74, 75, 76, 84, 89, 93, 94, 103, 113, 175, 191, 230, 240, 244, 291, 292, 309, 313, 319, 320, 323, 325, 332, 338, 346, 354 (top left), 361 (top), 395, 399, 403, 408, 443, 474, 500 ▪ photolibrary.com: pages 33/Science Photo Library; 310; 448 (top)/Mike Blank; 459/Brett Alatt ▪ Qantas Airways, page 264 (top middle) ▪ © Queensland Library Supplies, page 249 ▪ © Reebok, page 489 ▪ Rod Clement: pages 37, 82, 85, 429, 484/R. Clement, *The Economic Rationalist's Guide to Sex*, Harper Collins, 1997: figs 2.13, 3.14, 3.16, 19.13, 23.1 ▪ © Ron Tandberg: pages 303, 410 ▪ © Rubberball Productions, page 366 ▪ Sage Publications UK, page 380/ *Asia Pacific Journal of Human Resources*, © Australasian Human Resources Institute, by permission of Sage Publications Ltd ▪ © Scratch! Media: pages 70, 79, 93, 280, 352, 365 (left), 404, 490/ (www.scratch.com.au) ▪ Sony Australia, page 229/© Sony Australia, April 2004 ▪ Spiral Foods International, page 255/© Advertisement courtesy of Spiral Foods International ▪ Stephen Chapman: pages 224, 245 ▪ Steven Cargill, page 18/John Wiley & Sons Australia/Jo Patterson ▪ © Stockbyte, page 204 ▪ © Thinkstock, page 365 (right) ▪ Tourism New Zealand, page 269 (bottom right) ▪ Vero Insurance Ltd, page 122 ▪ © Virgin Money Australia, page 216 ▪ Wesfarmers Limited, page 25 ▪ © Westpac Banking Corporation: pages 180, 187 ▪ Wild & Woolley, page 284/R. Cobb ▪ © Woolworths Limited: pages 264 (bottom right), 272

Text:

▪ Angela MacRae, page 181–2 ▪ Dr Annabelle Duncan, page 47 ▪ © Anti-Discrimination Board NSW, page 410 ▪ Australian Bureau of Statistics: pages 370–1/Cat. no. 6322.0; 371/Cat. no. 63220.0.55.001 ▪ Australian Broadcasting Corporation, page 44/Extracts from Dorothy McRae-McMahon, *Daring Leadership for the Twenty-first Century*, ABC Books, 2001, pp. 72, 74 ▪ APESMA, page 314–15/This material is reproduced from the *Professional Network Magazine*, which is the journal of the Association of Professional Engineers, Scientists & Managers Australia, www.apesma.asn.au ▪ Billabong International Limited, page 485 ▪ Cambridge University Press, page 419/Dr John Wiseman, *Global Nation? Australia and the Politics of Globalisation*, Cambridge University Press, Melbourne 1998, pp. 13–14 ▪ Cameron England, page 138–9/*The Advertiser* ▪ © Commonwealth Bank, page 101 ▪ CCH Australia: pages 412, 413/Reproduced with the kind permission of CCH Australia Limited. For more information see www.cch.com.au ▪ Damien Lynch, pages 120–1/*The Australian Financial Review* ▪ © Dave Oliver, pages 297–8/Australian Manufacturing Workers' Union ▪ Egmont Books Ltd, pages 15–16/From *Winnie-the-Pooh on Management* © 1995 Roger E. Allen. Text by A.A. Milne and illustrations by E.H. Shepard. Copyright under Berne Convention. Published by Egmont Books Limited, London ▪ Export Magazine, pages 430–1/Katrina Clifford, Article extracted from *Export* magazine, May 2004, pp. 18–20, 22, www.exportmagazine.com.au ▪ FranklinCovey Co.: pages 20, 55 ▪ GM Holden Ltd, page 401 ▪ Houghton Mifflin Company Trade, page 46/ Excerpt from *Punished by rewards* by Alfie Kohn © 1993 by Alfie Kohn. Reprinted by permission of Houghton Mifflin Co. All rights reserved ▪ © InfoHRM Pty Ltd, page 339/for further information contact Info HRM by email at info@infohrm.com or go to the website ww.infohrm.com ▪ IBISWorld Business Information, page 499 ▪ Janine Perrett, pages 128–30/ *The Sydney Morning Herald* ▪ Journalists' Copyright: pages 186/Bruce Andrews, *BRW*, September 2004, by permission of Journalists' Copyright; 195/Kath Walters, *BRW*, September 2–8 2004, by permission of Journalists' Copyright; 333–5/Emily Ross, *BRW*, May 2004, by permission of Journalists' Copyright; 408/Gina McColl, *BRW*, October 21–27 2004, by permission of Journalists' Copyright; 435/ Amanda Gome, *BRW*, December 2–8, 2004, by permission of Journalists' Copyright ▪ Julian Lee, page 243/*The Sydney Morning Herald*, 15 July 2004 ▪ Kate McClymont, pages 396–7/Senior Writer/ *The Sydney Morning Herald* ▪ © Katie Lahey, pages 300–1/Business Council of Australia ▪ Lend Lease Development: pages 499, 501 ▪ Mercer Human Resource Consulting, page 337/© Sandy Hutchinson, Asia–Pacific Comunication, Consulting Leader, Mercer Human Resource Consulting ▪ Morris Kaplan, page 106–7/*The Daily Telegraph*, 9 November 2004 ▪ News Limited, page 113 ▪ Paul Robinson, page 340/*The Age* ▪ Pearson Education US, page 11/Henry Mintzberg, *The Nature of Managerial Work*, 1st Edition © 1980. Pearson Education Inc. Upper Saddle River, NJ ▪ © Reebok, page 489 ▪ Robert K. Critchley, page 309 ▪ Sage Publications UK, page 333/*Asia Pacific Journal of Human Resources*, © Australasian Human Resources Institute, by permission of Sage Publications Ltd ▪ Simon Evans, pages 191–2/*The Australian Financial Review* ▪ Steven Cargill, page 18 ▪ Sue Mitchell, pages 103–4/*The Australian Financial Review* ▪ Tim O'Brien, page 394 ▪ Wesfarmers Limited, page 25

Every effort has been made to trace the ownership of copyright material. Information that will enable the publisher to rectify any error or omission in subsequent reprints will be welcome. In such cases, please contact the Permissions Section at John Wiley & Sons, Australia, who will arrange for payment of the usual fee.

Introduction

At the start of a new millennium, the need for effective and efficient managers has never been greater. As the pace of change across all facets of business operation accelerates, and as the level of both domestic and global competition increases, managers face increasingly complex — yet exciting — challenges.

These changes are particularly pertinent for large-scale organisations, whose size and structure demand visionary and competent managers to effectively implement and communicate new ways of doing business. Successful managers will have a comprehensive understanding of the theoretical and operational frameworks underpinning best management practice in large-scale organisations, as well as an ability to anticipate and manage change — both within the business itself and in its operating environment. Equally important is an awareness of the vital role people play. They are the lifeblood of any successful business. Good personnel management requires a thorough grasp of human relations issues in a contemporary context, as well as skills in areas such as leadership, negotiation, motivation, conflict resolution and change management.

Businesses that survive and prosper in this new era will be managed by people who not only respond positively to rapid change, but also initiate it. Ultimately, the wellbeing of the country will depend on their success. Such managers will thrive on the unexpected, seamlessly integrating new technology and the needs and expectations of an increasingly diverse workforce into their areas of operation.

These challenges now being faced by Australian businesses were initially identified in 1995 in a report commissioned by the Australian Government — *Enterprising nation: renewing Australia's managers to meet the challenges of the Asia–Pacific century* (the Karpin Report). They include the need to:

- master a complex, fast-changing and competitive environment
- develop relationships with a wide range of stakeholders
- manage a more flexible and better educated workforce
- lead an organisation of a quite different structure from what was more the norm in past decades.

The report's key finding was that Australia's new generation of senior frontline managers must develop a very different profile of skills and knowledge. Proactively managing rapid change requires people who are adaptable, decisive and resilient, and who have the aptitude and judgement to take calculated risks, as well as the empathy and interpersonal skills to be highly effective communicators.

Meeting the challenges identified in the Karpin Report will mean that businesses will have to be structured and managed quite differently from the way they have been managed traditionally. Developing a new generation of business managers with the necessary leadership and management skills to meet the challenges and to guide Australia through this turbulent time will require changes in the way in which these managers are educated.

Topic 1

Business management and change

FOCUS AREA: To examine the nature and responsibilities of management within a changing business environment from a theoretical and practical perspective.

Outcomes

Students should be able to:

- describe and analyse business functions and operations and their impact on business success
- explain management theories and strategies and their impact on businesses
- evaluate the effectiveness of management in the organisation and operation of businesses and their responsiveness to change
- analyse the impact of management decision making on stakeholders
- critically analyse the social and ethical responsibilities of management
- evaluate management strategies in response to internal and external factors
- select, organise and evaluate information and sources for usefulness and reliability
- communicate business information and concepts in appropriate forms.

Mind map showing the specific aspects examined for the 'Business management and change' topic

Zara's approach to management

Zara examined the latest production figures. It was three years since she had joined Omega Engineering Limited. As Senior Production Manager she was responsible for the efficient operation of both the Sydney and Melbourne factories.

The weekly production statistics were one important tool she used to evaluate the business's performance. When the figures revealed a problem she was able to decide upon an appropriate course of action. Zara prided herself on having a wide overview of the company and the numerous production schedules and operations that she had implemented. She was a most competent planner and organiser.

On joining the company, Zara began implementing two management strategies to improve the company's production performance — work teams and Total Quality Management. She was a great believer in establishing work teams, with each team having responsibility for setting specific production goals. It had taken her 18 months to prepare the organisation for such a change in the workplace culture, but now the results were starting to be seen in the improved productivity figures.

After some initial teething problems, the teams were prepared to take on more responsibility and starting to become involved in long-term planning decisions. After suggestions from individual team members, Zara encouraged the teams to adopt responsibility for quality control as well as production. She was able to encourage, motivate and direct team members. In this sense Zara was adopting the characteristics of a leader.

Zara was well respected by the line managers who were responsible to her as well as team leaders and other senior managers. One of her greatest strengths was her ability to manage change. Instead of seeing change as a difficulty to overcome or a problem to avoid, Zara had the ability to manage change effectively. In this sense she was proactive. She was a passionate believer in the principle that all employees needed to understand the reasons for change. At all times she attempted to provide visionary leadership — a shared vision as to where the organisation was heading. By communicating this, she believed that employees would more readily 'own' the change rather than resist it. She based her ideas on some contemporary management theories: systems management and contingency theories. She was first introduced to these management theories at a conference.

Zara knew it was unlikely that one management theory would contain all the answers so she developed her own strategies based on a number of ideas. The one thing she wanted to avoid was being seen as a manager who could no longer effectively manage. Therefore, she read widely and attended a number of management workshops to keep up with the latest research, and always challenged her own ideas to evaluate their releto the present situation.

If the latest production statistics were any indication of her ability to manage, then Zara was indeed a very competent manager.

CHAPTER

1 The nature of management

1.1 Introduction

Have you ever been shopping and spent all your money on the first few things you saw only to later be disappointed when you came across something you would have liked more? What about the assessable task you left until the last minute only to find all the information resources had been borrowed from the library? Or the dental appointment for which you were half an hour late? In these cases you did not manage either your money, assessment requirements or time very well. These cases reveal that you have actually been practising the art of management for a number of years. Sometimes you have managed your affairs successfully; at other times you may have mismanaged them.

Managing is an essential skill that all people need to develop. How well you perform the task of management will often determine whether you achieve the goals you have set for yourself. In the world of business, just as in your personal life, management is a fundamental activity. It is what makes the business function.

*The **traditional definition of management** is the process of coordinating a business's resources to achieve its goals.*

***Human resources** are the employees of the business and are generally its most important asset.*

***Information resources** include the knowledge and data required by the business, such as market research, sales reports, economic forecasts, technical material and legal advice.*

***Physical resources** include equipment, machinery, buildings and raw materials.*

***Financial resources** are the funds the business uses to meet its obligations to various creditors.*

Zara, featured in the story at the beginning of this topic, is a good manager because she does five things particularly well:

1. She has a good understanding of the technical details of her job.
2. She has the vision to see how things could be rather than just accepting things the way they are.
3. She realises that she can accomplish most by empowering her employees and establishing work teams.
4. She has the skills to manage change.
5. She is extremely competent at coordinating a number of resources so the objectives of the organisation can be achieved.

The **traditional definition of management**, as shown in figure 1.1, is the process of coordinating a business's resources to achieve its goals.

As you learned in the preliminary course, the four main resources available to a business are:

- **Human resources.** These are the employees of the business and are generally its most important asset.
- **Information resources.** These resources include the knowledge and data required by the business such as market research, sales reports, economic forecasts, technical material and legal advice.
- **Physical resources.** These resources include equipment, machinery, buildings and raw materials.
- **Financial resources.** These resources are the funds the business uses to meet its obligations to various creditors.

BiZ FaCT

'For us, the core of management is the art of mobilising and pulling together the intellectual resources of all employees in the service of the firm . . . Only by drawing on the combined brain power of all its employees can a firm face up to the turbulence and constraints of today's environment.' Konoskue Matsushita, Japanese industrialist and executive adviser to Matsushita Electric Industrial Company, Japan

Source: S. R. Covey, A. R. Merrill and R. R. Merrill, *First things first*, Simon & Schuster, New York, 1994.

Manager — coordinates the business's resources

Human resources
- Players
- Equipment managers
- Cleaners
- Compere
- Ushers

Informational resources
- Musical scores
- Orchestra and cast selection reports
- Musician and cast reports
- Ticket sales reports

Physical resources
- Musical instruments
- Sound equipment
- Lighting equipment
- Costumes
- Props and sets

Financial resources
- Budget from the school
- Grant from local business

Goals to achieve
- Excellent performance
- Good reviews
- Increased ticket sales

Figure 1.1 The management of resources for a school musical

The skills and expertise of the management team in coordinating the business's resources largely determine whether the objectives of the organisation are achieved.

A **manager**, therefore, is someone who coordinates the business's limited resources in order to achieve specific goals.

*A **manager** is someone who coordinates the business's limited resources in order to achieve specific goals.*

Figure 1.2 A skilful and experienced management team is an essential ingredient for achieving business success.

BiZ WORD

*A more contemporary definition of **management** views management as the process of working with and through other people to achieve business goals in a changing environment. Crucial to this process is the effective and efficient use of limited resources.*

Contemporary definition

The past few years have seen a subtle, but significant modification of the meaning of the term management. More contemporary definitions emphasise that **management** is the process of working with and through other people to achieve the goals of the business in a rapidly changing environment, as shown in figure 1.3. Crucial to this process is the effective and efficient use of limited resources.

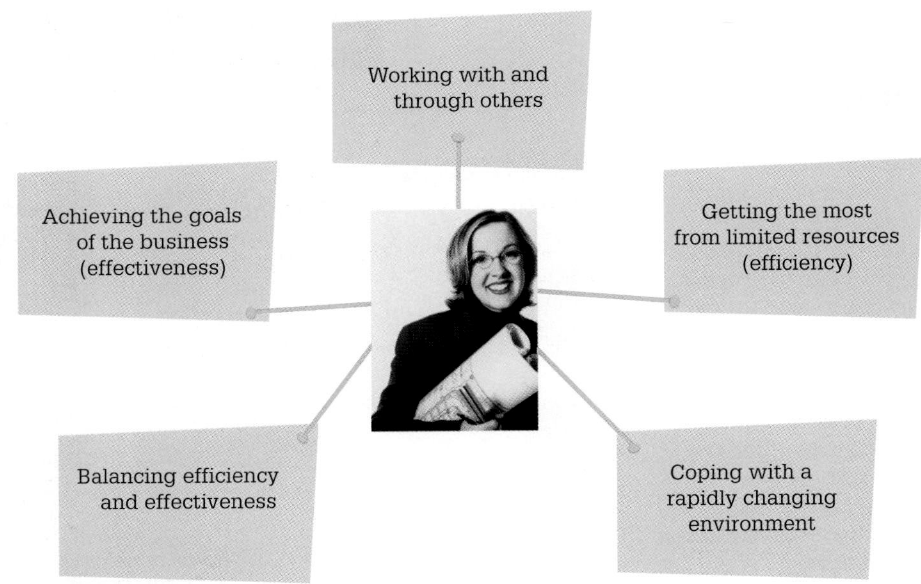

Figure 1.3 Key aspects of the management process

According to this definition, management requires:

- *Working with and through others.* Management is, above all else, a social process. Those managers who do not interact and communicate well with employees fail to achieve high levels of commitment from staff.
- *Achieving the goals of the business.* Without goals, the business would quickly lose direction. Employees would not understand the ultimate purpose of their work and managers would not be able to measure performance. **Effectiveness** measures the degree to which a goal has been achieved.
- *Getting the most from the limited resources.* All businesses face the problem of limited resources or scarcity. Consequently, managers need to coordinate the resources efficiently. Efficiency compares the resources needed to achieve a goal (the costs) against what was actually achieved (the benefits). The most efficient coordination of resources occurs when the benefits are greater than the costs.
- *Balancing effectiveness and efficiency.* Managers must usually balance both the effectiveness and efficiency of their decisions. For example, an effective way of preparing a shopping list may be to first purchase an expensive computer and set up a file that may be regularly updated. But, given the reality of limited resources, effectiveness is not the sole consideration. In this example, a simple notepad and pen would be both effective and efficient for the task.

  A balance between efficiency and effectiveness is the key to achieving a competitive position in today's challenging business environment.
- *Coping with a rapidly changing environment.* This is one of the most important tasks of all managers. Successful managers are those who anticipate and adjust to changing circumstances.

BiZ WoRD

***Effectiveness** measures the degree to which a goal has been achieved.*

BiZ FaCT

Managers' expectations have a direct impact on their employees' productivity. Managers with high expectations lead a more highly motivated and productive staff. Low expectations cause employees to behave in a manner that increases the possibility of failure.

Management within the business

Management is a complex task. It is an exciting, challenging, sometimes frustrating but usually rewarding experience. All organisations must be managed; they do not operate automatically.

The manager's role is similar to that of a musical conductor. It is the conductor who has to coordinate all the members of the orchestra so they stay in time, inspire and lead, encourage superior playing, develop the correct interpretation of the score and have the orchestra playing as a whole rather than as a group of individuals just playing notes.

When management is successful in performing this coordinating role, the end result is **synergy**. Synergy is the combined action that makes the whole (symphony or finished product) greater than the sum of its parts (the musicians or stages of production). Some call synergy the '1 + 1 = 3' effect. Well-coordinated and effective management always achieves a degree of synergy.

***Synergy** is combined action that makes the whole greater than the sum of its parts.*

Figure 1.4 A manager shares many similar features with a conductor.

1.2 The importance of effective management

Every business — whether it be profit or non-profit, small, medium or large — needs effective management to succeed.

Over the last century, there has been a shift in the way consumers satisfy their needs and wants. We no longer rely on a large range of small businesses for most goods and services but rather on a small range of large businesses. For example, the days of purchasing all your grocery needs from the corner store are long gone. Instead, consumers today rely on just a few national supermarket chains stocking items produced by large companies. We depend on some form of business for our housing, clothing, health care, transportation, recreation, entertainment and communication; in short, for the satisfaction of most of our individual needs.

This makes the task of management crucial. Managers are necessary because society could not function without businesses, and businesses cannot function without managers.

Effective management is usually the major factor influencing the success or failure of a business.

The important role of effective management is to make sure the joint efforts of employees are directed towards achieving the goals of the business. Producing all the goods and services demanded by consumers involves the combined efforts of many people. This combined effort must be effectively coordinated so that the greatest amount of goods and services can be produced for the least cost — that is, efficiently. This coordination needs to be managed on many different levels; for example, within businesses, between businesses and on a national and international level. Businesses must do more than meet the needs of individuals. They must also meet the needs of all the stakeholders in general.

Above all else, what is important to any business is not the number of managers it employs, or the prestigious titles it gives them, but the ability of these managers to achieve the business's goals. To do this effectively, a manager must perform a number of important roles as well as possess a range of skills.

EXERCISE 1.1 *Revision*

1. Read about Zara and her role (see page 3) and list five specific things Zara does that make her an effective manager.
2. What is the main function of management according to the traditional definition?
3. Briefly describe the four main resources available to a business.
4. How does the contemporary definition of management differ from the traditional definition?
5. Construct a mind map outlining the five key aspects of the management process according to the contemporary definition. The first one has been started for you.

Contemporary definition of management — key aspects

- Working with and through others
- A social process
- Communication essential

6. Outline the difference between effectiveness and efficiency.
7. 'The performance of managers is often evaluated according to two criteria: effectiveness and efficiency. Of the two, effectiveness is the most important.' Discuss.
8. What is meant by the term 'synergy'?
9. Suggest why synergy might exist in well-managed organisations.
10. Explain why effective management is so important in our society.

Extension

1. Consider the following statement: 'Management is often demanding, complex, stressful and exacting. Contributing to the complexity are globalisation, focus on quality, increasing competition, technological developments, and the rising demand for the ethical conduct of people and organisations. But at the same time it can be personally rewarding.' Research the positive and negative aspects of being a manager.
2. Identify a large business that competes globally and a local small business that serves only its surrounding region. Compare the management challenges facing these two businesses.
3. Some people argue that middle-level managers have a more difficult job than top/senior or lower/frontline managers. This is because the work of a middle-level manager is more varied in managerial and non-managerial duties. Discuss.

4. Which do you think is the more difficult management task: getting employees to work in teams rather than independently, or getting employees to accept change in the workplace? Provide reasons for your answer.
5. 'The main difference between employees and managers is that employees work and managers think.' To what extent does this statement reflect conditions in today's workplace? Compare your answers with other class members.

1.3 Management roles

Imagine you are the senior financial manager of a national furniture manufacturer. As a manager you are required to perform a number of different functions, specifically planning, organising, leading and controlling. These functions of management were first described early last century by a French engineer named Henri Fayol (see figure 1.5). His explanation of the functional approach to management provided a type of 'job description' for managers.

Fayol outlined four main functions that managers perform, as shown in figure 1.6. Fayol's explanation of the functions of management was so concise and easy to understand it formed the foundation of most management courses offered during the twentieth century. His explanation was often used as a definition of management itself.

Figure 1.5 Henri Fayol (1841–1925), a French engineer, pioneered the functional approach to management, focusing on the four main management activities.

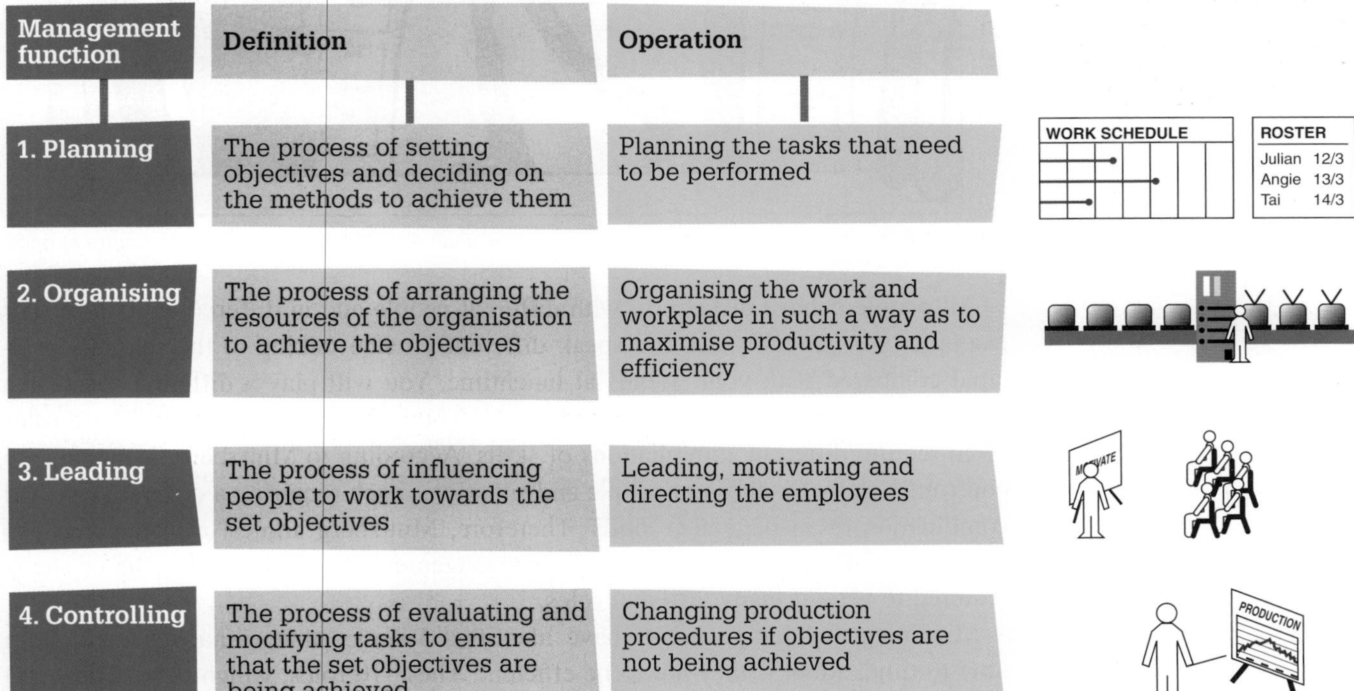

Management function	Definition	Operation
1. Planning	The process of setting objectives and deciding on the methods to achieve them	Planning the tasks that need to be performed
2. Organising	The process of arranging the resources of the organisation to achieve the objectives	Organising the work and workplace in such a way as to maximise productivity and efficiency
3. Leading	The process of influencing people to work towards the set objectives	Leading, motivating and directing the employees
4. Controlling	The process of evaluating and modifying tasks to ensure that the set objectives are being achieved	Changing production procedures if objectives are not being achieved

Figure 1.6 The four main functions of management, according to Henri Fayol

More recently, in 1973, a management researcher named Henry Mintzberg (see figure 1.7) criticised Fayol's traditional functional approach as too simplistic and therefore unrealistic. From his own observations of senior executive management, Mintzberg concluded that the functional approach does not provide enough information about what managers actually do.

According to Mintzberg, a manager, like an actor, must play many different roles. A **role** is a part that a person plays. However, unlike an actor who plays only one role at a time, a manager plays several roles in the same day and occasionally two or more at once (see figure 1.8).

Figure 1.7 Henry Mintzberg

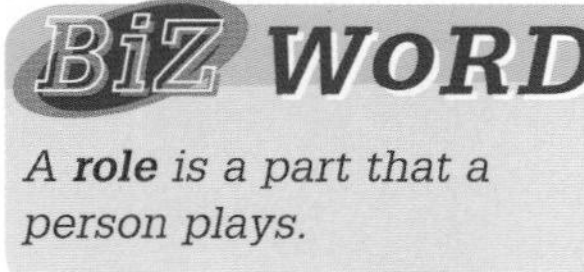

*A **role** is a part that a person plays.*

Figure 1.8 Managers must act out a number of roles each day and occasionally two or more at once.

All people behave differently with different people and in different situations. For example, you probably act and speak differently when talking to the school's principal compared with your friends at lunchtime. You will play a different role when working at your part-time job compared with your role in a sports team. These roles often require different combinations of skills. According to Mintzberg, managers are confronted daily by different people and situations, each requiring a different role and combination of management skills. Therefore, Mintzberg argues, a manager is not someone who rigidly performs just four management functions. Rather, he or she is required to act out many different roles.

Mintzberg and his adherents have identified 10 roles that managers must, from time to time, adopt if they are to be efficient. These 10 roles, which they believe are common to managers at all levels of a business, can be grouped into three categories: interpersonal, informational and decision making (see figure 1.9).

Category	Role	Description	Activity
Interpersonal	1. Figurehead	▪ Performs ceremonial duties ▪ Symbol of legal authority	▪ Signing documents ▪ Attending functions ▪ Receiving visitors
	2. Leader	▪ Motivates employees	▪ Communicating with subordinates
	3. Liaison	▪ Establishes and maintains a network of contacts ▪ Interacts with other organisations	▪ Interacting with outside people ▪ Answering letters, email, phone calls ▪ Attending conferences
Informational	4. Monitor	▪ Seeks and receives information from a wide variety of sources to gain better understanding of the business and its environment	▪ Dealing with all forms of communication and contacts ▪ Receiving all types of communication
	5. Disseminator	▪ Shares information with selected employees within the business	▪ Forwarding communication on to appropriate areas of the business
	6. Spokesperson	▪ Presents to outsiders information about the business's plans, policies, results and structure	▪ Attending board meetings ▪ Compiling newsletters ▪ Conducting media interviews
Decision making	7. Entrepreneur	▪ Scans the environment for opportunities ▪ Initiates projects to improve performance ▪ Brings about change	▪ Conducting review sessions ▪ Undertaking evaluation analysis ▪ Organising research
	8. Disturbance handler	▪ Deals with issues and crises inside and outside the business ▪ Takes corrective action	▪ Implementing strategies to resolve conflicts or deal with issues
	9. Resource allocator	▪ Decides who should get what resources ▪ Allocates the human, financial, physical and informational resources	▪ Preparing budgets ▪ Authorising requests and expenditure ▪ Programming employee tasks
	10. Negotiator	▪ Participates in negotiations with other parties (e.g. unions, suppliers)	▪ Negotiating ▪ Bargaining

Figure 1.9 Mintzberg's 10 managerial roles *Source:* Adapted from H. Mintzberg, *The nature of managerial work*, Prentice Hall, Englewood Cliffs, NJ 1980.

Mintzberg's categorisation of managerial activities into the 10 roles gives some insight into what managers actually do. The roles also provide some clues about the types of skills managers need to possess to perform effectively.

Interpersonal roles

An **interpersonal role** is one in which the manager deals with people.

Dealing with people, both inside and outside the business, is an integral part of a manager's job. An **interpersonal role** is one in which the manager deals with people.

Due to their authority and status within the business, managers need to adopt three distinct interpersonal roles. These are:

- *figurehead.* The manager may perform ceremonial duties such as signing a contract, giving awards or attending a public presentation.
- *leader.* The leader works to create an appropriate workplace culture, improving employee performance, developing the skills and abilities of subordinates, and recruiting and motivating staff.
- *liaison.* Individual managers often interact with other managers inside and outside the business.

Informational roles

An **informational role** is one in which the manager gathers and disseminates information within the business, also providing it to the outside world.

An **informational role** is one in which the manager gathers and disseminates information within the business, also providing it to the outside world.

Informational roles are important because information is the lifeblood of any business. There are three main informational roles that a manager must adopt. These roles are:

- *monitor.* In this role the manager seeks out and gathers information that may be valuable to the business. In this way the manager gains a better understanding of what is happening in the outside world.
- *disseminator.* As a disseminator, a person who spreads information, a manager provides information to other managers or employees.
- *spokesperson.* In this role the manager provides information to people and organisations outside the business, including the media and general public.

Decisional roles

A **decision-making role** involves solving problems and making choices.

In the **disturbance-handler role** the manager must make decisions necessary to keep the business operating under extraordinary circumstances.

The **resource-allocator role** requires the manager to share out or allocate the limited resources of the business.

The **negotiating role** requires the manager to arrange for, or bring about through discussions, the settlement of an issue.

As the name implies, a **decision-making role** involves solving problems and making choices. Through decisional roles, strategies are formulated and put into action. There are four main decisional roles. These are:

- *entrepreneur.* In the entrepreneurial role the manager looks for and implements new ideas that hopefully will make the business more efficient and effective.
- *disturbance handler.* The manager who finds a new supply of raw materials because of shortages or who deals with equipment failure is playing the role of **disturbance handler**. The manager must make decisions that allow the business to keep operating under extraordinary circumstances.
- *resource allocator.* Managers rarely have all the resources they would like. Therefore, the manager is forced to act as a **resource allocator**, sharing out the limited resources of the business.
- *negotiator.* The **negotiating role** requires the manager to arrange for, or bring about through discussions, the settlement of an issue.

Managers spend a great deal of time negotiating because they are usually the only ones with the information and authority to undertake such negotiations.

The interpersonal management role involves dealing with people.
The informational management role involves gathering and disseminating information.
The decision-making management role involves solving problems and making choices.

Figure 1.10 The three main management roles

Managerial 'facts of life'

Observations made of modern managers' work patterns suggest that Mintzberg is correct. Management is a difficult and demanding job. Most people, when asked to describe a manager, would probably use terms such as the following: power, privilege, status, authority and high income. This image of a manager is often reinforced through the media, especially through the stereotype of the 'mogul' or 'tycoon'. The reality, however, is quite different.

Mintzberg's observations highlighted the gap between the myths and realities of management (see table 1.1 on page 14). The hours are long, interruptions frequent, many conflicting interests have to be dealt with and each day follows a hectic schedule (see figure 1.11). It is predicted that future managers will confront an even more hectic pace of work. And yet, management can be a highly rewarding experience for those who develop their skills and strive for excellence.

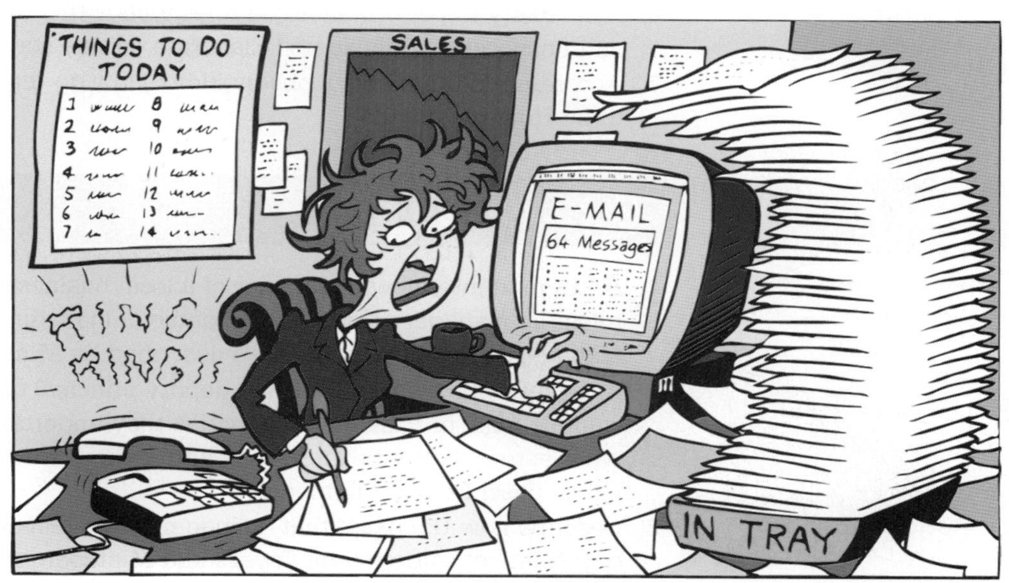

Figure 1.11 The facts of life in management — the real picture of a manager's day in the workplace!

TABLE 1.1	The myths and realities of a manager's job according to Mintzberg	
	Myth	**Reality**
1.	The effective manager is a methodical planner, reflects on what has been achieved, with time to systematically work through problems encountered throughout the day.	The typical manager is constantly interrupted, with no more than approximately 10 minutes spent on any one activity. The manager takes on a great deal and has little time for reflection.
2.	The effective manager has no regular activities to carry out. It is all a matter of coordinating other people's responsibilities and then sitting back to watch others do the work.	Although managers' days are constantly interrupted by both trivialities and crises, they still have regular duties to perform. They must interpret and analyse information, attend meetings and communicate regularly with other parts of the business.
3.	Management is a science and, as such, can be reduced to a formula and set of 'laws' that, if followed, result in goals being achieved.	The manager's job is more art than science. Managers rely heavily on judgement, past experience, perception and intuition.

EXERCISE 1.2 *Revision*

1. Examine figure 1.6 on page 9. List and briefly explain the four main functions of management according to Henri Fayol.
2. Suggest reasons why Fayol considered planning to be the 'first' function.
3. What is a management role? Explain the three general types of management role identified by Mintzberg.
4. Under the headings of 'interpersonal', 'informational' and 'decision making' outline the 10 roles that managers must adopt according to Mintzberg's observations.
5. Suppose that you have opened a music store in the local shopping mall that stocks CDs, tapes, videos, DVDs and other audio and video accessories. Assume that you have seven employees. Outline how you would perform the 10 roles in managing your business.
6. 'The ability to perform multiple roles well is the difference between successful and unsuccessful managers.' Elaborate on this statement.
7. According to Mintzberg's observations, how do the 'realities' of a manager's job differ from the 'myths'?

Extension

1. Arrange to interview a manager of a local business. Identify the management roles the manager adopts in the course of managing the business. Compare the manager's responses with those described by Mintzberg.
2. Interview either a head teacher, deputy principal or principal at your school and compile a list of managerial activities they undertake in the course of a day. To what extent do their experiences mirror the myths and realities of a manager's job as described by Mintzberg?
3. Describe how the belief that 'management is responsible for the performance of organisations' differs from Fayol's and Mintzberg's views about management.

1.4 Skills of management

So far we have discussed only the '*what*' of management. We have examined the following questions:

- What is management?
- What is its importance?
- What different roles must managers adopt to do their work?

However, as Winnie-the-Pooh reminds us (see the Snapshot 'Winnie-the-Pooh on management') most people agree on the 'what' of management but the 'how' is not so clear cut. In other words, how is the task of management actually done? What skills do managers need to possess?

Winnie-the-Pooh on management

'Man-age-ment,' said Edward Bear in the somewhat puzzled tone he used when he was thinking, or, as Eeyore might say, 'Trying to think.'

'Yes. Management.'

'That is a very long word.' Pooh reflected. 'It is the kind of long word that Owl uses. Does it stand for something good, like ah ummm honey?'

'Well, not exactly. It stands for something that some people called managers do. Management is neither good nor bad. It just is. You can have either good or bad management, depending on how managers do their job.'

'That seems very confusing. Almost everyone I know thinks that honey is good always.'

'Yes. Well, we are not talking about honey.'

'I am.' Pooh rubbed his tummy. 'In fact, I was looking for some but I found you instead.'

'We are talking about management.' . . .

'Now, the reason that management is a Very Important Subject is that if we didn't have management, most important things wouldn't get done, or if they did, they wouldn't get done very well.'

'Like going to visit Rabbit and his not having remembered to stock the larder with a pot of honey to put on the bread that he should serve to guests who just happen to drop by and might like to have a mouthful of something?'

'Exactly. That and many other important things.'

Pooh sat up straight, taking more of an interest in the subject of management. 'So why don't people who management —'

'—people who manage—'

'—manage learn how to do it properly?'

'That's the problem. Just about everybody agrees on what management is. "The art and science of directing effort and resources so that the established objectives of an enterprise may be attained in accordance with accepted policies" is one definition. It is the "How" that nobody is quite sure about.'

Pooh nodded, assuming his wise-bear look. '*How* is difficult,' he said. 'If you ask Eeyore how he is, he almost always says, "Not very how." Everyone has trouble with "How". I remember once when I heard a buzzing-noise from the top

(*continued*)

of a tree and decided that there might be honey there. I also decided that I would like to eat a little honey. It was the "How" to get the honey that was troublesome.'

'Well, it is the same thing with management. It seems that almost everyone has a theory about good management and how it can be achieved. There are stacks and stacks of books on the subject . . . Over the past twenty years or so, I think that many managers have been distracted by the theories in these books and by management fads. They have paid too much attention to trying the latest management theory and not enough attention to the real basics of managing. I think that most would improve their performance tremendously by concentrating on these basics of a manager's job.

'I think that many of your adventures illustrate those basic functions of a manager that, if practised consistently and properly, would help any manager do a really excellent job.'

'They would?' Pooh sounded surprised. 'Oh, yes. They would,' he said in a barely certain kind of voice.

Source: Roger E. Allen, *Winnie-the-Pooh on management*, Methuen, London, 1995, pp. 2–5.

SNaPSHOT Questions

1. According to this Snapshot, why is management a 'Very Important Subject'?
2. Use your own words to restate the definition of management provided in this Snapshot.
3. Suggest why most people agree on the 'what' of management, but offer many different suggestions on the 'how' of management.

In general, effective managers are those who:

- possess a range of specific management skills (see figure 1.12)
- are able to use these skills in a number of managerial roles.

FINANCE AND ADMINISTRATION MANAGER

State responsibilities

Our client is a division of one of Australia's top 50 companies and is highly regarded for its business success and status as an employer.

Your role will be to add value to management decision making through analysis of operational information and ensuring accurate and timely information is provided.

Degree qualified in Accounting or a business related discipline, you have strong general accounting skills. With a high level of leadership aptitude, you are adept at managing teams, applying your commercial instinct and developing solutions to broad-based business issues. This is an excellent opportunity to join one of the country's most recognisable organisations during a phase of substantial growth.

To enquire further, please telephone our Sydney office. Confidentiality is respected.

INTERNATIONAL SERVICE PROVIDER

PERTH • SYDNEY • MELBOURNE • BRISBANE

REPORTING AND ANALYSIS MANAGER

We currently have a vacancy for a Reporting and Analysis Manager based in our Sydney office. This position supports senior management and board of directors to effectively manage and track strategies and action plans which enable appropriate communication with internal and external parties.

Key responsibilities of this role are to:

- establish and maintain information flows on key business drivers between various business units
- develop analysis of monthly results and forecasts
- prepare monthly management and board reports
- support business units to meet specified information requirements
- support statutory reporting requirements by ensuring information received is in accordance with specified accounting policies and procedures

The successful candidate must be pro-active and energetic with strong analytical skills. High computer literacy and attention to detail is also required. You will need to be team oriented as you will be expected to initiate and participate in continuous process improvement work teams.

We would like to hear from applicants who possess strong interpersonal and communication skills. CA or CPA qualifications are required with a background of at least six years in finance with a focus on management reporting.

If you are interested in this position, please provide a written application detailing your qualifications, skills and work experience.

Figure 1.12 Managers are required to possess a range of specific management skills, as shown by these job advertisements.

Normally, no manager is required to use all these skills constantly or to play a particular role all the time. What is important is that these skills and abilities must be available when they are needed.

People skills

People skills *(interpersonal/human skills) are those skills needed to work and communicate with other people and to understand their needs.*

Managers get their work done through other people. Therefore, **people skills** are extremely important. Such interpersonal or human skills mean a manager can work and communicate with other people and understand their needs.

People skills centre on the ability to relate to people, being aware of and appreciating their needs and showing genuine understanding. People skills include the ability to communicate, motivate, lead and inspire.

A manager who lacks empathy, is arrogant, opinionated, unable to communicate or who has difficulty relating to people will not be able to develop positive relationships with employees. Employees may actually work more efficiently when such a manager is absent because the fear of intimidation or victimisation is reduced.

In 1995, an industry task force on leadership and management skills in Australia reported its findings. The report, Enterprising nation: renewing Australia's managers to meet the challenges of the Asia–Pacific century *(known as the Karpin Report), was commissioned by the Australian government. It identified eight 'ideal characteristics' (skills) managers should possess:*

- *people skills*
- *strategic thinking skills*
- *ability to be visionary*
- *ability to be flexible and adaptable to change*
- *self-management skills*
- *ability to be a team player*
- *ability to solve complex problems and make decisions*
- *ethical/high personal standards.*

Strategic thinking skills

Consider the following quotes:

'Who in the hell wants to hear actors talk?'
Harry Warner, founder of Warner Bros Studios, 1927

'I think there is a world market for about five computers.'
Thomas J. Watson, chairman IBM, 1943

'There is no reason for any individual to have a computer in their home.'
Ken Olsen, president, Digital Equipment, 1977

'Nothing has come along that can beat the horse and buggy.'
Chauncey De Pew, president of the New York Central Railroad, warning his nephew against investing in Henry Ford's new company

'Everything that could be invented has now been invented'
U.S. Patent Office circa 1900

With hindsight we laugh at these quotes. And yet, at the time, most people would have agreed with the speakers. It could be argued that their shortsightedness inhibited strategic thinking. Therefore, they were not able to perceive meaningful patterns in complex circumstances. **Strategic thinking** allows a manager to see the business as a whole — as a complex of parts that depend on and interact with each other, like the gears in a machine (see the Snapshot 'Steven Cargill' on page 18).

Strategic thinking *allows a manager to see the business as a whole — as a complex of parts that depend on and interact with each other, like the gears in a machine.*

The ability to think strategically lets the manager see the 'big picture'. The manager may then:

- visualise how work teams and individuals interrelate
- understand the effect of any action on the business
- gain insights into an uncertain future
- see the business in the context of events and trends, and identify opportunities or threats.

Overall, strategic thinking enables managers to anticipate how their decisions will affect and be affected by other parts of the business.

Steven Cargill

POSITION: Project Manager
COMPANY: PJM Engineering Pty Ltd
QUALIFICATIONS: Design Draftsman
Certificate of Airconditioning and Refrigeration, RMIT

As a project manager, I am responsible for ensuring projects are completed on time and within the estimated cost. It is also part of my job to ensure quality workmanship and safety (OH&S) on jobs.

A usual day for me consists of ordering and distributing materials, and visiting sites to oversee project progress. I organise placement of staff and liaise with clients, tradespeople and contractors. I also spend my time looking at costing of future projects, and problem solving.

PJM Engineering aims to provide quality mechanical services to industrial and commercial buildings. My part in achieving this objective is to ensure correct placement of staff for optimum use of individual skills. I also negotiate with unions, tradespeople and clients to meet the needs of all involved.

I used a number of management skills in a situation where staff began arriving late, leaving early and taking long breaks. I held a meeting with the site staff to discuss the impact on the cost of the job, company profit and individual employment, as well as the effect on other staff members. This resulted in improved productivity and a better understanding for all involved.

The rapid expansion of our company meant there was a need for new buildings and extra staff. I was involved in interviewing people for the new positions created and in developing a new structure within the company.

If you are interested in a career in business, complete the appropriate courses pertaining to your chosen path. Always maintain high standards of honesty and workmanship.

SNAPSHOT Questions

1. What management skills did Steven use when his staff arrived late to work?
2. The ability to think strategically lets the manager see the 'big picture'. How did Steven use strategic thinking when involved in his company's expansion?

Vision skills

In his book *Management: tasks, responsibilities, practices*, Peter Drucker explains that it is 'the first response of the manager . . . to give others vision and the ability to perform'. By **vision**, Drucker means the clear, shared sense of direction that allows people to attain a common goal.

__Vision__ is the clear, shared sense of direction that allows people to attain a common goal.

Drucker argues that vision is the essential contribution of management, for without it there can be no sense of cooperation and commitment, which makes achieving goals impossible. Drucker explains that the most effective way for managers to share their vision for the business is through the organisation's goals. Knowing where the business is headed and what it is trying to achieve helps employees understand where

Having to develop a vision for the business is most important during times of constant change. Without a vision, any business will ultimately fail.

***Proactive** refers to a management style that incorporates dynamic action and forward planning to achieve particular objectives.*

Effective managers have a range of management styles that they can use comfortably. They have developed some flexibility in using those styles in different situations. Effective managers also have a knack for being able to diagnose what their people need from them in order to build their skills and confidence in doing tasks they are assigned. Finally, effective leaders can communicate with their staff — they are able to reach agreements with them not only about their tasks but also about the amount of direction and support they will need to accomplish these tasks. These three skills — flexibility, diagnosis and contracting — are the three most important skills managers can use to motivate better performance on the part of the people with whom they work.

Source: K. Blanchard, P. Zigarmi and D. Zigarmi, *Leadership and the one minute manager*, Collins, London, 1986.

the manager wishes to take the business. A manager without a clear vision for the business is like a person who attempts to lead a bushwalk without any idea of where the group wants to go, without a compass or even a map. The walk would become aimless. The same thing happens in a business whose manager has not communicated clearly its vision. The business is without guidance.

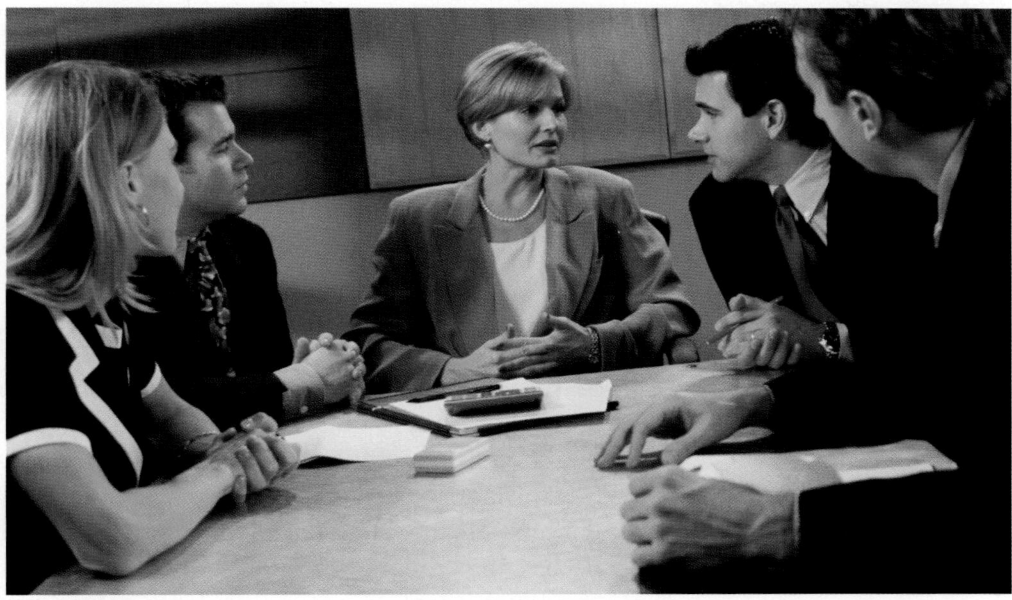

Figure 1.13 To share their vision with others, managers must possess the skill of leadership

Flexibility and adaptability to change skills

Not since the Industrial Revolution over 200 years ago has business experienced so much change. Over the next 10 to 20 years, the Australian business environment will dramatically change. How managers perceive and react to these changes will have dramatic consequences for their businesses.

Regardless of their level of management, successful managers are those who anticipate and adjust to changing circumstances. They must be flexible and adaptable, **proactive** rather than reactive (see the Biz Fact on the left). Those who are unprepared or passive in the face of change will not succeed.

Businesses today are recruiting and selecting managers who can cope with unfamiliar and unexpected circumstances. For example, Arthur Hancock, former Senior Human Resources Manager for Global Equities Limited, said:

> We are seeking managers who have learned how to learn and can adapt to changing situations. We do not want managers who are dogmatic and inflexible. Such a style of management may have been appropriate 50 years ago, but not for today's markets which are highly competitive, technologically driven and rapidly changing. We want to hire people who like surprises!

The topic of management and change will be examined in more detail in chapter 3.

Self-managing skills

Walk into any book store and you will be confronted with numerous self-help books. While some of these offer little real value, others provide powerful insights into management techniques and styles. Such books often focus on self-management strategies. Management is not confined simply to managing businesses or groups of people. Managing oneself is just as important. In fact, numerous management researchers and consultants argue that self-management is a basic prerequisite for effectively managing other people and organisations.

***Self-managing** involves adopting techniques that allow people to manage their own behaviour so that less outside control is necessary.*

Self-managing involves adopting techniques that allow people to manage their own behaviour so that less outside control is necessary. Examples include time management, delegation and stress management. It requires that people observe their own behaviour and identify areas for improvement.

Stephen R. Covey, in his book *The 7 habits of highly effective people*, provides a useful agenda for managers to help them improve their performance (see the Snapshot 'The 7 habits of highly effective people').

The 7 habits of highly effective people

1. Be proactive. You are responsible for your life. Decide what you should do and get on with it.
2. Begin with the end in mind. Think of how you want to be remembered. Use this as the basis for your everyday life.
3. Put first things first. Devote more time to what is important but not necessarily urgent.
4. Think 'win–win'. Have an abundance mentality. Seek solutions that benefit all parties.
5. Seek first to understand, then to be understood. Do not dive into a conversation. Listen until you truly understand the other person.
6. Synergise. Find ways to cooperate with everyone. Value the differences between people.
7. Sharpen the saw. Continually exercise and renew four elements of yourself: physical, mental, emotional, social and spiritual.

Source: Adapted from S. Covey, *The 7 habits of highly effective people*, Australian Business Library, Melbourne 1990.

SNAPSHOT Question

Examine Covey's seven habits of highly successful people. Identify the habits you consider most important. Suggest practical ways of adopting these habits.

Teamwork skills

The traditional hierarchical structure of many businesses is disappearing. Layers of management are being removed and replaced by work teams, resulting in 'flattened' management structures. These self-directed work teams will alter some of the traditional roles of management. One obvious change is that managers will have to work more closely with people over whom they have no apparent authority. They will be required to adopt a team approach, negotiating consensus decisions rather than imposing demands. The role of managers is changing from controller to facilitator. Without being able to impose their authority, managers will have to achieve their aims by balancing the needs of the team with those of the business. This can be accomplished by the manager attempting to understand the views of others, handling disagreements honestly and directly, and persuading others to adopt new ideas. Above all else, the manager must build a sense of trust, teamwork's key ingredient.

Figure 1.14 Managers require a good understanding of team/group dynamics.

Complex problem-solving and decision-making skills

People at all levels in a business must constantly solve problems and make decisions. The problem-solving and decision-making tasks are particularly important for managers. For problems large or small, it is usually the manager who has to confront the issue and decide the most appropriate course of action. The decisions made by managers may have enormous influence on the business and largely determine the actions and decisions of other employees.

BiZ WORD

Problem solving *is a broad set of activities involved in searching for, identifying and then implementing a course of action to correct an unworkable situation.*

Problem solving

We are all problem solvers. But this does not mean that all of us are good problem solvers, or even that we know how to solve problems systematically. Usually, when confronted with a problem we search for an answer, jump at the first workable solution and move on. Using this method to solve problems is quite haphazard. While it may be satisfactory when dealing with informal day-to-day activities, it is not appropriate in the world of management. Management requires a more systematic problem-solving process when confronted with difficult and unfamiliar situations.

Problem solving is a broad set of activities involved in searching for, identifying and then implementing a course of action to correct an unworkable situation.

Although managers have to deal with many problems in the course of a day, not all of the problems require such a systematic, formal process. One of the most important skills a manager can develop is the ability to decide the problem to which they should give their full attention.

Decision making *is the process of identifying the options available and then choosing a specific course of action to solve a specific problem. Decision making is a fundamental part of management because it requires choosing an alternative course of action.*

Decision making

The task of solving problems will obviously require making some decisions. **Decision making** is the process of identifying the options available and then choosing a specific course of action to solve a specific problem.

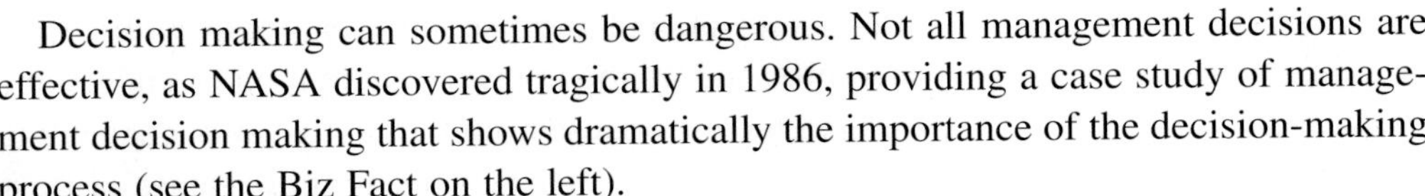

Decision making can sometimes be dangerous. Not all management decisions are effective, as NASA discovered tragically in 1986, providing a case study of management decision making that shows dramatically the importance of the decision-making process (see the Biz Fact on the left).

In 1986, NASA management had to decide whether to launch the space shuttle Challenger *even though temperatures at the launch site had fallen below the levels normally required for a safe launch. Lower-level engineers expressed their concerns. However, top-level NASA managers decided to go ahead with the launch, a decision that resulted in the deaths of all the astronauts on board.*

Managers today are often confronted with complex, challenging and stressful decision-making demands. Accelerating change often makes it difficult to accurately predict the full effect of any decision. Therefore, managers need to develop an effective decision-making environment within the business. This can be accomplished by tapping into the creative potential of employees.

High personal standards and ethics

Highly publicised accounts of corporate misconduct in recent years have led to a widespread cynicism about the personal and business ethics of people in management roles (see the Snapshot 'Ethical behaviour in the boardroom'). However, the news is not all bad. The majority of businesses and managers consistently conduct themselves with honesty and integrity.

Ethical behaviour in the boardroom

In Australia and overseas, there has been a recent spate of corporate scandals involving accusations of fraudulent conduct by senior managers and board members. HIH Insurance, WorldCom, Enron and One.Tel are examples of corporations where the senior managers and board representatives engaged in unethical and morally dubious conduct, including:

- intentional misrepresentation of financial information to stakeholders
- questionable approval of loans to senior executives
- non-declaration of conflicts of interest
- secret deals with companies owned by executives and board members
- deceptive and misleading media releases

Senior managers and directors from these organisations were found to have either knowingly engaged in unethical business behaviour or condoned such action by turning a blind eye to its existence. Whether by commission (an intentional act) or omission (failure to act), unethical behaviour will severely damage the reputation and financial viability of an organisation, no matter how large the organisation is. One.Tel, HIH and WorldCom have collapsed and Enron is struggling, and a number of their managers and directors involved in the unethical behaviour face financial ruin and/or prison sentences.

Without the commitment of an organisation's senior managers, including the board of directors, a program for ethical responsibility will fail. If senior management pay only lip service to the organisation's code of conduct, then such behaviour 'sets the tone' (one of noncompliance) and will serve as a guide for other employees.

SNaPSHOT Questions

1. Using the library, newspapers, magazines and the Internet, select one of the companies mentioned, and research and report on:
   (a) the unethical business practices conducted by the people involved
   (b) the consequences of the unethical behaviour to the individual
   (c) the consequences of the unethical behaviour to the stakeholders.
2. Why should an organisation be concerned about the ethical behaviour of its senior managers and board members?

Ethical behaviour is consistent with society's standards about what is morally acceptable and conforms to society's judgement about what constitutes right and wrong actions.

Ethical behaviour is consistent with society's standards about what is morally acceptable and conforms to society's judgement about what constitutes good and bad actions.

Managers act as role models and their actions have an impact on other employees. For example, a manager's strong ethical practices and honesty will spread throughout the entire work team and be reflected in employees' behaviour. Consequently, managers are one of the most important factors in the ethical or unethical running of a business. Ethical behaviour will not be achieved in a business until it becomes part of senior management's philosophy and practice.

Figure 1.15 Corruption undermines the integrity of the business.

Ethical business practices do not just happen; they are carefully planned and implemented. Such practices will filter through the entire business. In return, employees are more loyal, committed and proud to work for such a business.

EXERCISE 1.3 *Revision*

1. Examine figure 1.12 on page 16. List some of the desired skills needed to perform these management positions.
2. What characteristics should today's ideal manager possess? (Refer to the Biz Fact on page 17, to help you with your answer.)
3. Use a table format similar to the following to summarise details of the essential skills of management. The first one has been completed for you.

Skill	Definition	Importance in the workplace
People skills	The skills needed to communicate and work with other people	Managers get their work done through other people. Need to communicate, motivate and display empathy

4. Distinguish between ethical and unethical behaviour.
5. 'Ethical behaviour will not be achieved in a business until it becomes part of senior management's philosophy and practice.' Do you agree or disagree with this statement? Give reasons for your answer.

Extension

1. In groups of three or four, imagine you are members of the board of a large public company. The company manufactures electronic items for the domestic market. It has 5000 employees and its current turnover is approximately $1 billion. The company is well established in domestic and export markets but, due to increasing competition, sales and profits have been decreasing over the past few years.
   The board is preparing to hire a new chief executive officer to lead the company. In your group, establish a profile of the business leader that you are seeking. Consider qualifications, experience, skills and personality factors.
   Conduct a class discussion on the similarities and differences of each group's profile. Suggest reasons for any differences.
2. Research some of the advantages of ethical performance by businesses. Are there any potential disadvantages?
3. *Leader to Leader* is the Drucker Foundation's magazine featuring articles, management issues and management strategies. Go to www.jaconline.com.au/businessstudies3e and click on the Leader to Leader weblink for this textbook to access the online version of the magazine. Select an article that deals with an area of management that interests you. After reading the article prepare an executive summary of it.
4. You have been asked to make a three-minute oral presentation at the local chamber of commerce meeting. The topic you have selected is 'The essential skills of management'. Present your report to the class. You might like to use some audiovisual materials to complement your presentation.

1.5 Responsibilities of management to stakeholders

***Stakeholders** are groups and individuals who interact with the business and thus have a vested interest in its activities.*

There are a number of stakeholders in business. **Stakeholders** are groups and individuals who interact with the business and thus have a vested interest in its activities. Over the last four decades, there has been a significant philosophical shift in business conduct to meet society's expectations.

Society increasingly expects businesses to accept responsibility and accountability toward all stakeholders for the promotion and management of change. Businesses are expected to be enterprising, to comply with the law and be socially just and ecologically sustainable in their operations. The responsibilities of management to stakeholders are outlined in figure 1.16 on page 26.

Most enterprises are now extremely sensitive to public opinion and strive to be recognised as 'good corporate citizens' (see the Snapshot 'Wesfarmers Limited — community participation'). Businesses recognise that they increase their chances of success when they pursue goals that align with the interests and expectations of all stakeholders.

Wesfarmers Limited — community participation

From its earliest days as a farmers' co-operative, Wesfarmers has placed great importance on maintaining strong links with the communities in which it operates.

In practice, this means having open and honest dialogue at a local level and being prepared to provide direct assistance by way of sponsorships and donations. Wesfarmers believes that the greatest contribution a company makes will always be the economic benefits that flow from successfully and responsibly run business operations. But it accepts there is an obligation on companies to go beyond this through direct support of community-benefiting activities.

Across the group, businesses contribute to many causes and organisations. These contributions take the form of direct financial support and involvement by employees in fund raising events.

This significant commitment by business units is supplemented by Wesfarmers Limited's donations programme under which the Board has agreed to contribute up to 0.25 per cent of annual pre-tax profit.

During the year, Wesfarmers made its fifth and final payment of $1 million to the Western Australian Institute for Medical Research, which aims to establish a world-class centre of excellence for research into adult health issues. Assistance was also provided in a number of other areas, including remote medical services, education and indigenous advancement.

Wesfarmers welcomes opportunities to join with organisations involved in programmes addressing particular issues within the community. An example is its long-standing partnership (implemented mainly through the Bunnings business unit) with Edge Employment Solutions in helping to find jobs for disabled people.

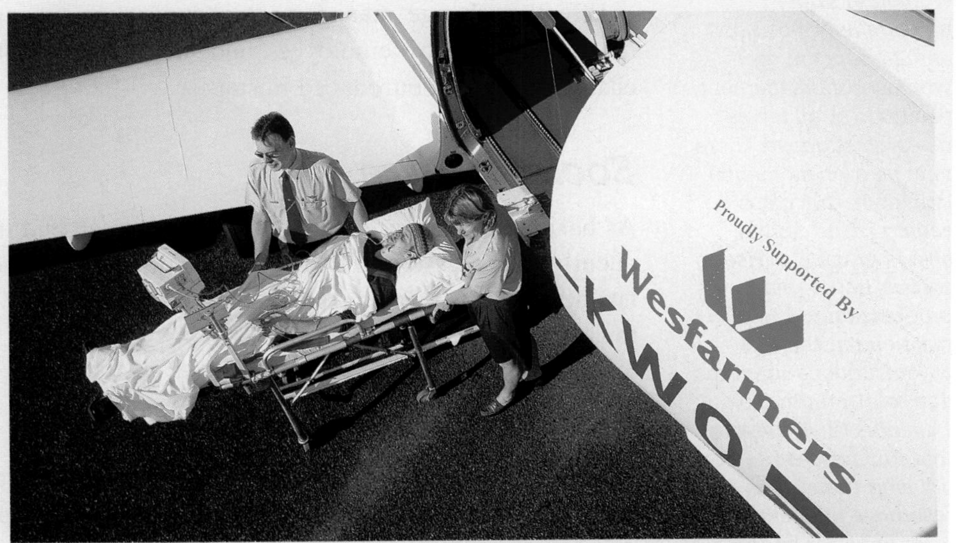

Wesfarmers provides financial assistance to the Royal Flying Doctor Service.

Source: Wesfarmers Limited, *Annual Report*, Perth 2003, p. 43.

SNaPSHOT Questions

1. How does Wesfarmers Limited fulfil its community obligations?
2. Go to www.jaconline.com.au/businessstudies3e and click on the Wesfarmers weblink for this textbook to access the company's annual report. Read about Wesfarmers' commitment to:
   (a) the environment
   (b) employee safety
   (c) public reporting
   (d) arts sponsorship.

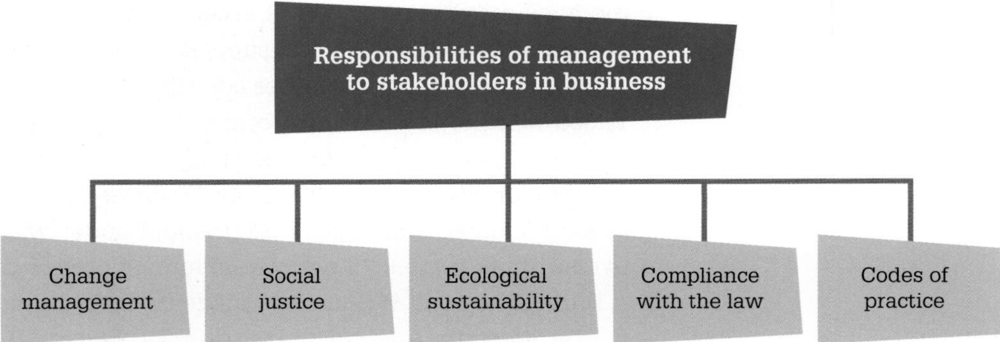

Figure 1.16 Responsibilities of management to stakeholders

Change management

The pace of change in the business environment has increased in the last two decades. Now well entrenched and likely to accelerate, change must be considered a fundamental aspect of an organisation's strategic planning. The ability to manage and, in many cases, embrace and adapt to change will increasingly determine a company's competitive advantage.

Effective change management occurs when management recognises that change must be owned by employees and, as people adapt to change in different ways, change should be introduced in stages.

Major social justice issues that have emerged over the last two decades include:

- *the glass ceiling: with less than 5 per cent of women in upper management positions and 23 per cent of women in management positions at all levels, research suggests there may be a phenomenon known as the 'glass ceiling'. This ceiling allows women to rise to certain levels, but progression to higher positions in the organisation is hindered due to discrimination. This effectively means that businesses are not utilising their human resources efficiently.*
- *discrimination in the workplace due to age, sex, disability, race or religion.*

Social justice

As businesses have access to substantial human and financial resources, they are frequently in possession of a large degree of market power. Society increasingly expects businesses to use their resources and market power responsibly, and to contribute toward the achievement of social justice goals.

Ecological sustainability

In response to concerns about climate change, the community increasingly expects businesses to adopt greenhouse-abatement measures and encourage the development of long-term sustainable strategies. Investors want companies to disclose details of their environmental performance.

Concerned consumers are also leading a move towards eco-design. Eco-design considers the impact of the raw material site, pollution caused by manufacturing, packaging, product use and eventual disposal. The widespread policy of the consumer industry known as '**planned obsolescence**', to encourage **consumerism**, will require replacement. Policies of planned obsolescence contribute to the generation of waste.

Planned obsolescence *refers to the built-in, predetermined life of a product that will thus require it to be replaced.*

Consumerism *is the act of buying goods and services.*

Figure 1.17 The Body Shop is committed to producing products that are sensitive to environmental concerns. It sells all its products in reusable or recyclable containers, many of which are refillable.

In Australia, many industries generate emissions of the most common greenhouse gas — carbon dioxide. The coal and power industries and resource projects have adopted a range of measures to reduce emissions, including the use of energy-efficient technology.

Compliance with the law

Many laws and regulations cover the operations of business. The amount, diversity and complexity of legal issues affecting the business environment have increased over the last two to three decades. Furthermore, society expects businesses to abide by the laws of the country. As a consequence, it is essential for businesspeople to have a sound working knowledge of the laws that will affect their operations and to understand and accept the legal responsibilities owed to all stakeholders.

Codes of practice

For good behaviour to occur at all levels of an organisation there must be a serious commitment by management. The promotion of respect for all stakeholders, employees and customers with clearly defined codes of behaviour, and fairness and honesty in all transactions will lead to improvements in productivity and public confidence.

For example in 2004, Australia's $11 billion general insurance industry released a new code of practice designed to lift the image of the industry. The code demands:

- better training for all general insurance industry participants
- greater professionalism in their dealings with the community.

The benefits for the community of the insurance industry code of practice will include faster claims handling, more understandable policies and access to a free dispute resolution system.

Reconciling conflicts of interest

All the stakeholders who interact with a business have a vested interest in its activities. However, all require something different; all place competing demands upon the business. Some of these expectations are compatible. For example, customers want quality for money. If the business meets this expectation then sales should increase, leading to greater profits. This in turn satisfies the business owners who are rewarded with higher dividends.

Industry safety is an area that is being increasingly scrutinised by employer groups and governments as poor or dangerous work practices can result in loss of life, permanent injury, rehabilitation and claims for workers' compensation. Employer groups have recently called for random breath testing in the workplace with the growth of alcohol and drug-related incidents occuring at work.

However, some expectations are incompatible; that is, they oppose each other. In this case satisfying one set of stakeholders will most probably result in other stakeholders being dissatisfied. For example, employees require safe working conditions and reasonable wages while customers want reasonably priced products. Providing safer working conditions or a wage rise will cost money in the short term. If the business wished to retain a high dividend to satisfy the shareholders' expectations then it may be forced to raise the prices of its products. This action will upset customers. On the other hand, the business may retain prices at the original level, reducing its profit. Doing this could cause disquiet among shareholders.

Reconciling these conflicting interests is not always easy. Senior management must assess constantly the actions of the business and attempt to satisfy as many stakeholder expectations as possible, while at the same time acting in a responsible manner.

Shareholders, society and future generations

The interests of society and future generations are very much reliant on the many decisions taken by businesses. Decisions concerning production processes, workplace practices, employment programs, product development and design, and business expansion will all have an impact on both present and future generations. Businesses have a responsibility to take into account the long-term effects of their current decisions.

Corporate social responsibility challenges each business to be accountable for the consequences of its actions. This means businesses must consider effects on all stakeholders while pursuing traditional economic goals.

One particular strategy that has been adopted by more enlightened businesses is to place greater emphasis on environmental practices. Adopting such a policy has benefits for both shareholders and society.

Professor Stanley Feldman of Bentley College in the United States joined researchers from ICF Kaiser International in an 18-month study to determine whether a business's good environmental performance results in a higher share price. Their research revealed that those businesses that adopted environmentally sound practices were rewarded with an increase in their share price. This increase occurred for two main reasons. First, society viewed favourably the business's environmentally friendly practices. This positive business image was perceived by the market as reducing the risk to investors, therefore encouraging more people to buy the company's shares. Second, share market analysts were more likely to notice and use the information about the environmentally friendly practices in their analysis of the company's financial performance, thus generating even more positive publicity. Therefore, even for purely pragmatic reasons, it is in a business's interest to consider its impact on the environment. In this way the conflicting interests of both shareholders and society are reconciled.

*The **triple bottom line** refers to the economic, social and environmental performance of a business.*

Many business analysts are now starting to refer to the '**triple bottom line**' — economic, social and environmental performance — where shareholder value increases through the careful management of stakeholder value. More businesses are realising that reconciling conflicting interests and increasing stakeholder value ensures long-term growth and survival.

Shareholder versus employee

Employee share acquisition schemes are one strategy used to reconcile conflicting interests between shareholders and employees. Such schemes provide the opportunity for eligible employees to purchase shares in a business, often at a reduced price. This aligns the interests of both groups as a number of employees become shareholders.

Another widely used strategy is to offer training and professional development to employees. An educated and skilled workforce works more efficiently, reducing production costs. This results in rising profits, which pleases shareholders. Also, better trained staff produce a higher quality product, thus satisfying customer expectations.

The more successfully a management team achieves the business's objectives, the more it will be able to satisfy a greater number of stakeholders. Therefore, to succeed in reconciling the conflicting interests of stakeholders a business needs competent, informed, ethical and socially responsible managers.

EXERCISE 1.4 Revision

1. What is meant by the term 'stakeholder'?
2. Prepare a mind map to provide a summary of the responsibilities of management to stakeholders. Copy and complete the example that has been started for you below.

3. Outline the difference between compatible and incompatible expectations of stakeholders. Provide examples.
4. 'Business is acutely aware that being out of step with community expectations can mean losing market share and poor employee morale and productivity, all of which can dramatically affect the bottom line' (Campbell Anderson, former President of the Business Council of Australia). Explain and discuss this statement, using examples from business.
5. In groups of three or four suggest methods a business could use to reconcile the following conflicting interests:
   (a) Consumers demanding cheaper products and employees wanting higher wages.
   (b) Shareholders desiring a higher return on their investment and society wanting a clean environment.

(c) Managers being required to keep costs of production down and the government demanding improvements in occupational health and safety practices.

6. You have been asked by a friend whether it is financially wise to purchase shares in businesses that have good environmental performance. What advice would you give to your friend after reading Professor Feldman's research (see page 28)?
7. Prepare a summary of this chapter. A summary condenses the important issues and concepts presented in the chapter. Go to www.jaconline.com.au/businessstudies3e to compare your finished summary with the one provided for this textbook.

Extension

1. In groups of three or four, investigate the likely impact of either the *Anti-Discrimination Act 1977* (NSW) or the *Sex Discrimination Act 1984* (Cwlth) on a workplace with which you are familiar. Present your findings as either a written or oral report.
2. Identify the major stakeholder groups often mentioned in relation to social responsibility. To what extent do these groups apply to your school? What other stakeholders might you add?
3. 'To be effective, corporate strategy must take into account the interests, needs, and expectations of all the business's stakeholders. Companies should have a strategy that combines business goals and broad social interests.' Elaborate.

2 Understanding business organisations with reference to management theories

2.1 Introduction

Like today's managers, the ancient Egyptian managers needed to:
- *develop plans*
- *acquire human and physical resources*
- *arrange finance*
- *analyse information*
- *keep records and prepare progress reports*
- *monitor performance and coordinate activities*
- *take corrective action whenever required.*

Management has been practised for thousands of years. The great pyramids of Cheops in Egypt, for example, represent the combined efforts of more than 100 000 individuals who worked on the project over a 20-year period. This remarkable achievement was the result of well-coordinated management practices.

Figure 2.1 Effective management practices were applied to building the pyramids of Egypt.

The development of management as a body of knowledge and a subject in its own right is much more recent. The Industrial Revolution of the late 1700s, which encouraged the growth of factories, acted as a catalyst for developing management theories. As the number of factories increased, there was a need to coordinate the efforts of many people in the continual production of goods and services.

A number of people began thinking and writing about ways of running factories more efficiently. These individuals were the first to develop theories of management and paved the way for the many management theorists who followed.

Over the last 200 years a number of influential business management theories have emerged (see figure 2.2) that have influenced management practices.

These theories or philosophies outline the main functions of management including planning, organising, leading, motivating, communicating, negotiating and controlling a group of individuals in an attempt to achieve specific goals. To a large extent, management theories have tended to reflect the customs and traditions of the society at the time. Consequently, as social and economic conditions changed new theories were developed. However, no single theory of management is universally accepted today. Rather, each theory offers something of value for today's managers.

BiZ FaCT

No one theory of management is universally accepted today. Rather, each theory offers something of value for today's managers.

The management philosophy adopted by a business will have an enormous impact on all aspects of the business's operation.

In particular, management theories influence:

- the organisation and allocation of tasks to staff
- the organisational structure
- levels of management
- management styles.

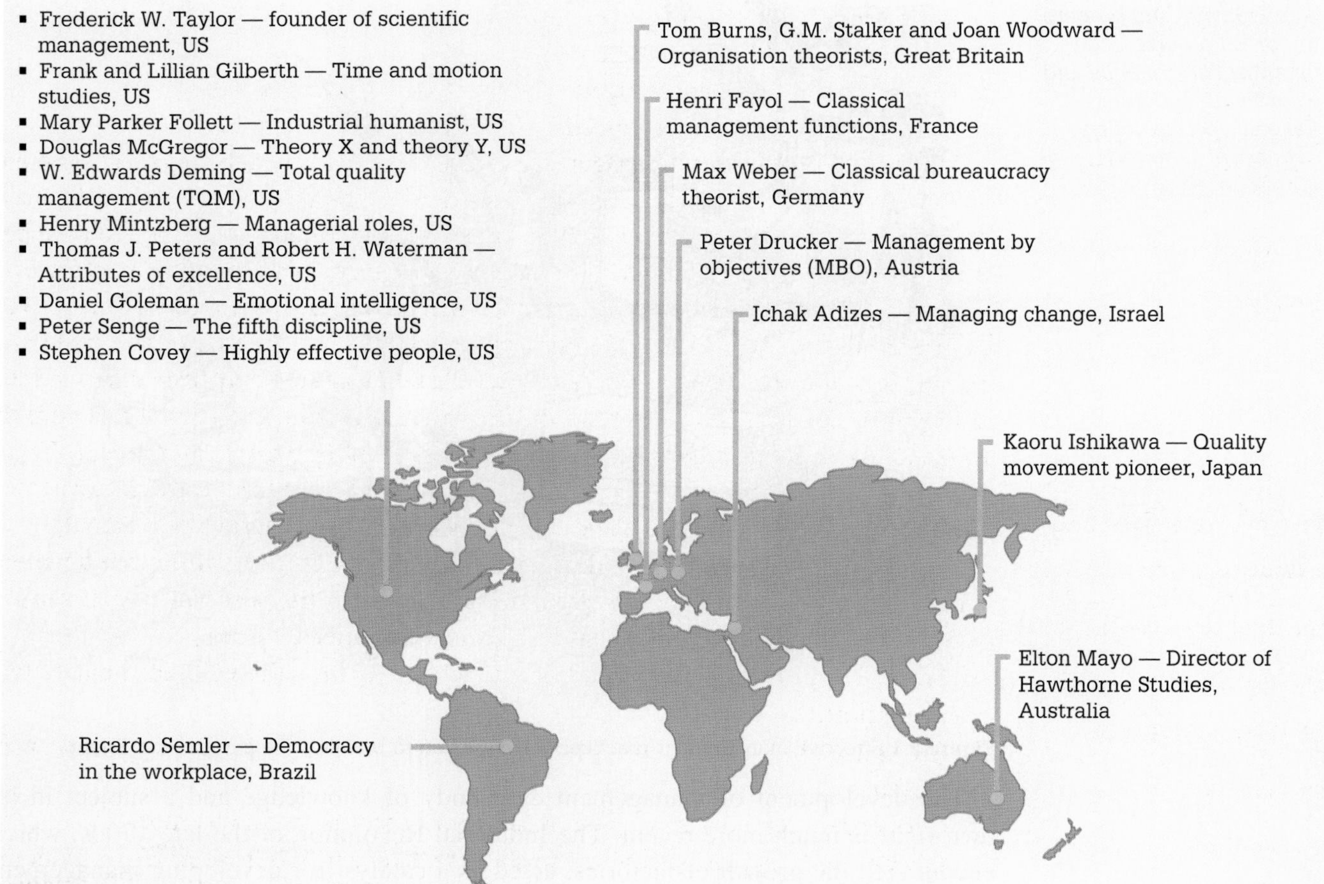

Figure 2.2 Theories of management — a global offering. Selected contributors to management theory and their contributions

2.2 Classical and scientific management theories

***Bureaucracy** is the set of rules and regulations that control a business.*

Figure 2.3 Max Weber (1864–1920), a German professor, coined the term 'bureaucracy' to identify large organisations that operated on a rational basis.

The classical approach was pioneered by Max Weber and Henri Fayol (see chapter 1). According to Weber (figure 2.3), a **bureaucracy** is the most efficient form of organisation and should have:

- a strict hierarchical organisational structure
- clear lines of communication and responsibility
- jobs broken down into simple tasks; division of labour and/or specialisation
- rules and procedures
- impersonal evaluation of employee performance to avoid favouritism and bias
- formal record keeping.

Fayol identified a number of management functions, including planning, organising, leading and controlling. He developed a number of principles to assist managers, including:

- discipline as a feature of leadership
- all activities should be directed to achieve a common goal
- the organisation's goals should take precedence over an employee's individual interests
- rewards for effort should be fair
- just treatment for all employees
- security of employment is essential
- teamwork should be encouraged
- every employee should be valued.

In the nineteenth century, management models were based on a hierarchical system of authority similar to the layered and somewhat rigid organisational structure of the major churches, educational institutions and the army. Such techniques were viewed as appropriate for the production line because they ensured effective control of the workforce.

One significant management theory that emerged during this period was that of Frederick W. Taylor (1856–1915). Taylor (figure 2.4) was an advocate of the production line method of manufacturing, which he viewed as the most efficient form of production. This production system was used in the industrialised countries of the world until the early 1970s and was based mainly on Taylor's scientific management ideas. Taylor adopted a **classical** perspective in his study of organisations; his ideas on management emphasise how best to manage and organise work so as to improve productivity.

*A **classical** perspective on management emphasises how best to manage and organise work so as to improve productivity.*

***Scientific management** is an approach that studies a job in great detail to discover the best way to perform it.*

Taylor, to assist his analysis, developed the principles of **scientific management**, an approach that studies a job in great detail to discover the best way to perform it.

Taylor's four principles of scientific management are as follows:

1. Scientifically examine each part of a task to determine the most efficient method for performing the task.
2. Select suitable workers and train them to use the scientifically developed work methods.
3. Cooperate with workers to guarantee they use the scientific methods.
4. Divide work and responsibility so that management is responsible for planning, organising and controlling the scientific work methods and workers are responsible for carrying out the work as planned.

Figure 2.4 Frederick W. Taylor (1856–1915) argued that productivity would be improved by preparing plans based on what needed to be done, designing each task scientifically and providing training and incentives for the workers. Some observers criticised Taylor for exploiting workers to get them to produce more.

To improve efficiency, Taylor attempted to systematise the way a job was done. He believed that a poorly skilled workforce could be trained to perform simple repetitive tasks effectively. He used time and motion studies to analyse the performance of a particular task, with the objective of reducing a task to an effective minimum standard. As well as reducing routine tasks into their most simple format, Taylor advocated the division of labour into function-related units; that is, tasks were divided into small, specialised activities.

Taylor also believed that employees follow their own self-interest and display a natural desire to avoid work. Such a situation, he argued, required tight control by supervisors and managers. He believed in the need for bureaucratic management to control workers and ensure they followed instructions. Taylor's scientific management theory is characterised by bureaucracy. It emphasises extensive and rigid rules and regulations based on a hierarchy of authority.

Figure 2.5 Taylor believed that dividing the task into smaller, specific activities would improve productivity.

One notable student of classical–scientific theory was Henry Ford (see figure 2.6) who was developing his car business at the time this theory was emerging. Being familiar with Taylor's work, Ford became an enthusiastic believer in scientific management and the use of machines. By combining these ideas, Ford developed his famous mechanised assembly line in 1913.

Figure 2.6 Henry Ford, one of the earliest believers in scientific management principles

McDonald's is another business that uses Taylor's scientific management approach in the preparation of its food. For example, a Big Mac is produced according to a set number of steps. The burger takes a predetermined number of seconds to cook, fixed amounts of lettuce, cheese and other ingredients are added precisely at the correct time and in exactly the same way. However, McDonald's adopts other management theories when dealing with its employees, theories that emphasise the 'human relations' aspect.

At the heart of the classical–scientific approach was the need for management to carry out the key activities of planning, organising and controlling.

According to classical–scientific thinkers, managers should constantly analyse all the activities performed within the business. They must teach effective methods to others, constantly monitor worker performance and plan responsibly while organising and controlling the work and the employees. Of course, the initial ideas of the classical–scientific theorists have been modified over time. However, modern managers realise that without motivated and committed employees empowered to analyse their own work habits and take responsibility for what they do, productivity will not improve.

EXERCISE 2.1 Revision

1. Explain why the practice of management is not considered a recent invention.
2. Outline the impact the Industrial Revolution had upon the development of management theory.
3. Henri Fayol and Max Weber advocated a classical application to organisational structures. Briefly list the features they believed needed to exist in an organisation for it to operate efficiently.
4. What is meant by the term 'scientific management'?
5. Briefly outline Taylor's four principles of scientific management.
6. Suggest why supporters of the scientific management theory established bureaucracies within their businesses.
7. Contrast Frederick Taylor's ideas on how to improve productivity with the ideas of Henri Fayol. Are there any ideas they have in common? You might like to present your information in the form of a Venn diagram, as shown in figure 2.7.

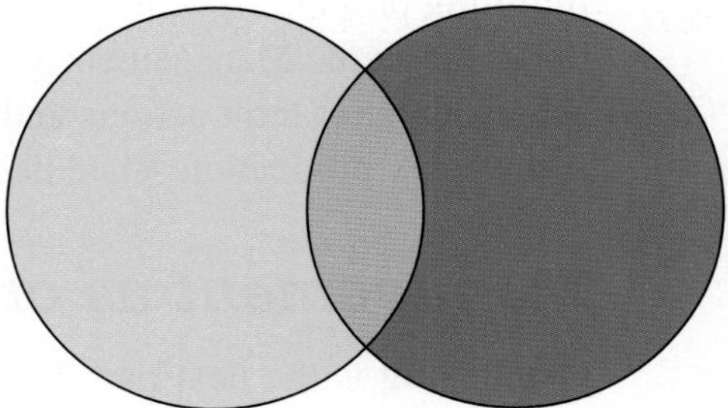

Figure 2.7 A Venn diagram is used to compare and contrast information. Points of difference are recorded in the outer parts of the circle and similarities are placed in the area where the two circles intersect.

Extension

1. In groups of three or four, prepare a list of advantages and disadvantages of a modern business adopting a purely classical–scientific management approach. Share your research with the class either as a written or oral presentation.
2. Research how classical–scientific management theory helped Henry Ford build the Ford Motor Company. What criticisms have been made of automated production line methods of manufacturing?
3. 'Classical management thinkers looked for the best way to do everything. Their tools were time and motion study and a scientific approach to studying work and work flow.' Elaborate.

Management as planning

Planning is often referred to as the primary management function. It provides the key to both the short-term and long-term success of a business. Effective planning provides a vision and objectives for a business, strategies to achieve the vision and objectives, and anticipation of future directions for change.

The ability of a manager to develop, implement and monitor plans will directly affect a business's success.

Planning is the preparation of a predetermined course of action for a business. It involves showing how the business will achieve its stated mission and organisational objectives.

__Planning__ is the preparation of a predetermined course of action for a business.

Levels of planning — strategic, tactical and operational planning

Once the organisational objectives have been determined, decisions have to be made about how they will be achieved. This requires detailed plans for activities at all levels of the organisation. Different types of plans will assist firms in achieving their objectives.

Strategic (long-term) planning is planning for the following three to five years. This level of planning will assist in determining where in the market the business wants to be, and what the business wants to achieve in relation to its competitors. **Tactical (medium-term) planning** is flexible, adaptable planning, usually over one to two years, that assists in implementing the strategic plan. Tactical planning allows the business to respond quickly to changes. The emphasis is on how the objectives will be achieved through the allocation of resources. **Operational (short-term) planning** provides specific details about the way in which the business will operate in the short term. Management controls the day-to-day operations that contribute to achieving short-term actions and objectives. Examples of operational plans are daily and weekly production schedules.

__Strategic planning__ is planning for the following three to five years. This level of planning will assist in determining where in the market the business wants to be, and what the business wants to achieve in relation to its competitors.

__Tactical planning__ is flexible, adaptable planning, usually over one to two years, that assists in implementing the strategic plan.

__Operational planning__ provides specific details about the way in which the business will operate in the short term.

__Organising__ is the structuring of the organisation to translate plans and the business's objectives into action.

Management as organising

Organising is the next part of the process when management puts into practice the objectives that were determined in the planning stage. Organising is determining what is to be done, who is to do it and how it is to be done. It is organising the financial, human and material resources to achieve the objectives of the organisation.

Management has to coordinate activities to **translate plans into reality** — that is, to ensure that the objectives of the strategic, tactical and operational plans are achieved.

__Translating plans into reality__ means using the strategic, tactical and operational plans to achieve the objectives of the business.

The __organisation process__ is the range of activities that translate the objectives of a business into reality.

The organisation process

The **organisation process** is the range of activities that translate the objectives of a business into reality. These activities include the following three steps:

1. *Determining the work activities.* The work activities required to achieve management objectives must be determined. Work activities are then usually broken down into smaller steps.
2. *Classifying and grouping activities.* Once the work activities of a business have been broken down into smaller steps, similar activities can be grouped together. This improves efficiency by enabling the most appropriate allocation of resources. For example, it is common practice to group activities into departments or sections and allocate employees and supervisors to each section or department.

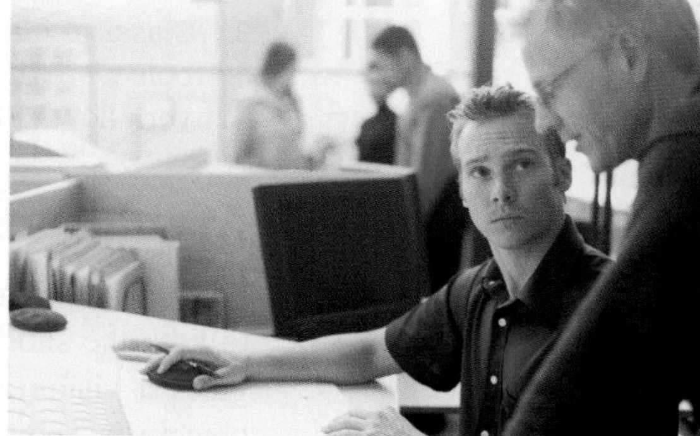

Figure 2.8 Effective delegation can increase productivity and efficiency, and increase job satisfaction for the employee.

The way that management views its employees will determine the level of responsibility and authority given to individuals for the purpose of achieving organisational objectives.

If a firm adopts total quality management (TQM) as its approach, it will emphasise teamwork and shared responsibility for achieving organisational objectives. If a firm adopts a more traditional approach, management may allocate supervisors who have direct control and authority to ensure that work processes are carried out.

Controlling *compares what was intended to happen with what has actually occurred.*

3 *Assigning work and delegating authority.* The next step in the organisation process is to determine who is to carry out the work, and who has the responsibility to ensure that the work is carried out. Delegation also involves ensuring that the person who has been given responsibility does carry out the processes.

Management as controlling

Controlling compares what was intended to happen with what has actually occurred. If there is a discrepancy between performance and objectives, changes and improvements can be made.

Traditional management control involves checking procedures and products at the *end* of the production process. The concept of control *throughout* the whole process is relatively new and is part of quality control practices developed and used extensively in Japan. Total quality management (TQM) and quality controls are now in place in many Australian businesses.

Control processes

As you learned in the preliminary course, there are three steps in the **control process** (see figure 2.9).

The control process

1. Establish standards in line with the firm's objectives and influences from employees, management, industry and government.

2. Measure performance and determine how comparisons will be made against standards or benchmarks.

3. Take corrective action — changing activities, processes and personnel to ensure that the objectives of the business have been met.

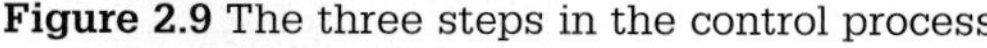

Figure 2.9 The three steps in the control process

The ***control process*** *involves establishing standards in line with the objectives of the organisation, measuring the performance of the organisation against those standards or benchmarks and making changes where necessary to ensure that the objectives of the organisation have been met.*

Benchmarking compares the strengths and weaknesses of an organisation against those of other businesses, with the aim of reforming those processes that are not achieving the organisation's objectives.

Figure 2.10 Sometimes managers lose sight of the reason for establishing standards.

Hierarchical organisational structure based on division of labour

Pioneering economist Adam Smith was the first to identify, in his famous book *The wealth of nations* (1776), the fact that when work activities are broken up into smaller and more specialised tasks productivity increases. Adam Smith called this the **division** or **specialisation of labour**.

Division of labour allows each employee to become more proficient by repeatedly doing the same specialised task. Overall, productivity improves compared to an organisational structure where the one person attempts to perform every task.

The division or specialisation of labour is not just a theory. Business organisational structures all over the world demonstrate specialisation. The way staff are organised and tasks allocated within a business depends on the management philosophy of the organisation — in this case, a traditional hierarchical organisational structure.

Think of a business as a three-storey pyramid (figure 2.11). This type of management structure is found in many businesses, and is based on the traditional managerial hierarchy. **Management hierarchy** is the arrangement that provides increasing authority at higher levels of the hierarchy. This means that senior managers have greater accountability, responsibility and power compared to those at lower levels of the pyramid.

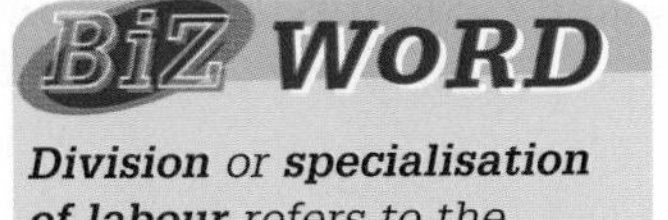

***Division** or **specialisation of labour** refers to the degree to which tasks are subdivided into separate jobs.*

***Management hierarchy** is the arrangement that provides increasing authority at higher levels of the hierarchy.*

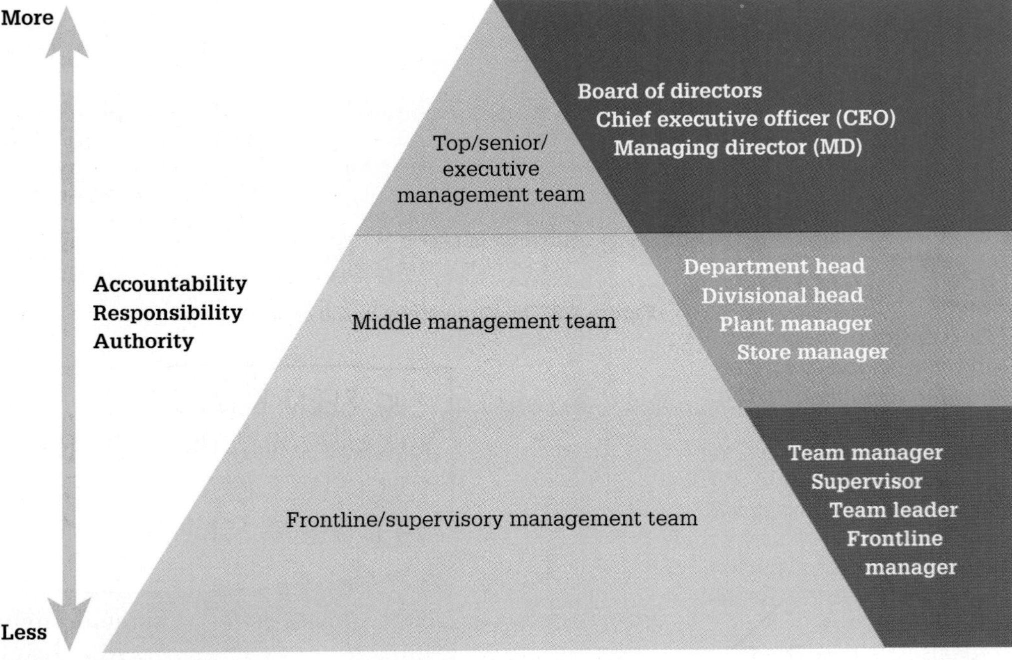

Figure 2.11 A management hierarchy. The coordinated effort of all three levels of management is required to achieve the goals of the business.

In The Wealth of Nations Adam Smith also discussed the disadvantages of the division of labour. The monotonous, mechanical regularity imposed on the worker stifled creativity. Gone was a sense of pride in his or her work. It was replaced by tedious, boring, and repetitive tasks, especially when there was too much specialisation.

The primary characteristic of traditional hierarchical organisational structures has been the grouping of people according to the specialised functions they perform (see figure 2.12). These may include marketing, finance, administration and production. Even within each of these functional areas tasks are further subdivided into specialised jobs. People within the marketing division, for example, have specialised tasks to perform, such as sales, administration, creative design, copyright and market analysis. The same principle applies to sporting teams. For example, a hockey team has members who specialise in certain positions, such as coach, captain, winger, goalie or centre. The team is organised in this way to offer the best combination of people's talents to achieve productivity, in this case, the team performing its best.

*A **chain of command** is a system that determines responsibility, supervision and accountability of members of the organisation.*

Characteristics of the pyramid-shaped organisational structure include:

- rigid lines of communication
- numerous levels of management, from managing director to supervisors
- clearly distinguishable organisational positions, roles and responsibilities
- hierarchical, linear flows of information and direction, with a large amount of information directed downwards
- a **chain of command** which shows who is responsible to whom.

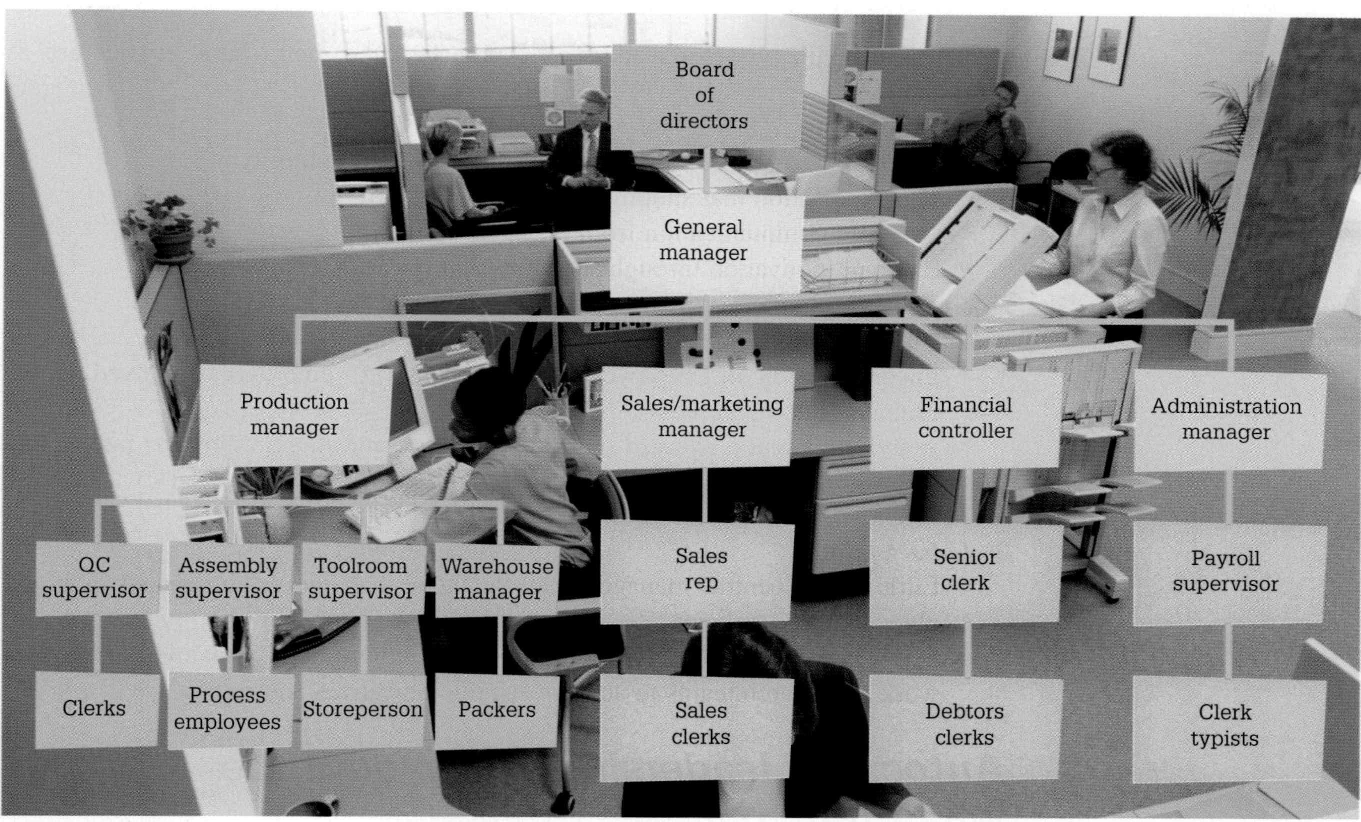

Figure 2.12 Typical pyramid-shaped, hierarchical organisational model

Leadership styles

There are a range of theories relating to leadership styles. One theory places the extremes of leadership style on a continuum (figure 2.13) with the autocratic manager at one end through to the laissez-faire manager at the other. An autocratic or authoritarian manager would be one who makes the decisions and tells employees what tasks to do and how to do them. A laissez-faire management style allows the workers to make the decisions and exercises very little authority over workers. The assumption is that all types of leaders would appear somewhere on that continuum.

Recent theories indicate that managers bring a range of styles to their leadership position that may change according to the situation. Most managers typically have a dominant style that they frequently adopt, and one or two 'backup' styles.

As figure 2.13 (on page 40) shows, leadership styles can vary from inflexible (autocratic/authoritarian) to flexible (laissez-faire).

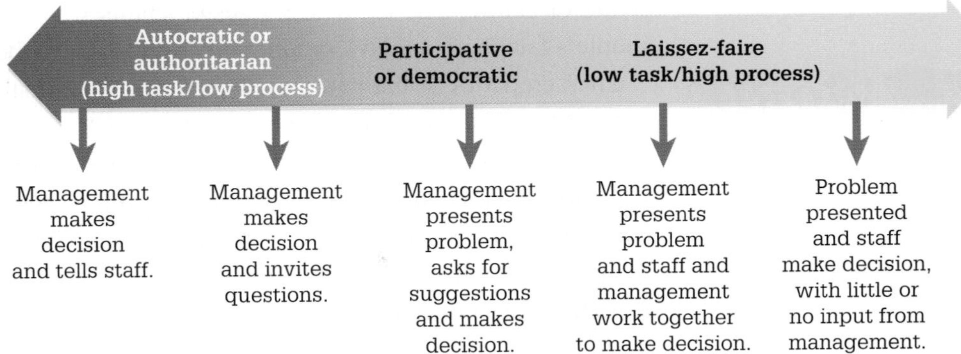
Autocratic or authoritarian (high task/low process)
Participative or democratic
Laissez-faire (low task/high process)
Management makes decision and tells staff.
Management makes decision and invites questions.
Management presents problem, asks for suggestions and makes decision.
Management presents problem and staff and management work together to make decision.
Problem presented and staff make decision, with little or no input from management.

Figure 2.13 One theory of leadership style — the continuum

The three main types of leadership approaches and their characteristics are as follows:

1 *Autocratic*
   - Strong, centralised control with a single source of authority
   - The expectation that subordinates follow orders
   - One-way communication from the top down
   - External motivation through sanctions and rewards
2 *Participative/democratic*
   - Authority and power decentralised throughout the organisation
   - Encouragement of employee empowerment (i.e. employees involved in the decision-making process)
   - A style frequently adopted by professional organisations where the intellectual abilities and skills of employees are similar and/or complementary
   - Employees are self-directed and intrinsically motivated
3 *Laissez-faire*
   - Little or no central management role other than the establishment of broad objectives and policies
   - A style frequently adopted in organisations where highly qualified employees work in research teams to achieve specific objectives and results.

Autocratic leadership style: 'do it the way I tell you'

BiZ WoRD

*A manager using an **autocratic leadership style** tends to make all the decisions, dictating work methods, limiting worker knowledge about what needs to be done to the next step to be performed, frequently checking employee performance and sometimes giving feedback that is punitive.*

Managers who adopt a strict classical–scientific approach commonly display an autocratic leadership style. A manager using an **autocratic leadership style** tends to make all the decisions, dictating work methods, limiting worker knowledge about what needs to be done to the next step to be performed, frequently checking employee performance and sometimes giving punitive feedback.

The autocratic manager generally provides clear directives by telling employees what to do, without listening to or permitting any employee input. This style of manager controls the people in the organisation closely and motivates through threats and disciplinary action. Such managers expect compliance and obedience, and give more negative and personalised feedback.

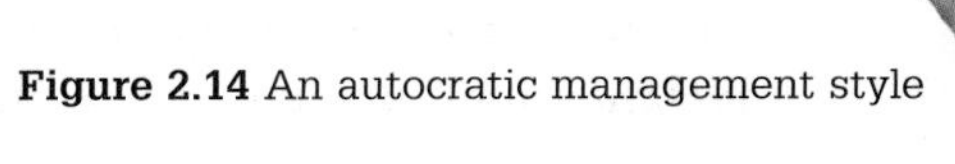

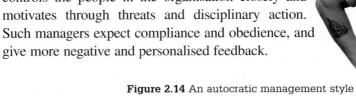

Figure 2.14 An autocratic management style

The autocratic style of leading can be effective in a time of crisis when immediate compliance with rules or procedure is needed, or in meeting an unexpected deadline when speed is important. An army officer, for example, would adopt this management style during military exercises. This approach is also effective when individuals lack skills and knowledge. A McDonald's crew trainer, for example, may adopt this style when supervising new employees. It is generally accepted, however, that this style does not encourage the best performance from employees.

EXERCISE 2.2 Revision

1. Explain the difference between strategic, tactical and operational planning.
2. Explain why the organising function is important to a business.
3. Explain why the controlling function is an important part of the management process.
4. How does controlling relate to the planning, organising and leading processes?
5. How and why have control procedures changed over time?
6. Why are management controls important?
7. Outline how the practice of division of labour has influenced the organisational structure of many businesses.
8. What is meant by the term 'management hierarchy'?
9. List the three main levels of management.
10. Describe the relationship between an organisational chart and an organisation's chain of command. If you were new to a business, how could an organisational chart help you become oriented?
11. Describe the leadership style of each of the following managers.
    - (a) The manager believes that once goals have been set, each person should have enough motivation to achieve them.
    - (b) The manager sets high standards of performance and has little sympathy for those who do not meet the standards.
    - (c) The manager takes care to explain why something must be done in a certain way.
    - (d) The manager tries to persuade staff to accept a decision.
    - (e) The manager rewards good work but does not punish poor performance.
    - (f) The manager believes that developing close personal relationships with staff is the mark of a good manager.
    - (g) The manager believes that job security and fringe benefits are important for employee job satisfaction.
    - (h) The manager persuades the employees to do their best.
12. Describe the situations when an autocratic management style would be appropriate.

Extension

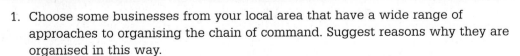

1. Choose some businesses from your local area that have a wide range of approaches to organising the chain of command. Suggest reasons why they are organised in this way.
2. 'The three levels of planning — strategic, tactical and operational — correspond to the three levels of management — top, middle and frontline.' Outline the relationship between the level of planning and the level of management.

3. Interview a manager of a business and find out the types of controls used in the business. Ask the manager to outline:
   (a) the difference between prevention, concurrent or feedback controls
   (b) the importance of control measures.
4. 'Managers who adopt a strict autocratic management style normally organise their business along traditional hierarchical lines.' Elaborate.

2.3 Behavioural management theories

Scientific management principles did not always lead to increased productivity due to the repetitive and boring nature of many jobs and the dehumanising structure of the workplace. Approximately 50 years after the emergence of scientific management ideas, behavioural or 'human relations' theories surfaced. The behavioural school recognised that, to make substantial productivity gains, worker participation in the production process was required. It acknowledged the workers' contribution to output.

*The **behavioural approach** to management stresses that people (employees) should be the main focus of the way in which the business is organised.*

Figure 2.15 Harvard professor Elton Mayo (1880–1949), founder of the behavioural approach to management

Advocates of the **behavioural approach** to management stress that people (employees) should be the main focus of the way the business is organised. They believe that successful management depends largely on the manager's ability to understand and work with people who have a variety of diverse backgrounds, hopes, desires and expectations. The development of this humanistic approach has greatly influenced management theory and practice.

One major contributor to behavioural management theories was Elton Mayo (1880–1949). Mayo (see figure 2.15), is considered the founder of industrial psychology. Through his revolutionary experiments, conducted at the Western Electric Hawthorne Company in Chicago (see the Snapshot 'Elton Mayo — the Hawthorne Studies (1927–1932)'), he discovered what became known as the 'Hawthorne effect', which demonstrates that meeting people's social needs has a significant impact on productivity. Two significant results from the research were that:

- worker satisfaction to a large extent is non-economic; that is, workers have social needs in addition to economic needs
- being made to feel part of a team increases job satisfaction and output.

Elton Mayo — the Hawthorne studies (1927–1932)

The Western Electric Company's Hawthorne factory manufactured a range of electrical components such as relay assemblies. Mayo wanted to find out what effect fatigue and monotony had on employee productivity. He selected six female employees from the assembly line, segregated them from the rest of the factory and placed them under the control of a supportive supervisor. The team was involved in assembling telephone relays. Mayo made frequent changes to their working conditions, always discussing and explaining the changes in advance.

To his amazement, Mayo realised that productivity had increased completely independent of any of the changes he made. The six individual employees had become a team and together eagerly participated in the experiment. They were happy knowing that they were working without coercion from senior managers or limitations from the workplace structure. They felt they were working under less pressure, not being pushed around or bossed by anyone. Under these conditions, they developed an increased sense of responsibility, with discipline coming from within the team.

Mayo's findings were at odds with F. W. Taylor's theory, which stated that workers are only motivated by self-interest. If Taylor was correct, the women's productivity should have decreased when Mayo returned them to longer working hours. However, Mayo realised that the women had formed a harmonious team and felt happier at work, which raised their self-esteem. The women talked, joked and began to meet socially outside of work. Mayo had discovered an elementary concept that seems obvious today: workplaces are social environments and employees are often motivated by much more than self-interest.

The section of the Hawthorne studies that examined the beneficial effects of positive and supportive supervision and the impact of teamwork became known as the Hawthorne effect.

Figure 2.16 Employees have social needs in addition to economic needs.

SNaPSHOT Questions

1. According to Elton Mayo's research, why did productivity increase even after the original working conditions were reintroduced?
2. What is the Hawthorne effect?
3. Imagine you are a manager for a small business. Explain what impact Mayo's research would have on:
   (a) how you organise your workplace
   (b) the management practices you would use.

A different value system emerged from the contributions of the behavioural theorists. Managers were now required to meet the social needs of their employees in addition to production efficiency. Skills in communication, social motivation and democratic leadership were quickly acquired.

__Leading__ is having a vision of where the business should be in the long and short term and being able to direct and motivate the human resources in an organisation to achieve its objectives.

__Delegation__ is the handing over of certain tasks or responsibilities to an employee who is suitably capable and qualified to carry them out.

Management as leading

Leading is having a vision of where the business should be in the long and short term and being able to direct and motivate the human resources in an organisation to achieve its objectives.

The type of leadership in a business depends on managers' attitudes and assumptions about people in the organisation, and the level of consultation and participation in the organisation.

A good leader is someone who:

- sets an example and earns the respect of employees
- listens to the opinions and ideas of others
- **delegates** tasks to suitable employees.

Management is:

- *coping with complexity*
- *planning and budgeting*
- *organising and staffing*
- *controlling and problem solving.*

Leadership is:

- *coping with change*
- *determining direction*
- *aligning people*
- *motivating people.*

- conveys the goals of the business to workers and motivates them to achieve those goals
- avoids 'jargon' when talking to employees and has an understanding of their needs
- demonstrates flexibility in dealing with situations and allows employees to take on responsibility when appropriate
- understands the technical aspects of the industry or business

Numerous books have been written about what makes a good leader. Some people believe that good leaders are 'born' rather than 'made'. They argue that the characteristics needed to be a good leader are part of an individual's unique personality and cannot be learnt from textbooks. Other people, however, argue that with appropriate training and coaching, the skills of leadership can be learned. Whichever the case, managers who display 'daring leadership' are best able to inspire their employees (see the Snapshot 'Daring leadership for the twenty-first century').

Daring leadership for the twenty-first century

A person who leads through management can be highly competent in organising people and enhancing their relationships in ways that enlarge their life and energy, or the manager can offer more to the role of leadership. Even in a management position, there is usually room for a new vision of the task, its environment and the possibilities that may lie dormant in those who work there. In other words, there is a choice to be made between being good at your job as a manager or inspiring in your job as manager. To choose the latter is to enter a life with more risks and adventure, but one that may move things forward in ways nobody had anticipated. This involves making decisions where there cannot, at that point, be any clarity. It is about wisdom and judgement when everything is not yet in place. This is the nature of leadership.

I believe that, although the manager has a grave responsibility to assume final responsibility for decisions, much of the envisioning of the future can also be corporate. It is about gathering people around you who will sit and spin ideas off each other, rather than competing for the best idea of their own to be the one. In my view, women managers often have a stronger cultural hold on this manner of working. We assume that to have our idea taken and reshaped by others so what emerges at the end is very different does not mean that we 'lost', but that we all created something together. A good manager allows this to happen by putting in his or her own idea to start things off and then modelling the process by genuinely letting that idea go or be changed and developed in response to the group. The manager also often has the capacity to keep summarising where the discussion is and 'value-adding' to what is happening without stopping the flow.

Source: D. McRae-McMahon, *Daring leadership for the twenty-first century*, ABC Books, 2001, pp. 72, 74.

BiZ FaCT

One contemporary, and somewhat controversial, viewpoint on the much-debated topic of effective leadership is that put forward by Robert K. Greenleaf. In the books Reflections on leadership *and* Insights on leadership, *he argues that a truly effective leader is a manager who serves. He outlines a practical philosophy of 'servant-leadership' which holds that people who choose to first serve, and then to lead, make the most effective leaders, because they expand services to others. Servant-leaders encourage collaboration, trust, listening, foresight and ethical use of power.*

SNaPSHOT Questions

1. According to Dorothy McRae-McMahon, what does the 'nature of leadership' involve?
2. What role should a manager play in developing new ideas?

Management as motivating

'Sometimes the most effective motivation is just to say "thank you".'

Zig Ziglar, motivator and trainer

Some people work harder than others. An employee with outstanding abilities may constantly be outperformed by someone with average skills. The difference between the two employees is their level of motivation. Motivated workers will always perform at a higher level than unmotivated workers. To some extent, a high level of employee motivation is determined by management practices. Efficient managers need to put in place work practices which motivate their employees; they must be aware of the *human factor* involved in the business organisation.

Elton Mayo's Hawthorne studies (see pages 42–3) highlighted the importance of the human factor in employee performance. Merely asking employees to participate in the research gave them a sense of involvement in their jobs. These employees — perhaps for the first time — felt as though they were of value and importance to the business. It was this sense of importance that acted as the motivating force that resulted in improved employee productivity.

Motivation *is the individual, internal process that energises, directs and sustains an individual's behaviour. It is the personal force that causes a person to behave in a particular way.*

Motivation is the individual, internal process that energises, directs and sustains an individual's behaviour. It is the personal force that causes a person to behave in a particular way.

The Hawthorne studies revealed that such human factors as recognition, self-worth and positive reinforcement are at least as important to motivation as external factors such as pay rates and working conditions. In some cases they may be more important. From this initial research came a flood of other behavioural management theories focusing on the area of motivation. Overwhelmingly, the research highlights the fact that management would do best to provide a work environment that maximises employee satisfaction. Good managers, therefore, should also be good motivators, encouraging employees and using positive reinforcement to influence behaviour. The overall success of the business largely depends on motivated and skilled employees who are committed to the business's goals — that is, everyone working towards a common purpose.

Figure 2.17 Placing trust in employees and providing them with the freedom to achieve success is fundamental to increasing staff morale and motivation.

How then does a manager go about the task of motivating the business's employees? This question is often asked and has resulted in a wide variety of answers. Numerous studies have identified such diverse factors as trust, respect for the individual, positive reinforcement, empowerment, enhancing self-esteem, employee participation, rewarding team performance, employee encouragement and so on. Managers can use a variety of techniques to improve employee motivation. However, what the majority of these motivation techniques have in common is the need to develop a workplace culture that fosters employee motivation. In his book *Punished by rewards*, Alfie Kohn suggests that the manager's primary role, if he or she wishes to motivate employees, is to create the appropriate *conditions* within the workplace (see the Snapshot 'Create the conditions for authentic motivation' on page 46).

Create the conditions for authentic motivation

Alan S. Blinder, a Princeton University economist, recently edited a research anthology entitled *Paying for productivity: a look at the evidence.* He summarised its findings as follows: 'Changing the way workers are *treated* may boost productivity more than changing the way they are *paid*.' This makes sense because treating workers decently allows them to become motivated, and motivation in turn boosts productivity. If motivation and productivity are in short supply in our workplaces, this may just have something to do with the way workers are treated there.

When employees are asked to describe the conditions they need, or when reflective and experienced managers are asked to describe the conditions they try to create, a variety of suggestions are offered. But there is substantial overlap in the ideas, a consensus that people in managerial positions ought to do these things:

Watch: Don't put employees under surveillance; look for problems that need to be solved and help people solve them.

Listen: Attend seriously and respectfully to the concerns of workers and try to imagine how various situations look from their points of view.

Talk: Provide plenty of informational feedback. People need a chance to reflect on what they are doing right, to learn what needs improvement, and to discuss how to change.

Think: If one's current managerial style consists of using extrinsic motivators, controlling people's behaviours, or simply exhorting them to work hard and become motivated, it is worth thinking carefully about the long-term impact of these strategies. It is also worth asking where they come from. A preference for using power in one's relationships with others, or a reaction to being controlled by one's own superiors, raises issues that demand attention.

Most of all, a manager committed to making sure that people are able and willing to do their best needs to attend to three fundamental factors. These can be abbreviated as the 'three C's' of motivation — to wit, the *collaboration* that defines the context of work, the *content* of the tasks, and the extent to which people have some *choice* about what they do and how they do it. ... The same model is also a useful way of thinking about what happens at school and at home.

Source: A. Kohn, *Punished by rewards*, Houghton Mifflin, New York, 1993, pp. 186–187

SNaPSHOT Questions

1. Describe the relationship between employee motivation and productivity.
2. Outline the four strategies managers can use to improve employee motivation.

***Communication** is the exchange of information between people; the sending and receiving of messages.*

Management as communicating

One of the most difficult challenges for managers is getting employees to understand and want to achieve the business's goals. Effective communication is at the heart of meeting this challenge. **Communication** is the exchange of information between people; the sending and receiving of messages.

Many managers talk too much; express themselves poorly; have difficulty writing a coherent letter or email, making an interesting speech or giving concise instructions.

Communication is one of the easiest and, at the same time, most difficult of management activities. This is because of the complex nature of communication. Unless managers are effective communicators and able to share their thoughts and plans, they will find it difficult to influence others.

Figure 2.18 Poor communication often leads to conflict in the workplace.

Effective communication is a crucial part of every manager's job (see the Snapshot 'Dr Annabelle Duncan'). It encompasses every management function and role. Without effective communication the most carefully detailed plans and brilliant strategies will most probably fail. Many studies have shown that the performance of both individuals and businesses improves when managerial communication is effective. This is especially so when open communication is used to motivate employees by providing them with information regarding the business's goals, plans and overall financial results. Whenever a manager operates on the communication principle of 'tell the employees only what they need to know and nothing else', then the workers will not be motivated to achieve common goals because they do not know what the goals are.

Dr Annabelle Duncan

POSITION: Associate Director, Bio 21 Molecular Science and Biotechnology Institute

ORGANISATION: The University of Melbourne

QUALIFICATIONS: BSc, Postgraduate Diploma of Science, MSc, PhD

I am responsible for the administration of the institute. This includes financial management, legal matters, science services, and development and implementation of business strategies and plans. I am also responsible for commercial and business developments and for liaising with corporate sponsors as well as with state, federal and government agencies.

Many paradigm shifting scientific breakthroughs come at the intersection of disciplines. The purpose of the institute is to bring together researchers from several different disciplines to work together to address major challenges. We hope to make major breakthroughs and to translate the research to application, either through existing companies, or through the development of new companies.

Given the breadth of my role, there is no typical day. I call upon my scientific background, especially the analytical skills acquired through a science education, but also rely on communication skills, diplomacy and people skills to carry out my job.

I would advise young people to obtain a broad education and wide experience in a range of roles.

SNaPSHOT Questions

BiZ FaCT

The 'flattening' of organisation structures at a local level can occur as part of restructuring towards a more global or 'vertical' reporting structure — a trend that is apparent in many multinational organisations today. For example, in the 1980s, Philips Electronics had 16 000 local employees working in more than 80 manufacturing and retailing subsidiaries. In the mid to late 1990s, it downsized its local operations, sold unprofitable sections of the business, removed the chief executive at the local level and restructured globally around the product divisions. In 2000, it employed 1200 people in eight product divisions that reported vertically to headquarters throughout the world.

__Flatter organisational structures__ have evolved due to a 'de-layering' of management structures resulting in the elimination of one or more management levels.

1. Why do you think reducing staff numbers would be a difficult management situation?
2. One of the basic roles of management is communication. Why would this be important to Annabelle's role?

Effective management communication is an area in which Australian managers compare unfavourably with their overseas counterparts. The Karpin Report, as well as other studies, has commented that this is a management task on which Australian managers constantly rate poorly.

Flat organisational structure

The demise of the traditional pyramid-shaped hierarchical organisational structure has been predicted for many years. Increasingly it was being seen by managers as obsolete. Initial changes were slow in coming and largely unnoticeable. However, the pace and degree of change has picked up dramatically in many businesses. Rapid advances in technology, especially the spread of the Internet, coupled with the significant pressures on businesses from increased competition due to the forces of globalisation, have resulted in changes to organisational structures. The traditional structure is now regarded by many as too slow and unresponsive to rapid change, expensive to maintain, stifling of creativity and too difficult to manage due to its many different layers. While the traditional organisational structure is still evident in many businesses, its value is being questioned. Hierarchical boundaries are breaking down and people and functions are mixing together to create more flexible and responsive companies. Such companies can adapt quickly to meet changing consumer needs and market conditions. These dramatic shifts are resulting in much **flatter organisational structures**.

Firms that adopt a flatter management structure reduce the number of levels of management, giving greater responsibility to individuals in the organisation (see figure 2.19). A flatter structure means that there is a wider span of control: individuals who have responsibility for others will have a larger number of people to supervise. However, the people in the flatter structure are given greater freedom and autonomy to carry out their tasks.

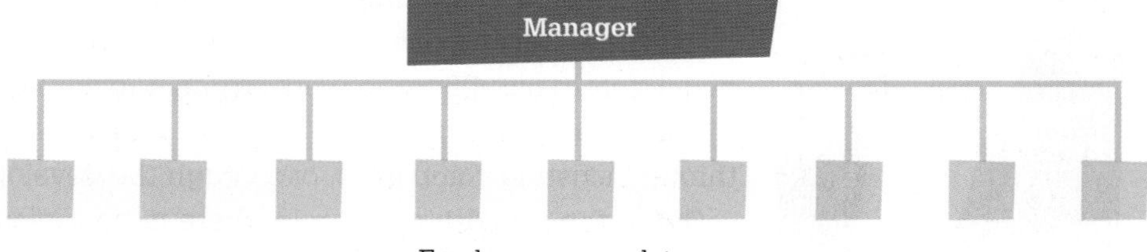

Figure 2.19 Flatter management structure — a typical organisation chart. The span of control is wider and management has more direct contact with employees.

The characteristics of flat organisational structures include:

- 'de-layering' of the traditional hierarchical structure at several levels; for example, middle-management and supervisory levels

- establishment of market-focused work cells, with concentration on one product, process or customer
- making each work cell responsible for a wide range of production functions, which encourages multiskilling, quality control and maintenance.

Teams

BiZ WoRD

Teamwork *involves people who interact regularly and coordinate their work towards a common goal.*

Coupled closely with the emergence of the flatter organisational structures is the development of work teams. **Teamwork** involves people who interact regularly and coordinate their work towards a common goal.

This not-so-quiet revolution is rapidly transforming workplace cultures, practices, operations and productivity levels. Many businesses are starting to realise that a team approach can be the catalyst for superior performance. Many businesses are replacing the traditional linear sequence of research, development, manufacturing and marketing with a process centred on teams of specialists from all these areas who work together as one unit (see figure 2.20).

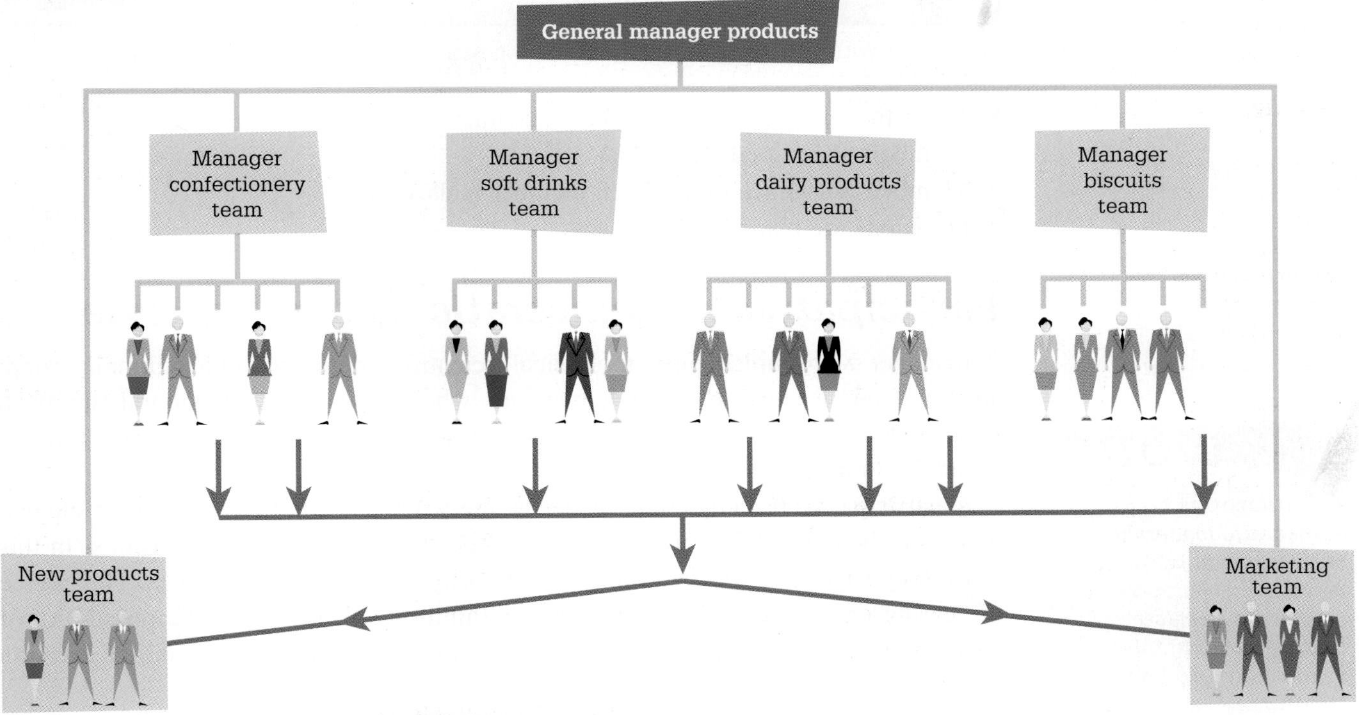

Figure 2.20 Team structure

Work teams can be organised in many different ways. These include self-directed work teams, quality circles, volunteer or nominated teams, project teams and task forces.

Understanding how such teams function, that is, understanding the group dynamics of teams and teamwork, is vital for managers operating in the modern workplace. It is essential that managers foster a sense of cohesion between team members, otherwise the team is no more than a collection of individuals all working separately. Such teams have no common purpose and therefore lack any sense of belonging to the organisation. In such cases it is quite common for conflict to develop between team members. Ultimately the team's effectiveness will be diminished.

As explained in chapter 1, as team structures are implemented, managers see their role change from that of controller to that of facilitator. This will require a significant change in how managers approach their jobs. At the core of this change will be a need for a high degree of trust between the team members themselves and between the team members and the manager. Trust is a key element in team effectiveness. To achieve it requires a move away from an autocratic leadership style to one that is more participative or democratic.

Figure 2.21 Without a sense of belonging and cohesion, team effectiveness is diminished.

Some of the characteristics of effective teams:

- Members share a common goal.
- Members trust each other. Each member feels valued.
- Decisions are made by concensus.

Participative or democratic leadership style

*A **participative** or **democratic leadership style** is one in which the manager consults with employees to ask their suggestions and then seriously considers those suggestions when making decisions.*

A manager who implemented a classical–scientific approach would normally adopt an autocratic leadership style; a manager who practised a behavioural approach would tend to use a more **participative** or **democratic leadership style** (refer to figure 2.13 on page 40).

A participative or democratic leader is one who asks employees for their suggestions and then seriously considers those suggestions when making decisions. In this sense they share their decision-making authority with their subordinates. The degree of sharing can range from the manager outlining a solution, with the possibility of changes being suggested, to allowing the team to participate in the initial decision making.

Sometimes referred to as the 'we' approach, participative or democratic managers recognise the strengths and abilities of employees and actively involve them in the decision-making process. This style is frequently practised in those organisations that have flatter management structures and work teams and is especially effective in situations where there are diverse groups to be coordinated. The contribution of employees is valued, and employees assist in the decision-making process through regular meetings. Employees have a commitment to the business's objectives because of their own input into the organisation. There is no simple answer to the question: 'What leadership style does a good manager possess?' Management is an art, not a science. This means that no simple management formula can be applied to deal effectively with all workplace situations (see the Snapshot 'Marc Lewis — management consultant').

Marc Lewis — management consultant

Marc Lewis, of Lewis Consulting Group (LCG), specialises in assisting organisations to improve the managerial skills of their frontline supervisors. As many organisations adopt flatter management structures, their frontline supervisors are being asked to undertake a greater range of management roles and leadership styles.

During Marc's presentation of one of these workshops, he met Sou Chen and Glenn Ravizza, two supervisors employed by a major food manufacturer based in Newcastle.

During the workshop, Marc asked the question: 'What skills and leadership style does a good manager possess?' While all the participants had an opinion, it was clear to Marc that Sou and Glenn had totally different views. According to Sou, good managers, above all else, must be technically proficient. They should know how to plan the required inputs and allocate resources effectively; they should understand production processes, workflow and job design; they should know how to control and monitor work performance and costs of production; and they should be able to make and implement decisions. Sou believed that a manager should direct her or his staff, tell them what was required, and monitor their performance closely. If employees did not perform to an acceptable standard, then they should be disciplined immediately. Sou did not believe in 'suitcase management' — carrying people who are not performing.

Glenn disagreed. According to him, good managers must know how to motivate employees; they must allow employees to be involved in the decision-making process and to take responsibility for implementing those decisions; and they must communicate effectively, empower team members, and understand human behaviour. Glenn believe that a manager should consult with his or her staff. If an employee was under-performing then he or she should be counselled and, if necessary, provided with training. If a manager is required to discipline someone, it should be done fairly and in accordance with organisational policy. Glenn also believed it is important to encourage employees and praise their efforts.

SNaPSHOT Questions

1. What is meant by the term 'flatter management structure'?
2. According first to Sou and then to Glenn, what leadership style should a good manager display?
3. Which leadership style would you prefer to work under, Sou's or Glenn's? Give reasons for your answer.

EXERCISE 2.3 Revision

1. According to behavioural management theory, what was required to improve worker productivity?
2. What is the Hawthorne effect?
3. Briefly outline the two significant results of Elton Mayo's Hawthorne studies.
4. What is meant by the term 'leading'? Do you think leadership skills can be learned? Give reasons for your answer.
5. In groups of three or four complete the following activities:
   (a) Prepare a list of five or six people who are effective leaders.
   (b) Against each name list the personal leadership qualities each person displays.
   (c) What leadership qualities do the individuals tend to have in common?
   (d) Compare your answers with other groups.
6. Explain the meaning of the term 'motivation'. What did the Hawthorne studies reveal about employee motivation?
7. Explain why effective communication is crucial within a business.
8. Draw a hierarchical and a flat organisational structure. Contrast the two diagrams by listing their differences.
9. Why are work teams becoming more common in today's businesses?
10. You have been appointed team leader of a new work group. Describe some of the strategies you could use to develop a sense of cohesion within the group.
11. You have been asked by your manager to prepare a report outlining the major differences between autocratic and participative or democratic leadership styles. In your report also list the advantages of each leadership style.

Extension

1. Research Douglas McGregor's 'theory X and theory Y'. What are the implications of these two theories?
2. 'Inefficient communication is the fault of the sender.' Provide reasons to support this proposition.
3. Why would employees favour the behavioural approach over the classical–scientific approach to management?
4. Why would the development of behavioural management theories be called a significant turning point in the evolution of management theories?
5. Reflect on what you have learned in this section. Prepare a report outlining the main ideas and concepts. Present your report orally to the rest of the class.

2.4 Political management theories

BiZ WORD

Politics *is the use of methods, sometimes unstated and/or unethical, to obtain power or advancement within an organisation.*

Have you ever been involved with a sports team and discovered that some team members tried to gain preference from the coach or captain? Or perhaps two members of your peer group engaged in a power struggle over who was going to be the group leader. In either of these situations you are witnessing some form of political behaviour. **Politics**, in this situation, is the use of methods, sometimes unstated and/or unethical, to obtain power or advancement within an organisation (see figure 2.22).

'It took me a long time to realise that power and politics are part of life in organisations everywhere. We have to learn to live with them and the more we understand them, the better we will be able to cope.'

Source: Charlies Handy, *Inside Organisations*, Penguin Books Australia, Melbourne, 1990, p. 115

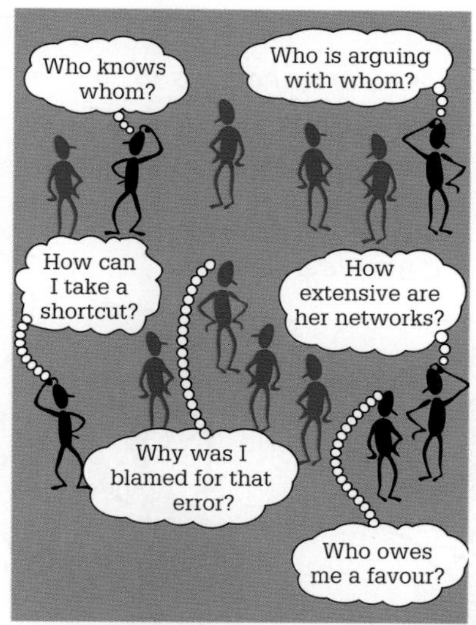

Figure 2.22 The politics of business

We are surrounded by political behaviour at work, school and home. Wherever people group together you will at some time be personally involved in the world of politics. It is an inescapable influence (see the Biz Fact on the left).

In an ideal world, everyone would be treated fairly. Lines of communication would be followed, the decision-making process would be transparent and understood by everyone, praise would be given on merit, desirable and not-so-desirable jobs would be divided equally and there would be no underhand or unscrupulous methods used to gain influence. Unfortunately, the world, and business organisations, are far from ideal. In reality, organisational politics is alive and well and how the business actually operates may be quite different from the formal organisational structure. Organisational life is often highly charged with political 'wheeling and dealing'. Such conduct within a business is referred to as the politics of the organisation.

***Organisational politics** are often the unwritten rules of work life. They involve the pursuit of self-interest through informal methods of gaining power or advantage.*

Organisational politics are often the unwritten rules of work life. They involve the pursuit of self-interest through informal methods of gaining power or advantage.

A business's structure, therefore, is the result of a power struggle by those within the organisation. In this sense, workplace behaviour can be equated to the behaviour sometimes displayed in the school playground, where a student or group of students will attempt to exert their influence over others.

Perceiving the workplace through a political philosophy highlights the need for managers to acquire new skills, such as understanding the role of power, negotiation and bargaining, identifying or forming coalitions, and managing conflict among various stakeholders.

Uses of power and influence

Power, and its use or abuse in influencing others, is the central theme in many forms of literature. **Power** is the ability to gather together resources to get something done.

***Power** is the ability to gather together resources to get something done.*

'Power tends to corrupt and absolute power corrupts absolutely' (Lord Acton, British historian, 1887). 'Power is the ultimate aphrodisiac' (Henry Kissinger, former Secretary of State, United States of America, 1973–1976).

Power, used correctly, can enable managers to achieve, for themselves and for others, individual success as well as the business's goals. However, when power is used incorrectly the organisation's goals will never be achieved. The use of power can either be the 'stuff of fantasies or the stuff of nightmares' (Thomas L. Quick, American management consultant, 1985). This means the use of power can influence others in either a positive and constructive way or a negative and destructive one.

According to Claire Polosak, human resources consultant and Managing Director of People First Consulting Group: 'When I use power effectively I can influence people within the organisation; the people I depend upon. I strongly believe managers should develop their own power so as to coordinate and more effectively influence and support the work of employees. Of course, power that is exercised by dictatorial methods is not real power. Quite the reverse. Whenever a manager has to resort to abusive power-play methods I know that this manager has no real power to bring about positive outcomes for the business or the employees' (see figure 2.23).

Figure 2.23 The abuse of power

If managers understand the nature of power and how it can be used to empower others, then they have an advantage when it comes to influencing others and getting things accomplished.

Why then do people accept the influence of a manager? Often, they do so because of the power base of the manager. The way in which this power to influence people is used depends on what the manager wants to achieve. Management can be about getting people to do what you want them to do, or about encouraging and supporting people to show initiative in achieving the goals of the business. There are a number of sources of power and these can be categorised as legitimate, expert, referent, reward or coercive:

- *Legitimate power.* Legitimate power is given because of the status or position of the person within the firm. Managers will normally have a certain amount of formal or legitimate authority.
- *Expert power.* Expert power emerges as a result of a person's skills and expertise, and it is usually the reason for which the person was employed.
- *Referent power.* Referent power comes from people's individual characteristics — their personality or charisma — and inspires and influences others.
- *Reward power.* Reward power relates to the rewards or compensation a manager distributes for doing a good job.
- *Coercive power.* Coercive power controls individuals in the organisation by the actions or words of the manager. For example, a coercive manager might threaten to fire an employee if deadlines are not met.

Matching sources of power to situations

Different situations may require the use of different types of power. Managers need to match their style to the situation. For example, if an organisation is about to introduce major changes, the use of expert and referent powers will be more effective than

BiZ FaCT

Legitimate power is effective in situations in which there is a need for the manager to be seen as the expert and when high-level decisions need to be made.

Expert power is effective in situations in which performance standards are important and each member of the organisation is working towards organisational objectives.

Referent power is effective when employees need inspiration to achieve performance objectives.

Reward power is effective when employees can participate in the organisation and there is an acknowledgement that employees are experts in their area.

Coercive power can be effective in times of crisis or danger when immediate compliance with instructions is required.

Social and workplace changes have led managers to rely less on the exercise of formal authority for getting the job done. Coercive power has been replaced by expert and reward powers.

Win–win

Win–win is a frame of mind and heart that constantly seeks mutual benefit in all human interactions. Win–win means that agreements or solutions are mutually beneficial, mutually satisfying. With a win–win solution, all parties feel good about the decision and feel committed to the action plan. Win–win sees life as a cooperative, not a competitive, arena. Most people tend to think in terms of dichotomies: strong or weak, hardball or softball, win or lose. But that kind of thinking is fundamentally flawed. It's based on power and position rather than on principle. Win–win is based on the paradigm that there is plenty for everybody, that one person's success is not achieved at the expense or exclusion of the success of others.

Win–win is a belief in the Third Alternative. It's not your way or my way; it's a better way, a higher way.

Source: S. R. Covey, *The 7 habits of highly effective people*, The Business Library, imprint of Information Australia, 1989, p. 207.

coercive power. If deadlines must be met and production is behind schedule, reward and coercive power may be more effective. However, there are no rules for the use of power, and an effective manager will identify and use appropriate power as needed for the situation.

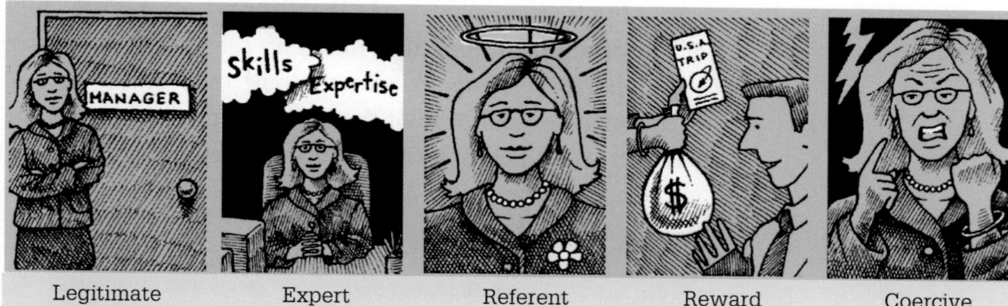

Figure 2.24 Sources of power in leading

Management as negotiating and bargaining

As previously explained, employees within all organisations often follow their own personal agendas; that is, they may put their own self-interest ahead of everything else. These agendas may sometimes run counter to or obstruct the overall goals of the business. Often the result of such a situation is conflict. At other times differences in attitudes, ideas and opinions between employees will require a mechanism for selecting the most appropriate course of action. It is in these situations that the manager is called upon to negotiate or bargain. **Negotiating** or **bargaining** is a decision-making process among people with different expectations. It attempts to bring about a solution that is agreeable to the greatest number of people.

Negotiating or bargaining is a fact of life for all managers. They are required to negotiate between the competing interests of the many stakeholders. Some 'give and take' may be required to satisfy all the competing interests. Negotiation or bargaining strategies are a crucial communication skill all managers need to develop and practise. One very successful strategy for effective negotiation that has gained prominence in recent years is the 'win–win' approach.

Stephen R. Covey, in his very successful book *The 7 habits of highly effective people*, outlines this method in the following way (see the Biz fact 'Win–win', on the left).

***Negotiating** or **bargaining** is a decision-making process among people with different expectations.*

Structures as coalitions

While the term 'politics' may offend many people because of its overtones of favouritism and sycophancy (or flattery), a manager needs to know about the politics of the workplace and the ways it influences the business. A manager adopting this management theory will be in a better position to view the organisation as a coalition of individuals or groups who are, for the most part, pursuing their own self-interest and personal agendas. Such a view allows the manager to be proactive and able to influence these coalitions.

A **coalition** is two or more people who combine their power to push or gain support for their ideas.

*A **coalition** is two or more people who combine their power to push or gain support for their ideas.*

Most organisations tend to have two distinct groups: those 'in power' and those 'out of power'. As well, those who want to be 'in power', if they cannot achieve this objective individually, will form coalitions. There is strength in numbers! Therefore, the structure of most businesses is based on the formal organisation, combined with the various coalitions and the informal interactions between the coalition groups.

Figuratively speaking, the formal groups are only the tip of the iceberg. The informal coalitions that make up the rest of the business's structure are formed by employees trying to achieve their own goals. In reality, these informal structures determine the future of the business just as much as the formal ones do. What a manager sees operating on the surface may in fact be a great deal different to what really happens (see figure 2.25).

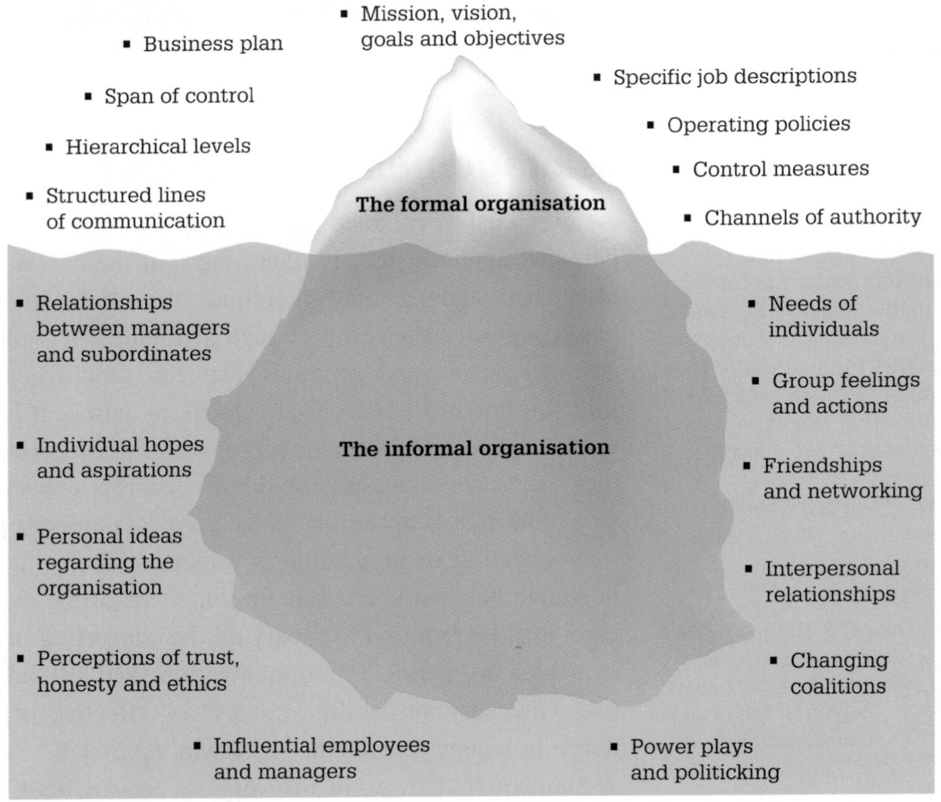

Figure 2.25 The organisational 'iceberg': formal and informal coalitions operate at and below the surface respectively.

Managers need to be aware of both the formal and informal coalitions within the workplace. Discussions held around the coffee machine, over a meal or via email could be just as meaningful and effective as formal meetings held in the conference room.

Stakeholder view

As outlined in chapter 1, there are a number of stakeholders in a business.

Stakeholders can form coalitions; however, these tend to alter over time. For example, the views of the employees and shareholders may sometimes be compatible and at other times incompatible. As well, stakeholders that are highly involved with the business today may be less involved tomorrow. To add further complexity, changes to stakeholder involvement may not occur uniformly in all sections of a large business. Modern managers are required to negotiate effectively between the various stakeholder groups.

A manager adopting a political perspective will view the success of the business as a balance between competing stakeholder demands. Such a manager sees his or her role as constantly identifying and monitoring any changes within the stakeholders' expectations. To assist in this role some businesses carry out a **stakeholder audit**. This involves identifying all the parties that could be affected by the business's performance and decisions.

*A **stakeholder audit** involves identifying all the parties that could be affected by the business's performance and decisions.*

Achieving a workable balance among the stakeholders is a never-ending challenge for all managers. Managers have an obligation to respond to stakeholders' needs.

2.5 Strengths and weaknesses of the classical, behavioural and political approaches

No one management theory provides *all* the answers. Each has its strengths and weaknesses as outlined in table 2.1.

A study of any business will reveal no one management theory is used exclusively. The practice of management does not fit so neatly into these theoretical ideas. As most managers are pragmatists, they will use whatever methods work. In doing so they will choose those ideas from a range of management theories, selecting the strengths and avoiding the weaknesses of each theory. A manager can also blend a number of different theories together as well as drawing upon past experience. In fact, many management experts argue that good management strategies are often the result of learning from past experience; successful managers learn from practice.

TABLE 2.1 The strengths and weaknesses of classical, behavioural and political management theories

Management theory	Strengths	Weaknesses
Classical–scientific	▪ Based on scientific principles ▪ Work methods may be improved through time and motion study ▪ Results in increased productivity ▪ Management may be trained ▪ Measurements may be analysed to verify improvements in output ▪ Individual's interests subordinated to the survival of the business ▪ Planning, organising and controlling are the central management functions ▪ Specialisation and division of labour ▪ Clear, orderly lines of communication and authority ▪ Emphasises the important role of money as a motivator	▪ Boredom resulting from production line approach ▪ Rigidity of autocratic leadership style ▪ Lack of employee empowerment ▪ Neglects the 'human' and social needs of employees ▪ Employees are motivated not only by material gain ▪ Today's better educated employees are less willing to accept formal authority ▪ Sense of impersonality and alienation between managers and employees ▪ Fails to acknowledge the informal organisational structures ▪ Overlooks employees' need for job satisfaction

(*continued*)

TABLE 2.1 *(continued)*		
Management theory	**Strengths**	**Weaknesses**
Behavioural	▪ Acknowledges the importance of the human dimension of work ▪ Integrates ideas from sociology, psychology and anthropology ▪ Outlines the importance of human resource managers ▪ Highlights the importance of communication, teamwork, group dynamics, motivation and leadership ▪ Stresses the importance of conflict resolution mechanisms ▪ Greater empowerment of employees due to flatter management structures ▪ Participative or democratic leadership style acknowledged ▪ By understanding basic psychology, managers are more able to prepare themselves for managing people.	▪ Complex theoretical concepts ▪ Positive results may not always be immediate ▪ Difficulty in accurately predicting human behaviour ▪ Some degree of conflict between the various behavioural theories ▪ No simple formulas can be designed to explain complex personal behaviour ▪ What motivates one individual may lessen another's motivation ▪ A management practice which was previously successful may not continue to work over time ▪ Many behavioural theories appear too abstract to apply to the 'real' world ▪ Vast amounts of research for managers to read, digest and apply
Political	▪ Recognises the 'power plays' within groups of people ▪ Acknowledges that individuals will pursue their own interests ▪ Explains the existence of hidden agendas ▪ Points out the existence and importance of coalitions ▪ Highlights the need for managers to adopt new skills in negotiating, bargaining and conflict resolution ▪ Explains power bases ▪ Argues that all stakeholders' views need to be taken into account ▪ Provides a mechanism for using power to achieve a wide range of stakeholder demands	▪ Provides only a superficial explanation of organisational politics and power ▪ Sources of real power are often difficult to locate and analyse ▪ Relies on personal observation and perception rather than scientific measurements ▪ Entrenched power positions are often overlooked ▪ Managerial dominance and control over employees may become acceptable behaviour ▪ Many view some of the strategies used as manipulative ▪ Managers may become hypersensitive about the strengths of coalitions which affect their performance ▪ Does not attempt to change the ▪ power relationships, only explain them

In reality, perhaps the most usual practice for managers is to adopt either a systems or contingency theory of management. This theory is discussed in the following section.

Figure 2.26 The theory and practice of management

'The theory of my book, set out in detail, is that successful managers learn from practice, not from reading the long-winded speculations of academics.'

2.6 Systems and contingency theories of management

While the classical–scientific, behavioural and political management theories continue to provide important lessons for managers, other ideas have also emerged during the last couple of decades. These contemporary management theories represent major innovations in ways of thinking about management and appropriate management practices. Two of the most important contemporary viewpoints are the systems and contingency theories.

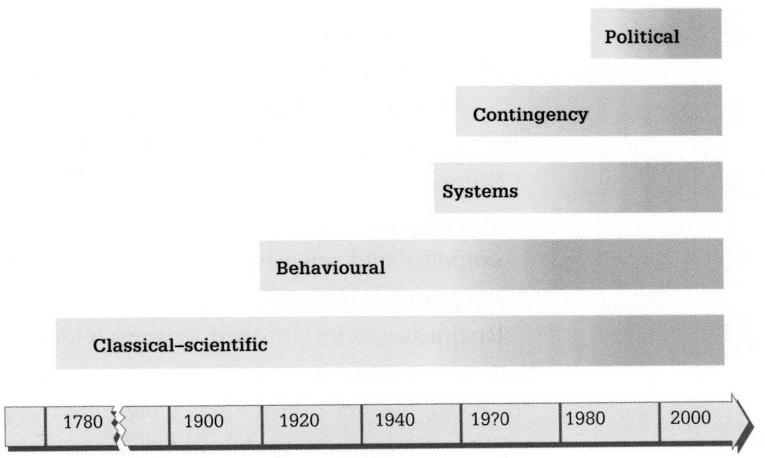

Figure 2.27 Timeline of management thought

Systems management theories

*A **system** is a set of interrelated parts that operate as a whole in order to achieve a common goal.*

*The **systems management approach** views organisations as an integrated process in which all the individual parts contribute to the whole.*

The systems theory approach is based on the idea that businesses can be viewed as systems. A **system** is a set of interrelated parts that operate as a whole in order to achieve a common goal.

For example, the human body can be viewed as a number of systems operating together to achieve a common goal — life. There is the skeletal system, blood system, central nervous system and so on. These individual systems operate autonomously but are all interdependent. That is, the human body will operate efficiently only when all the other contributing systems are functioning normally. The systems approach as applied to organisations is largely based on work in biology. The **systems management approach**, therefore, views organisations as an integrated process in which all the individual parts contribute to the whole. Each individual within an organisation is autonomous but at the same time interdependent.

According to the systems approach, an organisation is made up of the following four main components (see figure 2.28):

1 *inputs* — the various human, financial, material, equipment and informational resources needed to produce the products
2 *transformational processes* — the managerial and technological processes of the organisation that convert the inputs into a finished product
3 *outputs* — the products, as well as other outcomes (such as profits, employment and waste) produced by the organisation
4 *feedback* — information about how well the organisation has performed in relation to its stated goals.

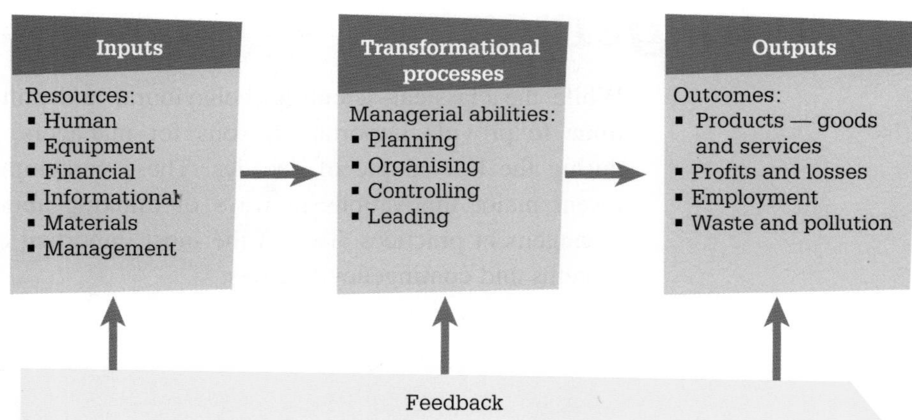

Figure 2.28 A systems view of organisations

Some of the characteristics of the systems approach include:

- commitment to a shared purpose and direction, supported by common values
- empathy and sensitivity towards the needs of all members within the group
- cooperative interaction between all groups within the organisation.

Businesses with an open systems view emphasise the need for openness to information, teamwork across functions, integrated systems and responsiveness to changing market conditions. Under this approach, the survival of the organisation requires individual members to understand and react to complex environmental change.

Contingency management theories

Contingency theory *stresses the need for flexibility and adaptation of management practices and ideas to suit changing circumstances.*

A relatively new approach to management is **contingency theory**. It stresses the need for flexibility and the adaptation of management practices and ideas to suit changing circumstances.

Contingency theorists point out to managers that no two situations are absolutely identical. Each situation, therefore, requires its own unique solution. For example, you may have used a particular strategy to complete a task for assessment. Although this strategy may have been quite successful for that particular task, another assessable task may well require a completely different approach.

Contingency theorists stress that traditional classical–scientific approaches to management were not necessarily wrong, but are no longer adequate for our needs today. They also urge managers to borrow and blend from a wide range of management practices.

Above all, advocates of contingency theory believe that managers need to be adaptable and flexible in their approach to solving problems. Because management is a discipline that is continually evolving, it frequently produces new ideas and theories, each with some relevance to practitioners.

Contingency theory, therefore, advocates that managers extract the most useful ideas and practices from a wide range, to best suit their organisation's present requirements. It stresses that an appropriate management response to one set of circumstances may be quite inappropriate to another. To adopt this approach, managers must sample all the past and present theories on offer; some refer to this as the 'smorgasbord' approach.

A manager adopting this theory will obviously need to apply the '10 commandments for the modern manager' (see figure 2.29).

THE 10 COMMANDMENTS FOR THE MODERN MANAGER

1. Share your vision with all relevant stakeholders.
2. Manage the relationships and the coalitions, not the employees.
3. Manage your own emotions and help others in the business to maintain an emotional balance.
4. Learn to thrive on diversity not conformity.
5. Lead, rather than simply managing, by inspiring trust and motivation.
6. Cultivate the ability to adapt to changing circumstances.
7. Learn how to access and use appropriate information and manage this knowledge effectively.
8. Be aware of how developments in technology can improve your effectiveness and efficiency.
9. Recognise and use the experiences and expertise of all employees.
10. Encourage ethical behaviour in order to promote pride and commitment in employees.

Figure 2.29 The 10 commandments for the modern manager

2.7 Summary and comparison of management theories

TABLE 2.2 Summary and comparison of management theories

Management theory	Organisation and allocation of tasks to staff	Organisational structure	Levels of management	Management styles
Classical–scientific management	▪ Based on 'scientific' analysis of work processes ▪ Highly programmed staff performing simple, repetitive tasks — single skilling, task specialisation ▪ Time and motion studies used to reduce inefficiencies ▪ Division of labour into function-related units, employees strictly controlled with tasks rigidly divided ▪ Prescribed limits on individual discretion ▪ Appraisal, reward and sanction of individuals based on achievement of production standards	▪ Hierarchical pyramid structure reflecting strata in church, army and school ▪ Hierarchical, linear flow of information, with a large amount of communication directed downwards ▪ Strict channels of responsibility from the top down and grouping into specialised activities based on function, product or process with considerable management and supervisory control at each level	▪ Many management and supervisory levels with clearly distinguishable and segmented organisational positions, responsibilities and roles ▪ Course of action decided by management with little or no consultation with workforce ▪ Bureaucratic management of authority believed to be the most effective means of controlling the workforce and ensuring that instructions are followed ▪ Workers believed to be prone to laziness and self-interest so tight control and external motivation necessary to achieve required organisational goals and objectives	▪ Autocratic
Behavioural management	▪ Recognition that workers have social needs in addition to economic needs ▪ Teamwork and informal work groups important for productivity	▪ Hierarchical pyramid structure ▪ More consultation with workforce but still not full participative partnership	▪ Many management and supervisory levels ▪ Development of people management skills, particularly communication and social motivation skills	▪ More democratic aspects emerging

Management theory	Organisation and allocation of tasks to staff	Organisational structure	Levels of management	Management styles
Political	▪ Need to manage the informal coalitions within the workplace ▪ Cross-functional teamwork and cooperation between coalitions within the organisation ▪ Need to recognise and deal with overlapping coalitions including external stakeholders	▪ May take the form of either a pyramid or flat management structure depending on the organisation's requirements	▪ Depends on the organisation's requirements; that is, the nature of the operations and the relationships between the coalitions	▪ Autocratic if the agenda of the coalitions is different from those of the organisation
Systems management	▪ Each individual in organisation is autonomous and at the same time interdependent ▪ Cross-functional teamwork and cooperative interaction between all groups within the organisation	▪ Flat organisational structure with participation and empowerment of all individuals ▪ Team accountability	▪ To survive, the system must acquire the ability to continuously transform itself. The need for greater flexibility means that positions, roles and responsibilities are flexible	▪ Democratic
Contingency theories	▪ Flexibility and adaptation of a variety of ideas and principles from a range of theories mean that a range of options may be pursued to suit the organisation's requirements	▪ May be pyramid, flat or federal decentralised organisational structure, depending on the organisation's requirements	▪ Depends on the organisation's requirements; that is, the nature of the operation and abilities of employees	▪ Depends on the requirements of the business

EXERCISE 2.4 Revision

1. What is meant by the term 'politics' in relation to organisations?
2. Identify and explain the central ideas of the political management theories.
3. What new skills does a manager need to acquire if adopting a political management theory approach?
4. Why does Claire Polosak regard power as an essential element in her organisation?

5. From your own experiences, find examples of the use of legitimate, expert, referent, coercive and reward power in situations.
6. Copy the mind map below and complete it, showing the different power bases of leadership. The first one has been started for you.

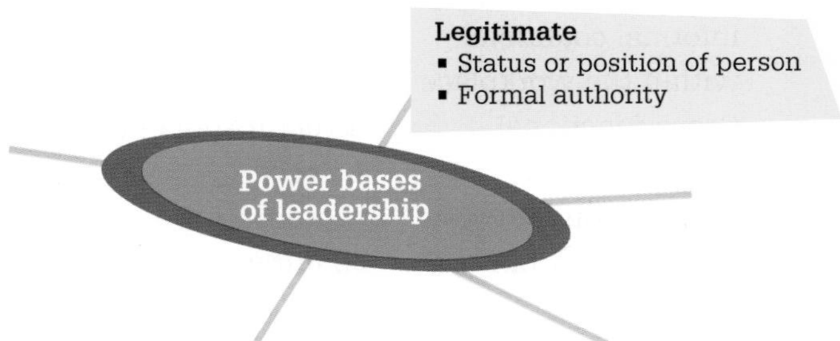

7. Recount a situation where you have been required to negotiate or bargain a solution to a problem. Outline the skills you needed to conduct the negotiation successfully.
8. Why is a 'win–win' attitude crucially important for negotiation in today's workplace?
9. What is meant by the term 'coalition'? How can a manager use his or her knowledge of coalitions in the workplace to achieve the organisation's goals?
10. Identify at least three strengths and three weaknesses of the classical–scientific, behavioural and political management theories.
11. Draw a diagram of your school showing how it operates as a system. List the inputs and outputs, describe the transformation process and explain how feedback occurs.
12. What important lessons does the contingency approach teach managers?
13. Prepare a summary of this chapter. A summary condenses the important issues and concepts presented in the chapter. Go to www.jaconline.com.au/businessstudies3e to compare your finished summary with the one provided for this textbook.

Extension

1. What is the purpose of management theory? Explain how knowledge and understanding of management theories can help a manager in his or her work. Use examples to illustrate your answer.
2. Reflect upon what you have learned from this chapter. Which management theory would you prefer to adopt if you were a senior manager? Present your answer as an oral report to the class.
3. Discuss the meaning of 'organisation' within the management process. Design a typical organisational structure based on the classical–scientific management approach. Design another organisational structure, this time based on behavioural principles. Outline the strengths and weaknesses of the two approaches.
4. Explain how each of the management theories discussed in this chapter affects the organisational structure, levels of management and management styles within a business.
5. W. Edward Deming, founder of the total quality management (TQM) movement, developed 14 management points outlining what managers should do to produce high-quality products. Research these 14 points. Analyse their influence on the way businesses have been organised over the last 20 years.

3 Managing change

3.1 Introduction

Some comments on the subject of change — 'Nothing is permanent but change'
Heracutus, Greek philosopher (c. 500 BC)

'It is always easier to talk about change than to make it'
Alvin Toffler, author (1994)

In Australia, over the past decade, there has been extensive and unprecedented change in the business environment. There is every indication that the pace of change will intensify during this decade. The prevailing attitude in business today can be summed up as follows: 'There is only one constant in business and that is change.'

To help guarantee the long-term survival of the business, managers must respond to these changes. Hoping that the changes will either go away or have no impact on their organisation is a recipe for disaster. Managers also find it frustrating to learn that as soon as they adjust to one change in the business environment, they must readjust to accommodate another. Some managers are fearful of change, seeing it as a destructive force. Others perceive change as an opportunity for creativity and openly embrace it.

Change is any alteration in the business and work environment; for example, change in consumer tastes, change in production methods, change in markets or products sold, or change in how employees perform their tasks. It could also be a change to the way things are perceived, or new ways of dealing with problems.

Change *is any alteration in the business and work environment.*

The rapidly increasing pace of change threatens to overwhelm many businesses. Adapting to change forced by the external environment is never easy for a business.

While change may be the most daunting challenge confronting management, the rewards are great for those who are prepared to accept the challenge and not only react to change but also initiate and manage it (see the Snapshot 'Change — will it ever end?').

Change — will it ever end?

One of the most challenging aspects of my role as a corporate manager is to initiate and implement change. For bad or worse, change keeps coming in business and in life. As the famous former English Prime Minister Benjamin Disraeli said in a speech in 1867, 'change is inevitable'. Yet change is not made without some inconvenience. Therein lies the challenge.

Previously, organisations faced one change at a time, and when it was over, people could rest for a while until the next change came along. In today's business environment, the problem is that most organisations have a number of major change projects occurring simultaneously.

A manager will ignore these changes at his or her own, and the organisation's, peril. *Alternatively*, well-managed changes can become the foundation for future growth and success. Five years ago, my organisation was facing increasing competition from cheap imports. Ultimately, the organisation

(*continued*)

was faced with two choices: scale back production and reduce the size of the business, or invest in new technology and training programs to improve productivity so as to reduce production costs. After much planning and evaluating of options, the organisation decided on the latter course of action.

From my experience, people will resist poorly implemented changes or changes that are suddenly imposed on them without any warning. Consequently, I had to create conditions and structures within the organisation so the necessary changes were perceived as an opportunity and not as a threat. I put in place a number of change management teams, encouraged people to apply knowledge in new ways, involved all employees in some decision-making processes and communicated the reason we needed the changes. To some extent, the changes were stressful and there was some initial resistance. However, five years later, the organisation has increased its market share by 15 per cent, productivity has improved by 18 per cent and production costs are down by 13 per cent. Most pleasing of all, however, is that the majority of employees adapted so well that morale has soared.

SNaPSHOT Questions

1. Why can change be difficult to manage?
2. What advantages can be gained by implementing well-managed change?
3. Identify the conditions and structures that the above manager put in place so the changes would be perceived as an opportunity.
4. Suggest some strategies that a manager can use to build on successes to ensure a change is implemented successfully.

In the words of Don Argus, former CEO of the National Australia Bank, the challenges posed to organisations by change are:

- *anticipating change*
- *understanding it*
- *responding to it*
- *initiating it*
- *communicating it*
- *managing it.*

As profitable opportunities can arise from change, it must be considered a fundamental aspect of an organisation's strategic planning. The ability to manage and, in many cases, embrace and adapt to change will increasingly determine a company's competitive advantage and survival. Successful managers are the ones who anticipate and adjust to changing circumstances rather than being passively swept along or, worse still, being caught unprepared. Such people are proactive rather than reactive.

The crucial management issue is *how* to manage change to make it as productive as possible, using it to renew and strengthen the business. However, to be constructive, change must occur at a pace at which it can be absorbed and integrated by the organisation.

Also, all changes should be thoroughly evaluated to assess their overall impact. Poorly managed changes normally result in employee resistance, tension, anxiety, lost productivity and, ultimately, decreased profits. Managing change is especially difficult when the pace and nature of change is largely beyond the control of the manager.

3.2 Nature and sources of change in business

It is said that if you stop moving, you die! The same applies to businesses. They must keep responding to the never-ending pressure for change. The forces driving change come from both outside (external) and within (internal) the business (see figure 3.1).

One of the most dramatic external forces acting on businesses is the rapid globalisation and integration of markets.

External change stems from the changing nature of markets and increased competition. It is also produced by economic, geographic, social, legal, political and technological developments. These forces are being experienced across all levels of business.

Internal change stems from identifying new methods, technology, systems and procedures. New business cultures also affect organisations internally.

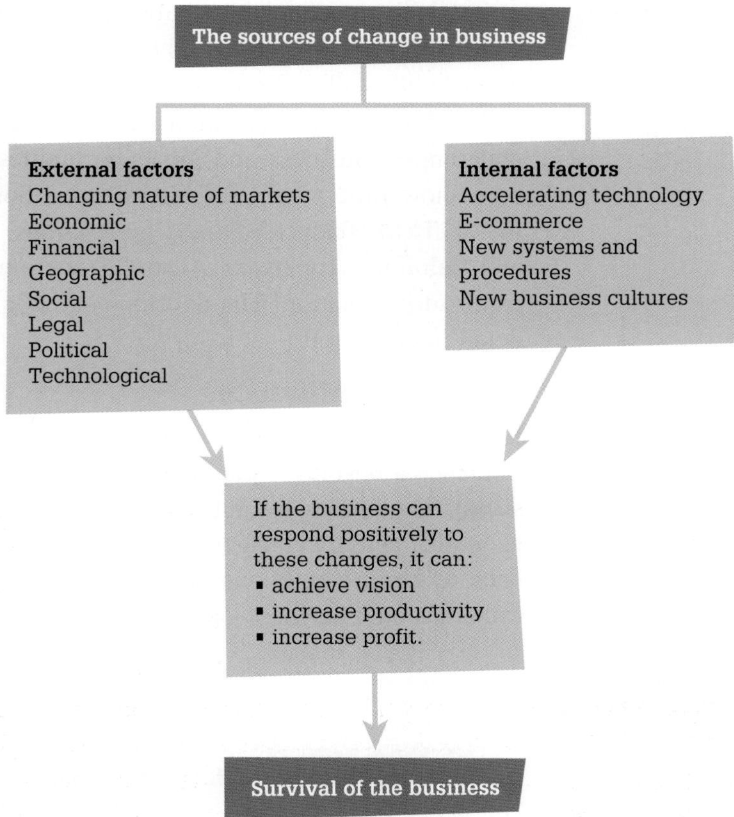

Figure 3.1 The sources of change in business

BiZ WoRD

The ***external business environment*** *comprises the factors and characteristics that are largely outside the direct control of owners, directors and managers.*

The ***internal business environment*** *comprises the factors and characteristics that are within the direct control of owners, directors and managers.*

The **external business environment** comprises the factors and characteristics that are largely outside the direct control of owners, directors and managers. The **internal business environment** comprises the factors and characteristics that are within the direct control of owners, directors and managers.

External influences

Changes within the external environment make it necessary for managers to make adjustments to business operations. For example, new government regulations may require a manufacturer to install pollution-control devices on a product or plant. Or a business, in response to changing social attitudes, may alter traditional work practices to accommodate more family-friendly or less discriminatory policies. The actions of competitors may force a business to reassess its operations and implement changes; this happened in Australia when one telecommunications company launched new low call rates. In response to this changed market condition other companies were forced to offer the same, or lower, prices.

The changing nature of markets

Globalisation is the process whereby hi-tech communications, lower transport costs, and unrestricted trade and financial flows are turning the whole world into a single market. This more integrated global economic system has altered the shape of world markets and the nature of the businesses that compete in them. Many Australian businesses must now compete against overseas products in the domestic market, in addition to competing in overseas markets when exporting. Australian businesses are increasingly meeting this challenge, and over the last decade have been forced to restructure their operations. The result has been significant **downsizing** in many operations, with staff reductions and the elimination of jobs and positions.

Downsizing *involves workplace staff reductions, with the elimination of jobs and positions.*

The forces of globalisation have created new opportunities, as well as increasing uncertainty. Business and job opportunities for those in senior executive positions now show little regard for international borders. Therefore, today's managers need the skills to conduct business transactions, and manage staff in multiple languages and cultural contexts as Australia continues to become an outward-looking and export-driven nation. The development of global business will be examined in more detail in chapter 19.

Economic influences

Economic forces have an enormous impact on both businesses and customers. They influence a business's capacity to compete and customers' willingness and ability to spend. Economies do not always experience constant growth. Rather, the level of economic activity changes from periods of growth ('boom') to recession ('bust') and back to boom conditions. Figure 3.2 shows the impact each phase of the business cycle has on a business's performance.

Economic growth is measured by comparing the level of real gross domestic product (GDP) achieved each year over a period of time. Real GDP is the GDP adjusted or deflated to remove the effects of inflation.

Peaks
Key features:
- GDP at high levels
- Firms operating at full capacity
- Wages and salaries at high levels
- Interest rates high
- Rising inflation

Troughs
Key features:
- GDP at lowest levels
- Consumer demand at lowest levels
- Unemployment at highest levels
- Sales and profits at lowest levels

Recession
Key features:
- Falling levels of GDP
- Consumption expenditure on consumer durables falling
- Rising levels of cyclical unemployment
- Sales and profit levels falling
- Business failures increasing
- Interest rates falling
- Rate of inflation slowing and may fall
- Investment expenditure declining

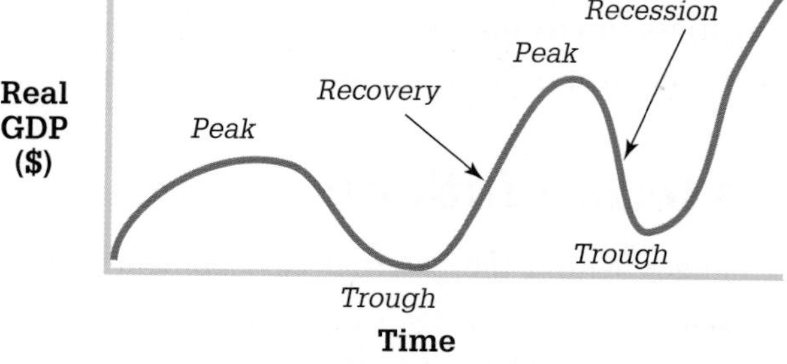

Recovery
Key features:
- Rising levels of GDP
- Increasing consumption expenditure
- Business expectations increasingly optimistic
- Employment opportunities increasing
- Increasing investment expenditure

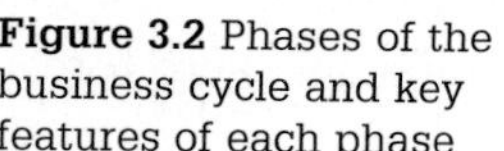

Figure 3.2 Phases of the business cycle and key features of each phase

Financial deregulation followed the Campbell Inquiry in the early 1980s. It led to a reduction in government intervention in the financial system, and an end to credit, interest rate and exchange rate controls. The result was increased competition within the banking sector. The Wallis Report in the mid 1990s recommended that the process of deregulation be extended even further, and resulted in the opening up of the financial industry to greater competition.

According to Professor Steve Dowrick of the Australian National University, about 1.5 percentage points of Australia's annual economic growth rate of 3.5 per cent have been the result of population growth.

***Demography** is the study of particular features of a population — its size, age, gender, income, cultural background and family size.*

Information on economic growth, inflation trends, average weekly earnings, consumer confidence, interest rates, consumer spending and unemployment data provide businesses with insight into economic trends. This information on the level of economic activity allows businesses to predict possible threats to, and opportunities for, business activity.

Financial markets

There have been enormous changes in global financial markets over the past 20 years.

Deregulation of Australia's financial system began in 1983 and it continues to undergo change. This has resulted in a more flexible, market-oriented approach across the financial sector. A substantial number of new banking products have emerged, aimed at the business sector. Some of the financial packages provide for funding against the existing and future market value of cash-generating assets (including the customer base, accounts receivables, inventory, plant and equipment) rather than finance secured against a mortgage.

Due to globalisation of the world's financial markets it is no longer necessary for many large Australian businesses to use only domestic financial institutions for the raising of finance. For example, News Limited, the Australian global media company, can access finance from worldwide sources.

Global financial markets themselves have undergone rapid change over the last decade. Developments in communications technology have enabled the phenomenon of global financial transactions. Global financial speculators may now easily make transactions spread across the globe.

Geographical influences

Two major factors that will have an enormous impact upon business activity over the next 10 to 20 years are Australia's geographic location within the Asia–Pacific region and the economic growth in a number of Asian nations. They provide challenging opportunities for business expansion, sales and profit.

Further changes that are likely to have a profound effect on business activity in Australia originate from changing demographic factors. **Demography** is the study of particular features of a population, including the size of the population, age, sex, income, cultural background and family size. Changes in any of these factors can lead to changes in demand levels and the nature of products and services.

Two major demographic issues that are likely to have a considerable impact on businesses are a slow-down in the growth of Australia's population and changes in the age structure of our population. A slow-down in population growth will have major implications for Australian businesses, as research shows there is a clear link between population levels and economic growth.

Social influences

Businesses that respond rapidly to social and cultural changes recognise that new demands and new opportunities can have a major impact on business success. The term 'social change' can incorporate any one or a combination of factors. These factors may include changes in beliefs, business ethics, work attitudes, cultural changes, spending habits and population changes.

Two social issues are leading to significant change or have the potential to influence major change in business practices. The first concerns a growing desire for family-friendly programs. Conflict between work and family responsibilities is a key factor causing women to leave businesses, and this high turnover is expensive for businesses. Consequently, businesses have been under pressure to implement family-friendly workplace practices that assist employees and, at the same time, reduce the associated costs to employers. The second social issue is the changing makeup of the workplace. Workplaces today are a mixture of different races, ethnic groups and cultures. (Cultural diversity is referred to later in the chapter.) Businesses need to have programs designed to assist understanding among diverse groups, not just tolerance of one another's existence.

Legal influences

BiZ WORD

***Deregulation** is the removal of government regulation from an industry, with the aim of increasing efficiency and improving competition.*

The processes of **deregulation** and regulation in Australia have led to significant change in the legal framework within which businesses must operate. Deregulation is the removal of government regulations from industry to enable businesses to perform more efficiently, enhance competition and reduce restrictive practices. This has led to considerable legislative reform. Simultaneously, the process of regulation — the introduction of government policies to promote fair conduct — has increased in some areas. Changes in legislation regarding environmental and consumer protection, occupational health and safety, industrial relations and trade practices reform will have major and increasing impacts on business conduct.

Figure 3.3 The deregulation of Australian labour markets will result in changes to working conditions.

Political influences

***Privatisation** is the process of transferring the ownership of government business to the private sector.*

All organisations are required to intereact with governments in various ways because they are subject to government regulation, and they are affected by issues such as deregulation and **privatisation**. Governments regulate by establishing rules of conduct that influence how organisations operate. These rules cover issues such as taxation, health and safety, competition within the industry, the environment, and trade practices. The Australian Competition and Consumer Commission (ACCC) and the Australian Securities and Investments Commission (ASIC) are two of the Australian Government's regulators, both responsible for the administration of the *Trade Practices Act 1974* (Cwlth) (see the Snapshot 'Government regulators').

Government regulators

THE AUSTRALIAN COMPETITION AND CONSUMER COMMISSION (ACCC)

The ACCC is an independent authority, established by government to administer the *Trade Practices Act 1974* (Cwlth). This Act deals with:

- anti-competitive and unfair market practices
- mergers and takeovers that have the potential to decrease competition within a market
- product safety and liability.

As well, the ACCC administers the *Prices Surveillance Act 1983* (Cwlth) and, in this role, acts as a watchdog on the pricing of goods and services — a role that has taken on added importance since the introduction of the goods and services tax (GST). The ACCC operates nationally for the enforcement and administration of competition and consumer protection laws, and to promote fair trading within the market.

THE AUSTRALIAN SECURITIES AND INVESTMENTS COMMISSION (ASIC)

ASIC is an independent statutory commission accountable to the federal parliament. It enforces and administers corporations law and protects consumers in Australia in the areas of investment, insurance, superannuation and banking. The aim of ASIC is to assist in reducing fraud and unfair practices in financial markets and financial products. The commission promotes honesty and fairness in securities and futures markets and in company affairs.

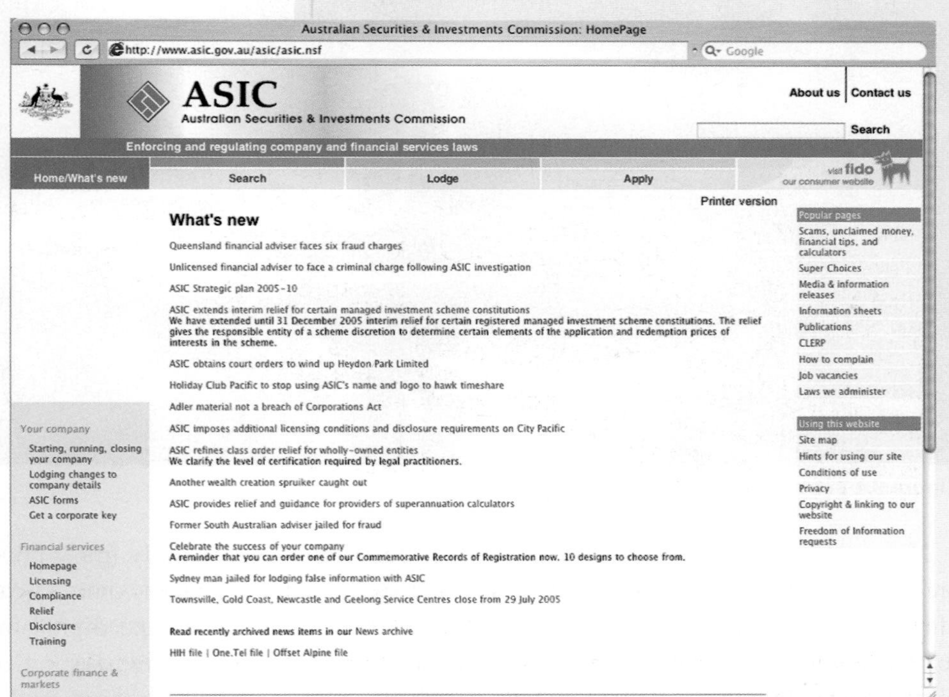

Source: The Australian Securities and Investments Commission, viewed 23 June 2005, www.asic.gov.au/asic/asic.nsf

SNaPSHOT Question

Outline the roles of the ACCC and ASIC.

Two political influences that are having an enormous impact on Australian business operations are:

1 *the goods and services tax (GST).* The **goods and services tax (GST)** is a broad-based tax of 10 per cent on the supply of most goods and services consumed in Australia. It was introduced in July 2000 in response to criticisms of Australia's wholesale sales tax system. The GST had a major impact on many aspects of business operations because businesses became responsible for collecting the tax on behalf of the government.

   The GST also requires all registered businesses to prepare a set of accounts at regular reporting intervals, either monthly or quarterly.

2 *free trade.* **Free-trade** policies could lead to cheaper foreign-made products entering the domestic market. Australian businesses will therefore face increased competition.

*The **goods and services tax (GST)** is a broad-based tax of 10 per cent on the supply of most goods and services consumed in Australia.*

***Free trade** is a policy of reducing or abolishing barriers to imports.*

Technological developments

Global technological innovation has increased at a remarkable pace, revolutionising the workplace and every aspect of daily life. With appropriate technology, businesses can increase efficiency and productivity, create new products and improve the quality and range of products and services. The use of hi-tech robotics in many manufacturing industries is improving productivity, reducing operating costs, and eliminating many boring and repetitious tasks.

Figure 3.4 Robotics — a technological revolution

New communications technologies allow information to be rapidly transmitted to an ever-increasing number of customers with a speed that now makes communication almost instantaneous. Since the introduction of fibre-optic cables and digital information transmission in the mid 1980s, the speed and capability of transferring communications data has allowed businesses to reorganise their structures and has fundamentally changed workplace practices.

A business that wants to be locally, nationally and/or globally competitive must adopt the appropriate technology. If slow to use and exploit technology, a business is likely to fail: the competition will strive to capture greater market share and develop a sustainable competitive advantage.

EXERCISE 3.1 *Revision*

1. Explain the meaning of the phrase, 'There is only one constant in business and that is change'.
2. In groups of two or three, select one source of change in the external environment.
   (a) Summarise the main points from the information provided in this book and prepare an outline of the main ideas in PowerPoint.
   (b) Present these ideas to the class and lead a discussion on the impact of the source of change on the business environment.
3. Refer to figure 3.2 (page 68). Discuss the economic conditions for consumers and businesses during each phase of the business cycle. Prepare an executive summary of the main points of your discussion.
4. Evaluate the accuracy of the following statement: 'One of Australia's main competitive advantages in terms of world trade is its geographic location within the Asia–Pacific region.'
5. Select two demographic features from those mentioned in the section on geographical influences (see page 69). How could changes in these features lead to opportunities and threats for businesses?
6. What are the full names of the ACCC and ASIC? What legislation do these bodies administer?
7. From newspapers, books, magazines and the Internet, research the advantages and disadvantages of free trade. Conduct a class discussion on the impact of free trade on Australian businesses.
8. Why is technology so crucial in terms of a business's success or failure?
9. Brainstorm the impact technology could have upon the organisation of your school over the next decade.

Extension

1. Using a business report format, discuss the following statement: 'Over the last 10 to 15 years, international influences have been instrumental in bringing about revolutionary change in the Australian business environment.'
2. *Newspaper portfolio*
   (a) Select four external factors that affect businesses. Collect eight to 10 articles on each factor from newspapers and journals over a 10- to 12-week period.
   (b) Paste the articles into a scrapbook under the four headings. Ensure that you date and acknowledge the source of each article.

   Reports
   (a) Write four reports of approximately 500 words on each of the external factors. Use a business report style with subheadings, graphs and diagrams to support your text.
   (b) A major focus within your reports should be an analysis of the impact of each of the four factors on either the manufacturing, primary or service industries, or a combination of those three industry types.
   (c) Your responses should synthesise the theory obtained from your teacher and textbooks with the information on current business conditions and factors from your newspaper and journal articles.
3. Go to www.jaconline.com.au/businessstudies3e and click on the ACCC and ASIC weblinks for this textbook. Find recent articles relating to investigations conducted by both organisations. Share and discuss these with other class members.

Figure 3.5 Information and communications technology — revolutionising human interaction

Internal influences

Internal change springs from the desire to develop new and improved ways of doing things. It may be in response to employee requests or the result of constantly striving for higher levels of efficiency and productivity. One example of major change in recent years is the accelerating rate of technological development, especially computerisation and e-commerce.

Effects of accelerating technological change

Advances in information and communications technology include electronic mail (email), voice mail, the Internet, videoconferencing, mobile Internet capabilities and pagers. These have reduced time delays and cost, and improved distance communication between suppliers and customers. As the diameter of the world 'shrinks' to one-quarter of a second — the time it takes to transfer information from one side of the globe to the other — many areas of business operations and management systems will be affected.

Many employees can now work from home, a practice known as telecommuting. Several major companies, including AMP, BP Australia, Caltex, Telstra and Pacific Power, provide work-from-home arrangements in a wide range of occupations.

However, merely purchasing computer equipment, adopting e-commerce strategies, reorganising work systems and procedures, and transforming the business culture will not automatically bring about improved productivity. What is equally important is how the new technology is used and managed.

Figure 3.6 New technology may not always deliver the promised results.

E-commerce

Electronic commerce (e-commerce) is the use of electronic communications to do business.

Electronic commerce (e-commerce) is the use of electronic communications to do business.

The term covers all transactions made by electronic methods, including phone, facsimile and the Internet. There are two main types of e-commerce:

1. *Business-to-consumer*. This covers products and services sold or distributed over the Internet with payment usually by credit card.
2. *Business-to-business*. This covers a business's electronic transactions with other businesses, including paying accounts, sending quotes and ordering supplies. The use of e-commerce in this way dramatically reduces the cost of doing business, especially internal processing costs. Communication expenses are also reduced and information sharing is greatly improved.

The real benefit of e-commerce is that it provides a mechanism to break with tradition and create new ways of operating by introducing new systems and procedures (see the Biz Fact on the left).

New systems and procedures

Historically, international trade has consisted mainly of goods, such as cars, electronics, raw materials and so on. However, the Internet has made it far easier to provide services of all types — such as education, banking and retailing — through a website that is globally accessible. This is forcing businesses to rethink many of their internal operating procedures. For example, Frito-Lay's salespeople each carry a hand-held computer that zaps data each night to computers in the head office. With this new system, Frito-Lay can tell how Doritos are selling not only in each state, but also in individual suburbs, rural stores and even at the end of aisle four on Monday!

The introduction of scanning systems is one example of a change in manufactured resources that has revolutionised business operations. Scanning systems that record prices at the cash register minimise price errors and save time. They have also had a significant impact on a range of essential but labour-intensive functions, such as stocktaking, purchasing, managing stock levels and updating prices. Stock orders can be automatically transmitted to suppliers. Stock levels can be adjusted rapidly and accurately to match patterns in demand. The sales and profit penalties of too little stock and the cost of maintaining too much stock are eliminated. Products are delivered just-in-time (JIT) to meet consumer demand.

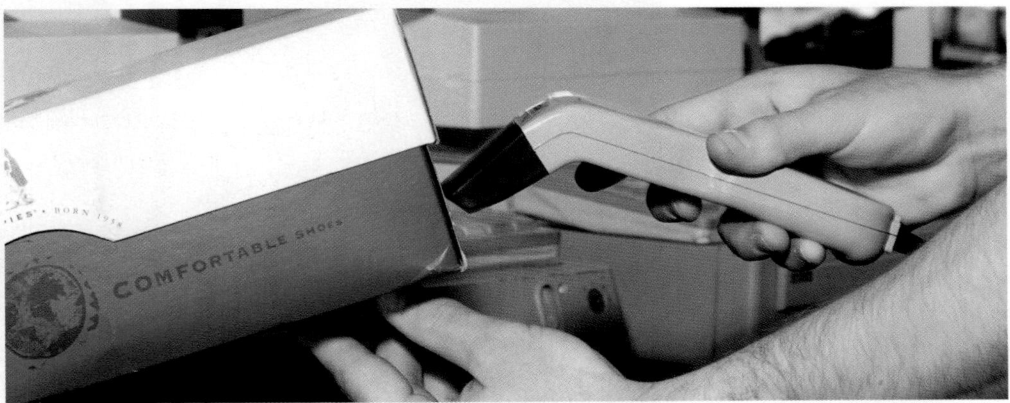

Figure 3.7 Information and communication technology — revolutionising operating procedures

The main changes to existing business systems and procedures brought about by technological development include:

- new business tools that assist in accessing and analysing information from a variety of sources
- the integration of business into the global market
- the cultivation of an outward-looking, export-oriented business culture
- improved methods of processing vast amounts of information
- the shift away from trading in goods to trading in information
- businesses being able to organise production to 'Internet time' schedules in which computerised stock controls reorder products and arrange delivery automatically

A **business culture** is a set of mostly unwritten or informal rules that spell out how people are to behave most of the time.

Management consultants Terrence Deal and Allan Kennedy believe that having a positive business culture is essential for an organisation's survival given:

- the rapid rate of social, technological and environmental change
- an increasingly competitive macroenvironment
- intensified global competition.

- being able to find the cheapest supplier from anywhere in the world
- the freedom to rapidly move information across international borders
- a dramatic slashing of the costs of everyday processes.

New business cultures

All businesses have their own **business culture** — a set of mostly unwritten or informal rules that spell out how people are to behave most of the time. These rules are based on the values, ideas, expectations and beliefs shared by members of the organisation. Each business develops its own particular way of doing things. The style or character of a business is consequently reflected in its culture.

The culture of an organisation is often evident in its organisational structure. Formal organisations with an emphasis on bureaucracy, line authority, hierarchical management structures, and defined job titles and areas of responsibility often have prevailing cultures that emphasise accountability, communication and cooperation. They also tend to conform to a culture of loyalty and respect for superiors (or, if not for superiors, at least for the positions they may hold). A culture that values and expects defined career pathways may be evident in formal organisations. Such organisations may also have a culture of resisting change. Change, therefore, must be managed carefully by providing new rules and processes regulating employees, or by changing the structure of the organisation itself.

Figure 3.8 A team culture is very responsive to change

Less formal organisations with flatter management structures, less departmentalisation and fewer defined spans of control often exhibit highly flexible, innovative and risk-taking cultures (see the Snapshot 'Creative culture — the Branson way'). Individuality and conflict are tolerated within this culture because it is often results driven. Individuals may exhibit loyalty to the team rather than the organisation. The culture is driven by a desire to achieve, and emphasis is placed on achieving results. This type of culture is common to a team organisational structure.

Creative culture — the Branson way

Richard Branson, chief executive officer and founder of the Virgin Group — which owns Virgin Music, Virgin Atlantic and Virgin Blue airways, and Virgin Mega stores, as well as having interests in radio and television production, railways, hotels and book publishing — is not your typical business leader. Informality extends throughout all the parts of the Virgin 'empire'. Formal board meetings are rarely held, and Branson encourages employees to contact him directly with their ideas. Rules and regulations are not the focus of the organisation. A person with a keen sense of adventure and humour, Branson is always open to new ideas.

Branson is a passionate believer in motivating employees by his enthusiasm and energy, as well as creating the right work environment for people to enjoy their work and flourish. Employees are encouraged to adopt an entrepreneurial flair, they are given responsibility and empowered to make decisions and take risks. This approach has allowed the Virgin Group to become a creative, high-performing organisation — a company that challenges the established way of doing things. Branson publicly attributes the organisation's success to the type of people employed and how they are motivated.

SNAPSHOT Questions

1. What type of culture has Richard Branson tried to develop at Virgin?
2. What do you see as being the advantages and disadvantages of this sort of culture?

EXERCISE 3.2 *Revision*

1. What is meant by the term 'technology'? Outline the main advantages and disadvantages of accelerating technology on a business's operations.
2. Briefly explain the two types of e-commerce.
3. Analyse how new technology has changed existing business systems and procedures.
4. Explain the nature of business culture.
5. Why is a positive business culture important, especially when new work methods are being introduced?

Extension

1. What factors will influence owners and managers to invest in new technology? Why are these important factors in the decision-making process?
2. Use magazines, books and the Internet to research your answers to the following questions:
   (a) What is e-commerce?
   (b) How important is e-commerce in terms of future growth for organisations involved in retail?
   (c) Critically analyse the social implications of e-commerce.
3. Research a business or industry that is experiencing considerable change due to accelerating technology. Business magazines or journals are an excellent source of information and frequently report on technological change in a variety of industries. Some recent examples that you may wish to explore include:
   - robotics and the car industry
   - banking
   - retail outlets.

   Write a brief report on the effects of accelerating technology on the internal business environment for your chosen industry.
4. (a) Rapid advances in information technology have led to global revolutionary changes. Consider the impact that the introduction of fax machines, mobile phones, answering machines and computers with modems have had on your life and the life of your family. Share your experiences with the class.
   (b) How have these changes affected the external and internal business environments in Australia? Record your ideas.
   (c) Write a half-page summary on possible opportunities and threats from accelerating technology and the potential impact on internal and external stakeholders.

Structural responses to change

Organisations need to continually improve and develop if they are to survive change. As the business environment changes, organisations examine and modify their business structures. Managers are involved with the structural changes taking place within the organisation. **Structural change** refers to changes in how the business is organised, that is, the organisational structure.

***Structural change** refers to changes in how the business is organised, that is, the organisational structure.*

Over recent years, the main structural changes have included:

- outsourcing
- flatter organisational structures
- development of strategic alliances
- network structures.

The aim of these changes is to make business operations run smoothly, improve efficiency, streamline coordination and control and empower employees to make their own decisions.

***Outsourcing** is the contracting of some business operations to outside suppliers.*

Outsourcing

A trend rapidly gaining support throughout the corporate world and government establishments is **outsourcing** — that is, the contracting of some business operations to outside suppliers.

Outsourcing has had a profound impact on business organisation, particularly on the mix of employees. Many businesses have rearranged their workforces to employ a minimum full-time staff, using as many people from outside the organisation on a contract, casual or part-time rate to keep costs to the lowest possible level. Obviously, outsourcing has both positive and negative social, personal and economic effects, many of which are presently being debated (see figure 3.9).

Figure 3.9 Outsourced labour

Flat structures

As was explained in chapter 2, flatter management structures have become more common in recent times. As middle-management positions are abolished, greater levels of responsibility and accountability are transferred to frontline staff or teams. Businesses need to develop a teamwork approach as well as becoming 'learning organisations' that respond positively to change. Such organisations are characterised by fewer formal reporting controls, sharing of 'best practice' methods, learning focused on business needs, a supportive learning environment and a focus on continuous improvement.

The contemporary workplace is seeing organisations evolve from formal, hierarchical structures with many levels to less formal, looser structures based on networked teams (see figure 3.10). This trend is likely to continue as workplace reforms filter through different industries

Figure 3.10 Hierarchical and networked organisational structures

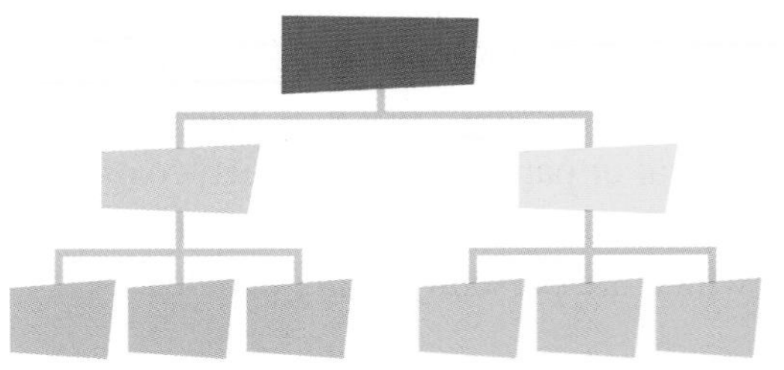

Hierarchical organisation (many levels)

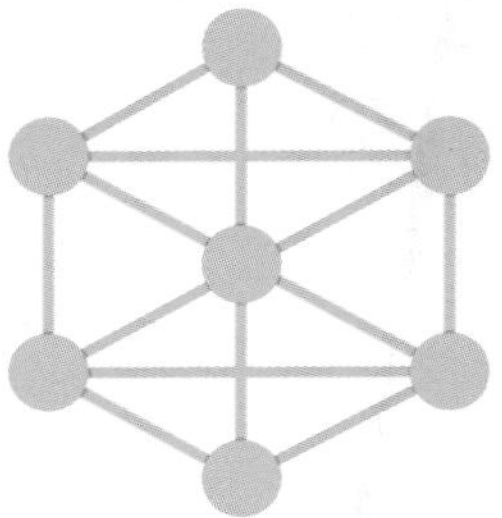

Network organisation (many teams)

Strategic alliances

One of the more complex methods of participation in global markets is the process of strategic alliance. A **strategic alliance** occurs when two or more businesses join together and pool or merge their resources. A business can pool its resources with one or more other businesses in either the domestic market or an overseas market. Forming a strategic alliance is considered to be a win–win strategy for businesses. The Ford Motor Company of the United States and Japan's Mazda Motor Corporation, for example, have established a successful strategic alliance by combining their individual strengths. The two cooperate on the production of new vehicles and exchange valuable information. In 2000, the music company EMI merged with Warner Music Group, part of the Time Warner business. This merger created the world's largest recording company, bringing together a group of well-known recording labels, including Virgin, Atlantic, WEA and HMV.

*A **strategic alliance** occurs when two or more businesses join together and pool their resources.*

Prior to their merger, Warner and EMI respectively were the fourth and fifth largest music businesses in the world. The merger rocketed them into global leadership.

Network structures

Another structural response to change is the formation of network structures. In such cases, the business does not actually produce what it sells. Instead, it relies on other businesses to perform the engineering, production and/or marketing functions under a contractual arrangement. The network structure's only function is the coordination of this subcontracted production or marketing. A **network structure** exists solely to provide administrative control of another business or set of businesses. For example, apparel companies Nike and Esprit use network structures to operate highly successful businesses, even though they do not own any manufacturing facilities and employ only a few hundred people.

In short, network structures buy a finished product with their brand name on it and then contract other businesses to distribute and sell it. To be successful, such organisations must have excellent relationships with their contractors. Their managers need a sophisticated level of conflict-resolution and negotiation skills.

*A **network structure** exists solely to provide administrative control of another business or set of businesses that perform all the functions needed to produce and sell the product.*

Figure 3.11 Nike relies on a network of businesses to produce and distribute its products.

EXERCISE 3.3 Revision

1. What is meant by the term 'structural change'?
2. Construct a mind map to summarise the four main structural changes that have occurred in the business environment over recent years.
3. Assess the possible impact of outsourcing on employees.
4. 'Flatter management structures often result in higher levels of responsibility and accountability for all employees.' Discuss.
5. What are the major advantages to businesses in forming strategic alliances?
6. List the possible advantages and disadvantages of a strategic alliance arrangement between an airline and a rental car company.

Extension

1. 'A business's environments present challenges, opportunities, uncertainties and change. Therefore, today's managers at every level in the organisation need to constantly monitor the business environment through a variety of means and activities. Managers also need to learn to adapt to the environmental changes they identify.' Discuss. In your answer refer to a business with which you are familiar.
2. Research how business culture influences organisational effectiveness. Analyse the factors that contribute to an effective business culture.
3. Consider the difficulties you have in your own experience of trying to predict how something will turn out. What can managers do to reduce these difficulties?

3.3 Reasons for resistance to change

Businesses, like individuals, find some changes difficult to cope with. When the pace of change is very rapid or coming from the external environment, then businesses may experience open resistance to the change. For example, consider where you sit in your Business Studies lesson and other lessons. It is likely that you and other students sit in the same seats in each lesson. Imagine now that all your classrooms were rearranged overnight without your knowledge. The next morning, you and your classmates may react with a mixture of annoyance, irritation, frustration, delight and/or anger. Perhaps you would be angry or upset at not being consulted or involved in the rearrangement process. You may have felt that you had no control over what you regard as your working conditions and organisational structure. Many of you may view the changes as a threat to the status quo.

Theories of human behaviour reveal that for most of us personal change is achieved only with a great deal of effort. Over the last decade, management has realised that change also represents a serious obstacle for businesses.

What does this tell us about resistance to change? This reaction is common among managers and employees. As individuals become accustomed to doing certain things and doing them in certain ways, so, too, do businesses. As a result, businesses and employees sometimes vigorously resist change.

Rapid, complex and turbulent change is now commonplace in most businesses. Australian businesses are becoming more aware of the problems that can emerge in the workplace when organisations face change. Strategies for managing change now occupy a prominent place in management education courses. The first step in managing change effectively is to ensure managers understand the main reasons for resistance to change (figure 3.12). Once these factors have been identified, each manager can put in place strategies to alleviate the resistance.

Figure 3.12 Reasons for resistance to change

Financial costs

A major reason for resistance to change is the financial cost of carrying out the changes. Even with access to finance, a business contemplating change must weigh up the costs and benefits of the change. Businesses need to make well-informed, calculated decisions to proceed with change in order to minimise risk and enhance long-term viability. The main financial costs include purchasing new equipment, possible redundancy payments, retraining expenses and reorganising plant layout.

Purchasing new equipment

The purchasing cost of new technology can be considerable. The decision to purchase new equipment should be made only after a detailed examination of all the alternatives. Such capital evaluation techniques should include a total breakdown of costs and benefits as well as the expected rate of return.

Redundancy payments

BiZ WoRD

*Employees are made **redundant** when their skills are no longer required by the business.*

Employees are made **redundant** when their skills are no longer required by the business. The employees who are retrenched (lose their jobs) because of the changes are entitled to financial compensation in the form of a redundancy payment. The total redundancy payout may be difficult to estimate. Inaccurate estimates may have detrimental consequences for a business.

Figure 3.13 Inaccurate 'guesstimates' can have serious consequences for any business.

Training and development *means changing employees' attitudes and behaviours; this may involve teaching them specific skills.*

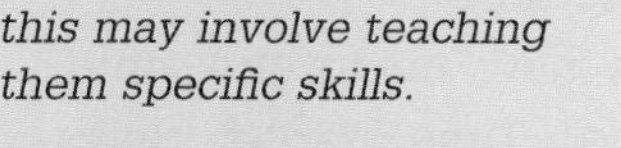

Plant layout *is the physical arrangement of people and machinery within the business.*

Retraining the workforce

As new technology is introduced, employees must be retrained, especially those whose existing skills are no longer required. **Training and development** means changing employees' attitudes and behaviours. It may involve teaching them specific skills, and allows existing employees to continually upgrade their skills. The full benefits of new technology cannot be realised without expenditure on training and development.

Reorganising plant layout

To improve efficiency and productivity, the installation of new equipment may require reorganisation of the plant layout. **Plant layout** is the physical arrangement of people and machinery within the business. Minor changes may have little or no effect on plant layout. However, major changes such as the complete re-engineering of systems often require extensive rearrangement of existing facilities.

Inertia of managers and owners

Inertia of management *refers to an unenthusiastic response from management to proposed changes.*

Inertia or inactivity is another reason for resistance to change. **Inertia of management** refers to an unenthusiastic response from management to proposed changes. Some managers and owners resist change because it requires moving outside and away from their 'comfort zones'. Many employees and managers of typical businesses desire a safe and predictable status quo. Such an attitude is summed up in the phrase, 'But we don't do things that way here'.

For example, the ungainly layout of the Qwerty keyboard was introduced in 1873 to slow down typists so the keys would not jam on their manual typewriters. Even though the inventor attempted to replace it with a more efficient keyboard once the original design fault had been removed, people were resistant to change. People had become too familiar with the Qwerty keyboard. The modern-day computer keyboard still has this inefficient design built into it!

Change entails risk and requires sound leadership skills and responsive management structures. Resisting change ultimately results in business failure. The long-term survival of all businesses depends on the ability of their managers to scan the environment, predict future trends and exploit change.

Cultural incompatibility in mergers and takeovers

When two companies join together, the resulting company may experience unpredictable 'culture clash'; this can be a powerful reason for employees resisting change. Recent research has revealed that businesses that had undergone a merger or takeover frequently failed due to incompatible organisational cultures.

Many mergers and takeovers are undertaken for financial or production reasons, generally driven by the expectation of improved long-term profits. However, the success of such strategies may hinge upon whether the two organisational cultures blend. Like oil and water, some types of organisational culture will not mix (see the Snapshot 'World's largest corporate loss — $A168 billion' on page 84).

World's largest corporate loss — $A168 billion

The supposed 'dream' corporate merger or strategic alliance between America Online (AOL) and Time Warner in 2000 has evolved into a financial nightmare. In January 2003, AOL Time Warner announced a net loss of $A168 billion for the previous year — the world's largest corporate loss to date.

The much publicised $A525 billion merger between the 'new' media and communications giant AOL with the 'old' media organisation Time Warner, was undertaken for financial and production reasons. However, it was generally driven by the expectation of improved long-term profits and greater market share. Instead, a number of factors combined to create a dramatic decline in revenue.

Firstly, as with many new-economy dotcom companies, the gap between reality and hype could not be bridged. AOL Time Warner's performance was severely restricted when revenues and subscriber numbers for its online business slumped shortly after the merger was announced. The decline continued during 2002. Secondly, the newly created organisation experienced a clash of business cultures; a common cause for failure among merged businesses. The incompatible business styles resulted in intense boardroom infighting and resistance to change.

In response to the poor performance, most of the senior management involved in the merger have resigned. The organisation is now in recovery mode, concentrating on reducing its debt by selling off some associated subsidiaries and trying to improve the performance of America Online.

SNaPSHOT Questions

1. Define the following terms:
   (a) merger/strategic alliance
   (b) business culture.
2. Identify the factors responsible for AOL Time Warner's 2002 financial loss.
3. What strategies has management adopted to limit future losses?

Staffing considerations

Any changes to a business organisation and its operating procedures will eventually impact on the level and type of staffing. Many human resource management consultants argue that staffing considerations are one of the most entrenched reasons employees will resist change. No matter how technically or administratively perfect a proposed change may be, staffing issues may make or break it. Employees may become fearful of changes if they threaten job status or security. As well, changes to the way jobs are performed may intimidate employees, causing them to doubt their own capabilities. Workers will, therefore, resist or disapprove of new processes because they feel that the result will be forced redundancies, loss of control or power and loss of skills.

***De-skilling** occurs when employees are no longer required to perform skilled tasks due to changes in work methods, usually resulting from new technology.*

De-skilling

De-skilling occurs when employees are no longer required to perform skilled tasks due to changes in work methods. Such changes usually result from new technology.

Figure 3.14 On an assembly line, a worker is given simple tasks to repeat throughout the day

In response to the loss of their skills, some employees may resist change by actively seeking to sabotage the new processes. Such people are nicknamed 'Luddites' (see the Biz Fact on the left). Others may refuse to have anything to do with the new technology.

De-skilling also happens at management level. When an organisation adopts a flatter management structure, many of the previous functions of management are performed by employees. As a consequence, middle management and line supervisors may find it particularly difficult to accept their changing roles. As they take up more of a coaching or guiding function they may feel that their power has been eroded and their skills are no longer required.

BiZ FaCT

Between 1811 and 1816, during the early stages of the Industrial Revolution, members of organised bands of craftsmen destroyed newly introduced machinery in the Midlands and north of England on the grounds that it took away their skills and livelihoods. Their leader was said to be Ned Ludd, and the groups became known as 'Luddites'. Today, people who resist new technology are called Luddites.

Acquiring new skills

While some employees are de-skilled, others are required to learn new skills. This too can give rise to resistance to new procedures or systems. Learning new processes requires rethinking or learning to think again; it is often hard work! This problem is made worse if training is not provided, because without adequate training an otherwise positive change may be perceived in a negative light; job satisfaction will decrease. For example, if the introduction of computerised financial management systems means that accountants will have to learn a new skill, some may fear that they will be unable to do so. They may, therefore, develop a negative attitude towards the new work systems.

Loss of career prospects or opportunities for promotion

Employees who perceive that new procedures or organisational structures may threaten their career prospects or promotional opportunities also resist change. For example, a salesperson may resist a territory change if he or she believes that the change will result in fewer opportunities to perform well; or a manager may view a corporate restructure with suspicion and fear because restructuring often involves the elimination of managerial jobs.

Often, the culmination of such situations is a decline in employee job satisfaction, which, in turn, has a negative impact on employee productivity.

Figure 3.15 Forced changes can often result in lower levels of employee job satisfaction.

EXERCISE 3.4 Revision

1. Complete the sentences below by choosing the correct term from the following list.

   Terms

   financial cost   common
   rapid   resistance
   turbulent   effectively
   strategies
   cultural incompatibility in mergers and takeovers
   inertia of managers and owners
   staffing considerations

   Sentences

   When change is too ________ or when managers and employees feel they have no control over it, then ________ to the change is to be expected. Resistance to change is ________ among individuals and businesses. This resistance needs to be managed ________. Rapid, complex and ________ change is now commonplace in most Australian businesses. ________ for overcoming resistance need to be developed by managers. The four main reasons for resistance to change are:

   (i) ____________________
   (ii) ____________________
   (iii) ____________________
   (iv) ____________________
2. Select a major change in your life and complete the following:
   (a) Reflect on the reasons why you liked or disliked the change. Share your thoughts with other class members.
   (b) List the reasons that were common among the group.
   (c) What does this tell you about the strategy a manager could best use to help overcome resistance to change?
3. Prepare a brief report outlining the main financial costs responsible for some businesses resisting change.
4. What kinds of resistance to change have you observed recently? How could they have been overcome?
5. What is meant by the term 'inertia management'?
6. When the new CEO for Bradley Southport Limited attempted to make some major changes, she encountered resistance among some senior level managers. Explain why these managers may have resisted the changes.
7. Explain why 'cultural incompatibility' is a major reason for the failure of businesses that have merged with or been taken over by other businesses.
8. Assume you are the human resource manager for a large financial organisation. You have been asked by the board of directors to prepare a report outlining the staffing considerations that may cause employees to resist workplace changes. Present your findings either as a written or oral report.

Extension

1. Based on the information from this section, explain why there was so much resistance by bank tellers when they were first required to use computers to process customer transactions.

2. Evaluate the accuracy of the following quotes concerning change:
   (a) 'Change for change's sake is not progress.'
   (b) 'Change is life. Life is change'.
   (c) 'Change what you can change. Accept what you cannot change.'
   (d) 'Those who ride the crest of the wave of change will profit from it. Those who resist change will be left behind in its wake.'
3. In small groups, produce a plan to solve the problems and manage a potentially difficult introduction to new technology. Present your plan to the rest of the class. Read the scenario below.

   Scenario

   You are a divisional manager of 30 loyal, long-serving employees. Fierce competition is threatening the long-term viability of the business. Sales and profits are in the process of declining due to the lower prices of your competitor. The business could compete if it introduced new technology. (It has the finance to purchase and install the machinery.) The introduction of the new technology is going to mean changes to your division and the current product.
   - Twenty employees are required to work the new technology so 10 will become redundant.
   - Even though sales have declined, you have a number of very loyal customers who have expressed satisfaction with the format of the current product.

   Problems requiring solution and action
   (a) Retrenching of 10 employees — what are some of the criteria you might consider regarding who should stay and who should go?
   (b) Training the remaining employees to understand and use the new and more complex technology (quite a radical change from the technology currently in use).
   (c) Managing the change with sensitivity: maintaining positive workplace morale and exhibiting leadership.
   (d) Communicating the change in the product format to the customers and convincing them to maintain their loyalty towards your brand and company.

3.4 Managing change effectively

'Employees who are not informed about why changes are necessary will ultimately resist such changes', says Russell McCulloch, a change management consultant. 'When they do not get the information they need, they turn to the rumour mill.' It is also essential, according to Mr McCulloch, that managers ask one fundamental question: 'Am I giving as clear a picture as I can of the what, when, how and why of the changes?'

Now well entrenched and likely to accelerate, change must be considered a fundamental aspect of an organisation's strategic planning. The ability to manage, and in many cases embrace and adapt to, change will increasingly determine a company's competitive advantage.

Strategies for reducing resistance to change

Businesses often fail to manage change well. The record tends to be poor because in the upheaval of a restructuring process the most crucial group of all, the employees, are often neglected. As well, existing communication channels are often inadequate when reporting progress. Such channels often break down in the highly emotional climate that surrounds a change program.

A great deal of research has been conducted on the most appropriate methods to reduce resistance to change. The majority of this research revealed that regardless of where or how a change originated, the environment created by the manager or supervisor can greatly affect employee acceptance. Figure 3.16 (on page 88) outlines several strategies for creating a positive environment for change.

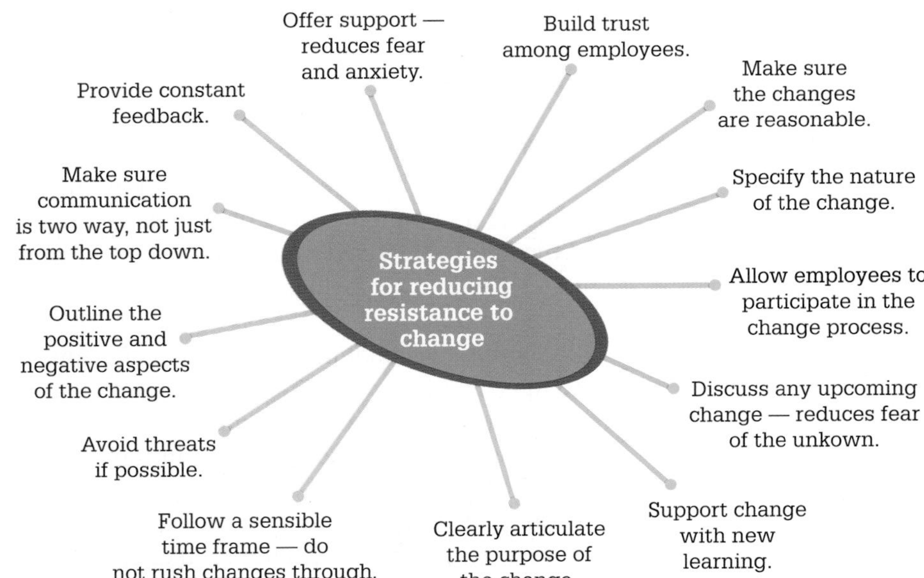
Strategies for reducing resistance to change
Offer support — reduces fear and anxiety.
Build trust among employees.
Make sure the changes are reasonable.
Specify the nature of the change.
Allow employees to participate in the change process.
Discuss any upcoming change — reduces fear of the unkown.
Support change with new learning.
Clearly articulate the purpose of the change.
Follow a sensible time frame — do not rush changes through.
Avoid threats if possible.
Outline the positive and negative aspects of the change.
Make sure communication is two way, not just from the top down.
Provide constant feedback.

Figure 3.16 Strategies for reducing resistance to change

Identifying the need for change

An effective manager should always be scanning the environment, attempting to understand factors that will have an impact on the business. In this way, he or she may better identify current trends and predict future changes.

Achieving such a vision requires a holistic view of the outside world and awareness of the potential impact on the business of a variety of factors. Correctly anticipating these factors greatly assists the manager in identifying the need for change. This strengthens the business so it may take full advantage of opportunities that favour its long-term survival in an increasingly competitive world.

BiZ FaCT

Analysing all information and observations using a 'strengths, weaknesses, opportunities and threats' framework (SWOT analysis) can be a particularly useful and powerful planning aid.

Setting achievable goals

A mission statement states the purpose of the business. It indicates what the firm does, and states its key aims. In conjunction with the mission statement a business establishes specific company goals that are measurable (usually set on a yearly basis). Reassessment of the mission statement and business goals may be required if management detects changes in the external business environment that may have a major impact on business activities. However, for change to be managed effectively it is essential that any new goals be achievable. This means goals that are attainable and realistic. Unachievable goals will only cause cynicism among employees and damage relationships between employees and supervisors.

On the other hand, achievable goals, devised after consultation with employees and communicated clearly by management, have a much greater chance of being realised.

Creating a culture of change — encouraging teamwork

Adopting changes to work procedures or organisational structures requires a degree of risk taking by the participants. For employees and managers to be prepared to take such risks the business culture needs to be supportive. One method to assist in this process is for the organisation to identify individuals who could act as supportive

A **change agent**, is a person, or group of people, who acts as a catalyst, assuming responsibility for managing the change process.

change agents. A **change agent** is a person, or group of people, who acts as a catalyst and assumes the responsibility for managing the change process. Such people fulfil a crucial role in helping to establish a positive and supportive workplace culture. Change agents may include members of the management team, employees of the business or outside consultants.

One highly effective change management strategy is for change agents to foster a workplace culture based on Peter Senge's concept of a learning organisation (see the Biz Fact on the left). To create a learning organisation culture requires a team structure, as these have been found to encourage employees and managers to better cope with the introduction of workplace changes.

BiZ FaCT

To survive increasingly turbulent and competitive environments, managers need to think differently about how to solve the problems they face. One way to do this is for managers to help their companies become 'learning organisations'. These are described as 'organisations where people continually expand their capacity to create desired results, where new patterns of thinking are nurtured and where people are continually learning how to learn together'. The learning organisation creates competitive advantages by:

- *adapting better to changing environments*
- *continually acquiring and building on new knowledge*
- *continually improving*
- *being able to absorb new concepts and innovations.*

Source: Adapted from M. Morrison, 'Learning about learning organisations', in *Management*, October 1994, pp. 26–27

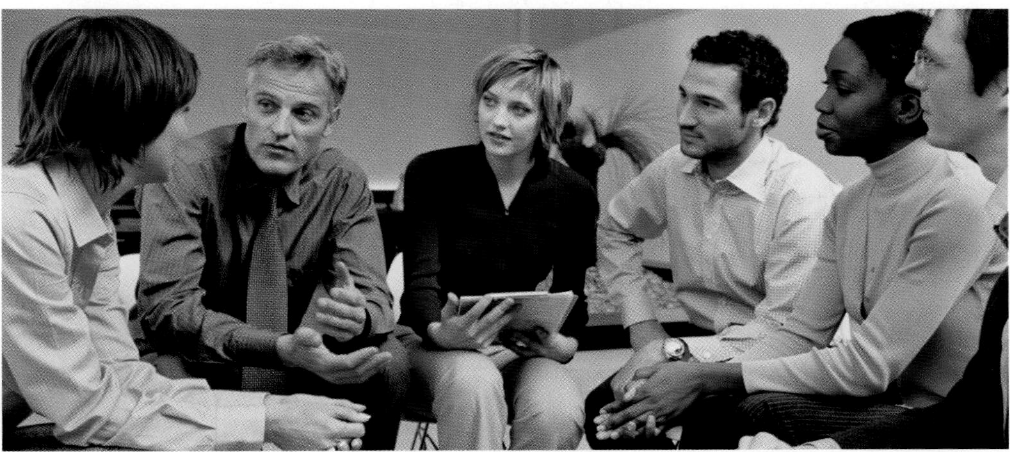

Figure 3.17 Teamwork encourages a supportive environment.

Change models

A **model** is a simplified version of reality. Models are useful tools when dealing with complex issues. For example, a street directory is a model of a highly complex geographical area that helps you get from one location to another.

Two very useful change models were developed in the late 1940s by psychologist Kurt Lewin. These models may assist managers in overcoming resistance to change. They are known as:

- force-field analysis
- unfreeze/change/refreeze.

Force-field analysis

As figure 3.18 shows, Lewin suggested that any organisational change program will experience two types of force that govern the effectiveness of the change. These are driving forces and restraining forces.

A **model** is a simplified version of reality.

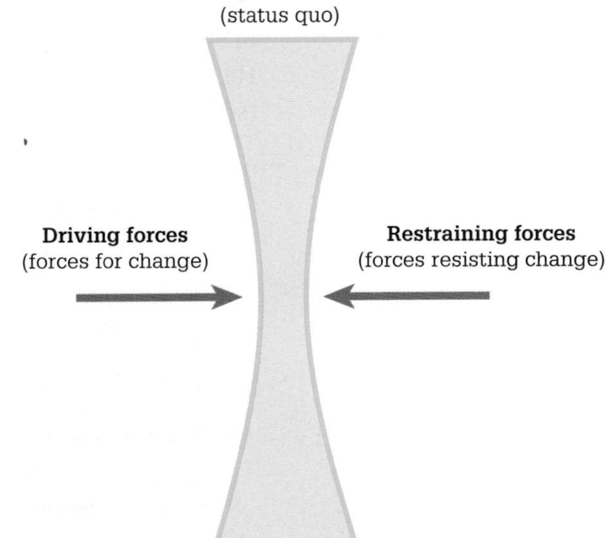

Figure 3.18 The forces that make up the organisation change 'force-field'

Driving forces are those forces that initiate, foster, encourage and support the change.

Restraining forces are those forces that work against the change, creating resistance.

Conducting a **force-field analysis** requires identifying, analysing and balancing the driving and restraining forces.

Driving forces are those forces that initiate, foster, encourage and support the change. They include the workplace culture, change agents, availability of training and other resources necessary to drive forward the change. **Restraining forces** are those that work against the change, creating resistance. They are the opposite to driving forces and hold the change back. The current conditions, or status quo, are a result of these two forces pushing in opposite directions.

According to this model, managers who are trying to implement a change must analyse and balance the driving and restraining forces. They need to conduct a **force-field analysis**. The manager must first identify the driving forces and make full use of them to help overcome any obstacles to the change. As well, the manager must also correctly identify the restraining forces and develop strategies to minimise their impact.

A force-field analysis for a change requiring students to sit in different seats for a Business Studies class is shown in figure 3.19.

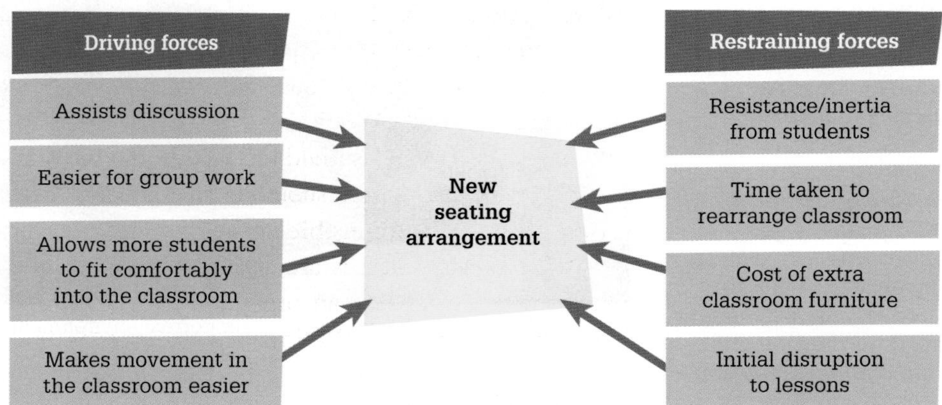

Figure 3.19 Force-field analysis for rearranged classroom seating

Unfreeze/change/refreeze

Suppose someone gave you a plastic cup filled with clear, solid ice. At the bottom of the cup is a twenty-cent piece lying heads up. Now, suppose you want the twenty-cent piece to be frozen in a tails-up position. What can you do to bring about this desired change? There is only one practical solution. You let the ice in the cup thaw (unfreeze), reach in and turn the coin over (change) and then freeze (refreeze) the cup of water. This is how Lewin recommended that change be handled in organisations. He advocated that change agents unfreeze, change and then refreeze the organisation (see figure 3.20).

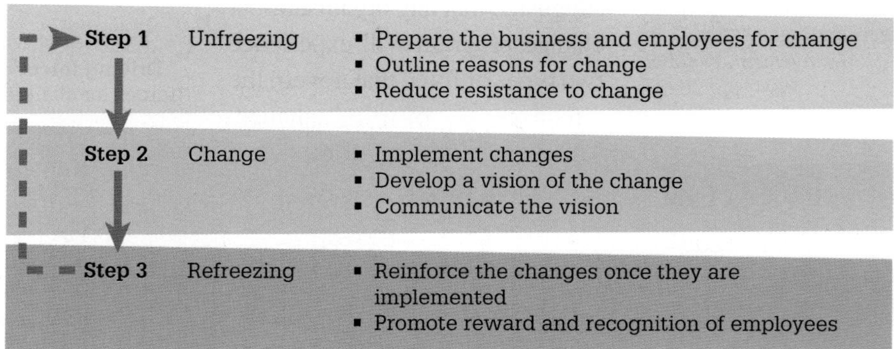

Figure 3.20 Lewin's unfreeze/change/refreeze change model

Lewin outlined each of the steps as follows:

1 *Unfreezing*. This process breaks down the forces supporting the existing system. It prepares the organisation for change as well as identifying the need for change.
2 *Change*. The change itself now begins. The new procedures, systems and behaviours must be identified, communicated, modelled and practised.
3 *Refreezing*. This requires that the changed behaviour be reinforced to make sure it lasts. The manager has a crucial role to play by offering praise and positively reinforcing employee efforts to change.

Lewin stresses that this three-step change process is continuous. It is not done once only.

3.5 Change and social responsibility

***Social responsibility** is how well a business manages the social, environmental and human consequences of its actions.*

Social responsibility is how well a business manages the social, environmental and human consequences of its actions. A socially responsible business will attempt to achieve two goals simultaneously: maximising profit (double bottom line) and providing for the greater good of society (triple bottom line). A central theme of social responsibility is that businesses should act 'above and beyond' making a profit and obeying the law. Therefore, businesses should always monitor any changes against this standard.

Being socially responsible makes good business sense — customers eventually find out which businesses are acting responsibly and which are not. Customers may react by ceasing to buy an organisation's product if they learn that the business is exploiting employees, polluting the environment or using inappropriate technology. A business, therefore, increases its chances of success when it pursues goals that align with the interests of its stakeholders, both internal and external (see the Snapshot 'Socially responsible companies').

Socially responsible companies

What do Westpac, Australia Post, Visy Industries and Alcoa have in common? They have all been selected as 'winners' in the first-ever rating of Australian companies' performance in social responsibility — the so-called triple bottom line.

The recent RepuTex Social Responsibility Rating assessed organisations on four categories:

1. Environmental impact (winner — Visy Industries)
2. Corporate governance (winner — Australia Post)
3. Social impact (winner — Alcoa)
4. Workplace practices (winner — Australia Post)

The survey produced some interesting results. Overall, Westpac was revealed as Australia's most socially responsible company of the largest 100. It was the only business to score the AAA 'outstanding' rating. The best-performing sectors were heavy industry, mining, utilities and transport. Traditionally, these sectors have come under scrutiny and received strong criticism

(continued)

for their environmental and social impacts. This survey shows that many organisations in these sectors have developed and implemented programs that account for their social responsibility. Such programs encourage employee involvement in decision making, are mindful of the work–life balance, respect human rights and adopt ethical management practices.

The survey also highlighted an interesting connection between an organisation's double bottom line (profit maximisation) and triple bottom line (social responsibility) performance. It showed that organisations' concern about the social impact of their decisions and actions has had a positive influence on the bottom line performance of those organisations. In other words, fulfilling social responsibility obligations actually improves an organisation's profit performance. Consequently, the notion that a company should aim to maximise its profit, regardless of any social responsibility, was shown to be counterproductive in the long term.

In a final note, the report pointed out that the corporate social responsibility of Australian organisations lags behind that of other developed economies, namely Europe and North America.

SNaPSHOT Questions

1. List the program that the best-performing sectors have developed and implemented to account for their social responsibility.
2. What relationship did the report find between an organisation's double and triple bottom lines?
3. Go to www.jaconline.com.au/businessstudies3e and click on the RepuTex weblink for this textbook. Provide an executive summary of the role of RepuTex.

Ecological sustainability

Concern for the environment has gradually increased since the mid 1970s. Current Australian research shows that an overwhelming majority of Australians consider themselves environmentalists. In fact, 65 per cent want to reduce pollution, even if it means paying higher prices. Some of the most pressing environmental issues businesses must address include global warming, waste disposal and pollution.

Economic development must be accomplished sustainably — that is, using methods of production that conserve the Earth's resources for future generations. Economic growth should not occur at the expense of polluting and degrading the air, water and forests that are essential to supporting life on this planet. There needs to be a balance between economic and environmental concerns — in other words, sustainable development.

Consequently, businesses are being asked to take increasing responsibility for the protection of the environment. The Earth is a fragile system, and needs high levels of support and informed intervention so that it may sustain itself. The social conscience of responsible business owners (and, increasingly, government legislation) has led them to adopt policies of conservation, recycling and restoration. The principle of ecological sustainability requires businesses to evaluate the full environmental effects of their operations.

Additionally, the growing consumer expectation that products should be 'clean, green and safe' is changing management practices in a number of Australian firms. By producing new and better products in an ecologically sustainable manner, the business focus coincides with stakeholder expectations.

Figure 3.21 Businesses that create pollution may risk losing customers

Quality of working life

The changing composition of the workforce and the need for increased business flexibility and productivity have meant that quality of working life issues must be taken into account when changes are introduced. The quality of employees' working lives can be improved by:

- programs to enhance employee dignity
- improvements to the physical and emotional wellbeing of employees
- efforts to enhance job satisfaction
- safe and healthy working conditions
- opportunities to use and develop talents and skills
- the right to personal privacy, free speech and equitable treatment
- family-friendly work arrangements; work schedules and job demands that do not regularly take up family time.

Figure 3.22 Family-friendly work schedules, an important quality of working-life issue

Technology

The introduction of new technology can often have both positive and negative effects. A socially responsible business will endeavour to contribute to the transfer of environmentally sound technology and management methods.

Technology also affects the design of work. As the use of technology increases, more and more people experience dramatic changes to the way they do their jobs. As the use of computer technology continues to accelerate, it is estimated that eventually all workers who perform a service for others (tertiary-related jobs) will have access to a personal computer, workstation or laptop. Such a change has enormous implications, especially in terms of interpersonal relationships, work design and communication. Some analysts forecast that the social aspect of work will be severely eroded, with negative consequences for many employees. Where once the office was a place for social interaction, many employees now work from home, their cars or at an isolated workstation and may experience a sense of isolation.

Globalisation and managing cultural diversity

Cultural diversity *means the multitude of individual differences that exist among people.*

As previously explained, the world economy is now extremely interrelated due to the process of globalisation. Globalisation has brought a change in the **cultural diversity** of workplaces. Cultural diversity means the multitude of individual differences that exist among people. With the pressure to globalise, organisations are having to find new approaches to staffing. Workplace diversity in terms of gender, race, ethnicity, religion, ability, sexual preference and age is a permanent feature of today's workplaces. Managers, therefore, are required to effectively manage a culturally diverse workforce.

The fostering of cultural diversity should be given a high priority because it brings many benefits, including:

- *better serving customers' needs*
- *enhancing a business's creativity, flexibility and responsiveness to change*
- *establishing new markets, especially those in which employees identify with the different cultures that support those markets.*

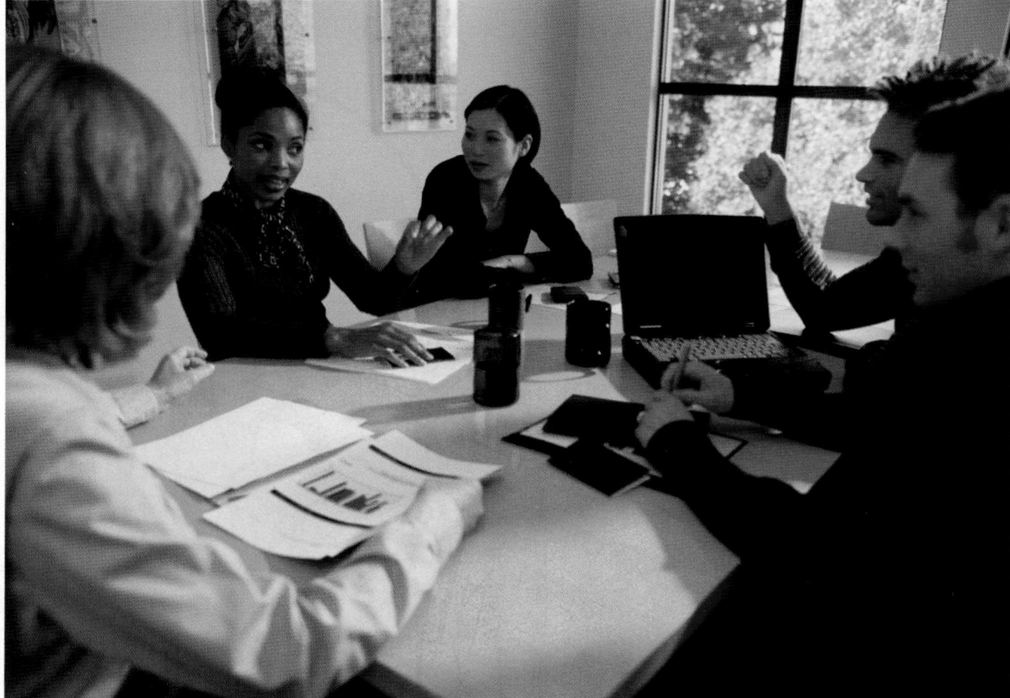

Figure 3.23 Workplace cultural diversity is now a key factor in Australia's international business success.

Fostering cultural diversity should be given a high priority because it brings many benefits. These include the following:

- Businesses may recognise their social responsibility to provide an equal opportunity environment.
- New markets may be more easily penetrated, especially by those employees who identify with the different cultures that support those markets.
- Customers' needs may be better served.
- Creativity, flexibility and responsiveness to change are enhanced.

Socially responsible business practices should, therefore, be designed to contribute to the quality of employees' working lives.

E-commerce

E-commerce, as previously outlined, is changing many facets of business organisations. The changes are rapid and diverse, affecting employees across a wide range of jobs. Some people argue that a business has a social responsibility to carefully monitor and minimise the negative impact of any such changes. They suggest that it is good business sense to devise programs that provide training and development opportunities, ergonomically designed workstations and procedures that assist employees in adapting to the changed work systems. Failure to do so may lead to loss of staff, lower rates of productivity due to a decline in employee job satisfaction or a compensation case brought about by inappropriate workplace design.

EXERCISE 3.5 Revision

1. Why should an effective manager continuously scan the business environment?
2. List two planning tools that can be used when trying to identify the need for change.
3. Outline why setting achievable goals can help managers implement change more successfully.
4. What is meant by the term 'change agent'?
5. Read the Biz Fact on page 89 outlining the concept of a learning organisation, and then discuss the following statement in the light of today's business environment.
   'The only sustainable competitive advantage is the ability to learn faster than your competitors.' (Peter Senge)
6. Distinguish between 'driving' and 'restraining' forces.
7. Explain force-field analysis.
8. Conduct a force-field analysis for changing the commencement time for your school from 9 am to 7 am.
9. Identify and briefly outline the three steps involved in Lewin's unfreeze/change/refreeze change model.
10. Why does a change program without proper 'unfreezing' have only a limited chance of success?
11. Because of recent changes to the Occupational Health and Safety Act you must implement some new safety procedures. You know that some of your employees are going to regard some of these changes as ridiculous. What might you do to get the employees to accept the changes?
12. Why should a business be concerned with its social responsibility?

13. Suggest a socially responsible change program to satisfy each of the following situations:
    (a) improving the quality of working life for employees
    (b) introducing new computer technology
    (c) making your employee mix more culturally diverse
    (d) integrating a number of business processing functions that use e-commerce.
14. Prepare a summary of this chapter. A summary condenses the important issues and concepts presented in the chapter. Go to www.jaconline.com.au/business studies3e to compare your finished summary with the one provided for this textbook.

Extension

1. (a) Explain the difference between change and innovation.
   (b) Think of some of the changes you have noticed within your school in the past year.
   (c) In each case, explain the extent to which the forces for change were internal or external.
   (d) List those changes that were implemented successfully.
   (e) Identify the factors that contributed to their success.
2. Assume you have been appointed managing director of an engineering business that is facing increased competition from products made overseas and needs, therefore, to improve productivity. Devise a plan for overcoming employee resistance to the changes that are necessary to increase production.
3. Think about a situation in which you would like to make a change, but one in which you face some resistance. The situations might involve improving your Business Studies results, changing the arrangement of your classroom or having greater use of the family car.
   (a) Write a brief outline of the status quo.
   (b) Write a brief description of the situation as you would like it to be if you could change it.
   (c) List the main driving forces.
   (d) List the main restraining forces.
   (e) Construct a force-field analysis diagram similar to figure 3.19 on page 90.
   (f) Devise strategies for reducing the impact of the restraining forces.
   (g) Present your diagram and your strategies to another class member for their evaluation.

Topic 2

Financial planning and management

FOCUS AREA: To develop an understanding of the role of financial planning within business operation and management and the interpretation of financial information.

Outcomes

Students should be able to:

- describe and analyse business functions and operations and their impact on business success
- evaluate the effectiveness of management in the organisation and operations of business and its responsiveness to change
- analyse the impact of management decision making on stakeholders
- critically analyse the social and ethical responsibilities of management
- evaluate management strategies in response to internal and external factors
- select, organise and evaluate information and sources for usefulness and reliability
- plan and conduct an investigation into a business to present the findings in an appropriate business format
- communicate business information, ideas and issues, using relevant business terminology and concepts in appropriate forms
- apply mathematical concepts appropriately in business situations.

Mind map showing the specific aspects examined for the 'Financial planning and management' topic

Gerry and Tony's computer business

Gerry and Tony established a computer business in the mid 1990s selling hardware and software for personal computers. The business was established as a partnership. Gerry had worked in the computer field for a number of years, while Tony had been a supervisor in the finance department of a large company. Both felt well qualified to run a business.

The business grew steadily in the first two years, but they were finding it increasingly difficult in their small premises. They wanted to expand into larger premises and employ staff to assist with sales and administration, but they were not sure how to go about it.

Having a large number of competitors, it was also important to keep abreast of the constantly changing and developing technology. But opportunities to 'grow' their business were limited with only two of them in the business. If one partner was away or sick there was no backup. They had noticed that if they were not able to give backup assistance their clients went elsewhere, usually to larger companies.

Sales of computer hardware and software fluctuate and, therefore, their cash flow varied quite significantly from month to month. They believed that this lack of regular cash flow was the main problem hindering the opportunities for growth.

Finally, Gerry and Tony visited their bank to discuss extra finance to help with cash flow and expand their business. This meeting made them realise that, although their business was growing in the short term, their lack of long-term vision and strategy was causing them problems in the longer term.

It was hard work — juggling the competing demands of:

- sufficient cash (liquidity)
- making profits (profitability)
- ensuring a good return on their investment (return on capital)
- increasing the size of their business (growth)
- achieving good use of their resources (efficiency).

They were determined that they would not go the way of many businesses — into bankruptcy through insufficient cash flows. Gerry and Tony realised and accepted that sound financial planning was the key to the growth and success of their business.

CHAPTER

4 The role of financial planning

4.1 Strategic role of financial management

 WORD

***Strategy** is the major tool adopted by an organisation to achieve its goals.*

*A **strategic plan** encompasses the strategies that an organisation will use to achieve its goals.*

Business organisations have specific goals they wish to achieve in relation to the investment in capital, training of staff and the expansion of operations. The **strategies** that an organisation adopts work towards achieving its goals both in the short and longer term. Developing a **strategic plan** as part of an organisation's financial management will ensure that the organisation survives and grows in the competitive business world.

Organisational goals and objectives

Organisations exist for a number of purposes that are translated into business goals. For example, a business's goals may include:

- to increase the dividends to shareholders
- to maintain an environmentally friendly organisation
- to be a market leader within five years.

These goals are translated, in turn, into **organisational objectives** that provide greater detail about the organisation's mission.

Organisational objectives break the business operations into achievable and manageable outcomes that can be measured and evaluated. Objectives give a clear indication to management of where the business wants to be.

Goals are the longer term outcomes of an organisation. The main purpose or goal for business organisations is usually to make a profit. An organisation can only make a profit if it has a carefully determined process by which it will achieve its goals. This process — its strategy — is the major tool that assists an organisation to achieve its goals. For example, to meet the goal of increasing the dividends to shareholders, an organisation will need to increase its profits. Its strategies might include opening up new outlets or expanding its marketing division.

 WORD

***Organisational objectives** break the business operations into achievable and manageable outcomes that can be measured and evaluated.*

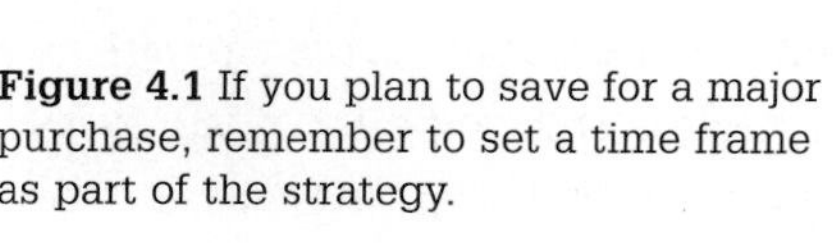

Figure 4.1 If you plan to save for a major purchase, remember to set a time frame as part of the strategy.

The Commonwealth Bank states its objectives this way: 'The Commonwealth Bank is one of Australia's leading financial institutions, with business in New Zealand, Asia and the United Kingdom. We are positioned for future growth, and aim to provide accessible banking and financial services for all Australians; fair, safe, challenging and rewarding employment for staff; and to reward all shareholders through dividends and capital growth.'

Strategic plans

Strategic plans are the most important plans for an organisation. They encompass a long-term view of where the organisation is going, how it will get there and a monitoring process to keep track of progress along the way. Strategic plans may cover periods of up to 10 years. The strategies that an organisation uses to achieve its goals are incorporated into a strategic plan. For example, if the strategic plan for Blue Green Skateboards is to be a market leader in the sale of skateboards, it might adopt the strategy of purchasing two new stores, one north and one south of its present location.

The goals of the strategic plan will be translated into short-term, specific objectives that make up the tactical (one to two years) and operational (day-to-day) plans of an organisation.

These short-term, specific objectives would be reviewed regularly to see if targets are being met and if resources are being used to the best advantage to achieve the objectives. For example, if management has a goal to achieve a 15 per cent increase in profit for the next 10 years, the tactical plans might involve purchasing additional machinery, updating old equipment with new technologies, expanding into new markets and providing new services. These objectives would be reviewed annually to see if the long-term goal of an increase in profit was being achieved.

Figure 4.2 The main elements of organisational planning

Managing financial resources

Financial resources are those resources of a business that have a monetary or money value. **Financial management** is the planning and monitoring of an organisation's financial resources to enable the organisation to achieve its financial goals.

Financial management is crucial if a business is to achieve its financial goals. The mismanagement of **financial resources** can lead to problems such as:

- insufficient cash to pay suppliers
- inadequate capital for expansion
- too many **assets** that are non-productive
- delays in accounts being paid
- possible business failure
- overstocking of materials.

Strategies for monitoring the financial resources of an organisation must be incorporated into its strategic plan. This involves:

- monitoring an organisation's cash flows
- paying its debts
- developing financial control techniques
- auditing of financial accounts
- continuing to make profits for its owners and shareholders.

Strategic planning of financial resources is essential to an organisation's success and growth.

Financial management *is the planning and monitoring of an organisation's financial resources to enable the organisation to achieve its financial goals.*

Financial resources *are those resources in a business that have a monetary or money value.*

Assets *are the property and other items and effects of a business, such as business premises, machinery, vehicles and cash (tangible assets) and patents, trademarks and goodwill (intangible assets).*

4.2 Objectives of financial management

For an organisation to achieve its longer term goals it must have a number of short-term, specific objectives. The objectives of financial management are to maximise the business's liquidity, profitability, efficiency, growth and return on capital. The responsibility of financial management is to make decisions about the best way to achieve those objectives (see figure 4.3). This will involve identifying and evaluating alternative courses of action and making recommendations.

How are we going to pay last month's accounts?
How profitable is the new line we introduced last March?
Is this the best use of our limited resources?
How can we do it better?
Why are our competitors able to sell the same product at a reduced price?
How will the new plant planned for 2008 be financed?
How can we ensure that our shareholders receive an increased dividend?

Figure 4.3 Some examples of the decisions that management might face, relating to its specific, short-term objectives. Sound financial management is about responding to such questions by choosing the most appropriate strategies to ensure that the financial objectives of an organisation are achieved.

Liquidity

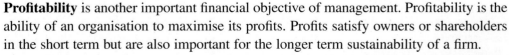

__Liquidity__ is the extent to which a business can meet its financial commitments in the short term.

Liquidity is an important financial objective of management. Liquidity is the ability of an organisation to pay its debts as they fall due. An organisation must have sufficient cash flow to meet its financial obligations or be able to convert current assets into cash quickly; for example, by selling inventory.

Controls over the flow of cash into and out of the business ensure that an organisation has supplies of cash when needed. Cash shortfalls and excess or idle cash must be avoided as both involve loss of profitability for a business.

Profitability

__Profitability__ is the ability of an organisation to maximise its profits.

Profitability is another important financial objective of management. Profitability is the ability of an organisation to maximise its profits. Profits satisfy owners or shareholders in the short term but are also important for the longer term sustainability of a firm.

To ensure that profit is maximised, an organisation must carefully monitor its revenue and pricing policies, costs and expenses, inventory levels and levels of assets.

Efficiency

***Efficiency** is the ability of a business to use its resources effectively in ensuring financial stability and profitability.*

Efficiency is the ability of an organisation to minimise its costs and manage its assets so that maximum profit is achieved with the lowest possible level of assets.

Efficiency generally relates to the operations or revenue-producing activities of the organisation. Achieving efficiency requires a firm to have control measures in place to monitor assets. An organisation that aims for efficiency must monitor the levels of inventories and cash and the collection of receivables.

Growth

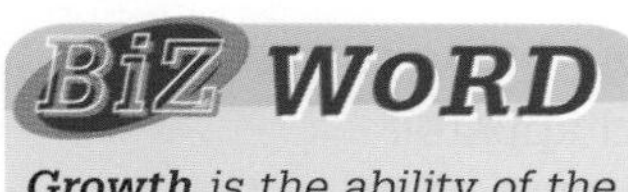

***Growth** is the ability of the organisation to increase its size in the longer term.*

Growth is the ability of the organisation to increase its size in the longer term. Growth of an organisation depends on its ability to develop and use its asset structure to increase sales, profits and market share. Growth is an important financial objective of management as it ensures that the organisation is sustainable into the future. An example of growth is shown in the Snapshot 'DJs follows golden thread of the young', which describes a strategy to increase profit levels adopted by the David Jones department stores.

Return on capital

***Return on capital** is the amount of profit returned to owners or shareholders as a percentage of their capital contribution.*

Owners and shareholders invest in an organisation through their contributions of capital. Their expectations are that profits will be maximised so that they receive a share of the profits. **Return on capital** is the amount of profit returned to owners or shareholders as a percentage of their capital contribution.

Owners and shareholders are interested in this financial objective as their return must be sufficient to make their investment worthwhile. Owners and shareholders assess their return on capital against other investment options. Shareholders are interested both in the amount of profit returned to them as dividends and the price of their shares.

DJs follows golden thread of the young

David Jones is putting the finishing touches to a marketing program aimed at enticing a younger generation of customers and driving sales of youth apparel.

The department store chain's youth-clothing business has grown fivefold over the last three years through the introduction of young Australian designer brands such as Sass & Bide, Fashion Assassin, Vicious Threads and Marcs Baby Doll.

For the last seven months, David Jones has been putting more resources into building its youth business, establishing a team to focus on ways to attract more 18- to 30-year-olds.

'We're enticing a customer with brands who wouldn't have been enticed before,' said David Bush, general manager men's and women's collections.

'Those brands are giving us a level of credibility we didn't previously have and giving us access to a customer that perhaps wasn't a department store shopper prior,' said Mr Bush, who heads the youth initiative. 'They'll find the same benefits as their mother finds shopping at David Jones.'

(continued)

The strategy involves adding more designer youth brands, establishing high-fashion concept areas housing seven or eight brands, and ultimately establishing an entire floor of fashion dedicated to young consumers.

'What it will do is give us more access to the younger customer and talk to them in a way that's a bit more relevant to them,' Mr Bush said.

Youth apparel now makes up 20 per cent of David Jones' clothing mix, compared with 4 per cent a few years ago, when it started signing up leading local and overseas designer brands as part of a strategy to differentiate its offering from that of Myer.

Mr Bush said David Jones' youth range would be more brand-driven than Myer's, which includes private labels as well as branded apparel.

'We see a very big difference between youth and [Myer's] Miss Shop,' Mr Bush said.

'This is far more design-driven, far more brand-driven — our customers respond to brands they see are credible, as opposed to price-pointed volume for the younger generation.'

In the past, David Jones' core demography has been consumers aged 35 plus — top-quartile earners who account for 50 per cent of discretionary spending. Now the retailer is extending its reach to younger consumers who might not have the same income but are prepared to pay for 'must-have' fashion.

Mr Bush said the retailer's youth business had not grown at the expense of its mainstream range.

'What we haven't seen is this business increase in dollar terms at the expense of something else, so we're still seeing the more established segments of our business growing very nicely,' he said.

Source: S. Mitchell, 'DJs follows golden thread of the young', *The Australian Financial Review*, 10 January 2005.

SNaPSHOT Questions

1. Why do you think the focus on 'youth apparel' is a valid strategy for achieving growth for David Jones?
2. Explain how David Jones aims to achieve this.

EXERCISE 4.1 Revision

1. Explain, with examples, the objectives of financial management.
2. Read the following strategy of Leading Bank and determine its objectives of financial management.

   Our strategy is to improve returns to proprietors by:
   - increasing the profitability of our retail business. We will do this by reducing costs substantially and by retaining and attracting valuable customer relationships through improved customer service.
   - reshaping our global institutional banking operations by changing our principal focus from corporate lending to a 'niche' global financial markets business

- reducing the impact of the problem asset portfolio on Leading Bank's performance
- improving returns from, or exiting, under-performing businesses
- reducing costs in, and improving the productivity of, the Corporate Centre.

Extension

1. The objectives of financial management sometimes conflict with each other. Explain this statement.
2. Examine the annual reports of a range of businesses and identify:
   (a) their goals
   (b) the strategies used to achieve their goals
   (c) the goals that were/were not achieved.

4.3 The planning cycle

Financial planning is essential if an organisation is to achieve its goals. Financial planning determines how an organisation's goals will be achieved. Figure 4.5 shows the main elements of the financial planning cycle.

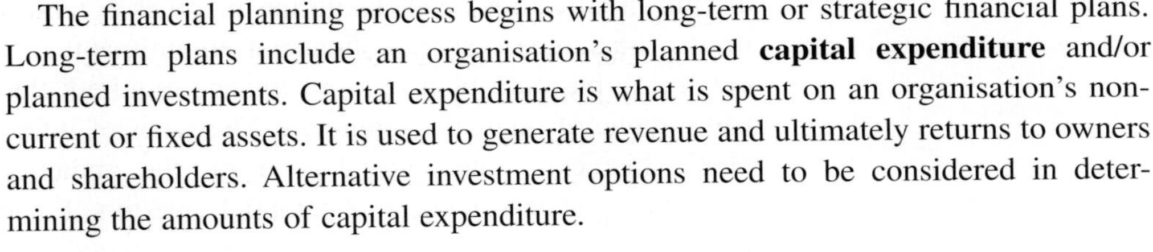

The financial planning process begins with long-term or strategic financial plans. Long-term plans include an organisation's planned **capital expenditure** and/or planned investments. Capital expenditure is what is spent on an organisation's non-current or fixed assets. It is used to generate revenue and ultimately returns to owners and shareholders. Alternative investment options need to be considered in determining the amounts of capital expenditure.

***Capital expenditure** is what is spent on an organisation's non-current or fixed assets.*

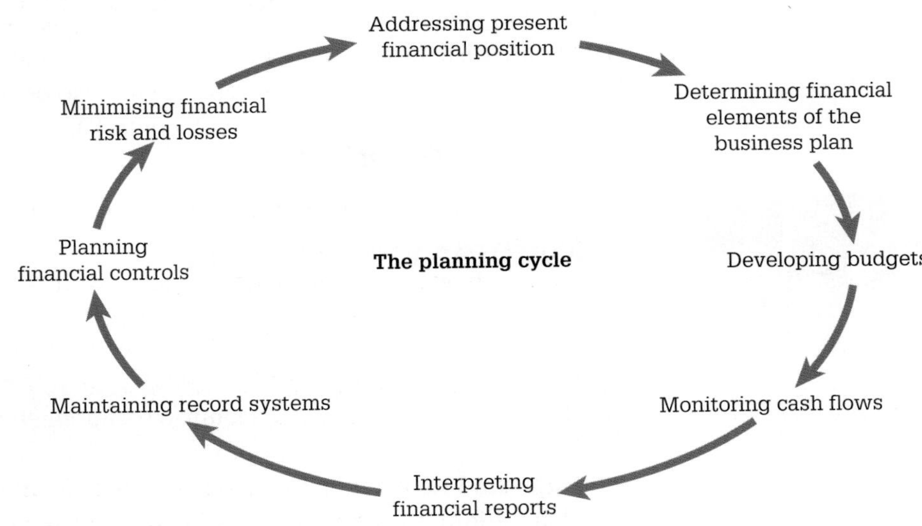

Figure 4.4 The planning cycle

The long-term plans also cover planned sources of finance, spending on research and development, marketing and product development activities. Long-term plans cover a time period of between two and 10 years. Long-term plans guide the development of short-term tactical and operating plans. Short-term plans are more specific and cover plans and budgets for periods of one to two years or one year or less.

Planning processes involve the setting of goals and objectives, determining the strategies to achieve those goals and objectives, identifying and evaluating alternative courses of action and choosing the best alternative for the organisation.

Planning processes involve the setting of goals and objectives, determining the strategies to achieve those goals and objectives, identifying and evaluating alternative courses of action and choosing the best alternative for the organisation.

Addressing the present financial position

In order to determine where an organisation is headed and how it will get there, it is important to know where it is positioned now. Important financial information needs to be collected before future plans can be made. This financial information includes balance sheets, revenue statements, cash flow statements, sales and price forecasts, budgets, bank statements, weekly reports from departments, break-even analysis, reports from financial ratio analysis and interpretation.

Determining financial elements of the business plan

As you learned in your study of the preliminary course, before any project is undertaken it is important that planning occurs and a business plan is drawn up. This ensures that the organisation knows what it aims to achieve, the processes it will use to achieve its aims and the benchmarks that show that it has been successful.

A business plan might be used when seeking finance or support for a project from a bank or other financial institution or other potential investors. These institutions need a guarantee that their financial commitment to the organisation will be successful. A business plan sets out finance required, the proposed sources of finance and a range of financial statements. The types of information included in a business plan's financial statements depend on the audience for the business plan — employees, owners, lenders or potential investors. Financial information is needed to show that the organisation can generate an acceptable return for the investment being sought and should, therefore, include an analysis of financial performance, revenue statement, cash flow statement, balance sheet and financial ratio analysis reports. Budgets and cost-volume-profit reports will also be included as part of the analysis of risk (see the Snapshot 'Conquer with control').

The form and content of the financial information in business plans vary but include some or all of the following:

- *revenue statement*
- *cash flow statement*
- *balance sheet*
- *cost-volume-profit analysis*
- *financial ratios.*

Conquer with control

Do you know exactly how much money from your last sale hit the bottom line? Suppose your competition suddenly drops their prices 10 per cent, what do you do?

Should you take a trade discount when applied?

My business is profitable but where's the cash?

How can I raise funds for my small business when the banks say no?

Can I afford my next big capital expenditure?

Questions like this come up every day for people in business and operators would dearly love to have the answers at their fingertips.

They can: it's called financial analysis and it's not rocket science.

A lot of small business owners think that by just keeping their noses to the grindstone and working like crazy, they'll prosper.

Despite headlines screaming a booming economy, success is not a given.

Competition is savage and costs tend to move like a runaway train.

A natural preoccupation with sales and growth tends to distract normally conscientious entrepreneurs, allowing financial mischief to undermine the best-laid plans.

But attention to key ratios such as sales-to-inventory is as much a part of business survival as getting the next widget out the door.

Ratios are about keeping control over the business.

Break-even analysis is one of the most basic financial tools used in management yet how many business owners apply this tool when planning, for example, to invest in expanding their business?

No expansion analysis is complete without a market analysis focusing on the (increased) sales you'll most likely get. You can then compare what you'll get — which the market analysis will tell you — with what you need to make the investment worthwhile from a financial analysis.

A basic analysis enables the business operator to calculate the sales volume necessary to cover costs including target or required profits — the break-even point.

If what you'll get is greater than what you need — it's a go.

If what you'll get is less than what you need — it's back to the drawing board.

Of course this may bewilder many operators not familiar with financial analysis.

Indeed many would say that you can simply work with your knowledge of the business costs to know when an investment is worthwhile.

Yet this would be akin to buying a property based on a photograph and no other data — hardly something a property investor or home buyer is likely to do.

Return-on-Investment (ROI), break-even points, inventory turns, receivables ratios, gross margin, are all financial indicators and ratios that many business operators will be familiar with.

Used to monitor daily, weekly, monthly or quarterly activity, every financial ratio opens a window into a specific aspect of the operation.

Taken together, ratios allow an owner to accurately understand how well the business is currently performing, whether productivity can be improved in specific areas and provide the financial justification behind growth plans.

Regular cash flow forecasting is another tool form the financial analysis toolkit.

That's what gives you time to react to fluctuations in the business.

If you forecast 12 months in advance, it will give you a pretty good idea of your potential to run out of cash.

Maybe the issue is faster turnover of your inventory, tightening accounts receivable or renegotiating the terms of a bank loan.

It gives you a chance to improve your cashflow so that you're not caught short six months from now when you realise there's not enough cash in the bank to meet the payroll.

The next stage of your business planning should be to undertake some financial analysis education. It's smart business.

Source: M. Kaplan, 'Conquer with control', *The Daily Telegraph*, 9 November 2004, p. 10.

SNaPSHOT Questions

1. Why is success not 'automatic' in a booming economy?
2. Why will attention to ratios be a more effective way to monitor the financial objectives of a business?
3. Why is regular cash flow forecasting also seen as a useful financial analysis tool?

Developing budgets

***Budgets** provide information in quantitative terms (facts and figures) about requirements to achieve a particular purpose.*

Budgets provide the facts and figures for planning and decision making, and enable constant monitoring of progress and problem areas. They signal where things are not going according to plan so that adjustments can be made, and show where achievement towards objectives has occurred.

Budgets provide information in quantitative terms (that is, as facts and figures) about requirements to achieve a particular purpose. Budgets can be drawn up to show:

- cash required for planned outlays for a particular period
- the cost of capital expenditure and associated expenses against earning capacity
- estimated use and cost of raw materials or inventory
- number and cost of labour hours required for production.

Budgets reflect the strategic planning decisions about how resources are to be used. They provide financial information for specific goals of a business and are used in strategic, tactical and operational planning.

Budgets enable constant monitoring of objectives and provide a basis for administrative control, direction of sales effort, production planning, control of stocks, price setting, financial requirements, control of expenses and production cost control.

Budgets are used in both the planning and the control aspects of a business. As a control measure, planned performance can be measured against actual performance and corrective action taken as needed.

A budget is an important part of the planning process and various factors need to be considered in preparing it, such as:

- review of past figures and trends, and estimates gathered from relevant departments in the business
- potential market or market share, and trends and seasonal fluctuations in the market
- proposed expansion or discontinuation of projects
- proposals to alter price or quality of products
- current orders and plant capacity
- considerations from the external environment; for example, financial trends from the external environment, availability of materials and labour.

***Operating budgets** relate to the main activities of an organisation and may include budgets relating to sales, production, raw materials, direct labour, expenses and cost of goods sold.*

***Project budgets** relate to capital expenditure and research and development.*

Budgets are often prepared to predict a range of activities relating to short-term and longer term plans and activities. Budgets can be classified as operating, project or financial budgets.

Operating budgets relate to the main activities of an organisation and may include budgets relating to sales, production, raw materials, direct labour, expenses and cost of goods sold. Information from operating budgets is used in preparing budgeted financial statements.

Project budgets relate to capital expenditure and research and development. Capital expenditure budgets in an organisation's strategic plan include information about the purpose of the asset purchase, life span of the asset and the revenue that would be generated from the purchase. Information from project budgets is included in the budgeted financial statements.

Financial budgets relate to financial data and include the budgeted revenue statement, balance sheet and cash flows.

Financial budgets relate to the financial data of an organisation. The predictions of the operating and project budgets are included in the budgeted financial statements. Financial budgets include the budgeted revenue statement, balance sheet and cash flows. The revenue statement and balance sheet reflect the results of operating activities and the cash flow statement shows the liquidity of an organisation.

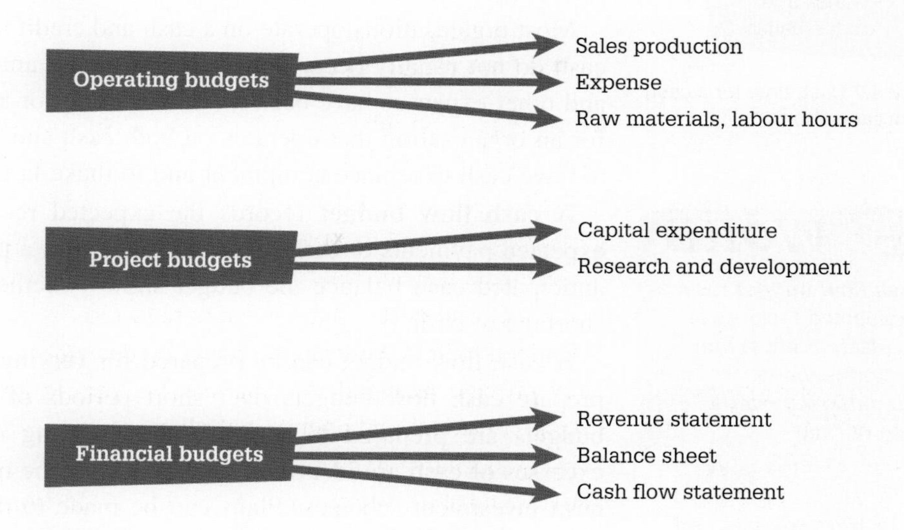

Figure 4.5 Operating, project and financial budgets

Budgeted Revenue Statement
for 3 months ended 30 June 2008

Sales	250 000
less cost of goods sold	195 000
Gross profit	55 000
less selling and administrative expenses	22 000
Net profit	33 000

Sales budget

	April $	May $	June $	Total $
Sales	85 000	90 000	75 000	250 000

Selling and administrative expenses budget

	April $	May $	June $
Fixed costs			
Advertising	2000	2000	2000
Rent	500	500	500
	2500	2500	2500
Variable costs			
Salaries	2800	3000	3400
Delivery	1500	2000	1800
	4300	5000	5200
Total	6800	7500	7700

Figure 4.6 Budgeted revenue statement including sales and expense predictions

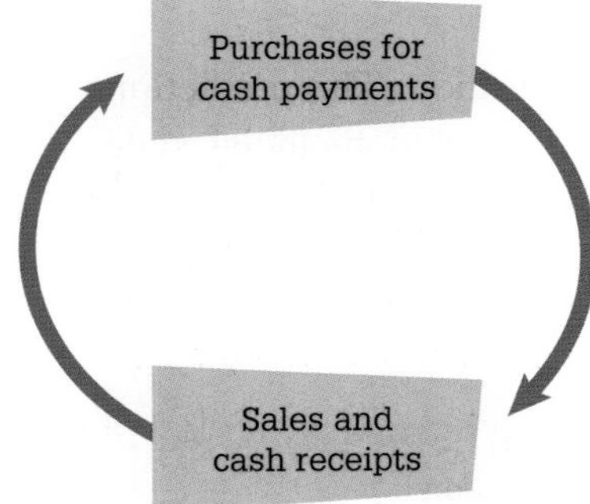

Figure 4.7 Cash flow for a cash only organisation

Cash flows

Cash is important in the planning cycle and sufficient supplies of cash are essential to ensure that financial objectives are met. Some organisations operate on a cash only basis. All transactions (purchases and sales) are paid for in cash. Their cash flows are easy to determine as cash receipts are generally sufficient to cover cash payments.

Most organisations operate on a cash and credit basis, which means that receipts of cash do not usually occur until the next month and usually after payments for stock and other expenses have been made. Planning for anticipated cash flows is important for an organisation that operates on both cash and credit. An organisation also needs to have cash to replace equipment and to make large sum payments.

*A **cash flow budget** records the expected receipts of cash (cash inflows) and expected payments of cash (cash outflows) over a period of time.*

A **cash flow budget** records the expected receipts of cash (cash inflows) and expected payments of cash (cash outflows) over a period of time. By determining the anticipated cash balance the budget shows whether the business has a surplus or a shortage of cash.

A cash flow budget can be prepared for varying periods of time but it is usual to prepare cash flow budgets over short periods of one to three months. Cash flow budgets are prepared to assist in the planning of short-term finance sources. If excesses of cash are identified, then plans can be made to place the surplus in short-term investment schemes. Plans can be made to determine how much and for how long cash surpluses can be invested to achieve the best return, for example, the short-term money market. If there is an anticipated cash shortage then short-term borrowing plans or changes to current assets can be made to overcome the shortfall. By anticipating cash shortfalls an organisation can investigate the cheapest method of financing these shortfalls, such as a bank overdraft or loan.

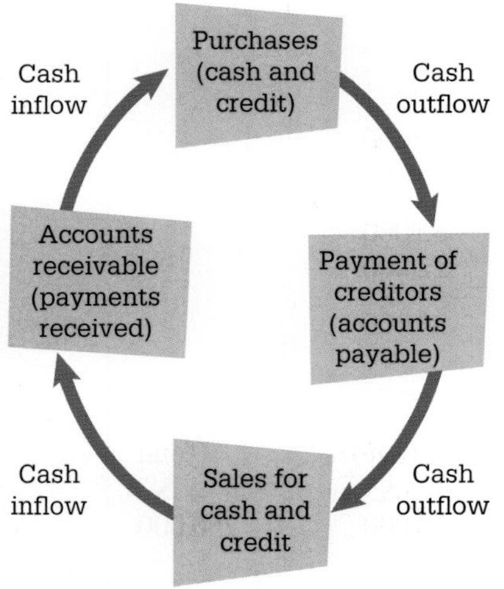

Figure 4.8 Cash flow for an organisation operating on credit and cash

Figure 4.9 shows the monthly cash flow statement. The budgeted cash flow statement shows the cash inflows for each month (from cash sales and accounts receivable payments) and projected outflows for each month (payments to creditors, employees, expenses, purchase of assets).

Budgeted Cash Flow Statement
for 3 months ended 30 June 2008

	April $	May $	June $
Cash receipts (accounts receivable)	38 000	52 000	48 000
Total receipts	38 000	52 000	48 000
Cash payments			
Purchases	15 000	16 500	17 800
Selling and administrative expenses	6 200	8 000	7 800
Purchase of motor vehicle	32 000		
Total payments	53 200	24 500	25 600
Net cash surplus/deficit	(15 200)	27 500	22 400
Opening cash balance	10 000	(5 200)	22 300
Closing cash balance	(5 200)	22 300	44 700

Figure 4.9 An example of a budgeted cash flow statement

Financial reports

Preparation of the budgeted financial reports is an important part of the planning cycle. Financial reports show what the organisation plans to achieve by the end of the period. Data from the operating and project budgets are used to prepare projected financial reports. The results or financial outcomes of an organisation's planning are reflected in a budgeted revenue statement, budgeted balance sheet and budgeted cash flows.

Budgeted Revenue Statement
for 3 months ended 30 June 2008

	$	$
Sales		350 000
less cost of goods sold		260 000
Gross profit		90 000
less operating expenses		
Selling	11 500	
Administrative	10 500	22 000
		68 000
less interest expense		2 500
Net profit		65 500

Figure 4.10 An example of a budgeted revenue statement

Budgeted Balance Sheet
as at 30 June 2008

	$	$
Assets		
Current Assets		
Cash	44 700	
Inventory	8 000	
Accounts receivable	15 000	67 700
Non-current Assets		
Motor vehicle	58 000	
Plant and equipment	104 000	162 000
Total Assets		229 700
less Liabilities		
Current Liabilities		
Accounts payable	5 800	
Non-current Liabilities		
Loan	22 600	
Total Liabilities		28 400
Capital		201 300

Figure 4.11 An example of a budgeted balance sheet

A cash budget (statement of budgeted cash flows) predicts the organisation's liquidity situation over the period. Cash shortfalls or cash surpluses enable decisions to be made about financing activities in the short term.

Interpretation

Budgets provide invaluable information in the planning process to achieve financial objectives and reflect the assumptions that an organisation makes about the future. Budgets provide warning signals and a realistic assessment of what is going to happen within the organisation.

Budgeted financial reports will be used to evaluate plans and to make changes if predicted results do not satisfactorily reflect the goals of the organisation. It must be remembered that the budgeted financial reports are estimates only and that the reality may be different to the plans.

Maintaining record systems

Record systems *are the mechanisms employed by an organisation to ensure that data are recorded and the information provided by record systems is accurate, reliable, efficient and accessible.*

Record systems are the mechanisms employed by an organisation to ensure that data are recorded and the information provided by record systems is accurate, reliable, efficient and accessible. Management bases its decisions on the information when needed and must have guarantees that the information is accurate and reliable.

Minimising errors in the recording process and producing accurate and reliable financial statements are important aspects of maintaining record systems. The double entry system of accounting is an important control aspect. By recording all items twice, the entries can be seen to balance, and checks to find errors can be carried out quickly.

Planning financial controls

Financial problems and losses prevent an organisation from achieving its goals. The most common causes of financial problems and losses are:

- theft
- fraud
- damage or loss of assets
- errors in record systems.

Theft and fraud include unnecessary or over-purchase of stock for personal use, conflict of interest, misuse of expense accounts, false invoices, theft of inventory or assets and credit card fraud.

Financial controls *are the policies and procedures that ensure that the plans of an organisation will be achieved in the most efficient way.*

Financial problems can be caused by both management and employees. **Financial controls** ensure that the plans that have been determined will lead to the achievement of the organisation's goals in the most efficient way.

The policies and procedures of an organisation are designed to ensure that they are followed by management and employees. Control is particularly important in assets such as accounts receivable, inventory and cash (see the Snapshot 'How to avoid a cash flow crisis' on page 113). Some common policies and procedures that promote control within an organisations are:

- clear authorisation and responsibility for tasks in the organisation
- separation of duties; for example, one person is responsible for ordering and another for receiving inventories; one person writes the cheques and another signs the cheques
- rotation of duties; for example, staff are skilled in a number of areas and can rotate duties

- control of cash, such as the use of cash registers, cash banked daily, no money kept on premises overnight, payments made by cheque not cash
- protection of assets; for example, buildings are kept locked, a registry of assets is maintained, regular checks of inventory are carried out and security surveillance systems are installed
- control of credit procedures, such as following up overdue accounts and credit checks of customers.

Budgets and variance reporting are financial controls used in businesses. Budgets are an important planning tool as they assist a business to estimate resource requirements for a specified future period to predict what will be achieved by an organisation. For example, preparing a cash budget enables an organisation to predict cash shortages.

How to avoid a cash flow crisis

Cash shortages can prevent you from meeting your financial obligations and might make it difficult to expand your business. It may even mean you have to close up shop. Follow these tips from the NSW Department of State and Regional Development to manage your cash flow:

- Account for every dollar and cent.
- Install an accounting system that produces relevant financial reports and meets tax requirements.
- Keep your financial records and bookkeeping up to date.
- Keep a detailed account of all your debtors and act promptly on overdue accounts and dishonoured cheques.
- Use the information in your accounting system to draw up a budget and cash flow forecast.
- Manage your cash inflow and outflow — be prepared for anticipated tax instalments and other payments.
- Do your banking regularly, both for security reasons as well as keeping track of your cash flow.
- Reconcile your bank statements regularly, double-checking receipts and payments with your own records.
- Remind your staff never to pay accounts if they have not been provided with a tax invoice bearing an ABN.
- Ensure you receive, record and retain all tax invoices for GST taxable purchases to support your claim for input tax credits.
- Consider visiting your accountant every three months to review your business performance.
- Bill your customers early and often.
- Consider offering discounts for cash sales or early payments of credit purchases.
- Keep a detailed list of amounts that you owe. Debts can soon mount up.
- If suppliers want to be paid early, ask about discounts for early payments.

Source: The Daily Telegraph, 11 January 2005.

SNaPSHOT Questions

1. Choose the three tips that are most important for managing cash flow. Give resons for your choices.
2. Choose three tips that you think small business owners might find difficult to implement. Give reasons for your choices.

Comparing other budgets with actual results is also an important financial control used by businesses. By determining the difference or variance between budgeted and actual results, changes can be made as needed. **Variance reports** show the difference between budgeted and actual performance. Variance reports can be prepared for sales, production, raw materials, direct labour, expenses and cost of goods sold.

***Variance reports** show the difference between budgeted and actual performance.*

Variance report — receipts and payments

	Budget $	Actual $	Variance $
Receipts			
Sales — cash	190 000	170 000	(20 000)
— accounts receivable	58 000	52 000	(6 000)
Total receipts	248 000	222 000	(26 000)
Payments			
Purchases — cash	120 000	140 000	+20 000
— accounts payable	78 000	68 000	(10 000)
Selling and administrative expenses	9 000	8 500	(500)
Interest expense	500	500	—
	207 500	217 000	+ 9 500

Figure 4.12 A variance report for cash receipts and payments

Minimising financial risks and losses

***Financial risk** is the risk to a business of being unable to cover its financial obligations.*

Financial risk is the risk to a business of being unable to cover its financial obligations, such as the debts that a business incurs through borrowings, both short term and longer term. If the business is unable to meet its financial obligations, bankruptcy will result.

There are many questions that a business must answer in relation to financial risk:

- Should the organisation borrow to expand its operations?
- Will shareholders/owners be prepared to contribute to the business or will expansion be financed through borrowings?
- Should the organisation use its excess funds to purchase assets or invest on the short-term money market?
- Will interest rates go up?
- What about changing exchange rates?

In assessing financial risk for a business, consideration must be given to:

- the amount of the organisation's borrowings
- when borrowings are due to be repaid
- interest rates
- the required level of current assets needed to finance operations.

If the business is financed from borrowings there is higher risk. The higher the risk, the greater the expectation of profits or dividends.

The low level of interest rates in the late 1990s meant lower risk for businesses. As interest rates rise, careful consideration must be given to the amount of debt incurred by the organisation and hence the risk.

To minimise financial risk, organisations must consider the amount of profit that will be generated. The profit must be sufficient to cover the cost of debt as well as increasing profits to justify the amount of risk taken by owners and shareholders. Consideration must also be given to the liquidity of an organisation's assets. If an organisation has short-term debt, it must have liquid assets so that debts including interest payments and the repayment of principal on loans can be covered. Careful consideration is needed to ensure that financial risk and losses are minimised for an organisation.

EXERCISE 4.2 Revision

1. Explain, with examples, the financial elements of the planning cycle.
2. Why is the preparation of financial information essential as part of the business plan?
3. Using the following information on Kennedy's Gardening Supplies, answer the questions below.

Kennedy's Gardening Supplies

	2006 $	2007 $	2008 $
Forecast cash position	85 000	150 000	185 000
Forecast profits	40 000	75 000	90 000
Forecast net assets	350 000	390 000	410 000

Kennedy's is requesting an increase of bank overdraft facility from 2006 of $80 000 and a loan of $50 000 to fund their expansion.

   (a) What further financial information would you require in the business plan of Kennedy's Gardening Supplies?
   (b) Suggest how Kennedy's might prepare their information for their funding application to the bank.
4. Explain the different types of budgets and their importance in financial planning.
5. Draw diagrams to represent the possible cash flow situation for each of the following different types of businesses.
   (a) William & Partners, solicitors
   (b) Slater's Plumbing & Gasfitting
   (c) Corbett Security, custom made and installed security doors
6. Prepare a budgeted cash flow statement from the following information. The cash balance for 1 October is $3500.

	October $	November $	December $
Receipts from sales	60 000	80000	95 000
Purchases	35 000	45 000	65 000
Selling expenses	12 000	15 000	20 000
Interest on loan payment	1 000	1 000	1 000
Sale of motor vehicle			8 000

7. Why are budgeted revenue statements and the balance sheet important to a business? Prepare a budgeted revenue statement using the information in question 6.

8. Write a memo to the manager of a fashion design company explaining how budget and variance analysis will assist the business.
9. Study the comparative report below and answer the following questions. (Note that a variance of 10 per cent is acceptable for this business.)
   (a) From the information in the comparative report, make recommendations where you think the performance of the business can be improved.
   (b) Suggest reasons for your recommendations.

Comparative Report — Receipts and Payments

	Budgeted	Actual	Variance
	$	$	$
Receipts			
Sales			
— Cash	3 000	3 000	—
— Accounts Receivable	8 000	8 800	+10%
Total receipts	11 000	11 800	+7%
Payments			
Purchases			
— Cash	1 500	1 400	–6%
— Accounts Payable	2 000	2 400	+20%
Wages	500	600	+20%
Insurance	100	100	—
Advertising	300	350	+17%
Total payments	4 400	4 850	+10%

10. Prepare a summary of this chapter. A summary condenses the important issues and concepts presented in the chapter. Go to www.jaconline.com.au/businessstudies3e to compare your finished summary with the one provided for this textbook.

Extension

1. 'Sound planning is crucial to achieving the financial objectives of an organisation.' Discuss.
2. Identify the stages in the planning cycle. Give a brief description of each stage using examples from your own knowledge of local businesses.
3. Prepare and conduct a survey of local businesses identifying the strategies employed by businesses for financial control.

5 Financial markets relevant to the financial needs of business

5.1 Introduction to financial markets

Figure 5.1 A person or business with surplus funds to invest is faced with many options.

***Financial markets** are made up of the individuals, institutions and systems supplying excess funds to those who require them. The term 'financial' relates to money, and 'market' indicates trading activity.*

The choices and decisions regarding the use of money, whether it is your own or that of a business, involve transactions and dealings in **financial markets**. Financial markets are made up of the individuals, institutions and systems that enable funds to be moved efficiently from those who have excess funds to those who require funds.

Financial markets are important for businesses because they provide:

- access to funds
- investment opportunities and contacts in managing funds
- expertise in financial market dealings.

Financial intermediaries *receive money from those with excess funds and provide finance to those wishing to borrow money.*

Exchange traded markets *are those traded on an authorised exchange, such as the Australian Stock Exchange (ASX) and Sydney Futures Exchange (SFE).*

Over-the-counter (OTC) markets *are not traded on an exchange, but transactions take place via telephone and other means of communication.*

Short-term debt instruments include cash, repos (repurchase agreements), deposits, bank bills, promissory notes, treasury notes, certificates of deposit and bonds with a fixed interest rate and maturity date of less than one year. Businesses use short-term debt instruments to invest their short-term cash excesses or to borrow to cover short-term cash shortages.

Long-term debt instruments include government bonds, corporate bonds, public authority securities and mortgage backed securities. These instruments usually have a fixed interest and have a maturity date of more than 10 years. Businesses use long-term debt instruments to fund their long-term capital requirements.

As part of its financial planning and management strategies, an organisation makes both financial and investment decisions. It needs initial finance or funds to establish itself, then the business must make investment decisions that enable it to operate and grow.

Financial management involves providing short-term funds for short-term needs and matching long-term funds with investments for capital projects. For example, if a business decided to build a new factory, long-term funding would be needed. Reliable cash flow would also be needed for a period of, say, 10 years until the project is completed. For the success of the project, provision must be made to guarantee that finance needs are met. The business would have to make important investment decisions that involve a range of dealings in financial markets.

The financial markets are made up of **financial intermediaries** such as banks, finance companies, merchant banks, building societies, insurance companies and superannuation funds. They receive money from those with excess funds, provide borrowers with access to funds and identify income-producing opportunities for savers; for example, through interest on deposits. They also provide advice and protection. Some participants in financial markets deal directly with each other. Some participants deal with intermediaries.

Financial intermediaries are able to provide large amounts of money to borrowers as money is pooled from different sources and they can spread the risk over a larger number of borrowers. This enables lower interest rates to be offered to those wishing to borrow. A greater range of financing options can be offered through the large number of borrowers and lenders with whom they deal.

Types of financial markets

Financial markets are either **exchange traded markets** or **over-the-counter markets**.

- Exchange traded markets are traded on an authorised exchange. The Australian Stock Exchange (ASX) and Sydney Futures Exchange (SFE) are examples of authorised exchanges.
- Over-the-counter (OTC) markets are not traded on an exchange, but transactions take place via telephone and other means of communication. OTC transactions are not subject to the rules and regulations of authorised exchanges and can be adapted to suit the needs of borrowers and investors. The OTC markets comprise four submarkets:
  - *Cash and securities markets*. These comprise both short-term and long-term debt instruments (see the Biz Fact on the left) usually with a fixed interest rate or yield. The range of financial instruments that exists for companies participating in the cash and securities market is summarised in table 5.1.
  - *Foreign exchange markets*. These involve the purchase and sale of currencies within Australia and overseas. Businesses normally use foreign exchange markets when undertaking financial transactions with overseas companies.
  - *Commodity markets*. These were developed in order to protect against changes in the price of commodities that businesses produce or purchase. Minerals, fuel and electricity are commonly traded in these markets.
  - *Derivatives markets*. These were developed to provide flexibility for business needs. Derivatives markets involve a number of financial instruments that can be interchanged and altered to suit the needs of participants.

Figure 5.2 Inside the Australian Stock Exchange

TABLE 5.1	**Cash and securities market — financial instruments**
Financial instrument	**Description**
Corporate bonds	A fixed interest security with a fixed maturity date
Junk bonds	Corporate bond issues of high-risk companies with low credit ratings
Eurobonds	Securities in another currency that are simultaneously issued in the major capital markets overseas. Eurobonds are fixed interest borrowings that mature in 5 to 10 years and are sold in countries with a different currency to the country in which the issue is made.
Unsecured notes	Issued by large companies with a strong financial reputation. Offer no security or priority to the value of the assets if a company defaults. As unsecured notes are a low priority for repayment, they offer higher interest rates.

5.2 Major participants in financial markets

The major participants in financial markets are banks, finance and insurance companies, merchant banks, superannuation, mutual funds (unit trusts) companies, public and private companies, and government (Reserve Bank of Australia).

Banks

Banks are the major operators in financial markets and are a most important source of funds for businesses. Their levels of profit and service often draw criticism from businesses (see the Snapshot 'Big banks work hard on small businesses' on page 120). Banks receive savings as deposits from individuals, businesses and governments and, in turn, make investments and loans to borrowers.

"My bank is committed to agribusiness"

Is yours?

When you're depositing your hard earned income it makes sense to invest with a bank that is committed to agribusiness - a bank that re-invests back into rural Australia.

Earn 5.35% pa

for 3 months on balances of $20,000 or more. Competitive rates are offered on lower amounts.

For more information please contact your local Elders branch, call 1300 660 115 or visit www.eldersruralbank.com.au

Elders Rural Bank
Committed to Agribusiness

Offer subject to change without notice. Terms, conditions, fees and charges may apply. This document has been prepared without taking into account your personal circumstances, objectives, financial situation or needs. Before deciding to acquire or hold the product, Elders Rural Bank recommends you read the relevant Product Disclosure Statement which is available by phoning our Customer Service Centre on 1300 660 115, by accessing our website at www.eldersruralbank.com.au, or by visiting your local branch. This product is issued by Elders Rural Bank Limited and distributed by Elders Limited. Elders Rural Bank Limited ABN 74 083 938 416 AFSL 238042. Registered office: 27 Currie Street, Adelaide SA 5000.

ERB236291 08/05

Figure 5.3 Competition between banks often focuses on interest rates.

Most of the funds provided through financial markets come from banks, which operate on their own behalf or on behalf of other corporations, although other financial institutions, credit unions and building societies also operate in the financial market.

Banks are the largest form of financial institution in Australia, although their share has declined as the financial markets have become deregulated. They perform an increasingly wide range of roles rather than specialising in one area, and have subsidiaries in superannuation and mutual and other funds. Banks are supervised by the Reserve Bank of Australia (see pages 123–4).

Big banks work hard on small business

Australia's top banks are rejecting claims made in a recent survey that they are slow to deliver on the banking needs of small and medium-sized enterprises, citing their own results and commissioned research as a defence.

A recent joint survey by JP Morgan and East & Partners found the major banks had treated **SMEs** as a 'low priority' for many years but it is understood at least one of the top banks says the survey's data doesn't tally with the data it has to hand.

East & Partners principal analyst Paul Dowling says the firm has no intention of debating the matter in the public arena.

Most of the market share and customer satisfaction data made public by the big banks themselves, on occasions such as the release of their results, tends to be very positive, if not flattering.

CPA Australia's business policy adviser, Judy Hartcher, says relationship management is a priority issue for SMEs.

A recent study of 859 small businesses by CPA Australia and Flinders University of South Australia showed slow and inefficient handling of bank accounts and an unsatisfactory relationship with management were the main reasons why 10 per cent of small businesses switched banks in the past three years.

The survey showed that, overall, most small businesses were satisfied with their banks, but about one-third of them have facilities at another institution.

'Many small businesses are hedging their bets, having a second bank as a back-up facility. About one-quarter have credit card facilities at the second bank most likely to extend their short-term credit options,' says Hartcher.

ANZ and Westpac are among those that talked up their relationships with SMEs last week.

Graham Hodges has been running ANZ's business banking division since it was established in July 2000. Since then, he has implemented a lot of changes at the bank, taking on a large number of extra staff, opening more business centres and creating new specialty areas for franchising and other industry-based sectors. He has also done a lot of work on how ANZ services its clients and he has simplified processes.

In keeping with its decentralised business model, ANZ recently appointed three managing directors to run its corporate banking, business banking and small business operations. The three will report to Hodges.

***SME** stands for small to medium-sized enterprise. Whether a business is an SME is determined by turnover, number of employees and asset value.*

'There has been a very considered investment in the SME part of the world for four years,' Hodge says. 'It is not a recent investment or a recent realisation that this is a valuable sector.'

At Westpac, Mike Pratt says the SME sector has been his focus as group executive, business and consumer banking, for the past $2\frac{1}{2}$ years. The bank lost vital ground to rival National Australia Bank in the mid- to late-1990s, but has been steadily recouping those losses in recent times.

Pratt says that renewed focus on SMEs has allowed Westpac to snare 12.5 per cent share of the market in Australia, up 70 basis points in the past year and up 3 per cent in the past five years.

He also cites TNS Business Finance Monitor results that show that, in New Zealand, Westpac has about 25 per cent of the SME market.

According to Roy Morgan Research, the percentage of Australian SMEs that are 'very or fairly satisfied' with the bank is 63 per cent, up 5 per cent on a year earlier.

In New Zealand, RNS Business Finance Monitor has found that the percentage of New Zealand SMEs that rate Westpac's service as either 'excellent' or 'very good' is 50 per cent, up 6 per cent on September 2003.

Source: D. Lynch, 'Big banks work hard on small business', *The Australian Financial Review*, November 2004, p. 52.

SNAPSHOT Questions

1. List the reasons (suggested in the Snapshot) for small businesses being 'unsatisfied' with banks.
2. Explain why you think these issues would affect business operations.
3. What changes are banks making to improve their performance with small to medium-sized enterprises? Give examples.

Finance and insurance companies

Finance and insurance companies are non-bank financial intermediaries that specialise in smaller commercial finance. These companies are regulated by the Australian Financial Institutions Commission.

Finance companies act primarily as intermediaries in financial markets. They provide loans to businesses and individuals through consumer hire purchase loans, personal loans and secured loans to businesses. They are also the major providers of lease finance to businesses. Some finance companies specialise in factoring or cash flow financing.

Finance companies raise capital through share issues (debentures). Debentures are for a fixed term and carry a fixed rate of interest. Lenders have the security of priority over the firm's assets in the event of liquidation. In other words, the finance company is entitled to sell the assets of the business to recover the initial loan if the business fails.

Insurance companies provide loans to the corporate sector through receipts of insurance premiums, which provide funds for investment. They provide large amounts of both equity and loan capital to businesses. Insurance can be general insurance (covering property or accident) or life insurance. The funds received in premiums, called reserves, are invested in financial assets. The premiums paid by investors provide for compensation should something adverse happen, such as injury or death, or for savings for future needs.

Life insurance companies are significant investors in financial markets. This is because they are able to invest in long-term securities as the mortality of their contributors is predictable and premiums collected involve significant amounts of savings. Life insurance companies also manage funds for other investors; for example, superannuation funds.

Fixed interest securities make up the majority of portfolios for insurance and superannuation companies because their investments are held to match long-term liabilities. As investments (assets) mature at the same time as securities (liabilities), protection is given in their portfolios.

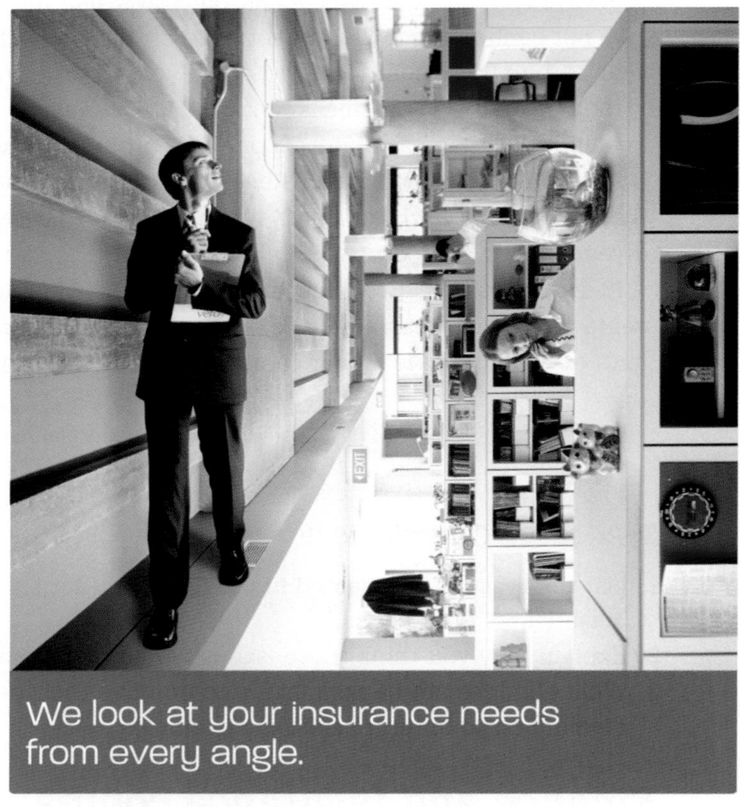

We look at your insurance needs from every angle.

From top to bottom, from inside and out, from micro to macro.
It's a way of looking at your business that gives us a much deeper understanding of your insurance needs. Combined with our structure of individual, expert business units, it means more thorough insurance coverage for you or your business.
To see how our range of products can help you, ask your broker about Vero or visit our website.
vero.com.au
Vero Insurance Limited ABN 48 005 297 807

a deeper understanding of your insurance needs.
that's our angle.

Figure 5.4 An example of an insurance company and the services it offers

Photographer © Chris Barlow/Sugar Love Pictures

Merchant banks must be licensed under the Securities Industry Code or the Futures Industry Code and they must meet financial and other requirements to deal in or advise on securities and future markets. Merchant banks make up the bulk of the non-bank financial institutions authorised to operate in foreign exchange.

Merchant banks

Merchant banks, or investment banks as many prefer to be known, make up one of the fastest growing sectors in the Australian financial system, providing services in both borrowing and lending, primarily to the business sector. Merchant banks:

- trade in money, securities and financial futures
- arrange long-term finance for company expansion
- provide working capital
- arrange project finance
- advise clients on foreign exchange cover
- advise on mergers and takeovers
- provide portfolio investment management services
- underwrite corporate and semi-government issues of securities

- operate unit trusts including cash management trusts, property trusts and equity trusts
- arrange overseas finance.

Superannuation funds

Superannuation funds have grown rapidly in Australia over the past 20 years due to tax incentives and compulsory superannuation introduced by the government. These organisations provide funds to the corporate sector through investment of funds received from superannuation contributions. Superannuation funds are able to invest in long-term securities as company shares, government and company debt because of the long-term nature of their funds.

Mutual funds (unit trusts)

Mutual funds take funds from a large number of small investors and invest them in specific types of financial assets. Mutual funds investments include the short-term money market (cash management trusts), shares, mortgages and property, and public securities. In recent years some mutual funds have also invested in gold, silver, oil and gas. Mutual funds are usually connected to a management firm that manages a diversified investment portfolio for its investors.

Public and private companies

Publicly listed and private companies participate in financial markets through:
- borrowing money to fund their operations
- investing their excess funds
- dealing in foreign exchange and commodities with overseas suppliers.

Companies issue securities on the primary market and buy and sell marketable securities. Companies participate in financial markets for a range of purposes — to manage their cash flows, foreign currency transactions and liabilities. For example, a company may invest in the cash market to earn a return on temporarily idle funds. The flexibility of the cash market enables a company to manage temporary shortages or excesses in cash flow. The cash market offers overnight (11 am repayment or renegotiation), 24-hour call or fixed-term periods investment and borrowing opportunities. Through the issuing of corporate bonds and debentures, companies have security of long-term funding for their activities.

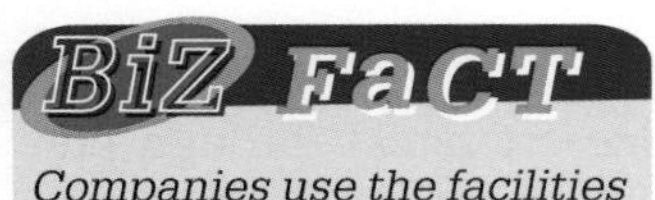

Companies use the facilities of financial markets to provide solutions to their financial problems and needs.

Government: the Reserve Bank of Australia

The government and its various departments and ministries, as well as statutory authorities such as Sydney Water, are participants in financial markets, operating through the Reserve Bank of Australia and commercial banks, providing funds for businesses and currency and interest rate swap services.

The Reserve Bank of Australia (RBA) is Australia's central bank and acts as banker and financial agent for the federal government. It supervises the financial system and manages monetary policy with the objectives of contributing to the stability of the Australian economy and to the welfare of the people. It is a vital and important component of the Australian financial market and participates as an end user in cash, securities and foreign exchange markets. The RBA uses its portfolio to influence market conditions to support monetary policy.

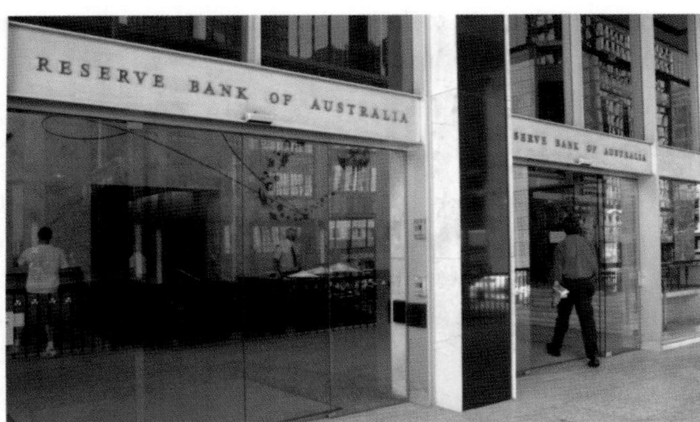

Figure 5.5 Reserve Bank of Australia, Martin Place, Sydney

The RBA holds its own portfolio of government securities and foreign exchange which are traded in the market. The sale of a security from the RBA's portfolio or the fresh issue of a government security affects the amount of money within the economy. The RBA operates in markets to manipulate the amount of money in the economy and thus influence interest rates.

Figure 5.6 The RBA sells securities to reduce the amount of money in the economy, thus increasing interest rates.

The Reserve Bank regulates and monitors banks and smooths the business cycle by influencing interest rates through the financial markets.

The RBA can also influence liquidity (and therefore interest rates) through purchases and sales of currencies. It enters the market from time to time to influence the level of the Australian dollar. If the bank buys Australian dollars from the market it tightens cash. If it buys foreign currencies in exchange for Australian dollars it adds to the pool of domestic cash.

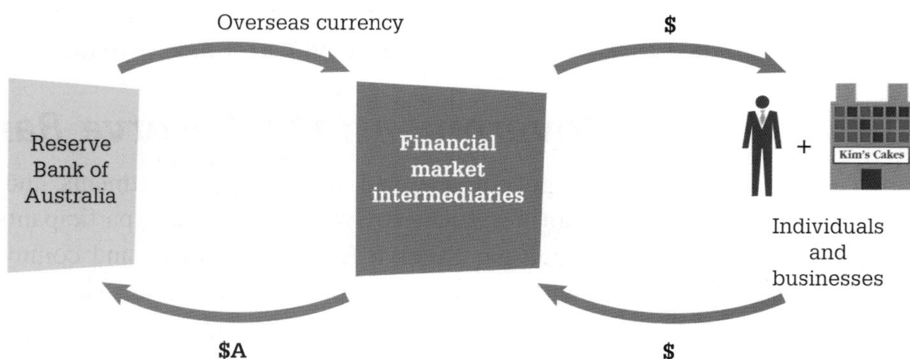

Figure 5.7 The RBA purchases foreign exchange to increase the money supply and decrease interest rates.

The RBA issues treasury notes and Commonwealth (treasury) bonds — bank bills or private sector bonds. Its activities are an important influence on business confidence and, hence, borrowing and investment.

EXERCISE 5.1 Revision

1. Explain the role of financial markets in meeting the needs of businesses.
2. Draw a table, as indicated below, to summarise the major participants in financial markets.

Institution	Financial instruments	Special characteristics

3. Choose three financial instruments. Research current interest rates, maturity dates, and terms and conditions from a range of institutions.
4. My business anticipates a cash flow excess of $100 000 over the next month. Suggest investment opportunities for the business. Justify your suggestions.

Extension

1. It has been said that financial markets drive the financial and investment decisions of businesses. Comment on this statement.
2. Choose one of the major participants in financial markets. Research the services offered to businesses. Find out current interest rates for borrowing and investing for businesses. Compare your investigations with other students.
3. Research the role of technology in improving financial market interactions for businesses. Write a report to management on how changing technology in financial markets can improve financial and investment decisions.

5.3 Australian Stock Exchange

The Australian Stock Exchange (ASX) is a listed company — in 1998 it became the first stock exchange in the world to demutualise and list on its own market. It comprises stockbroker corporations and partnerships, and provides a marketplace for the trading in shares. The ASX assists listed companies to raise funds from the public through share issues (equity) and trade in debt instruments.

The ASX regulates and monitors its members and their activities and ensures that listed companies meet the listing requirements. Members are subject to the rules and procedures laid down by the exchange, and all companies listed on the ASX must comply with the ASX's own listing rules.

Importantly for businesses, the ASX acts as a **primary market**. This primary market enables a company to raise new capital through the issue of shares and through the receipt of proceeds from the sale of securities.

The ASX also operates as a secondary market. The **secondary market** is where pre-owned or second-hand securities, such as shares, are traded between investors who may be individuals, businesses, governments or financial institutions. Transactions in this market do not increase the total amount of financial assets, but the secondary market increases the liquidity of financial assets and, therefore, influences the primary market for securities.

Primary markets *deal with new issue of debt instruments by the borrower of funds.*

Secondary markets *deal with the purchase and sale of existing securities.*

The ASX's rules cover matters relating to continuous disclosure, election of directors, dividends, division of power, executive share options, members, off-market transactions, options, preference shares, promoters, prospectuses, reduction of capital, rights issues, takeovers, restricted securities and voting rights.

1987

Australian Stock Exchange Limited is formed through the amalgamation of the six stock exchanges throughout Australia. This in effect creates one body to govern stock market trading throughout Australia and one national market.

Introduction of Stock Exchange Automated Trading System (SEATS)

1989

Introduction of Flexible Accelerated Security Transfer (FAST)

1990

Trading floors abolished
All trading conducted on SEATS

1991

The Australian Securities Commission (ASC) replaced the NCSC and national Corporations Law replaced cooperative legislation.

1992

Settlement system ensuring that all trades are settled within five business days (T+5) introduced

1993

Fixed interest securities added to the SEATS system

1994

First stage of an electronic clearing and settlement system (CHESS) introduced

1995

Major redevelopment of the trading system initiated (SEATS '97)

1996

Final stage of the CHESS clearing and settlement system and open interface to SEATS trading system introduced.
ASX members vote to demutualise.

1997

Computer-based trading introduced for options market.

1998

ASX becomes the first stock exchange to demutualise and list on its own market
Options trading automated
Enterprise Market for capital raising by unlisted companies launched

1999

Strategic alliance formed between ASX and the Nasdaq stock market
Settlement time reduced to three business days (T+3)

2000

ASX forms joint venture with Perpetual Registrars to form ASX Perpetual Registrars Limited (APRL).
ASX explores a number of international alliances (e.g. Singapore, North America).
Announcement of ASX Supervisory Review Pty Ltd

2001

Trading alliance with North America becomes operational.
ASX makes successful application to trade and clear futures products.
New platform launched for listing and trading of managed funds

Figure 5.8 Advances in computer technology have created rapid changes to systems at the Australian Stock Exchange since 1987.

Source: Adapted from information on the Australian Stock Exchange website, viewed 19 July 2005, www.asx.com.au

5.4 Influences on financial markets: implications for business

Financial markets are influenced by a wide range of political and economic factors from both overseas and within Australia (domestic).

Domestic market influences

Within Australia's domestic market there is a range of factors that influence the financial needs of businesses. These are shown in figure 5.9 and need to be closely monitored by businesses.

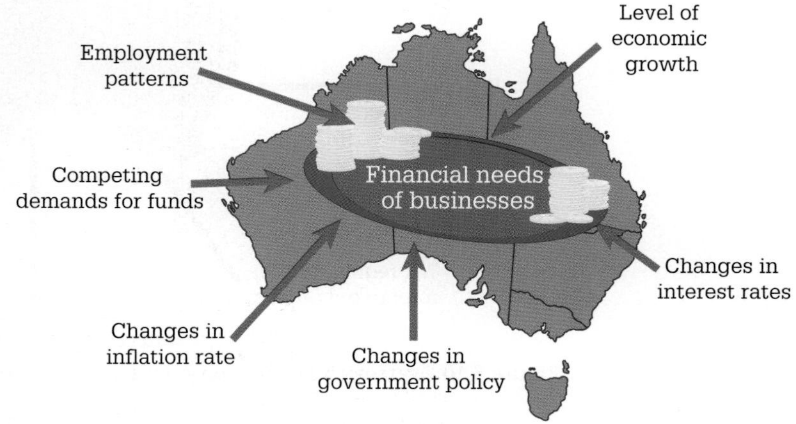

Figure 5.9 Domestic influences on the financial needs of businesses

The fluctuations in the business cycle require business managers to continually monitor how these factors will affect their businesses. Some businesses are more vulnerable to changes in interest rates and consumer demand. They tend to include retailers of the more expensive consumer items such as cars, jewellery and designer fashion. In periods of economic downturn (recessionary periods), consumers delay such purchases, which requires these businesses to adopt strategies to sustain them throughout an economic downturn period.

These strategies may include offering special deals to attract customers, such as offering extras when they buy a car or a holiday. Another strategy to encourage consumers to spend more on expensive items is to offer 'interest free' periods for payment. Retailers such as Harvey Norman and Domayne use this strategy. This allows the business to maintain a reasonable level of turnover in periods of economic downturn.

In 2005, Australia signed a free-trade agreement with the United States. This creates an opportunity for a broad range of Australian businesses to be exposed to a much larger market for their products and/or services. Businesses that may take advantage of this include manufacturers, the technology sector and education-based services. They may explore opportunities using their own resources and contacts in the United States, but many SMEs will rely on government agencies such as Austrade to guide and assist them in accessing the new markets.

Overseas market influences

Overseas influences on Australian business markets are summarised in figure 5.10 (see also the Snapshot 'Inventor wakes up to new strategy'). Governments are acknowledging the importance of Australia's political and economic relations with other countries, particularly those of the Asia–Pacific region. Improved understanding between nations and cultures has seen increased business opportunities emerge in the last decade.

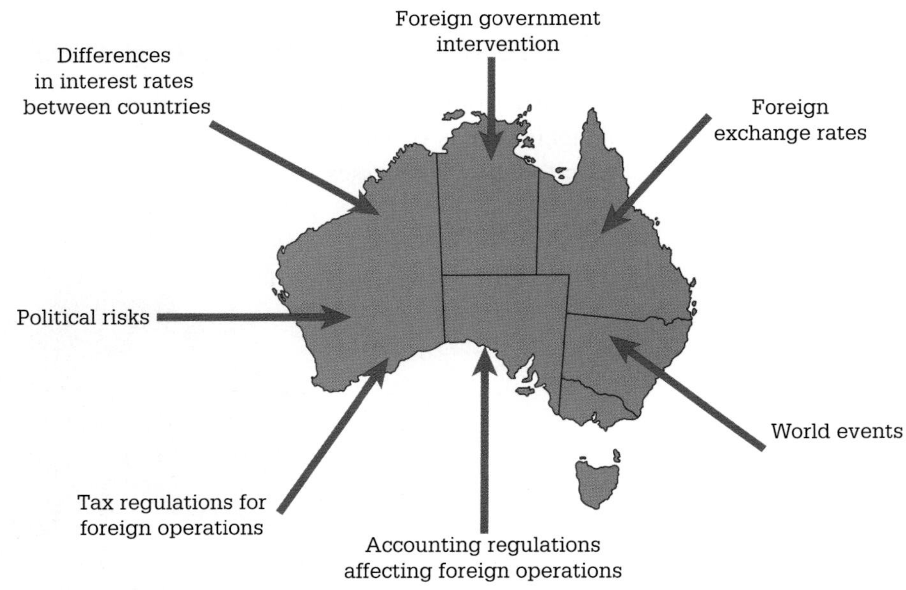

Figure 5.10 Overseas influences on Australian business and financial markets

To assist in managing risk and uncertainty associated with overseas influences (i.e. trade) caused through uncertain and unpredictable events, the financial markets have developed a number of strategies and instruments, one of which is derivatives.

Derivatives *are financial instruments used to hedge against risk by businesses that have to deal with uncertain prices of their own products or their purchases.*

Derivatives

Derivatives are financial instruments used to hedge against risk by businesses that have to deal with uncertain prices of their own products or their purchases.

Derivatives assist in managing risk. They were developed from the various traditional equity and debt instruments to better provide for the needs of the participants in financial markets.

Inventor wakes up to new strategy

Most people with a bright idea who finally get to start up a hobby business usually see volume build slowly and profits come even more gradually. Chris Thomas had the opposite problem.

When his bright idea became a small business reality it made an impressive $100 000 in the first year, but as sales have increased he has seen his profits evaporate to barely break even now.

His Hibermate business, which produces and sells innovative sleep masks, is heading backwards even as it grows.

The problem for Thomas is simple — currency. He sells 90 per cent of his product into the American market in US dollars. The collapse of the greenback and rise in the Australian dollar has presented him with an immediate challenge.

'The problem is the business relies too heavily on external things that are outside my control — like a weaker currency,' he said.

Sitting in the study of his Fitzroy, Melbourne, terrace where he stores, packages and posts out his product, Thomas explained how the innovation grew out of his own experiences.

A qualified cartographer, who spent many years working for the Lonely Planet guide book group, he travelled a great deal and in his early career spent a long period on night shift.

'I couldn't sleep during the day, and I wanted something to block the road noise and the phone, and I found traditional earplugs uncomfortable.

'I rang my brother, who is a manufacturer of foam, and asked him if he had something that could totally block out sound.

'None of the usual eyemasks could support the foam, so I mucked around and made a blindfold which wrapped around your head and put the cut-out foam ear muffs on the side. It was my first prototype.'

He let the idea drop for a number of years and then in 1999, while travelling through Asia, he once again found his sleep interrupted and wished he had brought his special mask.

On his return he was determined to get his idea to start-up phase so he prepared by doing a small business course for three months.

Having invented the mask, he recognised he needed to learn business skills, and to pass the course he had to do a professional business plan.

He sold his house and put about $15 000 of the profit into his new business because he 'didn't want to take a huge risk'. He found a professional seamstress and ran up his first 550 masks in 2001.

'Obviously I couldn't just take 550 masks to Myer or Grace Brothers, but I had to sell them and make as much money as I could so I looked at the Internet.'

Thomas admits that until then he had little interest in the Net but realised it was the answer to his marketing problems.

He went to Google and studied its webmaster search and researched how he could optimise his website.

'When people typed the term sleep-mask, I needed to be near the top. It worked, because within 18 months I was the world's No. 1 sleep-mask manufacturer on the Google website ranking.

'As for the site itself; when I built it the two things I wanted were trust and likeability. To brand yourself you had to stand behind your product and convince people to trust you. In fact I had my first order 20 minutes after I first put up the site. I packaged the order, posted it and was really excited. I thought this isn't work, it's good fun.'

Pricing was, and is, the key issue. In 2001, when he began, the Australian dollar was down to just above US50c and he charged $US21.95 for each mask with postage of $US6.95. As the unit cost was only about $11 a mask, in Australian dollar terms he was making between $40 and $50 per mask — a terrific margin.

(*continued*)

Hibermate's overheads were not huge. He sourced the foam from his brother and the Velcro, elastic and other materials locally. His main costs were merchant fees and the payments for credit card use on the Internet.

He decided against taking out a patent, as his main US competitor was in the process of getting one and it didn't seem to make much difference to them. While Thomas cites competition as one of his challenges, he doesn't seem too fazed by it.

'I ordered one of the masks from the US company and I got quite excited. I thought if he's doing well with that, I could beat him, because my quality was so much better.'

In the first full year of operation, Hibermate sold about 2000, making a handsome profit of $100 000. But by 2003 the currency was starting to cause concern — even though he was now selling about 3000 units per annum, profit had dropped to $70 000.

'Two things went wrong. First, Google, without notice, changed the way it ranked websites and we suddenly went from No. 1 to 90th. Then there was the Australian dollar starting to climb back over US70c.'

While Hibermate has managed to regain its Google ranking, the currency appreciation has seen profits in the current year cut to break-even point.

'We keep limping along, but over the summer I need to write a new business plan,' he said.

Faced with such a big challenge, Thomas will now have to decide on a couple of key new strategies. The first major issue is the perennial dilemma of saving costs by manufacturing overseas.

'Basically we are being driven offshore because it will halve our production costs, which could help double our profit. I've already looked at India, China, Thailand and Pakistan.

'The second part of the strategy is to move into the domestic market because the local market is one I've never touched before.'

Of course, it was the fact that the majority of customers are in the US which exacerbated his currency and banking issues.

'While we advertise the price in US dollars, we charge in Australian dollars and I had to do the conversions myself. One thing I always wanted was a US dollar bank account, but it was very difficult.'

Obviously opening a domestic market has distinct advantages but it also brings challenges such as picking retailers and marketing.

'I have to look at different marketing strategies, like advertising in health-related magazines. As it's aimed at the night-shift worker we could also do local radio on the midnight-to-dawn shift, which is only a few hundred dollars. The same with off-peak TV.'

Thomas certainly has plenty to keep him awake at night.

'Hibermate is only part-time and I'm also juggling a full-time job and a family life. My girlfriend helps out but it's just the two of us in the business.

'I always hoped Hibermate would move from a hobby business to full time and there was a point we talked seriously about taking the plunge, but that has gone on the backburner.'

Source: J. Perrett, 'Inventor wakes up to new strategy', *The Sydney Morning Herald*, 21 January 2005, p. 22.

SNaPSHOT Questions

1. Use the following questions to analyse the challenges that this business is facing. Place your answers in a table like the one below.
   (a) What is the name of the business?
   (b) What are the business's activities and operations?
   (c) What are the challenges or problems that this business is facing?
   (d) What strategies will the business adopt to deal with the challenges?
   (e) What challenges do you think the business will face in the future?

Name of the business	
Brief overview of the business's activities and operations	

5.5 Trends in financial markets

The activities of financial markets have grown and changed rapidly over the past 20 years. The market continues to change and the volume of activity continues to grow in record proportions. Businesses both small and large trade in the domestic and international market as part of their everyday operations.

The fast changing market has implications for the financial needs of businesses. New trading instruments continue to be developed to suit the needs of businesses. These financial instruments are required to be flexible and adaptable to suit the rapidly changing environment.

Changing technology continues to have an impact on the activities of businesses as they participate more actively in financial markets. The highly competitive nature of the marketplace enables businesses to be involved in domestic and international transactions via telephone and the Internet — 24 hours a day, 365 days a year. New packages that ensure quick and efficient transactions continue to be developed to suit businesses.

EXERCISE 5.2 *Revision*

1. Yung & Co. is anticipating a 10-year expansion plan involving the purchase of three new stores. Suggest how Yung & Co. could use financial markets to assist in this expansion.
2. Explain the factors that influence a business when it is deciding on investment options.
3. Explain how inflation and interest rate rises affect business activities.
4. Explain the methods used by businesses to take account of overseas and domestic market influences.
5. Prepare a summary of this chapter. A summary condenses the important issues and concepts presented in the chapter. Go to www.jaconline.com.au/businessstudies3e to compare your finished summary with the one provided for this textbook.

Extension

1. 'Today's businesses cannot survive without interaction with financial markets.' Do you disagree/agree? Give reasons.
2. Conduct an Internet search for websites of three financial institutions. Investigate how each financial institution meets the needs of businesses.
3. Go to www.jaconline.com.au/businessstudies3e and click on the ASX and the RBA weblinks for this textbook. Using the information from these two sites, write a report on how the ASX and RBA assist businesses.

6 Management of funds

6.1 Sources of funds

A business cannot establish itself and thrive without funds to enable it to pursue its activities. The range of activities in which a business is involved during its life cycle includes the initial set-up — whether establishing a new business or buying one that is already established — and might also include expanding its range of products, introducing a new product, expanding the number of outlets, upgrading its systems and technology, employing more staff, building a new warehouse, and so on.

In the establishment of a business, owners and/or shareholders usually contribute funds. When an organisation is considering growth and development in later years, a number of options can be considered regarding sources of funds and how those sources will be used. Sources of funds may be internal or external (see figure 6.1). Finding the appropriate source of funds for the business's needs involves **financial decision making**, which means that relevant information must be identified, collected and analysed to determine an appropriate course of action.

Financial decision making *requires relevant information to be identified, collected and analysed to determine an appropriate course of action.*

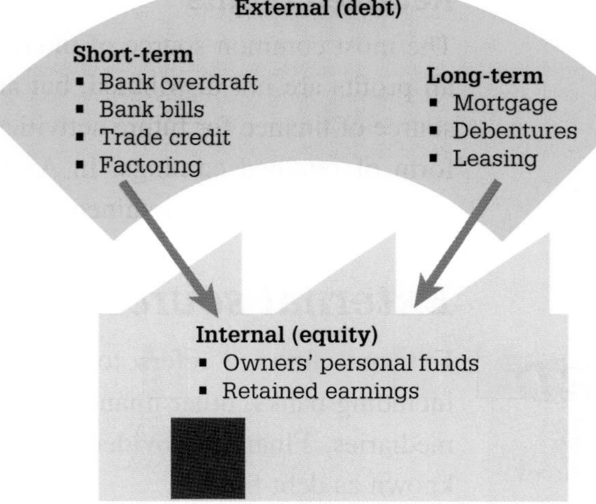

Figure 6.1 Internal and external sources of funds

BiZ WoRD

Internal finance *is the funds provided by the owners of the business (capital) or from the outcomes of business activities (retained earnings).*

Owners' equity *is the funds contributed by owners or partners to establish and build the business.*

Internal sources

Internal finance comes either from the business's owners (equity or capital) or from the outcomes of business activities (retained earnings).

Owners' equity

Owners' equity is the funds contributed by owners or partners to establish and build the business.

Owners' equity has a range of advantages and disadvantages that are outlined in table 6.1.

TABLE 6.1 **Advantages and disadvantages of owners' equity**

Advantages	Disadvantages
Does not have to be repaid unless the owner leaves the business	Lower profits and lower returns for the owners
Cheaper than other sources of finance as there are no interest payments	The expectation that the owners will have about the return on their investment (ROI)
The owners who have contributed the equity retain control over how that finance is used	
Low gearing (use resources of the owners and not external sources of finance)	
Less risk for the business and the owner	

Equity capital can be raised in other ways; for example, by taking on another partner or seeking funds from an investor who then becomes an owner or shareholder, selling off any unproductive assets or through the issuing of shares.

Retained profits

The most common source of internal finance is retained earnings or profits in which all profits are not distributed, but are kept in the business as a cheap and accessible source of finance for future activities. Most businesses keep some of their profit in the form of retained earnings. In Australian businesses, approximately 50 per cent of profits on average are retained to be reinvested.

External sources

***External finance** is the funds provided by sources outside the business, including banks, other financial institutions, government, suppliers or financial intermediaries.*

External finance refers to the funds provided by sources outside the business, including banks, other financial institutions, government, suppliers or financial intermediaries. Finance provided from external sources through creditors or lenders is known as debt finance.

Using debt as a source of finance means that the business relies on outside sources rather than the owners to finance the business. The increased funds for the business should mean increases in earnings and hence profits. Regular repayments on the borrowings must be made so firms must generate sufficient earnings to make the payments. There is an increase in risk for businesses using debt as the interest, and bank and government charges have to be paid, on top of the principal borrowed. However, Australia's tax system has promoted debt financing for businesses by providing generous tax deductions for interest payments. Some advantages and disadvantages of debt as a source of finance are given in table 6.2.

TABLE 6.2	Debt as a source of finance
Advantages of debt	**Disadvantages of debt**
▪ Increased funds should lead to increased earnings and profits ▪ Tax deduction for interest payments	▪ Increased risk if debt comes from financial institutions as the interest, bank charges, government charges and the principal have to be repaid ▪ Security is required by the business ▪ Regular repayments have to be made ▪ Lenders have first claim on any money if the business ends in bankruptcy

Types of external debt include short- and long-term borrowing (see figure 6.2). The type of debt must match the purpose of the loan. For example, bank overdrafts cover temporary cash shortfalls, while a term loan would finance the purchase of new plant and equipment.

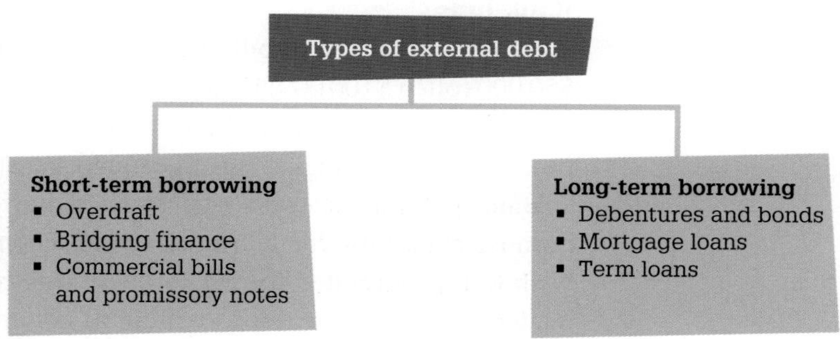

Figure 6.2 Types of external debt

Figure 6.3 Balance sheet showing sources of funds

Western Light Company
Balance Sheet as at 30 June 2008

	$ million	$ million
Current Assets		
Cash	1.0	
Receivables	10.5	
Inventories	6.0	17.5
Non-current Assets		
Property, plant and equipment		25.0
		$42.5
Current Liabilities		
Bank Overdraft	2.0	
Accounts Payable	3.2	
Borrowings	1.0	6.2
Non-current Liabilities		
Borrowings		10.0
		16.2
Shareholders' Equity		
Share Capital	21.0	
Retained Profits	5.3	26.3
		$42.5

Short-term borrowing

Short-term borrowing is provided by financial institutions through bank overdrafts, commercial bills and bank loans. This type of borrowing is used to finance temporary shortages in cash flow or finance for working capital. Short-term borrowing is generally those funds that will be repaid within one or two years.

Bank overdraft

> **BiZ WoRD**
>
> *With a **bank overdraft**, the bank allows a business or individual to overdraw their account up to an agreed limit and for a specified time, to help overcome a temporary cash shortfall.*

A **bank overdraft** is one of the most common types of short-term borrowing. A bank allows a business to overdraw its account to an agreed limit. Bank overdrafts assist businesses with short-term liquidity problems; for example, a seasonal decrease in sales. Costs for bank overdrafts are minimal, and interest rates are lower than on other forms of borrowing. As interest rates are usually variable, interest is paid on the daily outstanding balance of the account. Banks usually require the agreed limits to the overdraft to be maintained at a high level and require some security. Bank overdrafts are repayable on demand, although this is not common.

Many businesses prefer bank overdrafts to short-term bank loans as bank loans do not have the same flexibility as bank overdrafts.

Bank bills

Bank bills are a type of bill of exchange and are given for larger amounts, usually over \$50 000 (often \$100 000) for a period of between 90 and 180 days. The borrower receives the money immediately and promises to pay the sum of money and interest at a future time. The bank acting as agent guarantees that the money will be repaid when due.

Bank bills are an attractive form of borrowing for both lenders and borrowers, because bank bills can be traded in the secondary bill market. Borrowers who do not wish to be committed for the full period of the loan can trade on the bill market and lenders are, therefore, more willing to commit to this type of investment. Bank bills are also attractive to borrowers, because at the end of the term of the bank bill, for example, 90 days, the bank bill can be 'rolled over' or re-borrowed, extending the period of short-term borrowing.

Figure 6.4 Short-term debt finance is now possible via charge card and credit card facilities

Long-term borrowing

Long-term borrowing relates to funds borrowed for periods longer than two years. It can be secured or unsecured and interest rates are usually variable. It is used to finance real estate, plant and equipment. Long-term borrowing includes mortgages and debentures.

*A **mortgage** is a loan secured by the property of the borrower (business).*

***Debentures** are issued by a company for a fixed rate of interest and for a fixed period of time.*

Mortgage

A **mortgage** is a loan secured by the property of the borrower (business). The property that is mortgaged cannot be sold or used as security for further borrowing until the mortgage is repaid. Mortgage loans are used to finance property purchases, such as new premises, a factory or office. They are repaid, usually through regular repayments, over an agreed period such as 15 years.

National Australia Bank
Indicator Rates - Business

• **BENCHMARK RATE**	**9.20** %PA
• **BASE RATE**	**9.85** %PA
• **TERM BASE RATE**	**9.40** %PA
• **FARMERS CHOICE VARIABLE**	**7.85** %PA

• NATIONAL BUSINESS MORTGAGE*

Fully Drawn Advance		**7.55** %PA
Instalment Loan		**7.55** %PA
Overdraft		**8.40** %PA
Combination Loan – Fixed Instalment	1 yr **7.20** %PA	4 yrs **7.30** %PA
Eff. 4/07/05	2 yrs **7.20** %PA	5 yrs **7.35** %PA
	3 yrs **7.25** %PA	

• NATIONAL COMMERCIAL MORTGAGE*

Fully Drawn Advance	**8.50** %PA
Instalment Loan	**8.50** %PA
Overdraft	**9.40** %PA

For more information, call 13 13 12 8am-9pm 7 days a week

* These rates apply while the Bank's qualifying criteria are met, otherwise base rate/term base rate and customer interest margin may apply.

† On completion of Fixed Rate period, Business Mortgage Instalment Loan rate applies.

These indicator rates are used as a basis to individually determine the interest rates charged on all relevant loans. Fees and charges are payable. Full details of these and relevant terms and conditions are available on application.

National Australia Bank Limited A.B.N. 12 004 044 937
Web site: national.com.au hmaBlaze 108051

Figure 6.5 An advertisement for a business mortgage loan *Source:* © 2005 National Australia Bank Limited ('National'). This material must not be used in any way without the express prior written permission of the National. No warranties or representations are made in relation to the accuracy or currency of the information and therefore no reliance should be placed on the information.

Debentures

Debentures are issued by a company for a fixed rate of interest and for a fixed period of time. Debentures are usually not secured to specific property. Companies that borrow offer security to the lender usually over the company's assets. On maturity, the company repays the amount of the debenture by buying back the debenture. The amount of profit made by a company has no effect on the rate of interest as debentures carry a fixed rate of interest. Finance companies raise much of their funds through debenture issues to the public.

***Leasing** is a long-term source of borrowing for businesses. It involves the payment of money for the use of equipment that is owned by another party.*

Leasing

Leasing is a long-term source of borrowing for businesses. It involves the payment of money for the use of equipment that is owned by another party. Leasing enables an enterprise to borrow funds and use the equipment without the large capital outlay required. Costs and benefits of the financial asset are transferred from the lessor to the lessee. The lessee uses the equipment and the lessor owns and leases the equipment for an agreed period of time. A lease cannot usually be cancelled.

Since the 1960s, leasing as a source of finance has been used widely in Australia. The main participants in lease finance have been finance companies. Businesses choose the equipment, arrange for the finance company to purchase it, then lease it from the finance company, which retains ownership for the period of the lease. There are two types of leases, operating and financial.

A motor vehicle leased for two weeks would be leased as an operating lease. The leasing firm would be responsible for repairs to the motor vehicle and, if the vehicle was returned earlier than two weeks, there would be an adjustment to the lease payment.

A motor vehicle leased for three years would be leased as a financial lease. The firm leasing the motor vehicle would be responsible for insurance and maintenance of the vehicle and the term of the lease would be close to the economic life of the vehicle.

Operating leases

Operating leases are assets leased for short periods, usually shorter than the life of the asset. The owner carries out the maintenance on the asset. Operating leases can be cancelled, often without penalty.

Financial leases

Under the conditions of a financial lease, the lessor purchases the asset on behalf of the lessee. Financial leases are usually for the life of the asset. Lease repayments are fixed for the economic life of the asset, usually between three and five years. Plant, vehicles, equipment, furniture and fittings are leased as financial leases. There are usually penalties for cancellation of financial leases. Leasing assets for long periods as financial leases is cheaper than leasing them as operating leases.

Some of the advantages of leasing as a source of finance are as follows:

- the costs of establishing leases may be lower than other methods of financing
- if some assets are leased an organisation may be in a better position to borrow funds
- it provides long-term financing without reducing control of ownership
- it permits 100 per cent financing of assets
- repayments of the lease are fixed for a period so cash flow can be monitored more easily
- lease payments are a tax deduction
- payment usually includes maintenance, insurance and finance costs.

However, a disadvantage of leasing is that interest charges may be higher than for other forms of borrowing.

Corporations are required by law to reveal significant leases in their published financial statements or in notes to the financial statements.

Factoring

Factoring *is the selling of accounts receivable for a discounted price to a finance or factoring company.*

Factoring is a short-term source of borrowing for a business. It enables a business to raise funds immediately by selling accounts receivable at a discount to a firm that specialises in collecting accounts receivable (a finance or factoring business). Factoring is an important source of short-term finance as the business will receive up to 90 per cent of the amount of receivables within 48 hours of submitting its invoices to the factoring company. By having immediate access to funds, the business will improve its cash flow and leverage. The business does not have to worry about the collection of accounts and the costs involved in this process. However, it must be remembered that the full amount will not be received for accounts.

A factoring company may offer its services with or without recourse.

- 'Without recourse' means that the business transfers responsibility for non-collection to the factoring company.
- 'With recourse' means that bad debts will still be the responsibility of the business.

As an example of factoring, Harvey Norman has an arrangement with GE Finance whereby cash flow is provided for 12 months interest free without recourse.

Factoring involves greater risk than other sources of short-term borrowing such as bank overdrafts and bank bills because of the likelihood of unpaid debts. It is a relatively expensive source of finance as the business is usually responsible for debts that remain unpaid and commission is paid on the debt. In the past, factoring was used as a last resort, but this attitude has changed in the last decade and factoring is seen as a legitimate means of financing the activities of a business.

In order to avoid cash shortfalls, a business should take care when offering credit (see the Snapshot 'Sharp credit policies can save grief').

Sharp credit policies can save grief

Now is the time to get an appropriate credit policy in place, before interest rate rises and other economic pressures put the bite on cash flow.

Bronwyn Phillips of Bridgement Smith Collections says informal business arrangements should be tightened up to ensure businesses do not run into cash flow problems.

'There's no doubt that as interest rates increase in the coming years, more pressure will be placed on businesses to keep ahead of their debtors,' Phillips says.

'Cash will become tighter and bills will be left unpaid longer. Now is the time to get a cash management process in place.'

Phillips says all businesses need to recognise the inevitability of bad debts, without surrendering to them.

'Involuntary debt is a problem all businesses face. However, while debt recovery is the lifeline of a business, credit management is important to prevent greater financial crisis. In other words, prevention is better than cure.'

Embedding a few simple processes can help maintain a strong cash flow management system, she says.

These including ensuring all customers fill out a credit application, and checking the details in the application.

Credit checks for all customers are also vital, she says.

'I believe the three golden rules for credit applications involve understanding the legal entity behind the debtor, how long the entity has been trading and securing a signed director guarantee.

'We recommend if you've done your work and are still chasing debtors after 60 days, it's time to seek external help.'

Source: C. England, 'Sharp credit policies can save grief', *The Daily Telegraph*, 9 November 2004.

SNAPSHOT Questions

1. Describe what a 'sharp credit policy' means to businesses.
2. What are the three 'golden rules' for credit applications?

Trade credit

Trade credit is an important source of short-term funds for organisations. Trade credit is widely used by businesses for short-term borrowing as organisations are granted a period of time, from 30 days to 90 days, before payment is required. Trade credit is attractive for businesses as there is no interest charge, it is easy to obtain if a business has a good credit record and, as the business grows, purchases increase and trade credit is easier to obtain.

Trade credit is a cheap form of finance, although there is greater risk involved, especially if organisations postpone payments to beyond the agreed credit period. This postponement of payments is known as 'stretching' and is common in firms that experience seasonal fluctuations. Stretching is allowed by some suppliers, especially if an organisation is a regular customer. Businesses must have ongoing good relations with their suppliers and ensure that their credit rating is not affected by using trade credit as short-term borrowing.

Figure 6.6 'Stretching' is an act of goodwill offered by many suppliers, but there are some businesses that abuse this aspect of a business relationship.

Venture capital

Venture capital is funds supplied by private investors or specialist investment organisations, either to new businesses (sometimes referred to as 'seed capital') or to established businesses ready to grow or diversify.

Venture capital is funds supplied by private investors or specialist investment organisations, either to new businesses (sometimes referred to as 'seed capital') or to established businesses ready to grow or diversify. It is associated with risky but innovative schemes that have a high potential for profit. The investing company or individual becomes an owner (or shareholder) in the organisation and, because of the risks associated with their involvement, may expect to have an input into the management and direction of the organisation.

Several organisations specialise in supplying venture capital to firms; for example, the Australian Industry Development Corporation (AIDC). Information on sources of venture capital is available through the Australian Venture Capital Association. Some organisations now specialise in matching potential investors with entrepreneurs or businesses seeking venture capital for a specific purpose.

Grants

A grant is a sum of money made available to a business to be used for growth and development. The provider of this money, primarily the government, places conditions and restrictions on the use of the grant; for example it may be used for specific purposes, such as for the development of export markets or for research and development.

Funds can be obtained through both state and federal governments, and are administered through business development departments or small business development centres, which advise individuals on setting up and administering a business.

EXERCISE 6.1 Revision

1. Explain the difference between internal sources and external sources of finance.
2. Explain why equity finance can be the most difficult type of finance to obtain.
3. Why would Thomas, who owns a hairdressing business, prefer to use retained earnings to expand his business rather than taking on a new partner?
4. A bank overdraft is the most flexible type of short-term finance. Discuss.
5. Identify and explain the sources of finance from the following balance sheet.

Current Assets		
Cash	$33 000	
Receivables	12 000	
Inventories	4 700	$49 700
Non-current Assets		
Land and Buildings	98 000	
Plant and Equipment	18 000	116 000
Total Assets		165 700
Current Liabilities		
Creditors	8 700	
Non-current Liabilities		
Borrowings	12 000	20 700
Net Assets		145 000
Owners' Equity		
Capital	140 000	
Profits	5 000	145 000

6. Why is trade credit the most easily accessible external source of finance for a small business?
7. (a) What is factoring?
   (b) Why has factoring become an important source of finance for business?
   (c) What are the advantages and disadvantages of factoring?
8. Look through newspapers and magazines for advertisements for companies offering leasing to businesses and make a comparison of their services.
9. 'Leasing is a cheap, flexible and important source of finance for businesses.' Discuss this statement, outlining the uses, advantages and disadvantages of leasing.
10. BJs Supermarket is considering whether to purchase or lease a new supermarket. The lease requires that BJs pays for maintenance, insurance and rates if the store is leased. The annual lease payment is $100 000 (payable in advance) for four years. The purchase price of the supermarket is $350 000 and funds would need to be borrowed if the store was purchased. Discuss the factors that need to be considered before a decision is made on whether to purchase or lease.
11. Kim wants to expand her catering equipment and supplies business over the next two to three years. The business requires a number of cars for the salespeople who travel extensively, both in the city and in the country. Write a report for Kim on the best alternative for the business, outlining the advantages and disadvantages both of leasing and of purchasing motor vehicles.
12. Leo has purchased a number of computers and new software for his photographic equipment business in anticipation of increasing sales on the Internet. This has not occurred and Leo is having difficulties paying bills on time. Advise Leo on the best sources of finance for the business to overcome the problems. Give reasons for your answers.

Extension

1. Go to www.jaconline.com.au/businessstudies3e and click on the Austrade, NSW Government and Small Business, and Australian Venture Capital Association weblinks for this textbook. Search these websites to find out the sources of funds available for business provided by each organisation.
2. Examine a range of annual reports of organisations to determine their sources and applications of funds. Create a table to summarise your findings.

6.2 Financial considerations — matching source with purpose

We have seen that organisations are regularly faced with a number of financial decisions related to achieving their financial objectives — for example, offering credit to customers, the purchase of new equipment, the purchase of inventories, building new premises, extending current premises and buying another factory or motor vehicle. Organisations must find the source of finance that is most appropriate to fund the activities arising from these decisions.

The terms of finance must also be suitable for the structure of the business and the purpose for which the funds are required. For example, one of the options for short-term finance discussed earlier should be suitable to match the short-term purposes of the business, such as managing a temporary cash flow shortfall. The alternative methods of long-term finance should be assessed for long-term purposes, such as an expansion of the business overseas. The use of short-term finance to fund long-term assets causes financial problems because the amount borrowed must be repaid before the long-term assets have time to generate increased cash flow. The use of long-term finance to fund short-term situations or assets means that a business is still paying the mortgage long after the situation is resolved or the inventory has been sold, and profits will be reduced.

Small businesses have a number of sources available when seeking debt finance, but the range of sources is not as great as with larger businesses because lenders are concerned about risk and security. The larger the equity capital on a business, the more secure the financial structure of the business and the more likely will be the opportunities to borrow. Lenders prefer to lend to firms with strong equity capital because this is an indication of the stability of the organisation and the commitment of the owners.

The cost of each source of funding, whether from equity capital (share issues and retained earnings) or debt capital such as borrowings, must be determined. The required rate of return that can be expected is also taken into consideration and balanced against the costs of each source.

The structure of the business can also influence decisions about finance. Small businesses have fewer opportunities for equity capital than larger businesses. Equity for unincorporated businesses has to be raised from private sources or by taking on another partner. Corporate businesses can raise equity by the issuing of shares to the public. It is common for businesses to use reserves or retained earnings when they wish to expand their operations.

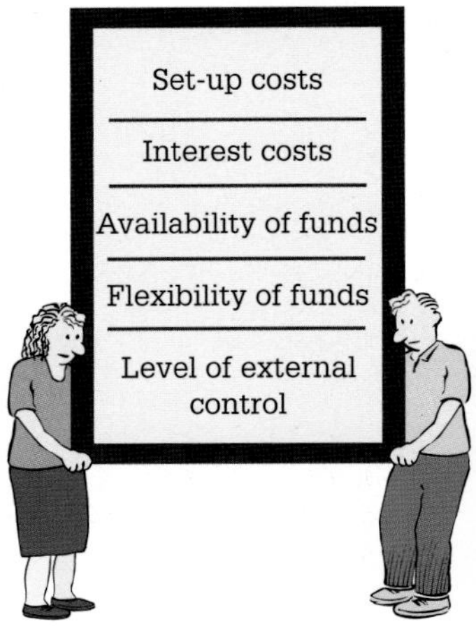

Among the many factors involved in financing the activities of a business, cost is probably the most important consideration. However, flexibility, the availability of funds and level of external control must also be considered.

Set-up costs
Interest costs
Availability of funds
Flexibility of funds
Level of external control

Figure 6.7 Factors to consider in financing business activities

Costs, including set-up costs and interest rates, must be measured for each of the available sources of funds, as costs fluctuate depending on market and economic conditions.

Flexibility of the source of funding is another important consideration. Organisations often require sources of funds to be variable so that, if firms have excess funds, borrowings can be paid off more quickly, increased or renewed as conditions change. Bank overdrafts provide greater flexibility for organisations than debentures and factoring.

Availability of finance is affected by a business's credit rating because the credit rating indicates the business's 'track record' in meeting its financial commitments. The higher the credit rating, the greater number of available sources. Banks are more willing to supply funds for organisations with a high credit rating.

The *availability of finance* cannot be taken for granted and is an important financial consideration. Too heavy a dependence on a small number of investors can increase risk if an investor pulls out and commitments cannot be met. Also, if an organisation has a low credit rating, it may need to look at alternative sources for funding (see the Biz Fact on the left).

The *level of control* maintained by an organisation is also an important consideration. If the lender requires security over an asset and other conditions of lending are imposed, a business's ability to consider future financing possibilities is reduced. For example, a mortgage over a building imposes restrictions on an organisation, and assets mortgaged cannot be used for further finance. Also, if receivables are factored then the liquidity of an organisation is reduced, and this may impact on the credit rating of the organisation.

6.3 Comparing debt and equity financing

Debt finance *relates to the short-term and long-term borrowing from external sources by an organisation.*

Equity finance *relates to the internal sources of finance in the organisation.*

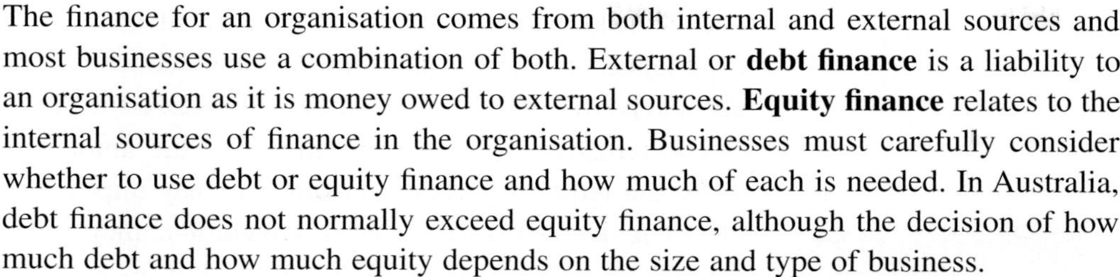

The finance for an organisation comes from both internal and external sources and most businesses use a combination of both. External or **debt finance** is a liability to an organisation as it is money owed to external sources. **Equity finance** relates to the internal sources of finance in the organisation. Businesses must carefully consider whether to use debt or equity finance and how much of each is needed. In Australia, debt finance does not normally exceed equity finance, although the decision of how much debt and how much equity depends on the size and type of business.

Figure 6.8 Organisations must determine the appropriate combination of debt and equity for their activities

BiZ FaCT

During the late 1980s and early 1990s, many businesses accumulated excessive levels of debt finance. The banks adopted a liberal lending policy and were willing to lend money to businesses on a dollar-for-dollar basis — that is, for every dollar invested by owners in the business, the banks were prepared to lend a dollar. The result for many businesses was insolvency and bankruptcy.

Debt finance

Debt can be attractive to businesses because funds are usually readily available and interest payments are tax deductible, therefore reducing the cost of debt financing. The amount of debt used by Australian businesses varies, but short-term borrowing (one year or less) is an important source of funding for businesses.

Risk and return must be carefully considered when determining whether debt or equity finance is used. For example, there is a greater level of risk associated with borrowing, and consideration has to be given to the impact of borrowing on the future profitability and financial stability of the organisation.

The costs to be considered in using debt financing are:

- repayment of principal
- interest payments
- timing of repayments
- administrative and legal costs associated with borrowing
- conditions and terms of borrowing
- tax considerations
- maturity date of the loan as refinancing may be required
- level of control by the lender.

A business must maintain sufficient liquidity or cash flow to ensure that commitments are paid as they are due. However, too much cash kept in a business reduces profitability and is an inefficient use of resources.

A business may experience solvency problems and bankruptcy because of cash flow problems, even though it is profitable. For example, if a business borrows money at 9 per cent interest and makes a return of 13 per cent in the dollar there will be a return for the owners from the excess of interest and return percentages. If interest rates rise to 15 per cent and returns remain at 13 per cent, there will be decreased returns for owners. In this case, the risk involved in using debt finance leads to problems for the business.

If an organisation uses a high level of debt finance it takes a greater risk than if it uses equity finance. The amount of risk is affected by how much the organisation has borrowed, when loans have to be repaid and the required level of current assets for the business. The higher the risk of an investment, the higher the return to the organisation. Risk and return are interrelated and determine what makes up the share prices of corporations.

In determining the type of capital structure for an organisation, the interests of stakeholders such as creditors, owners and lenders must be considered. Creditors seek the assurance that they will receive payment for their goods and services, and lenders must consider the likelihood of repayment of funds borrowed if an organisation experiences financial difficulties. The main concern of owners is the level of risk and, ultimately, the level of return they will receive for funds invested.

The terms of debt are determined by the amount of risk and return the lender takes and requires. Lending institutions may impose conditions during the period of the loan. Known as **restrictive covenants**, they tell borrowers what they can or cannot do while they hold the loan. For example, the lender may require the borrower to maintain a certain level of net worth (assets less liabilities) during the term of the loan, or that the business not be involved in purchasing major equipment or looking at a takeover bid without the lender's approval during the period of the loan.

__Restrictive covenants__ set down what a borrower can or cannot do for the period of a loan.

A simple example can illustrate the effective use of debt. Jai saved $500 of his own money to begin a skateboard company. He borrowed $1000 on short-term (30-day) loan to buy the parts to make the skateboards. He sold the skateboards for cash as soon as they were completed and made repayments on the loan. He then borrowed a further $2000, bought more parts, made more skateboards and paid off more of the loan. This process continued and the business grew. Jai matched the purpose of the finance to the appropriate source and used debt to finance his business success.

Figure 6.9 Using debt finance effectively (see the Biz Fact on the left)

Equity finance

In the case of equity finance, shareholders' funds represent the highest proportion of total funds to finance business operations and assets. Equity finance is the most important source of funds for companies because it remains in the business for an indefinite time, because funds do not have to be repaid at a set date as with debt financing. Equity is generally safer than debt, but equity requires sufficient profits to be made so that the organisation can continue to operate. Equity funds provide confidence to creditors and lenders, who are more willing to lend to an organisation if there are equity funds. They act as a safety net for unexpected downturns or changes in the business activities. Debt and equity funds are compared in table 6.3.

A highly leveraged or geared business offers greater potential for profit. For example, Ruby has $50 000. One financial institution is willing to lend her 50 per cent of the purchase price of a new clothing store. She has $100 000 to spend on a store. If another financial institution is willing to lend her 95 per cent she can buy a $1 000 000 store.
Scenario 1 — financial institution lends 50 per cent
Ruby's $50 000 = 50 per cent ($50 000 + $50 000 = $100 000)
Scenario 2 — financial institution lends 95 per cent
Ruby's $50 000 = 5 per cent ($50 000 + $950 000 = $1 000 000)
The more highly leveraged business of scenario 2 offers greater possibilities for Ruby as debt finance is tax deductible, she owns a larger asset and the increased size of the business will lead to increased business activity and profits.

***Leverage** is the proportion of debt (external finance) and the proportion of equity (internal finance) that is used to finance the activities of a business.*

TABLE 6.3 Comparison of debt and equity finance

Debt	Equity
▪ Lenders have prior claim in the event of liquidation	▪ Shareholders have a residual claim on assets
▪ Debt must be repaid by periodic repayments	▪ Equity has no maturity date
▪ Interest payments are tax deductible	▪ Dividends are not tax deductible
▪ Lenders usually require a lower rate of return	▪ Shareholders require higher return due to higher risk
▪ Interest payments are fixed	▪ Dividend payments are not fixed and may be reduced through lack of funds
▪ Debt providers have no voting rights	▪ Equity holders have voting rights

Gearing/leverage

The capital structure of a business is determined by the mix of debt and equity, and the proportion of each is known as leverage, or gearing. The term 'leverage' originated in the United States while the term 'gearing' is used in the United Kingdom.

Leverage (or gearing) measures the relationship between debt and equity. Leverage is the proportion of debt (external finance) and the proportion of equity (internal finance) that is used to finance the activities of a business. The degree of leverage depends on the type of industry and management of the business. An industry that carries higher risk but is likely to generate large profits (for example, mining) may have a higher debt-to-equity ratio; that is, it is highly geared. Manufacturing industries with strong markets often have high debt as the potential for profit is greater.

Gearing or leverage is an important consideration for businesses as the more highly geared the business (using debt rather than equity), the greater risk for the business but the greater potential for profit.

Debt affects stakeholders and potential investors, as high risk may discourage investment.

The level of leverage (or gearing) for the organisation is an important decision. Factors such as risk, return and degree of control over the enterprise influence the level of leverage that is appropriate for an organisation.

In balancing the leverage of an organisation, consideration must be given to the level of control by owners. For example, profits earned must be sufficient to cover interest payments. If funds are not available to meet interest charges and accounts are not paid, lenders and creditors have rights to claim payment from the organisation.

There is no optimal level of leverage for an organisation, although it is rare for a company to have no leverage. A business must consider:

- return on investment
- cost of debt
- size and stability of the business's earning capacity
- liquidity of the business's assets (the greater the cash flow and the more liquid the assets, the more likely the interest charges will be paid)
- purposes of short-term debt.

EXERCISE 6.2 *Revision*

1. Why is it important to match the term of a loan to the life of the asset for which the finance was obtained?
2. Why should short-term finance not be used to finance the expansion of a business?
3. Explain why cash flow problems might result from the use of a bank overdraft to finance the purchase of assets to fit out a new branch of Gloria's Hi-Class Shoes and Accessories.
4. How would the purchase of a new delivery vehicle with a 30-day bank bill lead to reduced profits?
5. James Young wishes to replace his fleet of courier vehicles. Explain to him the sources of finance available to finance the replacement vehicles.
6. Advise on the type of finance you would suggest for the following. Give reasons for your answer.
   (a) Payment of inventory
   (b) Purchase of a new motor vehicle
   (c) Diversification of the business over the next five years
   (d) Takeover of a competitor
   (e) Expansion to double the volume of sales
   (f) Purchase of new plant and equipment
7. Explain the cost and benefit factors that need to be considered by a business when using debt finance.
8. From the following information, match each item of anticipated expenditure to the source of finance you think is most appropriate. Give reasons for your choices.

Soo Lee Computer Systems — sources of finance

Anticipated expenditures	
Purchase of a property in Karalta Court	$200 000
Furniture and fittings	$9 000
Renovations	$18 000
Inventory	$8 000
Working capital	$12 000
Cash reserve	$3 000
Total	$250 000
Sources of finance	
Mortgage loan	$150 000
Term loan	$45 000
Unsecured loan	$15 000
Bank overdraft	$10 000
New investment from owners	$30 000
Total	$250 000

9. Use the summary on page 147 of a business's assets and liabilities to complete the following tasks:
   (a) identify the sources of debt finance
   (b) identify the sources of equity finance
   (c) identify which sources of debt and equity finance have increased or decreased between the years 2007 and 2008

(d) suggest reasons for the changes and comment on the change of leverage from 2007 to 2008.

	2007 $	2008 $
Assets		
Cash	—	5 000
Accounts Receivable	60 000	70 000
Inventory	95 000	115 000
Fixed assets	45 000	35 000
Total	200 000	225 000
Liabilities and Owners' Equity		
Overdraft	20 000	—
Accounts Payable	45 000	50 000
Accrued Expenses	15 000	15 000
Term Loan	35 000	50 000
Capital	35 000	35 000
Retained Earnings	50 000	75 000
	200 000	225 000

10. Prepare a summary of this chapter. A summary condenses the important issues and concepts presented in the chapter. Go to www.jaconline.com.au/businessstudies3e to compare your finished summary with the one provided for this textbook.

Extension

1. You have been in the mobile dog-washing business for two years and you are making a small profit. You see some opportunities to expand and make a bigger profit. Prepare a case to present to your local bank requesting finance for the expansion.
2. Using information from websites, magazines, banks and other financial institutions, collect five advertisements offering different types of finance and funding. Compare them under the following headings. Share your results with other class members.

Source	Interest rate	Borrowing limit	Terms	Other advantages

3. Examine a range of annual reports and note some examples of the matching of sources of funds to expenditure.
4. James operates a small graphic art business from home, but, with increased business activity, he is ready to expand into larger premises. He anticipates he

will need $100 000 for the expansion. Write a memo to James explaining the risk and return factors involved in expanding his business.

5. (a) From the information in the table below determine if the business is high-geared or low-geared.
   (b) What are the advantages and disadvantages for the business of its present gearing?
   (c) If the business decided to expand, what do you suggest would be the best method to finance this expansion? Give reasons for your answer.

	$	$	$	$
Current Assets				
Cash		17 000		
Receivables				
Trade Debtors	1 800			
Other Debtors	500			
Bills of Exchange	4 000	6 300		
Inventories		2 300		25 600
Non-current Assets				
Property, Plant and Equipment				18 000
Total Assets				43 600
Current Liabilities				
Creditors			5 000	
Non-current Liabilities				
Secured Loans		15 000		
Unsecured Loans		2 000	17 000	22 000
Net Assets				21 600
Shareholders' Equity				
Capital			20 000	
Retained Profits			1 600	21 600

CHAPTER

7 Using financial information

7.1 The accounting framework

BiZ WORD

*The **accounting framework** consists of raw data that is processed, stored and then summarised in a meaningful and accepted form.*

The **accounting framework** of an organisation provides most of the financial information for decision-making purposes. Effective decisions can come only from accurate and timely financial information that assists management and other interested parties in evaluating the organisation's performance.

The accounting framework consists of raw data that is processed, stored and then summarised in a meaningful and accepted form.

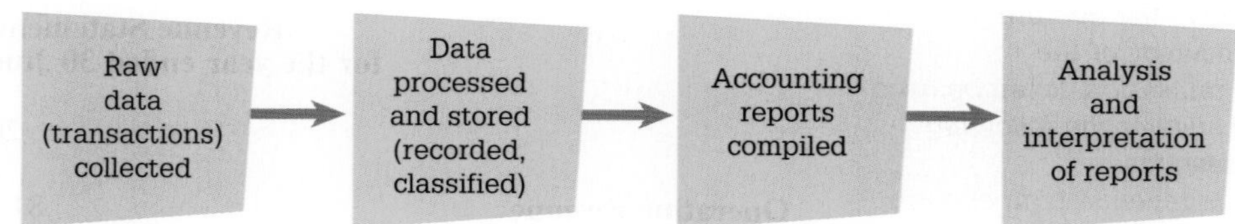
Raw data (transactions) collected
Data processed and stored (recorded, classified)
Accounting reports compiled
Analysis and interpretation of reports

Figure 7.1 The accounting framework

The output of data from the accounting process is communicated and reported to interested parties. Several million transactions can be summarised on one page of financial results in a company financial statement.

BiZ WORD

***Financial statements** summarise the activities of an organisation over a period of time.*

Financial statements

The end products of the accounting process are the **financial statements**, which summarise the activities of an organisation over a period of time. The information provided by financial statements is analysed and interpreted so that an organisation's performance can be monitored and future decisions made.

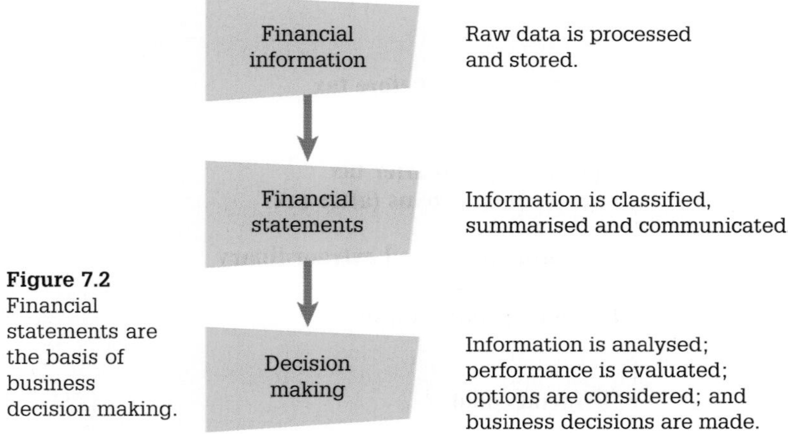
Financial information
Raw data is processed and stored.
Financial statements
Information is classified, summarised and communicated.
Decision making
Information is analysed; performance is evaluated; options are considered; and business decisions are made.

Figure 7.2 Financial statements are the basis of business decision making.

The key financial statements used by an organisation are revenue statements (profit and loss statements), balance sheets and statements of cash flows. Revenue statements and balance sheets are discussed in this chapter. Cash flow statements are discussed in chapter 8.

Revenue statements (statements of financial performance)

*The **revenue statement** shows the operating results for a period. It shows the revenue earned and expenses incurred over the accounting period with the resultant profit or loss.*

The **revenue statement** shows the operating efficiency — that is, revenue earned and expenses incurred over the accounting period with the resultant profit or loss. Revenue or income is the earnings from the main objectives of the business. Expenses are recurring amounts that are paid out while the business earns its revenue.

The revenue statement shows:

- operating revenue earned from the main function of the business, such as sales of inventories, services and non-operating revenue earned from other operations, such as interest, rent and commission
- operating expenses such as purchase of inventories, payment for services and other expenses incurred in the main operation of the business, such as advertising, rent, telephone and insurance.

The difference between the revenue and expenses is the profit or — if expenses exceed revenue — the loss.

The revenue statement shows the operating efficiency of the organisation. It can be used to answer the following questions:

- *Is revenue high enough to cover expenses?*
- *Is the mark-up on purchases sufficient?*
- *Is the organisation making a good profit?*
- *Are the expenses in proportion to the revenue they are earning?*
- *Is inventory turnover appropriate for the business?*

Revenue Statement
for the year ended 30 June 2008

	2006 $	2007 $	2008 $
Operating revenue	81 200	83 500	78 800
Cost of goods sold			
Opening inventory	11 280	11 300	11 240
Purchases	53 000	55 200	48 000
	64 280	66 500	59 240
Closing inventory	11 300	11 240	11 100
	52 980	55 260	48 140
Gross profit	28 220	28 240	30 660
Expenses			
Selling	7 800	9 200	8 900
Administrative	4 400	4 400	7 000
Interest	3 000	3 500	3 000
	15 200	17 100	18 900
Operating profit before tax	13 020	11 140	11 760
Tax	4 500	3 900	4 100
Operating profit after tax	8 520	7 240	7 660
Extraordinary items (after tax)	4 300	4 600	3 900
Operating profit and extraordinary items after tax	12 820	11 840	11 560
Retained profits (1 July)	25 000	31 000	35 000
	37 820	42 840	46 560
Dividends paid	3400	2 900	3 800
Retained profits (30 June)	34 420	39 940	42 760

Figure 7.3 An example of a revenue statement

By examining figures from previous revenue statements, managers can make comparisons and analyse trends before making important financial decisions. They can see whether expenses are increasing, decreasing or remaining the same, why profits have increased or decreased and in which areas there has been significant change.

Balance sheets (statements of financial position)

*A **balance sheet** represents an organisation's assets and liabilities at a particular point in time, expressed in money terms, and represents the net worth of the business.*

A **balance sheet** represents an organisation's assets and liabilities at a particular point in time and represents the net worth (equity) of the business. It shows the financial stability of the organisation. The balance sheet is prepared at the end of the accounting period.

The balance sheet shows the level of current and long-term assets, current and long-term liabilities, including investments and owners' equity.

- Assets represent what is owned by a business.
- Liabilities are claims by people other than owners against assets, and represent what is owed by the business.
- Owners' equity represents the owners' financial interest in the business or net worth of the business.

Balance Sheet
as at 30 June 2008

	Consolidated $m	Chief entity $m
Current Assets		
Cash	86.3	20.2
Receivables	578.5	414.0
Inventories	100.8	
Total Current Assets	765.6	434.2
Non-current Assets		
Investments	589.3	649.9
Property, plant and equipment	2182.2	46.7
Intangibles	189.8	
Total Non-current Assets	2961.3	696.6
Total Assets	3726.9	1130.8
Current Liabilities		
Accounts payable	438.3	4.5
Provisions	253.3	64.2
Total Current Liabilities	691.6	68.7
Non-current Liabilities		
Borrowings	1347.4	—
Total Non-current Liabilities	1347.4	—
Total Liabilities	2039.0	68.7
Net Assets	1687.9	1062.1
Shareholders' Equity		
Share capital	988.4	988.4
Reserves	75.2	3.3
Retained profits	624.3	70.4
Total Shareholders' Equity	1687.9	1062.1

Figure 7.4 An example of a balance sheet

The balance sheet shows the financial stability of the organisation. Analysis of the balance sheet can indicate whether:

- the organisation has enough assets to cover its debts
- the interest and money borrowed can be paid
- the assets of the business are being used to maximise profits
- the owners of the business are making a good return on their investment.

The balance sheet shows the return on the owners' investment, the sources and extent of borrowings, the level of inventories, and so on. The figures also show whether the business has sufficient assets to continue to make profits in the longer term, how much of the assets are financed from outside borrowings, whether the business can expect to meet its financial obligations in the short and longer term, and how the year's figures compare with the previous year.

It is important that the presentation of figures in the balance sheet allows clear interpretation so that interested parties can draw meaningful conclusions and make important decisions about the business. Figures from previous years' balance sheets can also be analysed and presented to show the decision makers the trends and changes in the business that need to be investigated.

Balance Sheet
as at 30 June 2008

	Consolidated		Chief entity	
	2007	2008	2007	2008
	$m	$m	$m	$m
Current Assets				
Cash	4.8	20.6	2.2	16.7
Accounts receivable	102.0	81.6	46.7	75.2
Investments	14.9	—	—	—
Inventories	36.0	31.5	—	4.9
Total Current Assets	157.7	133.7	48.9	96.8
Non-current Assets				
Receivables	59.3	64.7	931.0	792.3
Investments	284.7	293.5	313.9	358.3
Inventories	17.3	79.5	—	47.7
Property, plant and equipment	831.4	882.9	40.0	39.9
Intangibles	5.1	5.6	—	—
Total Non-current Assets	1197.8	1326.2	1284.9	1238.2
Total Assets	1355.5	1459.9	1333.8	1335.0
Current Liabilities				
Creditors and borrowings	190.0	118.2	125.4	71.1
Provisions	59.6	51.7	69.8	38.8
Total Current Liabilities	249.6	169.9	195.2	109.9
Non-current Liabilities				
Creditors and borrowings	238.7	417.6	258.4	391.6
Provisions	210.2	208.4	21.2	36.4
Total Non-current Liabilities	448.9	626.0	279.6	428.0
Total Liabilities	698.5	795.9	474.8	537.9

Net Assets	657.0664.0		859.0797.1	
Proprietors' Equity				
Share capital	132.3	182.7	276.5	265.7
Reserves	228.3	235.1	329.6	336.2
Retained profits	161.9	111.7	252.9	195.2
Equity attributable to proprietors of the chief entity	522.5	529.5	859.0	797.1
Reserve account	134.5	134.5	—	—
Total Capital and Reserves	657.0	664.0	859.0	797.1

Figure 7.5 An example of a comparative balance sheet

The accounting equation and relationships

*The **accounting equation**, which forms the basis of the accounting process, shows the relationship between assets, liabilities and owners' equity.*

The **accounting equation**, which forms the basis of the accounting process, shows the relationship between assets, liabilities and owners' equity.

Assets are what is *owned* by an organisation; liabilities and owners' equity are what is *owed* by an organisation. The business and the owner are separate; therefore, owners' equity is what is to be repaid (hopefully with increased profits) by the business to the owner. The accounting equation shows that the assets of the business may be financed by either the owners or by parties external to the business.

It is important to remember that the accounting entity assumption means that financial information records for a business are kept separate from those of the owner.

The balance sheet shows the outcome of the accounting process. The accounting equation can be represented in different ways but, because it is an equation, it must always be equal.

Assets = Liabilities + Owners' equity
Owners' equity = Assets – Liabilities
Liabilities = Assets – Owners' equity

The balance sheet can be displayed in different forms to show the different ways of expressing the accounting equation. In the first example (figure 7.6), the balance sheet represents the accounting equation Assets = Liabilities + Owners' equity.

Balance Sheet
as at 30 June 2008

	$	$
Current Assets		
Cash	30 400	
Inventories	4 100	92 500
Accounts receivable	58 000	
Non-current Assets		
Plant and equipment	68 000	
Land and buildings	85 000	153 000
		$245 500
Current Liabilities		
Accounts payable	82 000	
Non-current Liabilities		
Loan	25 000	107 000
Owners' Equity		
Capital	100 000	
Net profit	38 500	138 500
		$245 500

Figure 7.6 A balance sheet showing Assets = Liabilities + Owners' equity

In the second example (figure 7.7), the balance sheet represents the accounting equation Owners' equity = Assets – Liabilities.

Balance Sheet
as at 30 June 2008

	$	$
Current Assets		
Cash	30 400	
Inventories	4 100	
Accounts receivable	58 000	92 500
Non-current Assets		
Plant and equipment	68 000	
Land and buildings	85 000	153 000
		245 500
less Current Liabilities		
Accounts payable	82 000	
Non-current Liabilities		
Loan	25 000	107 000
		$138 500
Owners' Equity		
Capital	100 000	
Net profit	38 500	**$138 500**

Figure 7.7 A balance sheet showing Owners' equity = Assets – Liabilities

The accounting equation shows the effect of the business's operations on owners' equity. Owners' equity comprises two elements — capital, or funds contributed by the owner or owners to the business, and retained profits (see figure 7.8).

Owners' equity

Paid up capital	285 000
Reserve for contingencies	37 000
Retained profits	33 000
	$355 000

Figure 7.8 Owners' equity showing proportion of capital and retained profits

Profit is the difference between revenue and expenses. The revenue statement and balance sheet are produced to show the effects of revenue earned and expenses incurred on owners' equity. The accounting equation could more accurately be expressed as:

> Assets = Liabilities + Capital + Revenue – Expenses
> or
> Assets = Liabilities + Capital + Profit (Revenue – Expenses)

The balance sheet and revenue statement show the outcomes of the accounting process on the accounting equation. The revenue statement shows the resulting profit from revenue, less expenses. The profit (or loss) figure is transferred to the owners' equity as part of capital in the balance sheet.

EXERCISE 7.1 Revision

1. What is financial information? Who is interested in financial information and why?
2. Make a list of questions to which the following groups of people might seek answers from a business. The first one is done for you.

Group	Questions
Creditors	Is your cash flow sufficient to pay your account on time?
Bank	
Employee	
Owner	
Investor	
Customer	

3. How can a comparative financial statement assist in decision making?
4. Explain the relationship between the accounting equation and financial statements.
5. IBJ is a company producing steel products. The company has weathered economic fluctuations and has made increasing profits over the past two years. The company has been in existence for 10 years and has recently expanded into Malaysia and Thailand. What questions might the following groups ask about the organisation?
   (a) Walter Banking Corporation
   (b) Australian Government
   (c) IBJ shareholders
   (d) IBJ management
   (e) employees of IBJ
6. What financial information would you request in the following situations?
   (a) To determine whether the business is a good investment
   (b) To determine whether you would offer credit to the business
   (c) To determine whether you would lend money to this organisation
7. Answer the questions using the balance sheet below.

Balance Sheet of Biq & Son
as at 30 June 2008

Current Assets		**Current Liabilities**	
Cash at bank	3 000	Accounts payable	9 500
Inventories	2 500	**Non-current Liabilities**	
Accounts receivable	8 500	Loan	50 000
Non-current Assets		**Owners' Equity**	
Furniture	2 500		
Vehicle	16 500	Capital	100 000
Land and buildings	140 000	Profit	13 500
	173 000		173 000

   (a) Why is the balance sheet written 'as at 30 June 2008'?
   (b) Who are the owners of the business and what was their original investment?

(c) What is the value of the owners' investment on 30 June 2008?
(d) Suggest how the assets of the business were financed.
(e) How much is owed by the business?
(f) Suggest how the business will pay its debts.
(g) Would you offer credit to this business? Why or why not?
(h) Explain the relationship between the accounting equation and the balance sheet.

8. Your friends Tony and Yung have a small business making novelty party accessories. They have been running the business for three months and it appears to be going well. They want to know if they are making a profit or a loss. You agree to help them. They provide you with the following information. Prepare a revenue statement to determine their profit or loss.
   - Raw materials and supplies to make the novelties cost them $2000.
   - At the end of the month they still have $700 worth of raw materials and supplies.
   - During the month, they sold 1000 of their novelty products for $5 each.
   - They paid their friends Sandy and Max $300 to help them.
   - They sent flyers to department stores advertising their product, and this cost them $220.
   - They paid the telephone bill ($340) and courier for delivery ($90).
9. What is the difference between an asset and a liability?
10. Complete the following accounting equation:
    Assets = ______________ + ______________
11. What does owner's equity represent?
12. What is the difference between a balance sheet and a revenue statement?
13. Complete the missing amounts in the following table (financial year is 1 July–30 June).

	Business A	Business B	Business C
Assets 1 July	275 000	221 000	—
Liabilities 1 July	135 000	—	353 000
Owners' equity 1 July	—	114 000	206 000
Assets 30 June	293 000	—	481 000
Liabilities 30 June	141 000	153 000	—
Owners' equity 30 June	—	189 000	242 000
Sales	484 000	521 000	—
Cost of goods sold	385 000	—	292 000
Gross profit	—	174 000	145 000
Expenses	—	135 000	105 000
Net profit	39 000	—	—

14. Using the information from question 13, answer the following questions. Give reasons for your answers.
    (a) Which owner is making the highest gross profit?
    (b) Which owner is making the highest net profit?
    (c) In which business would you invest and why?
    (d) In what information would employees be interested?
    (e) Each business has applied for a loan of $50 000 from a bank. Which business is most likely to be successful in their application?

Extension

1. Financial management is concerned not so much with what has happened in the past but with what is going to happen in the future. Explain this statement.
2. Examine the financial reports of a number of businesses. For which business would you be most interested in working? What other information might be needed to help you make a decision?

7.2 Types of financial ratio

__Analysis__ involves working the financial information into significant and acceptable forms that make it more meaningful and highlighting relationships between different aspects of an organisation.

__Interpretation__ is making judgements and decisions using the data gathered from analysis.

Careful analysis can provide signals regarding the success of the business or impending problems. For example, management may be interested to know:
- *how effectively assets have been used in an organisation*
- *why an increase in advertising expenses has not generated more sales revenue than anticipated*
- *why sales have decreased over the past two years*
- *why bank overdrafts have continued to increase.*

Many important questions cannot be answered by simply 'looking' at the financial statements of an organisation. Financial statements summarise the activities of an organisation over a period of time and must be analysed to increase understanding of the implications of those activities.

Analysis is an important part of the accounting process. It involves working the financial information into significant and acceptable forms that make it more meaningful and highlighting relationships between different aspects of an organisation. Analysis involves comparing similar items in the revenue statement and balance sheet.

The main types of analysis are vertical, horizontal and trend analysis.

- Vertical analysis compares figures within one financial year; for example, expressing gross profit as a percentage of sales and comparing debt to equity.
- Horizontal analysis compares figures from different financial years; for example, comparing 2007 and 2008.
- Trend analysis compares figures for periods of three to five years.

The methods of analysis involve calculations of figures, percentages and ratios. Ratios are one of the main tools used to analyse financial information and assist in answering more clearly the questions relating to profits, solvency, efficiency, growth and return. But analysis without **interpretation** is meaningless. Interpretation is making judgements and decisions using the data gathered from analysis.

The type of analysis chosen will depend on the reasons that the information is required and the decisions to be made from the information. Users of information may be interested to compare figures, percentages or ratios for departments, different products, different branches or against the industry. They may also wish to monitor trends over a number of years or make comparisons between items within a financial statement, selling expenses and sales.

Analysis of financial statements is usually aimed at the areas of:

- financial stability (i.e. liquidity and solvency)
- profitability
- efficiency.

Liquidity

Liquidity is the extent to which the business can meet its financial commitments in the short term, which usually refers to a time period of less than 12 months. The business must have sufficient resources to pay its debts and enough funds for unexpected expenses. To assess a business's liquidity, its managers must assess whether the business can pay its debts when they are due. Is there sufficient cash and a level of assets and inventories that can be converted to cash quickly to repay the firm's debts — that is, the firm's accounts payable, interest and loans?

The holding of outstanding debts means the business has less cash to earn revenue. The quicker the firm receives cash from its accounts receivable, the quicker those funds can be used to earn revenue. Current assets and current liabilities determine the liquidity or short-term financial stability of an organisation. The firm must be careful to ensure that it has enough current assets that could be used to generate cash quickly, but not so much that the resources are not being used for producing revenue.

There are a number of ratios to show short-term financial stability, calculated from balance sheet figures. An example is the current ratio (or working capital ratio).

Many firms operate successfully with current ratios of less than 2:1. Firms that sell finished goods and keep large levels of inventories need a higher ratio than firms selling on credit rather than cash. Large businesses in the food industry, for example, Woolworths, use a lower ratio of approximately 0.6:1. Businesses in service industries, such as doctors and dentists who rely on cash payments for their services, also do not need as high a ratio and operate on ratios of less than 2:1.

Current ratio (working capital)

$$\text{Current ratio} = \frac{\text{Current assets}}{\text{Current liabilities}}$$

Current assets and liabilities are turned into cash within 12 months. For example, assets such as inventories and accounts receivable would be paid in a month or two, as would liabilities, such as the firm's own accounts payable. It is generally accepted that a ratio of 2:1 indicates a sound financial position for a firm. That is, the firm should have double the amount of assets to cover its liabilities.

However, an 'acceptable' ratio will also depend on a number of factors, such as the type of firm, how other firms in the industry are operating and factors in the external environment (see the Biz Fact on the left). In other words, the current ratio gives only a limited indication of the ability of the business to meet its liabilities. The nature and composition of current assets may vary considerably. It is not a good idea to give rule-of-thumb standards for the current ratio.

$$\text{Current ratio} = \frac{\text{Current assets}}{\text{Current liabilities}} = \frac{300\,000}{195\,000} = 1.54$$

Comment: This firm has $1.54 of current assets to cover $1 of current liabilities. A ratio of less than 1:1 indicates there are insufficient assets to pay current commitments or liabilities. If this firm has previously operated successfully, it may find a ratio of 1.54:1 acceptable. However, if this is not the case, the firm may have to sell non-current assets to cover liabilities, which will reduce its capacity to earn profits; or it may have to borrow in the short term and incur higher interest repayments. In most instances a firm would be unwise to allow this ratio to fall below 1.5:1.

$$\text{Current ratio} = \frac{\text{Current assets}}{\text{Current liabilities}} = \frac{450\,000}{150\,000} = 3:1$$

Comment: This firm has $3 of current assets for every $1 of current liabilities. This indicates that the firm is in a sound financial position — that is, it is liquid and will be able to pay for its debts in the short term. If the firm has a high demand for its product, for example, food products, there may be reason to reduce the level of its current ratio. Even for a firm that has a low demand, for example, jewellery, its working capital may be too high. Too high a ratio can mean that current assets are not being used fully. Action is needed to ensure that sufficient use is being made of the assets in the business.

Figure 7.9 Examples of current ratio

Solvency

Solvency *is the extent to which the business can meet its financial commitments in the longer term. Solvency is measured using leverage or gearing ratios.*

Solvency is the extent to which the business can meet its financial commitments in the longer term. The longer term generally refers to a time period greater than 12 months. Solvency is particularly important for owners, shareholders and creditors of an organisation because it is an indication of the risks to their investment.

Solvency indicates whether the firm will be able to repay amounts that have been used for capital investment; for example, the purchase of a new factory or an investment in new machinery that may have been financed from borrowings. The firm needs to determine whether it will be able to service these borrowings; for example, its mortgage repayments, over a sustained period of five to 10 years.

Leverage or gearing ratios measure the firm's solvency — that is, its ability to meet its financial commitments in the longer term. Potential investors and creditors are interested in leverage ratios, as they show whether the creditors will be paid or whether investors can expect a good return on their money.

The control of debt and equity — the relationship between them and how much or how little of each to allow — is an important decision for the management of a firm. As we saw in chapter 6, management has to determine whether capital investments for the firm will be financed through outside sources (debt) or from within the firm's capital structure (equity). Debt is attractive because the interest on the debt is a tax deduction. However, the interest and the principal have to be repaid at a later date, and interest has to be paid no matter what the financial position of the business. Equity is safer and carries fewer risks, but returns on equity will be less, as amounts have to be 'retained' from current earnings. Retained earnings, and hence dividends to shareholders, will vary depending on the profitability of the business. Shareholders expect a regular return on their investment so companies have to ensure they can provide it. If shareholders are not satisfied they may sell their shares, withdrawing their equity in the firm.

Debt to equity ratio

$$\text{Debt to equity ratio} = \frac{\text{Total liabilities}}{\text{Owners' equity}}$$

The debt to equity ratio shows the extent to which the firm is relying on debt or outside sources to finance the business. This ratio is an important control aspect for management because the relationship between debt and equity must be carefully balanced.

The higher the ratio, the less solvent the firm. That is, the higher the ratio of debt to equity, the higher the risk. The firm must look carefully at interest rates, business confidence and economic indicators to determine if the balance between debt and equity is appropriate for its particular business or industry. A highly geared firm — a firm that uses more debt than equity — carries more risk with regard to longer term financial stability. Investors would be less attracted to a firm with a higher debt to equity ratio because this indicates a greater financial risk.

The type of business will determine how highly geared or low geared a business can be. For example, a business that is less influenced by economic fluctuations can be more highly geared. A shop selling essential food items will not be affected by economic downturns so it can carry more debt than a business that sells luxury items.

An interesting question is posed by the debt to equity ratio. Should the owners of an organisation have as much at stake as the creditors (that is, should the ratio be at least 1:1)? Different firms have different financial structures and the attitude of the owners to financial risk determines what levels of debt to equity are appropriate for the business. Debt to equity ratio also has a direct effect on the short-term and immediate solvency of an organisation. The greater the owners' financial interest in the business, the more solvent in the short term the business is likely to be. Ultimately, the level of solvency in a business reflects its financial structure — that is, its control of debt and equity. This is important for the long-term survival of the business.

Balance Sheet 2008

	$	$
Current Assets		
Cash	20 000	
Accounts receivable	50 000	
Inventories	80 000	150 000
Non-current Assets		
Delivery vehicles		50 000
		200 000
Current Liabilities		
Accounts payable		20 000
Non-current Liabilities		
Mortgage		30 000
Owners' Equity		
Capital	140 000	
Add net profit	10 000	150 000
		200 000

$$\text{Debt to equity ratio} = \frac{\text{Total liabilities}}{\text{Owners' equity}}$$

$$= \frac{50\,000}{150\,000}$$

$$= 0.3{:}1 \text{ or } 33\tfrac{1}{3}\,\%$$

Comment: The firm has $0.33 in external debt (liabilities) for every $1 of internal debt (owners' equity). A ratio of 1:1 indicates a sound financial position so this company is in a safe position. Depending on the type of firm, the industry and past trends, the firm could possibly increase its rate of external debt.

Figure 7.10 An example of a debt to equity ratio

Profitability

Profitability is the earning performance of the business and indicates its capacity to use its resources to maximise profits. Profitability depends on the revenue earned by an organisation and the ability of the business to increase selling prices to cover purchase costs and other expenses incurred in earning revenue. The ability of the business to generate profits is its most important financial objective.

A number of parties are interested in a business's profitability:

- Owners and shareholders want to know whether the firm is earning an acceptable return on their investment.
- Creditors want to know whether they will be paid and should offer credit in the future.
- Lenders want to know whether the principal on the loan and interest will be repaid and whether to lend to the firm in the future.
- Management uses profitability to decide on the need for adjustments to policies.

The amount of profit is determined by a number of factors, such as the volume of sales, the mark-up on purchases and the level of expenses. Financial information must be examined to see where changes have occurred and where changes need to be made in the future.

*A **profit and loss statement** is a document that provides information for a particular period of time regarding sales, operating profit before and after tax and extraordinary items, as well as dividends to be paid and retained earnings.*

Profitability cannot be assessed in isolation. The amount of profit must be related to the assets of the firm. For example, we might hear that a firm has made a profit of $250 000, but we cannot interpret this as a good or bad result without relating it to the type of firm, its size and its asset structure.

The type of business will determine the amount of mark-up needed. A firm with quick turnover, for example, a bread shop, will have lower mark-ups. Firms with slower stock turnovers need higher mark-ups; for example, expensive and slow-selling items such as luxury cars.

The **profit and loss statement** is used to measure the profitability or earning capacity of the firm. Figures from the profit and loss statement are used to calculate:

- gross profit ratio
- net profit ratio.

Gross profit ratio

Gross profit represents the amount of sales that is available to meet expenses resulting in net profit. A fall in the rate of gross profit may mean a fall in the amount of net profit. The amount of that decrease depends on such factors as price reductions as a result of specials or sales, mark-downs on out-of-date stock, theft of stock, errors in determining prices, changes in the mark-up policies or changes in the mix of sales.

$$\text{Gross profit ratio} = \frac{\text{Gross profit}}{\text{Sales}}$$

The gross profit ratio shows changes from one accounting period to another, and indicates the effectiveness of planning policies concerning pricing, sales, discounts, the valuation of stock and so on. If the ratio is low, alternative suppliers may need to be sourced and competitors investigated.

Net profit ratio

Net profit represents the profit or return to the owners. For sole traders and partnerships, this represents a return for both their contribution to the firm in terms of labour and on the funds they have contributed to the business. It is usual for a company to return part of net profit to shareholders as dividends and retain part for future expansion.

$$\text{Net profit ratio} = \frac{\text{Net profit}}{\text{Sales}}$$

The net profit ratio shows the amount of sales revenue that results in net profit. The costs or expenses after gross profit must be low enough to generate a net profit. The amount of sales must be sufficiently high to cover the costs or expenses of the firm and still result in a profit. A firm would be aiming at a high net profit ratio. A low net profit ratio indicates that expenses should be examined to see whether reductions can be made.

Profit and Loss Statement for Young's Corner Store, 2008

	$	$
Revenue	100 000	
less Cost of goods sold	80 000	
Gross profit		20 000
less Selling expenses	3 000	
less Administrative expenses	1 500	
less Financial expenses	500	5 000
		15 000

Opening stock	$15 000
Closing stock	$25 000
Accounts receivable	$10 000

(a) Gross profit ratio $= \frac{\text{Gross profit}}{\text{Sales}}$

$= \frac{20\,000}{100\,000} \times 100$

$= 20\%$

(b) Net profit ratio $= \frac{\text{Net profit}}{\text{Sales}}$

$= \frac{15\,000}{100\,000} \times 100$

$= 15\%$

Figure 7.11 Examples of profitability ratios

Return on owners' equity ratio

$$\text{Return on owners' equity ratio} = \frac{\text{Net profit}}{\text{Owners' equity}}$$

The return on owners' equity ratio shows how effective the funds contributed by the owners have been in generating profit, and hence a return on their investment. The return for the owners has to be better than any return that could be gained from alternative investments, such as bank investments. If return on owners' equity rises due to increased leverage (debt) the improved result should be seen as carrying increased risk.

$$\text{Return on owners' equity} = \frac{\text{Net profit (after tax)}}{\text{Owners' equity}}$$

$$= \frac{10\,000}{150\,000}$$

$$= 0.06 \text{ or } 6.6\%$$

Comment: The higher the ratio or percentage, the better the return for the owner. In this example, a return of 6.6 per cent would not be seen as a good investment. Depending on other information, the owner would need to consider alternatives for investment, such as bank interest rates.

Figure 7.12 An example of a return on owners' equity ratio

Owners are interested not only in the return for the current year but also in comparing the current year's return with previous years and against industry averages. It is also useful to compare the return with alternative investment considerations; for example, interest earned through a financial institution.

If returns compare favourably, owners might consider expansion or diversification of the business. If the return is unfavourable, the owners would consider alternative options, including selling off the business.

Efficiency

Efficiency is the ability of the firm to use its resources effectively in ensuring financial stability and profitability of the business. Efficiency relates to the effectiveness of management in directing and maintaining the goals and objectives of the firm. The more efficient the firm, the greater its profits and financial stability.

Expense ratio

$$\text{Expense ratio} = \frac{\text{Expenses}}{\text{Sales}}$$

Each of the categories of expenses is compared with sales. The ratio indicates the amount of sales that are allocated to individual expenses, such as selling, administration, cost of goods sold and financial expenses. The expense ratios indicate the day-to-day efficiency of the business. A business aims to keep expenses at a reasonable level. Management needs to determine why expense ratios are too high or why they have decreased or increased. For example, if the selling expense ratio has increased, it may be that advertising costs have not generated the expected increase in sales. A decline in the financial expense ratio may be a result of lower interest rates or less debt being used by the firm.

Expenses should also be compared with budget in order to find reasons for differences. Expense ratios should be examined carefully. Some expenses will be fixed and some expenses will fluctuate according to the level of sales.

Accounts receivable turnover ratio

$$\text{Accounts receivable turnover ratio} = \frac{\text{Sales}}{\text{Accounts receivable}}$$

Accounts receivable turnover ratio measures the effectiveness of a firm's credit policy and how efficiently it collects its debts. It measures how many times the accounts receivable balance is converted into cash or how quickly debtors pay their accounts. By dividing the ratio into 365, businesses can determine the average length of time it takes to convert the balance into cash. If a firm's accounts receivable turnover is 84 days but its creditors allow 30 days before payment, the firm would need to examine its cash flow, its credit policies, its credit collection procedures and costs, and its policies relating to doubtful debts.

Profit and Loss Statement for Young's Corner Store, 2008

	$	$
Revenue	100 000	
less Cost of goods sold	80 000	
Gross profit		20 000
less Selling expenses	3 000	
less Administrative expenses	1 500	
less Financial expenses	500	5 000
		15 000

Opening stock	$15 000
Closing stock	$25 000
Accounts receivable	$10 000

(a) Expense ratio $= \dfrac{\text{Expenses}}{\text{Sales}}$

(i) Selling expense ratio $= \dfrac{2\,500}{100\,000} \times 100$

$= 2.5\%$

(ii) Administrative expense ratio $= \dfrac{1\,000}{100\,000} \times 100$

$= 1\%$

(iii) Financial expense ratio $= \dfrac{1\,500}{100\,000} \times 100$

$= 1.5\%$

(b) Accounts receivable turnover ratio $= \dfrac{\text{Sales}}{\text{Accounts receivable}}$

$= \dfrac{100\,000}{10\,000}$

$= 10\%$

$\left(\dfrac{365}{10}\right) = 36.5$ days

Comment: Depending on the type of business and past trends, the firm has made a reasonable gross and net profit. Selling, administrative and financial expenses are quite low.

Debt collection figures indicate relative efficiency in the collection of debts. Debts are being repaid on an average of 36.5 days (assuming that the firm has a billing cycle of 30 days).

Figure 7.13 Examples of efficiency ratios

TABLE 7.1	Types of financial ratio				
Ratio	**Formula**	**Example on page**	**Analysis of which aspect of the financial statement**	**What does analysis of this ratio show about a business?**	**Interpretations of ratio results**
Current ratio	$\frac{\text{Current assets}}{\text{Current liabilities}}$	158	Liquidity	Shows the short-term financial stability of a business (i.e. its ability to meet its short-term financial commitments)	It is generally accepted that a ratio of 2:1 indicates a sound financial position (i.e. a firm should have double the amount of assets to cover its liabilities).
Debt to equity ratio	$\frac{\text{Total liabilities}}{\text{Owners' equity}}$	159	Solvency	Shows the extent to which the firm is relying on debt or outside sources to finance the business	The higher the ratio, the less solvent the firm (i.e. the higher the ratio of debt to equity, the higher the business risk).
Gross profit ratio	$\frac{\text{Gross profit}}{\text{Sales}}$	161	Profitability	Shows the changes from one accounting period to another and indicates the effectiveness of planning policies concerning pricing, sales, discounts, the valuation of stock etc.	The higher the ratio the better. If the ratio is low, alternative suppliers may need to be sourced and competitors investigated.
Net profit ratio	$\frac{\text{Net profit}}{\text{Sales}}$ *(Net profit is gross profit less expenses)*	161	Profitability	Net profit ratio represents the profit or return to the owners.	A firm will be aiming for a high net profit ratio. A low net profit ratio indicates that expenses should be examined to look for possibility of reductions.
Return on owners' equity ratio	$\frac{\text{Net profit}}{\text{Owners' equity}}$	162	Profitability	Shows how effective the funds contributed by the owners have been in generating profit and so the return on investment (ROI)	The higher the ratio or percentage, the better the return for the owner.

Ratio	Formula	Example on page	Analysis of which aspect of the financial statement	What does analysis of this ratio show about a business?	Interpretations of ratio results
Expense ratio	$\frac{\text{Expenses}}{\text{Sales}}$	162	Efficiency	Each of the categories of expenses is compared with sales. The ratio indicates the amount of sales that are allocated to individual expenses such as selling, administration, COGS and financial expenses.	Expense ratios indicate day-to-day efficiency of the business. Expense ratios need to be kept at a reasonable level, and management must monitor each type of expense in relation to sales. Higher expense ratios may be the result of poor management.
Accounts receivable turnover ratio	$\frac{\text{Sales}}{\text{Accounts receivable}}$	163	Efficiency	Measures the effectiveness of a firm's credit policy and how efficiently it collects its debt.	High turnover ratios indicate the business has efficient debt collection.

EXERCISE 7.2 *Revision*

1. What is the difference between analysis and interpretation of financial reports?
2. Explain how financial reports are analysed and interpreted.
3. What are the purposes of analysing financial ratios?
4. Draw up a table listing the types of financial ratio under the following headings (the first one has been completed for you).

Financial management objective	Type of ratio	Financial statement	Purpose
Liquidity	Current ratio	Balance sheet	Short-term financial stability

5. What ratio would assist to determine the answers to the following questions?
   (a) Are assets being used efficiently?
   (b) Is the organisation able to pay its debts in the short term?
   (c) Is the organisation able to pay its debts in the long term?
   (d) Are owners/shareholders receiving value for their investment?

(e) Are credit policies of the organisation being used effectively?
(f) How is the organisation being financed?

6. Using the information below, write a report for Bobbie and Lee at the end of their first year in business as 'T-shirts and More', commenting on:
   (a) return on owners' equity (Bobbie and Lee invested $50 000 in the business)
   (b) gross profit ratio
   (c) net profit ratio.

Profit and Loss Statement
for T-shirts and More, 2008

	$	$	$
Sales of T-shirts			40 000
less Cost of goods sold			25 000
Gross profit			15 000
less Selling expenses			
Advertising	1 000		
Wages	3 300	4 300	
less Administrative expenses			
Telephone	1 400		
Rent of premises	1 500	2 900	7 200
Net profit			7 800

7. Using the following information, write a report commenting on the efficiency of accounts receivable of Blossoms Tyres. Suggest reasons for the trend. What comment would you make if the business was Blossoms Trucks rather than Blossoms Tyres?

Average days sales uncollected			
2005	2006	2007	2008
104 days	110 days	120 days	120 days

8. The gross profit percentages and net profit percentages of a firm for three years are as follows.

	Gross profit	**Net profit**
Year 1	45%	24%
Year 2	42%	22%
Year 3	38%	16%

Suggest reasons why these trends might have occurred.

9. Using the information from the revenue statement on page 167, answer the questions below.
   (a) What was the profit or loss for the business in 2007 and 2008?
   (b) What expenses (if any) would you recommend be cut in 2009? Give reasons.
   (c) What has been the trend in advertising expenses as a percentage of sales over the last two years?
   (d) Comment on the profitability of the business for the past two years. Give reasons.

Revenue Statement for year ended 30 June 2008

	2007 $	2008 $
Sales	130 000	135 000
less Cost of goods sold	80 000	82 000
Gross profit	50 000	53 000
less Expenses		
Advertising	20 000	23 000
Rent	13 000	13 500
Interest — short term	1 200	1 200
Motor vehicle expenses	8 500	10 100
Net profit	7 300	5 200

10. You have been given the following analysis of the financial reports of JY Enterprises. Prepare a report for management giving your interpretation of the data under the headings 'Liquidity', 'Solvency' and 'Profitability'.

	2005 $	2006 $	2007 $	2008 $
Current Assets				
Inventory	90 000	100 000	100 000	150 000
Accounts receivable	120 000	140 000	150 000	150 000
Non-current Assets	250 000	250 000	300 000	200 000
Total Assets	**460 000**	**490 000**	**550 000**	**500 000**
Current Liabilities				
Bank overdraft	40 000	50 000	60 000	60 000
Accounts payable	80 000	100 000	110 000	120 000
Non-current Liabilities	100 000	120 000	150 000	150 000
Total Liabilities	**220 000**	**270 000**	**320 000**	**330 000**
Owners' Equity				
Capital	150 000	150 000	150 000	150 000
Retained earnings	90 000	70 000	80 000	20 000
	240 000	**220 000**	**230 000**	**170 000**
Current ratio	$\frac{210\,000}{120\,000}$ = 1.75	$\frac{240000}{150\,000}$ = 1.6	$\frac{250\,000}{170\,000}$ = 1.48	$\frac{300\,000}{180\,000}$ = 1.67
Debt to equity	$\frac{220\,000}{240\,000}$ = 0.92	$\frac{270\,000}{220\,000}$ = 1.22	$\frac{320\,000}{230\,000}$ = 1.4	$\frac{330\,000}{170\,000}$ = 1.94
Return on owners' equity	$\frac{90\,000}{240\,000}$ = 0.38	$\frac{70\,000}{220\,000}$ = 0.32	$\frac{80\,000}{230\,000}$ = 0.35	$\frac{20\,000}{170\,000}$ = 0.12

11. In analysing the financial statements of Williams' Computing Services, the following ratios were calculated. What trends are indicated by the ratios? Comment on possible causes of the trends.

	2007	2008
Current ratio	2:1	1.5:1
Profit %	15	12
Debt:equity	1:1	1.5:1
Accounts receivable turnover	35 days	50 days

Extension

1. The objectives of financial management often conflict with one another. Explain this statement.
2. Financial analysis is the beginning of an investigation of a business. Discuss.
3. Examine a range of financial reports from a business.
   (a) Calculate solvency, liquidity, profitability and efficiency ratios using figures from the reports.
   (b) Prepare a report commenting on the ratios.
4. Use the Internet to find the most recent annual report and financial statements of three companies.
   (a) What are the operating profit (or loss), total assets and total liabilities?
   (b) Print screenshots of the sites where you found the results and share them with others in the class. Compare your results.

7.3 Comparative ratio analysis

Figures, percentages and ratios do not provide a complete picture for analysis. For analysis to be meaningful, comparisons and benchmarks are needed. Judgements are then made by comparing a firm's analysis against other figures, percentages and ratios. This is known as comparative ratio analysis and is important for firms. Comparisons can be made in a number of ways. Ratio analysis taken for a firm over a number of years can be compared with similar organisations and against common industry standards or benchmarks.

Ratios provide a 'snapshot' at a particular point in time and should be used carefully along with other information. Sales and stock levels may vary significantly throughout a year so financial information will also vary. It is important to look at trends in the financial information over several years. Figures from at least the previous two years can indicate directions or trends and make ratio analysis more meaningful.

Profit and Loss Statement

	2006		2007		2008	
	$	%	$	%	$	%
Sales	100 000	100	120 000	100	150 000	100
less Cost of goods sold	40 000	40	40 000	33	50 000	30
Gross profit	60 000	60	80 000	67	100 000	67
less Other expenses	20 000	20	30 000	25	45 000	30
Net profit	40 000	40	50 000	42	55 000	37

Although sales have increased steadily, cost of goods sold has risen only slightly over the three-year period. Cost of inventories may have decreased due to the suppliers being used or more efficient stock control methods being developed. Expenses have shown no great variation, with figures of 20 per cent, 25 per cent and 30 per cent of sales for the three-year period, resulting in a steady profit percentage (40 per cent, 42 per cent and 37 per cent respectively).

Figure 7.14 An example of profitability trends over a number of years

Analysis can also include budget figures so that predicted figures can be compared against actual figures, usually over short time periods such as per month. This information is usually available for interested parties within a firm rather than for external stakeholders.

Profit and Loss Statement

	Actual $	%	Budget $	%
Sales	75 000	100	100 000	100
less Cost of goods sold	42 000	56	55 000	55
Gross profit	33 000	44	45 000	45
less Other expenses	20 000	26	35 000	35
Net profit	13 000	17	10 000	10

Although actual sales is considerably less than budget, the reduced amount for expenses has led to an increased profit against sales (17 per cent rather than 10 per cent).

Figure 7.15 An example of comparing budget to actual figures

Comparison with other businesses and benchmarking — comparing results against standards that have been developed for a particular industry — are common. However, care must be taken to ensure that the same things are compared. Also, each firm has differences, and finding comparable firms may be difficult. Benchmarks are useful but are merely a guide. For example, financial leverage is often used to compare firms, so that if the industry average of debt to equity was 80 per cent and a particular firm had 40 per cent, then it would need to examine the risks and analyse the reasons for the differences.

In the past, Australian businesses have mainly used Australian standards but, with the globalisation of business, world standards are more commonly used for benchmarking.

Inter-business comparisons are useful and firms may access relevant business statistics from a number of sources, including the Australian Bureau of Statistics. They must ensure that information is up to date and accurately reflects the industry norms.

7.4 Limitations of financial reports

Ratio analysis provides information on the state of the business and indicates trends in its operations. However, caution needs to be exercised in reading the information. Misleading information impacts on business decision making and puts the business at risk. The following issues must be considered when analysing financial information.

Financial reports deal with monetary items only — that is, those items that can be expressed in money terms. Items that cannot have a monetary value attached to them are not taken into consideration. For example, the benefits of a large advertising campaign will not be shown in the financial reports.

Financial reports are summaries only, and further investigation and information may be required before judgements can be made. Financial reports cover activities over a period of time, usually one year. Therefore, the firm's financial positions may not be a true representation if the organisation has experienced seasonal fluctuations.

Ratios are taken at a particular time, so variations throughout the accounting period may not be truly represented.

Historical costs

***Historical cost accounting** states that values are stated at the cost incurred at the time of purchase or acquisition.*

There are accounting conventions and standards that are accepted practice for organisations. Historical cost accounting is one of them. **Historical cost accounting** states that values are stated at the cost incurred at the time of purchase or acquisition.

This means that figures in financial statements will be a mixture of different years' figures. For example, the following balance sheet shows a mixture of different years' figures.

When a business is purchased, the business receives benefit from the already established customer base if the customers continue to patronise that business. For example, a local garage has provided a service in the community for a number of years. It has many customers, both from within and outside the local area. Six months ago it changed hands. The purchase price of the business included an amount for goodwill. For a time, customers continued to come to the business but prices increased, some of the workmanship was not up to the previous standard and the customer base began to fall away. It would be unrealistic to continue to have goodwill in the balance sheet for the original amount and it is, therefore, reduced over a number of years.

Balance Sheet
as at 30 June 2008

Liabilities		**Assets**	
(2005) Long-term liability	50 000	(2008) Current assets	40 000
(2008) Current liabilities	20 000	(2003) Non-current assets	130 000
(2003) Capital	100 000		
	170 000		170 000

Figure 7.16 A balance sheet showing a mixture of different years' figures

The balance sheet represents historical cost values and, as the figures show, the values are mixed because of the different rates of acquisition.

Historical cost accounting is accepted practice and provides the following advantages:

- It is simple to prepare and understand (values are stated at the time of acquisition — no adjustment needed).
- It is safe (there is acceptance that figures have not been manipulated).
- It is unambiguous (non-accountants have less difficulty interpreting figures).

Historical cost accounting has been accepted and used for a long time and has worked well. However, it does mean that, in times of inflation, figures are distorted and figures in the financial statements do not represent an accurate picture of a firm's financial position. In times of inflation, organisations do make adjustments for the effects of inflation through a process of indexation.

Value of intangibles

***Intangible assets** are those assets that have value for a business but their value is difficult to measure and include licences, patents, trademarks, brand names, intellectual property and goodwill.*

Intangible assets include licences, patents, trademarks, brand names, intellectual property and goodwill. Intangible assets are either purchased from another party or internally generated through business operations. Purchased intangible assets such as licences are included in the balance sheet at their original cost. Other intangible assets, such as trademarks, brand names, patents and intellectual property, are often generated within an organisation. These have a value to the business but there is no uniform means of treating these intangibles in the balance sheet.

Some organisations write off these intangible assets, generally over a maximum period of 20 years, although many organisations retain these intangibles at their original value. The original value of the assets is determined as the lowest cost at which the asset could currently be purchased in the normal course of business.

Goodwill is a particularly difficult asset to measure. It is generally accepted that goodwill in the balance sheet is the residual value of the market value of the assets (purchase price) and the historical cost of assets. Goodwill is treated differently by different organisations. However, it is agreed that goodwill has a limited benefit for an organisation. Therefore, organisations usually write off goodwill over a period of time — being the period of time during which benefits will occur. Organisations usually reduce the amount of goodwill in the balance sheet over a number of years. The maximum period in Australia over which goodwill is to be written down is 20 years.

EXERCISE 7.3 Revision

1. Why do firms compare their results with industry standards and benchmarks?
2. Why is it often difficult to compare ratios for firms with industry averages?
3. Why is it difficult to compare businesses over time?
4. Why is it important for management to be aware of the limitations of financial reports?
5. Using examples, explain the limitations of financial reports.
6. Using the information below, compare Business X with industry standards. Write a report identifying significant differences, suggested changes and where further investigation is necessary.

	Business X	Industry standard
Profitability		
Gross profit	28.0%	29.2%
Net profit	1.2%	7.9%
Efficiency		
Wages (including owner)	17.4%	11.4%
Rent	5.7%	2.6%
Advertising	1.2%	0.8%
Total expenses	24.3%	14.8%
Credit collection		
Days outstanding	70 days	61 days
Staff productivity		
Sales per person	$50 000	$95 000
Sales per $ staff wages	$8.50	$9.30

7. The following is a summary of the performance of a leading Australian company.

	2008–07	2007–06	2006–05	2005–04	2004–03
Operating profit after tax ($m)	330.5	283.2	243.2	214.8	185.5
Annual increase (%)	16.7	16.5	13.2	15.8	20.3
Earnings per share (cents)	144.2	125.3	108.7	96.9	84.4
Annual dividend (cents/share)	78	74	71	69	65

Using the table, answer the following questions:
(a) Which has been its most successful year? Why?
(b) Which has been its least successful year? Why?

(c) In 2003 management set a target of 15 per cent annual growth rate to 2008. Has the company achieved this?
(d) If you had invested in this company, what would be your comment regarding your investment? Use data from the table.
(e) Give reasons why you would or would not invest in this company now.

8. Look at the revenue statement and balance sheet for Business Z.
(a) Comment on the profitability of Business Z.
(b) Comment on the solvency of Business Z.
(c) What recommendations would you make for the following year?

Revenue Statement, Business Z

	2006	2007	2008
Sales	80 000	74 000	95 000
less Cost of goods sold	57 500	54 000	73 800
Gross profit	22 500	20 000	21 200
less Administrative and finance expenses	16 500	15 000	16 500
Net profit	6 000	5 000	4 700

Balance Sheet, Business Z

Inventory	80 000	72 500	87 500
Non-current Assets	70 000	77 500	62 500
	150 000	**150 000**	**150 000**
Bank overdraft	35 000	38 000	32 000
Other Current Liabilities	35 000	32 000	38 000
Capital	80 000	80 000	80 000
	150 000	**150 000**	**150 000**

9. Use the balance sheet and the industry averages below to answer the questions that follow.

Balance Sheet
as at 30 June 2008

Current Assets			
Cash	300		
Accounts receivable	1 200		
Inventory	3 000		4 500
Non-current Assets			5 500
			10 000
Current Liabilities			
Accounts payable			1 000
Non-current Liabilities			5 000
Owners' Equity			
Contributed capital		1 000	
Retained earnings		3 000	4 000
			10 000

Industry averages	
Current ratio	2:3
Debt:equity	2:3
Accounts receivable turnover 55 days	
Return on owners' equity 30%	

(a) Calculate the current ratio, debt to equity ratio, return on equity ratio and accounts receivable ratio (sales $15 000 of which 60 per cent were on credit).

(b) Using the industry averages, identify the strengths and weaknesses of the firm's financial position and determine where improvements would need to be made.

10. Prepare a summary of this chapter. A summary condenses the important issues and concepts presented in the chapter. Go to www.jaconline.com.au/businessstudies3e to compare your finished summary with the one provided for this textbook.

Extension

1. Financial ratios have limited use in times of high inflation. Explain this statement.
2. 'Analysis of financial information identifies only symptoms, not causes.' Do you agree or disagree with this statement? Give reasons for your response.
3. Obtain recent copies of published annual company reports. Analyse the performance and financial position of the company, using liquidity, profitability, solvency and efficiency ratios. Write a report for the chairperson of the company stating your recommendations.

CHAPTER

8 Effective financial management

8.1 Working capital (liquidity) management

We saw in chapter 4 that short-term liquidity is important for organisations. It means an organisation can take advantage of profit opportunities when they arise, as well as meeting short-term financial obligations, paying creditors on time to claim discounts, paying tax and meeting payments on loans and overdrafts. An organisation must have sufficient liquidity so that cash is available or **current assets** can be converted to cash to pay debts. The lack of short-term liquidity could necessitate the sale of non-current assets, including long-term investments, to raise cash. In the longer term this can lead to reduced profitability for owners and shareholders.

Current assets *are assets that a business can expect to convert into cash within the current accounting period. They usually include cash, accounts receivable, inventories and short-term investments. (Current liabilities include overdraft, accounts payable and short-term loans.)*

Working capital *is the funds available for the short-term financial commitments of an organisation.*

Net working capital *is the difference between current assets and current liabilities. It represents those funds that are needed for the day-to-day operations of an organisation to produce profits and provide cash for short-term liquidity.*

Creditors place importance on an organisation's liquidity as they seek guarantees that their accounts will be paid. Failure to pay debts on time can alienate a business's creditors and suppliers who incur extra debt collection costs and lose confidence in the business.

Working capital is the term used in organisations to describe the funds available for the short-term financial commitments of an organisation. **Net working capital** is the difference between current assets and current liabilities. It represents those funds that are needed for the day-to-day operations of an organisation to produce profits and provide cash for short-term liquidity. The working capital cycle for businesses is illustrated in figure 8.1.

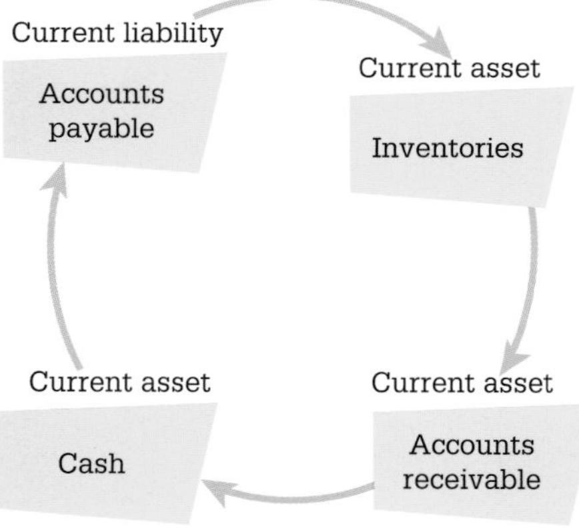

Figure 8.1 The working capital cycle

Through the operating cycle of an organisation, current assets are constantly changing as inventories are sold, cash is paid out and payments are received. Working capital is often the major asset of an organisation and current assets may make up approximately 40 per cent of a business's assets. Therefore, their use and management requires planning and constant monitoring.

Business failure can result from poor management of working capital. Insufficient working capital means there are cash shortages or liquidity problems and the situation forces businesses to increase their debt, find new sources of finance or sell off non-current assets. On the other hand, an excess of working capital means that assets are earning less than the cost to finance them.

Working capital management *is determining the best mix of current assets and current liabilities needed to achieve the objectives of the organisation.*

Working capital management involves determining the best mix of current assets and current liabilities needed to achieve the objectives of the organisation. Management must achieve a balance between using funds to create profits and holding sufficient funds to cover payments. The more efficient a business is in organising and using its working capital, the more effective and profitable it will be (see figure 8.2).

McDonald's retains its daily cash levels as close to zero as possible. The large daily cash collections provide the liquidity that enables it to operate with very low cash balances.

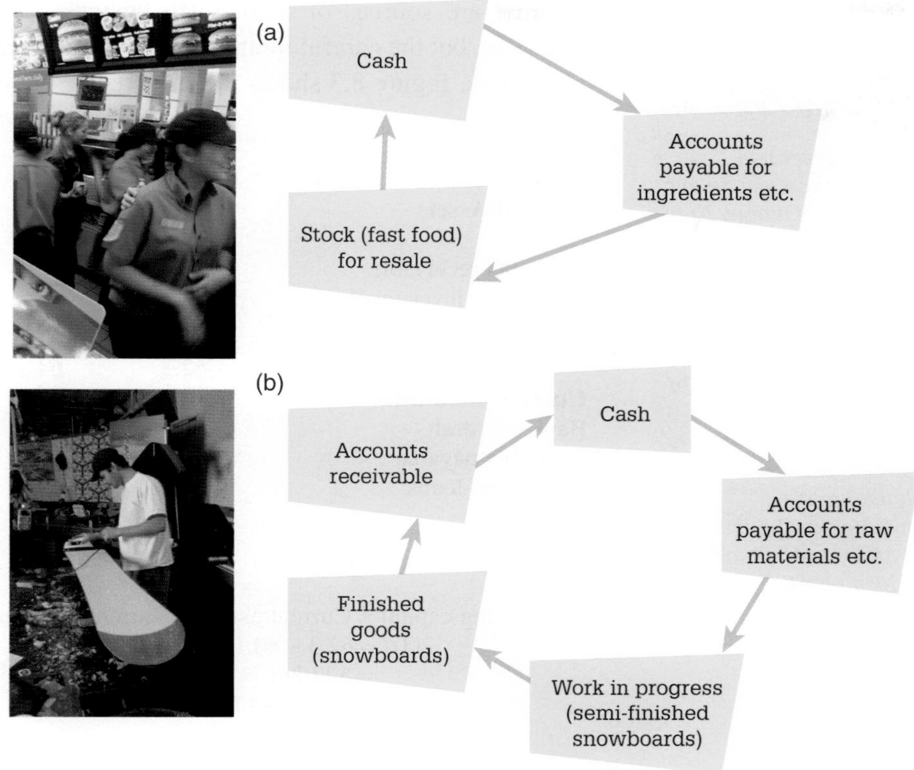

Figure 8.2 The requirements for working capital vary for each business. (a) A food outlet requires a relatively low level of working capital as its cash flow cycle is short. (b) A snowboard manufacturer requires a higher level of working capital as the cash flow cycle — between paying for raw materials and receiving payment for finished goods sold — is longer.

The working capital ratio

The working capital ratio shows if current assets can cover current liabilities. That is, it helps to determine whether a business is managing cash flows so that it can pay its immediate debts. The ratio indicates the amount of risk taken by an organisation in relation to profitability and liquidity and can help determine whether the organisation's financial structure is acceptable. For example:

$$\text{Working capital ratio} = \frac{\text{Current assets}}{\text{Current liabilities}}$$

$$= \frac{500\,000}{250\,000}$$

$$= 2:1 \text{ or } 200\%$$

In the above example, the ratio indicates that, within the next 12 months, twice the amount of assets need to be sold to generate cash to meet the short-term debts of the organisation for the same period.

A high working capital ratio may indicate the business has invested too much in current assets that bring in a small return. Profitability may be reduced as the business has chosen to reduce its risk of not being able to pay its debts by having a higher working capital ratio. A low current ratio may mean that the business is more profitable if it is investing its resources in longer term assets and generating more profits. However, there is a risk that the business may not be able to pay its current liabilities.

A working capital ratio of 2:1, or 200 per cent, is generally acceptable, but ratios vary depending on the industry, the type of business, the efficiency of the organisation in being able to convert current assets into cash and the relations with creditors and banks that are sources of cash. Each business determines an appropriate working capital ratio, but the careful monitoring of working capital is important for the survival of a business. Figure 8.3 shows the importance of working capital management.

Poor credit collection policies can increase delays in the receipt of money from accounts receivable and more working capital is needed to cover the shortfall. Non-current liabilities or owners' equity may be needed. The use of long-term liabilities to finance short-term liquidity problems may cause problems for the organisation in the longer term, as reduced finances mean less profit.

	2007	2008
Current Assets	$m	$m
Bank	3.4	0
Accounts receivable	30.6	34.8
Short-term investments	6.7	4.2
Inventory	21.6	25.1
	62.3	64.1
Current Liabilities		
Bank overdraft	0	4.6
Accounts payable	22.3	20.4
Short-term loans	17.8	19.2
	40.1	44.2
Working capital	22.2	19.9

Working capital = Current assets – Current liabilities
2007 = 62.3 – 40.1
= $22.2m
2008 = 64.1 – 44.2
= $19.9m

$$\text{Working capital ratio} = \frac{\text{Current assets}}{\text{Current liabilities}}$$

$$2007 = \frac{62.3}{40.1}$$

= 1.55:1 (155%)

$$2008 = \frac{64.1}{44.2}$$

= 1.45:1 (145%)

- Current assets have increased in total over the two periods but at a slower rate than current liabilities. Working capital has fallen by $2.3m ($22.2m – $19.9m).
- There has been an increase in current liabilities ($17.8m to $19.2m).
- Working capital ratio has changed from 1.55:1 (155 per cent) to 1.45:1 (145 per cent). Management must decide whether this ratio and trend is acceptable.
- Bank has moved from a surplus to an overdraft ($0 to $4.6m). This would need to be evaluated in terms of the costs.
- Accounts receivable has increased ($34.8m – $30.6m = $4.2m) by over 10 per cent ($4.2m/30.6m = 13.7 per cent).
- Accounts payable has fallen ($22.3m to $20.4m).
- Short-term investments have fallen ($2.5m from $6.7m to $4.2m).
- Short-term loans have increased ($1.4m from $17.8m to $19.2m).

It would appear that short-term loans are balanced by accounts payable and short-term investments with accounts receivable. Management must examine this in the light of past experience and business policy.

Inventories have increased significantly ($3.5 from $21.6m to $25.1m). The reasons for this change should be investigated.

Although the working capital ratio has declined a little, there is sufficient liquidity (current assets) to fund current liabilities.

Figure 8.3 An example of working capital ratio

Control of current assets

A business generally must spend cash on assets before it can produce goods or services and receive payments. It may need finance to do this. If sales increase, there will be an increase in accounts receivable and an increase in inventories. If there are delays before cash is received, there may be a need for financing to cover this.

Management of current assets is important for monitoring working capital. Excess inventories and lack of control over accounts receivable lead to an increased level of unused assets, leading in turn to increased costs and liquidity problems. Excess cash is a cost if left idle and unused. On the other hand, insufficient inventories and tight credit control policies may also lead to problems.

Control of current assets requires management to select the optimal amount of each current asset held, as well as raising the finance required to fund those assets. The costs and benefits of holding too much or too little of each asset must be assessed. Working capital must be sufficient to maintain liquidity and access to credit (overdraft) to meet unexpected and unforeseen circumstances.

Cash

Cash is critical for business success, and careful consideration must be given to the levels of cash receivables and inventories that are held by a business. Cash ensures that the business can pay its debts, repay loans and pay accounts in the short term, and that the business survives in the long term. Supplies of cash also enable management to take advantage of investment opportunities, such as the short-term money market.

Planning for the timing of cash receipts, cash payments and asset purchases avoids the situation of cash shortages or excess cash. Cash shortages can, however, occur due to unforeseen expenses and they are a cost to the business. Money may need to be borrowed, incurring interest and perhaps set-up costs.

Internal management procedures must be in place to ensure that cash is not lost through theft, fraud or mismanagement.

Businesses try to keep their cash balances at a minimum and hold marketable securities as reserves of liquidity. Reserves of cash and marketable securities guard against sudden shortages or disruptions to cash flow. A bank overdraft might also be arranged to allow a business to overdraw its account to an agreed overdraft amount.

Receivables

The collection of receivables is important in the management of working capital. The quicker the debtors pay, the better the firm's cash position. Procedures for managing accounts receivable include:

- checking the credit rating of prospective customers
- sending customers' statements monthly and at the same time each month so that debtors know when to expect accounts
- following up on accounts that are not paid by the due date
- stipulating a reasonable period, usually 30 days, for the payment of accounts
- putting policies in place for collecting bad debts, such as using a debt collection agency.

The disadvantage of operating a tight credit control policy is the possibility that customers might choose to buy from other firms. The costs and benefits must be weighed up carefully by management.

'Just-in-time' is one method used by some businesses to ensure that inventory is not lying idle. An arrangement is made with a supplier that orders will be supplied immediately. The firm carries little or no inventory and relies on the supplier to fulfil orders as soon as required.

Inventories

Inventories make up a significant amount of current assets, and their levels must be carefully monitored so that excess or insufficient levels of stock do not occur. Too much inventory or slow-moving inventory will lead to cash shortages. Insufficient inventory of quick-selling items may also lead to loss of customers, and hence lost sales.

Inventory is a cost of the business if it remains unsold: the holding of too much stock means unnecessary expenses (for example, storage and insurance costs). The rate of inventory or stock turnover differs depending on the type of business. For example, a fruit and vegetable merchant has a high turnover and pays for inventory close to the time of sale, whereas a motor vehicle dealer has a much slower stock turnover and usually pays for inventory well before a sale is made.

Firms must ensure that inventory turnover is sufficient to generate cash to pay for purchases and pay suppliers on time so that they will be willing to give credit in the future.

EXERCISE 8.1 *Revision*

1. Explain why working capital is important to a business.
2. 'Too much working capital is as bad as not enough working capital.' Explain this statement.
3. Draw a diagram to explain the working capital cycle of a firm selling computers and computer software and providing repair services for computer hardware. The firm generates $3 million in sales and $1 million in repair services annually.
4. Why is the management of cash so important to a business?
5. KJ Carpet Cleaning operates on a cash-only basis.
   (a) Describe the working capital cycle for KJ Carpet Cleaning.
   (b) What are the advantages and disadvantages of cash only for KJ?
6. Simon and Kim's Drafting Services has a wide client base and 90 per cent of their fees are on credit. Simon and Kim allow 90 days' payment of their drafting services.
   (a) What potential problems in relation to their credit policy might Simon and Kim's Drafting Services experience?
   (b) What recommendations would you make to the business?
7. Using the information for a soft toys manufacturer below, answer the following questions.
   (a) What is the amount of working capital for the business?
   (b) Comment on the apparent success of managing accounts receivable (all sales are on credit).
   (c) Comment on the amount of inventory in relation to working capital.
   (d) Comment on the amount of cash retained in the organisation.
   (e) What recommendations would you make to management in relation to the management of current assets?
   (f) Determine the working capital ratio and comment on the level of the ratio.
   (g) If the ratio for the previous two periods was, respectively, 220 per cent and 240 per cent, comment on the trend.

Financial status of soft toy manufacturer	
Cash	5 900
Inventory	2 800
Accounts receivable	2 500
Plant and equipment	45 000
Accounts payable	4 200
Long-term loans	20 000

8. Prepare a report to management with recommendations on controlling assets to manage working capital.

Extension

1. 'Over-investment in working capital ties up cash flow.' 'Under-investment in working capital reduces profits.' Explain these statements.
2. Explain how inflation and fluctuating business cycles impact on working capital.
3. Explain, with examples, how cash flow relates to working capital management.
4. Explain how a business may have a high working capital ratio but experience difficulties in finding cash to pay its suppliers.

Control of current liabilities

Current liabilities are financial commitments that must be paid by a business in the short term. Minimising the costs related to a firm's current liabilities is an important part of the management of working capital. This involves being able to convert current assets into cash to ensure that the business's creditors (accounts payable, bank loans or overdrafts) are paid.

Payables

Organisations view trade credit as cost-free finance. For example, if a business buys goods from a supplier and the account is due for payment in 30 days, the business has 30 days of cost-free finance.

A business must monitor its accounts payable and ensure that their timing allows the business to maintain adequate cash resources. The holding back of accounts payable until their final due date can be a cheap means to improve a firm's liquidity position, as some suppliers allow a period of interest-free trade credit before requiring payment for goods purchased. It may also be possible to take advantage of discounts offered by some creditors. This reduces costs and assists with cash flow. Accounts must, however, be paid by their due dates to avoid any extra charges imposed for late payment and to ensure that trade credit will be extended to the business in the future.

Control of accounts payable involves periodic reviews of suppliers and the credit facilities they provide, for example:

- discounts
- interest-free credit periods
- extended terms for payments, sometimes offered by established suppliers without interest or other penalty.

Alternative financing plans should be investigated with suppliers, such as floor plan and consignment finance. Motor vehicle sales businesses have slow stock turnover and often use floor plan or floor stock finance. This means that suppliers agree to provide the motor vehicles for a period of time before payment is due. Consignment financing is a similar arrangement — goods are supplied for a particular period of time and payment is generally not required until goods are sold. Goods supplied may also be returned if they are not sold within the designated period.

Bridging finance can be provided by banks to cover time periods when funds from the settlement of asset sales, such as property, have not been received but payment for another property is required. However, the costs in interest rates and charges associated with bridging finance are high.

As there are costs involved in providing and receiving credit, organisations may negotiate reduced prices if credit card facilities are used. Costs and benefits in using credit must be determined in the control of accounts payable.

Loans

Businesses may need to borrow funds in the short term for a number of purposes. Funds may be required to cover the sale and purchase of property, unforeseen circumstances, and import and export commitments. Short-term loans and bridging finance are important sources of short-term funding for business.

Management of loans is important, as costs for establishment, interest rates and ongoing charges must be investigated and monitored to minimise costs. Short-term loans are generally an expensive form of borrowing for a business and their use should be minimised. Control of loans involves investigating alternative sources of funds from different banks and financial institutions. Positive, ongoing relationships with financial institutions ensure that the most appropriate short-term loan is used to meet the short-term financial commitments of the organisation.

Overdrafts

Bank overdrafts are a convenient and relatively cheap form of short-term borrowing for a business. They enable a business to overcome temporary cash shortages. Features of overdrafts differ between banks, but generally involve an arrangement with the bank that the business's account can be overdrawn to a certain amount. Banks may demand the immediate repayment of the overdraft, although this is rare, especially if the business has a good record and a positive relationship with the bank.

Banks require that regular payments be made on overdrafts and may charge account-keeping fees, establishment fees and interest. Interest payable for a bank overdraft is usually less than that for a loan. Bank charges do, however, need to be carefully monitored, as charges vary depending on the type of overdraft established. Businesses should have a policy for using and managing bank overdrafts and monitor budgets on a daily or weekly basis so that cash supplies can be controlled.

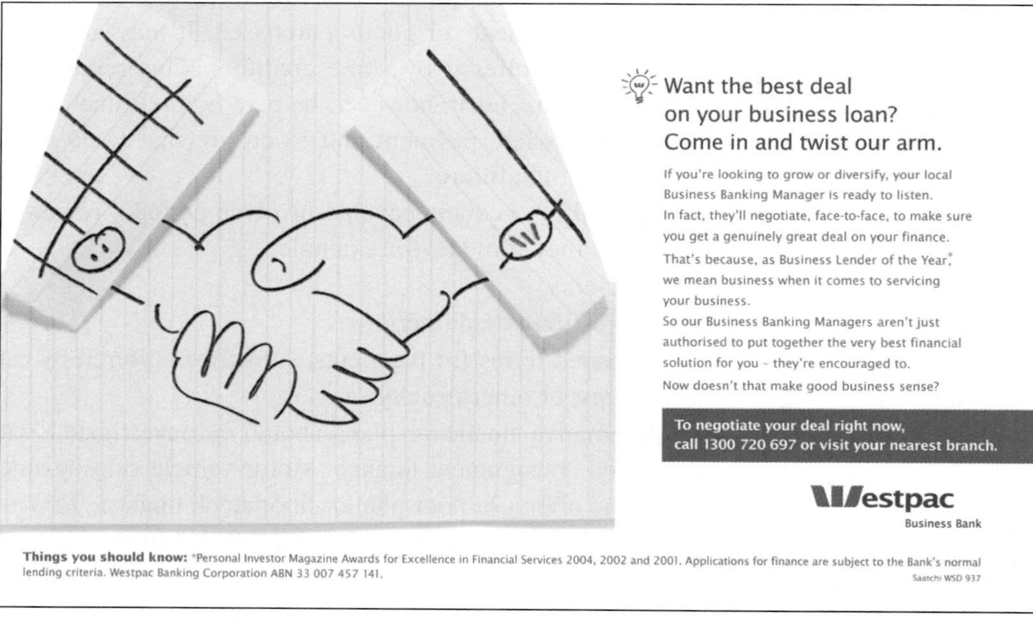

Figure 8.4 Examples of some of the services offered by Westpac to assist business customers with cash flow and management of funds

Strategies for managing working capital

Organisations use a number of strategies to manage working capital, which is required to fund the day-to-day operations of a business. Strategies for working capital management include:

- leasing
- factoring
- sale and lease-back.

Leasing

Leasing is the hiring of an asset from another person or company who has purchased the asset and retains ownership of it. Leasing 'frees up' cash that can be used elsewhere in a business, so the level of working capital is improved. It is an attractive strategy for some organisations as it is an expense and is tax deductible. Firms can also increase their number of assets through leasing and this means that revenue, and therefore profits, can be increased. Regular and fixed payments made for the lease can be planned to match the business's cash flow. While most loans require a deposit so that a firm can borrow only 90 to 95 per cent of the purchase price of the asset, leasing allows 100 per cent financing.

Factoring

Factoring is growing in popularity as a strategy to improve working capital. Factoring is the selling of accounts receivable, for a discounted price, to a finance or specialist factoring company. The business saves on the costs involved in following up on unpaid accounts and debt collection.

Sale and lease-back *is the selling of an owned asset to a lessor and leasing the asset back through fixed payments for a specified number of years.*

Sale and lease-back

Sale and lease-back is the selling of an owned asset to a lessor and leasing the asset back through fixed payments for a specified number of years. Sale and lease-back increases an organisation's liquidity because the cash that is obtained from the sale is then used as working capital. (See the Snapshot 'Buy, lease or loan?' for a discussion of advantages and disadvantages of using leasing, hire purchase or loans.)

SNAP SHOT

Buy, lease or loan?

Most businesses have to face the tricky question of how best to acquire new capital equipment. The key options involve a lease, hire purchase or loan. The decision is likely to be tax driven; however, the impact of options on the cash flow and capital position of your business and the flexibility of each will also be important.

For most small businesses the decision to lease, hire purchase or loan is likely to be tax driven.

Typically, the choice between leasing, hire purchase agreements and loans will depend on costs, prevailing interest rates and depreciation allowances. Depreciation is often the determining factor, though you usually have to write off your equipment over the term that you use it (the effective life) rather than the more generous accelerated rates that applied before recent tax reforms. As well, if your business is in a loss position for tax purposes, the value of any depreciation deductions will be deferred until you make a profit.

LEASES

Under a lease contract, the lessor buys equipment and leases it to you over a specified period, in return for periodic rental payments. At the end of the lease period, you can return the equipment to the lessor or buy it at an agreed price. However, if the arrangement is to be treated as a lease for income tax purposes, you must not have a right, express or implied, to purchase the equipment at the expiry of the lease. If such a right exists, it will be treated like a hire purchase arrangement for income tax purposes.

(*continued*)

The business making the lease rental payments is entitled to a deduction for those payments. The provider of the lease finance makes the depreciation claim, as they retain ownership of the equipment.

At the end of the lease period, you may buy the item at its residual value (the written down value after depreciation). Payment to acquire the equipment at the termination of the lease is not deductible, but will form the basis for claiming depreciation deductions.

HIRE PURCHASE

Under a hire purchase agreement, you hire the equipment with an option to purchase later. The financier retains ownership until you have paid for the equipment on a principal plus interest basis. The interest is tax deductible and, as the implicit owner of the equipment, you are also able to claim depreciation deductions.

Usually you, not the financier, are responsible for registration, insurance, maintenance costs, stamp duties and statutory fees.

LOANS

If you take out a loan to purchase equipment, the interest on the loan is tax deductible and you can also claim a tax deduction for the depreciation. The downside of a loan can be that financiers may not be prepared to provide a loan unless you are able to put up security, which can be a problem for start-ups in particular.

GST can also be an important factor. If you are registered for GST and the equipment is to be used fully for business purposes, then if you:

- take out a lease, you can claim 1/11th of each lease payment
- enter a hire purchase agreement you can claim 1/11th of the principal component of the payments, but there is no entitlement for the interest component. The input tax credit can be claimed upfront if you report for GST on an accruals basis, but can only be claimed when each payment is made if you report on a cash basis.
- take out a loan, you can claim an input tax credit on the purchase price, but there is no input tax credit entitlement on the interest paid.

Source: A. MacRae, 'Buy, lease or loan?', *My Business*, May 2004, p. 16.

SNaPSHOT Question

Use the information provided in the Snapshot to complete the following table.

Options for purchase of capital equipment	Features	Tax advantage	Advantages	Disadvantages
Leases				
Hire purchase				
Loans				

EXERCISE 8.2 Revision

1. Why is the control of liabilities important in the management of working capital?
2. Explain how taking advantage of credit can assist working capital.
3. Soulos Motor Cycles offers its goods for sale for cash and credit (28 days' credit is allowed). The sale of motor cycles is often slow. Explain how floor plan and consignment finance would assist the working capital of this business.
4. Soulos Motor Cycles is considering whether a loan or a bank overdraft would assist in the management of working capital. Make recommendations to the owner of Soulos and give reasons.
5. By visiting bank branches or using the Internet, investigate the types of short-term loans available for businesses. Draw up and complete a table similar to the one below.

Type of loan	Interest rate	Other charges	Term of loan

6. MG Farming contract their labour using a wide range of equipment (for example, trucks, tractors and harvesters). Capital outlay is high and repairs are often unexpected and expensive.
   Write a report to MG Farming explaining the advantages and disadvantages of leasing, the different types of leases and how leasing can increase working capital.
7. KS Jacobi Ltd is a timber merchant and had credit sales of $2 million for the previous year.
   (a) Explain how factoring would assist in the management of working capital.
   (b) What are the advantages and disadvantages of factoring for KS Jacobi Ltd?

Extension

1. 'It is inappropriate to say that the working capital ratio should not fall below 2 or 200%.' Do you agree or disagree with this statement? Give reasons.
2. Explain, using diagrams, the relationship between accounts receivable, accounts payable and the need for finance.

8.2 Effective financial planning

We saw in chapter 4 that effective financial planning is essential if a business is to achieve its goals. Most businesses' goals relate to profit, and decisions must be made to ensure that a business maximises its profits. In order for a business to survive in the short and longer term, it must have adequate cash flows. Profitability and cash flow management are two important and complementary aspects of financial planning.

Cash flow *is the movement of cash in and out of a business over a period of time.*

Cash flow management

Cash flow is the movement of cash in and out of a business over a period of time. If more money goes out than comes in, or if money must be paid out before cash payments have been received, there is a cash flow problem. Matching cash flow in with cash flow out is essential.

In the 1980s, Alan Bond was a successful businessman in Australia. His company Bond Corp grew into a large conglomerate through takeovers of Castlemaine Tooheys and Swan breweries, both of which had consistently strong cash inflows. Bond used the cash inflows of his brewery interests to diversify into property, more breweries and the media. He also purchased a mansion in England, original paintings, an office complex in Hong Kong and established Bond University in Queensland. Profitability was high.

Cash flow problems arose when the share market crashed in 1987, interest rates increased and property prices fell. Lack of cash meant that interest and loan repayments could not be met. Bond sold off some assets to improve cash flow but it was insufficient and many assets were sold at great losses. He was unable to raise sufficient finance to remedy the cash flow problems and the company went into liquidation in 1992.

By keeping records of cash flow, you know how much cash you have in your wallet or in the bank at a given time. However, this record does not tell you what debts you have or what is owed to you by others. The issue is the same for a business, which is why budgets are an important tool for managing cash flows. Examples of cash inflows and outflows are given in table 8.1.

TABLE 8.1 Some examples of a business's inflows and outflows of cash

Inflows	Outflows
Sales Accounts receivable Commissions Sales of assets Rents Interest (investments/loans, etc.) Dividends	Payments to suppliers — raw materials/finished goods, etc. Interest on loans Operating expenses — wages/salaries, raw materials/finished goods Drawings Purchase of assets Loan repayments

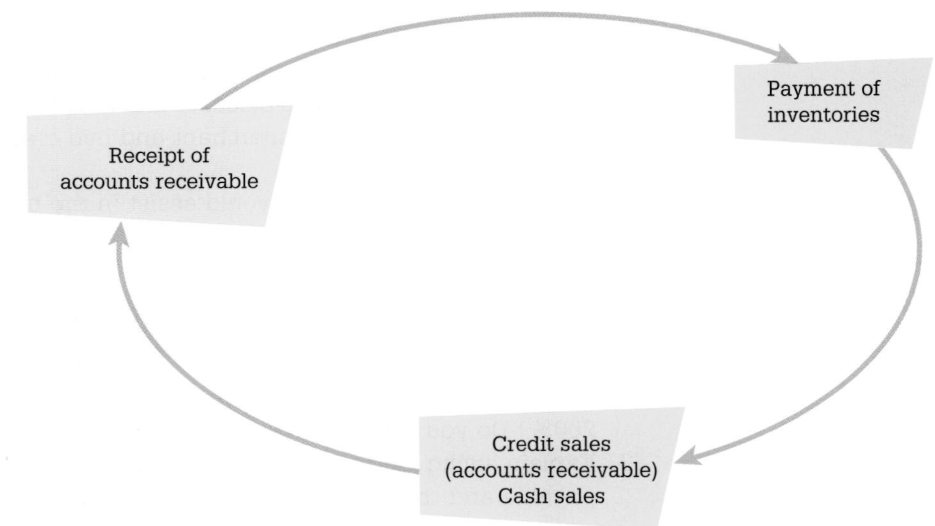

Figure 8.5 The cyclical flow of funds. Efficient management of cash flows is crucial to a business's success.

Cash flow statements

*A **statement of cash flows** is a financial statement that indicates the movement of cash receipts and cash payments resulting from transactions over a period of time.*

A **statement of cash flows** is one of the key financial reports that are part of effective financial planning. It provides the link between the revenue statement and balance sheet, as it gives important information regarding a firm's ability to pay its debts on time.

The statement of cash flows indicates the movement of cash receipts and cash payments resulting from transactions over a period of time. It can also identify trends and can be a useful predictor of change.

Users of cash flow statements include creditors and lenders of finance, as well as owners and shareholders, who can assess the ability of the business to manage its cash. Potential shareholders check that a business has had positive cash flows over a number of years. A fluctuating pattern of cash flows might point to difficulties in the business.

Cash flows can be a better predictor of a business's status than profitability. A statement of cash flows can show whether a firm can:

- generate a favourable cash flow (inflows exceed outflows)
- pay its financial commitments as they fall due; for example, interest on borrowings, repayment of borrowings, accounts payable
- have sufficient funds for future expansion or change
- obtain finance from external sources when needed
- pay drawings to owners or dividends to shareholders.

In preparing a statement of cash flows, the activities of a business are generally divided into three categories — operating, investing and financing activities.

Operating activities are the cash inflows and outflows relating to the main activity of the business — that is, the provision of goods and services. Revenue from sales (cash and credit) make up the main operating inflow plus dividends and interest received. Outflows consist of payments to:

- suppliers
- employees
- other operating expenses (insurance, rent, advertising, etc.).

Investing activities are the cash inflows and outflows relating to purchase and sale of non-current assets and investments. These assets and investments are used to generate revenue for the business. Examples include the selling of an old motor vehicle, purchasing new plant and equipment or purchasing property.

Financing activities are the cash inflows and outflows relating to the borrowing activities of the business. Borrowing inflows can relate to equity (issue of shares or capital contribution from owner) or debt (loans from financial institutions). Cash outflows relate to the repayments of debt and cash drawings of the owner or payments of dividends to shareholders.

A statement of cash flows is usually prepared from the revenue statement and balance sheet, as these summarise the transactions of the business. Remember that only cash transactions are included in the statement of cash flows. An example of a statement of cash flows is given in figure 8.6.

The statement of cash flows, revenue statement and balance sheet are used to show how effectively finance is being used in a business. They also provide information on whether the business has sufficient funds to meet unforeseen circumstances.

Burgess Enterprises Ltd
Statement of cash flows for year ended
30 June 2008

Cash flows from operating activities	
Receipts from customers	30 000
Payments to suppliers and employees	(25 000)
Dividends received	4 000
Interest received	8 000
Interest paid	(5 500)
Net cash provided by operating activities	11 500
Cash flows from investing activities	
Proceeds from sale of assets	85 000
Payment of plant and equipment	(150 000)
Net cash from investing activities	(65 000)

(continued)

Cash flows from financing activities	
Proceeds from issues of shares	90 000
Proceeds from borrowings	40 000
Repayments of borrowings	(15 000)
Dividends paid	(25 000)
Net cash from financing activities	90 000
Net increase in cash	36 500
Cash at beginning of year	15 000
Cash at end of year	51 500

Figure 8.6 An example of a statement of cash flows

BiZ FaCT

Financial flexibility is important, because a business must be able to adapt its finances to cover planned and unplanned changes. In times of reduced business confidence, organisations are usually more concerned with being able to pay their debts and remain solvent than their profitability. Economic climate is a factor in determining whether a business focuses on cash flows rather than profitability.

Management strategies

A business may have temporary shortfalls of cash (see the Snapshot 'Find the cash'). Many businesses use bank overdrafts to cover these shortages. Banks allow the business to overdraw their account to a set limit with the payment of competitive interest rates. Shortfalls of cash over longer periods are of greater concern for a business as insolvency or bankruptcy may result.

The receipt of cash into a business does not necessarily coincide with payments of cash coming in. Management must implement strategies to ensure that cash is available to make payments when they are due — for example, to the Australian Taxation Office, suppliers for accounts payable, employees for wages, owners and shareholders for profits and dividends, banks and financial institutions for interest on loans or overdrafts, and leasing payments.

An important strategy involves distributing payments throughout the month, year or other period so that cash shortfalls do not occur. A cash flow projection can assist in identifying periods of potential shortfalls and surpluses (an example is shown in figure 8.7).

Find the cash

Cash flow is the biggest headache for small and medium-size enterprises, according to a survey of 57 business owners in Australia and New Zealand conducted in late July 2004. The survey, by the accounting franchise CAD partners (formerly Computer Accounting Doctor), asked owners to list their three largest financial challenges. Cash flow topped the list at 29.8 per cent followed by falling margins (15.8 per cent) and tax (10.5 per cent). A further 21.1 per cent of owners said cash flow was their second-biggest cause of frustration.

The chief executive of CAD partners, Stuart Frost, says the problems that small business owners have with cash flow usually stem from not getting their customers to pay on time. 'They often do not have a system that enables them to get the money in and often customers will not pay until they get a phone call.' Frost suggests one problem is that bookkeepers and staff of small businesses tend to do the easy thing first: which is pay bills rather than chase customers to settle outstanding accounts.

Source: B. Andrews, 'Find the cash', *BRW*, September 2004.

SNaPSHOT Questions

1. List the three major financial challenges for small and medium-sized businesses as identified in the Snapshot.
2. Describe the main reason for cash flow problems in small businesses. Suggest one or two strategies a business might adopt to address this problem.

Business Cashflow Projection Worksheet *From*____________*to*____________

CASH IN	INITIAL FUNDS	MTH 1	MTH 2	MTH 3	MTH 4	MTH 5	MTH 6	MTH 7	MTH 8	MTH 9	MTH 10	MTH 11	MTH 12	TOTAL
Enter Month														
a. Cash sales														
b. Credit sales (trade debtors receipts)														
c. Cash from: sale of assets														
d. Finance obtained/monies borrowed														
e. Capital injections/personal funds														
f. Other (give details)														
g. **CASH YOU WILL RECEIVE FOR THE MONTH**														

CASH OUT	START UP COSTS	MTH 1	MTH 2	MTH 3	MTH 4	MTH 5	MTH 6	MTH 7	MTH 8	MTH 9	MTH 10	MTH 11	MTH 12	TOTAL
Enter Month														
h. Cost of goods/services – raw materials/stock														
production/handling distribution costs														
i. Payments of accounts owed to others (creditors)														
j. Expenses – accounting/legal fees														
– advertising														
– bank charges/interest														
– insurances														
– lease or hire purchase – payments														
– loan repayments														
– other professional services														
– packaging/postage/freight														
– power/light/heat/gas														
– rates, water														
– rent on premises														
– repairs/maintenance														
– stationery/office supplies														
– telephone/communications														
– travel/transport														
– wages/salaries														
Tax (sales, group, payroll)														
Drawings/dividends/directors fees														
Sundry														
k. Purchase of assets and capital items														
l. **CASH YOU PAID OUT FOR THE MONTH**														

FINAL POSITION	START UP PERIOD	MTH 1	MTH 2	MTH 3	MTH 4	MTH 5	MTH 6	MTH 7	MTH 8	MTH 9	MTH 10	MTH 11	MTH 12	TOTAL
Enter Month														
m. Bank balance at the beginning of the month														
Cash In (Figure in Row g)														
Cash Out (Figure in Row l)														
n. Sub total (CASH OUT subtracted from CASH IN)														
o. Bank balance at the end of the month (Sub total subtracted from beginning of month bank balance)														

ASSUMPTIONS – please provide details of how you calculated these figures

Figure 8.7 Completion of a cash flow projection worksheet such as this one can assist people setting up new businesses to plan and manage their cash flow. It also provides a useful summary for the bank or other financial institution to which a business may go to borrow or invest funds (*Source:* Westpac Banking Corporation).

Cash discount is a percentage deducted from the price if the account is paid by a specified time. The period is the number of days after the beginning of the credit period, which is usually from 5 to 20 days. To take full advantage of the cash discount, a firm pays its account on the last day of the discount period. If a business's cash flow situation is still tight when the discount period expires, it might choose to forgo the cash discount and pay the full amount at the end of the credit period (30–60 days). If the credit period is 30 days, the business receives 30 days of free credit.

Although a business may generate good profits, problems arise if the money generated is not received. Bad debts and late payments of accounts by debtors can cause shortfalls of cash for businesses at important times, and they are time-consuming and expensive to follow up. In order to overcome these difficulties, some businesses provide discounts as an incentive to debtors to pay by a certain date. The cash that the business forgoes by giving the discount is often a worthwhile sacrifice for the sake of receiving prompt payment.

Some organisations delay payment of their own accounts to suppliers and creditors as late as possible before the due date for cash flow reasons, without affecting their relationships with the suppliers or their credit rating. At the same time, businesses should take advantage of cash discounts offered by suppliers.

Some large organisations take advantage of smaller firms by extending the cash discount period beyond what is normally accepted. There are ethical issues involved in paying accounts payable as late as possible, known as 'stretching' accounts payable, and speeding up the accounts receivable.

EXERCISE 8.3 *Revision*

1. Why is a statement of cash flows so important for a business? What information can be obtained from it?
2. Classify the following transactions as operating, investing or financing.

Paid interest	$2000
Received cash from customers	$25 000
Took out a short-term loan	$10 000
Paid a dividend	$3200
Sold furniture and fittings	$1700
Paid tax	$4500
Purchased equipment	$12 000
Paid wages to employees	$4000
Purchased a 90-day Treasury bill	$3000
Mortgage repayments	$5000

3. Using the information from question 2, prepare a statement of cash flows for Johnson Ltd for the year ended 30 June 2008. Cash at 1 July 2008 was $7500.
4. Using the information in question 3, what changes to cash management would you recommend?
5. For the following transactions, complete the table below:

Transaction	Operating/ investing/ financing	Cash inflow/ outflow
(a) Repaid loan of $80 000 and interest $9000		
(b) Purchased bonds for $50 000		
(c) Paid suppliers $65 000		
(d) Paid income tax $12 000		
(e) Purchased machinery for $20 000 cash and mortgage for $75 000		
(f) Received $70 000 from accounts receivable		
(g) Received $20 000 from investments		

6. State which of the following are cash inflows and which are cash outflows.
   (a) Cash sales

(b) Office furniture purchased for cash
(c) Cash received from owner as capital
(d) Cash purchases
(e) Rent revenue
(f) Withdrawal of cash from business by owner
(g) Loan repayment made
(h) Accounts receivable payment received
(i) Commission received
(j) Cheque received from Better Finance Ltd for loan
(k) Accounts payable paid
(l) Administration expenses

7. Partridge Motor Cycle Tours runs both short and long trips throughout the year, although the warmer months, from September to April, generate the most revenue. Cash flow problems often arise in July, as repairs are carried out to the bikes and registration and insurances fall due. What suggestions can you make to Partridge Motor Cycle Tours to assist it in managing cash flow?
8. Vadia runs a landscape gardening business and has come to you for financial advice. You find that she is reluctant to offer discounts for cash. Explain the reasons for and against offering discounts for cash and make some recommendations for Vadia's business.

Extension

1. 'Profit is not the same as cash in the bank.' Explain this statement.
2. In the long term, is it more important for a business to have positive cash flows from its operating activities, investing activities or financing activities? Give reasons for your answer.
3. Examine cash flow statements from a number of organisations and determine the source of their cash flows. Comment on the management of cash flow for each business.

Profitability management

With the objective of earning profits, management must control both the business's costs and its revenue. Data and reports are essential tools for effective profitability management.

Cost control

Most business decisions — for example, to open a new store, introduce a new product or buy a new piece of machinery — are influenced by costs. The costs associated with a decision need to be carefully examined before it is implemented. For all organisations, costs must be:

- identified
- analysed
- controlled.

Fixed costs are costs that are not dependent on the level of operating activity in a business.

Variable costs are costs that change proportionately with the level of operating activity in a business.

Before a business can control its costs, management must have a clear understanding of what those costs are. Businesses generally have **fixed costs** and **variable costs**.

Fixed costs are not dependent on the level of operating activity in a business. Fixed costs do not change when the level of activity changes — they must be paid regardless of what happens in the business. Examples of fixed costs are salaries, depreciation, insurance and lease. (In reality, fixed costs can change — for example, if new premises are needed then leasing costs will increase — but, once the changes are made, the costs again become fixed.)

Variable costs are those that change proportionately with the level of operating activity in a business. For example, materials and labour used in the production of a particular item are variable costs, because they are often readily identifiable in a business and can be directly attributable to a particular product.

(a) Fixed costs

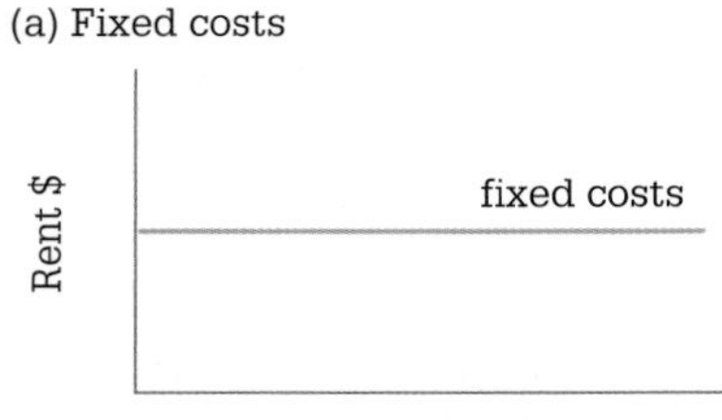

(b) Variable costs

Figure 8.8 A simplified illustration of (a) fixed costs and (b) variable costs

Monitoring the levels of both fixed and variable costs is important in a business. Changes in the volume of activity need to be managed in terms of the associated changes in costs. Comparisons of costs with budgets, standards and previous periods ensure that costs are minimised and profits maximised.

A business's costs and expenses must be accounted for, and management needs to be able to identify their source and amounts. A number of costs can be directly attributable to a particular department or section of a business, and these are termed **cost centres**. A cost centre in a retail store or service organisation would be called a service cost centre. A cost centre in manufacturing would be called a production cost centre.

Cost centres *are particular areas, departments or sections of a business to which costs can be directly attributed.*

Cost centres have direct and indirect costs. Direct costs are those that can be allocated to a particular product, activity, department or region; for example, depreciation of equipment used solely in the production of one good. Indirect costs are those that are shared by more than one project, activity, department or region. For example, the depreciation of equipment used to make several products would have indirect costs allocated on some equitable basis.

Profits can be weakened if the expenses of an organisation are high, as they consume valuable resources within an organisation. Guidelines and policies should be established to encourage staff to minimise expenses where possible. Savings can be substantial if people take a critical look at costs and eliminate waste and unnecessary spending.

Budgets and cost-volume-profit analysis are the tools used in the control of revenue.

Revenue controls

Revenue is the income earned from the main activity of a business. For most businesses, revenue comes from sales or, in the case of a service organisation, from fees for professional services or commission. In determining an acceptable level of revenue with a view to maximising profits, a business must have clear ideas and policies, particularly with regard to:

- the sales objectives
- sales mix
- pricing policy.

Sales objectives must be pitched at a level of sales that will cover costs, both fixed and variable, and result in a profit. A cost-volume-profit analysis can determine the level of revenue sufficient for an organisation to cover its fixed and variable costs to break even, and predict the effect on profit of changes in the level of activity, prices or costs.

Changes to the sales mix can affect revenue. Businesses should control this by maintaining a clear focus on the important customer base on which most of the revenue depends before diversifying or extending product ranges or ceasing production on particular lines (see the Snapshot 'Holeproof campaigns to sock it to shoppers'). Research should be carried out to identify the potential effects of sales-mix changes before decisions are made.

Pricing policy affects revenue and, therefore, affects working capital. Pricing decisions should be closely monitored and controlled. Overpricing could fail to attract buyers, while underpricing may bring higher sales but may still result in cash shortfalls and low profits. Factors that influence pricing include:

- the costs associated with producing the goods or services (materials, labour, overheads)
- prices charged by the competition
- short- and long-term goals — for example, if the business aims to improve market share over a five-year period, prices may be reduced
- the image or level of quality that people associate with the goods or services
- government policies.

Holeproof campaigns to sock it to shoppers

Holeproof is planning to double its rate of sales growth in Australia's $600 million sock market to a consistent 10 per cent-plus within three years.

Part of Pacific Brands, which has 45 per cent of the sock market in Australia, Holeproof is to accelerate its advertising and marketing campaign spending to change shoppers' perception of socks as a replacement purchase.

Stephen Audsley, the general manager of Pacific Brands' underwear and hosiery division, which includes Holeproof, said socks were not commonly viewed as inspiring by consumers.

'The product has very low interest', he said.

The company's sock advertising and marketing budget represents about 98 per cent of the total spent on promoting the sock market in Australia. That includes the services of troubled business celebrity Donald Trump, who appears in television advertisements for Holeproof Computersocks.

Mr Audsley said the agreement with Mr Trump would run for 12 more months but declined to say how much he was being paid.

The group's advertising spend on socks in 2001 was $3 million and rose to $10 million last year. It is projected to reach about $12 million in 2004–05.

Holeproof has culled the number of product lines it makes under a brand makeover. It has stripped the number of stock-keeping units from 16 000 to 10 000 by weeding out unprofitable lines and short-run items such as making small batches of socks in stipulated colours for various schools.

Mr Audsley said Holeproof's headline sales growth rate last year was about 5 per cent. The aim now was to increase sales to above double-digit growth in two to three years.

'We've set our sights at growing our sock business at double-digit rates', he said.

One of the top performing lines in the Holeproof stable has been the Holeproof Explorer socks, which retail for about $10 a pair.

Mr Audsley described the Explorer as the sock market's equivalent of a top-selling Australian beer.

'The Explorer is our Victoria Bitter, a tried and true performer', he said.

The Explorer had delivered 'better than 30 per cent growth' in 2003–04 and thus far in 2004–05 has been able to retain sales at that level and make additional gains, albeit at a 'more modest rate'.

(continued)

About 20 per cent of socks and underwear sales in Australia are through department stores, such as Myer and David Jones, 60 per cent in discount department stores, such as Big W, Kmart and Target, and 20 per cent in supermarkets.

Mr Audsley said new technology was being implemented at Holeproof's plant in Nunawading, Melbourne, with the aim being to produce a sock from start to finish entirely by machines, within 15 months. The plant already turns out 55 000 pairs of socks a day.

Mr Audsley said 35 per cent of Holeproof products were still made locally, which gave the company advantages in being able to respond quickly to market changes and new orders.

But competition from China, where the remainder of the Holeproof range was made, was fierce.

'It would be very easy to simply wave the flag and say "we're off to China".

'But we're not.'

Source: S. Evans, 'Holeproof campaigns to sock it to shoppers', *The Australian Financial Review*, 10 January 2005.

SNAPSHOT Questions

1. Outline how Holeproof plans to double its rate of sales growth.
2. What changes have been made to the product line? Discuss the effect of these changes on the company's profitability.
3. Identify the product Holeproof sees as its 'top performer'. Outline its current sales rates.
4. Outline the role of technology for the company's future growth and development.
5. Identify the major threats to the company's profit levels as identified in the Snapshot.

EXERCISE 8.4 Revision

1. Why is it important to manage costs and revenues in a business?
2. Explain, with an example, the difference between fixed and variable costs.
3. Indicate whether the following are fixed or variable costs. Give a reason for your answer.

Factory rent	Direct labour
Advertising	Office wages
Wages of factory staff	Lease payments
Administrative expenses	Packaging
Insurance	Delivery costs
Sales discounts	

4. Marco and Betty have just purchased the local corner shop. The business is well established, but profits have been falling for a number of years despite the same number of customers. Suggest reasons why profits have been falling. What advice would you give to the new owners on how to manage costs and revenues effectively?
5. What is a cost centre and why do organisations use them?

6. From the following revenue statement, make suggestions to Georgia on managing costs.

Georgia's Real Estate **Revenue statement for the month ended** **30 June 2008**		
Sales commission		20 000
less Expenses		
Advertising	9 500	
Salaries	12 000	
Telephone	4 000	
Rent	1 500	
Office expenses	1 200	28 200
Profit/loss		(8 200)

8.3 Ethical and legal aspects of financial management

Organisations have ethical and legal responsibilities in relation to financial management. In recent years, unethical practices have been highlighted and increasingly questioned. There are growing calls for codes of behaviour to regulate the activities of businesses in relation to financial management.

It is generally accepted that financial management decisions must reflect the objectives of an organisation and the interests of owners and shareholders. For example, an area in which ethical considerations are important is in the valuing of assets, including inventories and accounts receivable. Such valuations influence the level of working capital and, hence, the short-term financial stability of an organisation. If inventories and accounts receivable are overvalued (the business makes no provisions for bad or doubtful debts), working capital will be high and indicate an untrue working capital figure for an organisation.

If debt funds are used extensively to finance activities in a business, although debt funds may be used to increase profits, there is added risk for shareholders. The impact of debt funds on risks to shareholders is an ethical issue that must be considered.

In preparing budgets, the expenditures and revenues are estimated. The common practice in business of overestimating expenditures and understating revenues to allow for unexpected and uncertain events is an ethical issue for an organisation.

Figure 8.9 The information contained in financial statements should be accurate and truthful.

Investment in long-term capital expenditure impacts on future operating activities, and ethical considerations arise if all alternatives are not evaluated. Ethical considerations also arise when a business chooses an alternative investment that favours another business with which it is likely to have future dealings.

Ethical considerations are closely related to legal aspects of financial management. Legislation is in place to guard against unethical business activity but there is often a time lag between the recognition of a problem and its implementation through law.

Laws relating to corporations include the responsibilities of directors and requirements for disclosure for corporations. For example, in relation to financial management, directors have a duty to:

- act in good faith
- exercise power for proper purpose in the name of the corporation
- exercise discretion reasonably and properly
- avoid conflicts of interest.

BiZ WoRD

***Corporate governance** is the way companies are directed and controlled.*

The Sarbanes–Oxley Act of 2002 changed the way business was conducted in the United States for the first time since the US securities laws of the early 1930s. It affects **corporate governance**, financial disclosure and the practice of public accounting. Corporate leaders who embrace the 'spirit of the law' — strong ethics, good governance, reliable reporting — should reap the benefits of a 're-energised company and reassured investors'.

The Australian Stock Exchange (ASX) corporate governance council officiates the requirements of corporations listed with the ASX and their responsibilities in regard to compliance with law, disclosure and transparency of company details to shareholders and the public.

Audited accounts

BiZ WoRD

*An **audit** is an independent check of the accuracy of financial records and accounting procedures.*

In all activities of an organisation the goals of the organisation remain paramount. Planning, monitoring, control and corrective action are all part of the process. The **audit** is an independent check of the accuracy of financial records and accounting procedures, and it has an important role in this process. Audits help protect the resources of an organisation and improve efficiency in achieving its goals (see the Snapshot 'Risk neglected' on page 195).

Potential users of information include financial institutions, owners and shareholders and potential investors who rely on the independent check of the auditor before making decisions about the organisation.

Audits are an important part of the control function and are generally used to examine the financial affairs of a business. There are three types of audits:

1. *Internal audits*. These are conducted internally by employees to check accounting procedures and the accuracy of financial records.
2. *Management audits*. These are conducted to review the firm's strategic plan and to determine if changes should be made. The factors affecting the strategic plan may include human resources, production processes and finance.
3. *External audits*. These are a requirement of the *Corporations Act 2001* (Cwlth). The firm's financial reports are investigated by independent and specialised audit accountants to guarantee their authenticity. The auditor issues a statement indicating that the firm's records and financial reports are accurate, to the best of the auditor's knowledge, and give a true and fair view of the state of affairs, and that they comply with Australian auditing standards. In 2005, businesses were required to adopt new international

Internal auditors can assist in improving efficiencies and often make recommendations about improved practices. For example, when an audit revealed that an organisation could be paying cheaper rates for packaging and postage, this change in practice alone resulted in a saving of over $10 000 a year for the business.

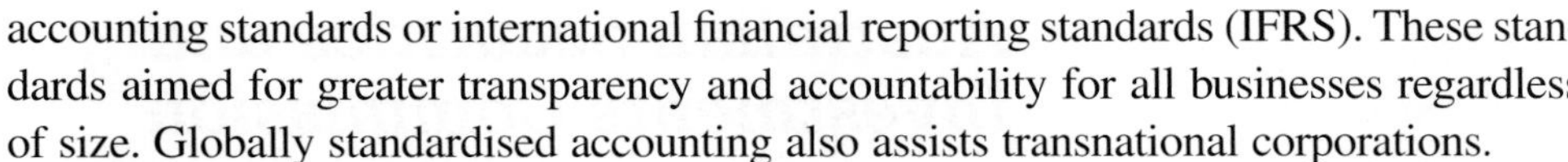

accounting standards or international financial reporting standards (IFRS). These standards aimed for greater transparency and accountability for all businesses regardless of size. Globally standardised accounting also assists transnational corporations.

Internal and external audits assist in guarding against unnecessary waste, inefficient use of resources, misuse of funds, fraud and theft. Audits are carried out on the financial records of a business to see if they are prepared in line with accepted accounting standards and that records provide accurate information for users. They check the control procedures of an organisation by physically checking assets. For example, cash is counted, the condition and amount of the inventory is checked, and accounts receivable and non-current assets are checked. Records are checked to see if they match the physical count.

External auditors are used to provide an annual audit of accounting practice and procedures. In small businesses, external auditors are usually used only if the business is for sale or as a check against theft and fraud.

Risk neglected

About 40 per cent of Australia's top 300 listed companies made little or no mention of their internal audit or risk-management functions in their last annual report, says Deloitte partner John Trotter.

'It surprised me a lot when we started to go through it', he says. 'We keep monitoring the top 300 through their annual reports and phone calls. In the latest statistics we have, 40–50 per cent make no mention of internal audit functions and haven't got a level of sophistication about their governance or risk management.'

The Australian Stock Exchange corporate governance guidelines, released on March 31, 2003, have put pressure on boards to ensure that internal audit and risk management are working well. The guidelines require boards to 'safeguard integrity in financial reporting' and to 'recognise and manage risk'. Many Australian companies that have subsidiaries in the United States must also comply with the US Sarbanes–Oxley Act, which has strict rules regarding internal audit and risk management.

A global survey of financial services companies released by PricewaterhouseCoopers in August [2004] shows that 72 per cent of respondents say most change is the result of regulatory pressure.

The survey report says financial institutions are too focused on quantifiable risk, such as policies, procedures and systems, but not enough is being done about the soft risks, such as the companies' internal cultures.

Trotter says that about 70 of the top 300 listed companies outsource or cosource their internal audit to professional services firms, according to their 2002–03 reports. The remaining 230 or so have the function totally in-house or have nothing at all, he says.

Source: K. Walters, 'Risk neglected', *BRW*, 2004.

SNaPSHOT Questions

1. Why do you think internal audits and risk management functions are so important for all companies to undertake? (Consider the effect on all stakeholders.)
2. The ASX guidelines for corporate governance require company boards to 'safeguard integrity in financial reporting'. What do you think this means?

Australian Securities and Investments Commission

The Australian Securities and Investments Commission (ASIC) is an independent statutory commission accountable to the Commonwealth parliament. It enforces and administers the Corporations Act and protects consumers in the areas of investments, life and general insurance, superannuation and banking (except lending) in Australia. The aim of ASIC is to assist in reducing fraud and unfair practices in financial markets and financial products. ASIC ensures that companies adhere to the law, collects information about companies and makes it available to the public. This includes the financial information that companies must disclose in their annual reports.

In 1998, the responsibilities of ASIC were broadened to cover supervision of the retail investments industry as well as overseeing the Corporations Act. ASIC assumed some of the previous functions of the Insurance and Superannuation Commission, the Reserve Bank and the Australian Competition and Consumer Commission.

Corporate raiders and asset stripping

Entities that use outdated asset values can become targets for takeovers and for asset stripping. Asset stripping describes the practice of organisations that identify and sell off for a profit the readily separable assets of a company, especially one that has been acquired through a recent takeover. Entities that take over other companies and sell off the assets are known as corporate raiders. The term also applies to organisations or individuals who purchase large blocks of a company's shares, thus appearing to threaten a takeover, but in reality hoping to profit by their increase in value when the company, or its associates, attempts to secure control.

EXERCISE 8.5 Revision

1. Why are ethical aspects important to consider in financial management?
2. A firm decides to undervalue its inventories and accounts receivable to indicate a favourable working capital ratio and, therefore, the short-term financial stability of an organisation. Discuss the advantages and disadvantages of this decision and its ethical implications.
3. Is it ethical to overestimate budgets to allow for uncertain or unknown risks? Give reasons for your answer.
4. What role do audits play in financial management?
5. Explain the role of ASIC in the supervision of business.
6. Go to www.jaconline.com.au/businessstudies3e and click on the ASIC weblink for this textbook. Find recent articles relating to investigations conducted by ASIC. Share and discuss these with other class members.
7. Increasing debt increases long-term and unnecessary risk for shareholders. Discuss the ethical implications of this statement.
8. Prepare a summary of this chapter. A summary condenses the important issues and concepts presented in the chapter. Go to www.jaconline.com.au/businessstudies3e to compare your finished summary with the one provided for this textbook.

Extension

1. In pairs, use newspapers, business magazines and the Internet to research and report
   on businesses that are involved in some form of legal action due to their unethical financial management practices. Explain how the business might have avoided this litigation if it had acted ethically.
2. 'Timely and valid internal and external audits are a primary safeguard against unethical financial behaviour.' Discuss

Topic 3

Marketing

FOCUS AREA:

The principal focus of this topic is the nature and role of marketing in a business, and the main elements involved in the development and implementation of successful marketing strategies.

Outcomes

Students should be able to:

- critically analyse the role of business in Australia
- describe and analyse business functions and operations and their impact on business success
- evaluate the effectiveness of management in the organisation and operations of businesses and its responsiveness to change
- critically analyse the social and ethical responsibilities of management
- select, organise and evaluate information and sources for usefulness and reliability
- plan and conduct an investigation into business to present the findings in an appropriate business format
- communicate business information, ideas and issues, using relevant business terminology and concepts in appropriate forms.

Mind map showing the specific aspects examined for the 'Marketing' topic

Michelle Giles and Quick-Fire Clay

Michelle had never lost faith in the idea. Three years of hard work was now about to be rewarded. By the end of the day the patent application would be finalised, which would give her sole rights to her invention, 'Quick-Fire Clay'.

As a potter Michelle had always been conscious of the high cost of operating a kiln. She had tried alternative energy sources, but the best she could manage was to reduce the energy bill to 38 per cent of total costs. It was at this stage she decided to think a little more creatively. If she could not reduce the energy costs any further, then perhaps she could reduce the time the clay needed to be in the kiln. Inventing a clay that required only half as much firing time would reduce her operating costs.

So, after three years of experimentation and having to mortgage her house to help pay for research and development, Quick-Fire Clay was about to become her exclusive product. Michelle had managed to develop a clay-based material that required only half the normal firing time. Another unexpected benefit was that the material became less fragile and did not shatter when dropped. Michelle knew she had a product that would be in great demand and make her a lot of money. Not wanting to lose the right to her invention she decided to apply for a patent. She left the Patents Office feeling optimistic about the future and enjoyed a celebratory meal at the Harbourside Restaurant. She believed her product to be a great success.

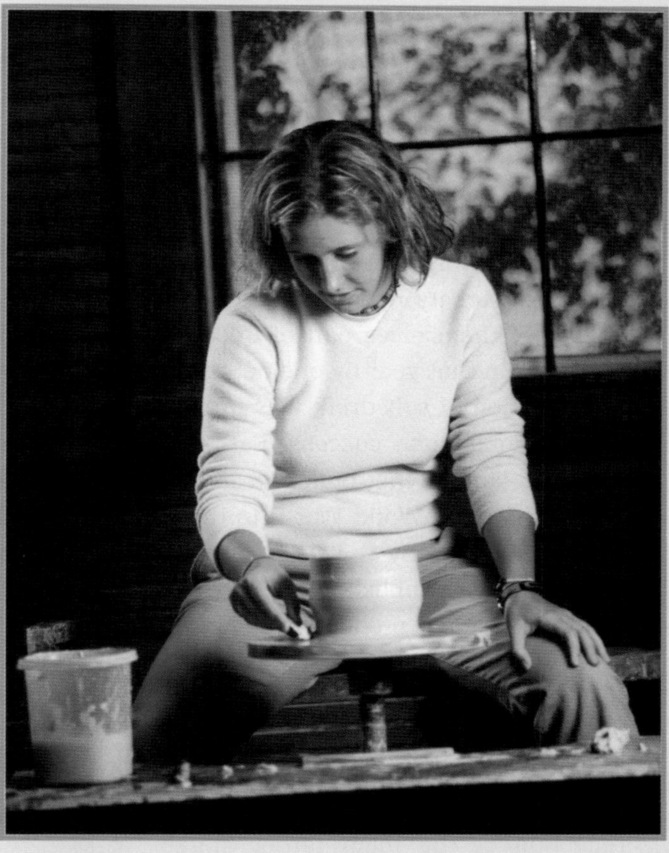

What Michelle failed to realise was that, although the first stage, developing a new product, was complete, the second stage was just about to begin — the successful marketing of her product. Even though she had a world-first, proven product, very few people knew about it. Michelle was about to discover that products do not 'sell themselves'. Without customers, a product — even though revolutionary, efficient, record-breaking, exciting and so on — is useless. Many inventors like Michelle have failed even though they had an excellent product. They lacked customers, and no customers means no profit.

Michelle had a lot to learn about successfully marketing her product.

CHAPTER

9 Nature and role of markets and marketing

9.1 Introduction

Contemporary society is bombarded by marketing strategies, which are vital to the existence of business. Even the best-designed or most revolutionary product may fail in the marketplace without a suitable marketing strategy. Research has shown that 70 per cent of all new products fail within a year of being launched, mainly as a result of poor marketing. Consequently, for a business to achieve its main objective of maximising sales and profit, it must develop and implement an effective marketing plan, as shown by Coca-Cola's success (see the Snapshot 'Coke — a successfully marketed product').

Coke — a successfully marketed product

Coca-Cola's Coke soft drink was released onto the Australian market in 1938, 50 years after its release in the United States. The first distinctively shaped bottles — themselves part of Coca-Cola's overall marketing strategy — were produced in that year by one of Sydney's oldest soft-drink factories. Australian consumption of soft drink was growing, but that did not guarantee the Coke product immediate success. Early sales representatives for Coca-Cola were lucky if a store owner bought a single bottle, let alone a case.

The spread of World War II to the Pacific region in the early 1940s was the impetus needed by the Australian producers of the soft drink. With the US armed forces established in Australia and the region, a ready-made market was in place and production greatly increased to satisfy this demand. Conditions were right for a post-war boom in sales. It was time for the marketing plan to be fully implemented, with advertising campaigns being the most visible marketing strategy.

Advertisements for Coke were initially aimed at older age groups — a reflection of the main target market selected in the United States. Over the years, the target market was modified to concentrate on teenage and young adult consumers. The company's marketing plan was so successful that the product has become Australia's market leader in the soft-drink market.

Figure 9.1 Coca-Cola's advertising has always adopted a message — that Coke is a part of life, associated with fun and pleasure (as the advertisements here, spanning many decades, demonstrate).

Contemporary Coke advertisement

SNaPSHOT Questions

1. What macroenvironmental factors provided the impetus for Coca-Cola to increase sales in the Australian market?
2. How has Coca-Cola's target market changed over time?
3. 'Coke's successful formula is not the ingredients of the drink but its superior marketing strategies.' Do you agree or disagree with this statement? Give reasons for your answer.

In 2002, for the first time in 17 years, Coca-Cola launched a new variety of its main brand: Vanilla Coke was mass marketed across the United States, with a launch budget of about $20 million.

Through its sophisticated marketing plan, Coca-Cola has built on its highly recognisable brand name (see the Biz Fact on the left). In its first year, about 10 servings of Coke were sold per day. Today, one billion servings are consumed every day. Marketing is, therefore, a powerful strategy available to help achieve a business's objectives.

9.2 What is marketing?

***Marketing** is 'the process of planning and executing the conception, pricing, promotion and distribution of ideas, goods and services to create exchanges that satisfy individual and organisational objectives' (American Marketing Association). More simply, marketing is a total system of interacting activities, designed to plan, price, promote and distribute products to present and potential customers.*

The most commonly accepted definition of **marketing** comes from the American Marketing Association: 'Marketing is the process of planning and executing the conception, pricing, promotion and distribution of ideas, goods and services to create exchanges that satisfy individual and organisational objectives.'

A more simplified definition is that marketing is a total system of interacting activities designed to plan, price, promote and distribute products to present and potential customers. At the heart of these activities is the most fundamental question that all businesses should continually ask: 'What do customers want to buy — now and in the future?' This is the essence of marketing: finding out what customers want, then attempting to satisfy their needs.

A successful business develops a marketing plan based on careful research and design. The customer should always be the central focus of the marketing plan. Any business that does not develop and maintain a customer base soon goes out of business. It is the role of the marketing plan to make sure a customer base is created and maintained.

9.3 The role of marketing in the business and in society

Businesses today place a strong emphasis on customer-oriented marketing. A market-focused business will want to create products that customers want to buy. The business needs to see itself as a customer-satisfying process rather than a production process.

In the opening story, Michelle was totally absorbed in developing a new product, her Quick-Fire Clay. She was product-focused. She gave no thought to a marketing plan. It was not until the product was patented that she started to think about how it could be sold. If she wished to achieve her financial goals and make a profit, her product would have to generate sales, and this would require her to develop a marketing plan.

To bring the buyer and seller together, the business needs to be able to identify:
- *where the market is*
- *who will buy the product*
- *why they will buy the product.*

To achieve the goal of profit, the marketing plan should be the focus of all short-term planning for three reasons:

1. The marketing plan outlines the strategies to be used to bring the buyer and seller together. The business needs to be able to identify:
   - where the market is
   - who will buy the product
   - why they will buy the product
   - how often they will buy the product.
2. The core of marketing is satisfying existing customer wants, which should lead to repeat sales.
3. Marketing is the revenue-generating activity of any business. Nothing is achieved until a sale is made.

A business must, therefore, determine what the customers want, then develop a product and marketing plan to satisfy these wants.

EXERCISE 9.1 Revision

1. What is the main reason for approximately 70 per cent of all new products failing shortly after their launch?
2. What is meant by the term 'marketing'?
3. How does the definition of marketing provided in this chapter differ from your previous understanding of the term?
4. Explain why Michelle Giles must develop a marketing plan for her Quick-Fire Clay (page 199).
5. Complete the following sentences. The words can be found by reading section 9.3.
   (a) The main emphasis of marketing today is the __________-oriented approach.
   (b) This means the business wants to __________ customers' needs and wants rather than merely produce products.
   (c) Michelle Giles is an example of a __________-focused businessperson.
   (d) To achieve the __________ goals and make a __________ a business needs to __________ sales.
   (e) A __________ plan helps in achieving __________ goals.
6. Write a brief, half-page report on how your views about marketing have changed since beginning this topic.

Extension

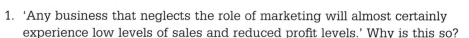

1. 'Any business that neglects the role of marketing will almost certainly experience low levels of sales and reduced profit levels.' Why is this so?
2. Use the Internet to research the marketing of Pepsi. Go to www.jaconline.com.au/businessstudies3e and click on the Pepsi and Coke weblinks for this textbook. In what ways is Pepsi's marketing similar to and different from Coke's marketing?
3. 'Selling is merely getting rid of existing stock, whereas marketing takes a much broader view. Successful marketing involves bringing the buyer and seller together and making a sale.' Elaborate.

9.4 Types of market

A **market** is a group of individuals, organisations or both that:

- need or want a product
- have the money (purchasing power) to purchase the product
- are willing to spend their money to obtain the product
- are socially and legally authorised to purchase the product.

For the purposes of this topic, a **market** is defined as a group of individuals, organisations or both that:

- need or want a product
- have the money (purchasing power) to purchase the product
- are willing to spend their money to obtain the product
- are socially and legally authorised to purchase the product.

A group that does not have these four features is not considered to be a market.

In general use, the term 'market' usually refers to the total population, or mass market, that purchases products. Our definition is more specific and refers to individuals or groups who wish to buy *specific* products. There are many markets in an economy. Based on the characteristics of the individuals and groups that make up a specific market, it is possible to divide markets into six main types as shown in figure 9.2.

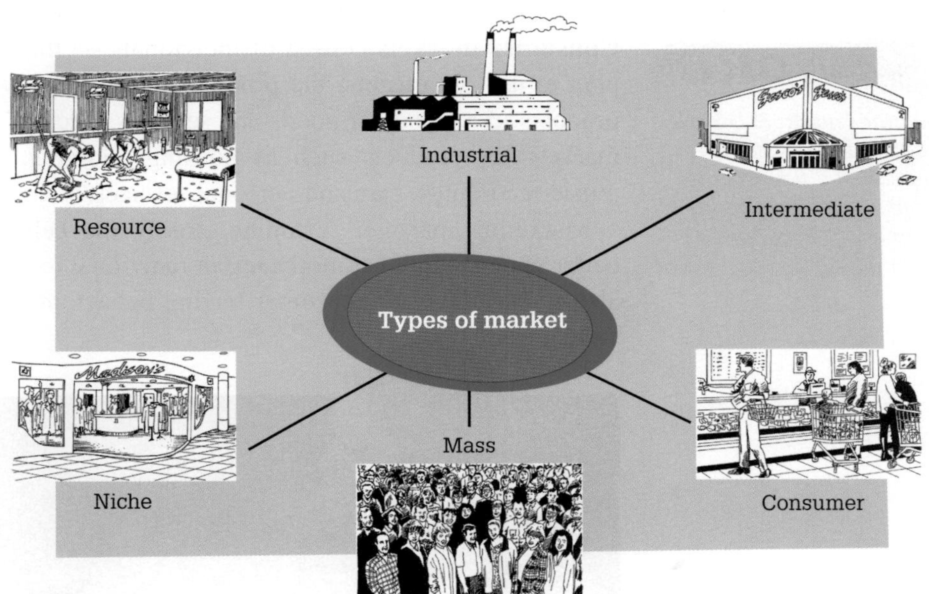

Figure 9.2 The six main types of market

Because marketing plans and strategies vary depending on the intended market, marketing managers need to understand the main characteristics of these six different types of market.

The **resource market** consists of those individuals or groups that are engaged in all forms of primary production, including mining, agriculture, forestry and fishing.

The **industrial market** includes industries and businesses that purchase products to use in the production of other products or in their daily operations.

Resource market

The **resource market** consists of those individuals or groups that are engaged in all forms of primary production, including mining, agriculture, forestry and fishing.

As a group, this market in Australia is made up of approximately 118 000 enterprises or customers and has a large purchasing power. Farmers, for example, purchase machinery, seed and fertiliser.

Industrial market

In Australia there are more than 930 000 businesses in the industrial market; these businesses are either secondary or tertiary. An **industrial market** includes industries and businesses that purchase products to use in the production of other products or in their daily operations. Tip Top Bakery, for example, buys flour to make bread and Sony buys plastics and metals to produce televisions.

Intermediate market or resellers

An **intermediate market** consists of wholesalers and retailers who purchase finished products and resell them to make a profit.

The **intermediate market** consists of wholesalers and retailers who purchase finished products and sell them again to make a profit. The vast majority of goods sold to consumer markets are first sold to an intermediate market.

In Australia, the total intermediate market is made up of approximately 160 000 retailers and 40 000 wholesaling intermediaries. Subway, for example, is a retailer that buys goods to make into sandwiches and salads for sale to consumers.

Consumer markets

Consumer markets consist of individuals — that is, members of a household who plan to use or consume the products they buy.

Consumer markets are the markets with which we are most familiar. Each time we go shopping at the local supermarket we are operating within the consumer market. **Consumer markets** consist of individuals — that is, members of a household who plan to use or consume the products they buy. Consumers do not intend to use the products to make other goods and services. Each of us is part of numerous consumer markets for products such as housing, clothing, food, entertainment, appliances, music recordings, cars and personal services.

Marketing managers examine closely the behaviour of consumers so they can better understand what motivates an individual to purchase a particular product. They also try to influence consumer buying behaviour by developing a mix of marketing strategies.

Figure 9.3 The consumer market

BiZ WORD

*In **mass markets**, the seller mass-produces, mass-distributes and mass-promotes one product to all buyers.*

Mass market

Fifty years ago, marketing managers commonly spoke about the 'mass market'. In other words, there was a large demand for a standard product. In **mass markets**, the seller mass-produces, mass-distributes and mass-promotes one product to all buyers. The Model T Ford was the first motor vehicle to be mass-produced and sold to the mass market (see figure 9.4).

When the Model T Ford was first released onto the American market in 1908, production could not keep up with demand. Henry Ford changed the production methods so that the assembly process was cut from 12.5 hours to 93 minutes. Henry Ford's 'famous' marketing slogan was that the customer could have the car in any colour he or she wished, 'as long as it was black'. This meant customers' wishes were not considered. A business could adopt this attitude in the early periods of industrialisation because consumers' wants could not be fulfilled; most items that were produced could easily be sold.

Figure 9.4 Early automobile manufacturers used mass-production techniques to sell their products to the mass market.

Very few products today are marketed to the mass market. Due to greater choice, higher personal incomes and customers seeking more individualised products, the mass market has been replaced by segmented or niche markets.

Niche markets

BiZ WORD

*A **niche market**, also known as a concentrated or micro market, is created when the mass market is finely divided into smaller markets consisting of buyers who have specific needs or lifestyles.*

At the other end of the spectrum to the mass market is a **niche market**, also known as a concentrated or micro market. The mass market is divided into smaller markets consisting of buyers who have specific needs or lifestyles. This smaller group of consumers becomes the 'target' market, toward which marketing managers 'aim' their marketing efforts. For example, in any newsagent you will see row upon row of magazines, each appealing to a specific niche market — male, female, young, old, high income, low income, urban, rural, outdoor lifestyle, indoor lifestyle and so on.

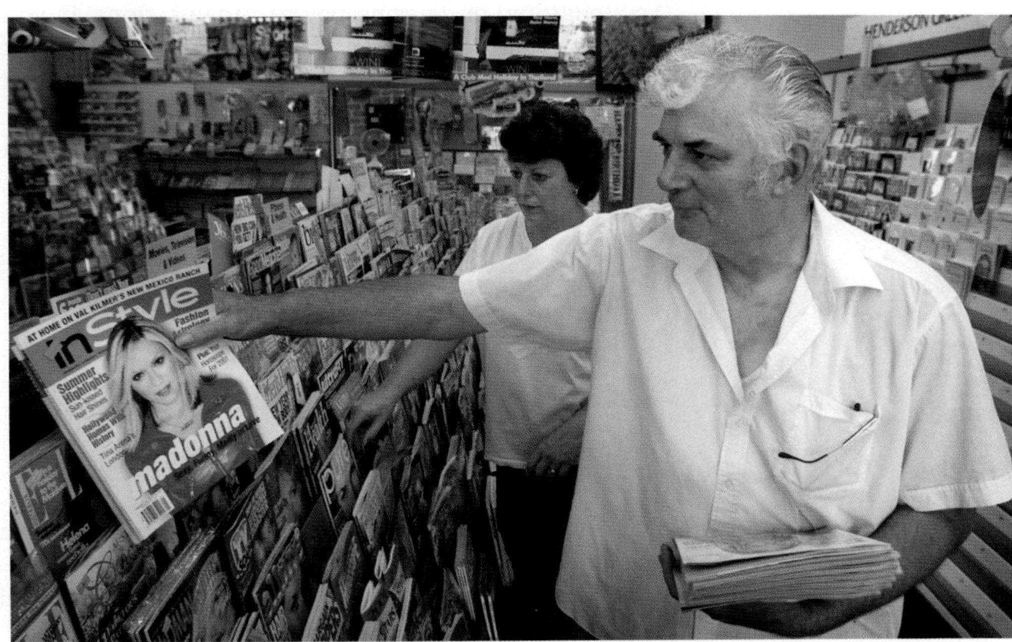

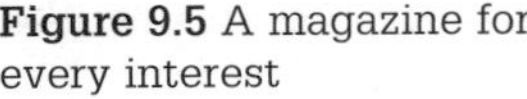

Figure 9.5 A magazine for every interest

EXERCISE 9.2 Revision

1. According to marketing managers, what is meant by the term 'market'?
2. What four conditions need to exist for a group of individuals, organisations or both to be considered a market?
3. Outline the difference between the resource and industrial markets.
4. Why is Subway considered to be part of the intermediary market?
5. Complete the following sentences. The words can be found by reading the 'Consumer markets' section on page 204.
   (a) When we shop at a local ________ we are part of the ________ market.
   (b) Consumer markets consist of ________, that is, ________ who plan to use or ________ the products they buy.
   (c) Marketing managers examine closely the ________ of consumers so they can better understand what ________ an individual to purchase a product.
   (d) Marketing managers also try to ________ consumer buying ________ by developing a mix of marketing ________.
6. Outline the difference between the mass market and a niche market.
7. Indicate, using an 'M' or 'N', whether the following products are sold in a mass or niche market.
   (a) Rolls Royce cars
   (b) Coca-Cola soft drink
   (c) *BRW*
   (d) Fruit and vegetables
   (e) BP Petrol
   (f) Rip Curl wetsuits
   (g) PlayStation games
   (h) Sunbeam shearing combs

Extension

1. 'Regarding purchasing power, organisational buyers such as businesses and government departments are generally considered to be more rational than ultimate consumers.' Suggest reasons why this is so. Compare your answers with other members of the class.
2. Compare and contrast the main features of a mass market and a niche market.
3. Would a furniture manufacturer need a different marketing strategy for a large retail chain, such as Myer, than for a single furniture store owned and operated by one person? Why or why not?

9.5 Production, selling and market orientation — approaches to marketing

The focus of businesses today is to develop a marketing plan based on the marketing concept — that is, an emphasis placed on customer satisfaction. However, marketing did not always have this as its main aim. As figure 9.6 shows, the focus of marketing strategies has changed dramatically over the years.

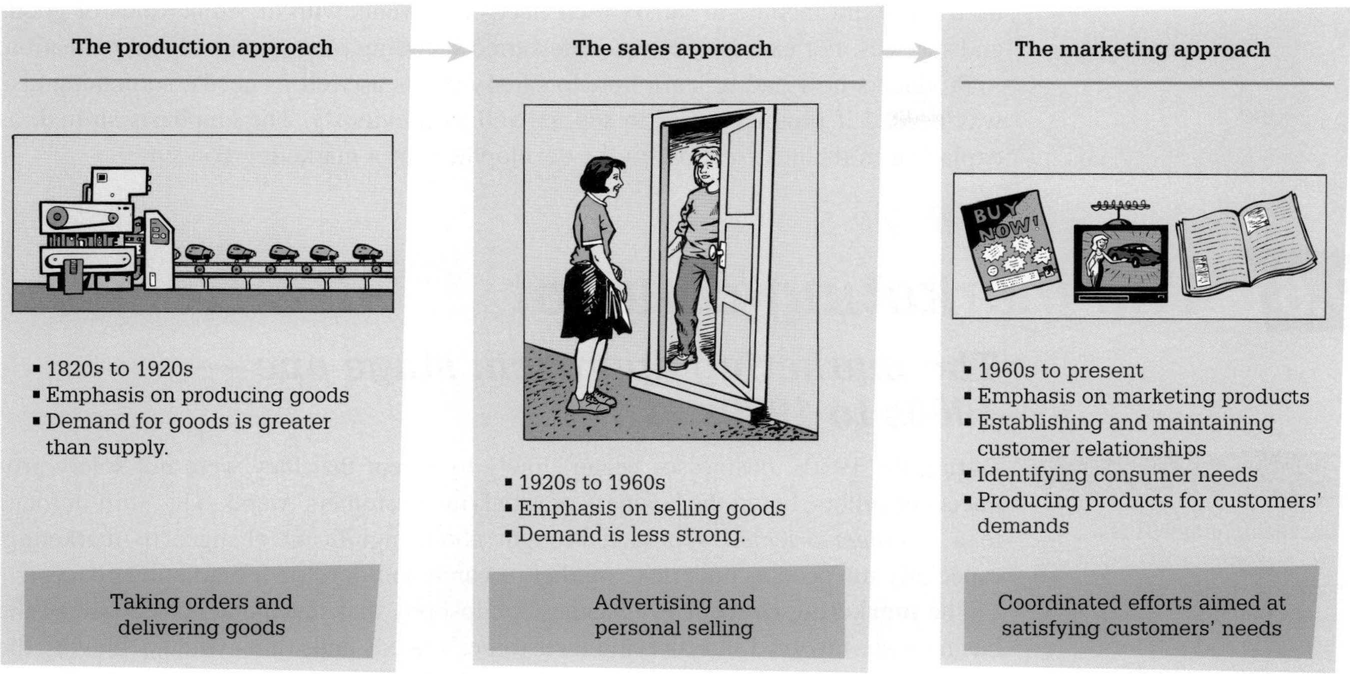

The production approach
1820s to 1920s
Emphasis on producing goods
Demand for goods is greater than supply.
Taking orders and delivering goods
The sales approach
1920s to 1960s
Emphasis on selling goods
Demand is less strong.
Advertising and personal selling
The marketing approach
BUY NOW!
1960s to present
Emphasis on marketing products
Establishing and maintaining customer relationships
Identifying consumer needs
Producing products for customers' demands
Coordinated efforts aimed at satisfying customers' needs

Figure 9.6 The evolution of marketing

The idea of the marketing concept evolved only in the early 1960s. Prior to this there were two different approaches to marketing: *production* and *sales*.

The production approach — 1820s to 1910s

The Industrial Revolution began in Britain over 170 years ago. This burst of industrial growth saw demand for products exceed the production capabilities of many businesses. Up until World War I, businesses concentrated their efforts on the production of goods and services. Businesses were usually able to sell all their output. Marketing consisted of simply taking orders and delivering the products. Business was *production-oriented*.

The sales approach — 1920s to 1960s

After World War I, production became more efficient and productivity increased. Slowly the output of businesses started to catch up with demand. High-quality, mass-produced products came on to the market and competition between businesses increased. No longer could a business rely on selling all it produced.

Because customers' basic needs were satisfied, businesses had to develop a new marketing approach — one that was *sales-oriented*. Businesses increased their advertising, making use of newly developed electronic communications systems, such as radio and film. Businesses faced the challenge of persuading customers to buy a specific brand. Sales representatives were hired and trained, and marketing departments took a more dominant role in the organisation.

Discretionary income *refers to disposable income that is available for spending and saving after an individual has purchased the basic necessities of food, clothing and shelter.*

The marketing approach — 1960s to present

The marketing era that began with the economic boom after World War II has continued to the present. For the first time, most Australian families had **discretionary income**, more income than what was needed to obtain the necessities of life. They used this extra income to satisfy their needs and wants with different kinds of goods and services. For example, consumers started spending more on travel and recreation.

Producers now had to learn how to satisfy wants as well as needs; something else was needed if products were to sell as well as previously. The emphasis shifted, as explained in the next section, to the development of a marketing concept.

9.6 The marketing concept

The marketing approach: stage one — 1960s to 1980s

Marketing concept is a business philosophy that states that all sections of the business are involved in satisfying a customer's needs and wants while achieving the business's goals.

During the 1950s, businesses began slowly to accept that they were not solely producers or sellers, but in the business of satisfying customers' wants. This shift in focus to a *customer-oriented* approach brought about significant changes to marketing, especially the need to undertake market research and develop a marketing concept.

The **marketing concept** is a business philosophy that states that all sections of the business are involved in satisfying a customer's needs and wants while achieving the business's goals. The business should direct all of its policies, plans and operations to achieving customer satisfaction. Therefore, the marketing plan needs to become integrated into all aspects of the business, as shown in figure 9.7.

The marketing concept is based on four principles. It must be:

- *customer-oriented*
- *supported by integrated marketing strategies*
- *aimed at satisfying customers*
- *integrated into the business plan so as to achieve the business's goals.*

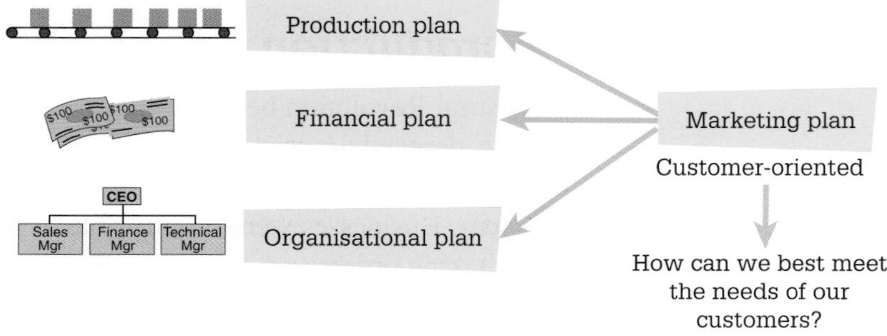

Figure 9.7 The integration of the marketing plan

The marketing approach: stage two — 1980s to present

To disregard the 'quality of life' issues when developing a marketing plan could lead to a customer backlash. Businesses need to stay in tune with the changing political, economic and social scene and modify their marketing plans accordingly.

Changing economic and social conditions over the last two decades have seen a modification to the marketing approach. With growing public concern over environmental pollution and resource depletion came a shift in the emphasis of marketing plans. Marketing managers now realise that their organisations have a social responsibility. External pressure from customers and environmental organisations, as well as political forces, is presently influencing the marketing plans of many businesses. One major change has been the increase in demand for ecologically sustainable products.

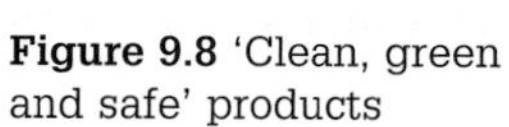

Figure 9.8 'Clean, green and safe' products

Customer orientation

For businesses that adopt a marketing concept philosophy, the customer relationship does not end with the sale; it begins there. These companies will strive continuously to not only simply meet but also exceed customer expectations.

To be effective, the marketing concept must be adopted by all employees of the business, not only those involved in marketing activities. This means that at every level of the business, employees should work towards customer satisfaction by establishing positive relationships with customers.

BiZ WoRD

***Customer orientation** occurs when a business bases its marketing decisions and practices on its customers' wants.*

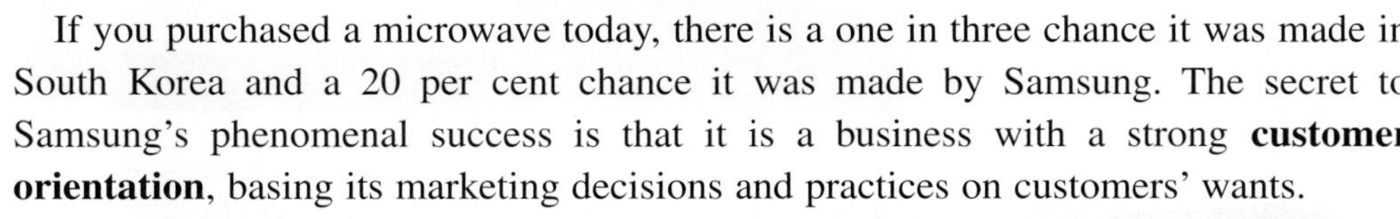

If you purchased a microwave today, there is a one in three chance it was made in South Korea and a 20 per cent chance it was made by Samsung. The secret to Samsung's phenomenal success is that it is a business with a strong **customer orientation**, basing its marketing decisions and practices on customers' wants.

A market-focused business such as Samsung wants to create products that customers want to buy. The business, therefore, needs to see itself as a customer-satisfying process rather than a production process.

Figure 9.9 All employees need to adopt the marketing concept philosophy, wanting to genuinely satisfy customer needs.

Relationship marketing

***Relationship marketing** is the development of long-term and cost-effective relationships with individual customers.*

The '80–20' principle says that 80 per cent of sales comes from 20 per cent of a business's customer base. Therefore, a strong relationship with this loyal group of customers should be developed and maintained.

Customers want more individualised treatment. In response, businesses are looking for ways to develop long-term, cost-effective relationships with individual customers, a process known as **relationship marketing**.

This marketing philosophy is the practical component of the marketing concept. Gone are the days of mass catalogue mail-outs, done in the hope of a one-off sale. Businesses want, instead, to forge strong relationships with their best customers. The ultimate aim is to create customer loyalty by meeting the needs of customers on an individual basis. Relationship marketing, therefore, emphasises customer retention — creating reasons to keep customers coming back

A highly successful relationship marketing strategy introduced during the early 1990s was loyalty reward programs such as Fly Buys and ABC Reward Card (see figure 9.10 on page 210). These schemes offer 'rewards' to those 'loyal' customers who purchase specified amounts or make repeat purchases. Relationship marketing can provide a business with a competitive advantage (see the Snapshot 'Maintaining the relationship' on page 210).

Figure 9.10 Loyalty programs help maintain a customer relationship.

Maintaining the relationship

Enticing new customers to purchase our product is about five times more expensive than maintaining our existing customers. Consequently, at Stellar Productions Ltd we work hard at establishing and maintaining good relationships with our existing clients. We have implemented a customer relationship marketing (CRM) program to monitor the long-term relationship with individual customers to evaluate their lifetime value to our business.

Stellar uses three elements to implement the CRM program successfully:

1. *Personalised service.* By focusing on satisfying our customers' needs and delivering more 'personalised' service, we have been able to maintain our competitive edge. Our sales representatives are encouraged to build long-term relationships with their clients by providing service above and beyond customer expectations.
2. *Personalised communication.* We use innovative media to communicate with our customers on a one-to-one basis. Salespeople distribute letters, emails and reports to their customers. Customers are invited to conferences and trade shows where relationships can be renewed and extended.
3. *Customer database.* We continuously update our database to store relevant information about current and potential customers. This provides us with important information about customer buying behaviour, including repeat sales and value of transactions.

SNAPSHOT Questions

1. What is the objective of the CRM program?
2. Why is it important to provide 'personalised service' and 'personalised communication' as part of a CRM program?
3. How does information technology support the CRM program?

9.7 Marketing planning process

***Strategic marketing planning** is the process of developing and implementing marketing strategies to achieve marketing objectives.*

A business should draw together all the market research available and use it to develop a strategic marketing plan. **Strategic marketing planning** is the process of developing and implementing marketing strategies to achieve marketing objectives, which in turn helps to realise the business's goals. With this strategic marketing plan, objectives can be identified and strategies or action plans developed to achieve them. Such a plan will consist of five steps, as shown in figure 9.11.

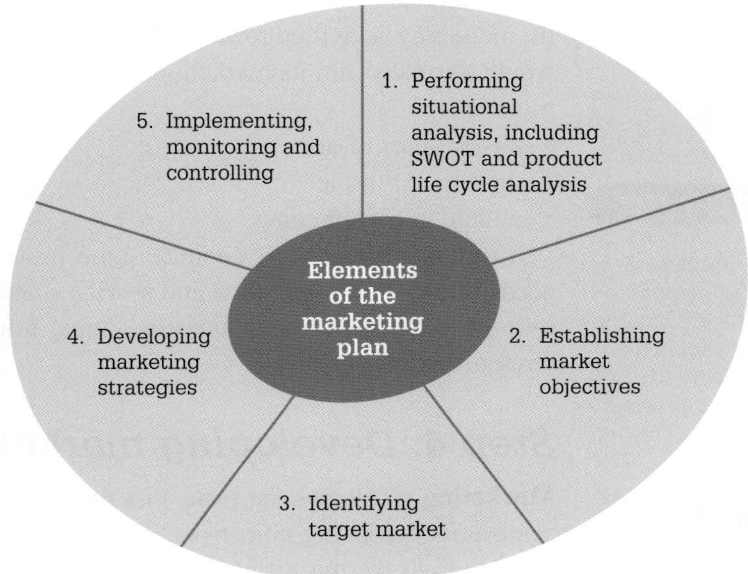

Figure 9.11 The five steps involved in the strategic marketing planning process

The following is a brief explanation of each of the five steps involved in the marketing planning process. Combined, these five elements form the entire marketing plan. Chapter 10 examines the marketing plan and explores these five steps in more detail.

Step 1: Performing situational analysis

BiZ WORD

*A **situational analysis** investigates the marketing opportunities and potential problems.*

The starting point for any marketing plan is an assessment of the business's present position. This is best achieved by conducting a **situational analysis**, which investigates the marketing opportunities and potential problems. To do this, market research is used to gather all the available information about the market environment. The data is then analysed by marketing managers.

Situational analysis attempts to answer two broad questions:

- Where is the business now?
- Where will the business be in the future?

Step 2: Establishing market objectives

BiZ WORD

*A **marketing objective** is a statement of what is to be achieved through the marketing activities.*

A **marketing objective** is a statement of what the business expects to achieve through its marketing activities. These expectations become the business's objectives. Clear objectives are essential for any marketing plan to be effective. Determining these objectives is the most important step in the marketing planning process. Some examples of marketing objectives might include:

- increase market share by 5 per cent
- improve existing product range.

Step 3: Identifying target markets

Sales are the lifeblood of any business, so it is important for businesses to have a good understanding of their target market.

*The **target market** is the group of customers to which the business intends to sell its product.*

Target market refers to the group of customers to which the business intends to sell its product. Once the target market has been identified, the business concentrates its marketing activities towards that group. For example, a rural supplies business would normally aim its marketing strategies at the following type of customer:

- male
- 25–60 years of age
- rural based/farmer
- middle to high income.

Any business that does not have a clear understanding of why its customers buy its product will be unable to decide the best way to promote, price and present the product.

Business owners must conduct some basic research to identify their customers' needs in order to tailor stock and service standards to the group's expectations. Data may be collected through questionnaires, informal interviews with customers and written surveys.

Step 4: Developing marketing strategies

***Marketing strategies** are plans that outline how a business will use its resources to achieve its marketing objectives.*

*The **marketing mix** refers to the combination of the four elements of marketing, the four Ps — product, price, promotion and place — that make up the marketing strategy.*

Marketing strategies are plans that outline how a business will use its resources to achieve its marketing objectives. The four main strategies a business can pursue are referred to as the marketing mix.

The **marketing mix** is the combination of the four elements of marketing, the four Ps, that make up the marketing strategy. They are:

1. product, including brand name, packaging, positioning and warranties
2. price, including list price, discounts, credit terms and payment period
3. promotion, including advertising, sales promotion and publicity
4. place, including location of markets, warehousing, distribution, transport and inventory.

Once the four Ps have been established, the business must then determine the emphasis it will place on each of the variables. This will largely be determined by where the product is positioned or its stage in the product life cycle. For example, a product that is being marketed with an image of exclusivity and prestige will require a marketing mix totally different from a no-frills, generic item. A different marketing mix will also be required for a product in its introductory stage than when it reaches the decline stage.

Step 5: Implementing, monitoring and controlling the marketing plan

***Marketing management** is the process of monitoring and modifying the marketing plan.*

The marketing plan will not operate effectively unless it is well managed. **Marketing management** is the process of monitoring and modifying the marketing plan.

Monitoring involves comparing actual performance with predetermined performance standards. By using performance standards, such as market share analysis and profitability by product or territory, management can assess the effectiveness of the marketing plan. If the plan is found to be failing, then modifications can be made. Modifications may be minor, such as a small change in price, or they could mean a major shift involving the development of a completely new marketing strategy.

Marketing — an evolutionary process

We have seen that marketing is concerned with customer satisfaction and ensuring maximum profit for the business. The marketing plan must focus the business's activities towards optimising customer satisfaction in the market. However, markets are not static — they are dynamic. Markets change and the marketing plans must evolve and adapt to new circumstances. Inflexible plans result ultimately in dissatisfied customers, lost sales and reduced profits.

EXERCISE 9.3 Revision

1. What is meant by the term 'marketing concept'?
2. Prepare a point summary of the marketing approach as it moved through two stages from the 1960s to the present.
3. The marketing concept is a business philosophy adopted by many modern businesses. Read the following five pairs of statements and write into your notebook the statement that represents the business that has adopted the marketing concept philosophy.
   (a) Business A: 'We offer a means of transport, reliability and customer service.'
   Business B: 'We make cars.'
   (b) Business A: 'If you order today we can attempt to deliver it by next Monday.'
   Business B: 'If you order today we can deliver in time for you to meet your sales quota.'
   (c) Business A: 'Perhaps we should start stocking Clear View Mineral Water again. A lot of customers are asking for it.'
   Business B: 'We will only stock Clear View Mineral Water when they decide to give us a better deal than Natural Springs.'
   (d) Business A: 'Our sales are falling. We will have to think about laying off someone.'
   Business B: 'Our sales are falling. We will have to undertake some market research to find out why.'
   (e) Business A: 'Please give generously with your donations, no matter how small. You never know when you or your children may need some help.'
   Business B: 'Please help with your donations. Our charity is short of money.'
4. Suggest reasons why a business would want to adopt a customer-oriented approach to marketing.
5. What is the aim of relationship marketing?
6. 'Relationship marketing is only successful if the business has access to detailed information about its customers.' Discuss.
7. Conduct a class survey to establish the number of loyalty programs that class members belong to. Discuss their effectiveness from the customers' viewpoint. Prepare a brief report of the discussion.
8. What is the purpose of strategic marketing planning?

9. List the five steps involved in the strategic marketing planning process.
10. Define each of the following terms, then use it in a sentence.
    (a) Situational analysis
    (b) Marketing objectives
    (c) Target market
    (d) Marketing strategies
    (e) Marketing mix
    (f) Marketing management
11. Explain why marketing plans and strategies should continue to evolve over time.
12. Prepare a summary of this chapter. A summary condenses the important issues and concepts presented in the chapter. Go to www.jaconline.com.au/businessstudies3e to compare your finished summary with the one provided for this textbook.

Extension

1. Explain why the marketing concept is difficult for some businesses to implement.
2. Prepare a list of service businesses that, in your opinion, do a good job of marketing their services. Now prepare another list of service businesses that you think do a poor job of marketing their services. Give reasons why you chose these businesses.
3. Explain the purpose of each of the three elements needed to implement and maintain a relationship marketing strategy.
4. 'Marketing is not the sole responsibility of the marketing manager, but all managers.' Discuss.

10 Elements of a marketing plan

10.1 Introduction

The acronym SEIDI will help you remember the elements of a marketing plan.
***S**ituational analysis*
***E**stablishing marketing objectives*
***I**dentify target markets*
***D**evelop marketing strategies*
***I**mplementation, monitoring and controlling*

A marketing plan gives a purpose and direction to all the business's activities. Everyone in the business needs to know the plan, so all departments are working towards achieving the goal. For this reason, it is referred to as an *integrated* marketing plan. The marketing plan needs to 'mesh' with the business's operational plan, financial plan and cash flow forecasts.

The elements involved in developing a marketing plan are shown in figure 10.1.

1. Situational analysis
(What is the present state of the business?)

2. Establish market objectives
(What do we want the business to achieve?)

3. Identify target markets
(To whom does the business presently sell? To whom could the business sell?)

4. Develop marketing strategies
(How is the business going to achieve these objectives?)

5. Implementation, monitoring and controlling
- Developing a financial forecast (How much is the marketing plan going to cost?)
- Comparing actual and planned results (Is the business achieving what we thought it would?)
- Revising the marketing strategy (Is the plan working? Does it need changing?)

Figure 10.1 Elements involved in developing a marketing plan

Strategic marketing planning provides a mechanism for businesses to gain a clear picture of where the business is at present, and where it could be in the future. In this sense it is the 'road map' for marketing.

There is no set format for developing a marketing plan. Each plan will reflect the individual characteristics of the business. However, all marketing plans should have two features in common. They should be:
- realistic in the light of the situational analysis
- achievable within the business's resources and budgets.

10.2 Situational analysis — SWOT analysis and product life cycle

The most crucial element of the marketing plan is that management has a precise understanding of the business's current position and a clear picture of where it is heading. That is, a situational analysis must be undertaken, based on meaningful market research.

SWOT (strengths, weaknesses, opportunities and threats) analysis

Changes in the external environment can dramatically alter the course of a business. For this reason, a business must constantly monitor these changes, looking for any opportunities to exploit and any threats to avoid.

The use of a SWOT exercise (strengths, weaknesses, opportunities and threats) provides the information needed to complete the situational analysis and gives a clear indication of the business's position compared with its competitors.

Internal forces operate from inside the organisation and are largely within the control of the business. These internal forces are unique to each business and, by analysing them, management can assess the strengths and weaknesses of the business.

To develop a clear understanding of both the external and internal environments, a SWOT (strengths, weaknesses, opportunities and threats) analysis should be conducted and the marketing plan modified to reflect this information.

Once the SWOT analysis has been conducted, an assessment of the product's position on the product life cycle should be carried out. This is necessary because different marketing strategies will need to be used at different stages of a product's life.

Product life cycle

Markets are constantly changing. New technology, variations in customers' tastes, fluctuations in the level of economic activity and shifts in customer spending habits require that the marketing of a new product be carefully planned and managed (see the Snapshot 'It's on the cards').

It's on the cards

Richard Branson, the chief executive officer and founder of the Virgin Group is an expert at identifying new business opportunities. In 2003, the Virgin Group launched Virgin Money — a new-look credit card, one with a curved edge.

The Australian credit card market is an established one with intense competition between the existing companies. Branson did not perceive this as a threat but an opportunity. He was lured by the challenge of introducing an innovative and popular product.

The credit card has specific characteristics to make it tempting, especially to young people: a lower interest rate, no annual fees and a loyalty rewards program. Innovative and entertaining advertising supports the product. The marketing campaign, which featured Branson dressed as a surgeon, was a success. Within the first week of its launch about 50 000 customers applied for the unusual looking card. After six weeks it had attracted more than 300 000. The Virgin credit card reflected the success of the Virgin Group — creative and high performing.

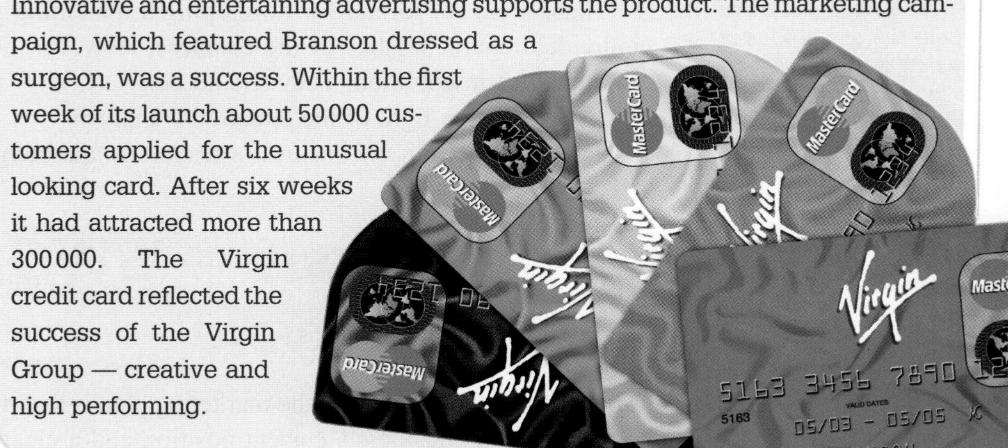

SNaPSHOT Questions

1. Who was the target market for the Virgin credit card?
2. What was the significance of the innovative shape of the card?
3. Identify the features that made this card appeal to its target market.

> **BiZ FaCT**
>
> *A business must be able to launch, modify and delete products in response to changes in the product life cycle.*

In addition, at each stage of the product's life cycle a different marketing strategy is necessary. A business must be able to launch, modify and delete products in response to changes in the product life cycle. Failure to do so will result in declining sales and reduced profits. Each of the separate stages in the product life cycle will require different marketing strategies (see figure 10.2).

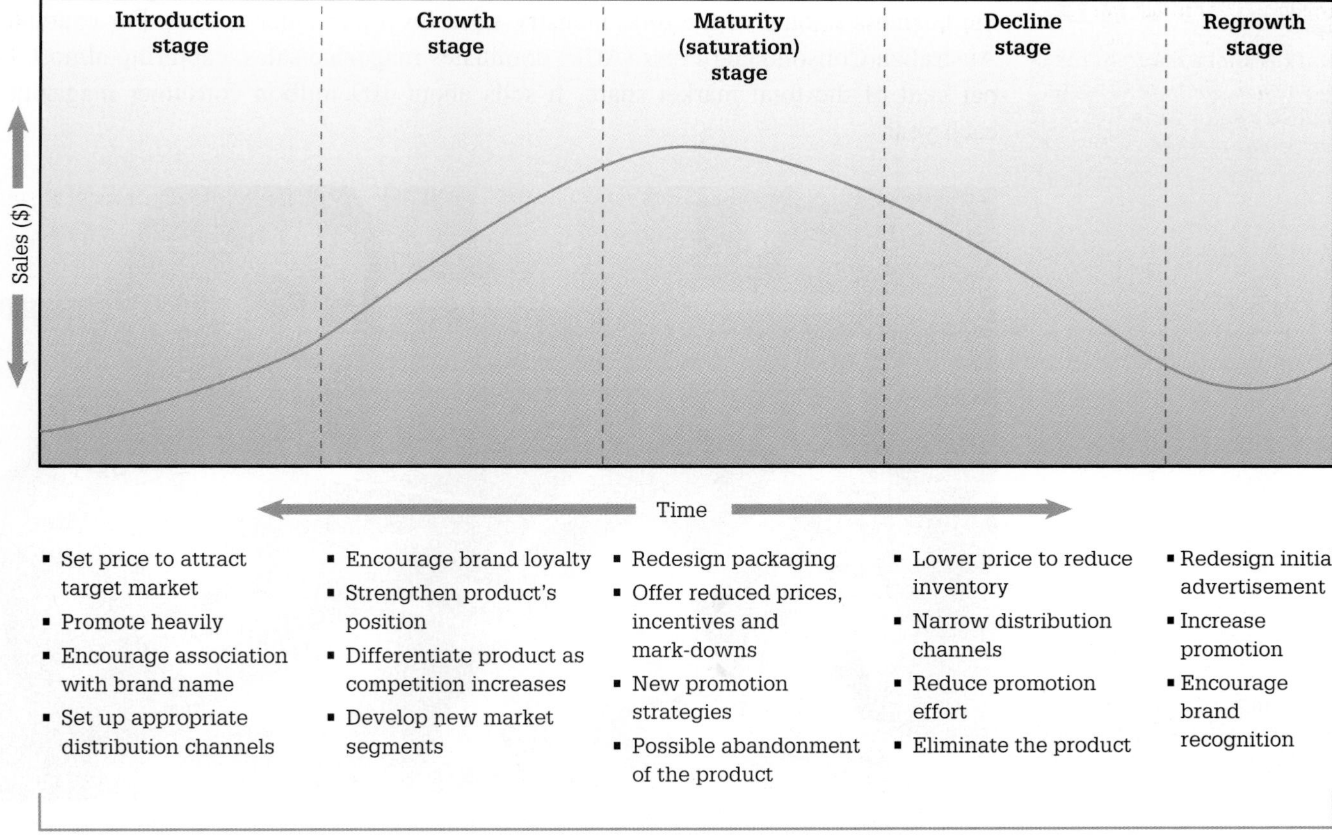

Figure 10.2 Product life cycle and appropriate marketing strategies for each stage

10.3 Establishing marketing objectives

The next element in marketing planning is the formulation of marketing objectives, considered to be the single most important step in the marketing planning process. These marketing objectives should be closely aligned to the overall business objectives. For example, to achieve a business objective of, say, a 10 per cent return on shareholders' funds for the next year may require the achievement of the marketing objective of an increase in the market share of 7 per cent.

Marketing objectives should be more customer oriented than the objectives for the entire business. They are also concerned with products and markets. Four common marketing objectives include:

- increasing market share
- expanding the product range
- expanding existing markets
- maximising customer service.

Such objectives can be measured, and should include specific targets to be met — for example, ‘increase market share by 10 per cent within the next 12 months’.

Increasing market share

BiZ WoRD

***Market share** refers to the business’s share of the total industry sales for a particular market.*

All marketing plans aim to achieve a specified market share. **Market share** refers to the business’s share of the total industry sales for a particular market. For example, Australian Consolidated Press (ACP) dominates magazine sales, capturing almost 49 per cent of the total market share. It sells about 109 million consumer magazines each year.

Figure 10.3 ACP publishes more than 120 magazines and has brand leaders in a number of categories.

In any market that is dominated by only a few large businesses, increasing market share is of prime importance for each of the companies involved.

Expanding the product range

***Product mix** is the total range of products offered by a business.*

The total range of products offered by a business is referred to as the business’s **product mix** (see figure 10.4). Businesses are usually keen to increase their product mix, as this will increase profits in the long term. The same product mix will not remain effective for long because customer’s tastes and preferences change over time, and demand for a particular product may decrease.

To develop the ideal product range, businesses must understand customers’ needs. Each item in a product line should attempt to satisfy the needs of different target markets.

As examples of companies that have increased their product mix, Procter & Gamble introduced Pampers nappies, Continental launched its Lite Cup-a-Soup containing only 39 calories, and Yamaha successfully brought onto the market its home theatre amplifiers and receivers.

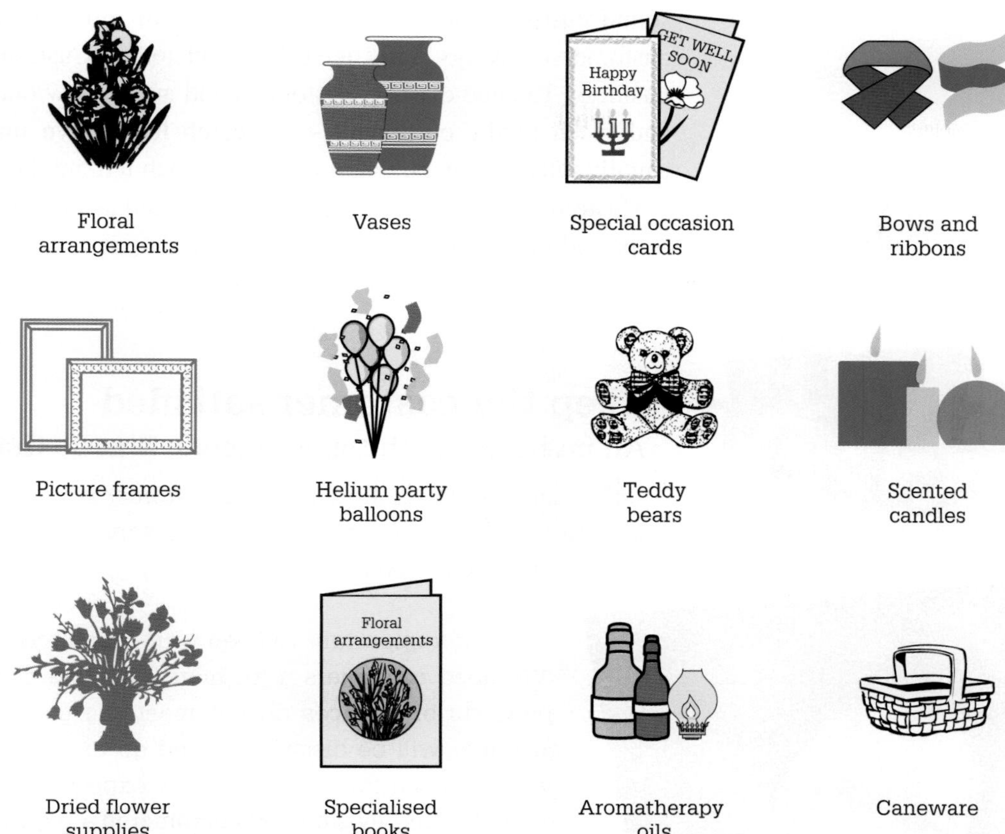

Figure 10.4 The product mix of Beau's Floral Studio (see the Snapshot 'Marketing plan for Beau's Floral Studio', pages 230–7)

Expanding existing markets

The demand for some products varies greatly from one geographic region to another. Differences in climate, landforms or customs can combine to influence customers' tastes and preferences. For example, the demand for swimwear in the Snowy Mountains area during winter is virtually non-existent, in contrast to the demand for ski equipment. Ski equipment, however, would have a very restricted geographical representation across the country.

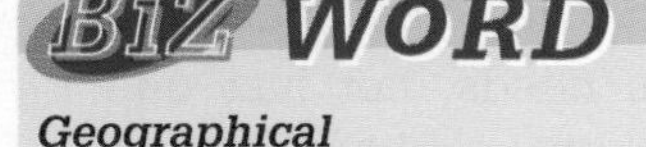

Geographical representation *refers to the presence of a business and the range of its products across a suburb, town, city, state or country.*

Geographical representation refers to the presence of a business and the range of its products across a suburb, town, city, state or country.

To be near their customers, large businesses usually place factories, sales offices and service agencies in a number of market areas. This allows the business to service customers quickly. BlueScope Steel, one of Australia's largest businesses, has a worldwide geographical representation due to its size and nature of operation. It presently has 76 operating sites in over 16 countries.

Maximising customer service

Customer service *means responding to the needs and problems of the customer.*

Of all the objectives examined so far, perhaps maximising customer service is the most important. **Customer service** means responding to the needs and problems of the customer. High levels of customer service will result in improved customer satisfaction and a positive reaction from customers towards the products they purchase (see the Snapshot 'Keep the customer satisfied' on page 220). This establishes a sound customer base with the possibility of repeat purchases. The old saying 'the customer is always right' is still correct today. Customers are the lifeblood of any business. To keep existing customers and attract new ones, the business needs to talk and listen to the customers — research has shown that one dissatisfied customer usually tells 11 others, who in turn will each tell another five.

Customer service can no longer be regarded as merely explaining the refund policy or providing a complaints department. Rather, it is an attitude that should be adopted by all departments within the business.

Keep the customer satisfied

An interview with Dana Cateora, Kinetic Graphics Pty Ltd

Do customers expect high levels of customer service?

Yes. Demand for high-quality customer service is increasing. I think this is because people are so busy.

Why is it important to keep your customers satisfied?

We need customers a lot more than the customers need us. If our products or services do not meet the customer's expectations, the customer will be dissatisfied and go to one of our competitors. However, if our performance matches expectations, the customer will be satisfied. A highly satisfied customer is a happy customer, and a happy customer generates a healthy profit. This is because customers will remain loyal to our business, make repeat purchases and generate word-of-mouth business. Therefore, customer satisfaction must be the central aim of all that we do.

What tactics do you use to deliver high levels of customer satisfaction?

Kinetic Graphics' philosophy is to exceed the customer's expectations. We aim to delight customers. To do this successfully we must provide outstanding levels of service. We train our employees in the 'above and beyond' principle of customer service — do those extra things to show the customer we care about them. We believe that customer satisfaction is achieved when employees are customer-oriented and not sales-oriented. Our employees are encouraged to focus their attention on the customer's needs, not just on making a sale. This lets our staff build long-term relationships with our customers. Of course, outstanding customer service occurs only when senior management provides leadership and demonstrates commitment. You will quickly lose customers if you cannot deliver what you promise.

To maximise customer service businesses need to:

- *train the staff in how to deal with customers*
- *review the product mix*
- *maintain customer contact*
- *anticipate market trends by reading and conducting research*
- *find out what the competitors are offering*
- *reward staff for excellent customer service*
- *ask the customers what they want.*

SNaPSHOT Questions

1. Explain the relationship between customer satisfaction and profits.
2. Briefly outline the strategies Kinetic Graphics uses to provide high levels of customer service.
3. Why is it important to deliver the level of service promised?

EXERCISE 10.1 *Revision*

1. What is the purpose of a marketing plan?
2. What two features should all marketing plans have?
3. Examine figure 10.1 (page 215), then copy the table below into your notebook. Complete the table by writing against each step the appropriate statement from those given below. The first step has been completed for you.

   Statements

   (a) The business will design a new promotional campaign featuring younger women. Direct selling methods will also be introduced.

   (b) The market share percentage will be examined every three months. If the results are negative, then the objectives will be reviewed.

   (c) The business is to increase its market share to 35 per cent within the next 12 months.

   (d) The business presently sells to 35- to 45-year-old females across all income groups. However, the product could be made to appeal to the 25 to 35 age group.

Developing a marketing plan	Statement
Step 1: Situational analysis	Business currently has a market share of 28 per cent. The market is growing but new competitors are likely to enter the market.
Step 2: Establish market objectives	
Step 3: Identify target markets	
Step 4: Develop marketing strategies	
Step 5: Monitor and modify the plan	

4. Outline the value of a SWOT analysis when reviewing the business's situation.
5. Why should the marketing strategies change as a product advances through the stages of its life cycle?
6. List the four most common marketing objectives.
7. Why do businesses wish to increase their product mix?
8. Outline the reasons why some businesses wish to increase their geographical representation.
9. Why is it important to maximise customer service?
10. Construct a mind map summarising the strategies a business can use to achieve the four main marketing objectives. The first one has been started for you.

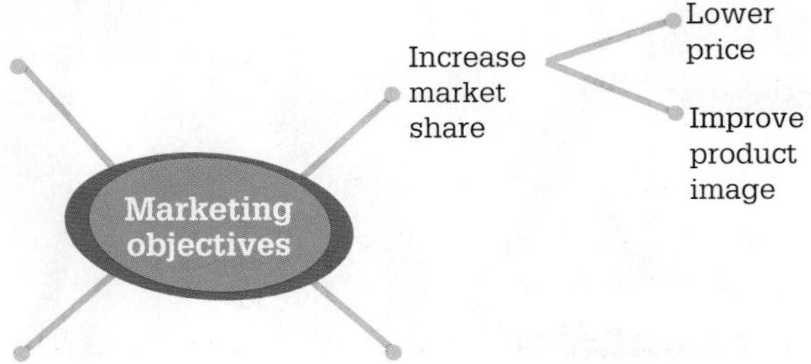

Chapter 10: Elements of a marketing plan

Extension

1. 'The most important step in the marketing planning process is the formulation of the marketing objectives.' Evaluate.
2. Develop a strategic marketing plan for your school's canteen. Outline how it could increase its geographical representation. What major problems would it face in trying to expand off-campus?
3. 'There are only two ways to create and maintain outstanding business performance. First, take exceptional care of the customer and, second, develop new products. It is that simple.' Evaluate.

10.4 Identifying target markets

The total market is normally too large and fragmented to be a viable target for a firm's marketing efforts. Therefore, a business will select a target market, a group of customers with similar characteristics who currently, or who may in the future, purchase the product.

Market segmentation approach

A firm that is marketing motor vehicles would not direct its marketing efforts towards every person in the total motor vehicle market. Some people might want only a sports car. Others might want a four-wheel drive. The business would thus direct its efforts towards a particular part, or 'segment', of the total market for motor vehicles. **Market segmentation** occurs when the total market is subdivided into groups of people who share one or more common characteristics.

BIZ WORD

Market segmentation *occurs when the total market is subdivided into groups of people who share one or more common characteristics.*

Marketing managers use four main variables when segmenting the total market. These are:

- demographic — age, gender, ethnicity, income, occupation, education level, religion, family size and social class
- geographic — urban, suburban, rural, region, climate, landform
- product-related — regular user, first-time user, brand loyalty, price sensitivity, end use
- psychographic — personality, motives, lifestyles.

Market segmentation will be explained in more detail in chapter 12.

Figure 10.5 The youth market

10.5 Developing marketing strategies

Once the business has established the marketing objectives and selected a target market, the next element of the marketing plan is to develop marketing strategies to achieve the objectives. A marketing strategy is a plan that outlines how the business will use its resources to achieve its marketing objectives.

Marketing involves a number of strategies designed to price, promote and distribute products to the marketplace. This section will provide a brief introduction to the main marketing strategies based on the 'four Ps' of marketing. This information will be examined in greater detail in chapter 12.

Marketing mix — the four Ps

One of the most useful ways of understanding how to develop a marketing strategy is to examine each of the elements of the marketing mix. The marketing mix refers to the combination of the four Ps: product, price, promotion and place.

The firm has control over these elements and uses them to reach its target market. As well, the business has control over other organisational resources, such as information, finances and employees. These resources may also be used to achieve marketing goals. However, the business's marketing activities are also affected by a number of external, and largely uncontrollable, forces, as illustrated in figure 10.6. These forces influence decisions about the various combinations of the marketing mix.

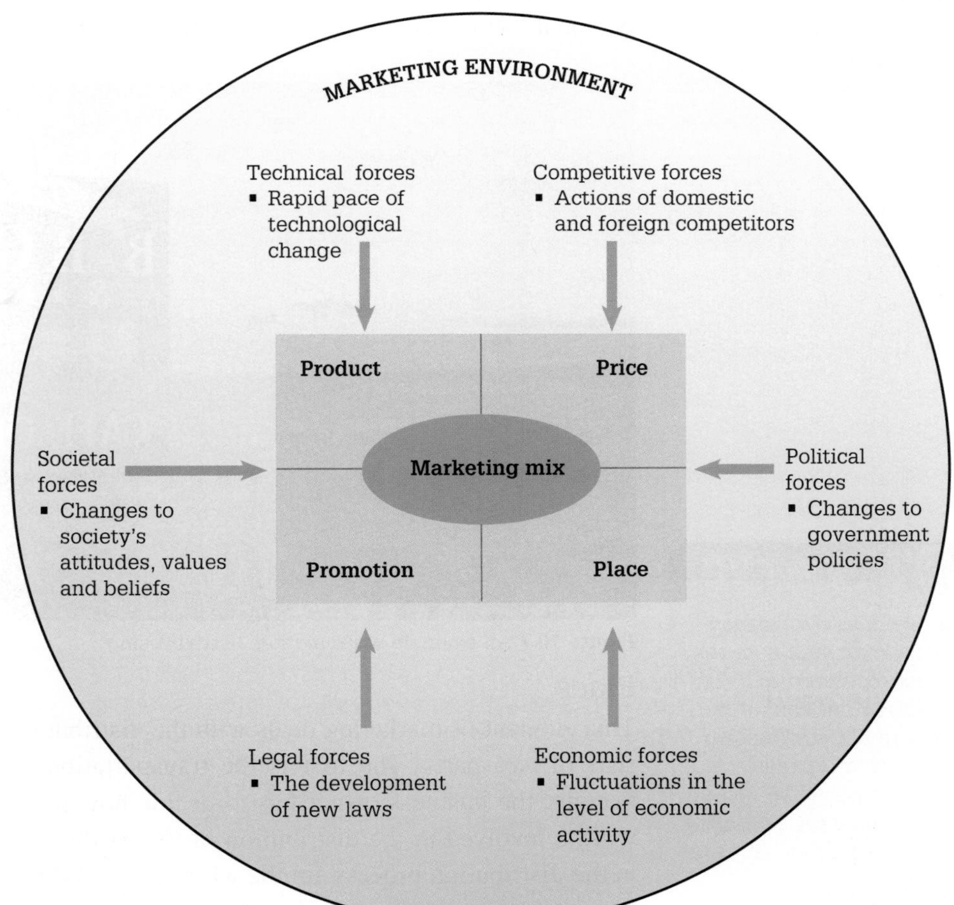

Figure 10.6 The marketing environment and its influence on the marketing mix

See also chapter 12, pages 262–3, for coverage of product.

Product

This element of the marketing mix involves much more than just deciding which product to make. The business owner needs to determine the product's:

- quality
- design
- name
- warranty and guarantee
- packaging
- labelling
- exclusive features.

The product is a combination of all these variables. Customers will buy products that not only satisfy their needs but also provide them with a number of intangible benefits such as a feeling of security, prestige, satisfaction or influence. Much careful planning needs to be undertaken when developing the product.

See also chapter 12, pages 266–7, for coverage of price.

Price

Business owners have difficulty in selecting the correct price for their product. A price set too high could mean lost sales, unless superior customer service is offered. A price set too low may give customers the impression of a 'cheap and nasty' product. Therefore, correct pricing is important.

The forms of promotion are also discussed in chapter 12, pages 268–73.

Promotion

A promotion strategy details the methods to be used by a business to inform, persuade and remind customers about its products. The main forms of promotion include personal selling, advertising, below-the-line promotions and public relations.

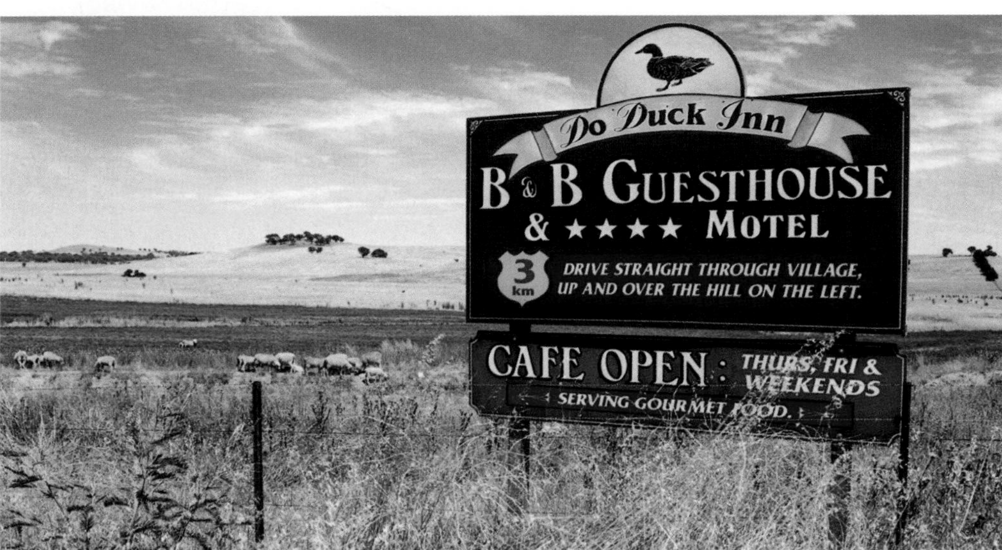

Figure 10.7 An example of promotion — advertising

The business owner may wish to keep supply of the product restricted to a few specialised outlets. Alternatively, distribution may be as wide as is practically possible. (See also chapter 12, pages 273–5 for coverage of place.)

Place

This element of marketing deals with the distribution of the good or service and consists of two parts. The first is the transportation and storage of finished products. Second, the business owner has to decide how many intermediaries (middle agents) will be involved in the distribution of the product. The most common intermediaries in the distribution process are the wholesalers and retailers. The number of intermediaries chosen will determine how widely the good or service will be distributed.

EXERCISE 10.2 Revision

1. Complete the following sentences. The words can be found by reading section 10.4.
   (a) A __________ market is a group of customers with __________ characteristics who currently, or who may in the __________, purchase the product.
   (b) Market __________ occurs when the total market is __________ into groups of people who share one or more common __________.
   (c) Marketing managers use __________ main variables when segmenting the total market. These are:
   (i) __________ (ii) __________ (iii) __________ (iv) __________.
2. What is meant by the term 'marketing mix'?
3. Examine figure 10.6 on page 223. Select two environmental factors and briefly explain how each influences the marketing mix.
4. 'A product consists of both tangible and intangible features.' Elaborate.
5. The 'place' element of marketing consists of two parts. Explain their importance to the overall marketing mix.
6. 'The four Ps are the variables that marketing managers can control, unlike the variables in the marketing environment.' Discuss.

Extension

1. Arrange to interview two people involved in marketing. Areas to investigate include:
   (a) possible changes to marketing in the future
   (b) reasons for these changes
   (c) the future role of marketing.
   Prepare a report, including an executive summary.
2. 'Marketing is a system of business activities designed to plan, price, promote and distribute something of value for the benefit of the customer at a profit.' With reference to a business you have studied, discuss and develop this statement.
3. Prepare a list of several businesses that seem to have effective marketing. Now prepare another list of businesses that seem to have a poor marketing approach. Give reasons for your choices.

10.6 Implementing the marketing plan

Implementation is the process of putting the marketing strategies into operation.

A marketing plan is a meaningless piece of paper until the plan is implemented. **Implementation** is the process of putting the marketing strategies into operation. Implementation involves the daily, weekly and monthly decisions that have to be made to make sure the plan is effective.

Whereas the previous elements of the marketing plan outlined *what* had to be done and *why* it had to be done, the implementation stage is the *how*, *where* and *when* it is to be done. This is a crucial part of the process.

To implement the marketing plan effectively, a number of basic questions need to be answered:

- Is the plan fully integrated with all other sections of the business?
- How should the business be structured and organised?
- Have effective lines of communication between the marketing department and all other departments been established?
- Who are the best people for the various tasks needed to implement the plan?
- Are the marketing personnel motivated and focused on achieving the marketing objectives?
- Are all other employees familiar with the marketing objectives and marketing strategies?

The implementation stage is quite difficult, especially as unforeseen situations may arise that put in jeopardy the success of the entire marketing plan.

10.7 Monitoring and controlling

***Monitoring** means checking and observing the actual progress of the marketing plan.*

*A **performance standard** is a forecast level of performance against which actual performance can be compared.*

Once the marketing plan has been implemented, it must be carefully monitored and controlled. **Monitoring** means checking and observing the actual progress of the marketing plan. This requires the marketing department personnel as well as other employees to gather information and report on any important changes, problems or opportunities that arise during the life of the marketing plan.

The information collected during the monitoring stage is now used to control the plan. Controlling involves the comparison of planned performance against actual performance and taking corrective action to make sure the objectives are attained (see figure 10.8). To achieve this, the marketing manager needs to constantly ask two questions regarding the marketing plan:

1 What does the business want the marketing plan to achieve; that is, what are the objectives?
2 Are these objectives being achieved?

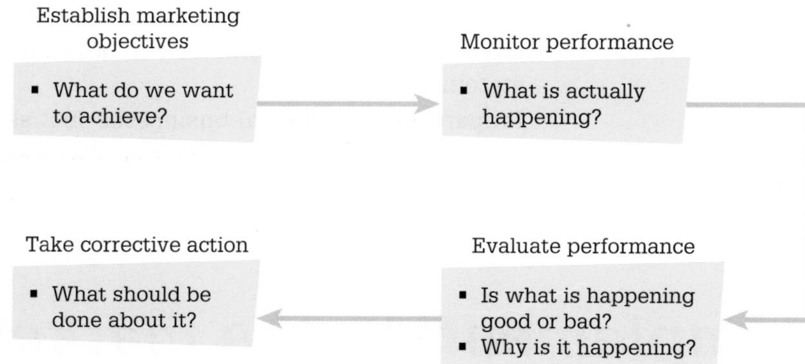

Figure 10.8 The control process

At radio station Triple J, the general manager evaluates the marketing strategies and performance on the basis of performance objectives, which include meeting budgets, reaching target ratings and a required rural/urban listener mix.

The first step in the controlling process requires the business to outline what is to be accomplished; that is, to establish a performance standard. A **performance standard** is a forecast level of performance against which actual performance can be compared. For example, a performance standard could be:

- increase monthly sales by 5 per cent
- improve sales revenue per salesperson by 10 per cent over the next six months.

The second step in the controlling process is to compare or evaluate actual performance against the performance standard. Budgets, sales statistics and cost analyses can be used to evaluate results. For example, a marketing manager could compare each salesperson's results with his or her sales quota. It is only by establishing performance standards and then comparing them with actual performance that a marketing manager can evaluate the effectiveness of the marketing plan.

Developing a financial forecast

When evaluating alternative marketing strategies, a business must develop a financial forecast that details the costs and revenues for each strategy. By measuring the sales potential and revenue forecasts (benefits) for each strategy and comparing these with the anticipated expenditures (costs), a business is in the best position to decide how to allocate its marketing resources. Once this information has been gathered, it is possible to determine the most appropriate course of action using a cost–benefit analysis.

Although financial forecasting allows the marketing manager to undertake a cost–benefit analysis, the results are always open to individual interpretation (see figure 10.9).

Figure 10.9 Forecasts are open to individual interpretation.

Until a detailed analysis of the forecast cost and revenue is undertaken, a business is making decisions based merely on 'gut feelings', which is an inappropriate approach in today's competitive environment.

Developing a financial forecast requires two steps:

1 *Cost estimate.* How much is the marketing plan expected to cost? Costs of the marketing plan can be divided into four major components: market research; product development; promotion, including advertising and packaging; and distribution.

2 *Revenue estimate.* How much revenue (sales) is the marketing plan expected to generate? Forecasting revenues will be based on two major components: how much consumers are expected to buy and for what price; and what sales staff predict they will sell. As time goes by, actual revenue can be compared with the forecast revenue data to determine the effectiveness of the marketing strategy.

Marketing costs are easier to forecast than revenue, because these activities are largely controlled by the business. Calculating the projected marketing revenue is much more difficult because of changes in the external environment, over which the business has little or no control. However, being able to accurately analyse both projected costs and revenues allows the business to forecast profit levels.

Research costs will include researcher, executive personnel and support staff time, computer usage, interviews, printing, testing, special equipment and any incentives to be offered to interviewees.

Comparing actual and planned results

Three performance indicators used to measure the success of the marketing plan are:

1 sales analysis
2 market share analysis
3 marketing profitability analysis.

Sales analysis *is the comparing of actual sales with forecast sales to determine the effectiveness of the marketing strategy.*

Sales analysis

A **sales analysis** uses sales data to evaluate a business's current performance and the effectiveness of a marketing strategy. The more the sales figures are broken down, the clearer the picture becomes, as can be seen by examining figure 10.10.

Sales revenue by territories — 1st quarter				
Sales territory	**Sales quota $**	**Actual sales $**	**Difference $**	**% change (– decrease + increase)**
1	50 000	58 000	8 000	+16.0
2	80 000	85 000	5 000	+6.3
3	70 000	76 000	6 000	+8.6
4	65 000	72 000	7 000	+10.8
5	90 000	94 000	4 000	+4.4
Total sales revenue	355 000	385 000	30 000	+8.4

Figure 10.10 Sales analysis

BiZ FaCT

The use of computerised sales has made the collection, storage, retrieval and analysis of sales data much easier. Computerised sales reports can be prepared, showing:

- *daily, weekly, monthly, quarterly and yearly sales reports*
- *product line sales*
- *credit as opposed to cash sales analysis*
- *sales reports for individual sales representatives*
- *company division sales reports*
- *any combination of the above.*

A cursory glance at the bottom line of figure 10.10 shows that the total sales revenue has increased by $22 000 or 6.2 per cent above the quota — a pleasing result and confirmation that the marketing plan is a success.

The main strength of sales analysis is that sales figures are relatively inexpensive to collect and process. Their main weakness, however, is that data for sales revenue do not reveal the exact profit level; such information can only be gleaned from further investigations of total expenditure.

Market share analysis/ratios

Just as sales can be analysed, so too can a business's market share. By undertaking a market share analysis, a business is able to evaluate its marketing strategies as compared with those of its competitors. This evaluation can reveal whether changes in total sales, either increases or decreases, have resulted from the business's marketing strategies or have been due to some uncontrollable external factor. For example, if a business's total sales revenue declined but its market share remained stable, then the marketing manager can assume that overall industry sales have fallen, perhaps due to a downturn in the economy. However, if a business's total sales revenue and market share have declined, then the marketing strategies need to be reviewed. Businesses place a great deal of importance on analysing market share statistics — a 1 per cent fall in market share can represent millions of dollars in lost sales.

Marketing profitability analysis

Sales and market share analyses, while useful, do not present the full picture. This can only be done by analysing the marketing costs involved with each marketing strategy. Using a **marketing profitability analysis**, the business breaks down the total marketing costs into specific marketing activities, such as advertising, transport, administration, order processing and so on.

Marketing profitability analysis *is a method in which the business breaks down the total marketing costs into specific marketing activities.*

By comparing the costs of specific marketing activities with the results achieved, a marketing manager can assess the effectiveness of each activity. This evaluation also helps in deciding how best to allocate marketing resources in the future.

Revising the marketing strategy

Once the results of the sales, market share and profitability analysis have been calculated, the business is now in a position to assess which objectives are being met and which are not. Based on this information, the marketing plan can be modified.

Modification of the marketing plan is equally important as all the other steps involved in creating successful marketing strategies.

Changes in the marketing mix

Because the marketing plan is operating in a dynamic business environment, the marketing mix will constantly need to be modified. Changes that could be introduced include the following:

- *Production modifications*. No product is perfect. Businesses that continually upgrade their products will be able to maintain a competitive advantage.
- *Price modifications*. Prices fluctuate due to a variety of reasons. Therefore, the price component of the marketing mix will need to be modified in response to changes in the external business environment.
- *Promotion modifications*. Promotion costs will be high when a new product is first launched onto the market. During the later stages of the product's life cycle, promotion costs may stabilise and even fall during the decline stage. Promotion strategies will, therefore, need to change over time, corresponding to the life cycle of the product.
- *Place modifications*. As a product's success increases, the distribution channels will need to be expanded to cater for the growing market. New overseas markets may be tapped, while old markets may decrease due to demographic changes. With the development of electronic communications, new distribution channels, such as the Internet, may be used.

If a firm wants to achieve long-term growth, it must continually introduce new products.

New product development

The product life cycle tells us that all products have a life span of somewhere between five to 10 years. Therefore, if a firm wants to achieve long-term growth, it must continually introduce new products. For example, if Sony had stopped product development at the transistor radio it would probably be out of business today. However, Sony, like many other large businesses, spends vast amounts on research and development to stay at the forefront of technology and introduce new products (see figure 10.11).

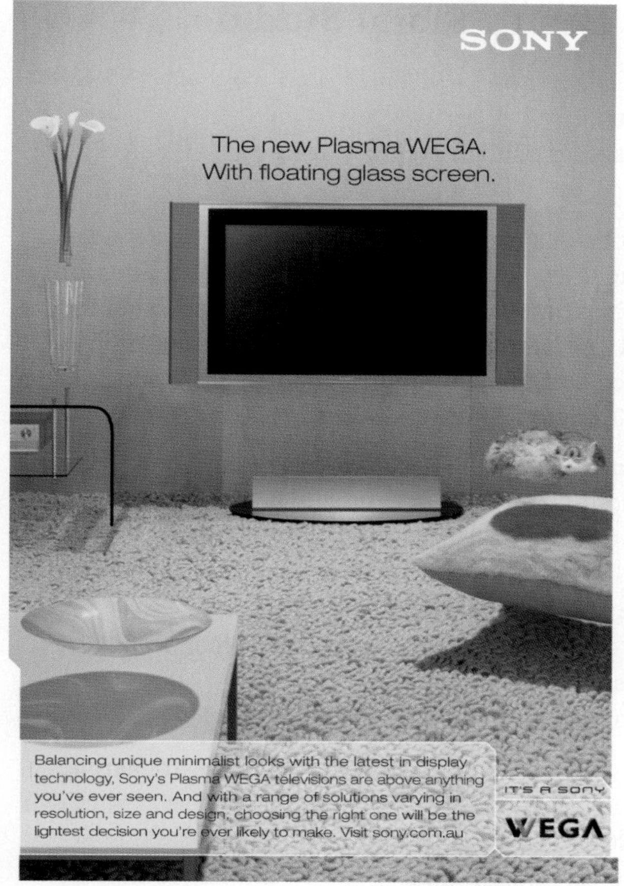

SONY
The new Plasma WEGA.
With floating glass screen.
Balancing unique minimalist looks with the latest in display technology, Sony's Plasma WEGA televisions are above anything you've ever seen. And with a range of solutions varying in resolution, size and design, choosing the right one will be the lightest decision you're ever likely to make. Visit sony.com.au
IT'S A SONY
WEGA

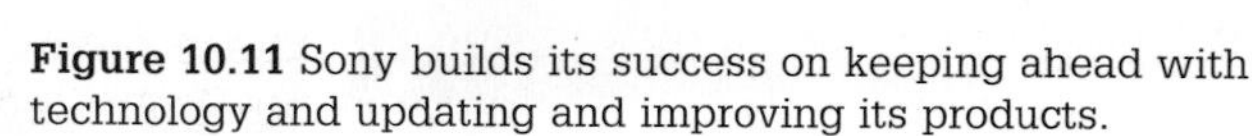

Figure 10.11 Sony builds its success on keeping ahead with technology and updating and improving its products.

Source: Sony Australia, April 2004.

Product deletion

To maintain an effective product mix, a business will have to eliminate some lines of products. This is called **product deletion**. Outdated products may create an unfavourable image and this negativity may rub off on other products sold by the business. Most businesses find it difficult to delete a product, especially if it has been successful for a long time. However, when a product is in the decline stage, a decision will eventually have to be made to either delete or redevelop the product.

***Product deletion** is the elimination of some lines of products.*

10.8 Elements of the marketing plan — an overview

In this chapter we have presented the five elements that make up the marketing plan. It is important that each section of the plan be comprehensively researched. A hastily prepared plan will only result in failure.

Although the majority of marketing plans contain a large amount of data and sometimes run to hundreds of pages, they all have one thing in common — they are organised around the same five elements discussed here. For a more detailed examination of a marketing plan based on the five elements, refer to the Snapshot 'Marketing plan for Beau's Floral Studio'.

Marketing plan for Beau's Floral Studio

EXECUTIVE SUMMARY

Purpose of the marketing plan

To provide an operational marketing plan for control purposes.

Description of the business

Beau Wilkes is owner-operator of a retail florist store called Beau's Floral Studio. The business provides fresh and dried flowers and associated product lines for all occasions. The business markets to a wide cross-section of the population within the surrounding suburbs but particularly to females aged 15 to 65 and males aged 15 to 25. Beau established the business in 2004 and operates it as a sole trader.

The needs the business will satisfy

The benefits sought by customers can be divided into four distinct categories. Customers associate the product with:

- comfort — giving gifts for condolence, sympathy and sickness
- beauty — brightening the house, office or workplace
- happiness — celebrating important events such as weddings and birthdays
- affection — showing friendship, fondness and love.

Products and services the business will offer to satisfy these needs

Beau's Floral Studio offers:

- a diverse range of fresh and dried, high-quality exotic and native flowers presented in original arrangements
- a wide range of complementary gift lines
- a welcoming, pleasant and fragrant environment in which customers may browse and select either prepared arrangements or individualised bunches of flowers
- friendly, efficient service and expert advice
- prompt delivery, including after-hours ordering and delivery

- access to a worldwide distribution network through membership of the 'Petals Network'
- easy access to parking
- various payment options, including EFTPOS and major credit cards.

Competitive advantage

Beau's competitive advantage is derived from a number of individual factors including:

- the freshness and quality of flowers in comparison to competitors
- a wide and diverse range of exotic and native flowers
- friendly, welcoming, personalised service and advice
- a pleasant, visually appealing and fragrant environment
- floral arrangement classes specialising in the Japanese technique of ikebana
- a convenient central location with parking
- membership of the 'Petals Network' distribution system, to which no other local florist belongs.

Sustainability of the competitive advantage

Beau has responded proactively to the existing competition by differentiating her products and services. She has provided:

- a more diverse range of exotic and native flowers (product mix)
- floral arrangement classes
- after-hours service
- both traditional and contemporary floral arrangements.

Mission statement

To provide the best quality and largest variety of fresh and dried flowers at all times.

THE MARKET

The floristry market is intensely competitive, and small owner-operated outlets face competition from both direct and indirect sources. Direct competitors of Beau's Floral Studio include florists located within and servicing the local suburbs. These are:

- Floral World Florist
- All Occasions Flowers and Gift Baskets
- Flowers in the Mall.

Indirect competitors include those businesses that offer floral arrangements as part of their overall product lines. Although these businesses are not located near Beau's Floral Studio, they are located at convenient points within the local suburbs and include the following supermarket outlets:

- Woolworths
- Coles.

Sales through these indirect competitors tend to be impulse purchases.

As flowers are a product that is difficult to differentiate, Beau's Floral Studio has added extra services and complementary product lines to provide the business with a degree of individuality. Beau's Floral Studio is the only local florist to offer flower arrangement classes.

(*continued*)

SWOT ANALYSIS

Strengths

- Beau's creativity and training in the industry
- Access to a reliable source of fresh and dried flowers
- 'Petals Network' enables customers to send flowers worldwide
- Ability to diversify and innovate
- Wide range of exotic and native flowers
- Traditional and contemporary floral arrangements displayed in a pleasant environment
- Central location with parking
- Differentiated complementary product lines
- Floral arrangement classes

Weaknesses

- Late entry into the local floral market — Beau's store was the last to open in the area.
- The store has been operating for only 18 months and is still in the establishment phase.
- The customer base is not fully developed.

Opportunities

- To develop a separate business unit specialising in wedding functions
- To improve market penetration through the use of a flower kiosk located within a popular location, capitalising on the popular range of fresh flowers already sold through the shop. Such a strategy would generate impulse purchases and help offset the indirect competition faced from the supermarkets.
- To establish a website for business-to-business and business-to-customer transactions. The site could also be used to link floral arrangement lessons to other sites.

Threats

- Three other direct competitors within the same shopping precinct
- Changes in customer tastes and preferences
- Increase in Internet sales by larger wholesale florist businesses

ESTABLISHING MARKETING OBJECTIVES

This marketing plan has been devised to achieve the following marketing objectives:

1. To increase sales by 12 per cent each year over the next three years.
2. To increase market share from the present 18 per cent to 30 per cent over the next three years.
3. To increase the studio's turnover of wedding-associated products by 150 per cent over the next three years by developing a subordinate business activity specialising in wedding functions.
4. To increase the product mix, through the introduction of a new line of products.
5. To implement marketing strategies targeted at increasing the number of male customers from the 15 to 25 age group.

TARGET MARKET

Size of target market

Potential

Beau's potential target market consists of approximately 54 000 people who live in the surrounding suburbs.

Actual

Beau's primary target market consists of three subdivisions:

- females between the ages of 25 and 65 who decorate their homes with floral displays
- females between the ages of 15 and 25 who purchase flowers for special occasions
- males between the ages of 15 and 25 who purchase flowers for their partners.

These target markets are important as they represent repeat customers who are essential for the business's long-term survival. The primary target market consists of approximately 31 000 people.

Presently, Beau's Floral Studio has an 18 per cent market share of fresh and dried flower sales within the surrounding suburbs. Estimates of the market share for floral arrangement classes are estimated to be 25 per cent of the target market.

The primary target market can be further subdivided according to the benefits sought by the customer (see table 10.1).

TABLE 10.1 Subdivision of primary target market

Benefits sought by customer	Customer characteristics
Comfort (sickness and sympathy)	Males and females aged 15 years and above
Beauty (floral displays)	Predominantly female, aged 25–65
Happiness (weddings and parties)	Predominantly female, aged 25–50
Affection	Predominantly male, aged 15–25

Description of market segments

Geographic

Beau's Floral Studio targets the residents of the local area. Although there are occasional sales to customers from outside the surrounding suburbs, these are not on a regular basis and, as such, do not constitute an important segment for the purposes of this marketing plan.

Demographic

Customer research data collected over the last 12 months reveal that 67 per cent of customers were female and 33 per cent male. Females within the 25 to 65 age group were the most common type of customer, making up 83 per cent of the total female customer base. Males within the 15 to 25 age group made up 78 per cent of the total male customer base.

Purchase decision maker

Predominantly, fresh and dried flower arrangements are considered a gift purchase, either for the individual or another person. The experience of a floral purchase should be considered within this context.

(*continued*)

Beau's Floral Studio has established a computerised database of regular customers' individual preferences. This service is frequently used by both male and female customers when making gift purchases.

Income level

Beau's Floral Studio caters for the middle to high income groups. These groups consist of individuals and households with high levels of disposable income. They do not perceive the buying of flowers as an infrequent luxury expenditure but, rather, as a regular (weekly or fortnightly) purchase.

However, Beau's Floral Studio will introduce a new range of lower-priced fresh flower and gift products to cater for males aged 15 to 25 years as this market segment tends to have less disposable income.

DEVELOPING MARKETING STRATEGIES

Product range and product mix

Beau's Floral Studio presently has a wide product mix, offering a diverse range of fresh and dried exotic and native flowers. Complementary product lines include teddy bears, balloons, porcelain ornaments, friendship gifts, plant holders, floral arrangement materials and instructional books.

It is intended to increase the width of the product mix with the introduction of a range of aromatic candles, fragrant oils and oil burners. This expanded product mix will allow the business to diversify its existing products and appeal to new segments in the market. Each item in the new product mix will be evaluated as to its ability to satisfy the needs of the different target markets.

As mentioned previously, Beau's Floral Studio has the opportunity to expand into wedding supplies. This is a logical extension of the current product range and will allow the business to penetrate further into the market. Market research will be undertaken over the next six months and a separate marketing plan developed for this business activity.

However, at the core of the product range is the belief that Beau's Floral Studio will stock only products of the highest quality. In this way, the customer base is protected and the business's image strengthened.

Branding

Beau's Floral Studio purchases its fresh and dried flowers from a number of wholesale suppliers based at the Sydney Flower Markets. Non-flower products are sourced from four wholesale gift suppliers.

As flowers cannot be identified as being sourced from a specific wholesale supplier, Beau will implement a number of strategies to identify purchases from the Floral Studio.

These strategies include:

- introducing distinctively coloured and environmentally friendly gift wrap and packaging. The name of the business, with its logo, telephone and facsimile numbers, and the address of its website will be prominently displayed.
- providing a complimentary sachet of 'Euro Fleur', (a special food for cut flowers), with every purchase of fresh flowers. The sachet will also carry the name and all contact details of the business.

- placing a distinctively coloured and designed sticker on all items sold
- designing a new and distinctive business logo.

Positioning and image

Beau's Floral Studio will continue to develop a high-quality image for the business. All other elements of the marketing mix will be used to shape and maintain this image. The maintenance of this product positioning is important if the business wishes to exploit its differentiation. Successful positioning of the product will allow for increased profit margins without loss of customers.

A customer survey will be distributed to all account holders to assist with monitoring the positioning of the business.

Beau's Floral Studio will not attempt to compete directly with the other three florist businesses within the shopping precinct. Beau's will differentiate itself in terms of its quality and 'exclusive' image (see figure 10.12).

Pricing

Beau's Floral Studio is presently a price follower because it is the most recent entrant into the flower market in the area. Setting prices too high will result in customers being lost to competitors. If the prices are too low it will damage the image of the business and give the impression that the quality of the products is inferior.

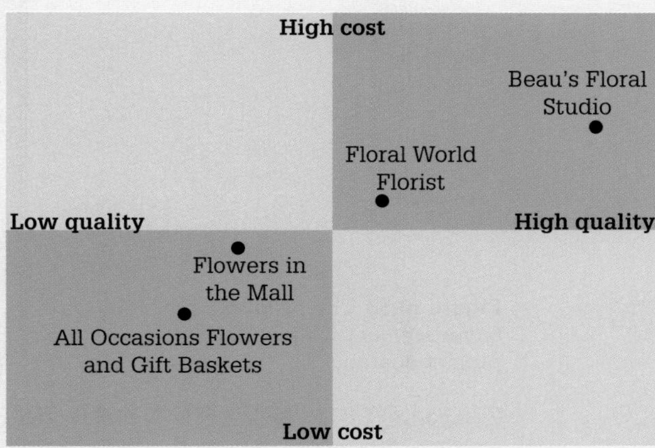

Figure 10.12 The market positioning of the four florist businesses

As a result of the strategies that make up this marketing plan, Beau's Floral Studio will be able to raise its prices and, therefore, increase its profit margin by an average of 35 per cent over the next 18 months. It is not expected that these price rises will lead to a significant loss of customers, due to the increased product range, product differentiation, accurate positioning and the high quality of the products and service.

Promotion

Presently, Beau's Floral Studio relies on the following five methods of promotion:

- local newspaper advertisements
- word-of-mouth recommendation
- packaging displaying the business name and logo

(*continued*)

- a *Yellow Pages* advertisement
- eye-catching window displays.

Three new promotional strategies are planned within the next six months. These are:

- the use of the website to promote contemporary floral arrangements and the new product lines
- a personalised direct-mail campaign to existing account holders with exclusive offers for special occasions such as Mother's Day, Easter, Christmas and Valentine's Day
- an enlarged and updated *Yellow Pages* advertisement (see figure 10.13).

Expenditure on all forms of promotion will be increased by 15 per cent in the next 12 months and a further 10 per cent over the following two years. This increased promotional expenditure is required during the establishment phase of the business.

Figure 10.13 The *Yellow Pages* advertisement is an important promotional tool.

PROJECTED REVENUE AND EXPENSES

The following projected expenses (costs) and revenue (income) will be used to assist with the monitoring of the marketing plan. Projected expenses and revenue will be compared against actual performance to determine the degree of success or failure.

Expenditure breakdown

These estimates detail how much will have to be spent on each part of the marketing plan (see figure 10.14). Total costs are subdivided into the individual expense items, which combine to make up the total marketing plan.

Revenue breakdown

Figure 10.15 reveals the projected revenue that should be generated due to the successful implementation of the marketing plan. As time goes by, actual revenue will be compared with the projected revenue data to determine the effectiveness of the marketing plan.

Marketing plan Beau's Floral Studio — Projected expenditure schedule			
		Year	
Expenditure item	**2006**	**2007**	**2008**
Fixed costs	550 000	550 000	550 000
Variable costs			
1. Market research	22 000	20 000	18 000
2. Advertising	35 000	30 000	28 000
3. Packaging materials	15 000	17 000	20 000
4. Direct mail campaign	8 000	6 000	5 000
Total	630 000	623 000	621 000

Figure 10.14 Marketing plan — expenditure forecast schedule

		Year	
	2006	**2007**	**2008**
Sales	700 000	750 000	800 000
Costs			
Fixed	550 000	550 000	550 000
Variable	80 000	73 000	71 000
Total costs	630 000	623 000	621 000
Profit	70 000	127 000	179 000
Return as % of sales	10.0	16.9	22.3

Figure 10.15 Marketing plan — revenue forecast schedule

MONITORING AND CONTROLLING OF THE MARKETING PLAN

All stages of the marketing plan will be monitored by comparing planned and actual results on a monthly basis.

A ratio analysis including current ratio, gross profit ratio, net profit ratio, return on owners' equity and accounts receivable turnover ratio will also be undertaken at the end of each month.

Beau's Floral Studio plans to introduce a full product-range analysis using the 'Mind Your Own Marketing' computer program. The data supplied from this program will assist in the decision-making process by providing a detailed and up-to-date analysis of each product's financial performance. Under-performing products may need to be deleted from the overall product mix.

Ultimately, the success of this marketing plan will be judged on whether the five specific marketing objectives have been achieved over the stated time frame.

SNaPSHOT Questions

1. Why is it necessary for Beau to conduct a SWOT analysis on her business?
2. Identify the primary and secondary target markets for Beau's Floral Studio.
3. How does segmenting the total market help Beau achieve her long-term business goals?
4. Outline the branding strategies Beau's Floral Studio implemented.
5. Predict the success of the three new promotional strategies.

EXERCISE 10.3 Revision

1. Explain why the implementation stage is as important as developing marketing objectives.
2. Outline the difference between 'monitoring' and 'controlling'. Discuss how the two processes are linked.
3. Why is it easier for a business to forecast marketing costs than revenue?
4. A business has a sales potential of $90 000 but achieves actual sales of only $25 000. What does this signify? What should the business do next?
5. 'Any business that fails to conduct a sales analysis will not be able to assess the effectiveness of its marketing strategies.' Discuss.
6. Examine the following market share results for Electronic Appliances Ltd.

Year	Sales revenue ($ million)	Market share (%)
2006	28	18
2007	25	18
2008	33	14

   (a) Explain how it is possible for sales revenue to decrease but market share to remain the same.
   (b) If you were the marketing manager, with which year's results would you be most pleased? Give a reason for your answer.
7. Briefly outline four changes that could be made to modify the marketing mix.
8. Distinguish between 'new product development' and 'product deletion'. Provide examples in your answer.
9. Prepare a summary of this chapter. A summary condenses the important issues and concepts presented in the chapter. Go to www.jaconline.com.au/businessstudies3e to compare your finished summary with the one provided for this textbook.

Extension

1. Outline the reasons why a business's marketing performance should be constantly evaluated. Describe some methods that can be used to measure the effectiveness of a marketing plan.

2. You have just been appointed marketing manager for Apollo Tracksuits Pty Ltd. One of your first tasks is to analyse total industry sales, territory sales and product line sales revenue breakdown, as shown in tables 10.2, 10.3 and 10.4.

TABLE 10.2 Apollo Tracksuits Pty Ltd — company sales and total industry sales, 2006–2010

Year	Apollo sales ($ millions)	Industry sales ($ millions)	Apollo market share (%)
2006	5	38	—
2007	7	44	—
2008	10	81	—
2009	9	70	—
2010	12	89	—

TABLE 10.3 Apollo Tracksuits Pty Ltd — territorial sales, 2006

Territory	Sales quota ($ millions)	Actual sales ($ millions)	Difference ($)	Difference (%)
A	4	3	—	—
B	2	2	—	—
C	5	4	—	—
D	1	1	—	—

TABLE 10.4 Apollo Tracksuits Pty Ltd — product line sales, 2006

Product	Sales quota ($ millions)	Actual sales ($ millions)	Difference ($)	Difference (%)
Techno Tracks	2	1	—	—
Weekenders	3	1.5	—	—
Sports Plus	2	2	—	—
Image Track	2	2.5	—	—
No Sweat Tops	3	3		

(a) Perform a market share analysis by completing table 10.2. Prepare a report on your results.

(b) Prepare an actual sales versus sales quota analysis for 2006 by completing table 10.3. What does this analysis show?

(c) The actual sales and sales quota figures for each product are shown in table 10.4. Complete the table. What do these figures indicate?

(d) What suggestions would you make to improve the actual sales performance?

CHAPTER

11 Market research and customer and buyer behaviour

11.1 Introduction

Imagine you have just been given an assessable task for your Business Studies class. If you want to achieve satisfactory results it is important that you undertake some type of research. The research could consist of reading books and magazines, conducting surveys, accessing Internet sites, carrying out experiments and talking to people. Marketing managers also have to undertake research of their market.

Market research is the process of systematically collecting, recording and analysing information concerning a specific marketing problem.

Market research is the process of systematically collecting, recording and analysing information concerning a specific marketing problem.

Figure 11.1 Surveying customers provides valuable information about customer buying behaviour.

The main purpose of market research is to gather information. Just as a well-researched assessable task will lead to better results, marketing strategies perform best when they are based on accurate, up-to-date, detailed and relevant information. Being well-informed about all aspects of the market, especially the buying behaviour of existing and potential customers, places the business in a stronger position.

For every successfully launched new product, there are at least four that fail.

Releasing a new product onto the market is risky. To help minimise the risk is the main purpose of market research. By collecting and assessing information about the needs and wants of consumers, a more accurate and responsive marketing plan can be designed and, therefore, reduce the risk of market failure. Market research attempts to identify and outline both marketing opportunities and problems as well as evaluating the implementation of the marketing plan.

Without adequate, reliable and correct information, businesses expose themselves to market embarrassments, which could result in the product failing to sell.

The three steps of the market research process

To obtain accurate information, marketing managers usually follow a three-step approach (see figure 11.2).

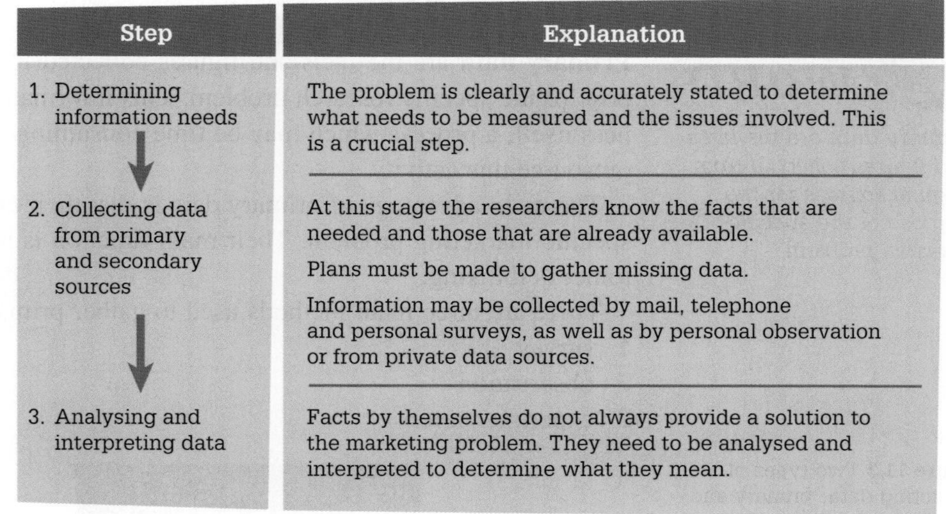

Step	Explanation
1. Determining information needs	The problem is clearly and accurately stated to determine what needs to be measured and the issues involved. This is a crucial step.
2. Collecting data from primary and secondary sources	At this stage the researchers know the facts that are needed and those that are already available. Plans must be made to gather missing data. Information may be collected by mail, telephone and personal surveys, as well as by personal observation or from private data sources.
3. Analysing and interpreting data	Facts by themselves do not always provide a solution to the marketing problem. They need to be analysed and interpreted to determine what they mean.

Figure 11.2 The three steps of the market research process

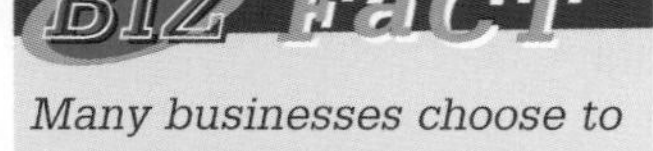

Many businesses choose to outsource their marketing research to companies such as ACNielsen Company and AGB McNair.

You will probably be familiar with this process as it uses similar steps to those needed to complete a research assignment.

11.2 Determining information needs

In the late 1950s, Xerox Corporation's marketing research study recommended only a small market existed for an automatic photocopier. Luckily for Xerox, management had a 'gut feeling' that the researchers' conclusions were wrong and they decided to launch the product anyway. The photocopier was an instant success and the rest is history.

It is often said that the recipe for effective decisions is 90 per cent information and 10 per cent inspiration. However, the information must be relevant to the situation or problem.

The best method to determine the relevance of data is to constantly ask questions concerning its ultimate use. Information is useful if it:

- results in marketing strategies that meet the needs of the business's target market
- assists the business to achieve its marketing objectives
- may be used to increase sales and profits.

Determining specific information needs from the market research process is a crucial first step in the overall process.

Ideally, marketing managers should treat information in the same way as other resources within the business, and weigh up the costs of collecting information against the benefits it provides.

More businesses are undertaking marketing research activities. This represents a shift from intuitive 'gut-feeling' decisions to scientific problem solving. However, sometimes even the most sophisticated statistical and logical methods do not produce the correct answer (see the Biz Fact on the left).

11.3 Data collection (primary and secondary)

***Marketing data** refers to the information, relevant to the defined marketing problem.*

Marketing data refers to the information, usually expressed as facts and figures, relevant to the defined marketing problem.

Market researchers may use two types of data: primary and secondary data, as shown in figure 11.3 (page 242). Normally market researchers use a combination of both types of data.

Primary data

Primary data are the facts and figures collected from original sources for the purpose of the specific research problem.

Primary data are the facts and figures collected from original sources for the purpose of the specific research problem. This information can be collected by the business itself, a process which may be time consuming and expensive. Many businesses outsource this activity.

The main advantage of primary data is that their collection is directed at solving a specific marketing problem. Their main function is to find out exactly what the customer is thinking.

There are three main methods used to gather primary data:

1 survey
2 observation
3 experimentation.

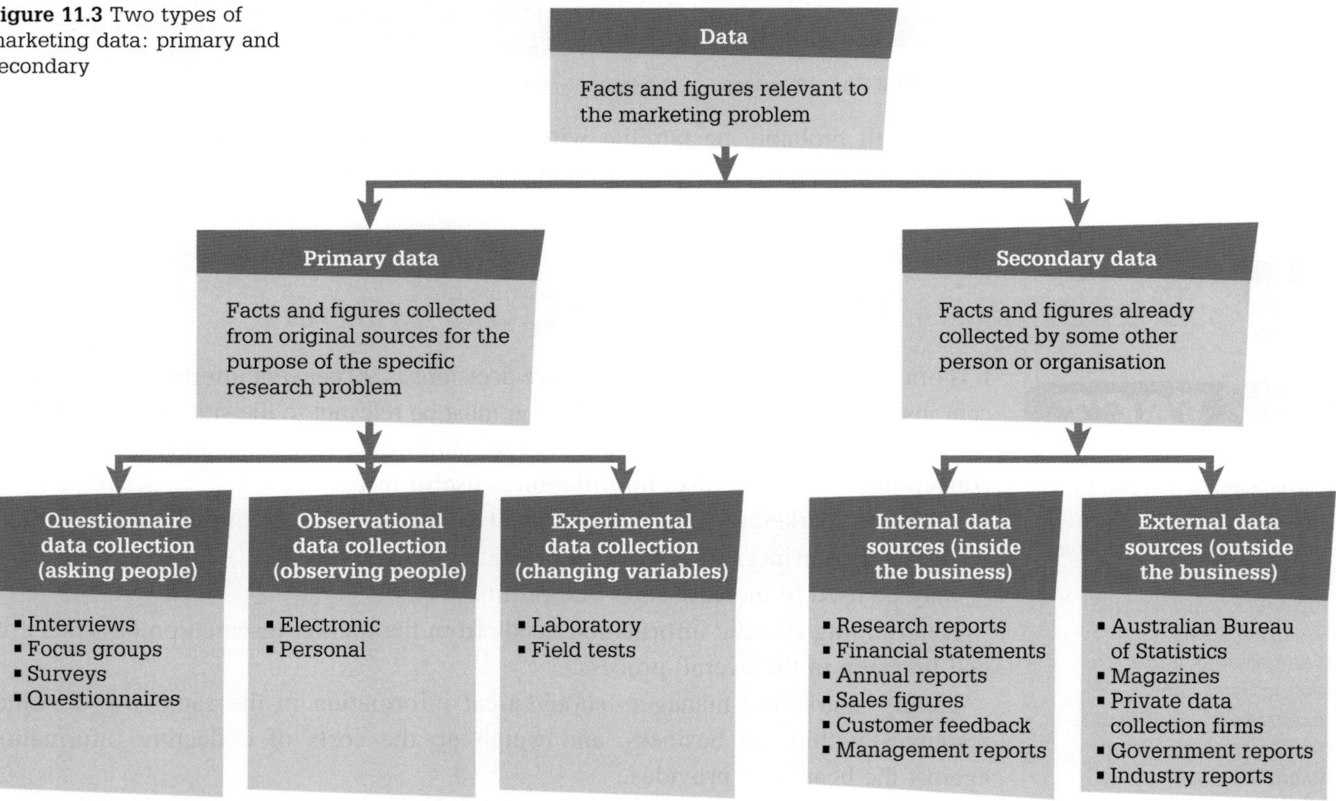

Figure 11.3 Two types of marketing data: primary and secondary

The survey method

*Conducting a **survey** means gathering data by asking or interviewing people.*

*The use of 'sugging' — **s**elling **u**nder the **g**uise of market research — has contributed to increased consumer reluctance to respond to surveys.*

Conducting a **survey** means gathering data by asking or interviewing people. Surveys may be carried out by:

- personal interviews — face-to-face interviews conducted in public places
- focus groups — small groups of people who meet with the researchers
- electronic methods of collection — telephone, mail and Internet
- questionnaires — a set of specific questions requiring a response from the person.

The main benefit of a survey is that it gathers first-hand information that provides details of customers' opinions. However, gathering information through surveys is becoming more difficult because respondent rates are declining. To overcome this problem, marketing companies are testing the use of electronic methods of collecting information about consumer behaviour (see the Snapshot 'Tracking the moods, hour by hour').

Tracking the moods, hour by hour

Sydney is to be the venue for a new method of market research which aims to record consumer moods and media consumption at hourly interviews throughout the day.

Prompted by an alarm every hour, study participants will key answers to a series of questions into personal digital assistants (PDAs), a move that researchers say will give them a snapshot of what that person is doing and feeling at any particular time of the day.

Rather than limit the scope of questions to media consumption, the media agency behind the project, MindShare, says it wants to measure consumer moods and actions in order to be able to get a more complete picture of consumer behaviour.

The portability of the PDAs allows the agency to record every aspect of media consumption as well as the time the media was seen and, more importantly, what the person was doing when they viewed it.

Up to 60 media channels from beer coasters and point of sale to billboards and TV are included in the survey.

At the end of the two-day research period the PDAs are handed back and the information downloaded.

. . .

Liz Harley, MindShare Australia consumer insights director, who is running the Mindset program, said she expected to recruit smaller groups of consumers who fitted into particular demographics rather than go for a larger and more general omnibus.

'This is not about casting the net wide but rather getting a richness of certain consumer behaviour,' she said. 'The novelty factor could also help us get to those high value customers that would not ordinarily participate.'

Rather than bombard participants with lots of questions every hour she would prefer to keep questions to a minimum.

'That way they will feel as though they are in control a bit more and it won't seem as intrusive.'

Top questions on the hour

- Where are you?
- How do you feel?
- What are you doing?
- What can you see?
- How often do you do this?
- To what extent would you normally have noticed it?

The hope is that the new method will collect information about media consumption that is not recorded by other media-specific research tools. 'We are not trying to supplant those methods but rather fill in the gaps', she said.

MindShare, which is owned in Australia by STW and London's WPP Group, is pitching the idea to clients such as Nestlé and Kellogg's.

Source: The Sydney Morning Herald, 15 July 2004, p. 29.

SNaPSHOT Questions

1. What is the aim of the Mindset program?
2. What does the expression 'high value customers' mean?
3. Why do you think the market researchers want to measure the 'moods' (How do you feel?) and 'actions' (What are you doing?) of consumers?

The observation method

Observation involves recording the behaviour of customers. No interviews are involved and direct contact with respondents is avoided. Instead, the actions of the customers are systematically observed. Such methods can raise serious ethical issues, especially with regard to privacy.

Information may be gathered through:

- personal observation, such as when a researcher poses as a customer in a store
- mechanical observation, using camera, tape recorder or counting machines. For example, the scanner and cash register at a store checkout counter can record data on sales and customers' purchase patterns.

The Queen Victoria Building shopping precinct uses security monitors to evaluate foot traffic into and past shops at different times of day.

This method of data collection has become very popular over recent years, especially with the development of computerised technology. It is now possible for a business to access its loyalty program, customer spending habits and customer database all at once, through the use of smart cards and bar coding (see figure 11.4).

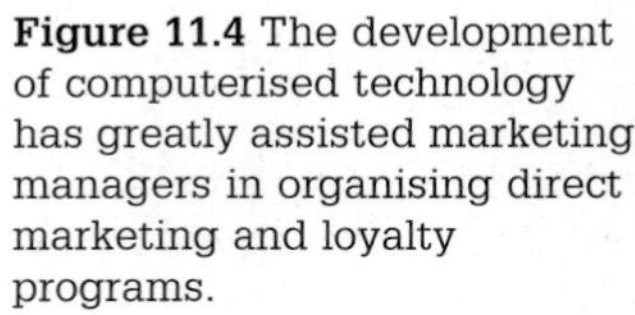

Figure 11.4 The development of computerised technology has greatly assisted marketing managers in organising direct marketing and loyalty programs.

Such observation methods can be highly accurate, but their main limitation is that they explain only *what* happens, not *why* it happens.

Experiments

Experiments involve gathering data by altering factors under tightly controlled conditions to evaluate cause and effect. Market researchers do this to determine whether changing one of the factors (a cause) will alter the behaviour of what is being studied (the effect).

Experiments may be carried out in either the laboratory or in the field. This is called test marketing.

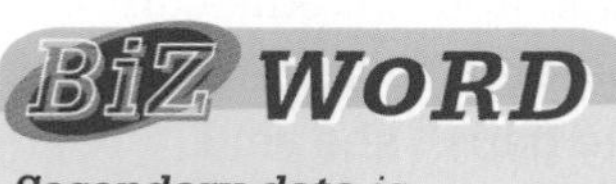

***Secondary data** is information that has already been collected by some other person or organisation.*

Secondary data

Secondary data comprises information that has already been collected by some other person or organisation. It is referred to as secondary because it is information that has been collected for some other purpose; for example, census data and household expenditure surveys gathered by government and private organisations (see figure 11.5).

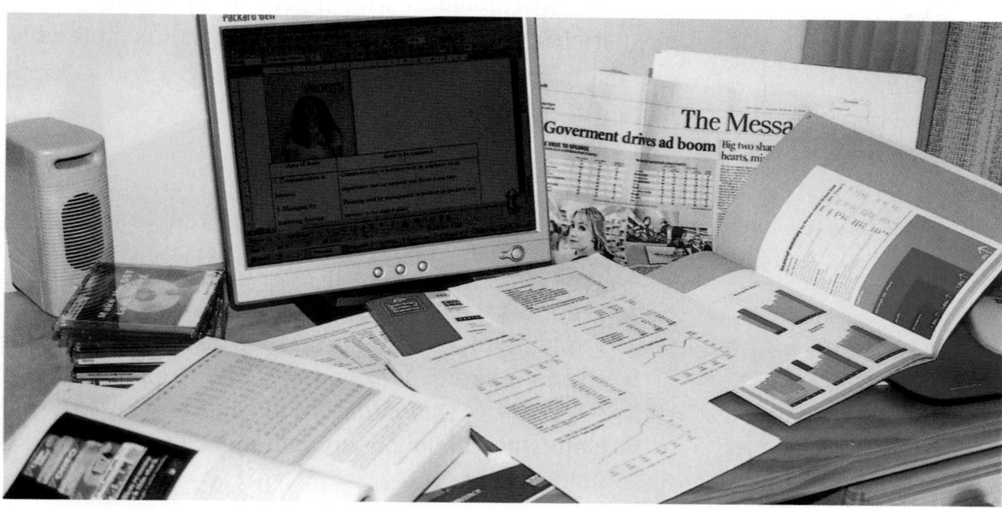

Figure 11.5 Secondary data market research

With the advent of computer databases, there is an abundance of secondary data available to market researchers.

There are two types of secondary data. These are:

- ***internal data***. This is information that has already been collected from internal sources — that is, from inside the business. Such data include financial statistics, annual and management reports, research reports, customer feedback and sales reports.
- ***external data***. This is published data from sources outside the business. Examples include magazines, industry association newsletters, government reports, Internet sources and private data collection agencies. Probably the best known are the numerous reports produced by the Australian Bureau of Statistics (ABS).

BiZ WORD

Internal data *refers to information that has already been collected from inside the business.*

External data *refers to published data from outside the business.*

Private firms such as AMR Quantum and ACNeilsen compile market research and prepare business reports covering a wide range of industries within the Australian economy. The Ray Morgan Research Centre monitors consumer and business spending, and compiles attitude data on 3000 Australian households. This organisation also monitors what a targeted group of customers read, when and what they watch on television, what they buy, where they buy and what they think of the different products.

Usually, market researchers will make use of both internal and external sources of data.

Businesses should begin all research efforts by collecting internal secondary data, which is the least expensive form of data to obtain.

11.4 Data analysis and interpretation

Once the data has been gathered, conclusions need to be drawn. Raw data is of little value until it has been analysed and interpreted. **Statistical interpretation analysis** is the process of focusing on the data that represents average, typical or deviations from typical patterns.

Statistical interpretation analysis *is the process of focusing on the data that represents average, typical or deviations from typical patterns.*

The first step in drawing conclusions (analysis and interpretation) is to tabulate the data — that is, display the information in table format. The use of a spreadsheet computer program greatly simplifies this task. Cross-tabulation will allow comparisons to be made between individual categories. For example, cross-tabulation could show

how men and women display different shopping habits, or the differences between the purchasing behaviour of high and low income earners.

This interpretation will largely be based on the marketing manager's judgement, experience and intuition. For this reason it is preferable to involve a number of people in the interpretation of data so as to gain a wider perspective and, therefore, avoid the error of personal bias.

EXERCISE 11.1 Revision

1. What is meant by the term 'market research'?
2. Explain why is it important for businesses to undertake market research.
3. Examine figure 11.3 on page 242. Create a mind map to show an outline summary of this information.
4. Complete the following sentences by selecting the correct term from the following list.

   relevant achieving information
   investigated resources objectives

   (a) Marketing managers should treat _________ in the same way as other _________ within the business.
   (b) Information collected must be _________ to the problem being _________.
   (c) Ultimately, relevant information will assist the business in _________ its marketing _________.
5. What is meant by the term 'data'?
6. Distinguish between primary and secondary data.
7. Identify each of the methods for gathering survey data. Under what circumstances should each be used?
8. Account for the increased use of electronic scanners to compile data.
9. Distinguish between surveys, observation and experimental methods of data collection.
10. Outline the difference between internal and external secondary data.
11. If a business were interested in cinema attendance within Australia, what secondary data sources could it access to locate this information?
12. Explain the purpose of analysis and interpretation of data.
13. Go to www.jaconline.com.au/businessstudies3e and click on the ACNielsen weblink for this textbook. What services does ACNielsen offer its clients?

Extension

1. Explain how you might use different types of market research (surveys, focus groups, observations and experiments) to determine customer reaction to a new kind of ice-cream.
2. Think about your school, or a business for which you work part-time.
   (a) Outline how the organisation collects and processes marketing information.
   (b) What is the information used for?
   (c) What secondary sources could be used to supplement this data?
3. Go to www.jaconline.com.au/businessstudies3e and click on the ABS weblink for this textbook. Find a set of market-related data available from the ABS. How might a business use this secondary data? List the data sources on a separate page.

4. As the owner of a supermarket, you believe you could sell more strawberries by displaying them loose on a tray, rather than packaging them in punnets.
   (a) Describe an experiment to test this idea.
   (b) Outline the difficulties in conducting the experiment.

11.5 Customer and buyer behaviour

Buyer behaviour *may be defined as the decisions and actions of people involved in buying and using products.*

Successful marketing begins with understanding why and how customers and buyers behave as they do. **Buyer behaviour** may be defined as the decisions and actions of people involved in buying and using products.

While market research asks questions such as 'Who are our customers?', 'What do they buy?', 'When do they buy?' and 'How often do they buy?', customer behaviour asks the question: 'Why do they buy?'

Marketing managers are better able to predict how customers may react to particular marketing strategies if they are aware of the factors that influence the buying behaviour of different types of customer

Figure 11.6 Understanding customer behaviour involves examining why customers buy particular products.

11.6 Types of customer

There are four types of customer, as shown in figure 11.7.

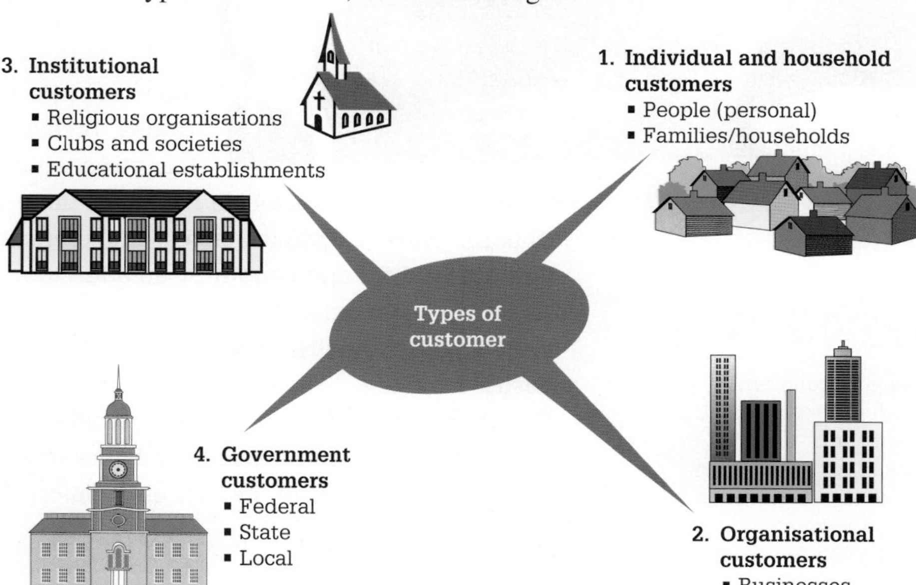

Figure 11.7 The four types of customer

Individual and household customers

Personal spending *refers to consumer purchases by individuals.*

Household spending *(or family spending) refers to the combined purchases of individuals living together.*

Personal spending refers to consumer purchases by individuals. **Household spending** (or family spending) refers to the combined purchases of individuals living together. This type of spending includes food, electricity and rent. Together these two groups make up the total consumer market, which consists of goods and services purchased for personal consumption. Many of the more visible marketing strategies, especially print and electronic advertising, are directed at this large buying group.

Children as customers

The 'kids' market, a subset of the individuals and households customer segment, currently attracts a great deal of marketing attention. Despite their fickle buying patterns, children interest marketing managers because of their surprising purchasing power and the influence they exert over many household purchase decisions (see the Snapshot 'KGOY — Kids Getting Older Younger').

KGOY — Kids Getting Older Younger

Who has an income of about $1.5 billion, spends $490 million and influences 67 per cent of all household spending each year? Answer: young people between the ages of 8 and 12, who marketing managers refer to as 'tweens'. Tweens today are exposed to a wider range of media messages than ever before. On average they will watch 22 000 television commercials a year. This, coupled with puberty happening earlier, results in these children taking on the behaviour of older teenagers. They are becoming much more consumer aware. Tweens are conscious of wearing clothes with the 'right' label and buying 'cool' products that have peer approval. Tweens, consequently, have enormous influence over their family's buying habits regarding soft drinks, breakfast cereal, ice-cream, clothes, leisure activities and even the household car.

Children influence household buying in three ways.

1. Children have individual tastes and preferences for particular products that are paid for and bought by an adult family member.
2. As children get older they begin to have their own income, usually in the form of pocket money. They, therefore, become buyers of the products they desire.
3. Children often influence the household's choice of products that are for shared use (for example, the family vacation) or even products used only by adults (for example, hi-tech electronics). Marketing managers refer to this as the 'nag' factor!

A research company, Brainchild, found that 30 per cent of the 600 children it surveyed said their parents asked them for advice when choosing the family car.

Marketing managers are aware that today's children are tomorrow's consumers. Many businesses, therefore, want to develop children as users of their products so that they will buy as adults.

There is a worrying side, however, to the millions of dollars spent annually marketing to young children. Children lack the sophistication and maturity to withstand the subtle effects of carefully targeted commercial messages. Some people argue that the intrusive nature of the marketing, and the large increase in the intensity that businesses use to sell their products to children, has resulted in the commercialisation of youth. They argue that children have become 'victims' of brands, which influence what they wear, eat, watch, read, listen to and talk about with each other.

SNaPSHOT Questions

1. What influences are causing young children to take on the behaviour of older teenagers?
2. Outline how children can influence household buying.
3. Marketing to young children raises what ethical issues?

Business customers

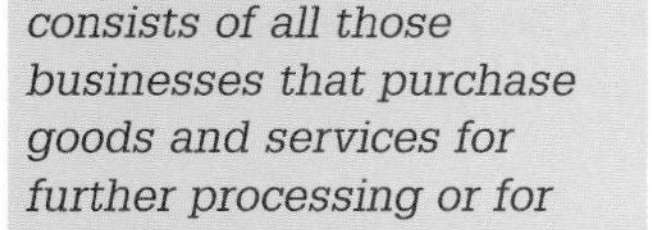

*The **business market** consists of all those businesses that purchase goods and services for further processing or for use in their production process.*

The **business market** consists of all those organisations that purchase goods and services for further processing or for use in their production process. For example, a manufacturer buys materials and component parts to use directly in the production of products.

Although this market has fewer customers than the individuals and households market, it is of much larger volume in terms of dollars spent and products purchased.

Most firms, especially large businesses, have a number of experienced, well-trained buyers. Their purchasing is usually more professionally handled than that of ordinary consumers. Overall, firms' buying decisions are much more detailed and formal than buying by individuals and households.

Institutional customers

***Institutional customers** consist of schools, hospitals, clubs, churches and other non-profit organisations.*

Collectively, these customers are referred to as institutional customers. **Institutional customers** consist of schools, hospitals, clubs, churches and other non-profit organisations. These institutions purchase millions of dollars' worth of products annually to provide goods and services to students, patients, congregations, club members and others.

Because institutions often have limited budgets and different objectives, marketing managers need to devise special marketing strategies to serve these customers.

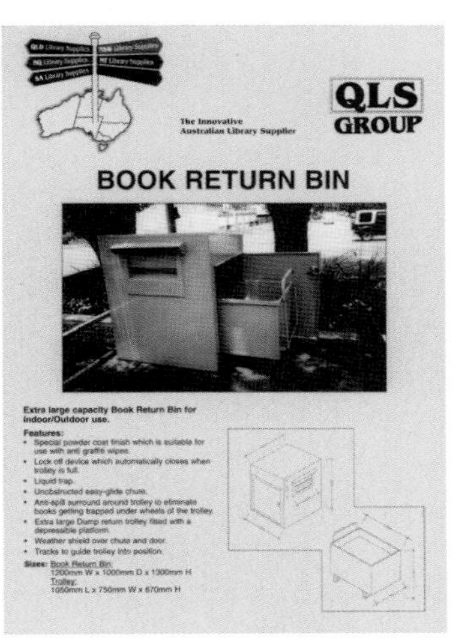

Figure 11.8 Queensland Library Supplies markets to institutional customers.

Government customers

Governments spend billions of dollars each year for a wide variety of goods and services, ranging from paperclips to battleships.

Because government agencies spend public funds to buy the products needed to provide services, they are accountable to the public. Therefore this accountability requires a much more formalised set of buying procedures (often referred to as 'red tape').

***Tendering** is a process whereby firms submit quotes to supply a good or service. The lowest bid that meets the specifications is usually accepted.*

Governments make many of their purchases through a process called **tendering**, where firms submit quotes to supply a particular good or service. The lowest bid that meets the specifications is usually accepted. However, the lowest price tender does not necessarily have to be selected if the business submitting the tender cannot comply with other terms of the contract, such as delivery dates or technical support.

EXERCISE 11.2 Revision

1. What is meant by the term 'buyer behaviour'?
2. List the four types of customer.
3. Distinguish between individual and household customers.
4. Examine a range of advertisements aimed at children. In groups of three or four, discuss the ethics of marketing to children. Record your ideas and present them to the rest of the class.
5. Outline the main difference between business customers and household customers.
6. Identify the main organisations that make up institutional customers.
7. Describe the process of tendering.
8. Draw a table in your notebook similar to the one below. Use it to classify the following customers.
   (a) Mulwaree High School
   (b) The Tai Long family
   (c) St Patrick's Church
   (d) Fine Foods Pty Ltd
   (e) Megan Holmes
   (f) Mulwaree Shire Council
   (g) CSR Ltd
   (h) Department of Health
   (i) Crookwell RSL Club
   (j) Geissler Motors Pty Ltd

Types of customer			
Individuals and households	**Businesses**	**Institutions**	**Government**

Extension

1. Identify the reasons why a government customer would use a tendering process.
2. Select four advertisements for business goods and services, and identify the buying motives they appeal to.
3. 'Effective marketing is of increasing importance in today's competitive environment.' Examine how businesses can market more effectively to other businesses.

11.7 The buying process

All customers tend to follow common steps in the buying process, as revealed in figure 11.9.

It is important to remember that when a customer purchases a product, it is not an act but a *process*. A consumer, therefore, usually undertakes a number of these steps when deciding on a purchase. However, consumers' buying behaviours differ when they buy different types of products. For example, when purchasing low-cost, frequently purchased items, most consumers carry out a routine response involving very little research or decision-making effort. When expensive items are purchased, the consumer usually undertakes extensive decision making, including price, product, warranty, after-sales service and delivery costs comparisons. The steps involved in this process are very similar to the buying behaviour of organisations.

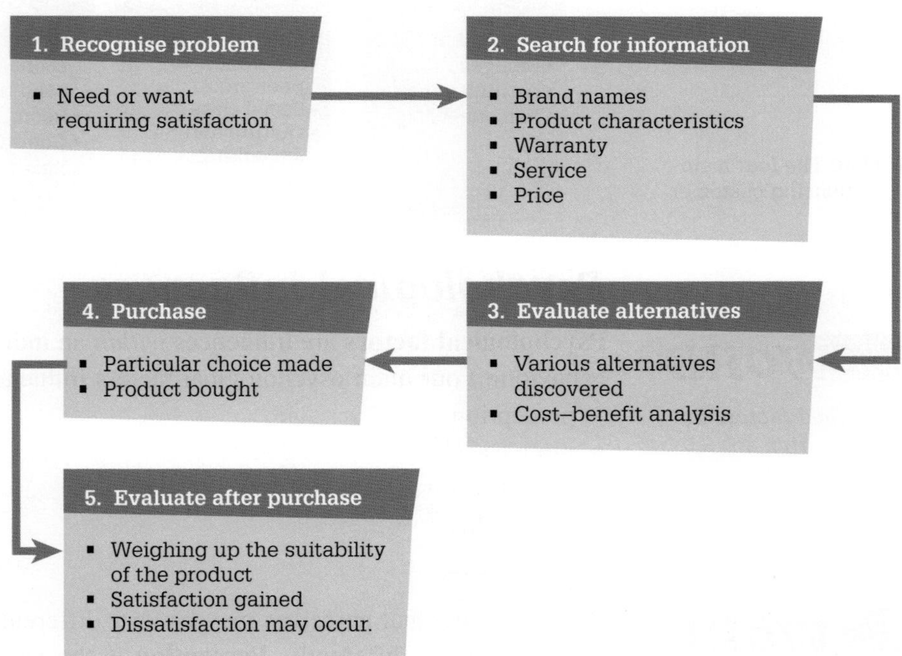

Figure 11.9 Common steps in the buying process

Organisational buyers consider a product's price, its quality and the back-up service provided by the supplier. Usually, a committee or group of people, rather than a single individual, decides which product to purchase. The purchaser's decision normally includes inspection, sampling and negotiation.

Buyers and users

A **buyer** is the individual or group who purchases the product.

A **user** is the individual or group who actually uses the product being purchased.

One important difference between the buying process of the consumer and organisational groups is the distinction between buyers and users. A **buyer** is the individual or group who purchases the product. A **user** is the individual or group who actually uses the product being purchased. In the vast majority of consumer purchases, the individual is both the buyer and the user. The consumer buys the product for his or her own immediate use.

Organisational purchases, however, are quite different. Buyers, sometimes called purchasing agents, select suppliers and negotiate the terms of purchase. The users are the individuals in the organisation who actually use the product being purchased. While they may have commenced the purchasing process, they usually do not act as the buyer. It is important that the buyer has a clear understanding of the needs of the user so that appropriate products are purchased.

11.8 Factors influencing customer choice

Four main factors influence both consumer and organisational purchasing decisions (see figure 11.10).

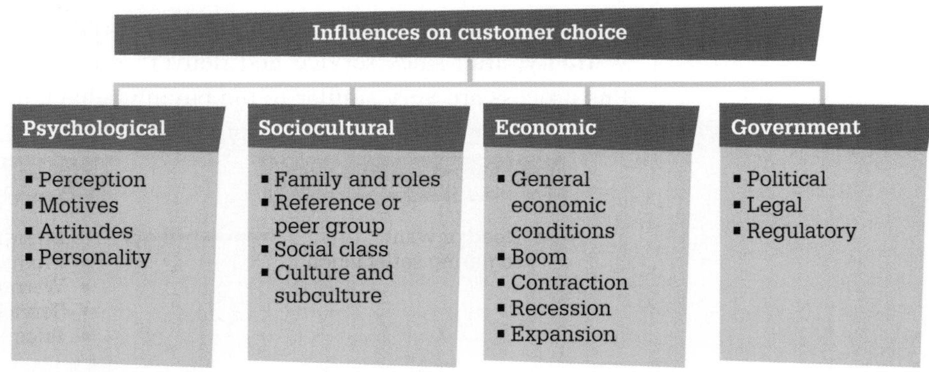

Figure 11.10 The four main factors influencing customer choice

Psychological influences

BiZ WoRD

Psychological factors *are influences within an individual that affect his or her buying behaviour.*

Psychological factors are influences *within* an individual that affect his or her buying behaviour. Four main psychological factors influence customer choice. These are:

- perception
- motives
- attitudes
- personality.

Perception

Perception *is the process through which people select, organise and interpret information to create meaning.*

What an individual perceives may be very different from reality; people see and hear the same things differently. **Perception** is the process through which people select, organise and interpret information to create meaning. Usually there is a range of perceptions across different individuals. An example of how one image can be perceived in two different ways is revealed in figure 11.11. Does drawing (a) show an old or young woman? The interpretation of drawing (a) depends on whether you have been previously exposed to drawings (b) or (c).

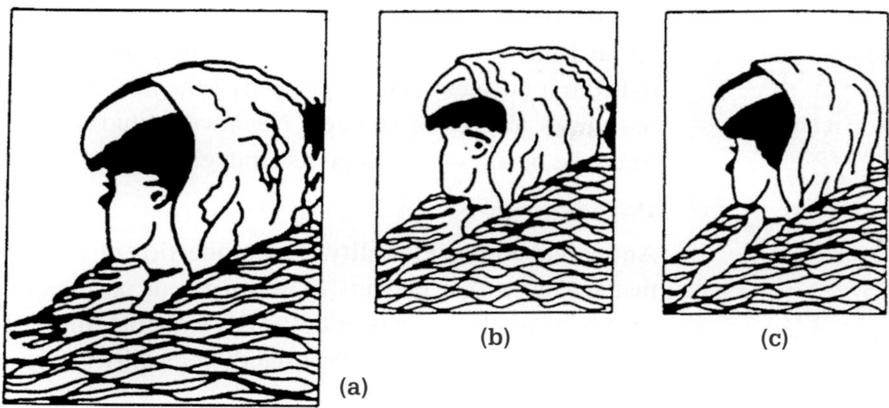

Figure 11.11 One image — two perceptions

As individuals we often act on our perceptions of reality rather than reality itself. Consequently, marketing managers are extremely aware that they must create a positive or favourable perception about their product in the mind of the customer. Customers will not normally purchase a product that they perceive as poor.

Obviously advertising attempts to create a positive perception about the product. For example, the perception you have of a product is often the result of some type of advertising, which attempted to create a certain 'image' of the product — images such as trendy, luxurious, classy, fun and rebellious. In reality, the product may not necessarily have such qualities. It may be more to do with how consumers perceive the product.

Motives

> **BiZ WoRD**
>
> *A **motive** is the reason that makes an individual do something.*

A **motive** is the reason that makes an individual do something. The main motives that influence customer choice include comfort, health, safety, ambition, taste, pleasure, fear, amusement, cleanliness and the approval of others. As with the customer's perception of the product, advertising also attempts to influence an individual's motives (for instance, the desire to emulate a sporting hero). That is, advertising attempts to motivate the customer to buy the product.

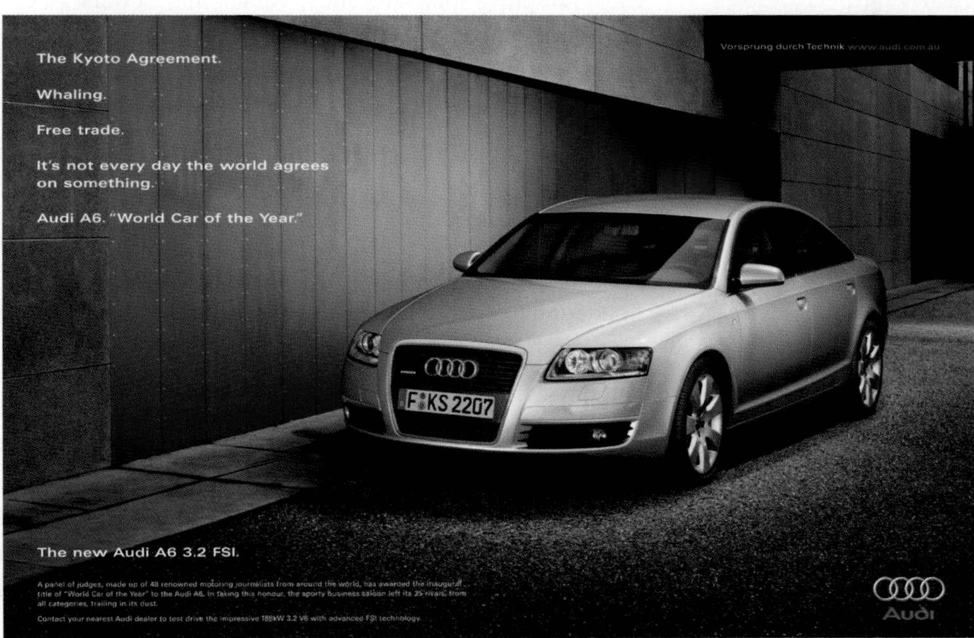

Figure 11.12 Advertising attempts to influence both perception and motives.

*An **attitude** is a person's overall feeling about an object or activity.*

*An individual's **personality** is the collection of all the behaviours and characteristics that make up that person.*

***Sociocultural influences** are forces exerted by other people and groups that affect an individual's buying behaviour.*

Attitudes

An **attitude** is a person's overall feeling about an object or activity. Customer attitudes to a business and its products generally influence the success or failure of the business's marketing strategy. Negative attitudes to a business or its products often force the business to change its strategies.

Personality

An individual's **personality** is the collection of all the behaviours and characteristics that make up that person. To some extent personality will influence the types and brands of product a person buys. For example, the style of car, clothing or jewellery that a person buys may reflect their personality.

Sociocultural influences

Whereas psychological influences are internal forces, **sociocultural influences** are forces exerted by other people and groups that affect customer behaviour. There are four main sociocultural factors. They are:

- family and roles
- reference (peer) group
- social class
- culture and subculture.

Family and roles

All of us occupy different roles within the family and groups within the wider community. These roles influence buying behaviour. For example, although women's roles are changing, market research shows that most women still make buying decisions related to health-care products, food and laundry supplies. Also, as we noted in section 11.6, children are making and influencing many household purchasing decisions.

Reference (peer) groups

*A **reference** or **peer group** is a group of people with whom a person closely identifies, adopting their attitudes, values and beliefs.*

A **reference** or **peer group** is a group of people with whom a person closely identifies, adopting their attitudes, values and beliefs. A customer's buying behaviour may change to match the rest of the group's beliefs and attitudes. For example, if a close friend tells you of a bad experience at a particular shop you will probably change your buying behaviour based on this information. Alternatively, if your peer group wears distinctive clothing you probably make clothing purchases based on this influence.

Social class

In our society, the factors generally used to classify people are education, occupation and income. Social class, therefore, influences the type, quality and quantity of products a customer buys. For example, higher income earners may purchase luxury cars that symbolise their status, and are more likely to shop in upmarket retail stores.

Culture and subculture

Culture is all the learned values, beliefs, behaviours and traditions shared by a society. Culture influences buying behaviour because it infiltrates all that we do in our everyday life. It determines what people wear, what and how they eat, and where and how they live. For example, in response to the greater desire for nutritious and healthy foods, many low-fat, sugar-free and fibre-enriched processed food products are now marketed.

Figure 11.13 The desire for a healthy lifestyle has led to the marketing of a wide range of organic products.

Economic influences

Economic forces have an enormous impact on both business and customers. They influence a business's capacity to compete and a customer's willingness and ability to spend. Economies do not always experience constant growth. Rather, the level of economic activity fluctuates — from boom to contraction to recession to expansion and back to boom conditions. Each of these four distinct phases influences the marketing environment in the following ways.

Boom

A boom is a period of low unemployment and rising incomes. Businesses and customers are optimistic about the future. Businesses increase their production lines, and attempt to increase their market share by intensifying their promotional efforts. Customers are willing to spend because they feel secure about their jobs and source of income. This phase can be referred to as the 'good times'. The marketing potential during such a phase is large, with sales responding to all forms of promotion.

Economies fluctuate from boom conditions (the 'good times') to contraction (the 'cautious times') to recession (the 'pessimistic times') to expansion (the 'quietly hopeful times') and back to boom conditions.

Contraction

A contraction is a period of slowly rising unemployment with incomes stabilising. The mood changes from optimism to one of caution and if this phase lasts for a long time, customers and businesses become pessimistic. Such caution and pessimism result in customers reducing their spending. Customers become more price-conscious. They look for value and products that are functional and long-lasting.

Marketing plans should, therefore, stress the value and usefulness of a product. This phase is often referred to as the 'cautious times'.

Recession

A recession sees unemployment reach high levels and incomes fall dramatically. Customers and businesses lack confidence in the economy and a mood of deep pessimism persists. Customer and business spending reach very low levels. The marketing plan during this time should concentrate on maintaining existing market share. Survival becomes the main business objective. This phase can be referred to as the 'pessimistic times'.

Expansion

In the expansion phase, unemployment levels start to fall slowly and incomes begin to rise. During the expansion phase, marketing managers need to modify their marketing plans to tap into this rising prosperity. Increasing market share once again becomes an important objective. This phase can be referred to as the 'quietly hopeful times'.

Government influences

Government economic policies directly or indirectly influence business activity and customers' spending habits, and, as such, will influence the marketing plan.

Governments use a number of economic policy measures to influence the level of economic activity. Depending on the prevailing economic conditions, the government will put in place policies that expand or contract the level of economic activity. These policies directly or indirectly influence business activity and customers' spending habits and, as such, will influence the marketing plan.

Of more direct and immediate impact on the marketing plans of a business is the influence of government regulations. Regulatory forces consist of laws and regulatory bodies that can influence business behaviour. Such regulatory forces exert a significant influence over the marketing activities of businesses because the breaking of these laws or regulations may result in financial penalties.

A number of laws, such as the *Trade Practices Act 1974* (Cwlth), *Sale of Goods Act 1923* (NSW) and the *Fair Trading Act 1987* (NSW), have been passed that influence marketing decisions. Marketing managers need to be fully informed about the regulations that directly influence their marketing plan, especially fair trading laws regarding misleading, deceptive or unconscionable conduct.

EXERCISE 11.3 *Revision*

1. Give an example of a situation in which you have been both the buyer and user. Now describe a situation in which you as the buyer will not be the user.
2. Which of the four psychological influences that affect buying behaviour do you think is the most important? Provide reasons for your answer.
3. What is meant by the terms 'perception' and 'motive'? Why would market researchers study customer perceptions and motives?
4. How and why do marketing managers attempt to alter consumer perception?
5. Distinguish between the sociocultural and psychological factors that influence customer choice.
6. Collect a number of print advertisements from a magazine. Suggest the psychological and/or sociocultural influence to which each advertisement is appealing.
7. Explain how roles affect buying behaviour.

8. Identify the different types of reference group. How do they influence buying behaviour? Name some of your own reference groups.
9. In what ways does social class affect a person's buying behaviour?
10. Describe a subculture to which you belong. Identify purchases that are unique to your subculture.
11. Copy the following table into your notebook. Show the impact that economic conditions may have on the marketing plan by completing the table. The first phase has been completed for you.

Economic phase	Economic conditions	Impact on the marketing plan
1. Boom	▪ Low unemployment ▪ Rising incomes ▪ Sense of optimism ▪ Production increasing ▪ Consumers willing to spend	▪ Marketing potential large ▪ Luxury items ▪ Promotion and sales are relatively easy
2. Contraction		
3. Recession		
4. Expansion		

12. Why is it important for a business to monitor economic conditions?
13. Explain how government policies and regulations influence the marketing environment.
14. Go to www.jaconline.com.au/businessstudies3e and click on the NSW Office of Fair Trading weblink for this textbook and then answer the following questions.
    (a) What is the main requirement of the Fair Trading Act?
    (b) What is the role of the Office of Fair Trading?
15. Prepare a summary of this chapter. A summary condenses the important issues and concepts presented in the chapter. Go to www.jaconline.com.au/businessstudies3e to compare your finished summary with the one provided for this textbook.

Extension

1. Provide an example of a recent purchase in which you followed in full all the steps in the buying process. What sources of information did you use to help you make the decision? As a marketing manager, how could you make use of the steps in the buying process model?
2. Research the tasks undertaken by an organisation's buying centre. Who are the individuals who make up a typical buying centre? Outline their functions.
3. 'Through knowledge of customer buying behaviour, marketing managers can learn to manipulate customers to purchase their products.' Write a paragraph examining the validity of this statement.
4. 'Perception is reality; what we think is true about a product does not matter.' Critically analyse this statement.

CHAPTER 12

Developing marketing strategies

12.1 Introduction

The marketing mix may be varied when a business wants to reach different target markets.

A business controls four basic marketing strategies to reach its target market. These four strategies or tools of marketing (the four Ps) are:

1. product — anything that satisfies a need or want and can be offered in exchange
2. price — the value placed on what is exchanged
3. promotion — activities used to communicate to a target market persuasive, positive information about a business and its products
4. place — methods used to get the product to the customer.

Together these strategies form the marketing mix, as shown in figure 12.1. The marketing mix is the centrepiece of the marketing plan.

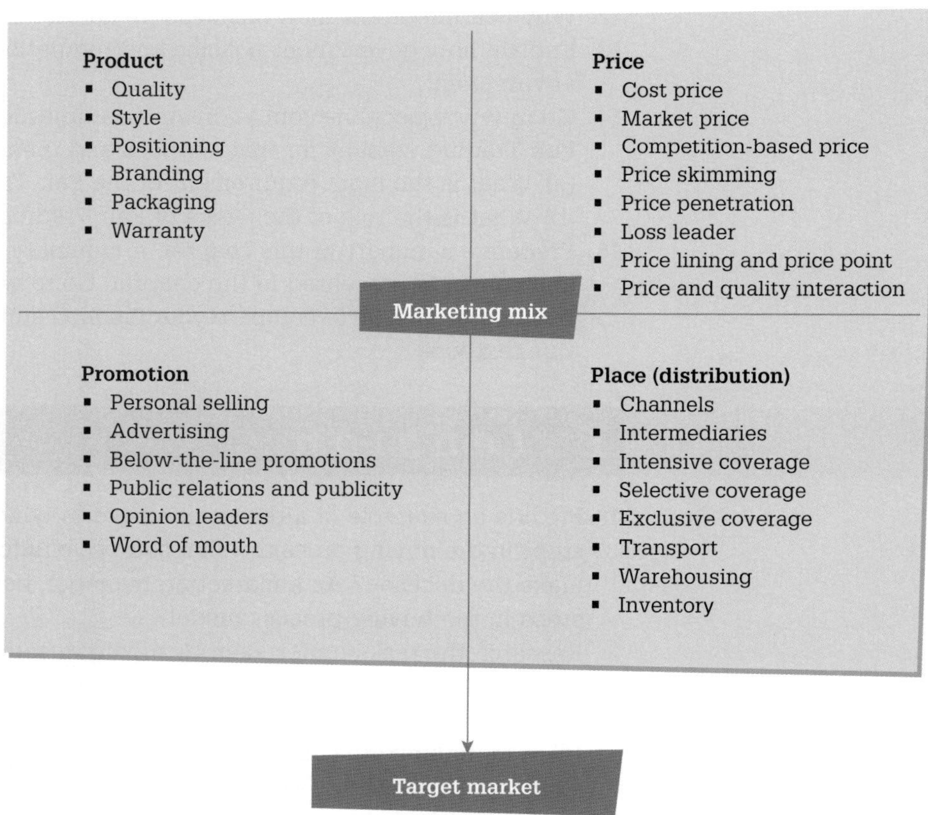

Figure 12.1 The four Ps of the marketing mix

A business can alter its marketing mix by varying any one or more of the four marketing strategies. Consequently, a business may adopt one marketing mix to reach one target market and a different marketing mix to reach another target market.

12.2 Market segmentation and differentiation of products and services

The ultimate aim of market segmentation is to increase sales and profits by better understanding and responding to the desires of the target customers.

A business segments its markets so it can direct its marketing strategies to specific groups of customers rather than the total market. This allows the business to better satisfy the wants and needs of a targeted group. This occurs because the business is able to:

- use its marketing resources more efficiently
- understand the buying behaviour of the target market better
- collect data more effectively and make comparisons within the target market over time
- refine the marketing strategies used to influence customer choice.

Few businesses can sell their products to the entire market — the market is just too big. Therefore, a business will divide the total market into distinct market segments. Once the market has been segmented, the marketing manager selects one of these segments to become the target market (see figure 12.2).

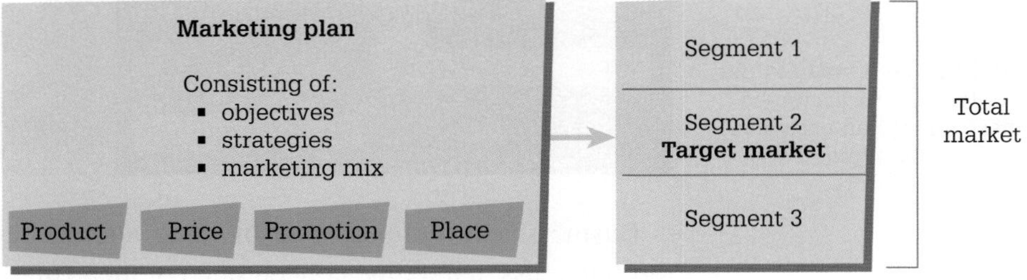

Figure 12.2 Selecting a market segment to be the target market

The total market can be segmented into one of two very broad types: consumer (household) markets and organisation/business markets.

The total market can be segmented into one of two very broad types: consumer (household) markets and organisation/business markets. Each of these broad segments can be further segmented. For example, the consumer market can be segmented according to demographic, geographic, lifestyle and behavioural variables (see table 12.1).

TABLE 12.1 Common variables for segmenting customer markets

Demographic	Geographic	Lifestyle	Behavioural
▪ Age ▪ Gender ▪ Education ▪ Family size ▪ Family life cycle ▪ Occupation ▪ Social class ▪ Religion ▪ Ethnicity	▪ Region ▪ Urban ▪ Suburban ▪ Rural ▪ City size ▪ Climate ▪ Landforms	▪ Lifestyle ▪ Personality ▪ Motives ▪ Socioeconomic group ▪ Consumer opinions and interests	▪ Purchase occasion ▪ Benefits sought ▪ Loyalty ▪ Usage rate ▪ Price sensitivity

The ability to choose the correct target market is an important marketing function because it will influence the entire marketing mix.

Sometimes a business may be able to identify a primary and a secondary target market. A **primary target market** is the market segment at which most of the marketing resources are directed. A **secondary target market** is usually a smaller and less important market segment.

*The **primary target market** is the market segment at which most of the marketing resources are directed.*

*A **secondary target market** is usually a smaller and less important market segment. For example, customer research conducted by Sportsgirl revealed a primary target market of 18- to 25-year-old females and a secondary target market of 26- to 40-year-old females.*

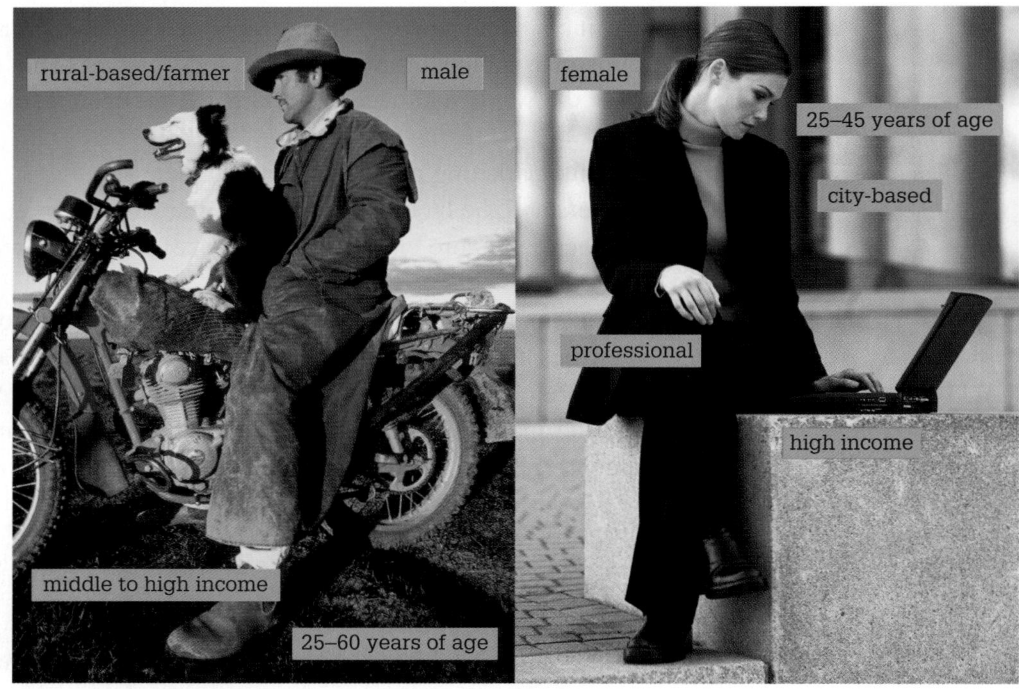

Figure 12.3 The primary target market for (a) a rural supplies business and (b) an exclusive city fashion boutique

Businesses can choose one of three approaches to selecting a target market — through mass marketing, concentrated or niche marketing, or differentiated marketing.

Mass marketing approach

***Mass marketing** or a **total marketing** approach seeks a large range of customers. Products that can be marketed using the mass marketing approach include basic food items, water, gas and electricity.*

*A **concentrated market approach** requires the business to direct its marketing mix towards one selected segment of the total market.*

A **mass marketing** or **total marketing** approach seeks a large range of customers. With this approach, the business's marketing mix is aimed at a wide customer market. The mass marketing approach assumes that individual customers in the target market have similar needs and, therefore, a single marketing mix will satisfy all. The single marketing mix will have one type of product, one standard price, one promotional strategy aimed at all customers and one method of delivery.

Concentrated or niche markets

This approach is the opposite to the mass marketing approach. The **concentrated market approach** requires the business to direct its marketing mix towards one selected segment of the total market. For example, although the automobile market consists of numerous segments, Mercedes-Benz concentrates on the 'luxury segment'. By using this concentrated market approach, the business is able to analyse its customer base more closely, design strategies to satisfy this select group's needs and develop particular products based on customer feedback.

An extension of the concentrated approach is that of the niche market, which is a narrowly selected target market segment. In a sense it is a segment within a segment, or a 'micromarket'. For example, an exclusive fashion boutique can carve out a niche market and, therefore, avoid direct competition with large department stores. In the last few years, some hotels have developed a niche market for their own 'boutique' beers, brewed on the premises.

The needs of customers in these markets are often neglected by large businesses because it is rarely profitable for them to alter their marketing mix for very small groups.

Differentiation of products and services

The existence of targeted markets has caused businesses to implement a marketing strategy of product differentiation. **Product differentiation** occurs when products that are the same or similar are made to appear different and/or better than those of their competitors (see figure 12.4). The difference could be as simple as changes to the packaging or labelling, or more complex, such as offering top quality service, greater convenience, more features, better value for money or products that are environmentally friendly. These factors all play a part in persuading consumers to perceive the product as being superior to all similar products and, therefore, influencing them to buy it. Examples include jeans with designer labels, washing detergent with brightener additives and sports shoes with specific brand names.

BiZ WoRD

***Product differentiation**, in its broadest sense, is the process of developing and promoting differences between the business's products and those of its competitors.*

Figure 12.4 Freedom Foods, a producer of a wide range of healthy foods, highlights the specific product characteristics of its Rice Puffs with Psyllium to differentiate it from competitors' products.

The marketing mix is greatly influenced by the nature of the selected target market and the specific product characteristics that the business wishes to highlight.

EXERCISE 12.1 Revision

1. Identify the four marketing strategies that make up the marketing mix.
2. What is meant by the terms 'market segmentation' and 'target market'?
3. Look back at table 12.1 (page 259) and explain what is meant by the terms 'demographic', 'geographic', 'lifestyle' and 'behavioural'.
4. Explain the difference between primary and secondary target markets.
5. Determine the primary target market for the following products or stores:
   (a) Coca-Cola
   (b) Rolls Royce
   (c) Levi's jeans
   (d) Year 11 mathematics textbook
   (e) David Jones

6. Elaborate on the difference between mass, concentrated and niche markets. Provide examples of products that would be found in each of these markets.
7. Here are five different market segments:
   (a) Young married couple, no children
   (b) Female teenager, part-time worker
   (c) Older single person, female, retired
   (d) Younger single person, male, working
   (e) Male teenager, full-time student

   Listed on the next page are 10 products. Copy the list into your notebook and, beside each item, write the most appropriate market segment letter for that product. In some cases you may want to write more than one letter. Compare your answers with those of the rest of the class.
   (a) Financial advice ________
   (b) Ballet tickets ________
   (c) Bus tour ________
   (d) *Dolly* magazine ________
   (e) Health insurance ________
   (f) Sony MP3 player ________
   (g) Rover lawnmower ________
   (h) School textbook ________
   (i) Computer ________
   (j) Furniture ________
8. Outline the purpose of product differentiation.
9. For four specific products with which you are familiar, illustrate how they are differentiated from their competitors.

Extension

1. Provide reasons explaining why the mass marketing approach has declined in recent years. Does this mean there is no place for mass marketing? Explain your answer.
2. Once the total market is segmented, a business selects a target market. Outline the different ways in which a market may be segmented. Explain why having a clear understanding of the target market improves the efficiency of the marketing plan.

12.3 Products and services

A ***product*** *is a good or service, an idea or any combination of the three that can be offered in an exchange.*

A **product** is a good or service, an idea or any combination of the three that can be offered in an exchange. When you buy a CD you are purchasing a *good*. It is a real, physical object that can be touched; it is tangible. The advertising campaign for the CD is an *idea*. The sales assistant at the music store provides a *service*. Ideas and services are intangible. Therefore, when customers purchase products, they buy both the tangible and intangible benefits (attributes) — a *total product concept*.

The term 'product' is a much broader concept than most people understand. Usually when people talk about products, they refer to what a company produces, such as motor cars or video recorders. And yet the intangibles that come with these products are also important. They can be used to differentiate one business's product from that of its competitor.

When customers purchase products, they buy both the tangible and intangible benefits — a total product concept.

Often, with mass-produced products, it is on the differences in the intangible benefits that product competition is based. For example, cars are basically a means of transportation used to get from one place to another. If this was all they were, then there would be only one model. But a car contains a vast array of intangibles that are used to differentiate each model, such as image, reputation, style, and safety record. Viewing the car in terms of a total product concept clearly shows that no two cars are exactly the same. All products, then, are a combination of tangible and intangible attributes.

Positioning

***Product positioning** refers to the development of a product image as compared with the image of competing products.*

Some brand names, such as Rolex, Ferrari, No Frills and Trax, can immediately evoke an image of the product's quality. This image gives the product its position within the market. **Product positioning** refers to the development of a product image as compared with the image of competing products.

In highly competitive markets, sales may be difficult to secure. For this reason, a business will attempt to create an image that differentiates its product from the others. Many businesses invest considerable resources in the positioning of their product. The business will decide on the image it wishes to create for a product and will use other elements of the marketing mix to shape and maintain this image.

Whenever a new product is launched, the marketing manager needs to have clearly determined the desired positioning of the product. This will be achieved through the product's name, price, packaging, styling, promotion and channels of distribution. Combined, these individual characteristics create the image of the product (see the Snapshot 'A well-positioned, and "sophisticated" product').

A well-positioned, and 'sophisticated', product

Recently, Ferrero Australia, maker of Ferrero Rocher and Nutella, launched Bueno, a wafer and hazelnut cream chocolate bar, onto the Australian market. Bueno will compete with Mars Bar, Cherry Ripe and Kit Kat for a slice of the $610 million chocolate bar market.

Prior to the national launch, Ferrero Australia undertook extensive market research, including product sampling, concentrated on the Gold Coast. Much of the market testing was to gather information to accurately position the new product. Over the 18-month test period Bueno successfully gained a place in the top 10 per cent of chocolate bar sales.

Ferrero Australia decided to position its product as a 'sophisticated taste experience'. At the centre of this 'experience', and what differentiates Bueno from the other chocolate bars, is the unique light, crispy wafer and the creamy hazlenut filling the parent company in Italy developed. This allowed the company to market something completely different, not just an imitation of its competitors. An extensive advertising campaign will reinforce the perception of the product's unique taste experience. As a result of correctly positioning the product Ferrero Australia is able to sell Bueno for a slightly higher price than its competitors.

SNaPSHOT Questions

1. Why was it important for Ferrero Australia to correctly position Bueno?
2. What is the purpose of the advertising campaign?

Branding — symbols and logos

Popular brand names

Levi's	Uncle Tobys	Holden	Colgate
Kellogg's	Arnott's	Sorbent	Cadbury
McDonald's	Mars	Telstra	Qantas
Coca-Cola	Reebok	KFC	Mambo
Vegemite	Weet-Bix	Speedo	Sony

Figure 12.5 Examples of brand names — how many do you recognise?

*A **brand** is a name, term, symbol, design or any combination of these that identifies a specific product and distinguishes it from its competition.*

*A **brand name** is that part of the brand that can be spoken.*

*A **brand symbol** or **logo** is a graphic representation that identifies a business or product.*

Read the list of brand names in figure 12.5 and test yourself: what products do you associate with each brand name? Your score was probably 20 out of 20. You have just experienced the power of *brand name recognition*. The 20 businesses that market these brands have spent a lot of money making sure customers instantly recognise their brand name and the products associated with them. A brand name can be a powerful marketing tool. A **brand** is a name, term, symbol, design or any combination of these that identifies a specific product and distinguishes it from its competition. A **brand name** is that part of the brand that can be spoken. It may include letters (BMW motor vehicles); numbers (4711 perfume); numbers and letters (3M tapes); or pronounceable symbols, like the ampersand in Johnson & Johnson. A **brand symbol** or **logo** is a graphic representation that identifies a business or product, as shown in figure 12.6.

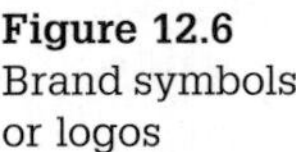

Figure 12.6 Brand symbols or logos

A brand symbol does not have to duplicate the words in the brand name. The three-pointed star of the Mercedes-Benz and Coca-Cola's distinctive narrow-waisted bottle are famous brand symbols. Some businesses encourage the instant recognition of their brand symbol rather than their brand name. Perhaps the most famous example of this technique is the 'golden arches' symbol used by McDonald's. Nike's 'swoosh' symbol has also become a brand symbol with a high recognition value. Notice how in some advertisements the brand name does not appear at all, only the brand symbol. This is a clever and subtle method used to reinforce the meaning of the symbol and associate it with a brand name.

***Manufacturer's** or **national brands** are those owned by a manufacturer.*

Brands are usually classified according to who owns them. When a manufacturer owns a brand name it is referred to as a **manufacturer's brand** or **national brand**.

A **private** or **house brand** is one that is owned by a retailer or wholesaler.

Generic brands are products with no brand name at all.

A **trademark** signifies the brand name or symbol is registered and the business has exclusive right of use.

Packaging involves the development of the container and the graphic design for a product.

Common examples of manufacturer's brands include Sunbeam appliances, Kraft Foods and Mambo Clothing. These brands have high appeal with customers because they are recognised across the country, are widely available and offer reliability with constant quality.

A **private** or **house brand** is one that is owned by a retailer or wholesaler. These products are often cheaper because the retailer or wholesaler can buy at lower costs. For example, Myer sells its own label products including Reserve, Basque, Urbane, Blaq, Bauhaus, Wild Rhino and Miss Shop.

Generic brands are products with no brand name at all. Carrying only the name of the product and in plain packaging, these generic brands have been available in supermarkets since the mid 1970s. Examples include Black and Gold (Davids Holdings), No Frills (Franklins), Home Brand (Woolworths) and Farmland (Coles).

To guard against other businesses using its brand name or symbol, a business can apply to have the name registered. This gives the business exclusive rights to use the name or symbol and protect it from infringement. The symbols TM or R at the end of a brand name signify that the name or symbol is a registered **trademark**.

Packaging

If the brand name becomes well recognised, the business will also enjoy a carry-over effect when new products are introduced. This gives it a distinct competitive advantage.

Packaging involves more than simply putting the product in a container or placing a wrapper around it. **Packaging** involves the development of a container and the graphic design for a product.

The packaging of a product is sometimes as important as the product itself to assist sales. Well-designed packaging will give a positive impression of the product and encourage first-time customers. For example, tasteful packaging can create an image of luxury, sensuality and exclusiveness, helping to promote the product. In addition, packaging helps preserve, inform, protect and promote the product (see figure 12.7).

Recent years have seen significant changes in the range of packaging available. Product tampering has become a problem for marketing managers, and safer packaging is required. Child-resistant caps, safety seals and pop-top openings have been introduced to lessen the problem. Blister packaging was introduced to help reduce shoplifting.

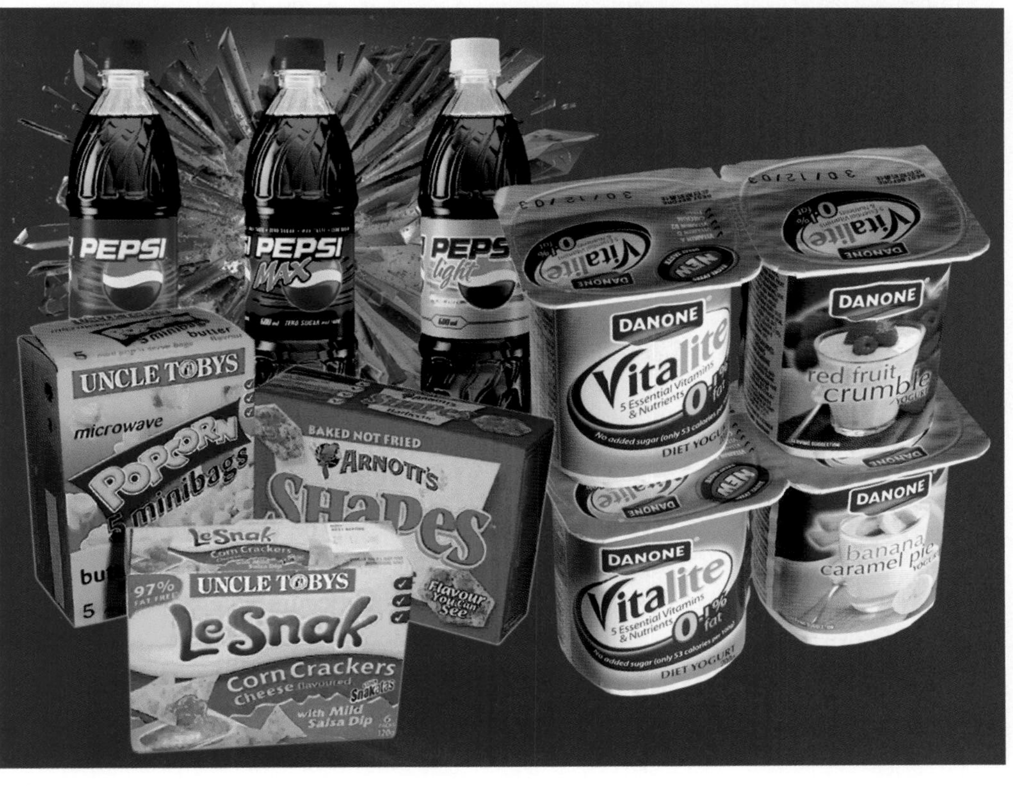

Figure 12.7 Packaging helps to preserve, inform, protect and promote the product.

With increasing community awareness of environmental pollution, marketing managers must also be sensitive to the problems caused by throw-away packaging. Approximately half of all household garbage consists of discarded packaging.

12.4 Price and pricing methods

***Price** refers to the amount of money a customer is prepared to offer in exchange for a product.*

Many factors affect the price of a product. **Price** refers to the amount of money a customer is prepared to offer in exchange for a product. Many businesses have difficulty selecting the 'correct' price for their products. A price set too high could mean lost sales unless superior benefits are offered. A price set too low may give customers the impression that the product is 'cheap and nasty'. Somewhere between these extremes is a correct price for a product.

In any market, businesses will attempt to gain some control over the price by differentiating their products. Once this happens, the business has more leverage over the price. For example, clothes with designer labels, such as Levi's, Country Road and Billabong, are the result of product differentiation strategies. These labels can set higher prices for their garments than clothing sold under the Target or Kmart brand labels.

Pricing methods

Levels of supply and demand for accommodation in the snow fields, for example, fluctuate dramatically between summer and winter seasons, and prices rise and fall accordingly.

Once a business has decided on its objectives, it must then select a pricing method. There are three main pricing methods — cost plus margin, market and competition-based.

Cost plus margin

This is the simplest method. The business determines the total cost of production and then adds an amount for profit. This extra margin is referred to as the mark-up.

Market

Instead of using costs to determine price, businesses sometimes set prices according to the level of supply and demand — whatever the market is prepared to pay. When demand is high, prices are high. When demand is low, prices fall.

Competition-based

This method is often used when there is a high degree of competition from businesses producing similar products. A business can choose a price that is either below, equal to or above that of the competitors.

***Price skimming** involves charging the highest price possible for innovative products.*

***Price penetration** occurs when a business charges the lowest price possible for a product or service so as to achieve a large market share.*

Pricing strategies

A number of strategies can be used by a business when determining the price of the product, including the following:

- ***Price skimming***. This occurs when a business charges the highest price possible for innovative products — that is, they 'skim the cream' off the market.
- ***Price penetration***. This occurs when a business charges the lowest price possible for a product or service. The strategy aims to quickly achieve a large market share for a product and is sometimes called 'mass-market pricing'.

Being a **loss leader** involves deliberately selling a product below its cost price to attract customers.

Price lining is a pricing strategy used mainly by retailers where a limited number of prices, or price points, are set for selected lines or groups of merchandise.

- ***Loss leader***. For a special promotion many businesses, especially retail stores, deliberately sell a product below its cost price to attract customers to the shop. Although the business makes a loss on this product, it hopes that the extra customers will buy other products as well.
- ***Price lining***. Price lining (or price points) is a pricing strategy used mainly by retailers. The business chooses a limited number of key prices or price points for selected product lines. For example, a jeweller may offer a line of watches priced at $35, and a more expensive line of watches at $55.

Price and quality interaction

You have probably heard the expression 'You get what you pay for'. To marketing managers, this saying describes the price–quality relationship. Normally, products of superior quality are sold at higher prices. This is usually due to the higher manufacturing cost involved in producing them.

This perceived price–quality relationship helps determine the image customers have of products or brands. Therefore, if a business charges a low price for a product, customers may perceive the product as 'cheap'. Charge a high price and the product develops an aura of quality and status. This pricing strategy is referred to as **prestige pricing** and is designed to encourage status-conscious consumers to buy the product. Rolls Royce cars and Cartier accessories are products sold at prestige pricing. Sometimes, the price is set artificially high to imply a prestigious or quality image when, in reality, the quality may not be much superior to cheaper alternatives.

Prestige pricing is a pricing strategy where a high price is charged to give the product an aura of quality and status.

This price–quality relationship does not apply to all products. Usually, high-priced and infrequently purchased items such as cars, homes and furniture display a stronger price–quality relationship than frequently purchased products such as grocery items. As well, consumers may believe that high prices reflect either expensive packaging or market exploitation. This may lead to a reduction in sales because the consumer perceives there to be little actual difference between the quality of a low- and high-priced item.

Figure 12.8 You get what you pay for!

EXERCISE 12.2 Revision

1. Explain why marketing managers prefer to use the term 'total product concept' rather than simply 'product'.
2. What is meant by the term 'product positioning'?
3. What image do the following products convey?
   (a) *Cosmopolitan* magazine

(b) *The Australian Financial Review*
(c) Country Road clothing and accessories
4. Suggest reasons why businesses spend so much money attempting to establish a brand name and brand symbol.
5. Describe the functions of packaging. Why is packaging critical to the success of a product?
6. What is meant by the term 'price'?

Extension

1. Explain why some customers are prepared to pay a high price for a product while other customers would not buy the product, even if the price was low. What does that tell you about the relationship between price and customer tastes and preferences?

12.5 Promotion

__Promotion__ describes the methods used by a business to inform, persuade and remind a target market about its products.

__Promotion mix__ is the various promotion methods a business uses in its promotional campaign. Methods include:
- *personal selling*
- *advertising*
- *below-the-line promotions*
- *publicity and public relations.*

People usually associate promotion with marketing because it involves the business communicating directly with the customer. **Promotion** describes the methods used by a business to inform, persuade and remind a target market about its products.

To achieve these objectives of informing, persuading and reminding, a promotion campaign attempts to:
- attract new customers by heightening awareness of a particular product
- increase brand loyalty by reinforcing the image of the product
- encourage existing customers to purchase more of the product
- provide information so customers can make informed decisions
- encourage new and existing customers to purchase new products
- change individuals' behaviour through information or persuasion.

Many people confuse promotion with advertising because of its visibility and frequency. However, advertising is just one of the four elements of the promotion mix. A **promotion mix** is the various promotion methods a business uses in its promotional campaign.

Elements of the promotion mix

When developing a promotional campaign, businesses can choose from four methods: personal selling, advertising, below-the-line promotions, and publicity and public relations. Examples of each of the promotion methods are shown in figure 12.9.

Personal selling

__Personal selling__ involves the activities of a sales representative directed to a customer in an attempt to make a sale.

Personal selling involves the activities of a sales representative directed to a customer in an attempt to make a sale. The major advantage of this method is that the message can be modified to suit the individual customer's circumstances. Complex and technical products, in particular, require the personal contact of a sales representative to familiarise the customer with the product.

The success of the marketing plan often depends on the competency of the business's sales force, without which sales and revenue would soon decrease.

PUBLICITY

What's new?

Software news and reviews by **Ita Chen**

The Executive Drive (TED)

Amid the avalanche of new computer products released onto the market each day comes an exciting new software package from Integrated Logistics (IL) — The Executive Drive, affectionately known as TED.

Targeted at the novice computer user, TED is a fully integrated, self-paced instructional package designed to equip business executives for careers in the computer age.

This Australian-made product is the result of extensive market research and has been three years in development. TED will meet the needs of a wide range of potential customers.

As with other IL computer products, a 24-hour help line is available, a feature many competing products cannot match. TED has been approved by the Australian Computer Users Network and comes with a full guarantee. Retail price is $89.95. For more details contact your local computer retailer or visit IL's website at www.intlogistics.com.au.

BELOW-THE-LINE PROMOTION

PERSONAL SELLING

ADVERTISING

Figure 12.9 The promotion mix: examples of publicity, below-the-line promotion, personal selling and advertising

Advertising

Advertising *is a paid, non-personal message communicated through a mass medium.*

Advertising is a paid, non-personal message communicated through a mass medium. Because of the myriad of products available, advertising is an essential tool for successful marketing. In Australia, businesses spend approximately $9 billion a year on various forms of advertising.

The form and presentation of advertisements have changed over time, but the purpose of advertising — to inform, persuade and remind — has remained constant.

Advertising is one of the main forms of promotion used to attract potential customers by creating a demand for the product, informing, and communicating essential information.

Advertising may take many forms, from buying time on national television to inexpensive leaflets or posters. All businesses need to develop the most cost-effective means to advertise their products. **Advertising media** is a term for the many forms of communication used to reach an audience. The five main advertising media and the advantages and disadvantages of each are summarised in figure 12.10.

***Advertising media** refers to the many forms of communication used to reach an audience.*

Other types of advertising media include:

- *direct mail*
- *catalogues*
- *billboards.*

TELEVISION

Advantages	Disadvantages
▪ Large audience reach ▪ Select time spot to reach specific audience	▪ High cost ▪ Remote control and channel-hopping ▪ Short life span

RADIO

Advantages	Disadvantages
▪ Specific programs to reach selected audience ▪ Most accessible medium ▪ Cheaper than TV	▪ Radio 'noise' — uncritical listening ▪ Small area coverage

NEWSPAPERS

Advantages	Disadvantages
▪ Reasonable cost — depending on circulation ▪ Local and national coverage ▪ Timely — can be placed the day before	▪ Short life span ▪ Cannot target specific market ▪ Usually only black and white

MAGAZINES

Advantages	Disadvantages
▪ Specific target markets ▪ Colour ▪ More prestigious than newspapers ▪ Longer life span	▪ High cost ▪ Lack immediacy

ONLINE (Internet)

Advantages	Disadvantages
▪ Gaining in popularity ▪ Global reach ▪ Live banners ▪ Richer interaction with customers ▪ Colour and movement	▪ Web surfers do not click through ▪ High establishment and maintenance costs ▪ Slow downloads ▪ Consumer resistance

Figure 12.10 Advantages and disadvantages of selected advertising media

Below-the-line promotions

Below-the-line promotions *are promotional activities for which the business does not make use of an advertising agency.*

Below-the-line promotions are promotional activities for which the business does not make use of an advertising agency. The promotional activities are designed and developed 'in-house'. These activities include exhibitions, point-of-sale material, demonstrations and direct marketing.

The 'line' is an imaginary boundary between those businesses that pay a commission to external advertising agencies and those that do not. Two types of below-the-line promotional activities that are increasing in popularity include direct-mail catalogues and telemarketing.

Publicity and public relations

Publicity *is any free news story about a business's products.*

Publicity is any free news story about a business's products. It differs from advertising in that it is free and its timing is not controlled by the business.

As with the other promotion methods, the main aim of publicity is to enhance the image of the product.

A business will use publicity to raise awareness of a product, highlight the organisation's favourable features and help reduce any negative image that may have been created.

Public relations *are those activities aimed at creating and maintaining favourable relations between a business and its customers.*

Public relations are those activities aimed at creating and maintaining favourable relations between a business and its customers. It is the role of public relations personnel to design, implement and manage the publicity events of the business.

Figure 12.11 The difference between advertising and publicity

The communication process

A ***channel*** *is any method used for carrying a message.*

Noise *is any interference or distraction that affects any or all stages in the communication process.*

The main role of promotion is to communicate with consumers or organisations directly or indirectly so as to influence their buying behaviour.

Marketing managers must be able to communicate clearly, efficiently and succinctly to their target markets. If the communication process becomes distorted or inefficient then the message becomes distorted. The resulting miscommunication may mean lost sales. Without effective communication, promotion is wasted.

Marketing managers can use a variety of channels to deliver a message. A **channel** is any method used for carrying a message. Two of the most common channels used for promotional communication include print and electronic media advertising. Any

With the advent of the remote control many consumers are 'channel-hopping' during commercial breaks. This habit is of concern to marketing managers as it is a type of 'noise' that is difficult to overcome.

interference or distraction that affects any or all stages in the promotional communication process is referred to as **noise**. Examples of noise include faulty printing, competing messages, inappropriate language or images, jargon, misinterpretations or — perhaps one of the most common — people having conversations and fetching refreshments during commercial breaks.

To determine the effectiveness of the communication process, the marketing manager needs some form of feedback. However, marketing managers may not receive immediate feedback in the form of increased sales or changed consumer behaviour. To overcome this problem, marketing managers use a variety of strategies. Asking the consumer to complete a survey provides the marketing managers with a basic level of feedback.

Often customers may be more willing to purchase a product if the message comes via a respected and trusted channel, such as an opinion leader, or by word of mouth.

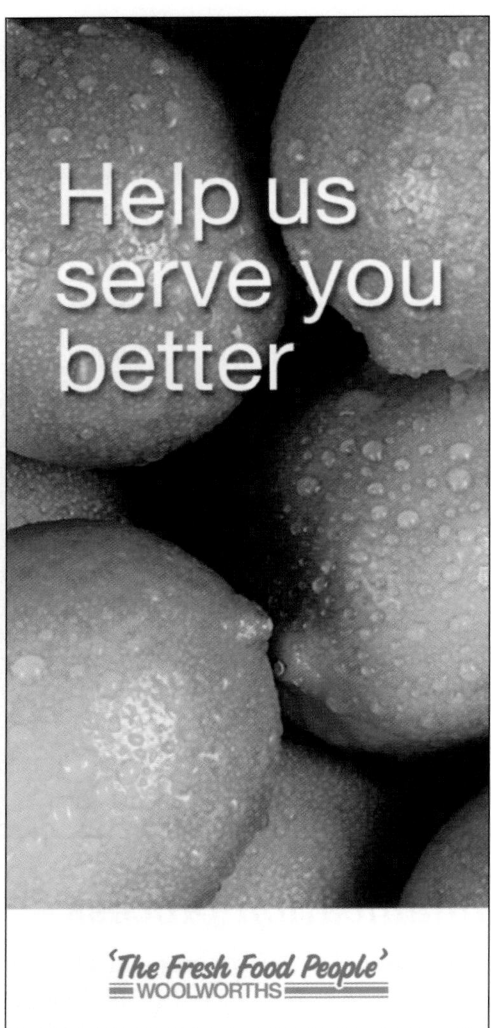

Figure 12.12 Encouraging feedback from the consumer

Opinion leaders

*An **opinion leader** is a person who influences others.*

An **opinion leader** is a person who influences others. Their opinions are respected, and they are often sought out for advice.

Marketing managers use opinion leaders as information outlets for new products or to endorse an existing one. Actors, athletes, musicians and models are regarded by some groups as opinion leaders.

Word of mouth

Word-of-mouth communication *occurs when people influence each other during conversations.*

Consumers tend to trust word-of-mouth communication more than business-sponsored commercials, especially if the message is being communicated by a friend or opinion leader. This is because the receiver places more trust in someone they know as opposed to a business advertising its products. When people influence each other during conversations it is called **word-of-mouth communication**.

Friends' recommendations are very important, especially for the purchase of services. Often we will use the services of a mechanic, dentist or hairdresser if they have been recommended by a friend.

12.6 Place (distribution)

Distribution channels and reason for intermediaries

Channels of distribution *or* ***marketing channels*** *are the routes taken to get the product from the factory to the customer.*

The final 'p' of the marketing mix (product, price, promotion and place) is 'place', or channels of distribution. **Channels of distribution** or **marketing channels** are the routes taken to get the product from the factory to the customer. This process usually involves a number of intermediaries, such as the wholesaler, broker, agent or retailers. Apart from the retailer the other intermediaries are often 'invisible', with the customer knowing very little about their role and operation.

The four most commonly used channels of distribution are described below.

1. *Producer to customer.* This is the simplest channel and involves no intermediaries. Virtually all services, from tax advice to car repairs, use this method.
2. *Producer to retailer to customer.* A retailer is an intermediary who buys from producers and resells to customers. This channel is often used for bulky or perishable products such as furniture or fruit.
3. *Producer to wholesaler to retailer to customer.* This is the most common method used for the distribution of consumer goods. A wholesaler is an intermediary who buys in bulk, from the producer, then resells in smaller quantities to retailers.
4. *Producer to agent to wholesaler to retailer to customer.* An agent distributes products to wholesalers but never owns the product. Agents are paid a commission by the producer. Usually agents are used for inexpensive, frequently used products. A business that does not have any sales representatives will often use an agent instead.

Channel choice — including intensive, selective and exclusive

Market coverage *refers to the number of outlets a firm chooses for its product.*

How a business chooses the channel of distribution best suited to its product depends largely on the location of the business's market or market coverage. **Market coverage** refers to the number of outlets a firm chooses for its product.

A business can decide to cover the market in one of three ways as follows, the difference being the intensity of coverage:

1. *Intensive distribution.* This occurs when the business wishes to saturate the market with its product. Customers can shop at local outlets and be able to purchase the

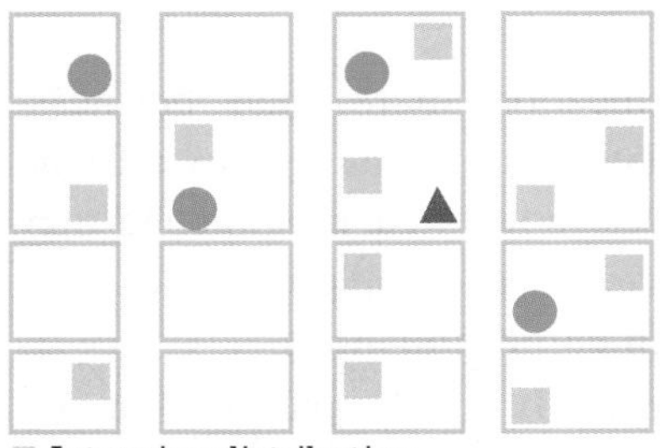
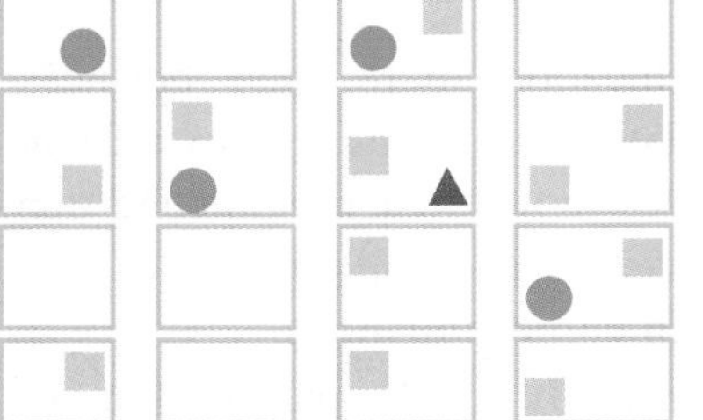

■ Intensive distribution
● Selective distribution
▲ Exclusive distribution

Figure 12.13 Market coverage

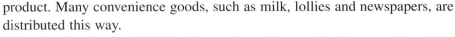

product. Many convenience goods, such as milk, lollies and newspapers, are distributed this way.

2. *Selective distribution.* This involves using only a moderate proportion of all possible outlets. Clothing, furniture and electrical appliances are often distributed using this method. The customer is prepared to travel and seek out a specific retail outlet that stocks a certain brand.
3. *Exclusive distribution.* This is the use of only one retail outlet for a product in a large geographic area. This method of distribution is commonly used for exclusive, expensive products.

Figure 12.13 illustrates the three levels of market coverage.

Physical distribution issues

BiZ WoRD

Physical distribution *is all those activities concerned with the efficient movement of the products from the producer to the customer.*

Physical distribution is all those activities concerned with the efficient movement of the products from the producer to the customer. Physical distribution is, therefore, the movement of the products themselves through their channels of distribution. It is a combination of several interrelated functions including transportation, warehousing and inventory control.

Transport

An intricate network of transportation is required to deliver the vast array of products on supermarket shelves. Developments in packaging and transportation now permit Australian native flowers, for example, to be picked then sold in Tokyo within 24 hours.

The method of transportation a business uses will largely depend on the type of product and the degree of service the business wishes to provide. The four most common methods of transportation are rail, road, sea and air.

Figure 12.14 Transporting and warehousing are important aspects of the physical distribution process.

***Warehousing** is a set of activities involved in receiving, storing and dispatching goods.*

Warehousing

Warehousing is a set of activities involved in receiving, storing and dispatching goods. A warehouse acts as a central organising point for the efficient delivery of products.

***Inventory control** is a system that maintains quantities and varieties of products appropriate for the target market.*

Inventory

Customers find it frustrating when a product they wish to purchase is 'out of stock', and a business that repeatedly allows this to happen will lose sales and market share. To avoid this, businesses may implement an **inventory control** system. If a business carries too much stock on its inventory, it will experience high storage costs. However, too little stock results in lost sales or 'stock-out costs'. The goal of inventory is to find the correct balance between these two situations.

12.7 Environmental effects on distribution

Businesses need to choose specific distribution methods carefully. They need to be aware of those forces in the total marketing environment that will directly influence the distribution of their products, especially technology and local government regulations.

Technology

***Non-store retailing** is retailing activity conducted away from the traditional store.*

Businesses are always looking for different ways to distribute their products. The purchasing of products from a store or a supplier is the oldest and most common form of distribution. **Non-store retailing** — that is, retailing activity conducted away from the traditional store, is gaining in popularity. Methods such as door-to-door selling, mail-order catalogues, party-plan merchandising and vending machines have been used for a number of years. However, with rapid changes in electronic communication businesses are beginning to exploit types of electronic marketing as alternative methods. Two of the most rapidly developing methods are telemarketing and Internet marketing.

Telemarketing

'But wait, if you ring this number in the next 15 minutes we'll throw in a set of steak knives absolutely free.' Does it sound familiar? This is just one example of telemarketing, which is the use of a telephone to make a sale. The logical extension of telemarketing is the area of interactive technology, which will allow customers to purchase via their television or personal computer.

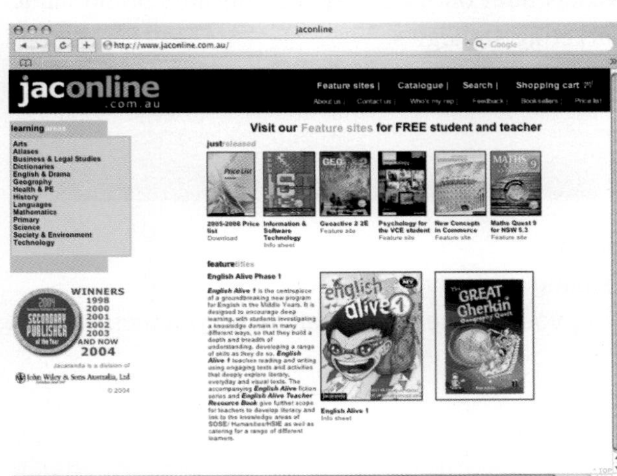

Figure 12.15 Internet shopping is changing the traditional distribution channels.

Interactive technology and Internet marketing

There is a current rush by businesses to use the World Wide Web as a promotional tool. US research suggests that businesses are moving away from the telephone and onto the Internet for product communication. It is now relatively easy for any business to obtain a domain name and a website and begin marketing its products via the Internet (see the example in figure 12.15).

Predictions are that the younger generation (14- to 17-year olds) who have grown up with the Internet will access it more frequently when they want to shop.

As more people use the Internet for shopping, the traditional distribution channels will be modified. Some retailers and wholesalers may be bypassed as customers deal directly with manufacturers. Electronic, post and parcel delivery channels will be used more extensively to meet the increasing demand.

Local government

Business owners sometimes feel they are overregulated. Licences, permits, approvals and authorities must all be taken into account. All business owners have a legal obligation to observe the statutory regulations when setting up and operating a business. Fulfilling all legal obligations may be frustrating at times. Local government regulations will have a direct impact on the distribution channels.

Many business owners overlook the importance of local government regulations. Any business using premises or land must first seek local government approval. Commencing to trade before approval is obtained could result in the closure of the business. Local governments have control over the following business activities: determining land zoning and the purpose for which a building or land can be used; approving new development applications and alterations to existing premises; fire regulations, especially the provision of adequate fire-prevention facilities; parking regulations governing the number of spaces that need to be provided; health regulations; and the size, shape and location of business signs.

12.8 Marketing techniques of the Coca-Cola company — an overview

The Coca-Cola Company uses a wide variety of marketing techniques to maximise sales (see figure 12.16). In the last year, 1.6 billion litres of Coca-Cola were sold in Australia, out of total worldwide sales of 17.1 billion litres. Since the early 1950s, teenagers and young adults have grown up believing that this product truly is a part of their lives: 'Coke is it'. Through its sophisticated promotion strategies and selling techniques, the Coca-Cola Company has built on its highly recognisable brand name by constantly implementing new marketing strategies.

EXERCISE 12.3 Revision

1. What is the main role of promotion?
2. Distinguish between personal selling and advertising.
3. Which advertising medium would you choose for the following products? Give reasons for your choices.
   (a) IBM computers
   (b) Toys for children
   (c) Nike sports shoes
   (d) School textbooks
   (e) A hairdressing salon

Figure 12.16 Marketing techniques used by the Coca-Cola Company

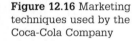

4. Suggest reasons why below-the-line promotion is increasing in popularity among marketing managers.
5. 'Advertising is what you pay for and publicity is what you pray for.' Explain.
6. Explain why efficient communication is important to marketing managers.
7. Devise a marketing channel for the sale of:
   (a) a daily newspaper
   (b) a washing machine
   (c) an imported motor vehicle
   (d) office furniture.
8. What is meant by the term 'market coverage'?
9. From the following products, determine those that are intensively, selectively or exclusively distributed.
   (a) Coca-Cola
   (b) Ferrari motor vehicles
   (c) Billabong clothing

(d) Streets ice-cream
(e) Samsung televisions
(f) compact discs
(g) rare coins
(h) Arnott's biscuits
(i) Dairy Farmers milk

10. Suggest reasons why a business would select an exclusive rather than an intensive distribution strategy.
11. Which method of transportation would be most appropriate for the following products? Give reasons for your answer.
    (a) Coal to Japan
    (b) Wheat to the silo
    (c) Sheep to the market
    (d) Fresh fruit to Tokyo
    (e) Iron ore from the mine to the port
    (f) Pepsi to the supermarket
12. List the activities involved in warehousing.
13. 'Holding either too little or too much stock is to be avoided.' Elaborate. What system can a business adopt to prevent either situation?
14. List four examples of traditional non-store retailing.
15. In groups of three or four, brainstorm the advantages and disadvantages to a business of selling via the Internet. Select a spokesperson to share the group's comments with the rest of the class.
16. Prepare a summary of this chapter. A summary condenses the important issues and concepts presented in the chapter. Go to www.jaconline.com.au/businessstudies3e to compare your finished summary with the one provided for this textbook.

Extension

1. Why is it important to identify the target market when designing an advertising program?
2. 'Advertising creates unrealistic expectations that many consumers can never attain.' Comment.
3. As technological advances continue, how would you expect smaller businesses, less able to afford to update their technology, to compete against larger, more efficient businesses?
4. Online shopping is predicted to grow rapidly during this decade. One particular business gaining an increasing market share of online shopping is Yahoo! shopping. Go to www.jaconline.com.au/businessstudies3e and click on the Yahoo! Shopping weblink for this textbook. Evaluate the ease of navigating this site.

13 Ethical and legal aspects of marketing

13.1 Introduction

In marketing, as with all business practices, there are ethical and legal dilemmas involved. Although the many laws regulating marketing strategies prescribe legal standards, ethical standards are more difficult to define.

In a recent survey of 350 Australian and overseas marketing managers, 64 per cent responded 'yes' to the question: 'Is it reasonable behaviour to bend the law if you do not actually break it?' How would you answer this question?

Most marketing decisions can be judged ethical or unethical, legal or illegal. Sometimes, however, it is not so clear cut. For example, some individuals may argue that if a certain marketing practice is within *reasonable* ethical and legal limits, then it is not really illegal or unethical. The difficulty with this approach is that what may be considered reasonable by one person could appear totally unreasonable to another. The concept of 'reasonable' limits lends itself to interpretation.

As figure 13.1 reveals, there are four basic positions a marketing manager can adopt.

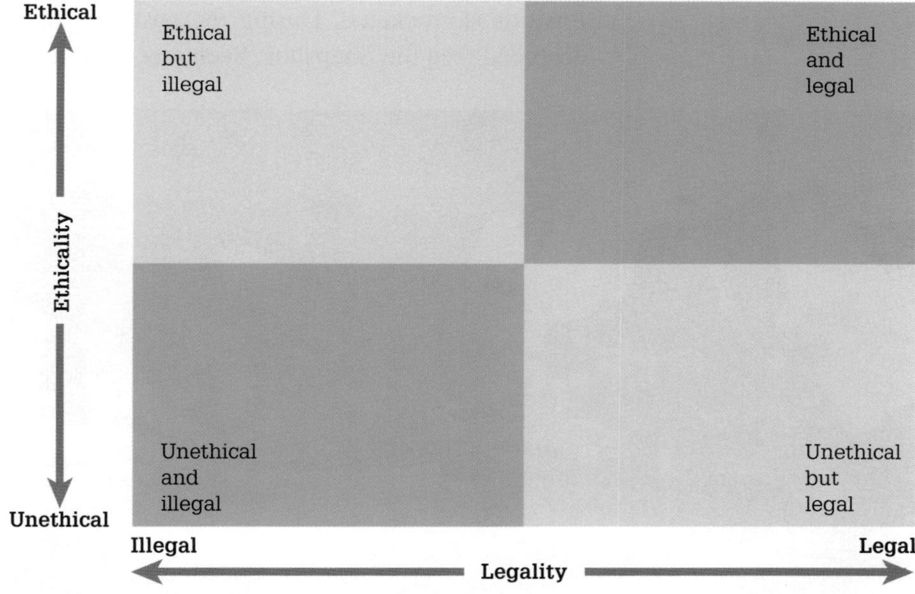

Figure 13.1 The four basic legal and ethical positions

Some marketing managers still believe that being ethical costs money and that there is conflict between ethics and profits. However, more research suggests the opposite. Aligning business values and operations to a high moral philosophy actually improves the bottom line.

The ethical and legal position adopted by a marketing manager is ultimately determined by individual judgement. Judgement is influenced by:

- an individual's personal moral philosophies
- an organisation's culture and code of ethics
- the marketing environment.

Marketing managers should never forget that the business exists because of its customers. By satisfying customers a business may operate profitably. Dishonest or unethical marketing managers ultimately drive customers away.

Two marketing strategies that have raised the concerns of many commentators relate to the ethics of sponsorship deals and product placement.

Figure 13.2 The ethical dilemmas of sponsorship

The ethics of sponsorship deals

One area receiving a great deal of attention is the ethical issues related to company sponsorship arrangements, especially those involving schools. It is not unusual to have a sportsground named after a team's sponsor or for the players to wear the sponsor's logo on their uniforms. However, it would be considered unusual to have pupils attending a school named, for instance, Coca-Cola Primary School!

Sponsorship arrangements open up a variety of ethical problems, such as:

- over-commercialisation of schools
- direct marketing to children
- health implications of promoting some food and drink products
- influence on the school curriculum.

The ethics of product placement

***Product placement** is the inclusion of advertising into entertainment.*

Chances are that you, along with thousands of other film-goers, have seen the films *Matrix Reloaded*, *Minority Report* or *GoldenEye*. All these movies used a promotion strategy referred to as **product placement**: the inclusion of advertising into entertainment. For example, in *Matrix Reloaded*, when the characters travel through time (teleport) they do so through a Samsung mobile phone with the Samsung logo clearly visible. In the first *Matrix* film, teleporting was via Nokia phones, sales of which afterwards skyrocketed. During the past few years, product placement has become widespread (see the Snapshot 'Seen any good movies lately?').

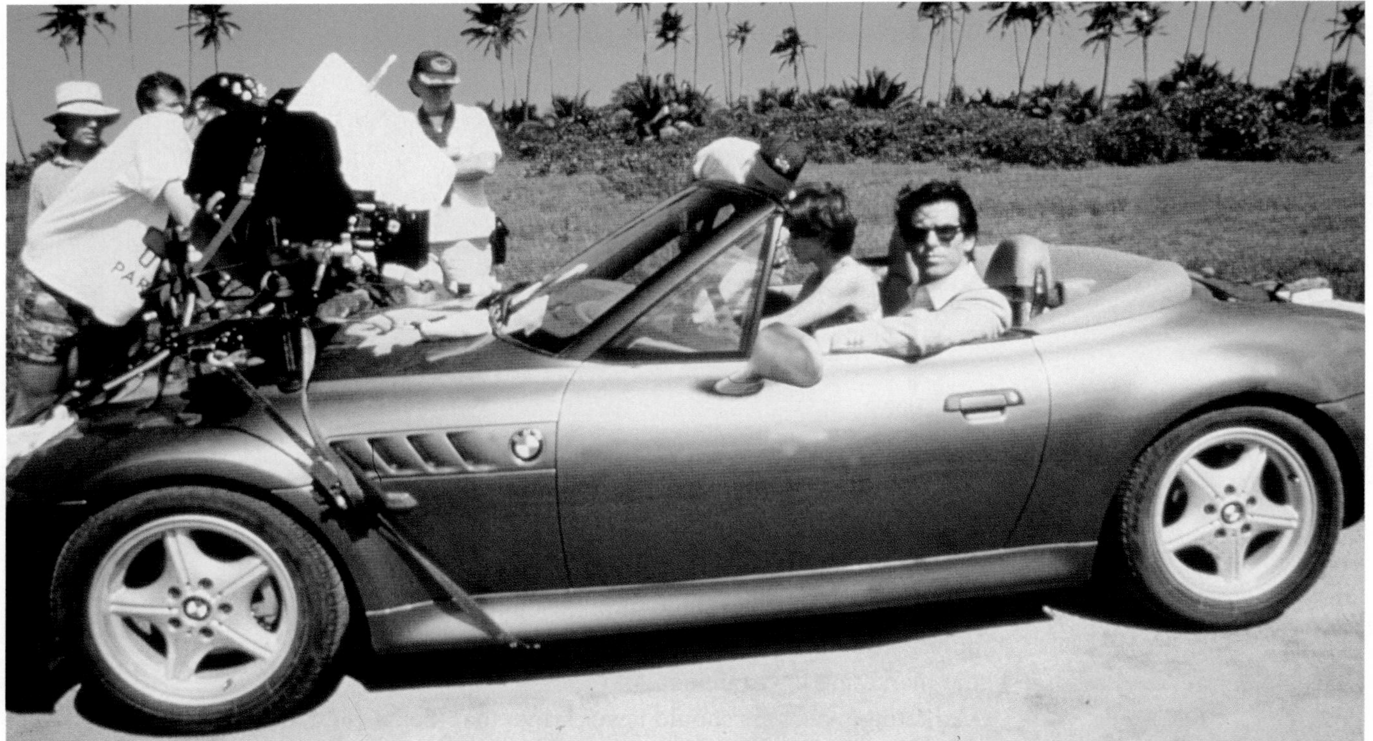

Figure 13.3 Product placement, especially of the motorised variety, is a traditional part of the James Bond films. In *GoldenEye*, the BMW Z3 roadster was prominently featured.

Seen any good movies lately?

Movies (and television programs) are being used by businesses as a channel to market products. Product placement, the seamless integration of advertising into entertainment, is becoming widespread. Even though the sci-fi movie *Minority Report*, for example, actually satirised the technique of product placement, 15 brands including Gap (clothing) and Lexus (motor vehicles) were prominently placed throughout the movie, earning the producers approximately $A43 million.

Samsung arranged a sponsorship deal with the producers of the film *Matrix Reloaded* to use product placement to redefine its brand, especially with its primary target market of 18- to 35-year-olds, as a manufacturer of leading edge 'cool' technology. To complement the appearance of its technology in the film, Samsung planned a $A5 million advertising campaign featuring *Matrix* characters. The television commercial was aired to coincide with the opening of the *Matrix* sequel, as well as before screenings at cinemas.

LG, the South Korean electronics manufacturer, formerly known as Lucky Goldstar, also used *Matrix Reloaded* to market one of its products. In one action-packed scene Keanu Reeves and Hugo Weaving fought against a wall of $A500 000 worth of LG hi-tech plasma television screens. Because LG is known as Zenith in the United States, the fight scene had to be shot twice: one scene displaying the LG brand name and the other the Zenith logo and name. Different product placement scenes for different audiences!

Marketing managers are keen to use this promotional technique because it allows them to reach advertisement-weary, but savvy consumers. To have the celebrity endorsing a product by wearing certain clothing, driving a particular make of car or using a branded mobile phone is a marketing manager's 'dream'.

Critics of product placement argue that because of its 'concealed' nature, this type of advertising blurs the line between what is advertising and what is entertainment. Consequently, product placement may be seen as subliminal, or, in the words of marketing managers 'getting under the radar of consumers'.

SNAPSHOT Questions

1. What is the main role of product placement?
2. Why are marketing managers keen to use this promotion technique?
3. Do you consider product placement an ethical or unethical marketing strategy? Give reasons for your answer.

13.2 Environmentally responsible products

Society's environmental concerns create both threats and opportunities for marketing managers. For example, two of society's biggest environmental problems are the disposal of packaging (especially of plastic materials that are not biodegradable, and that use CFC gases in their manufacture) and air pollution and the resultant destruction of the ozone layer.

In response to these problems, state and federal governments have passed legislation banning certain packaging materials. This has created problems for some businesses, especially those in the fast-food industry.

Other firms, however, see environmental constraints as opportunities. For example, The Body Shop is committed to marketing practices that are responsive to environmental concerns. It markets all of its products in recyclable or reusable packaging and a lot in refillable containers. It also uses recycled paper and cardboard for packaging. Furthermore, its production processes are rigorously self-monitored to guarantee minimal harm to the environment. The Body Shop also produces an externally verified environmental audit and report.

Misleading advertising claiming a product has environmentally friendly qualities is not only unethical but also may actually be illegal. For example, labelling that states a product has '50 per cent more recycled material than before' is misleading if the recycled content has increased only from 2 per cent to 3 per cent.

Figure 13.4 The Body Shop views environmentalism as a marketing opportunity.

Green marketing

Green marketing refers to the development, pricing, promotion and distribution of products that either do not harm or have minimal impact upon the environment.

BiZ WoRD

***Green marketing** refers to the development, pricing, promotion and distribution of products that either do not harm or have minimal impact upon the environment.*

Green marketing provides many new opportunities for businesses. However, research shows that consumers:

- may not be prepared to pay higher prices to protect the environment
- still want to use convenience products
- are confused about which products are environmentally safe.

Whether businesses will begin to market more environmentally responsible products to meet ethical or legal considerations depends upon society and its continuing concern for a cleaner physical environment. Indications are that growing consumer expectation that products should be 'clean, green and safe' will continue to change marketing practices over the next decade.

EXERCISE 13.1 Revision

1. Why is it sometimes difficult to decide whether a marketing strategy is ethical or unethical?
2. Provide arguments for and against business sponsorship arrangements involving schools.

3. What is meant by the term 'product placement'?
4. What ethical issues does product placement raise?
5. Outline the impact environmentalism has had upon marketing practices.
6. 'Green marketing is just a clever marketing strategy to make purchasers feel good.' Evaluate this statement.

Extension

1. To research the code of ethics for the following professional bodies, go to www.jaconline.com.au/businessstudies3e and click on the weblinks for:
   (a) American Marketing Association
   (b) Marketing Association of Australia and New Zealand.
   What is the purpose of a code of ethics?
2. You have been asked by your manager to place a 'special' sign on a number of items but the price is not to be lowered. Is this an ethical or unethical practice? As an employee what could you do? Compare your answers with other class members.
3. If you were the marketing manager for a food company, which would you prefer: government regulation of food additives or a voluntary industry code? In your answer provide advantages and disadvantages for each alternative.

13.3 Other marketing ethical and legal issues

There are a number of other ethical and legal issues confronting the nature and practice of marketing. Many have criticised businesses for encouraging materialism and pursuing misleading or dishonest strategies to gather information or win sales.

Creation of needs — materialism

Does marketing make people buy products they do not need? The answer to this much-debated question depends largely upon your own experiences, beliefs and values. While many people believe that the marketing system has evolved in *response* to consumers' increasing materialism, others contend that marketing has *created* today's materialistic society.

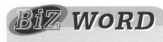

***Materialism** is an individual's desire to constantly acquire possessions.*

Materialism is an individual's desire to constantly acquire possessions. Those who argue that marketing does not encourage materialism, point out that marketing merely satisfies existing needs of customers; it does not create those needs. They argue that marketing practices aim simply to help meet existing consumer demands and provide consumers with a valuable service.

However, critics of marketing feel that most businesses, especially large businesses, use sophisticated and powerful promotional strategies (particularly advertisements) to persuade and manipulate customers to buy whatever the firm wants to sell. These critics argue that marketing creates needs, many of which are artificial, by playing upon an individual's emotions. The result is higher levels not only of materialism but also personal debt within society.

Figure 13.5 Marketing — satisfying existing needs or creating new ones?

These critics believe marketing has created a practice in society of judging people by what they own rather than who they are. The subliminal message behind much advertising is that a successful person owns a large home, two cars, numerous electronic items and wears the 'latest' fashions. Critics see these as false wants, created by marketing strategies such as advertising.

The supporters of marketing argue that customers are not puppets. They cannot be manipulated to buy everything a business chooses to produce. For example, a consumer who buys an ice-cream product that tastes terrible will not buy another of that brand no matter how often it is advertised. Supporters believe that marketing is most effective only when it responds to existing needs, rather than creating new ones.

Non-store retailing is growing faster than in-store retailing. More than 60 per cent of Australian retailers say global shopping via the Internet is an area of retailing they wish to exploit. Online shopping threatens to cause some problems for customers and government regulators, since the consumer protection laws that apply in the buyer's country may not be applicable in the country from which the product was sold.

Impact of retail developments

Within the last 50 years retailing has undergone enormous change.

Retailing will further evolve with developments such as:

- linking of direct marketing to electronic databases
- introduction of automatic checkout scanning systems that do not require an operator
- use of in-store television presentations
- provision of Internet ordering services
- transformation of shopping malls into entertainment centres.

Along with these developments will come increased competition between retailers. The pressure to survive in this intensely competitive environment may result in some retailers using questionable marketing practices. For example, government regulatory agencies and consumer organisations are concerned about some retailers advertising special sale items to attract customers to the store, in the knowledge that stocks are low and will quickly sell out.

Sugging

***Sugging**, **s**elling **u**nder the **g**uise of a survey, is a sales technique disguised as market research.*

Have you ever been approached by someone in a shopping centre and asked to complete a short survey? Perhaps you have been contacted by telephone and surveyed about a particular product only to discover the person was really trying to sell you something? If so, then you have just been 'sugged'. **Sugging**, **s**elling **u**nder the **g**uise of a survey, is a sales technique disguised as market research.

Although this technique is not illegal, it does raise several ethical issues, including invasion of privacy and deception.

13.4 Role of consumer laws

Since the 1960s, the broad area of business law that relates to dealings between consumers and businesses has been subject to radical and fairly continuous change. Governments, both federal and state, have introduced statutes (laws), such as the Sale of Goods Act, Trade Practices Act, Fair Trading Act, Consumer Credit Act, Door-to-Door Sales Act and the Consumer Claims Tribunal Act. These statutes have been implemented to continually try to improve the protection and rights of consumers, and to clarify the rights and responsibilities of businesses.

Trade practices

BiZ WoRD

***Monopolistic power** occurs when only one business operates in a market and, therefore, controls prices in that market.*

The *Trade Practices Act 1974* (Cwlth) is one of the most important pieces of legislation in Australia and has two major purposes:

- to protect consumers against undesirable practices, such as misrepresenting the contents of products or their place of production (this is covered in Part V of the Act)
- to regulate certain trade practices that restrict competition, hence the term 'restrictive trade practices'. The government also wants to ensure that a number of businesses are operating at any one time in the same market, to avoid the problem of **monopolistic power**.

Figure 13.6 Consumers are now protected, under the Trade Practices Act, against misleading advertising or false representations on the part of businesses.

13.5 Consumer laws and specific marketing practices

In the case of Makita (Australia) v Black & Decker (Australasia) Pty Ltd *(1990), Black & Decker began a series of advertisements comparing one of its drills with one of Makita's. The court found that the comparison of the two drills was not accurate and, because of this, the advertisement was 'misleading and deceptive'. Black & Decker was not allowed to use the advertisement and had to correct its advertising.*

Businesses must ensure that they are up to date with the current laws and that they apply them to all marketing practices.

Deceptive and misleading advertising

Of all the unfair trading practices, false or misleading advertising can be the most serious because of the influential nature of advertising. Even though the Trade Practices Act makes false or misleading advertising illegal, a number of methods are still used by some retailers. The most common include:

- *fine print*. Important conditions are written in a small-sized print and are, therefore, difficult to read.
- *before and after advertisements*. Consumers may be misled by 'before' and 'after' advertisements where the comparison is distorted so that 'before' images are worsened and 'after' images enhanced.
- *tests and surveys*. Some advertisements make unsubstantiated claims; for example, stating '9 out of 10 people' prefer a product when no survey has been conducted.

- *country of origin*. Accuracy in labelling is important; for example, 'made in Australia' and 'product of Australia' have two distinct meanings.
- *packaging*. The size and shape of the package may give a misleading impression of the contents.
- *special offer*. Advertisements may be misleading or deceptive if they imply that a special offer is available for only a limited period when, in fact, the offer is continuously available.

Bait and switch advertising *involves advertising a few products at reduced and, therefore, enticing prices to attract customers.*

Two of the most common false and misleading advertising techniques are:

- ***bait and switch advertising***. This involves advertising a few products at reduced and, therefore, enticing prices to attract customers. When the advertised products quickly run out, customers are directed to higher priced items (see figure 13.7).

Figure 13.7 Bait and switch advertising is often misleading and deceptive.

In the case of Doherty v Traveland Pty Ltd *(1982), a travel agent continued to display brochures advertising a holiday for 13 days when it had been reduced to 11 days. The travel agency was penalised $2200 for 'misleading the public'.*

- *misleading advertising*. Advertisements must not use words that are deceptive or claim that a product has some specific quality when it does not. Such actions convey a false impression of the exact nature of the product (see the Biz Fact on the left). As well, price reduction, specials or free-gift offers must all be genuine. Advertisements that could deceive, even though no-one may actually be deceived, are also to be avoided.

Figure 13.8 Deceptive advertising

Price discrimination

Price discrimination is the setting of different prices for a product in separate markets.

Price discrimination is the setting of different prices for a product in separate markets. The difference in price is possible because:

- the markets are geographically separated; for example, city and country prices
- there is product differentiation within the one market; for example, different electricity prices for domestic and business users
- separate discounts and allowances are being offered.

Section 49 of the Trade Practices Act prohibits price discrimination if the discrimination could substantially reduce competition.

Implied conditions

***Implied conditions** or terms are the unspoken and unwritten terms of a contract.*

***Merchantable quality** means that the product is of a standard a reasonable person would expect for the price.*

***Fitness of purpose** means that the product is suitable for the purpose for which it is being sold. That is, it will perform as the instructions or advertisement implies.*

Implied conditions or terms are the unspoken and unwritten terms of a contract. These conditions are assumed to exist regardless of whether they were especially mentioned or written into a contract. The two most important implied terms relating to customer purchases refer to the merchantable quality and fitness of purpose of the product.

- **Merchantable quality** means that the product is of a standard a reasonable person would expect for the price. Merchantable quality applies to most consumer contracts.
- **Fitness of purpose** means that the product is suitable for the purpose for which it is being sold. That is, it will perform as the instructions or advertisement imply.

It is a breach of the law to suggest that a product has a particular characteristic that it does not have (see figure 13.9). It is illegal, for example, to state that a washing machine is automatic, when it is not or that a motor vehicle has a certain fuel-consumption performance, when it does not.

Figure 13.9 It is misleading to suggest that a product has certain characteristics when it does not.

Warranties

*A **warranty** is a promise by the business to repair or replace faulty products.*

All businesses have certain obligations with regard to the products they sell. These obligations are designed to offer a degree of protection to the customer if the product is faulty or if the service is not carried out with due care and skill. One important obligation is to provide a warranty (guarantee). A **warranty** is a promise by the business to repair or replace faulty products.

Signs such as 'no refunds given' or 'no refunds on sale items' are meaningless. The Trade Practices Act gives consumers certain rights (such as the right to be supplied with products that are of merchantable quality and fit for their purpose) and remedies (for example, to return the goods and seek a refund of money). A more accurate sign would read either 'no refunds given if you change your mind' or 'no refunds or exchanges unless your purchase is defective'.

***Resale price maintenance** occurs when the manufacturer or supplier insists that a retailer sell the product at a certain price.*

In recent years, government legislation has made it necessary for businesses to state, clearly and simply, the terms and conditions of the warranty. A warranty assures the customer that the business has confidence in the quality of its product and will repair or replace any faulty items. A warranty can also be used as an aggressive marketing tool, if it includes superior options to those of a competitive product.

False or misleading statements concerning the existence, exclusion or certain conditions of the warranty are prohibited under the Trade Practices Act. In particular, the legislation clearly outlines the rights of consumers with regard to refunds and exchanges (see the Biz Fact on the left).

Resale price maintenance

This is a very rigidly enforced provision of the Trade Practices Act. **Resale price maintenance** occurs when the manufacturer or supplier insists that a retailer sell the product at a certain price. For example, if a distributor of television sets forced a retailer to charge a set price for a product, this would be viewed as an incidence of resale price maintenance and, therefore, a breach of the Act. Retailers have the right to set their own prices and offer discounts. Companies have been prosecuted for engaging in resale price maintenance.

Manufacturers and suppliers can *recommend* a resale price as long as it is made clear that it is only a recommended price. However, suppliers can specify a *maximum* price for resellers without breaking the law.

EXERCISE 13.2 Revision

1. 'Marketing creates needs, it does not satisfy existing ones.' Discuss.
2. What is meant by the term 'sugging'?
3. Suggest reasons why sugging may be an unethical marketing practice.
4. What are the two main aims of the Trade Practices Act?
5. In each of the following examples, state whether there has been a breach of the Trade Practices Act:
   (a) A company advertises a particular brand of television and states that it is at a cheaper price than a competitor. This statement is false.
   (b) A company advertises jumpers and claims that they are made in Australia when, in fact, they are made in Hong Kong.
   (c) A company offers its customers a 10 per cent discount if they provide the names and addresses of five potential customers for the company.
   (d) A company advertises that the special deal is for one week only, when, in fact, it plans to extend it to two months.
   (e) A company advertises a motor vehicle as having low mileage when, in fact, it has travelled 200 000 kilometres.
6. Provide a brief description of:
   (a) bait and switch advertising
   (b) misleading advertising
   (c) price discrimination.

7. Distinguish between a 'warranty' and a 'refund'? Why do you think disagreements over warranties and refunds are a common source of consumer complaints?
8. Prepare a summary of this chapter. A summary condenses the important issues and concepts presented in the chapter. Go to www.jaconline.com.au/businessstudies3e to compare your finished summary with the one provided for this textbook.

Extension

1. Go to www.jaconline.com.au/businessstudies3e and click on the Australian Competition and Consumer Commission (ACCC) weblink for this textbook. Access the 'quick guide' dealing with advertising and selling (section 2). Suggest how a knowledge of this information would influence marketing promotion practices.
2. 'Advertising can get people into a store, but it can't make them buy.' Discuss.
3. Arrange for a representative from the Consumer Claims Tribunal or the New South Wales Department of Fair Trading to address your class about the role of consumer laws and their impact upon marketing strategies. Prepare a list of interview questions and send them to the representative before the visit. After the visit, compile a report and arrange for a copy to be sent to the representative.
4. In groups of three or four, critically analyse the ethical issues involved in:
   (a) advertising to young children during morning television programs
   (b) using sexual overtones and imagery in advertisements.
5. Should a marketing manager or a business refuse to produce a product that could have harmful side effects, even though many consumers are demanding it?

Topic 4

Employment relations

FOCUS AREA: To understand the nature of effective employment relations and their importance to business operation and society.

Outcomes

Students should be able to:

- describe and analyse business functions and operations and their impact on business success
- evaluate processes and operations in global business
- evaluate the effectiveness of management in the organisation and operations of business and its responsiveness to change
- analyse the impact of management decision making on stakeholders
- critically analyse the social and ethical responsibilities of management
- evaluate management strategies in response to internal and external factors
- select, organise and evaluate information and sources for usefulness and reliability
- plan and conduct an investigation into businesses and present the findings in an appropriate business format
- communicate business information, ideas and issues, using relevant business terminology and concepts in appropriate forms
- apply mathematical concepts appropriately in business situations.

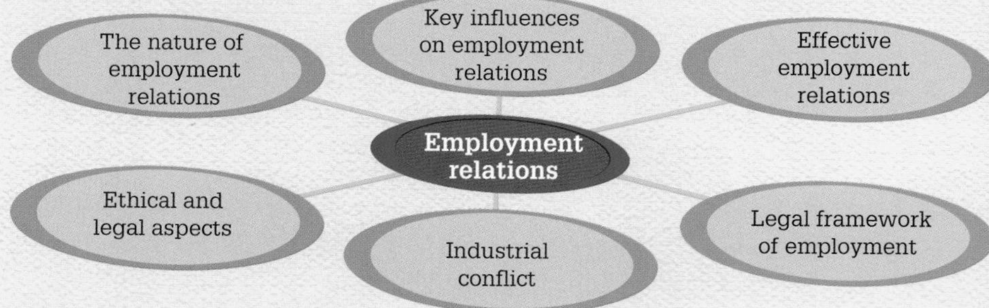

Mind map showing the specific aspects examined for the 'Employment relations' topic

Trouble cooking in the kitchen

Christina is an apprentice chef in a modern beachside restaurant, Zeus. Currently working over 50 hours per week, she is finding her work stressful, as the head chef, Dimitrius, is so demanding. He is often heard screaming at new staff and apprentices; as a result, new staff don't stay for very long. As she is nearing the completion of her apprenticeship, Christina is hanging on, and trying to avoid upsetting Dimitrius. She also really likes his modern Australian–Greek cooking style, and is keen to pick up more ideas.

Dimitrius is frustrated because his employers are a group of lawyers with lots of money but no experience in the industry, and they are not responding to his concerns, particularly the need for more marketing, modern equipment and safety improvements. Staff are often not paid on time and casuals all receive cash with no statement of earnings. The kitchen is chronically understaffed and absenteeism is high. Two employees received minor injuries this year, but as they were not on the books, and were casuals, the owners just reduced their hours till they stopped turning up. The two employees took no action because they would have had their student allowances reduced if their income was officiallly documented. Other employees are on awards and are often paid late.

The owners are constantly pressuring Dimitrius to find ways to cut costs, as profitability is in single figures.

The restaurant has a loyal following, but people always tell him they have never seen the restaurant advertised. Although the internal décor is great, the poor lighting and small signage outside doesn't help.

Dimitrius also works more than 50 hours per week, and was recently divorced, his wife citing his job as the cause of the break-up.

Christina is paid nearly half the wage of a fast-food employee, and her friends think she is a fool to stay. She has a plan to start her own restaurant using funds she saved in her previous job in sales, but needs her qualification to really be effective in managing a restaurant.

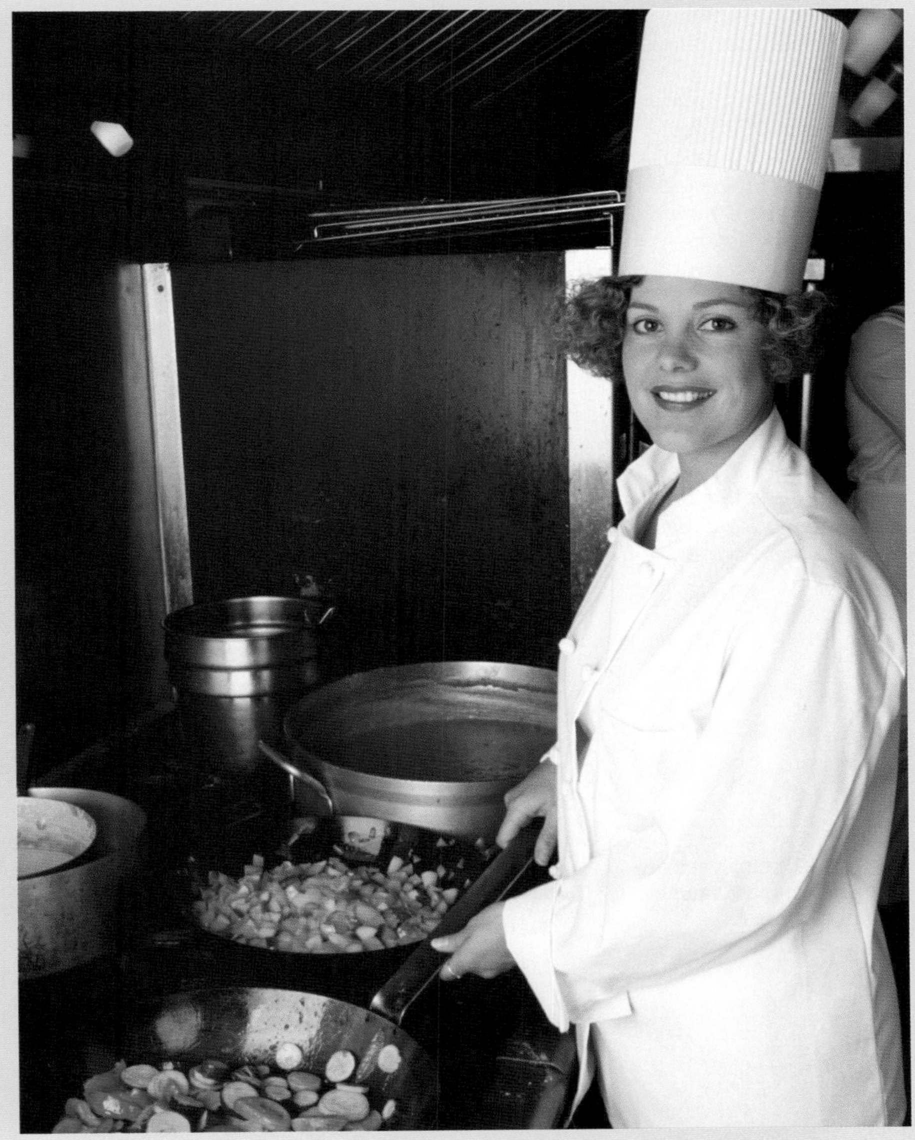

CHAPTER

14 Employment relations: its nature and key influences

14.1 The nature of employment relations

Employment relations *refers to the total relationship between an employer and employee. An* ***employer****, for legal purposes:*
- *exercises control over employees*
- *has responsibility for payment of wages*
- *holds the power to dismiss employees.*

An ***employee*** *is a worker under an employer's control. Control may involve:*
- *the location of the workplace*
- *the way in which the work is performed*
- *the degree of supervision involved.*

These criteria are critical in determining legal disputes over the employment contract.

Employment relations refers to the total relationship between an **employer** and **employee** — the two major participants or parties in the workplace. The term employment relations is often used as a substitute for industrial relations, human resource management or workplace relations. Although these terms are similar, employment relations is an approach that incorporates all the aspects of the employer–employee relationship in the workplace, including recruitment, equal opportunity, training and development, and organisational structure.

Employment relations sees an employee as an asset rather than a cost, and encourages open communication and goal orientation. It accepts that legitimate differences exist in workplaces but aims to reduce conflict through effective procedures and relationships.

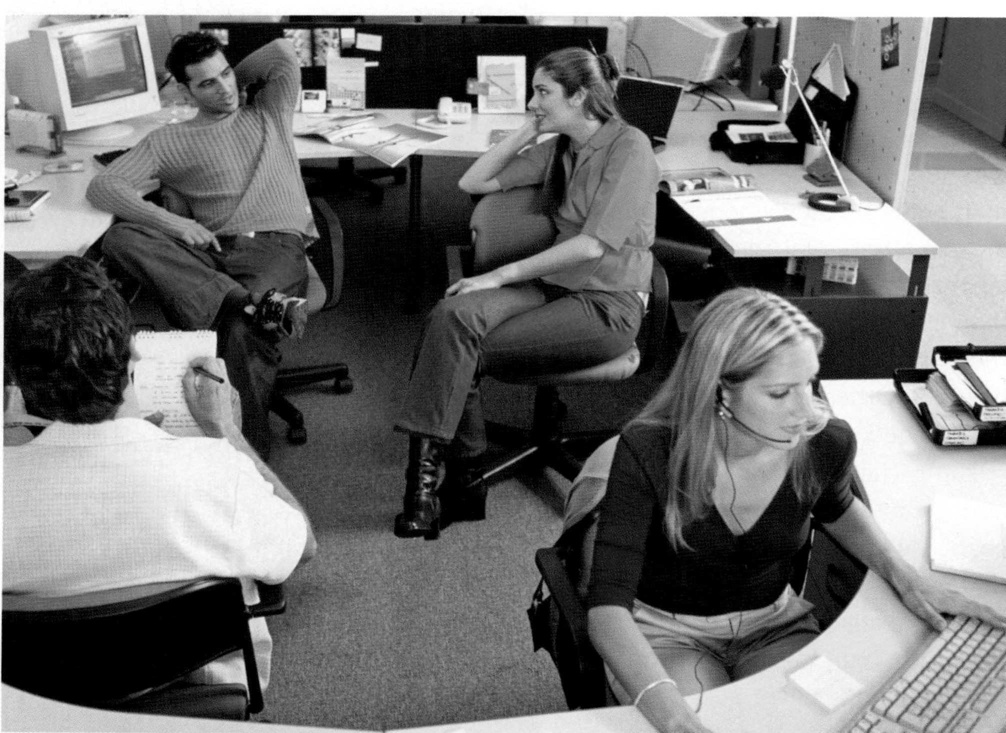

Figure 14.1 Employees are a business's most valuable resource or asset.

Businesses are continually examining ways to improve competitiveness and profitability. An increasing number take a strategic (or big picture) approach to managing employment relations, by:
- seeing an effective workforce as a way of adding value to all areas of their business performance

- focusing on the use of specific employment relations strategies to retain, reward and motivate effective and skilled employees to achieve the organisation's objectives.

Businesses with effective employment relations practices manage change more effectively, and this enhances their ability to gain a sustainable competitive advantage. In recent years, governments have also tried to assist businesses in becoming more competitive by creating a more flexible legal framework for employment relations.

14.2 Stakeholders in the employment relations process

Employers and employees are the major stakeholders in a business, but the nature of their relationship is strongly influenced by other stakeholders; for example, employer associations (representing owners/management) and unions, governments and the courts that establish the legal framework under which the parties operate.

Stakeholders have a common interest in the survival and success of the business. However, not all their interests are shared — conflict can arise due to differences and competing interests (see figure 14.2).

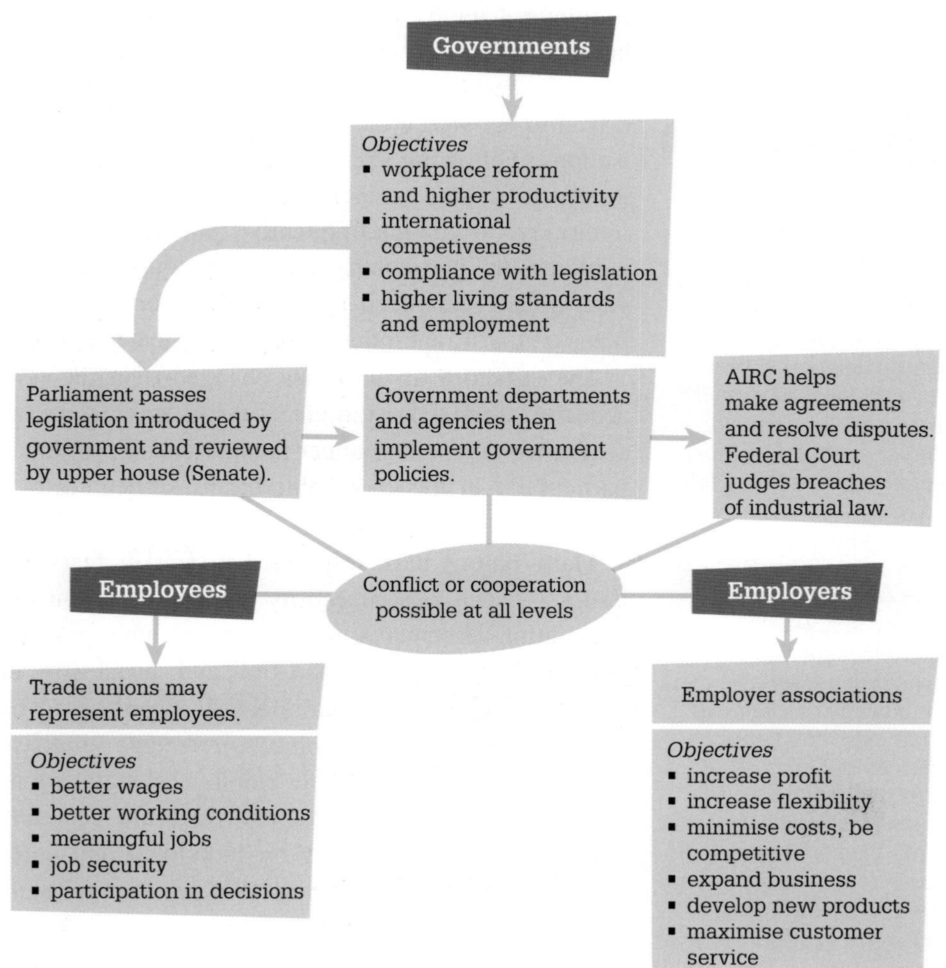

Figure 14.2 Stakeholders in employment relations and their interests

Coles Myer is Australia's largest employer, with over 165 000 employees.

The most common method of settling pay overall in 2004 was a collective agreement. In the private sector, the most common method was individual arrangement, (40.7 per cent) while in the public sector it was collective agreement (93.1 per cent).

A recent survey of employees from 32 countries, published by Walker Information Global Network and Hudson Institute (reported in The Australian Financial Review*), found that worker loyalty was low in Australia, for example:*

- *28 per cent of Australian employees said they felt an obligation to stay with their company, compared with an average of 44 per cent of employees in other countries*
- *36 per cent of Australians considered their employers' problems as their own, compared with 60 per cent internationally*
- *Australian employees are more likely than not to move to a different company within two years.*

Employers

Employers and managers handle employment relations issues on a daily basis, some spending over half their work day on matters related to this area, including involvement in developing programs that focus on improving business performance (see the Snapshot, 'Employment issues and trends for employers and managers'). Employers' responsibilities are increasing, as recent legislation today encourages them to negotiate agreements and resolve disputes at the individual workplace or individual employee level. However, employers have been widely criticised in many management surveys for failing to tackle issues in managing employees effectively. Improving management training in Australia is, therefore, important in improving employment relations.

Under recent legislation, employers have gained more power to make agreements relevant to the individual workplace or enterprise. Not all employers support government policy enough to engage in full confrontation with unions and employees as the costs of such confrontation may be very high, as seen in the Waterfront dispute (1997–98). A 2004 survey of more than 7600 people found 'people management' to be the most serious failing of Australian leaders, and was cited 2.5 times more frequently than any other management failing.

Employees

Employees today are, on average, more highly educated than in the past. They become bored very quickly and demand more challenging, interesting work, involvement in decision-making processes and autonomy at their workplace. Many feel driven to build their career through a succession of jobs in a range of different organisations. Following the extensive downsizing that occurred in the 1990s, they no longer trust one business to look after their needs. As a result, the practice of 'churning' — moving frequently from one job to another in different organisations — is increasing, particularly in service industries. Businesses hoping to retain and motivate skilled staff need to put extra effort into developing staff career and training plans, rewards, and opportunities for greater employee involvement.

The structure of work has changed over the last decade and affects employees' access to work. For example, many older workers retrenched from the manufacturing sector, women, and younger inexperienced people are unable to obtain full-time jobs, particularly in the knowledge-based service sector. These people have become our 'flexible', casual workforce.

Many unions have responded to worker fears and have made some employment issues — such as job security and limitation on the use of casuals — a priority in negotiating agreements. A significant number of employees do, nevertheless, enjoy the flexibility of job sharing, part-time and casual work in managing family commitments.

The move from a predominantly award-based bargaining system towards enterprise and individual workplace agreements (discussed in chapter 16) has had mixed effects on employees. Where employees' skills are in demand, or where they are represented by strong unions, employees are generally achieving excellent wage and non-wage outcomes. Many on individual and enterprise agreements are achieving higher wage outcomes (around 4–5 per cent per annum).

Many employees in less secure bargaining situations are under pressure to accept individual agreements. Employers, who are also under pressure to reduce costs, see such agreements as a strategy to improve flexibility and competitiveness in global markets. When the survival of a business is threatened, even hard-line unions are having to face the option of wage concessions to keep their members in work, and in some cases, to keep their jobs from going offshore. For many employees today, agreements involve significant trade-offs in working hours and conditions, and this has led to higher stress levels and a number of industrial disputes in recent years.

Trade unions

Trade unions are organisations formed by employees in an industry, trade or occupation to represent them in efforts to improve wages and the working conditions of their members. The key factors and stages in their development in Australia are summarised in figure 14.3.

***Trade unions** are organisations formed by employees in an industry, trade or occupation to represent them in efforts to improve wages and the working conditions of their members.*

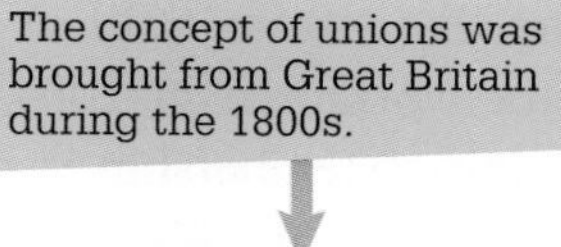

The concept of unions was brought from Great Britain during the 1800s.

Gold rushes create a time of prosperity, which leads to formation of unions and demands for shorter hours. Stonemasons win first 8-hour day in 1856. Other unions call for 8-hour day.

Late 1800s — unions organise on broader scale, on waterfront, in mining, manufacturing and shearing. They form a framework in Trades and Labor Councils from 1871.

Recession develops and major strikes break out in 1890s. Unions defeated by combined power of colonial governments, employers, the military, police and non-union workers (referred to by unionists as 'scabs').

Unions decide to take a political vote to survive, and form Labor Party in 1891. Labor Party comes to power in 1901, after Federation.

Constitution is established. *Conciliation and Arbitration Act 1904* enshrines power of unions and employer associations.

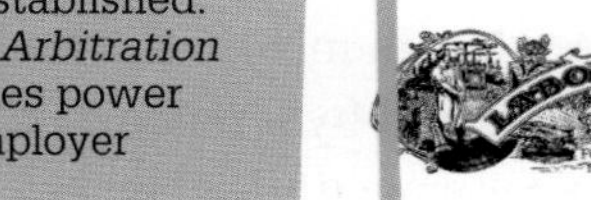

1907 — famous Harvester case establishes principle of basic wage for a family. This leads to other awards, establishing principle of comparative wage justice (where wage gains are spread across the wage system to other workers).

By 1926, 55 per cent of the workforce was unionised and, in 1927, ACTU was established. Further test cases establish principles including sick leave, long service leave, 40-hour week and, in 1969, equal pay for equal work.

White collar unions boom in the 1970s, fostered by 'closed shop' arrangements (compulsory union membership imposed by certain unions in particular industries). These are now some of the largest unions in Australia.

Unions use power to lobby on political, social and environmental issues.

Union membership falls rapidly in 1990s — a global pattern in high-income countries.

Figure 14.3 The development of trade unions and their role in employment relations in Australia since 1800

In 2004, 23 per cent of full-time employees were trade union members, while only 17 per cent of part-time employees were members.

The term **social wage** refers to improvements in social benefits, such as better health care, education, welfare and taxation reform, that act like a wage increase.

The system for resolving industrial disputes, established in 1904 in Australia, gave unions a powerful role in employment relations (discussed in detail in chapter 16). It provided unions with an official bargaining position in the making of industrial agreements. Through test cases, unions won major improvements in terms and conditions of employment. These established key principles that flowed on to other workers.

Union power reached its peak with the establishment of the Accord — an agreement between the Australian Council of Trade Unions (ACTU) and the new Labor government in 1983. Following a decade of unrest, unions agreed to exchange wage restraint for policies that would provide an improved **social wage** and reduce unemployment. When the Hawke Labor government later introduced award restructuring (1987) and supported enterprise bargaining (1991) to improve the competitiveness of Australian firms, unions were given an important role.

Union membership peaked at 51 per cent in 1976, falling to 46 per cent of all employees in 1986 and reaching the current level of 23 per cent of the workforce (17 per cent of the private sector workforce in 2004). Today, only 11 per cent of teenage employees belong to unions. Membership is highest among full-time males in the public sector (47 per cent), and in the 45–59 age group. Nevertheless, unions are still represented in around two-thirds of workplaces with more than 20 employees (see figure 14.4).

Figure 14.4 Unions have achieved improved working conditions for their members.

Unions are expanding their range of services and becoming more active in recruiting to regain membership numbers. As well as providing representation in disputes, the range of services offered by a union to members might now include free or discounted legal services, superannuation schemes, cheap home loans, training programs through TAFE, insurance, cheap holiday units to rent, income protection against illness or accident, occupational health and safety advice, and many more.

The major reasons for the decline in union membership are shown in figure 14.5.

The peak trade union body is the Australian Council of Trade Unions (ACTU). Some of the larger unions include:

- *Australian Services Union (ASU)*
- *Australian Workers' Union (AWU)*
- *Australian Manufacturing Workers' Union (AMWU)*
- *Construction, Forestry, Mining and Energy Union (CFMEU)*
- *Finance Sector Union (FSU)*
- *Maritime Union of Australia (MUA)*
- *Transport Workers' Union of Australia (TWU)*
- *Community and Public Sector Union (CPSU).*

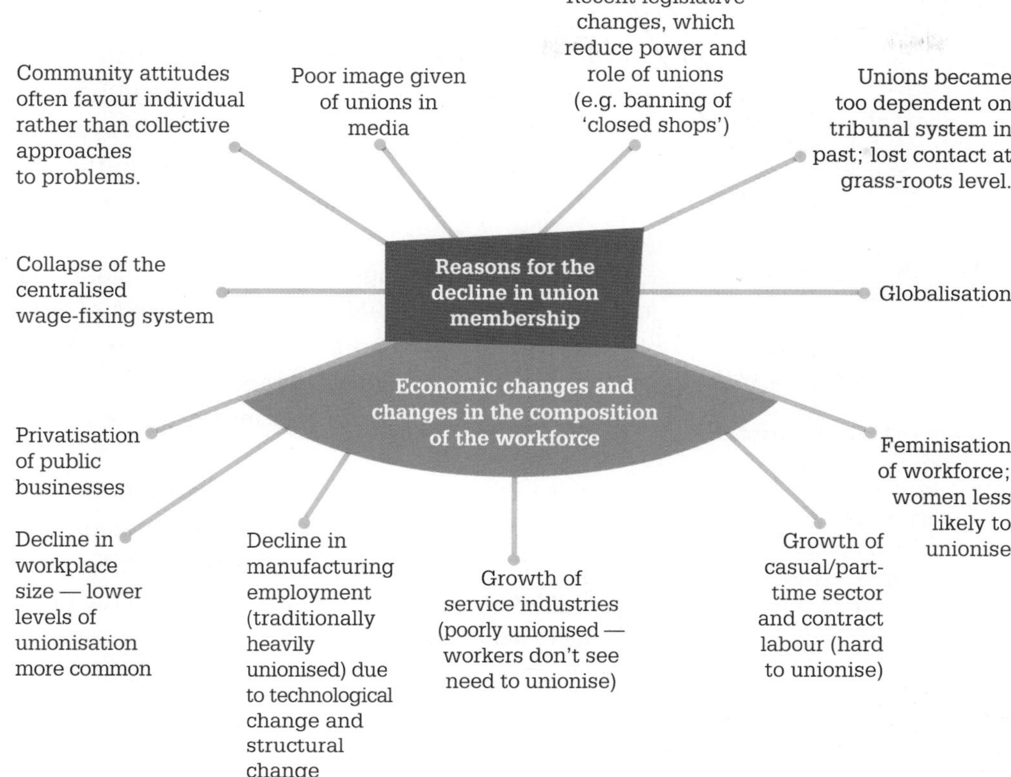

Figure 14.5 Reasons for the decline in union membership

From the mid to late 1990s, the policies of the Liberal–National party coalition government and recent legislation have led to reduced union power.

Awareness of these trends has increased on a global scale. Unions are developing global unions to counterbalance the power of global corporations and globalisation of business.

Employees who are members of unions with international links and strong bargaining power, such as the Australian Manufacturing Workers' Union (AMWU) (see the Snapshot 'An interview with Dave Oliver'), often obtain higher wage increases through enterprise bargaining than those on other agreements.

An interview with Dave Oliver

Dave Oliver is the Victorian secretary of the Australian Manufacturing Workers' Union (AMWU) and national secretary of the Metal and Engineering Division.

What is your view of the current system of industrial relations?

The current system is designed to weaken the collective strength of workers and restrict the ability of unions to organise. It is promoting individual bargaining under the guise of an employer and employee bargaining on an equal footing. It is, of course, utter nonsense to believe that an individual employee has the same bargaining power as an employer. AWAs [Australian workplace

(*continued*)

Research by Essential Media Communications has found that:

- young Australians don't even consider unions when discussing the workplace, despite being more likely to be working in workplaces in which conditions are poor
- seventy per cent of Australians believe the country is better off with unions
- more than 50 per cent say they would join a union if they could.

Unions are examining new ways to operate in the changed work environment. Some of these include providing a blanket union organisation for people who are job mobile; allowing people to transfer membership between unions when they change jobs; and establishing a 'think tank' as a balance to conservative think tanks to provide intellectual credibility based on research for the union movement. They realise that people don't join unions because of a philosophy about unions; they need to be attracted by advice on careers, industry trends, ethical and high-quality employers and unethical employers. Unions need to be more relevant to a future where young people will have four or five careers, and may not want to work five days a week, or specific hours, anymore.

Source: R. Wainright 2004, 'Comrades no more', *The Sydney Morning Herald*, 5 November 2004.

agreements] are offered to workers on a 'take it or leave it' basis — that is, if you want the job it's under these conditions — whereas collective agreements enable employees to bargain with collective strength to regulate common wages and conditions. The current system is also designed to erode the safety net even further through award stripping. This widens the gulf between collective wages and conditions and award rates.

Enterprise bargaining has been worthwhile. It has delivered, without doubt, real benefits in respect of wages and conditions. However, as a result of isolated enterprise bargaining we have seen the erosion of industry standards. The number of casuals and contract employees in our industry has increased by 250 per cent over the last five years.

Despite achieving a 38-hour week more than a decade ago, workers in the manufacturing industry are working, on average, 44 hours per week. We have a declining workforce, fewer workers working more hours and more people working fewer hours. The only way to stem the growth of casuals, contractors and increasing hours is to address it across the industry. The AMWU has been very successful in delivering significant wage increases under enterprise bargaining while restricting the impact or penetration of AWAs in the manufacturing industry.

What are the key issues for unions at the moment?

The key issues are to improve wages and conditions while maintaining and improving the social safety net. Unions must be campaigning in the field of job security, protection of entitlements and conditions that will allow workers to balance their work and family commitments. Globalisation has impacted severely on our manufacturing industry as a result of governments reducing protection through tariffs. The unions must be campaigning to maintain a real manufacturing base in this country that will provide real jobs for our children.

Why should young people join unions?

If it wasn't for unions, young workers would not be enjoying the benefits of entitlements such as annual leave, penalty rates, shift loadings, meal breaks, sick leave, skills development, industry superannuation, workers' compensation and other provisions. The difference in wage rates between a unionised and a non-unionised workplace is about $90 per week. Young people need to be protected. In the future they may be forced to negotiate their wages and conditions 'one out' with an employer who, in a lot of cases, would be backed by lawyers or an employer association.

SNaPSHOT Questions

1. Discuss the union's view of the impact of current legislation on employees.
2. Suggest reasons why younger employees have a low rate of union membership.
3. Would you enjoy being a union representative? Give reasons for your answer.
4. Suggest strategies unions could use to be more effective in attracting members.

Role of the ACTU

Trade unions are represented at the workplace or 'shop' level, state branch level and federal level (see figure 14.7). Most unions are linked to the peak national trade union body, the Australian Council of Trade Unions (ACTU). Through its affiliations and member unions and councils, the ACTU acts on behalf of 90 per cent of trade unionists.

Cooperation between unions is maintained through meetings held by the ACTU and its state branches. This peak trade union body:

- formulates and coordinates union policy and practice at a national level
- represents the union movement and/or lobbies on its behalf in dealings with the federal government, industry and trade organisations and the media
- helps affiliated unions manage disputes and represents them before the Australian Industrial Relations Council (AIRC) and other tribunals
- maintains contacts with international trade union and labour organisations, such as the International Labour Organization (ILO), and lobbies in world forums on labour issues
- provides legal and other advice to member unions
- writes submissions and research papers on issues affecting employees, such as health and safety issues and enterprise bargaining.

Federal Level — ACTU

The peak national union body, the ACTU (Australian Council of Trade Unions), formulates and coordinates union policy and practice at a national level; represents the union movement, internationally or nationally, in courts and tribunals and in dealings with the government and other organisations; and helps affiliated unions settle disputes.

State branches

These key operating units of unions have full-time staff members dealing with matters within their state. Disputes are often referred to state branches by shop stewards. Full-time union members often handle negotiations of agreements at the management level of business and provide advice and information. Most state unions are affiliated to State Labor Councils, which are the state branches of the ACTU.

Shop level

Union members elect a delegate to represent the union, handle minor workplace issues and grievances and keep watch for breaches of awards or agreements. Delegates are increasingly involved in enterprise bargaining.

Figure 14.7 Trade union structure

Figure 14.6 Sharan Burrow is the president of the ACTU, which is the peak union body in Australia. (See the Snapshot 'Role of the ACTU').

SNaPSHOT Questions

1. What do the letters ACTU represent?
2. Suggest reasons why most unions are linked to the ACTU.

Employer associations

BiZ WoRD

Employer associations *are organisations that represent and assist employer groups.*

A ***log of claims*** *is a list of demands made by workers (often through their union) against their employers. These demands cover specific wages and conditions. Employers may also serve a counter-log of claims on the union.*

Employer associations were originally created by employers as a counter-party to unions, to represent employers in the making of awards through the conciliation and arbitration system established in 1904. They assisted employers in formulating policies and processed **logs of claims** served on their members by unions. Their main role today is to act on behalf of employers (especially small businesses) in collective bargaining sessions and before industrial tribunals, courts, commissions and committees. They:

- provide advice (especially to small business) on such matters as awards, unfair dismissals and discrimination issues
- make submissions to safety net wage cases
- negotiate agreements
- lobby governments and other organisations with the views and interests of employers, industries and trade.

Unlike unions, employer associations represent employers on a broader range of issues (see the Snapshot 'An interview with Katie Lahey'); industrial relations matters make up just one aspect of their role.

Employer associations may function as professional bodies, such as the Australian Medical Association, or as marketing bodies, for example, dairy cooperatives and the Meat and Livestock Corporation. Others are associations with an industrial relations function within their services, such as the Australian Chamber of Commerce and Industry (ACCI), and the Australian Industry Group (AIG) representing the Australian Chamber of Manufactures and the Metal Trades Industry Association.

An interview with Katie Lahey (Chief Executive of the Business Council of Australia)

What role does the Business Council of Australia play in workplace relations?

The Business Council of Australia (BCA) represents the chief executives of Australia's Top 100 companies. The council's role is to promote policies that help the economy to be prosperous and competitive. The BCA has identified the importance of workforce participation in supporting economic growth and individual prosperity. It is essential to have a workplace relations environment that provides the opportunity for people to work.

The BCA works with a range of organisations across government and the community to promote these outcomes. These include:

- presenting reform proposals to the federal government
- liaising with Commonwealth and state departments on workplace relations policies
- liaising with other industry groups such as the Australian Chamber of Commerce and Industry and the Australian Industry Group on areas of mutual interest in workplace relations.

What role do you play within the organisation?

As chief executive I manage the organisation, manage policy development, administer the work for the council and lead the process of engagement with our members, the government and the wider community.

What do you enjoy about this role?

The subject matter is always interesting and stimulating. It also gives me the opportunity to meet a range of prominent people across the corporate sector, politics, community organisations, the media and the general public.

You recently participated in the 'Principal for a Day Program'. What attracted you to the program?

The 'Principal for a Day Program' is a great way for businesspeople like me to see first-hand the demands and challenges that a principal of a school manages today. I participated in the program at Gilmore College for Girls in Melbourne's inner west. The teachers were very dedicated and skilled. I also admired the students for their hard work and discipline. The standards were high, with a strong value placed on learning and knowledge.

How did you find the job compared to your own?

There were strong parallels. Many jobs now require employees to have multiple skills, but the job of the principal is really multiskilling at its best. The principal has to manage the school organisation, control its operations and its finances all at the same time. In business these roles would usually be allocated to several individuals. At Gilmore College, the principal also had to be a counsellor and a role model for the students. Also, because a school plays a role in developing young people, a principal is very much a member of his or her wider community. So it is a very broad and complex role that carries a lot of responsibility.

SNaPSHOT Questions

1. Who does the BCA represent?
2. What is the role of the BCA?
3. Which other industry groups (employer associations) does the BCA liaise with?
4. In what ways is a school principal's job similar to that of a senior business manager?

Governments and government organisations

Governments are important stakeholders in the employment relations process (see the Snapshot 'What have the government and courts got to do with my job?' on page 304–5). Over time, they have significantly affected the industrial relations system as a result of their key roles as follows:

- *Legislator.* Our elected representatives pass laws in parliaments (state and federal), which provide the legal framework for industrial relations. Legislation has also led to the growth of the judicial system, and the institutions and processes used by employers and employees to conduct bargaining and resolve disputes.

- *Employer.* Federal and state governments employ almost one-third of Australian workers, as teachers, nurses, clerks, police officers, postal workers, transport workers, and in other roles. They are often regarded as pacesetters in terms of responsible industrial relations policies, having introduced practices such as maternity leave, flexitime and affirmative action for women that were eventually adopted in the private sector.
- *Responsible economic manager.* Governments, operating at the macro level, are keen to ensure non-inflationary, stable economic growth and a high standard of living for all Australians. At times there may be conflict between governments' economic goals, which impact on industrial relations. For example, a decision to cut spending through reductions in the size of the public service to reduce a budget deficit may conflict with its desire to maintain employment. The decision could also spark widespread industrial unrest.
- *Administrator of government policies on industrial relations.* Through the departments and agencies established, governments are able to implement the legislation they enact. This is achieved through publishing information and guidelines providing advice to the government and the public (see the Biz Fact on the left) and investigating breaches of legislation.
- *Representative of Australia in the international arena, in foreign affairs, trade and international labour matters.* Australia is a foundation member of the International Labour Organization and has been represented on its governing body. As a result of its membership of such organisations, the government generally implements legislation based on the treaties and conventions it signs with international organisations. Social justice legislation passed in relation to discrimination and human rights originated in these treaties and conventions.

The federal department responsible for industrial relations is currently the Department of Employment and Workplace Relations. The department:

- *represents the government in national wage cases and in other cases before the Australian Industrial Relations Commission*
- *conducts research and disseminates information*
- *provides advice*
- *promotes good industrial relations practices*
- *investigates breaches of awards and certified agreements.*

Figure 14.8 Governments (both state and federal) perform many roles that impact on the employment relations process; for example, the roles of legislator, employer, economic manager, policy administrator and representative of Australia on the international stage.

The AIRC can sit in any location, refer a matter to an expert, summon witnesses and do whatever is required to give a just, fair, speedy hearing and determination.

***Awards** are legally enforceable, formal agreements made collectively between employers and employees and their representatives at the industry level. They are determined by an industrial court or tribunal and set out minimum wages and conditions of employees.*

***Award simplification** is the process of reducing the number of 'allowable matters' in each award to 20, and eliminating inefficient work practices.*

***Enterprise agreements**, known as **certified agreements** at the federal level, are agreements about wages and conditions made at the enterprise level. Each agreement is made between an employer and a union or a majority of employees in the workplace.*

***Safety net increases** are increases in wages awarded by the AIRC to all employees on awards who are not covered by enterprise agreements, to ensure that they do not miss out on the economic gains achieved or fall too far behind.*

Governments have attempted to increase their power to regulate the industrial relations system through use of the External Affairs and Corporations powers (among others) given under the Constitution of Australia. Recent government policy has focused on reducing the powers of industrial tribunals and encouraging decentralised bargaining in the workplace (enterprise).

Industrial tribunals and courts

Industrial tribunals exist at the federal and state levels to enforce laws established by governments. The Australian Industrial Relations Commission (AIRC), formerly the Australian Conciliation and Arbitration Commission, was first established in 1904 to assist in the resolution of industrial conflict following the extensive Shearers' and Maritime Workers' Strikes in the late nineteenth century. It is a federal tribunal established to resolve disputes of an interstate nature. Its decisions, especially the national wage cases, dominate the industrial relations system, determine wage-fixing principles and are generally duplicated by state tribunals.

The commission is an administrative tribunal. Its primary functions today include settling disputes through conciliation, supervising the making of agreements or **awards** and **award simplification**, hearing appeals and handling unfair dismissal cases. Through these functions it is also, in effect, determining questions of future rights in the workplace.

Figure 14.9 A cartoonist's interpretation of the role of tribunals

Much of the work done by the AIRC is conducted by individual members or groups of members of the commission who are responsible for specific industries or disputes. Full-bench decisions (three members present, two must be presidential members) are reserved generally for matters of significant national or industry interest and national wage cases. Only a full bench can:

- hear matters of significant national interest such as test cases on matters concerning family leave, superannuation and public holidays, and establish principles about the making and varying of awards
- provide award **safety net increases** for workers not covered by **enterprise** (or **certified**) **agreements**. It must also ensure the maintenance of an effective safety net of minimum conditions.
- certify multiple business agreements
- hear appeals against orders, or cancel and suspend awards and orders
- arbitrate after a bargaining period is terminated.

The commission also has the power to:

- deregister a union. In such cases it does not recognise the union for bargaining and arbitration purposes.
- determine whether a federal or state authority should hear a dispute and order joint proceedings or consultations with state authorities.

The role of the AIRC, particularly in dispute resolution (its original constitutional role), diminished significantly after the introduction of enterprise bargaining in 1991. The *Workplace Relations Act 1996* (Cwlth) limited its role to managing award/safety net matters and hearing unfair dismissals, to encourage employees and employers to bargain directly and resolve disputes at the enterprise level. A legal ruling by the full bench in June 2000 gave the AIRC new powers to intervene and take a more active role in workplace disputes; however, the Howard government and business associations are moving to reduce these powers.

What have the government and courts got to do with my job?

Eddie and Min Mei are watching TV at home. Eddie's mum, Jan, is watching Question Time *in federal parliament.*

Eddie: Mum, do we have to watch this?

Jan: Yes, Eddie. I want to know what the minister has to say.

Eddie: It won't make much difference to your life, Mum!

Jan: Is that what you think, Eddie? You are wrong. If this new law goes through, I may not get my entitlements if our company goes broke!

Min Mei: Look at them, Mrs Smith! They're screaming at each other and the ones at the back are out of control! Look at that one standing up and booing!

Eddie: They don't even stop when the speaker says 'Order Order'.

Eddie: My Design and Technology class never behaved this badly. We'd have been suspended for this!

Jan: Yes, such hypocrites! Ah well, all that policy must get boring. Anyway, be quiet. I need to know about their industrial relations policy. Go and feed Blackie — he's pinching the cat's food again.

Min Mei: He's saying he has the right to make laws about employees in any corporation in Australia. Does that mean the new laws will cover me too?

Jan: Yes. Under the Constitution, the founding fathers also gave the Commonwealth the power to make laws to prevent and settle disputes, and other powers to sign treaties with other countries, which is why we now have laws to protect you from discrimination because you are young and pregnant!

Min Mei: What were the founding mothers doing?

Jan: They didn't get much of a look in. Women didn't get equal pay until 1969, and other rights didn't come till much later. When Grandma was a teacher, she was forced to resign when she got married.

Min Mei: Is law made in parliament the only way the government influences our work?

Eddie: No. Remember how WorkCover came around and shut down Firat's workshop until he fixed the hoists and put some windows in his workshop, because it wasn't safe? He's lucky the Office of Industrial Relations inspector didn't check on the wages he was paying, because I think there were a few gaps. He could have been taken to court on a number of counts!

Jan: His workers could have worked that out if they had gone on the Net and looked up their wages on the department's website.
Eddie: Yeah. The department's website gave me good advice on my apprenticeship. Those guys spend all their time showing off in their cars at night — they couldn't be bothered. Cars are their life!
Jan: Silly boys! Your dad loved his FJ too.
Eddie: So what else does the government do that affects my work?
Jan: (watching one of the front benchers, who is speaking) Oh look at him making a fool of himself! To think we pay his salary! Oh yes, dear, don't forget the public service! Today, governments also employ around a third of all Australians. And they often are the ones who bring in better conditions, such as maternity leave! That kept me going with you, Eddie. They let me have flexitime so I could pick you up early and get you to soccer on time. You would never have made it to soccer without that. Don't forget the government's role in managing taxes and inflation — all these things affect your wages. When I was young, we went on strike all the time because inflation was up to 15 per cent! You're lucky you don't have to face that. Strikes would go on for weeks, and then the commission would finally make a decision and we'd be back to work!
Eddie: Mum, that's great! You know that apple pie you offered? It would be great now. Can we please turn over to the tennis?

SNaPSHoT Questions

1. Identify all the roles played by governments and courts in this Snapshot.
2. Discuss the advantages and disadvantages of the role of courts and tribunals in the employment relationship.

Federal Court

Judicial power *refers to the power of courts to interpret and apply laws.*

The Federal Court of Australia is a judicial court. Under the Constitution, only courts have the **judicial power** to determine disputes about existing rights and to make decisions about these matters. The Federal Court (which was merged with the Industrial Relations Court in 1997) enforces industrial relations legislation by administering court actions that arise under Australian industrial laws. It handles cases relating to industrial action and breaches of industrial laws, interprets industrial legislation, and is able to impose penalties for the breach of an award or order, and discrimination or victimisation under industrial and human rights legislation. It also has the power to approve the disamalgamation (splitting up) of unions, declare unauthorised action taken during a dispute and hear cases under the *Corporations Act 2001* (Cwlth) (more detail can be found at the Federal Court's website).

Australian workplace agreements are not supported by organisations such as the ACTU, which believes the individual and secret nature of the agreements leave workers open to exploitation.

The Employment Advocate

The Employment Advocate (EA) is a federal agency established to oversee the implementation of Australian workplace agreements (AWAs) introduced with the Workplace Relations Act. It provides advice, maintains records, checks AWAs, investigates breaches of their terms, and may refer them to the AIRC for consideration if they do not meet requirements. It also publishes statistics on AWAs, which are otherwise secret agreements — that is, free from public scrutiny.

Other government agencies

Some federal government agencies are also stakeholders in the employment relations process. For example, the roles of the Human Rights and Equal Opportunity Commission, the Equal Employment Agency (formerly Affirmative Action Agency) and state organisations such as the Anti-Discrimination Board are to implement particular areas of government legislation.

In the area of occupational health and safety (discussed in detail in chapter 18), the federal *National Occupational Health and Safety Commission Act 1985* established the National Occupational Health and Safety Commission (Worksafe Australia) to develop and promote national standards of occupational health and safety. Due to constitutional limitations, it is currently state rather than federal legislation and agencies that actually regulates business activity in terms of occupational health and safety, for example, the *Occupational Health and Safety Act 1983* (NSW) and WorkCover.

14.3 Managing the employment relations function

Line management and specialist

Employment relations is seen as an increasingly important aspect of a business's overall human resources strategy. In large organisations, responsibility for managing employment relations is often the sole function of a specialist human resources or employment relations manager. In smaller companies, the general manager and junior managers may share these responsibilities.

The scope of the employment relations function depends not only on the size but also on the nature of the business, the level of industrial action and unionisation in the industry or business.

In larger enterprises, **line managers** are also increasingly trained in general employment relations issues, including legal compliance in such areas as occupational health and safety, equal employment opportunity and workplace resolution of conflict.

*A **line manager** is responsible for the management of staff contributing to the prime function of the business; for example, a production manager, service manager or sales manager.*

Line managers play a greater role in employment relations in organisations in which activities are spread across diverse business activities and knowledge of issues relevant to the specific business unit is more important. In organisations with one market/product/service range and a large head office function, the specialist employment relations manager is more commonly involved.

Half of all Australian businesses employ a specialist employee relations or human resources manager. Multinational organisations, particularly those based in the United States, are more likely to have a specialist manager, and to train line managers, than Australian businesses. Australian line managers are more reluctant to take on people-management responsibilities.

Most specialist managers are responsible for:

- recruitment and selection
- induction and training
- separation
- managing the implementation of equal employment opportunity and affirmative action legislation.

They are also more involved in negotiation with unions, establishing/negotiating agreements and preparing for tribunals than they were in the past.

In many businesses, the employee relations manager is now part of the senior executive and is consulted before decisions about strategic issues, such as a change in product, service or organisation of work, are made. This role will increasingly involve high level organisational and human resources auditing, advising on risk, and developing an HR strategic plan, which is then translated into operational plans. In the future, many specialist human resources functions will be outsourced to consultants with these skills.

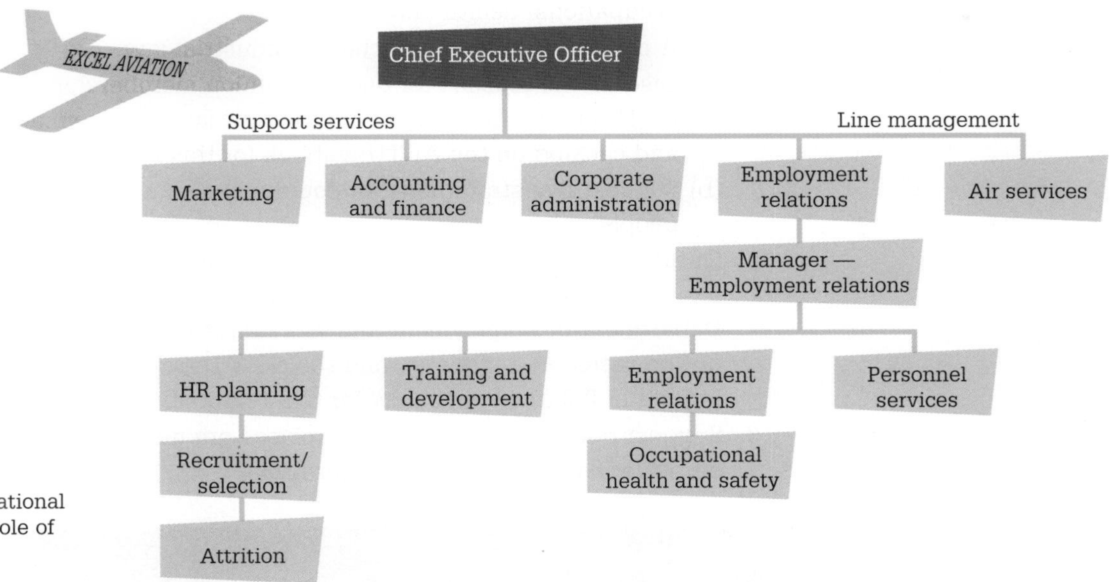

Figure 14.10 An organisational chart that includes the role of employment relations specialist

Employment relations is, therefore, evolving from a support function increasingly to assist managers in improving their strategies for managing staff in order to achieve business goals.

EXERCISE 14.1 *Revision*

1. Read the topic opener story on page 291 and use the text to help you carry out the following tasks.
   (a) Draw up a table listing the major problems faced by this restaurant that relate to managing staff.
   (b) Outline any additional strategies you would advise management to consider in improving this business.
   (c) Imagine that Christina and other staff join a union. Write a letter to the employer from the union explaining:
      (i) the issues that are of concern to the staff
      (ii) ways in which the business may be breaching employment law
      (iii) the risks involved and likely effects of breaching employment law
      (iv) recommendations for resolving the problems.
2. Draw up a table that summarises all the participants in employment relations and their main roles. Write a paragraph explaining why conflict may occur between two of the participants.
3. Match each of the following terms with one of the descriptions: Federal Court, parliament, Worksafe Australia, award, ACTU, AIRC.
   (a) An organisation that is the peak union body

(b) A formal agreement about wages and conditions determined by an industrial court
(c) Legislation originates from this place
(d) Major decisions about industrial issues and test cases are made by this organisation
(e) An organisation that develops and promotes national standards for occupational health and safety
(f) A court that judges breaches of industrial law

4. (a) Discuss the reasons for declining union membership levels. (The view of the ACTU can be found by going to www.jaconline.com.au/businessstudies3e and clicking on the ACTU weblink for this textbook.
   (b) Suggest five strategies that could increase union membership among young people.
5. Outline the major functions of employer associations today. For more information, go to www.jaconline.com.au/businessstudies3e and click on the Department of Employment and Workplace Relations, the Australian Chamber of Commerce and Industry, and the NSW Department of Commerce Office of Industrial Relations weblinks for this textbook.
6. Suggest reasons why single workplaces are more likely to be members of employer associations than larger firms.

Extension

1. A recent Labor Council survey of 1200 people in New South Wales revealed the following attitudes to unions:
   - People think Australia would not be better off if unions disappeared.
   - Unions have lost their way and are stuck in the past, but should continue to exist.
   - Union officials are more interested in their political careers than in serving members' needs.

   (a) Do you agree with these views?
   (b) Develop and conduct your own survey into young people's attitudes to unions, using the attitudes above to help you devise questions. Do your results match those above?
2. Survey a businessperson who is a member of an employer association. Ask what the benefits are for employers. Some examples are the NSW Employers Federation, Metal Trades Industry Association, Australian Shipowners Industry Association and the Pharmacy Guild of Australia.

14.4 Key influences on employment relations

Recent surveys of managers, employees and employment relations specialists have indicated that many factors significantly influence employment relations in Australia today (see figure 14.11 and the text below). Change is the only constant factor in the business environment. Successful businesses now see the value in recruiting and retaining a flexible, adaptable, committed, highly trained workforce. Many use their employees' skills and abilities to gain an edge over competitors.

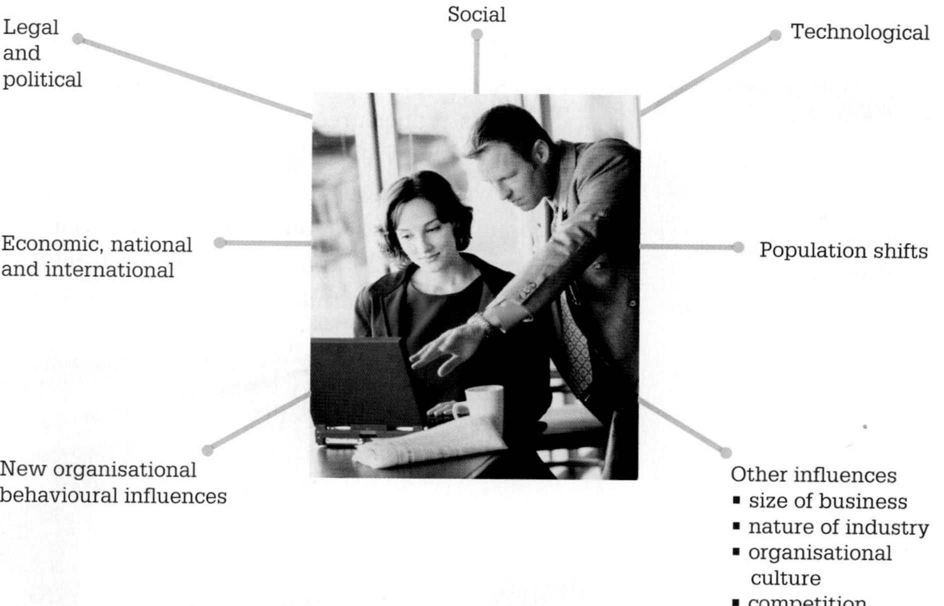

Figure 14.11 Influences on employment relations

Social influences

Changing work patterns

> **BiZ FaCT**
>
> *A recent ACTU survey of occupational health and safety delegates from 800 workplaces in Australia reported that 78 per cent of employees sometimes work more than five days in a row, 78 per cent complain of fatigue and 42 per cent report that working hours contribute to accidents and 'near misses'.*

As we saw in chapter 3, traditional work patterns are changing rapidly. The idea of a 'job for life' is disappearing and employees in the future will tend not to have a clear career path. Some forecasters predict the term 'employee' will disappear over the next few decades. Many people today have periods as full-time employees followed by periods of casual, part-time or contract work, and sell their skills to different businesses (see table 14.1).

TABLE 14.1 Old and new approaches to work

Old view	New view
Job	Work
Employee	Vendor
False sense of security	Sense of personal comfort
Employment	Employability
Job titles	Competencies
Career ladder	Career lattice
One career	Portfolio career

Source: Adapted from R. Critchley in R. Kramar, *Human resource management in Australia*, 3rd ed., Addison Wesley Longman, Melbourne, 1998, p. 239

> *Employers believe using casuals is one of the few ways they can reduce fixed costs to compete in globalising markets.*

Many changes in work patterns today appear to be driven by businesses' need to reduce costs and improve productivity. Some changes include:

- the rapid growth of contracting out or outsourcing. Outsourcing is frequently used to obtain a better service or product quality than would be obtained internally. Contracting, particularly offshore, may significantly reduce costs for some manufacturers.

- a preference of many businesses to have a smaller permanent core workforce and casual/temporary employees as a flexible workforce to meet demand at peak times. As a result, part-time and casual employees make up 27 per cent of the workforce today. This reduces recruitment and other labour 'on costs', such as long service leave and holiday pay that are applicable to full-time or part-time positions.
- flexible working hours, opportunities for flexible working arrangements including telecommuting and annualised salaries. Such arrangements are allowing businesses to operate 24 hours a day and on weekends, if required.
- increasing use of internal networking, team and project-based approaches to work.

Almost 25 per cent of full-time employees worked more than 50 hours per week in 2002, up from 20 per cent in 1982.

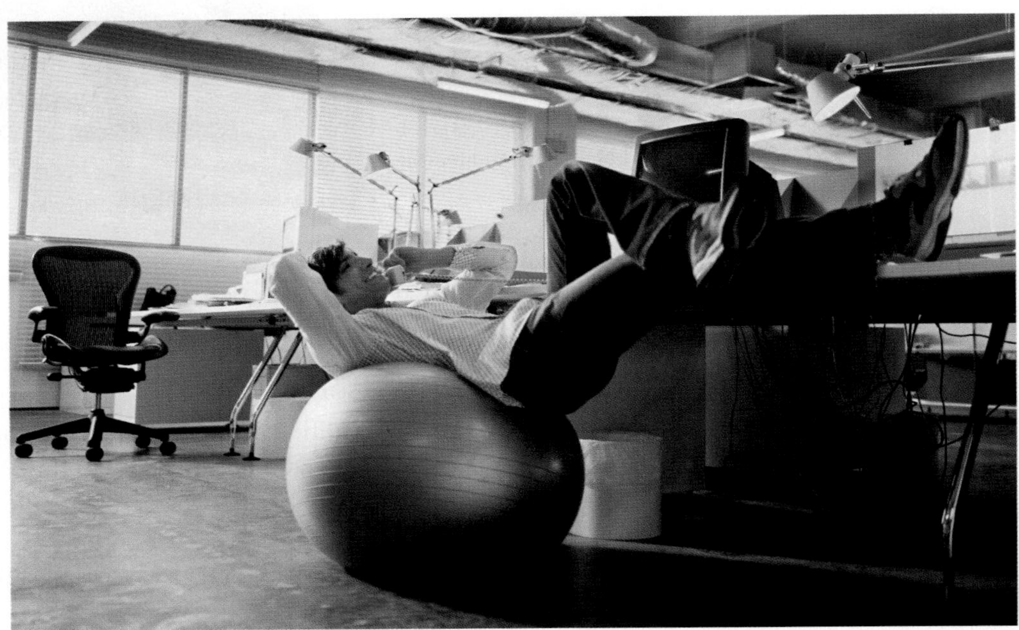

Figure 14.12 Work patterns are changing.

Full-time employment increased by 7 per cent between 1998 and 2003, while part-time employment and casual employment increased by over 22 per cent during the same period, largely due to growth in the finance, retail and hospitality industries and community services. Most casuals are either young males in a transitory stage of their working life, students or older females.

Careers are much more flexible today. Workers are looking after their own interests and careers. Around 14–16 per cent of employees are considered job mobile, and only 44 per cent of full-time employees have worked for their current employer for more than five years. The most mobile employees are aged 20–24, Australian-born, or of English-speaking background, and are found in retail or hospitality industries.

Population shifts

The female **participation rate** (52.3 per cent in 2004) has risen rapidly in recent decades. Women comprise 44 per cent of the workforce, 70.5 per cent of the part-time workforce and 33.7 per cent of the full-time workforce.

*The female **participation rate** refers to the proportion of women aged 15–69 employed or actively looking for work.*

Employers are increasingly recognising the cost savings and benefits of 'family friendly' practices (discussed in chapter 15) in retaining skilled staff. The workforce in developed nations is ageing, and labour shortages are emerging. Governments, concerned about the economic impacts of skills shortages, and the growing health burdens related to age, are keen to encourage employers and employees to postpone retirement and remain in the workforce.

Compulsory retirement is now illegal unless someone is on a federal award/ agreement that states a compulsory retirement age.

Early retirement from full-time work is popular today. The average age of retirement from full-time work is 49 (58 for males and 41 for females); however, participation in part-time work is much higher, suggesting older employees are using a gradual withdrawal approach to retirement.

In this environment, it is important for employers to develop succession and training plans to allow younger staff to move into management positions, and strategies to retain older staff. Effective strategies may include more flexible working hours and arrangements, opportunities to update skills, greater job variety and challenges, and targeted health and safety programs.

Changing attitudes

The workforce today is well educated and employees increasingly want challenging work, greater responsibility and autonomy. Employees are more aware of occupational health and safety issues and the effects of stress, often due to long working hours. With more women in the workforce, many employees are seeking increased equity in employment opportunities and trying to find a balance between work and family. Such matters are only being addressed in around 8 per cent of industrial agreements. Recent legislation, including the Workplace Relations Act, provides some support, as discussed in chapters 15, 16 and 18.

Legal influences: major employment legislation

The employment contract creates obligations for both employer and employee, and all businesses operate within a legal framework of common law and statute law — that is, law passed by federal and state parliaments in Acts (discussed in chapter 16).

***Social justice** in the workplace involves businesses being responsible or behaving in a fair and ethical manner towards their employees, customers and the broader community.*

*A **centralised industrial relations system** is a collectivist approach in which disputes are referred to industrial tribunals, such as the AIRC, for conciliation and arbitration.*

*In a **decentralised industrial relations system**, employers and employees negotiate wages and working conditions in the individual workplace through collective or individual bargaining without the involvement of tribunals.*

Legislation covers the nature of employment contracts and agreements; dispute-settling methods (as a result of our international agreements); protection of human rights in employment; and employer responsibilities for tax payments on behalf of employees. Employee welfare is provided for through occupational health and safety legislation and specific legislation such as the Superannuation Guarantee, under which all employers are obliged (either under awards or the legislation) to pay superannuation contributions for employees, whether or not they are on awards. They are charged at 9 per cent of their payroll for a base year multiplied by the employee's earnings 'base', which is deposited into a superannuation fund of the employee's choice.

Changing community and worker expectations on **social justice** (equal employment opportunity, anti-discrimination), safety and environmental issues are increasingly reflected in legislation and work practices, explored in more detail in chapters 16 and 18.

In recent years, governments have implemented policies to deregulate the economy and decentralise the industrial relations system to increase the competitiveness of firms in global markets. Our industrial relations system now allows employees to negotiate industrial agreements either on an individual basis, a collective basis without unions, or on a collective basis with unions at the enterprise level. We have, therefore, moved from a **centralised system** to a **decentralised system**, based increasingly on bargaining at the workplace level (see also chapter 16).

Research suggests that government policy and the economic environment are the most significant influences on the workplace today. Significant changes to government policy and legislation are generally the result of differing political and economic philosophies held by successive governments.

New organisational behavioural influences

Flat management and team structures

Businesses encouraging worker participation experience fewer industrial relations problems, as workers tend to develop a shared identity with, and commitment to, the goals of the firm. Businesses are transforming their organisational structures to create flatter, more responsive, adaptable management structures and networks of self-managing teams that encourage innovation, participation, improved productivity and greater efficiency.

However, promotional opportunities are more limited, particularly where layers of management are removed or new technology introduced. Employment relations managers, therefore, need to develop alternative motivational strategies for such staff. **Job enlargement**, **job rotation** (multiskilling), **job enrichment** and ongoing training help ensure that staff are retained and motivated to contribute to the organisation's success.

BiZ WoRD

__Job enlargement__ involves increasing the breadth of tasks in a job. __Job rotation__ involves moving staff from one task to another over a period of time. __Job enrichment__ involves increasing the responsibilities of a staff member.

Best practice organisations are responding by becoming 'learning organisations' that continue to develop employees and utilise their key competencies to remain competitive. Knowledge and employee skills are increasingly seen as a source of power and future wealth for businesses.

Team structures have become popular in recent years. They typically involve employees sharing some management functions, planning rosters or work schedules, and monitoring and evaluating their own performance. Teams offer employers greater flexibility, tap into employee experience and create opportunities for innovation, employee empowerment and leadership.

BiZ FaCT

All businesses in New South Wales must pay payroll tax of 6 per cent of their annual wages bill, over a tax-free threshold of $600 000 in annual wages.

Economic influences

The economic cycle

The demand for labour (employees) is determined by the demand for goods and services within the economy. If labour shortages develop during periods of economic growth, employers compete for employees by offering higher wages. Unions may use their stronger bargaining power to demand significant wage increases, which may then put upward pressure on costs and prices, creating inflation. During downturns in the economic cycle, demand for goods and services falls. Businesses are forced to reduce the size of their workforce (downsize) and limit their capacity to provide significant wage increases.

Strategies used by businesses when a labour shortage develops during a high growth period include:

- *tap into referral networks among staff*
- *find ways to reduce turnover*
- *recruit constantly*
- *consider your business structure — outsource recruitment or other functions, or automate simple tasks*
- *be prepared to recruit overseas*
- *reward loyalty.*

Structural change occurring in the economy has led to a rapid growth in employment in the services sector, which accounts for 82 per cent of total employment.

Employment is growing in property and business services, retailing, trades, tourism, educational services, hospitality, and community and personal services. Some of these industries have been traditionally dominated by women. As each sector grows, recruitment, selection and remuneration become important industrial issues. Effective training and staff empowerment are also critical to business success in such competitive customer service-based industries.

In manufacturing, removal of protective tariffs and quotas has increased business exposure to international competition. The subsequent fall in manufacturing employment has been hastened by rapid technological change.

Figure 14.13 Tourism is a rapidly growing industry.

Figure 14.14 Jobs of the twenty-first century — the growth areas

Globalisation

Unions are also responding to the globalisation of business by developing global union networks as a counterweight to the power of transnational corporations. Union leaders believe transnational corporations too often play workers of one nation off against those of another. The International Federation of Chemical, Energy, Mine and General Workers' Unions (ICEM) is a democratically run global union representing 20 million workers, now affiliated through the federation. The federation's aims include providing support for member unions during disputes, campaigning for human rights, union building in countries where unions are weak or non-existent and providing advice on industrial matters including health and safety standards.

Other global unions include the International Transport Workers' Federation (ITF), covering 5 million workers in 500 affiliates around the world, and FIET (International Association of Commercial, Clerical, Professional and Technical Employees) with links in many industries.

Globalisation of business has increased the level of international competition. Australian businesses compete every day with 'local' subsidiaries of transnational corporations. Many restructure, outsource non-core functions or subcontract production, in order to compete effectively. Corporations, both domestic and transnational, are increasingly prepared to relocate production units in other cities, states or countries where dispute levels, labour and regulatory costs are much lower (see the Snapshot 'Burger for burger'). In such an environment, there is an increased need to attract and retain motivated and effective core staff, and make continuous improvements in productivity, costs, innovation, quality and customer service. Productivity has increased by 3 per cent per annum in recent years as businesses invested in new technologies and manufacturing approaches, such as just-in-time and total quality management. Enterprise bargaining has allowed many employers to trade off restrictive/inefficient work practices for wage increases in industrial agreements. Business profitability has improved significantly.

Some transnational companies are introducing standardised global management employment contracts for all the countries in which they operate. They have found that to maintain harmony within the organisation and to attract the best managerial talent, they need to provide internationally competitive and standardised packages covering salary, housing, children's schooling, return trips and other resettlement costs.

Training in the management of multicultural workforces with differing approaches to power, authority and the role of groups/individuals is increasing with the globalisation of business.

International experience and research in employment relations influences policies adopted in Australia. The 'Japanisation' of employment relations is reflected in the focus on continuous improvement and total quality management. The 'Americanisation' of employment relations is reflected in more strategic holistic approaches to personnel management or what is known as human resource management. This approach recognises the strategic value of well-trained, motivated staff as a source of a firm's sustainable competitive advantage.

There is also an increasing role for international institutions, in a global market, such as the International Labour Organization (ILO) and trade blocs (for example, the European Union and the World Trade Organization), in promoting trade between countries that adhere to social justice principles (such as bans on child labour).

Burger for burger

The international business magazine *The Economist* uses the price of a McDonald's Big Mac as a benchmark for comparing the cost of living in countries around the world.

The Association of Professional Engineers, Scientists and Managers Australia's (APESMA) Big Mac Index compares graduate engineer salaries internationally by calculating the minutes of work required for a graduate engineer to pay for a Big Mac. It assumes a 40-hour week.

Country	Minutes	Local Big Mac price	Graduate salary	Salary in $A (approx)
Australia	9.9	A$3.20	A$41 000	$41 000
Canada	8.4	C$3.20	C$47 000	$47 500
Denmark	13.5	DKr24.75	DKr230 000	$51 000
India	31.3	Rupee 55	Rupee 220 000	$6 500
Italy	16.2	Lira 2.75	Lira 21 000	$35 000
Japan	7.0	¥270	¥4 800 000	$58 500
Malaysia	21.3	M$5.10	M$30 000	$10 500
New Zealand	12.8	NZ$3.95	NZ$38 500	$34 000
Singapore	13.3	S$3.30	S$31 000	$24 000
South Africa	17.5	Rand 14	Rand 100 000	$20 000
Sweden	13.6	SKr30	SKr280 000	$51 000
UK	13.3	£2	£19 000	$45 000
US	7.2	US$2.65	US$46 000	$59 500

SNaPSHoT Questions

1. In which countries are graduate salaries lowest?
2. Go to www.jaconline.com.au/businessstudies3e and click on the Gradsonline weblink for this textbook and research salaries for other professionals.
3. Why do some firms choose not to outsource work to lower-cost locations when others do?

Figure 14.15 Technological change underpins productivity improvements.

Other influences on employment relations

Other factors that influence employment relations practices include new technology, the nature of the industry, the actions of competitors and internal factors such as the size and nature of the business.

Technological change

Technological change is the major source of improvements in productivity, communication and competition between firms. It is causing the nature of production and services to change, resulting in the need for ongoing training programs. Many organisations are re-engineering and restructuring as networks. New jobs are created utilising new technology and its applications, while others become redundant.

Competitors

The actions of competitors are important in determining employment relations strategies used, particularly if the supply of potential staff is limited, leading to poaching problems. Retention of good staff is improved through good management of the employment relationship, and not just financial incentives.

Communications technology can change the workplace structure. For example, a cleaning company that relies totally on mobile communication with staff may be able to virtually eliminate its main office, but may need to increase its social activities, or plan special team meetings to promote commitment and communication to the organisation and an organisational identity.

EXERCISE 14.2 *Revision*

1. Draw a mind map to show all the influences on the employment relations function.
2. The influences on employment relations include economic influences, globalisation, legislation and many more. Read the following scenarios, which each describe a change in workplace employment practices. Discuss the type of influence that may have caused each change and the likely impacts each may have.
   (a) An agreement is introduced to allow continuous production and changes in work practices.
   (b) Affirmative action awareness is made a criterion for promotion to management positions.
   (c) Training in the recording of near misses and accidents is introduced.
   (d) Older staff are given a bonus for undertaking more training and mentoring.
   (e) Three hundred assembly-line workers are being retrenched as their jobs are redundant. The employment relations manager may offer younger staff the opportunity to 'up-skill' for jobs in other areas of the business.
   (f) Staff in the Vietnam office are increasing their cultural awareness.
3. Match the terms with the appropriate definitions:
   multiskilling, restructuring, downsizing, outsourcing, productivity, feminisation of workforce, flatter management structure, decentralisation of industrial relations, enterprise bargaining, social justice, globalisation, job design, award restructuring.
   (a) Occurs when a firm changes its organisational structure and functions, often closing down sections or removing jobs that are no longer needed, or too expensive for the business to operate.
   (b) Involves employees learning new tasks, which allows them to carry out a wider range of tasks in the workplace.
   (c) Occurs when firms are forced to retrench staff in order to improve efficiency, reduce costs or survive.
   (d) The increasing integration of financial and product markets, the increasing operation of business in global markets, and the opening up of economies to global influences.
   (e) The efficiency of production of goods and services; officially output per unit of input per employee.
   (f) The increasing participation of women in the workforce. Approximately 50 per cent of married women work.
   (g) Firms hire businesses or consultants to carry out tasks such as accounting or marketing for them on a contract basis.
   (h) Disputes over pay and conditions being resolved more and more by employers and employees in the workplace without the involvement of industrial tribunals.
   (i) The increasing trend of employers to make agreements about wages and conditions with their own employees in the workplace. These are then certified by the AIRC.
   (j) The practice of removing outdated or unnecessary provisions in awards.
   (k) Grouping a number of related tasks to be carried out by an employee. Today these need to be varied and challenging.

(l) Employers making decisions that consider the welfare of employees and the community.

(m) Redesigning the structure of a business to allow closer contact between management and subordinates and customers.

4. Prepare a summary of this chapter. A summary condenses the important issues and concepts presented in the chapter. Go to www.jaconline.com.au/businessstudies3e to compare your finished summary with the one provided for this textbook.

Extension

1. Collect information from annual reports to illustrate how more businesses today are using an employment relations approach to managing people. To find the annual reports, go to www.jaconline.com.au/businessstudies3e and click on the Selected Company Websites weblinks for this textbook. Using the information, draw three cartoons that show an employment relations approach to managing people and three cartoons that show where an employment relations approach is not being used.
2. Rachel is an employee relations consultant. Pretend you are Rachel and write a response to each letter. Compare your answers with your classmates.

> Dear Rachel
>
> I have just taken over my parents' piggery. I have been away studying physics at uni and have no idea about managing a pig farm. There are eight staff members, and some of them have slackened off a lot over the last few months. Two had a big punch-up yesterday. I'm at my wit's end. How do I start managing all these people? One employee has been trying to manage the place, but wants to leave as soon as I can start work. Who can help me?
>
> Peter

> Dear Rachel
>
> I recently got work in a shop selling take-away food. They told me I had to do two days' trial to see if I was any good at the job, and then they took me on probation for six months. They have not paid me for those two days, and I have only been paid twice. I am often expected to stay back, and the owner often screams at me if I'm not quick enough. He does the same thing with the other employees too. He doesn't make this much fuss about the cockroaches!
>
> I really need this job, but I want to be paid on time and not be yelled at by my boss. What do I do?
>
> Latife

> Dear Rachel
>
> The toy company I work for is outsourcing the production of electronic dogs to India. Luckily, I am being retrained, but some will lose their jobs. Why doesn't the government stop this?
>
> Victoria

CHAPTER

15 Effective employment relations

15.1 The role of employment relations

Reflect on either a part-time job you enjoyed doing, or a class you liked attending. What made these experiences so worthwhile? Your enjoyment was probably due to a combination of factors:

Figure 15.1 Better work relationships begin with an understanding of how people interact.

- You believed you were treated fairly and honestly.
- Your work was appreciated.
- Positive reinforcement, in the form of praise, was given for a job well done.
- Your involvement gave you a feeling of self-worth.
- Criticism, when given, was constructive.
- Conflicts, when they arose, were dealt with sensitively and appropriately.
- There was a harmonious atmosphere in the workplace/classroom, with positive work relationships between the staff.
- You felt part of a team working together to achieve a specific goal.

When you think about it, a sporting or debating team, emergency workers at the scene of an accident, the crew of an aircraft or sales assistants serving at the checkout all have one thing in common: they are part of a team that requires the interaction of a large number of individuals to achieve a common objective.

Most organisations that are successful in the long term maintain a balance between concern for success (expansion or profit) and regard for their employees. Better work and employment relationships begin with an understanding of how people interact.

People are an organisation's most valuable resource or asset. It makes sense, therefore, to develop cooperative and effective working relationships. Without dedicated, trained and motivated employees, the best organised plans will never be achieved. The human factor is crucial in all organisations. In its broadest sense employee or human relations covers all types of interaction among people: conflicts, cooperative efforts and interpersonal and group relationships.

Fortune magazine recently analysed the top 100 businesses in the United States. It believes they make the greatest investment in training (average of 43 hours per employee) and have a formal or informal commitment to job security (no retrenchments).

The employment relations function aims to manage the relationship between employer and employees effectively in order to develop competent, flexible, productive employees committed to the organisation (see figure 15.1). Employees must also be empowered to respond quickly and positively to change. Managers in the best-performing companies are increasingly recognising that retaining loyal, experienced staff is a priority in a competitive global marketplace and effective employment relations is a key factor.

Commitment from top-level management and collaboration of all staff are essential to ensure effective implementation of a strategic approach to employment relations.

Effective employment relations, therefore, involves a proactive, strategic approach. Management decides how the employment relationship will be best managed so that it is cost-effective, ethical, achieves the organisational objectives, and contributes to the 'bottom line'. A holistic, long-term view is taken of the importance of specific employment relations practices to the success of the enterprise.

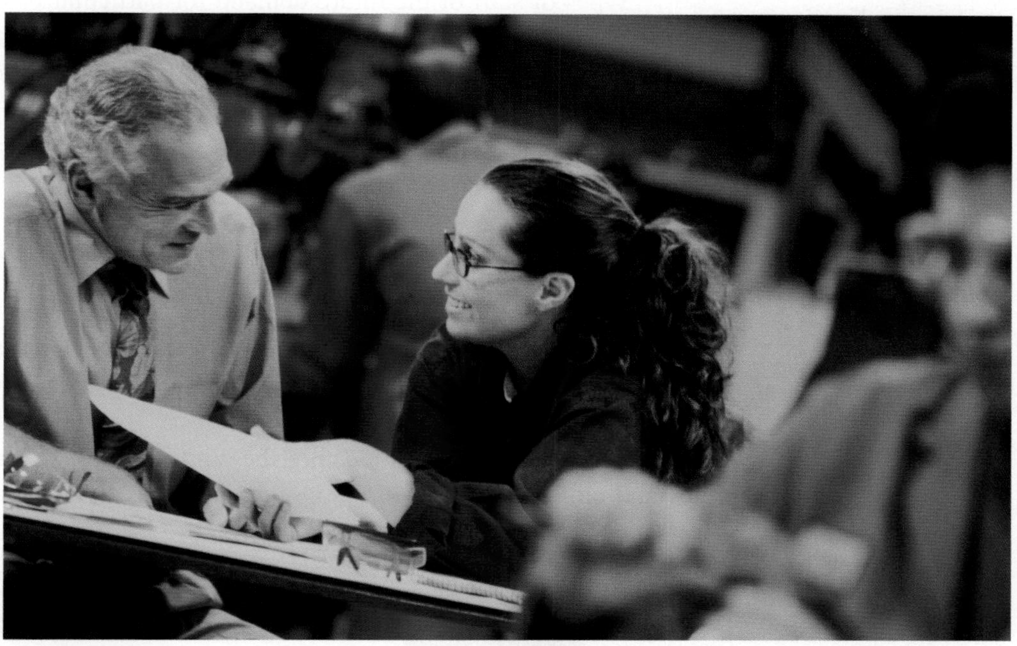

Figure 15.2 Effective employment relations is proactive.

Managing the employment relations role effectively

Managing the role of employment relations effectively may involve coordination of line management, the employment relations manager and even external consultants. Each may share in managing these practices shown in figure 15.3.

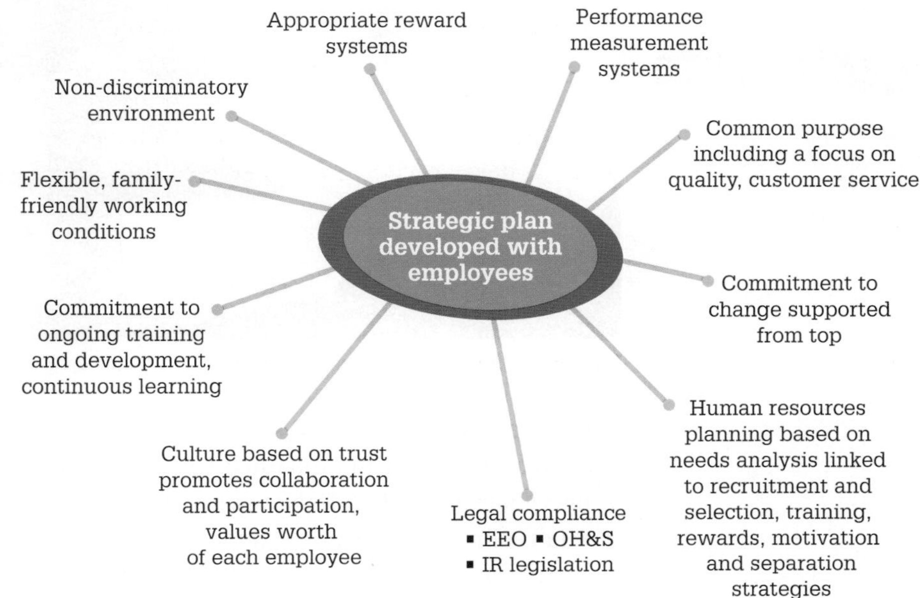

Figure 15.3 Key principles of effective employment relations

Labour costs are around 70 per cent of all operating costs of businesses. They include the direct wages cost and the labour 'on-costs' (often an additional 25–30 per cent) such as entitlements, leave allowances, superannuation contributions and fringe benefits.

***Recruitment** is the process of locating and attracting the right quantity and quality of staff to apply for employment vacancies or anticipated vacancies at the right cost.*

***Employee selection** involves gathering information about each applicant and using that information to choose the most appropriate applicant.*

***Placement** involves locating the employee in a position that best meets the needs and utilises the skills of the individual in the organisation.*

The median age of the labour force will be 39 in 2011.

Human resource planning

Human resource planning involves analysing:

- the internal environment, particularly the organisational goals, such as cost containment, stability, growth, downsizing, improved customer service or quality, and other internal influences on the business, such as the supply or skills of particular types of staff or the future demand for particular products or services
- the external environment, including economic conditions, competition, social and legal factors such as an ageing population, which influences the demand for or supply of potential employees.

Once the needs have been determined, the specific aspects of human resource management, such as recruitment or training, can be planned to meet these needs.

Recruitment, selection and placement

Recruitment is the process of locating and attracting the right quantity and quality of staff to apply for employment vacancies or anticipated vacancies at the right cost.

Employee selection is a screening or sifting process. It involves gathering information about each applicant for a position and then using that information to choose the most appropriate applicant.

Placement involves locating the employee in a position that best meets the needs and utilises the skills of the individual in the organisation.

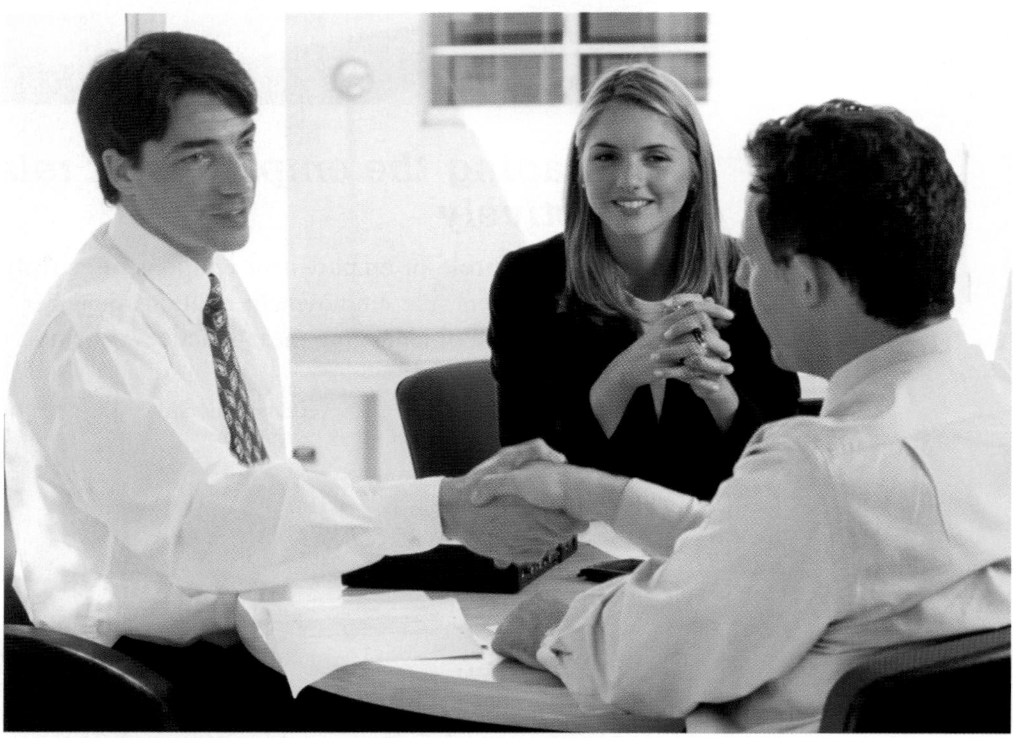

Figure 15.4 Employers need to plan selection policies carefully.

Effective recruitment and selection involves:

- evaluating and hiring qualified job applicants who are motivated and have values and goals aligned with the organisation
- a fair, non-discriminatory and legally compliant selection policy and process
- giving applicants a realistic understanding of their job description and responsibilities from the information provided to them in the process

The cost of a poor recruitment decision is generally believed to be around two or three times the annual salary of the person recruited.

A poor selection process leads to increased costs and lower productivity by increasing (among other things):

- *training costs (if poorly qualified staff are selected)*
- *job dissatisfaction, lower performance, industrial unrest/labour turnover if the organisation or the job does not meet the expectations of candidates selected*
- *the absenteeism rate if staff feel inadequate for the job/organisation or feel excessive work pressure*
- *accident or defect rates, fines or claims if inappropriate/untrained staff are selected.*

- using strategies that will prove useful for later selection and placement decisions. For example, a tool such as WEPP (Work Environment Preference Profile) can be an effective placement and development tool, as it allows an individual's work environment preferences to be compared with an actual work environment.
- using strategies that are aligned with other employment relations strategies and the business's needs. If the business is seeking to increase gender equity, there should be female representation on the selection panel and equitable remuneration and benefits packages, training and promotion opportunities.

The sources and methods used will depend on the recruitment goals and policies of the organisation (such as a preference for internal recruitment), the conditions of the labour market, the location of the business, the financial or other resources of the business and the specifications of the job to be filled. Internal recruitment may be used as a strategy to motivate and reward employees. Most businesses use a mix of internal and external recruitment.

Training and development

Training aims to develop skills, knowledge and attitudes that lead to superior work performance (discussed further on pages 328–31). Development focuses on enhancing the skills of the employee to allow them to take advantage of opportunities to develop a career with the organisation. The organisation benefits through the employee's experience and knowledge of the business through this process.

Rewards management

A well-planned reward system (discussed further on pages 326–8) providing both monetary and non-monetary rewards is a key strategy in attracting, motivating and retaining employees.

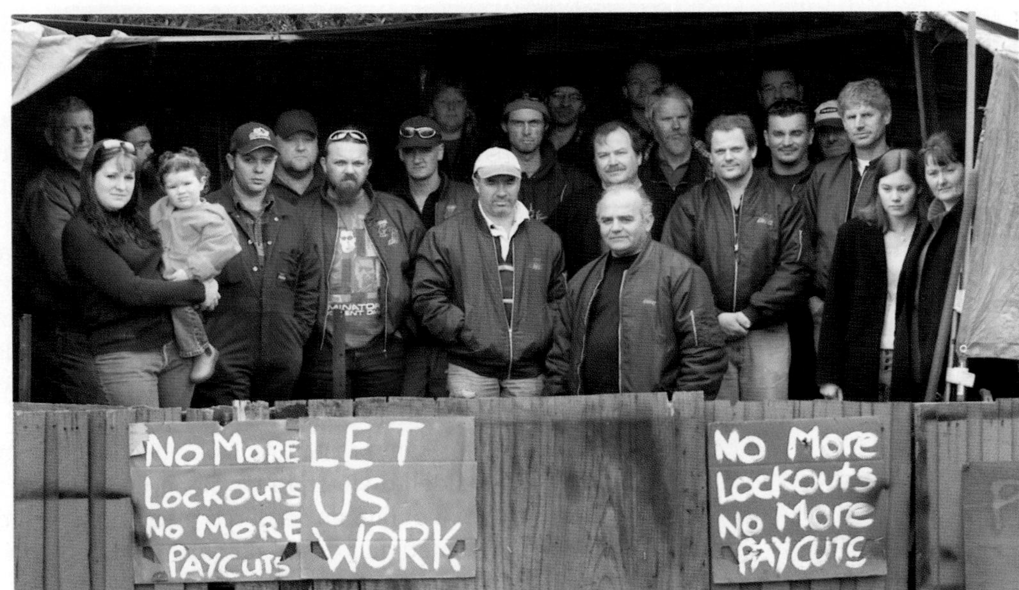

Figure 15.5 Managing industrial conflict is an important employment relations function.

Conflict resolution and management of industrial agreements

Conflict between stakeholders is inevitable in managing the employment relations function, and the level of conflict varies within and between industries and businesses. Some employers seek to minimise conflict, others stifle it through tough tactics while others manage it constructively through the use of collaborative

Much employee turnover in Australia occurs in newly recruited staff with less than one year in the job. This reinforces research that suggests most Australian management selection processes are unplanned, subjective, unsophisticated, highly susceptible to error and not supported with effective induction programs.

approaches to employment relations. Developing effective industrial agreements is a key role of this function and is discussed in chapter 17.

Legal compliance — occupational health and safety and social justice

All employers are required by law to ensure that employment relations procedures and policies comply with existing legislation, including occupational health and safety, taxation, social justice legislation and industrial relations legislation and agreements (discussed further in chapters 16 and 18).

Separation

Separation may take the form of resignation, relocation, voluntary redundancy, contract expiry, retrenchment or dismissal (summary and performance based). It must be managed carefully by employment relations managers to avoid claims of discrimination and adverse effects on the morale and productivity of remaining staff.

When an employee's employment is terminated, the employer must provide a written statement confirming the termination and reasons for the termination (if requested). It is important to use a range of strategies in determining who will be retrenched, and the mix may include such factors as length of service, standard of performance, future potential and whether some staff may be willing to leave voluntarily. Notice must be given complying with the relevant state or federal award or legislation. Managers should consult with staff prior to termination, and support them with outplacement to ensure a smooth transition that does not adversely affect the remaining employees' morale.

With a shortage of skilled staff looming in Australia, firms will need to work harder to motivate and retain staff to reduce separation rates or 'employee churn'.

EXERCISE 15.1 *Revision*

1. Outline the key functions of the employment relations manager.
2. Explain why effective employment relations is so important to business success today. Explain why staff other than employment relations staff might be involved in this area.
3. Outline the difference between the strategic and management roles of employment relations.
4. Identify problems that may arise if a business does not undertake human resource planning in some form. Give examples from businesses you have studied.
5. Identify the types of costs that may result from a poor recruitment and selection policy. Give examples.
6. Prepare a PowerPoint presentation on effective employment relations. Identify two strategies considered effective for managing each of the following employment relations functions: human resource planning; recruitment, selection and placement; training and development; rewards management; conflict resolution and management of industrial agreements; legal compliance; separation.

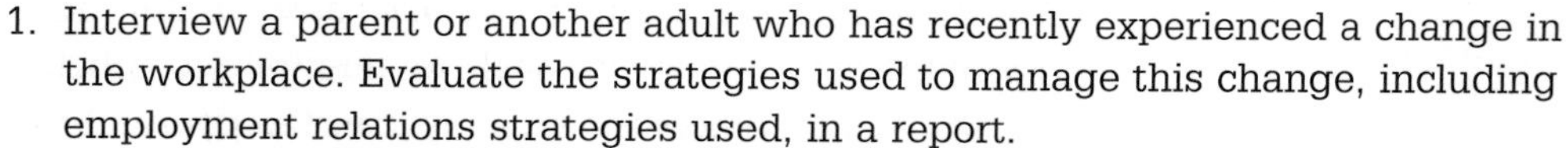

1. Interview a parent or another adult who has recently experienced a change in the workplace. Evaluate the strategies used to manage this change, including employment relations strategies used, in a report.

15.2 Importance of communications systems

Effective employment relations depends heavily on the strength of an organisation's communications systems. Methods of communication between employers and employees might include a daily 'walk around' by management; regular meetings between managers or supervisors and employees; staff bulletins and newsletters; staff seminars, including videos; social functions; suggestion boxes and surveys of staff; and use of email and intranet.

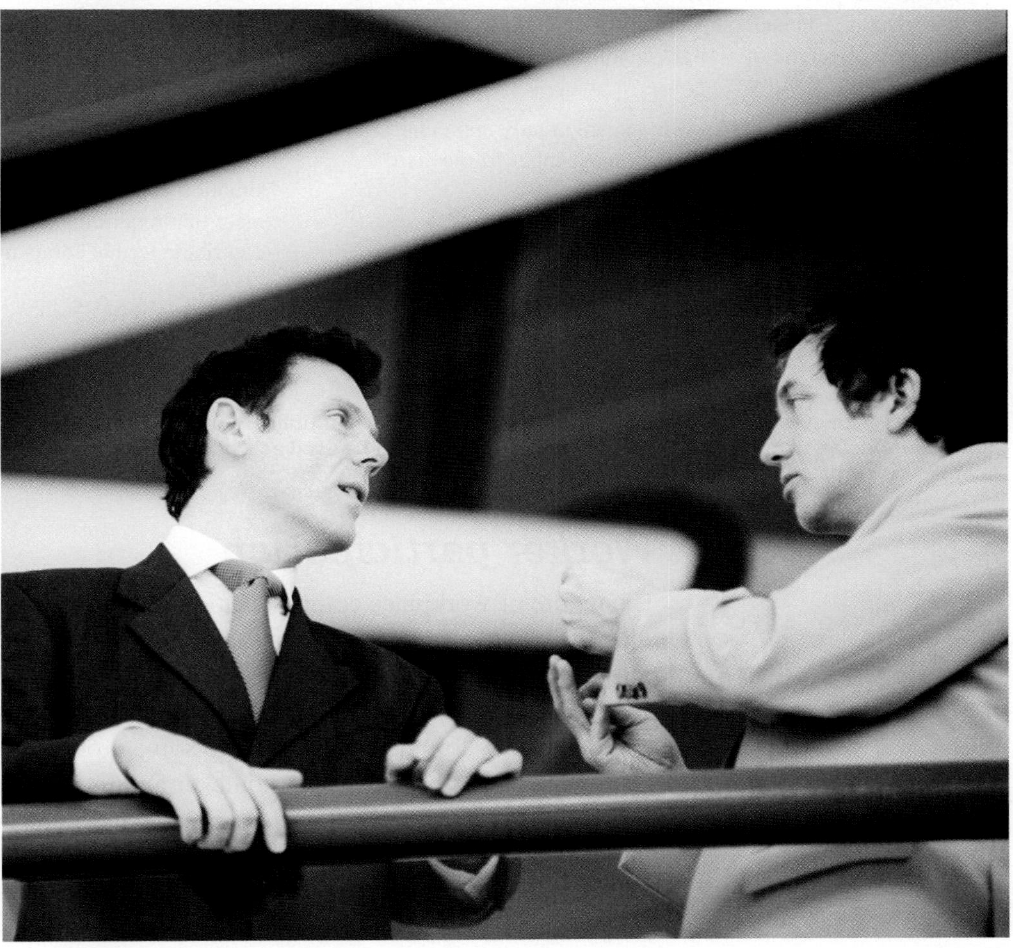

Figure 15.6 Effective communication is critical to business success.

Grievance procedures

Grievance procedures are formal procedures that an employer and employees have agreed to use to deal with issues or conflict in the workplace. Grievance procedures acknowledge that employment relations is a two-way communication process — that is:

- employees need avenues to communicate problems and air conflicts
- employers must be able to reprimand staff for unsatisfactory work or conduct.

They can help prevent a workplace issue from developing into a serious dispute. Most firms have established formal processes to manage grievances, whether due to requirements of awards or agreements or a management requirement, because ignoring complaints may lead to serious legal consequences.

Grievance procedures are mainly used to deal with personality conflicts and bullying, and disciplinary matters.

(a)

Letter of praise

TO: Terri Lee
Production Supervisor
FROM: Kim Jenkins
Managing Director
DATE: 6 October 2007

I am writing to convey our company's gratitude and my thanks for your hard work over the last year. You have demonstrated outstanding organisational skills and have striven to meet the often tight deadlines that the company has set.

Your special skills and knowledge are greatly appreciated and I look forward to your continued input to our hard-working team.

Kind regards,

K. Jenkins

(b)

Letter of reprimand

TO: Terri Lee
Production Supervisor
FROM: Kim Jenkins
Managing Director
DATE: 6 October 2007

The company has always regarded you as a valuable member of our team who strives to meet difficult deadlines and motivate others. However, you were recently responsible for a breach of company policy, which resulted in the loss of a valuable customer account.

In future you must abide by company policy and inform me of any complaints from customers before the situation escalates. I will make every effort to help you meet this requirement and trust that you will continue to contribute to this company's success.

Yours sincerely,

K. Jenkins

Figure 15.7 Examples of communications with staff: (a) a letter of praise, a useful management tool for boosting morale, and (b) a letter of reprimand which, under unfair dismissal laws, could be used as evidence that management gave an employee the required number of warnings of unsatisfactory conduct.

Worker participation

Figure 15.8 Employee participation provides a constructive path to business success.

The nature of workplace communication is changing with the increasing use of email and the increased opportunities for employee participation. Firms encourage employee participation to improve communication, empower employees and develop their commitment to improving quality and efficiency. Staff are being trained to make some decisions 'on the spot', either to solve problems or provide incentives to retain customers, as customers demand quicker and more efficient service.

Firms benefit from employee experience and knowledge on the job and improvements they suggest are often critical to a firm's competitiveness and success.

The value and effectiveness of employee participation depends on the training, knowledge and skills of the employees involved. The use of suggestion boxes is often included as an example of employee participation. However, true participation is fostered through regular team meetings/briefings to discuss company trends and issues — these build a sense of shared purpose and company identity.

Joint consultative committees

Joint consultative committees, or works committees, are formally established groups consisting of employees and management representatives, and may or may not include union representatives. Their original purpose was to provide management with the views of employees on a range of issues, enhance communication and improve efficiency or productivity.

The committees have become vehicles for sharing mutual concerns in the workplace, but surveys suggest they rarely give employees control or influence over a firm's objectives. They function best when substantial and relevant issues are discussed and where there is a cooperative management approach towards union and employee involvement. They are less effective where they become 'gripe sessions'. To be effective, members need to be trained and given adequate time and sufficient information for meetings.

Team briefings

A range of team strategies are employed in businesses today, from project teams who work together for the duration of a project to quality circles and semi-autonomous and self-managed work teams.

Quality circles

Quality circles involve employees meeting voluntarily on a regular basis to discuss, analyse and resolve specific problems, such as safety, quality, work processes and productivity issues in a workplace. Teams present their suggestions in reports to management and the groups then disband.

Semi-autonomous teams/self-managing work teams

A semi-autonomous team is a form of participative work organisation in which a group of employees assumes a high degree of responsibility for a task or group of tasks. More workers are being trained and empowered to make decisions on the spot to either solve problems, or provide incentives to retain customers, as customers increasingly demand quick and efficient service.

Effective team building by management must include development of conflict resolution skills, preparation for issues which may arise, careful selection of a balanced team, and opportunities for problems and feedback to be shared.

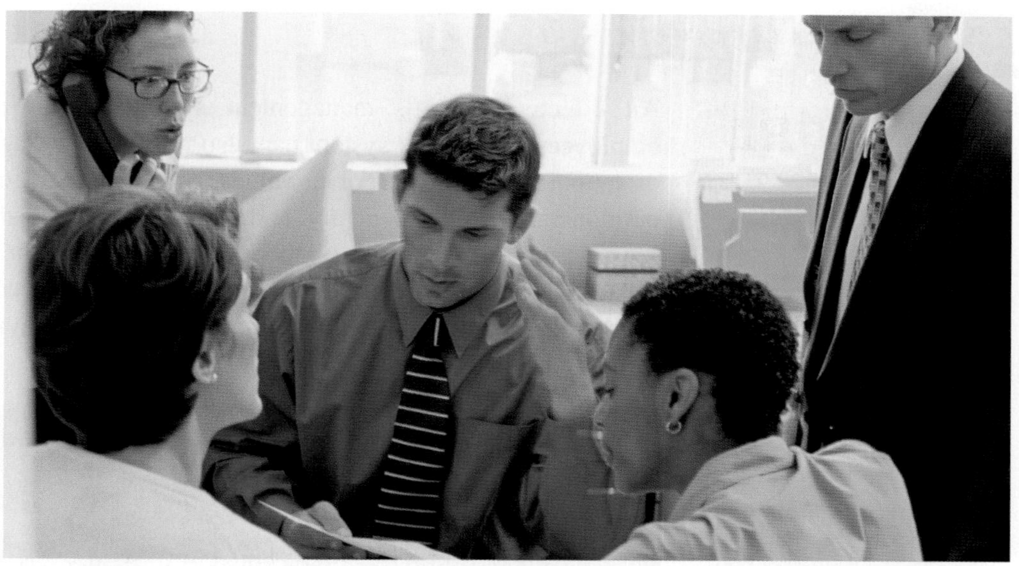

Figure 15.9 Worker participation is achieved through regular team meetings at the workplace.

Over time, teams may become self-managing and even rotate leadership roles. Such teams have been introduced in organisations as varied as Intel and the Swedish Volvo Company. In a self-managing work team (SMWT), the employees take responsibility for planning and organising their work, including the allocation of tasks within their group. They are also accountable for the results of the team. This approach reduces the need for managerial supervision, and fosters self-management, multiskilling, teamwork and problem solving by the group.

EXERCISE 15.2 *Revision*

1. What is the purpose of a grievance procedure? Describe the typical grievance procedure.
2. Try to use all the following terms to write *a few sentences only* that describe the benefits of worker participation and team structures: ideas, experience, shared purpose, company identity, process improvement, productivity, motivation, responsibility, accountable, better customer service.
3. Interview someone you know who works in a team.
   (a) Identify the benefits of implementing work teams.
   (b) Identify factors which may hinder the effective operation of work groups and teams.
   (c) Outline ways in which the effectiveness of teams may be improved.

Extension

1. Suggest reasons why the critical issues identified by businesses for effective employment relations today are high productivity, customer satisfaction, quality, and linking employment relations business practices to business goals.
2. Explain how specific employment relations strategies, such as employee participation, teamwork, flexible working conditions, training and rewards strategies, may help achieve each of the objectives in question 1.

15.3 Rewards

***Intrinsic rewards** are those that the individual derives from the task or job itself, such as a sense of achievement. **Extrinsic rewards** are those given or provided outside the job itself. They may be monetary, for example, incentive payments, or non-monetary, for example, flexible work schedules.*

Executive remuneration averaged 74 times average weekly earnings.

An effective rewards management system should *attract*, *retain* and *motivate* employees. A rewards system can also reinforce strategies that will facilitate change or support desirable corporate values, such as a focus on the customer. Rewards can be monetary or non-monetary, and **intrinsic** or **extrinsic** (see figure 15.11). Intrinsic rewards are those that the individual derives from the task or job itself, such as a sense of achievement. Extrinsic rewards are those given or provided outside the job. They may be monetary, for example, incentive payments, or non-monetary, for example, flexible work schedules.

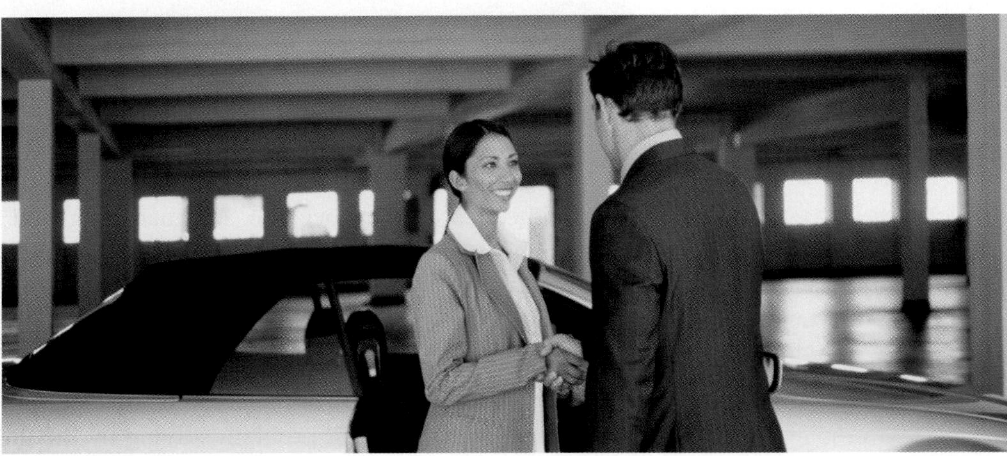

Figure 15.10 Rewards are important motivators.

Total reward system

Intrinsic rewards associated with job (non-monetary)

Job
- Interesting work
- Challenge
- Responsibility
- Recognition/feedback
- Promotion
- Autonomy in job
- Sense of achievement

Environment
- Good policies and practices
- Effective leadership/supervision
- Good relationships with co-workers
- Safe and healthy work environment
- Fair treatment
- Club membership
- Social activities
- Recognition, praise

Extrinsic rewards associated with job (monetary/non-monetary)

Direct (cash)
- Wages
- Salary
- Commissions
- Incentive and performance
  - bonus plans
  - share plan
  - pay increase
  - group profit sharing (gainsharing)

(non-cash)
- Individual awards
- Group awards

Indirect (fringe benefits)
- Insurance
- Holidays
- Child care
- Medical/health costs
- Employee assistance
- Flexible work schedules
- Free legal advice
- Personal loans at cheap rates
- Moving expenses
- Training expenses/time off
- Company car
- Parking space
- Discount purchases and privileges

Figure 15.11 Features of reward systems

Around 90 per cent of Australia's public companies offer share ownership schemes. With profit sharing, employees may be offered shares, annual bonuses or performance payments based on output, sales, profits or other indicators. The federal government has set a target to increase the proportion of employees with shares in the company they work for to 11 per cent by 2009.

Some of the most effective motivational strategies include:
- *providing opportunities for advancement*
- *job security*
- *challenging and interesting work*
- *showing respect for employee efforts*
- *employee recognition for performance and value to business.*

Profit sharing or employee share plans are often used to boost commitment and to promote a culture that values quality, customer service, participation or teamwork. Reward systems are also increasingly linked to performance management through enterprise bargaining and individual contracts.

Many tools can be used by the employment relations manager in developing a reward system. For example, a grid or matrix could be drawn up to assess the objectives of each reward and the overall effectiveness of the system (an example is shown in table 15.1).

TABLE 15.1 A rewards matrix for a business

	Reward objectives					
Reward component	**Attract**	**Retain**	**Productivity**	**Individual contribution**	**Employee security**	**Company performance**
Base salary	✓	✓				
Gainsharing plan			✓			
Performance incentive		✓	✓	✓		
Corporate profit share	✓					✓
Superannuation	✓	✓				
Other benefits		✓			✓	
Career planning		✓	✓		✓	

Workers in 2004–05 received wage increases averaging $2000 per year, while executive increases averaged $140 000.

*An **equitable reward** is seen as fair or deserved by employees. Equity may be seen from an internal (inside the business) or external (in comparison with other businesses) viewpoint.*

The reward system should aim to motivate staff and be equitable, clearly communicated, defensible, consistent, relevant, cost-effective and integrated with corporate strategy. Managers can also link rewards with performance and skills recognised in the marketplace using job evaluations (based on job descriptions, specifications and performance appraisals), comparisons with other similar employers, and analysis of statistics and surveys compiled by recruitment agencies.

Some argue that businesses may use performance incentive systems as a substitute for more important motivation strategies, such as improved job design, employee participation and feedback to employees about their work.

Performance-based rewards may lead to problems if some individuals believe they work harder than others in teams, without recognition of their efforts. They may also lead to competition between workers rather than cooperation. For other employees, productivity or job performance may be difficult to measure and reward. Employees must see the system as fair and **equitable** or increases in industrial unrest or employee turnover may result.

15.4 Training and development

Statistics on training indicate that:

- *51 per cent of the labour force has a post-school qualification*
- *85 per cent of employees in organisations with more than 10 employees are given some form of training*
- *84 per cent of full-time employees have undertaken some form of training*
- *training is most common for management and professional employees aged 25–44*
- *82 per cent of training is primarily formal, in classroom/seminar format*
- *employers' support is greater for persons with post-school qualifications.*

The aim of training is to seek a long-term change in employees' skills, knowledge, attitudes and behaviour in order to improve work performance in the organisation. Most organisations today offer training in some form, whether as a requirement for competency in the role or as a tool to develop and expand workers' skills. Around half of employees who have worked for their employer for one year or more receive some kind of education or formal training. The majority who attend a formal course or who study for an educational qualification receive some assistance from their employer.

Many enterprise agreements focus today on improving the functional flexibility of the workforce through multiskilling, job rotation, removal of restrictive work practices, reductions in work classifications and demarcations, job enlargement and job enrichment. Ongoing training and development are key ingredients in this process.

Lack of training can have long-term implications for businesses in remaining competitive and could lead to higher turnover rates as staff seek development in other firms.

Induction

An effective induction program is carefully planned to introduce the new employee to the job, their co-workers, the organisation and its culture. Supervisors, co-workers and the human resources department (if a larger business) may be involved in the process. Most employees who leave an organisation depart in the first three months; therefore, the need for support is greatest when an employee is in a new job. A well-prepared induction program:

- gives employees a positive attitude to the job and the organisation
- builds a new employee's confidence in the job
- stresses the major safety policies and procedures and explains their application (see figure 15.12)
- helps establish good working relationships with co-workers and supervisors.

INDUCTION

Induction of new employees into positions is a vital part of the OH&S process because it is at this point that the safety aspects of the plant and the job can be outlined. The following is a sample checklist.

OH&S INDUCTION CHECKLIST

Employee's Name: .... **Starting Date:** .... / ..../.............

Department:.. **Position:** ....

All boxes to be marked off where applicable

Occupational Health & Safety

- ☐ Safety rules and procedures
- ☐ Safety regulations
- ☐ Supply of uniforms and specialised clothing

About the company

- ☐ Annual leave entitlements
- ☐ Sick leave
- ☐ Long service leave
- ☐ Special leave
- ☐ Retirement
- ☐ Company policies and procedures
- ☐ Company organisation charts
- ☐ Superannuation
- ☐ Workers' compensation
- ☐ Current staff telephone lists
- ☐ Affirmative action policy statement
- ☐ Promotion and recruitment
- ☐ Quality statement

Conditions of employment

- ☐ Salary and wages
- ☐ Methods of payment
- ☐ Employment Tax Declaration
- ☐ Tax File Notification form
- ☐ Review/appraisal procedures
- ☐ Award payments
- ☐ Hours
- ☐ Overtime
- ☐ Shift arrangements
- ☐ Incentive and bonus schemes
- ☐ Safety rules and procedures
- ☐ Company facilities

Floor plans

- ☐ Location of facilities: First Aid Room, canteen, tea room, staff notice boards
- ☐ Parking

Work procedures

- ☐ Position description
- ☐ Work instructions
- ☐ Care of company property
- ☐ Supply and maintenance of tools and equipment
- ☐ Protective clothing
- ☐ Lifting and handling
- ☐ First aid facilities
- ☐ Relevant legislation explained

Introductions

- ☐ To appropriate managers and supervisors
- ☐ To co-workers
- ☐ To employee representative
- ☐ Other relevant personnel

Building emergency procedures

- ☐ Tour of premises
- ☐ Explanation of fire warning system
- ☐ Fire alert action plan
- ☐ Escape exits
- ☐ Assembly points after evacuation
- ☐ Training in use of fire-fighting and alarm equipment
- ☐ No smoking rule
- ☐ Out of bounds areas
- ☐ Maintaining clearance of exits and gangways
- ☐ Closing fire doors
- ☐ Protective clothing
- ☐ Legislation
- ☐ First aid officers

Feedback opportunities

- ☐ Progress in job — after first day; after first week; after first month
- ☐ Matters requiring further clarification
- ☐ Any other concerns

Figure 15.12 A plan for the induction of new employees is a vital aspect of a company's Occupational Health and Safety program.

The most common reasons for providing training include improving job performance, responding to new technology, improving quality of goods/services, safety needs and to build greater flexibility in the workforce.

Training programs

An effective training program is planned, is integral to the business strategy and to maintaining or developing a business's sustainable competitive advantage. It is essential in overcoming business weaknesses, building on strengths and maintaining staff commitment. A focus on acquiring new skills and knowledge helps a business adapt to change and stay ahead of the competition.

Ongoing training for all employees is increasing in importance due to rapid technological change and global competition, leading many organisations to promote

*A **learning organisation** monitors and interprets its environment, seeking to improve its understanding of the interrelationship between its actions and the business environment. All of its employees are involved in developing knowledge and insights that allow the organisation to continuously grow and improve.*

***Performance appraisals** are strategies used by management to evaluate the performance of employees. In some cases, employees evaluate the performance of managers too. Performance appraisals are commonly undertaken annually or biannually and may be conducted using such methods as staff surveys, ratings and reports based on observations, interviews and analysis of critical incidents.*

the concept of a '**learning organisation**' within their business. All employees are involved in developing and regularly updating, knowledge and insights that allow the organisation to continuously grow and improve.

Key features of an effective training program include the following.

Step 1

Assess the needs:

- of the individual (skills, knowledge, attitudes, both long and short term)
- of the job (competencies required)
- of the organisation (for example, culture, goals, standards, service levels).

This information may be provided from trend analysis (production or financial), safety records, **performance appraisals**, staff surveys, feedback from customers or supervisors, exit interviews or observation.

Step 2

Determine the objectives of the training program for the organisation, job and individual. Management input and support at this stage is critical to a successful training program.

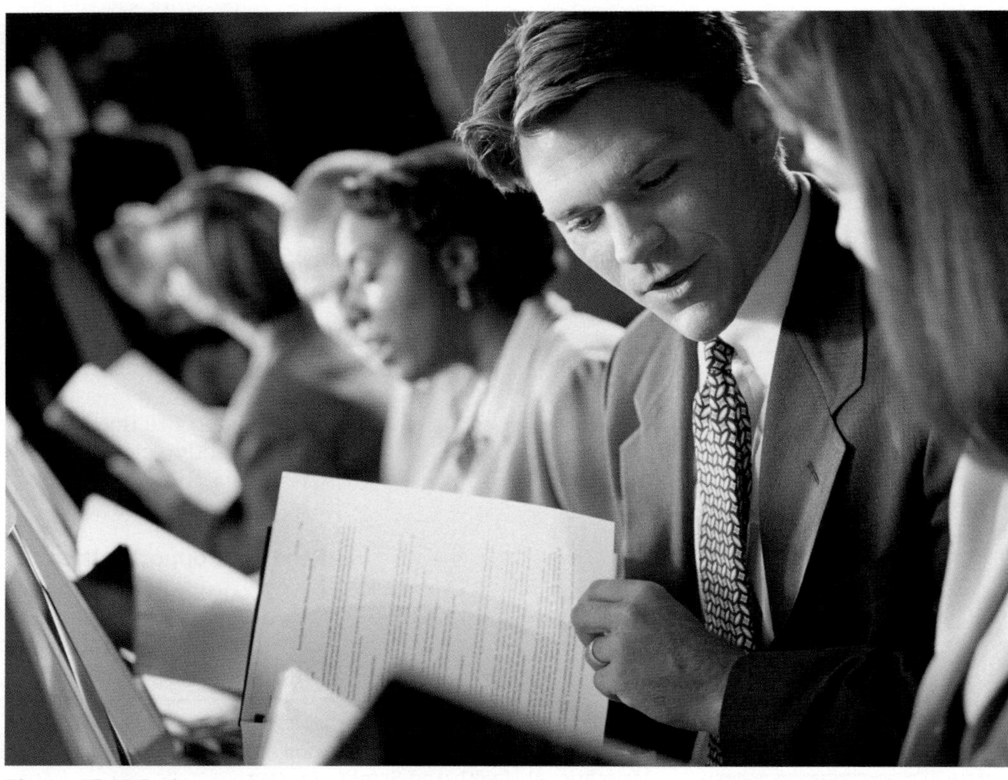

Figure 15.13 Self-paced learning is popular in some firms.

Step 3

Consider the internal and external influences. Internal influences include the attitude of employees to training, and staffing, financial and physical resources available to operate the program. Sometimes the outsourcing of aspects of the program is required. External influences include any new research on relevant training issues and government programs or support available for training. Key influences also include competitor behaviour and training programs in the local or global market, current industrial relations legislation and technological change.

Figure 15.14 Training keeps businesses competitive.

Key skills needed by employees today are:

- *communication*
- *teamwork*
- *problem solving*
- *initiative and enterprise*
- *self-management*
- *technology*
- *planning and organising.*

Management development programs focus increasingly on providing challenge and opportunities to develop skills in facilitation, goal and action management, leadership, and management of people. Key features of effective management training techniques are the use of job rotation, mentoring and formal business training through programs such as the MBA (Master of Business Administration).

A recent leadership survey conducted by Leadership Management Australia found the major issues for employees in the workplace today are:

- *added work responsibilities*
- *pressure to perform*
- *work–life balance through workplace flexibility.*

Employers were generally considered unaware of the importance of these issues.

Step 4

Determine the process — that is:

- the content of the training program
- learning principles to be applied, including participation, repetition, demonstration and feedback
- the learning methods to be applied, such as simulation training, lectures, job rotation, apprenticeship
- the location of the training program, whether on-site or off-site (for example, TAFE or seminar)
- the participants involved — employees, supervisors, employment relations manager, external consultants.

Step 5

Evaluate the training program. Strategies include tests and surveys, both prior to training and after training; performance appraisal; observation; benchmarking of key indicators, such as defects, customer complaints and accident rates. The training program can be evaluated over time in terms of the changes in key indicators, including cost of sales, sales volumes/employee, profits and productivity absenteeism, overtime and labour turnover. The program should also be evaluated for its cost-effectiveness and the time involved in the training program (see figure 15.15).

The general impact on employee behaviour, in terms of skills or relationships with customers or other employees, should be monitored and evaluated by management over the longer term. Employees also require regular feedback to reinforce their progress.

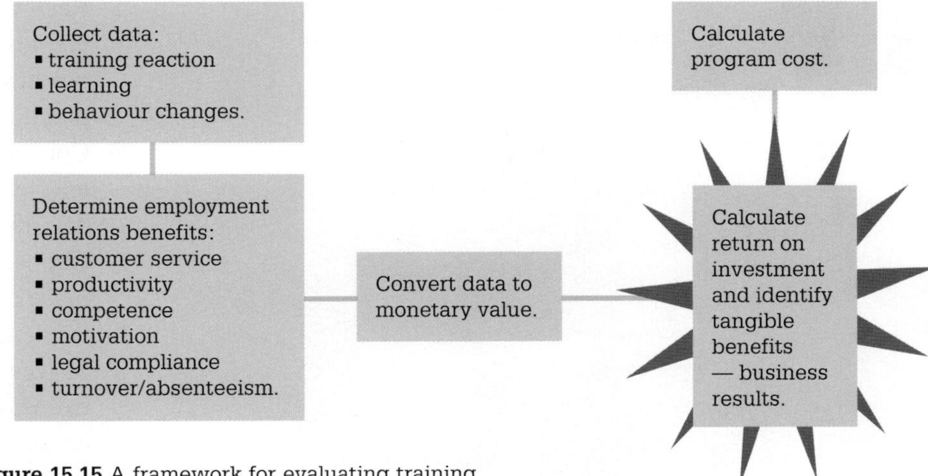

Figure 15.15 A framework for evaluating training

Development

Businesses need to plan for future human resource needs both at the managerial and entry level. Effective development programs ensure that all experienced and talented staff — male and female — are retained, and that motivation and commitment are enhanced through promotion opportunities for all employees over the longer term. Training and development needs change as an employee's career develops. In the early stages, employees may focus on gaining qualifications. As they move from one employer to another, younger employees focus on experiencing a variety of roles to determine their interests and talents. Later, the developing of specialist or managerial competencies may become important as employees move into senior positions. For over-40s, the focus may be on upgrading knowledge and work–life balance issues.

15.5 Flexible working conditions

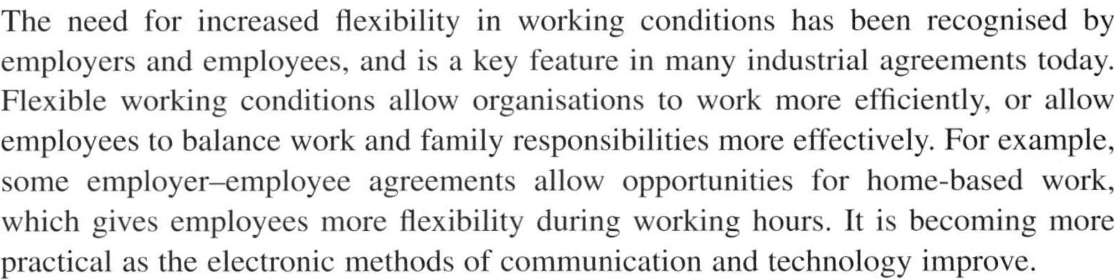

The need for increased flexibility in working conditions has been recognised by employers and employees, and is a key feature in many industrial agreements today. Flexible working conditions allow organisations to work more efficiently, or allow employees to balance work and family responsibilities more effectively. For example, some employer–employee agreements allow opportunities for home-based work, which gives employees more flexibility during working hours. It is becoming more practical as the electronic methods of communication and technology improve.

Figure 15.16 Family-friendly working hours allow workers to balance work and family responsibilities more effectively.

Typical flexible working conditions include flexible remuneration (reward) options, flexible working hours, flexible study/work arrangements, career break schemes, job sharing, family leave, work from home arrangements (rostered days off, telecommuting, a compressed work week), and part-year work arrangements, which often suit competitive sportsmen and women.

The following steps to implementing flexible practices are recommended for businesses:

1. Review the nature of the workforce, employee behaviour and areas of the business that will benefit from such practices.
2. Consult with staff, unions and external advisers, such as government bodies, to determine the practices needed.
3. Choose the best options for the workplace and ensure legal compliance.
4. Implement the new practices.
5. Survey staff, review practices for effectiveness and modify them, if required, on an ongoing basis.

BiZ WoRD

Profit sharing *refers to the practice of calculating an employee's portion of a monthly profit pool.*

Productivity sharing *refers to the practice of rewarding employees for productivity levels above specific targets.*

Flexible remuneration agreements

Some organisations offer employees flexible remuneration arrangements in an integrated package in their agreements, often as a motivational tool (see the Snapshot 'Life work'). They allow employees to see how their efforts are important and relate to the improvements in the performance of the company. These arrangements may include conditional pay increases (for achieving objectives), bonuses, performance pay, employee share ownership, **profit sharing** and **productivity sharing**. These arrangements are often related to the business achievement of key performance indicators. Figure 15.17 shows a mathematical formula used by many businesses to determine the total wage payments of an enterprise agreement.

The following is an example of a model used to establish the enterprise wage component of the total wages bill for a company. Its complexity indicates the range and types of issues that companies must consider in arriving at their enterprise agreements.

$$E = LYP(1 + CPI) - \left[\frac{(\Delta A^*WA) + (\Delta B^*WB) + (\Delta C^*WC) + (\Delta D^*WD)}{r}\right]$$

where:

E = wage determined at the enterprise
LYP = last year's enterprise wage component
CPI = consumer price index for the year previous
A = the indicator for accidents
B = the indicator for absenteeism
C = the indicator for consumer complaints
D = labour ratio
r = ratio of division between the firm and employees
W = weighting of indicator (in dollars)

Source: Asia Pacific Journal of Human Resources, vol. 35, no. 3, p. 55

Figure 15.17 Mathematical formula for calculating total wage payments of an enterprise agreement

Life work

Australian companies have poor policies about work–life balance or they are not interested in promoting themselves as employers of choice. These could be conclusions to be drawn from the number of entries in this year's National Work & Family Awards. . . .

The Australian Chamber of Commerce and Industry (ACCI) has a national network of more than 350 000 businesses, so it would be reasonable to assume that the judging panel for the awards would have received thousands of entries. Not so. The record number of entries was 74 — only 74 companies were keen to be scrutinised on their achievements in providing for the work–life needs of employees. It seems that companies are not interested in having their policies on work–life balance put under the microscope.

. . .

The winners have important traits in common: the leaders of these organisations are determined to retain staff; they are trying to embrace the idea that staff, particularly those with families, often need flexibility to do their jobs properly; and they are continually surveying staff to find out what they want in terms of flexibility, and then acting on it. . . .

Australian Federal Police (AFP), the Gold award winner this year, has dramatically changed its approach on work and family policy since Commissioner Mick Keelty took over in 2001. After an organisation-wide survey, sweeping changes have been introduced to help staff find a balance between work and family life. Keelty says: 'The demands on police, particularly parents in the force and the hours that police have to work, mean that it was quite a challenge to find a way of promoting work–life diversity and make family life a focus.' . . .

(*continued*)

In the surveys, staff asked for more flexible hours, the option of working from home, job sharing, part-time options, carer's leave and paternity leave. In emergencies, such as the Canberra bushfires, the AFP now pays for Dial-An-Angel care for staff that need child care. Keelty says: 'People want to come to work and contribute to these major operations but are often hindered because of a lack of child-care arrangements. Or . . . you have both partners in policing, and it meant that one could and one couldn't.' The AFP now provides a carer's room and facilities so that staff can bring in their children when necessary.

The AFP has introduced a Finding your Rhythm program to help staff cope with the demands of their jobs and keep a semblance of balance in their lives. At the heart of the strategy is an intranet site that outlines what support assistance, services and emergency care are available for AFP staff and provides ways for managers and workers to develop flexible work arrangements and information on policies and protocols.

. . .

The law firm Minter Ellison is this year's joint winner of the Rising Star award. The firm's human resources manager, Robert Marriott, says it has taken three years to start to change the culture of long hours and gruelling workloads. 'It has been difficult', he says. The results include board approval for part-time partner positions, seminars for all levels of staff on issues such as how to deal with teenagers, and paid parental leave (which, after 12 months, has resulted in 78 per cent, rather than 40 per cent, of staff returning to work after having children).

Despite the Rising Star award, Marriott is modest about the firm's progress. 'We don't see ourselves as advanced. We know we have a big way to go.'

One of the big shifts for Minter Ellison, says Marriott, has been to benchmark the firm's work–life policies not against other law firms, but against the best-in-all-sectors employers of choice. Minter Ellison employed a consultancy, Hewitt Associates, to measure the attitudes to the firm of Minter Ellison's 1788 staff. After that, committees were formed to look at ways to introduce work–life policies throughout the firm. Initiatives included programs to keep in touch with staff on parental leave or leave of absence, health and relaxation support, subsidised yoga and gym, discounts on child care and health insurance, language classes, flu shots and parental leave.

. . .

Winning an award for being an employer of choice has its benefits: recognition, the potential to recruit the best talent, and the slap-up awards night. But it is also a tough standard to live up to. Many times, awards such as the Work & Family Awards inspire whistleblowers to reveal unfair or inconsistent work practices within a company, exposing departments and managers that do not want to be a part of a new ethos.

Perhaps this is why so many companies do not want to expose themselves to the outside world; they are not ready for the open-for-inspection, and have a lot of tidying up to do before they can show off their human resources prowess.

WHAT THE BEST COMPANIES ARE DOING

- Surveying staff about the flexible policies they would like.
- Approaching the issue of workplace flexibility as a 'win-win' situation rather than employee win/employer lose.
- Remembering that, when it comes to work–life balance, actions speak louder than words.
- Looking at the cost of implementing policies as a staff incentive rather than a financial drain on the company.
- Acknowledging the importance of staff retention, particularly after maternity or long service leave.
- Seriously investigating how to make paid maternity leave possible if the organisation does not already offer it.
- Making leave allowances for illness in the family or special family events.

. . .

Source: E. Ross, 'Life work', *BRW*, 6 May 2004.

SNaPSHoT Questions

As CEO of Pets Play, a manufacturer of pet accessories with a turnover of $50 million and 150 employees, you are finding it hard to keep your young staff once they begin having families.

1. Draw up a list of family-friendly initiatives you may be able to afford to offer.
2. Explain how four of these initiatives may help you retain staff.
3. Outline the processes you would use to become a more family-friendly workplace
4. Identify and justify three policies a firm could implement to reduce absenteeism.
5. Outline strategies you could implement to promote your family-friendly initiatives and become an employer of choice.

Flexible working hours

Flexible working hours are a common feature of enterprise agreements and individual contracts today. They allow some firms to operate shifts at much more intensive levels during peak seasons, with the benefits passed on to employees all year round; for example, in the form of longer holidays in the quieter parts of the year.

Job sharing involves two employees voluntarily sharing one permanent full-time job. This arrangement is now popular with women returning to the workforce after having children, but requires commitment and communication between the two job-holders to be effective.

Flexible working hours may take the form of:

- variable working days/weeks, with the core hours specified as required, but with the starting and finishing times flexible
- extension of ordinary hours to weekend work and public holidays
- lengthening of shifts to 10 hours
- flexitime, which allows employees to nominate starting and finishing times to suit their needs
- maxiflex, which allows employees to build up sufficient hours or overtime to take time off
- **job sharing**, which allows two workers to share the hours required for one job.

Part-time work

Many businesses offer part-time work in order to retain skilled and valued staff with family or study commitments. Part-time work allows employees to work fewer than full-time ordinary hours (less than 35 hours per week). In 2004, 28.5 per cent of all

Casual employees may be classified as full-time. Around 60 per cent of casual employees are part-time.

Women represent around 71 per cent of part-time workers.

Twenty-five per cent of Australian employees have children under the age of 12.

employees in Australia were working part-time, compared with the OECD average (2002) of 14.3. The benefits include continuity of employment and accrual of pro rata benefits (the proportion of normal full-time benefits provided is related to the hours worked). Businesses benefit from the productivity of part-time workers, who may be more motivated than full-time employees, and the ability to employ people specifically for peak periods. Most part-time employees are females.

Family-friendly programs

Conflict between work and family responsibilities is a key factor causing high-performing women to leave organisations.

Recent surveys of the Australian workforce have found that:

- working parents take around nine days off from work per year to care for children
- about three of those days are to care for sick children
- almost half of the parents surveyed had taken time off work in the previous 12 months to care for sick children or relatives
- women take more time off to care for family members than men; often without pay.

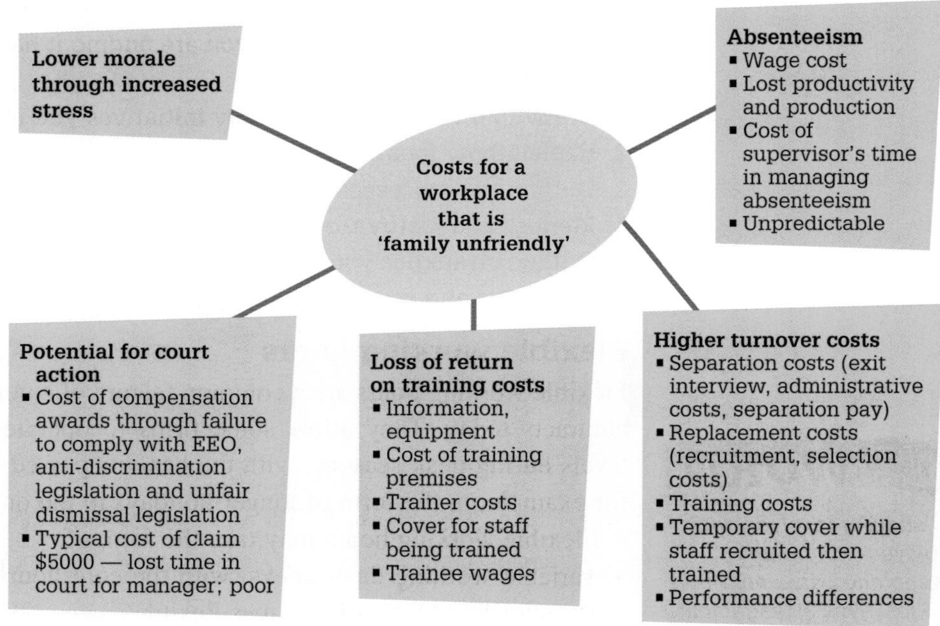

Figure 15.18 Costs for a workplace that is 'family unfriendly'

Common family-friendly policies include provision of job sharing, flexible working hours/conditions, family leave, planning for spouses/children within overseas career postings and assistance with child care or provision of child-care facilities.

Family-friendly programs are effective in retaining staff in the longer term as they recognise the interdependence of work and family life, and reduce problems involved in managing family responsibilities. Staff are able to leave and later re-enter the workforce, thus reducing separation, recruitment and training costs for new employees (turnover costs are discussed in chapter 17). Such programs also create a positive image of the firm in the community.

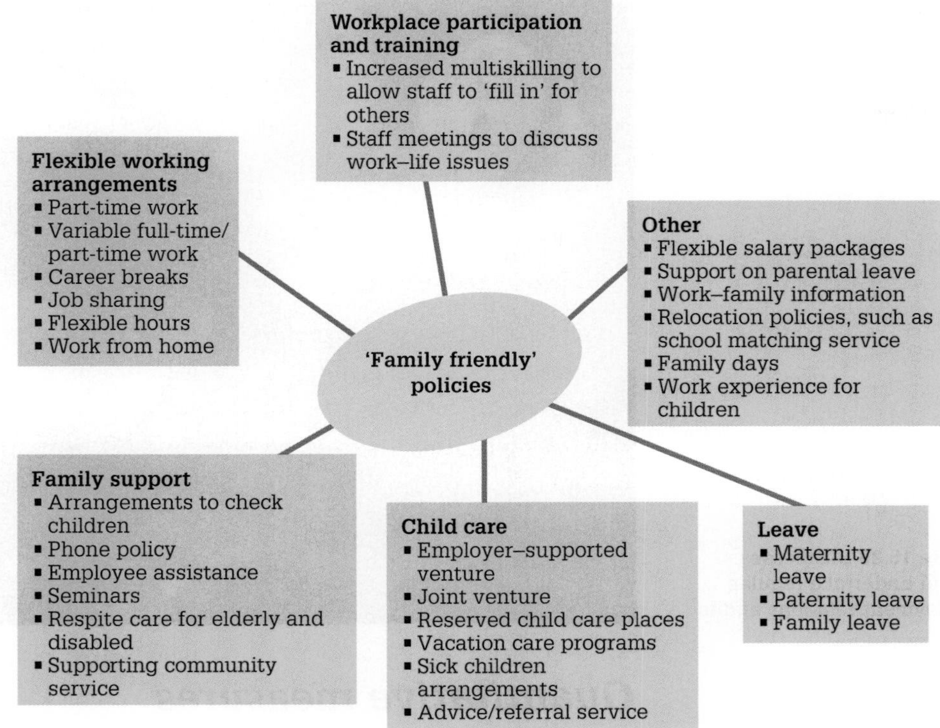

Figure 15.19 Features of a family-friendly workplace

15.6 Measures of effectiveness

To ensure the effectiveness of employment relations strategies, evaluation is essential. The approach used should be chosen for its suitability to the organisational needs. Quantitative evaluation based on key indicators and trends should be combined with qualitative evaluation based on analysis and feedback from staff and customers. The impact on the 'bottom line' (i.e. valued in terms of profits/costs) must be justified if the employment relations function is to be seen as effective.

A What's Working study of Australia at work by Mercer Human Resource Consulting has found that Australian employees:

- *who don't receive adequate training, or are not treated fairly by their manager will leave their organisation*
- *do not believe good performance is rewarded*
- *are more committed when their employer encourages two-way communication and keeps them informed about matters that affect them.*

Employment relations audits

An employment relations/human resource audit can be used to systematically analyse and evaluate employment relations activities and their effectiveness. This audit can be performed in a number of ways:

- Performance of one division or the firm itself against another is benchmarked to determine areas of weakness.
- An outside consultant conducts research to analyse problems and suggest solutions.
- Key performance indicators are evaluated by management.
- A legal compliance analysis may be undertaken to determine areas of variance from laws and company policies. High levels of fines, workers' compensation claims and unfair dismissal claims would indicate this type of audit was required.
- A management by objectives (MBO) approach can be used to determine areas of poor performance against targets established.

Figure 15.20 Businesses should undertake regular employment relations audits

Quantitative measures

Quantitative measures to be analysed are shown in table 15.2. These should be able to demonstrate the actual effect of indicators in economic terms — that is, in terms of costs and profits. Key measures often include variances in labour budgets, time lost/costs of injuries and sickness, and performance appraisals completed compared with targets and percentage of goals achieved.

TABLE 15.2 Employment relations effectiveness indicators

Area	Indicators (/ means 'as a proportion of')
Human resources planning	Number of staff/budgeted staff
Recruitment and selection	Applicant rejections Recruitment costs Vacancies filled within target time
Training and development	Training days/hours per employee Training time/budgeted time Cost of training Test outcomes — changes in skills, quality accidents, output, productivity
Employee rewards and benefits	Costs of rewards and benefits Labour turnover rates Absence rates/total hours worked Rewards and benefits compared with other organisations
Industrial relations	Grievance records Industrial disputes, work stoppages Time lost through disputes

Area	Indicators (/ means 'as a proportion of')
Occupational health and safety	Accident rates Lost time injury incidence rates Workers' compensation costs/payroll
Performance appraisal	Appraisals undertaken Goals achieved/not achieved Disciplinary interviews/people employed Improvements in quality and productivity (turnover rate)
Separation/termination	Separation rate Dismissal rate Resignation rate Unfair dismissal claims
General ER effectiveness	ER costs/sales and gross profit per employee Growth in market share

Benchmarking of indicators is undertaken frequently by businesses seeking to operate at world's best practice, or in accordance with standards in quality assurance programs (see the Snapshot 'Summary of key human resources benchmarks (median)').

Summary of key human resources benchmarks (median)

	2000	2001	2002	2003	2004
Return on human investment ratio	$0.30	$0.38	$0.32	$0.19	$0.47
Managerial/ professional male to female staffing rate	1.96	1.79	1.82	1.43	1.60
Unscheduled absence per employee	7.03 days	7.25 days	7.74 days	7.87 days	8.22 days
Employee-initiated separation rate	8.39%	8.29%	7.36%	7.61%	7.26%
Total separation rate	15.16%	16.01%	13.59%	15.06%	13.24%
Training investment per employee*	$635	$817	$898	$1021	$1111

* excluding trainees' remuneration

Source: CCH, 'HRM Consulting, managing HR effectiveness summary of key HR benchmarks', *Human Resources Management*, 2003, vol 2, pp. 35–792.

SNaPSHOT Questions

Imagine you are the human resources manager of a major fashion store. When you examine your key indicators for the last year, you find your return on human investment is $0.16, absenteeism is 12 days per employee, your separation rate is 40 per cent and your ratio of internal to external recruitment has fallen from 60 per cent to 30 per cent.

1. Write a report which analyses possible causes of, and solutions to, these problems.
2. How does your business compare to the 2002 human resources benchmarks?

Qualitative evaluation

Qualitative evaluation involves detailed feedback and research on key issues, which allows judgements to be made about changes in behaviour or quality of service provided. Key areas for analysis may include the following:

- Careful analysis of industrial disputes and the issues raised may provide useful feedback about the business to management.
- Feedback from performance appraisals will provide information useful in planning for training, recruitment and selection, development, rewards and separation.
- Exit interviews are useful sources of feedback as there are fewer conflicts of interest for staff leaving in providing honest views on the organisation.
- Feedback from supervisors, consultative committees, customers and employees in organisational surveys.

Research by external organisations and institutions also provides valuable information for analysis and comparison. Recent research on trends in employment relations shows that employers are benefiting through lower labour costs and through improvement and flexibility in work practices, working hours and times, resulting in improved productivity (up to 3 per cent per annum in the last decade) and healthy profits.

Businesses, therefore, need to consider domestic and international trends and management practices when planning strategies for improving the effectiveness of employment relations and business performance.

Teachers and scientists are the happiest employees — and forget about poor pay and long hours as the pet hates of working Australians.

A national study of 6000 workers found that most were contemptuous of management quality, with more than 63 per cent suggesting the boss just couldn't be trusted. Yet, the second annual survey of employee satisfaction and motivation by employment market analyst SEEK found that relationships with co-workers had strengthened, with 62.5 per cent saying they 'love the people they work with'.

SEEK chief executive Paul Bassat said a lack of trust in management was endemic, ranking ahead of gripes about salary, stress and the variety of work. 'This survey should serve as a fairly significant wake-up call to employers', he said.

The study showed that 41 per cent of people working in education and science were very happy — compared with 29 per cent in general.

Source: P. Robinson, 'Bosses get thumbs-down', *The Age*, 28 October 2004.

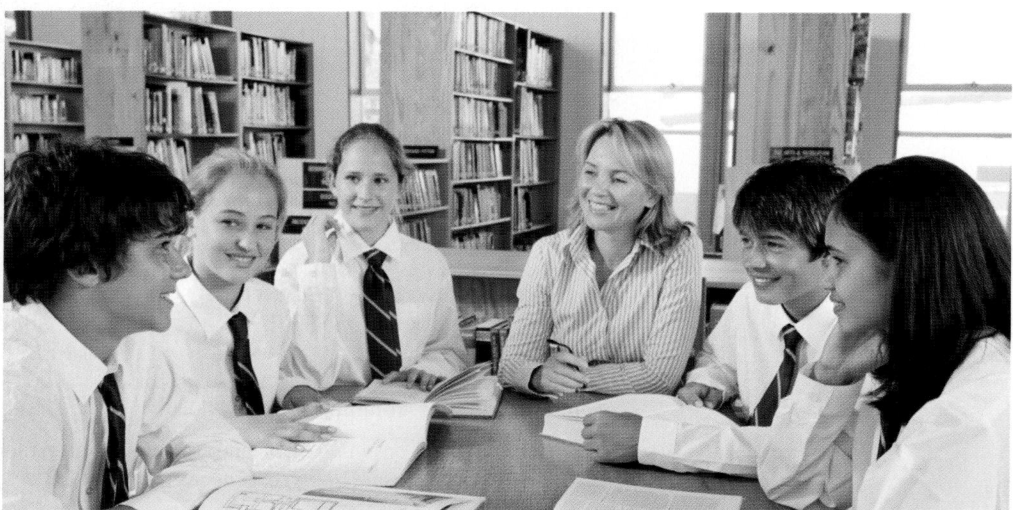

Figure 15.21 Most people working in education were happy with their employment.

EXERCISE 15.3 Revision

1. List the key features of an effective employment relations approach. Rank, then justify each feature.
2. The AWIRS Survey has revealed that most workplaces with more than 20 employees use these practices:
   - formal disciplinary procedures
   - training for supervisors
   - EEO and AA policies
   - performance appraisal of non-managerial employees
   - productivity improvement systems, such as key indicators and benchmarking.

   Discuss the possible benefits to be gained from the use of each of these practices.
3. Interview an adult about the system of rewards and benefits used in their workplace. Evaluate the rewards system. Identify the criteria you would use. Discuss your results with your class.
4. Develop a flow chart that outlines the process that businesses should undertake in designing an effective training program. Use your desktop publishing skills to develop this flow chart.
5. Identify the costs of a poor induction program (consider your induction into your school to give you ideas). Develop an induction program for your school or a local large business.
6. Justify four family-friendly practices you would use if you were a CEO.
7. Identify advantages and disadvantages of the range of flexible working conditions available in many organisations.
8. Explain why the effectiveness of employment relations in a business cannot be evaluated using a quantitative approach alone.
9. Develop and conduct a survey on the effectiveness of employment relations in a local workplace. (Survey one member of the staff; e.g. your parent.)
10. Develop a series of linked web pages for an automotive business wishing:
    (a) to provide information on employment policies
    (b) to retain and promote females through its EEO program.
11. Prepare a summary of this chapter. A summary condenses the important issues and concepts presented in the chapter. Go to www.jaconline.com.au/businessstudies3e to compare your finished summary with the one provided for this textbook.

Extension

1. Jasmine manages a printing business, which is now merging with a large stationery business. The new business location is half an hour's drive north of the current location. This current location is in an inner suburb of a large city, close to public transport. Jasmine and her new partner Paul will both reduce their workforce by one-third and merge their staff into one with several sections, including printing, customer sales, accounting and finance, warehouse and distribution sections. Significant change will occur.
   (a) Discuss some of the employment relations issues which will arise during the change.

(b) Break into groups. Discuss the ways in which employment relations may be involved in each step. Consider all the things that will need to change, such as production systems, and 'people management' issues involved in merging two workforces, such as teamwork, communication and resistance to change.

(c) Recommend a communication strategy for Jasmine in the merger and identify its benefits.

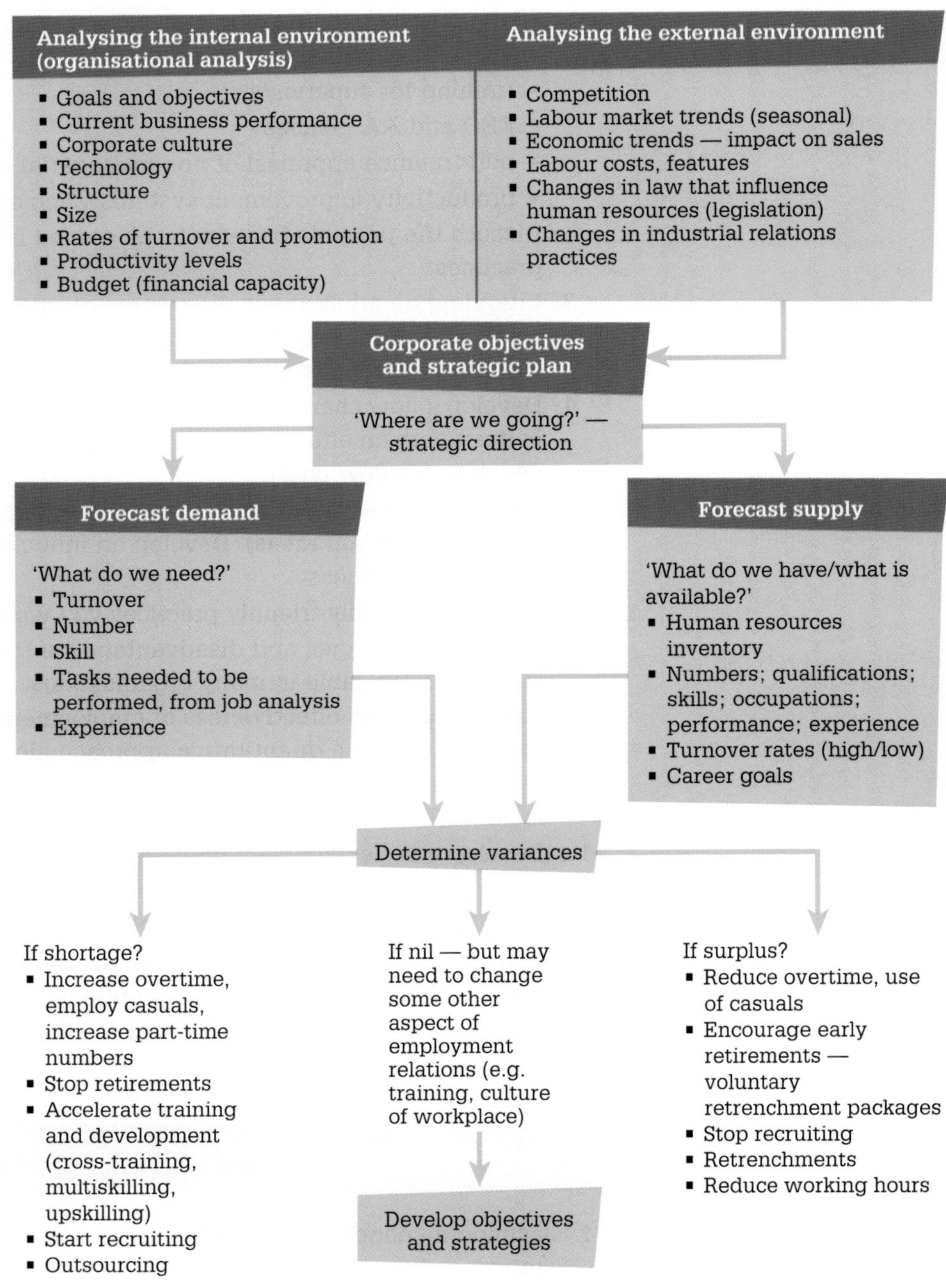

Figure 15.22 Human resource planning (adapted from R. J. Stone, *Human resource management*, 3rd ed, John Wiley & Sons Australia Ltd, Brisbane, 1998, p. 53)

2. You operate a travel agency, Worldover, employing 50 staff in a flat management structure. You employ four managers, responsible for customer service/sales, administration, marketing, and finance/accounting. Staff turnover in sales and customer service is 45 per cent, in administration and marketing it is 10 per cent,

while the accounting and clerical staff has remained largely intact over the past decade. Staff turnover is high during the first weeks of employment. Staff in customer service are frequently involved in disputes with administration and marketing staff. Although there has been no real decline in customers 'walking through the doors', sales have fallen 30 per cent in recent years. Feedback from customers indicates that frequent errors are made in bookings, and that service is not consistent.

(a) Identify possible reasons and suggest solutions for your business's problems.
(b) Describe a process you could use to more effectively plan for your staffing needs. (Use figure 15.22 to assist you.)
(c) Draw up a grid-based rewards system (see table 15.1, p. 327) showing the short- and long-term financial and non-financial rewards that may help you improve customer service.

3. Write a logical structured report on the following topic. (Refer to business examples or case studies in your response.)

   'A key aspect of effective employment relations is the monitoring, evaluation and modification of plans and performance. Explain how these tasks assist in a strategic approach to employment relations, and analyse the benefits of this approach.'

CHAPTER

16 Legal framework of employment

16.1 The employment contract

*An **employment contract** is a legally binding, formal agreement between employer and employee.*

The most basic relationship in employment and the workplace is between employer and employee. An **employment contract** is a legally binding, formal agreement between employer and employee. Every employee has a contract with an employer. A written contract gives more protection to both parties than a verbal contract, as disputes often occur over contracts if working arrangements are not clear and it is one person's word against another. A written contract encourages the parties to clarify the key duties and responsibilities of a job (see figure 16.1).

Dear Blake,

This letter confirms your appointment to the Overboard Surf Store as its new Manager. Your employment commences on 25 July 2006 under the following conditions:

1. Your conditions of employment as full-time Manager are established in the Overboard Enterprise Agreement.
2. You will carry out all duties as a manager (as attached) within the store, together with any other duties as may reasonably be directed and requested by the employer.
3. Your wages will be subject to review by the company on the basis of individual performance assessment undertaken on a six monthly basis. Your annual salary will commence at $40 000 per annum.
4. During the first month of probationary employment, your employment may be terminated by either party giving immediate notice.
5. You will be given half a day's paid absence per week for six weeks to complete our management course.

Please complete the acceptance of this offer on the attached form.

Our store's policies and Enterprise Agreement are attached for your information. Please note the termination provisions.

We look forward to a rewarding relationship in the future and welcome you to our organisation.

Yours faithfully,

I Tuncay

Irem Tuncay
General Manager,
Overboard Surf Company

Figure 16.1 An example of an employment contract

The contract need not be written but is valid and legally enforceable when:

- the parties involved intend to create a legal relationship
- one party offers and the other accepts the offer
- both parties obtain a benefit
- both parties have the capacity to contract; for example, they are old enough to make the contract

Independent contractors are typically self-employed and have a contract for services (between a principal and a contractor) as opposed to the contract of service that employers have with employees on individual contracts of employment. Independent contractors do not have the same rights as employees, are responsible for their own tax payments and may work for a number of businesses. By using independent contractors, firms bypass many of the requirements of a contract of employment, such as sick leave entitlements and maternity leave provisions.

In the event of a dispute between a business and a contractor, a 'control test' is used by the courts in cases where the extent of the employer/employee relationship is unclear. If an independent contractor is working for a company and the company clearly had the right of continuous, dominant and detailed control over the contractor, the company could be seen as acting as an employer. Further evidence of the employer–employee relationship can be found in regular payments of salary or wages, regular and specific hours of work, and deduction of PAYG tax.

The **common law** is developed by courts and tribunals.

Equity in the workplace is the provision of equal opportunities for all employees to gain access to jobs, training and career paths in the workplace.

- consent is genuine and not pressured
- the offer does not contravene any public interest.

Other employment relationships that can exist include voluntary working relationships and the relationships between independent contractors or subcontractors and businesses (see the Biz Fact on the left).

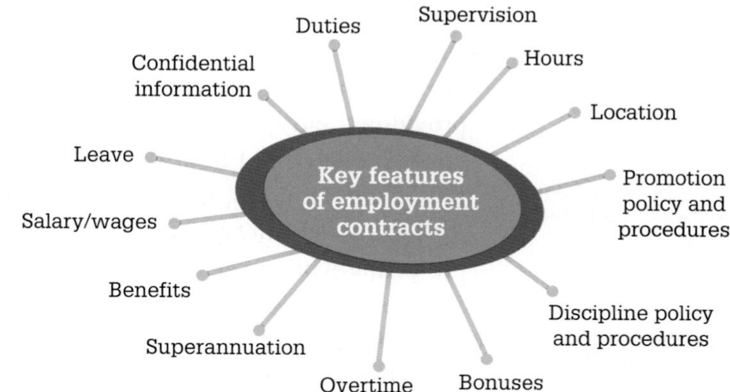

Figure 16.2 Key features of employment contracts

Source: Adapted from R. J. Stone, *Human resource management*, John Wiley & Sons Australia Ltd, Brisbane, 1998, p. 98

Employment relations in the workplace is governed by:

- common law
- statutes — federal and state legislation
- awards and agreements, with awards and collective agreements determined through, or ratified by, industrial tribunals.

Common law

The **common law** is developed by courts and tribunals. Unlike statutes, it is not made by a parliament. Under common law, judges make decisions based on the facts of a case, guided by precedent (decisions made in the past). The body of common law ('case law') is, therefore, developed from decisions made over time by judges.

Under common law, both parties — employers and employees — have basic obligations in any employment relationship, regardless of whether it is in a formal or informal contract.

Employer responsibilities include the following:

- *Providing work.* Employers are not allowed to 'stand down' employees if there is no work. They are not generally required to provide work if there is none; however, they must pay the correct wages.
- *Payment of income and expenses.* Employers are required to pay the income (including wages, commission, fees) stipulated in the award, enterprise agreement or contract, and reimburse employees for expenses legitimately incurred as a result of performing their work.
- *Meeting requirements of industrial relations legislation.* This includes:
  - providing a workplace and work practices, such as **equity** policies and promotion, which are free from discrimination, as required by the sex discrimination, anti-discrimination and equal employment opportunity legislation of the federal and state governments

- ensuring that workers are protected against unfair dismissal, where this legislation applies. Employers only have the right to dismiss employees who do not obey lawful instructions (insubordination); neglect their duties; are guilty of theft or dishonesty; exhibit wilful or serious misconduct; fail to meet the conditions of the employment contract; and fail to perform satisfactorily over time.

Employers do not have to give references to employees or give them medical care at work (unless there is an accident in which case the employer must seek medical care). Employees do not have to undertake any work for which they are not contracted.

- *Duty of care*. Employers are legally bound under the federal and state Occupational Health and Safety Acts, to provide reasonable care for the safety of the employees by:
  - providing a safe system of work, without risks to health
  - providing and maintaining premises that do not unreasonably expose an employee to risk of injury
  - providing resources, information, training and supervision necessary to ensure the health and safety of workers
  - protecting workers against risks arising out of their work activities.

All employees are obliged to observe the following:

Before you start work you should find out:
- *what your duties and conditions are*
- *whether your job is full-time, part-time or casual*
- *what your wages and allowances are*
- *your job classification/ title*
- *if there are any uniform requirements*
- *what the training requirements are*
- *whether there is a probationary period.*

You should not generally be required to work for a trial period if you will not be paid for that period, unless it is part of an approved training course.

- *Obey lawful and reasonable commands* made by the employer. Where employees do not obey such orders they place themselves at risk of dismissal. 'Reasonable' orders are those that do not expose employees to physical danger or contravene awards or existing laws.
- *Use care and skill* in the performance of their work activities — that is, they must not behave in a negligent manner.
- *Act in good faith* and in the interests of the employer. Taking confidential information or trade secrets from one employer to another, especially to a competitor, when an employee changes jobs may be an example of failing to act in good faith.

Figure 16.3 Employers and employees have common law duties for occupational health and safety.

Statutes

Statutes are laws made by federal and state parliaments; for example, laws relating to employment conditions, wage and salary determinations and dispute resolution.

Statutes are laws made by federal and state parliaments about employment conditions, wage and salary determinations, and dispute resolution. These statutes require employers to:

- meet occupational health and safety requirements
- maintain workers' compensation insurance
- provide all employees with superannuation, annual leave and long service leave
- ensure employment practices in the workplace, such as recruitment, remuneration, promotion and termination, are free from discrimination on the basis of age, sex, physical or mental disability, marital status, family responsibility, pregnancy, union membership, political opinion, race or social origin.

Figure 16.4 Statutes are laws made by parliaments.

Statutes have also provided the framework for awards and agreements that cover employees at both the state and federal levels.

The statutory framework in Australia today

A dual system of industrial relations

Australia has a dual system of federal and state industrial relations, a result of the powers allocated under the Constitution in 1901.

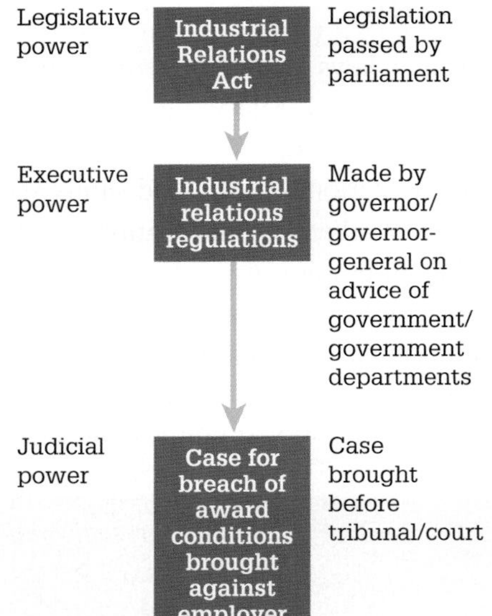

Figure 16.5 The functions of government (state or federal) in workplace relations

Section 51 (xxxv), the most important section for industrial relations, gave the federal government the power to: '... make laws for the peace, order and good government of the Commonwealth with respect to: ... (xxxv) Conciliation and arbitration for the prevention and settlement of industrial disputes extending beyond the limits of any one State'. The effect of this Section was that:

- *a dispute (actual or pending) must exist before the tribunal could intervene*
- *the dispute must be an 'industrial matter'*
- *the dispute must extend beyond one state.*

Section 51 (see the Biz Fact on the left) and other sections of the Constitution were used to delegate dispute resolution to industrial tribunals, such as the Australian Industrial Relations Commission (AIRC).

The power to settle disputes limited federal power to make laws about terms and conditions of employment, and only allowed it to handle disputes extending beyond one state. It could only, therefore, prevent and settle disputes involving parties (unions and employer associations) representing employees and employers who were registered as national bodies, or matters relating to Commonwealth government employees.

The Constitution gave the Commonwealth powers that have been used to pass additional legislation on industrial relations, particularly through the external affairs and corporations powers, as indicated in table 16.1.

TABLE 16.1 Federal legislation

Law or test case	Date	Features
Conciliation and Arbitration Act	1904	Gave the Conciliation and Arbitration Commission power to prevent and settle industrial disputes extending beyond the limits of the state.
Harvester case	1907	Established the basic wage for full-time male worker with wife and two children.
Equal Pay case	1969	Principle of equal pay for equal work established for women.
Trade Practices Act	1974	Secondary boycotts (provisions) made illegal. Jurisdiction for this later moved to AIRC, as ILO (International Labour Organization) report suggested it interfered with the right to strike.
Racial Discrimination Act	1975	Discrimination in employment on the basis of race, colour, national or ethnic origin prohibited.

Law or test case	Date	Features
Maternity Leave case	1979	Test case on maternity leave won by ACTU.
Sex Discrimination Act	1984	Prohibited sexual harassment and discrimination on basis of sex, marital status and pregnancy.
Affirmative Action (Equal Opportunity for Women) Act	1986	Required all private sector employers and all higher education institutions to implement affirmative action programs for the employment of women and to submit annual reports on their progress.
Industrial Relations Act	1988	Award restructuring introduced under the structural efficiency principle (SEP).
Parental Leave test case	1990	Federally covered male employees given opportunity to take leave to mind newborn children, etc.
Industrial Relations Reform Act	1993	Improved safety net provisions for employees, through the award system and minimum entitlements. Improved arrangements for direct bargaining through both certified enterprise agreements (between employers and unions) and enterprise flexibility agreements (non-union agreements). Protection against unfair dismissal.
Workplace Relations Act	1996	Revised arrangements for enterprise bargaining, allowing for collective and individual agreements, with or without union involvement. All agreements subject to no disadvantage test. Tighter restrictions on industrial action. Limited arbitration role for AIRC. Focus of AIRC is on award simplification to 20 allowable matters and safety net provisions. No new paid rates awards, only minimum rates awards. 'Fair go all round' — unfair dismissal system revised.

States were given the power to make concurrent legislation about industrial matters, or matters not covered by the Constitution, leading to the body of legislation indicated in table 16.2. Disputes not covered by federal legislation or agreements were managed at the state level in a parallel tribunal system, under state awards. Today around 60 per cent of employees are under federal agreements and awards, and the other 40 per cent are under state agreements.

Evolution from a centralised to a more decentralised system

From 1904 until 1991, Australia's industrial relations system was a centralised system, with most employees covered by awards. Industrial tribunals handled disputes and the wage determination process, which generally began with the serving of a log of claims; for example by a union on an employer association, to create a 'paper dispute'. The tribunal would hear submissions of both parties and an award, or variation, was achieved by conciliation or arbitration.

Over time, national wage cases, heard by the AIRC (called the Conciliation and Arbitration Commission prior to 1988) made adjustments to wage levels, which flowed on to all employees, leading to 'comparative wage justice'.

Constitutional powers used to develop federal industrial relations legislation include the:
- *exclusive power (to make laws relating to the public service employees)*
- *defence power*
- *external affairs power of the federal government to make laws in relation to its international treaties (the source of legislation against discrimination in employment)*
- *corporations power (the source of laws with respect to the internal affairs and industrial relations activities of foreign and trading or financial corporations)*
- *trade and commerce power (to make laws related to trade and commerce between Australia and other countries or between states)*
- *taxation power (used to introduce the Superannuation Guarantee Act in 1992)*
- *inconsistency rule (used to allow federal law to override state law in the case of a conflict, although it was amended in the* Workplace Relations Act 1996 *(Cwlth) to stop switching from state to federal awards).*

TABLE 16.2 Major New South Wales industrial relations legislation

Law	Date
Annual Holidays Act	1944
Long Service Leave Act	1955
Factories, Shops and Industries Act	1962
Anti-Discrimination Act	1977
Employment Protection Act	1982
Occupational Health and Safety Act	1983 (1990, 2000)
Workers' Compensation Act	1987
Essential Services Act	1988
Industrial Arbitration (Enterprise Agreements) Amendment Act	1990
Industrial Relations Act	1991
Industrial Relations Act	1996
Workplace Injury Management and Workers Compensation Act	1998

Through international agreements and test cases on such issues as equal pay for women, a body of federal employment legislation developed. Often this legislation reflected the impact of social changes, such as the feminisation of the workforce.

It became apparent in the late 1980s that labour market reform was needed to improve Australia's international competitiveness. Both unions and employers recognised:
- the disadvantages of a 'one size fits all' system of wage determination, which does not recognise the differences in the 'capacity to pay' for different employers or industries
- that many employers and employees and their representatives wanted to negotiate agreements appropriate to the business, without reliance on a third party or tribunal
- that greater flexibility and incentives and rewards for increased efficiency were needed
- that awards needed to be simplified to promote greater efficiency and flexibility

Both unions and employers pushed for enterprise bargaining, which was approved by the AIRC in 1991, and extended further to non-union enterprise agreements in 1993 with the Industrial Relations Reform Act.

Further decentralisation after the Workplace Relations Act

Successive governments have continued to decentralise the system, as table 16.3 on page 351 shows. An early priority of the newly elected Howard government in 1996 was further industrial relations reform. The Workplace Relations Act extended workplace bargaining to individual workplace agreements (Australian workplace agreements), and shifted the primary responsibility for determining the employment relationship in favour of the employer and employees in the workplace. (A light-hearted look at workplace agreements is taken in the Snapshot 'All this legal stuff is giving me a headache' on page 357.)

The role of the AIRC in dispute resolution was restricted to conciliation for certified agreements and arbitration only in cases of 'national interest' or for awards, or the handling of unfair dismissal claims.

TABLE 16.3 Changes in the framework for employment relations in Australia

Year	Change	Features of each stage
1983	Accord Agreement (ALP and ACTU)	ALP government. Social contract — new centralised approach to industrial relations; wage restraint in exchange for national wage decisions and social wage. Wage indexation through National Wage case.
1987	Accord modified — two-tier system	ALP government. Partial decentralisation of wage determination, allowing wage increases for reform through restructuring, efficiency and flexibility changes. National Wage case retained.
1991	National Wage case decision	ALP government. Pressure by employers and unions for flexibility grows. The AIRC endorsed introduction of enterprise bargaining.
1993	Industrial Relations Reform Act	ALP government. Enterprise bargaining spreads, and includes a new stream of non-union agreements, but both are under supervision of the AIRC and must pass no-disadvantage test and include consultation and conflict resolution procedures.
1996	Workplace Relations Act	Liberal–National government. New focus on decentralisation, reduced role for the AIRC in disputes, individual bargaining allowed with AWAs, awards simplified, union power reduced. Youth wage approved.
2004–05	Workplace Relations Act amendments proposed	Liberal–National government re-elected with majority in both houses of parliament. Further restrictions on union power, exemption of small and medium-sized businesses from unfair dismissals, possible steps to harmonise state/federal industrial relations system proposed.

Union rights were reduced, particularly in terms of right of entry into workplaces, and the prohibition of compulsory union membership in workplaces (known as 'closed shops'). Industrial action other than for genuine bargaining for agreements (generally at the expiry of existing agreements), secondary boycotts (industrial action in support of another union), and payment or acceptance of strike pay was made unlawful.

Further reform during the fourth term of the Howard Liberal government 2004 onwards

The Howard government, having gained a majority both in the Senate and the House of Representatives in 2005, is keen to use this unique opportunity to reform industrial relations to further remove 'structural impediments' to labour market flexibility. The government's key strategies and their features are listed in table 16.4.

Figure 16.6 One view of the intent of the Howard government Reform Program

TABLE 16.4 Proposed reforms to legal framework of employment relations

Area of reform	Explanation
More decentralised system of wage determination based on enterprise and individual agreements, possible reduction in awards	▪ Rules on jury service, notice of termination and long-service leave removed. Business sector keen to reduce number of awards or remove awards. ▪ Streamlining of enterprise agreements by limiting the scope of matters included in enterprise agreements, and extended expiry to five years. ▪ Expansion of individual contracts in the public and private sectors. ▪ Employment Advocate to handle all agreements — both enterprise and Australian workplace.
Further stripping of awards	▪ Award matters reduced from 20. ▪ Redundancy, penalty rates, annual leave and sick leave minimums likely to be reduced. This could increase the power of employers to exert pressure on unions in negotiations over enterprise agreements, if back-up is reduced.
Modest safety net increases	▪ Award safety net increases seen as being too generous; decisions may need to take unemployed into account. Increases to be set by Fair Pay Commission.

Area of reform	Explanation
Reduced role of AIRC in disputes	▪ Possible further limitation on the AIRC role to award simplification. ▪ Use of alternative dispute resolution mechanisms and voluntary mediation role for the AIRC.
Harmonising federal and state systems	▪ Systems could be streamlined or harmonised to create one system to reduce compliance costs. ▪ Political interests, such as states rights issues, and opportunities for businesses and unions to switch systems if needs arise, reduce the likelihood of change. ▪ Concern about powers of future ALP governments.
Exemption from unfair dismissals for businesses with up to 100 employees	▪ Removal of possible barriers to hiring of staff through exemption of businesses with up to 100 employees from unfair dismissal claims; however, this could reduce protection for up to 90 per cent of workforce.
Further limitation of union power	▪ Protection for independent contractors against being forced to join a union. ▪ Restrictions on the ability of unions to stop negotiation of individual agreements in workplaces with collective agreements in force. ▪ More restrictions on union activity, including introduction of secret ballots prior to strike action, limitations on industrial action during the life of, and towards the expiry of, certified agreements, restrictions on union right of entry. ▪ Stronger secondary boycott laws and sanctions applied to breaches.

Commentators note that with an ageing population and a growing labour shortage, benefits flowing from cuts in labour costs arising from these changes are likely to be limited. Facing a labour shortage, business is much more likely to reconsider relationships with employees and negotiate benefits that attract and retain staff, and promote increased flexibility for all parties.

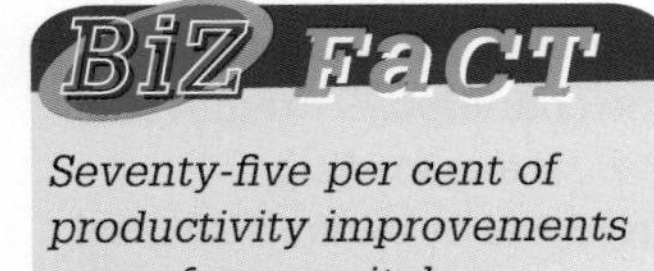

Seventy-five per cent of productivity improvements come from capital investment, rather than reductions in wage costs.

The most recent reform process began with *the Workplace Relations Amendment (Agreement Validation) Act 2004* (Cwlth). This Act supports a 2 September 2004 High Court decision in *Electrolux Home Products Pty Ltd v AWU and Others* (2004) HCA 40 *(Electrolux)* where the High Court found that agreements can only contain matters (pertaining) related to the employment relationship. As a result of the Act, non-pertaining matters in existing agreements are invalid. In the Electrolux case, unions had sought to charge a bargaining fee. Non-pertaining matters include deduction of union dues or other payments to third parties from earned income and restrictions on the use of contract or agency labour. Other matters that remain unclear include salary sacrificing, union right of entry on matters not directly related to enforcement of employment obligations, and other union features including training leave and facilities such as noticeboards.

Figure 16.7 Views of some employers supporting reform of the industrial relations system

The possible impact of the industrial relations reforms on the major stakeholders is outlined in table 16.5.

TABLE 16.5 The changing world of employment relations

Party	Objectives	Possible impact of proposed IR reforms 2005
Employee	▪ Job security ▪ Increased wages ▪ Improved working conditions ▪ Meaningful jobs ▪ Good working relationships	▪ Wages to fall in real terms with Fair Pay Commission ▪ No disadvantage test for agreements to be dropped ▪ Non-union employees under pressure to move onto AWA, with worse conditions — removal of overtime, penalty rates, leave loading ▪ Less job security — removal of unfair dismissal protection for most ▪ Probationary period for employees increased from three to six months ▪ Minimum working conditions to be enshrined in law

Party	Objectives	Possible impact of proposed IR reforms 2005
Trade unions	▪ Job security for employees ▪ Reduce casualised workforce ▪ Protect/improve working conditions	▪ Further restrictions on power, especially pattern bargaining, restrictions on right of entry. Removal of wage case to Fair Pay Commission, and reduced powers of AIRC ▪ Secret ballots required to delay industrial action ▪ Pressure to move to individual agreements, aimed at reducing power of unions in specific industries ▪ More industrial conflict likely, but could be expressed more in publicity campaigns than in pressure to strike
Line manager	▪ Maximise productivity ▪ Reduce costs ▪ Resolve minor disputes ▪ Implement company policy ▪ Ensure legal compliance	▪ Increased pressure to resolve disputes ▪ More power to dismiss staff
Human resources manager	▪ Ensure supply of qualified, competent staff meets the demands of the organisation through planned and cost-effective acquisition, induction, development, rewards, EEO, workplace relations and termination strategies	▪ Increased need to understand legal implications ▪ Easier to dismiss unsatisfactory staff. ▪ Awards likely to be stripped to 16 matters, taking out jury service, termination notice, long-service leave, superannuation — left to individual or enterprise bargaining.
Employer	▪ Reduce costs, including unfair dismissal claims ▪ Maximise profits and productivity ▪ Maximise competitiveness and flexibility	▪ Increased power to hire and dismiss ▪ Increased role in dispute resolution ▪ Exempted from unfair dismissal if fewer than 100 employees
Employer association	▪ Advise employers ▪ Reduce costs ▪ Increase flexibility for employers to increase competitiveness	▪ More power for employers ▪ Interests/views more likely to be considered
Federal government	▪ International competitiveness ▪ Low unemployment ▪ Legal compliance ▪ Higher living standards ▪ Workplace reform	▪ Federal government may have more power over IR if states hand over IR powers, creating national, unitary system. Will use hostile takeover of states' powers if required. ▪ Keen to reduce cost to business of multiple systems, and to lower unemployment through unfair dismissal exemption ▪ High levels of state–federal conflict likely. Constitutional challenge a likelihood ▪ Will create Fair Pay Commission to oversee wage increases for award-based employees ▪ Will set in law, using Corporations Power, minimum conditions of employment including annual leave, carer's personal leave, maximum hours of work

(*continued*)

TABLE 16.5	*(continued)*	
Party	**Objectives**	**Possible impact of proposed IR reforms 2005**
AIRC	▪ Legal compliance ▪ Fair outcomes for parties involved	▪ Reduced role for AIRC in dispute resolution and unfair dismissal claims ▪ Fair Pay Commission will handle minimum wage adjustments ▪ Reduced union involvement (only one seat on Fair Pay Commission) likely to lead to reduced real wages long term. ▪ Will continue to handle award simplification
Employment advocate	▪ Vetting of AWAs	▪ Will approve all agreements — certified agreements and AWAs ▪ No longer required to assess every AWA before approval ▪ No disadvantage test to be dropped ▪ Comparison to be made against minimum wage and five basic working conditions alone.
Federal Court	▪ Enforce industrial law	▪ Likely to see more work as common law actions increase due to removal of rights under other workplace legislation
HREOC	▪ Ensure workplaces are free from discrimination and harassment	▪ Little change foreshadowed except for issues related to unfair dismissal
EOWA	▪ Ensure workplaces are free from discrimination and harassment based on gender	▪ Little change foreshadowed except for issues related to unfair dismissal
WorkCover	▪ Ensure workplaces are safe	▪ No change in short term — state organisations ▪ Federal government keen to remove 'blame' focus attached to employers, and would like to reform aspects of OH&S ▪ OH&S reform options may be limited by Constitution

For further information on the implementation of these reforms go to www.jaconline.com.au/businessstudies3e and click on the Workplace Legislation and Policy and Reviews weblinks for this textbook.

The NSW Department of Industrial Relations administers state employment legislation, investigates breaches of legislation and provides advice to the government and the public on employment issues.

Legal framework in New South Wales

State agreements cover 40 per cent of employees in New South Wales. Similar agreements are available to state employees (awards and enterprise agreements) as are provided at the federal level. Employees on individual agreements other than AWAs are covered by state legislation.

The Industrial Relations Commission (IRC) was established by the *Industrial Relations Act 1996* (NSW) to:

- resolve industrial disputes through conciliation and arbitration
- handle award matters, inquiries and reports on matters referred to it by the State Minister for Industrial Relations.

Unlike the federal AIRC, which is restricted by its constitutional powers, the IRC has the power to make awards and agreements without a dispute being present. Awards are ratified by the IRC once the employer organisation and the union have reached an agreement. These awards then bind all employers in an industry or occupation, even if they were not a party to the award, unless they are involved in a federal award.

The IRC hears unfair dismissal claims and ratifies collective union or non-union enterprise agreements. Non-union agreements are subject to a secret ballot before being submitted to the IRC.

All this legal stuff is giving me a headache

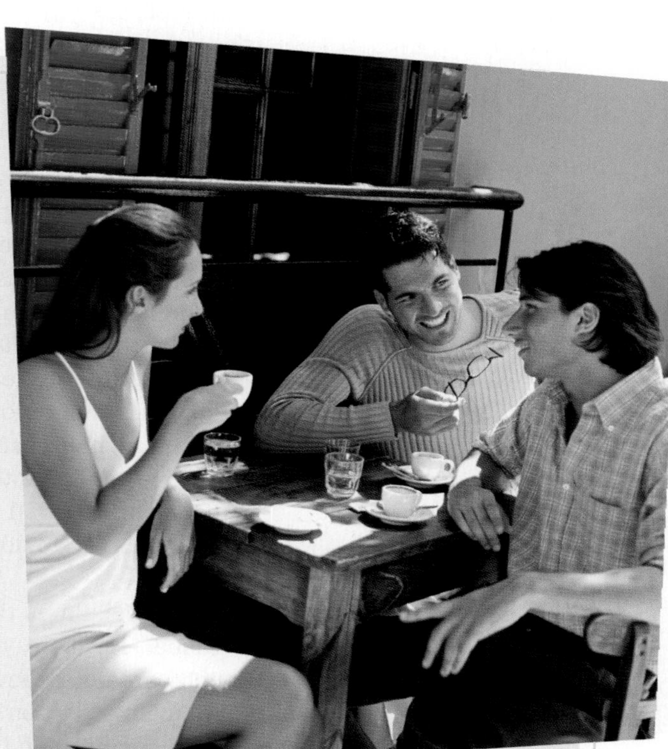

Fifi, Moshe and Ozkan, old high school mates, are having a coffee in a local shopping centre, and are discussing issues related to their jobs. Moshe works as a casual for a video store and is studying full-time at university. Fifi is a supervisor at the local bank, and Ozkan runs the local pet shop and boarding kennels.

Ozkan: All this legal stuff is giving me a headache!

Fifi: What legal stuff?

Ozkan: I have to make sure all my staff are being treated as it says in the award or we will be fined again.

Fifi: Why is it such a problem?

Ozkan: Have you seen an award? It goes on for pages, with lots of details about hours, rates for juniors, leave arrangements, shift length (which got us into trouble last time), grievance procedures and arrangements for managing change (which I must admit I ignored last time). I was given a very hard time by my boss for not paying attention to the details, so I'm reading up on the topic now. I've also got to worry about OH and S all the time, like arm strain from dogs who think they are champion racers, and slips and trips. What kind of work arrangements have you got?

Fifi: I'm on an AWA, an individual agreement. It's great because I'm paid more than the other supervisors. That's because I'm prepared to work long hours and the customers like my style, apparently.

Ozkan: How much did you pay the customers to tell the bank that?

Moshe: What do the other supervisors think?

(*continued*)

Fifi: Well, they don't really know I'm paid more, because an AWA is not made public. It's not on the Internet, unlike an award or enterprise agreement. Some of them seem to think I get more, but I haven't told them how much I'm getting. I feel great: valued and appreciated! I've earned the right to be paid more! I get good performance appraisals because I'm good at my job and bring in a lot of customers!

Ozkan: I bet the others would love to know that. They must be so cooperative with you at work!

Fifi: Well, they gossip a bit, but I just get on with my work. I don't care about the others that much, they're not that friendly, and they don't talk to me much.

Ozkan: (rolls eyes) I wonder why! Do you think any others get paid more?

Fifi: No, someone in management told me I'm the highest paid.

Ozkan: Do you think any deserve more?

Fifi: There is one guy who does a great job, but his English is not quite where it needs to be so he is not paid the extra yet.

Moshe: That sounds like a bit of discrimination to me! I bet if he were a union member the union would sort that out.

Fifi: Oh, they just make trouble!

Moshe: Mate, the reason your safety and leave conditions are so good is due to all the groundwork unions did in the past! There was a time when you could have been sent to jail for going on strike, when you were the servant and your employer the master! You just take it all for granted!

Fifi: Yes we needed them then. But I don't see the need for them now, in this sort of job. It would be different if I were a miner. How does it all work in your job?

Moshe: Well I'm in the union just in case I need help one day, even though I'm a casual. How are you going to cope if you have a problem? You've not got much bargaining power. What if you and Eren have kids? How will your great AWA help you then? I'm on a casual rate which is okay as I get 20 per cent more per hour than full-timers to make up for all the benefits I miss out on, like sick and long service leave. There is no way I would stay a casual anyway, long term, because you can't get credit easily, so there goes the car or a home loan.

Ozkan: You don't get training or career development either. We've found that if you have too many casuals coming and going no-one knows what's going on, mistakes happen and can't be followed up!

Moshe: Yeah. It's hard to survive on a yo-yo income too! If your employers don't need you they don't call you and you have to eat baked beans for days! If they don't want you anymore they just reduce your hours and you can't do anything about it. And of course if you get sick, bad luck! At least my boss is nice. He thinks I'm okay so I do get regular shifts. I'll stay for a while because he is fair, honest and slips me ice-creams, and videos to watch at home. His wife even makes me souvlaki, because she thinks I eat poorly!

Ozkan: Well, maybe awards and agreements aren't so bad after all. At least all my staff get on, their hours are regular and they get safety net increases regularly. I wouldn't have the time or resources to manage individual contracts anyway, and at least we know what the going rates are for staff. Getting awards right is hard enough, without the hassle of individual agreements.

Fifi: Yeah, but you know workers on awards are the lowest paid workers of all! Lots of them are women too — women just seem to often work in award-based, poorly paid occupations.
Ozkan: The owner is talking to the union about developing an enterprise agreement for all the staff, so we can add more than the basic allowable matters and provide some incentives, such as flexible working hours for employees who are parents or carers. I must admit we try to be helpful, anyway. Sarita is allowed time off when her dad needs to be taken to the hospital, and I'm sure Jenna uses most of her sick days to look after her kids. It's tough at times because the animals bark and whine if we don't feed them on time!
Fifi: Yeah, yeah — a likely story!

SNAPSHOT Questions

1. Research the topic of industrial agreements on the Internet. You may like to use keywords such as award, employment contract, enterprise agreement, Australian workplace agreement and certified agreement.
2. Use the information given in the Snapshot and your Internet research to complete this table.

Agreement	Main features	Advantages	Disadvantages
Award	Legally binding document stating minimum terms and conditions of employment Collective agreement		
Enterprise agreement		Can be tailored to fit needs of employee(s) and employer	
Australian workplace agreement			Secret
Individual common-law employment contract	Informal agreement or letter of contract	No effort required by employer	

3. Prepare a PowerPoint presentation that compares the major types of agreements, and provide examples of situations in which each may be commonly used.

EXERCISE 16.1 Revision

1. Draw a mind map to show the main components of the legal framework of employment relations.
2. What has been the most important factor shaping this legal framework for employment relations?
3. The letter of appointment in figure 16.1, page 344, follows the procedure generally recommended by employer associations. Suggest reasons for:
   (a) putting the appointment in writing
   (b) including the store's policies and termination provisions in the contract
   (c) including the job description
   (d) requesting a written acceptance from the employee.
4. How can you generally tell whether someone is an employee or a subcontractor?
5. Examine legislation covering the employment relationship on pages 348–51. In what ways does the state legislation differ from the federal legislation? Suggest reasons for these differences.
6. Go to www.jaconline.com.au/businessstudies3e and click on the Australian Workplace weblink for this textbook and summarise and evaluate the latest employment relations legislation.
7. Got to www.jaconline.com.au/businessstudies3e and click on the Office of Industrial Relations weblink for this textbook to find out the most up-to-date information on the issues discussed in this section.

Extension

1. Argue the case for and against moving to a federal (only) system of employment relations.
2. Go to www.jaconline.com.au/businessstudies3e and click on the Department of Employment and Workplace Relations and the NSW Department of Commerce Office of Industrial Relations weblinks for this textbook.
   (a) List the key features provided on each website.
   (b) Evaluate each website from the perspective of an employee or an employer.

Awards

At the federal level, awards are one of three types of agreements available to businesses and employees: two are **collective agreements** such as awards and enterprise agreements (certified agreements) and the other is individual agreements, Australian workplace agreements (AWAs).

Collective agreements *are made between a group of employees or one or more unions representing employees, and an employer or group of employers.*

Awards:

- are legally binding documents, setting out minimum wages and conditions of employees in an industry or occupation, made by the Australian Industrial Relations Commission (AIRC). The process for making an award (as shown in figure 16.10 on page 362) requires lodgement of a dispute ('paper' or real) by a union, or employer association, as the Constitution only allows for dispute settlement at the federal level.
- are used as a benchmark for comparison with other agreements in a test of minimum wages and conditions.

The most common method of setting pay for employees is by collective agreement, such as an award or enterprise agreement. Forty-two per cent of employees are covered by collective agreements, which dominate the hospitality, administration, defence and government sectors, and are common among larger businesses, as figure 16.9 shows. In the private sector the most common method is by individual arrangement (40.8 per cent), while in the public sector it is by collective agreement (98 per cent).

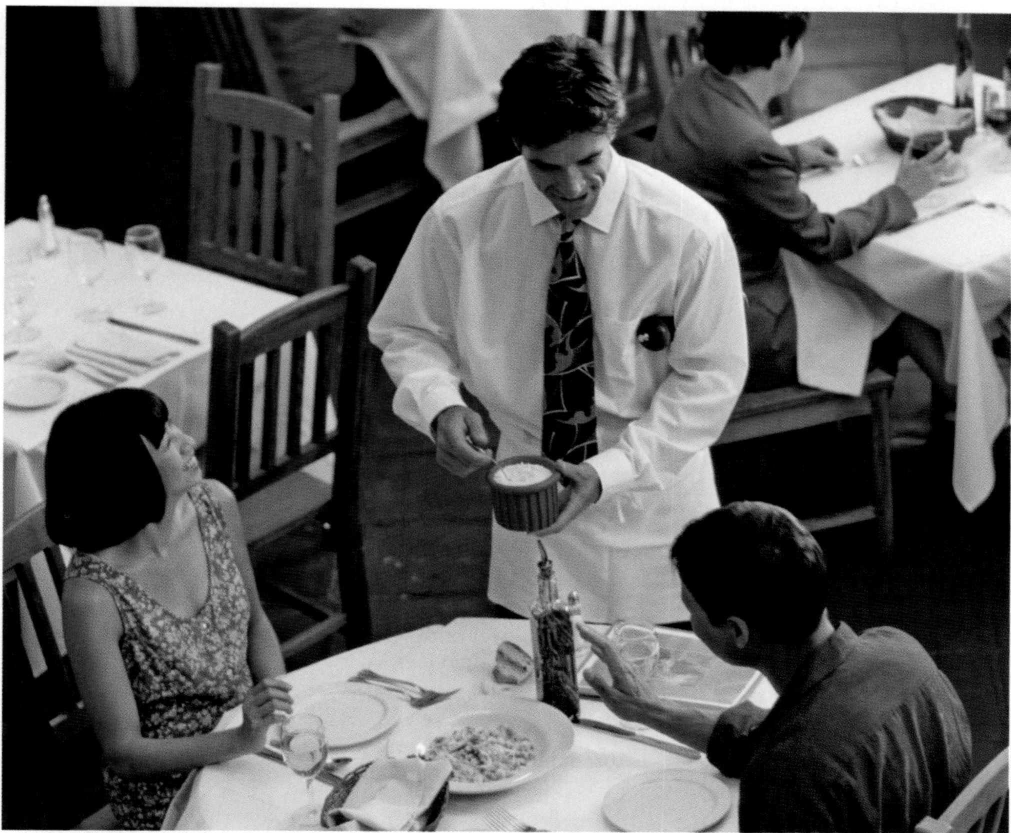

Figure 16.8 Award coverage is high in hospitality, retail and community services

Employers are ***respondent*** *to an award when they are cited in the award, either after a successful log of claims and an AIRC hearing, or if they are a member of a federally registered employer association. Unions are respondent in the same way.*

- are adjusted for increases awarded in annual national wage cases, known as 'Safety Net Reviews' conducted by the AIRC. This function will now be taken over by the Fair Pay Commission.
- operate at state and federal level. The main difference is the way in which they apply to employers. State awards apply by 'common rule' to all employers in an industry or occupation. Federal awards are binding to all employers **respondent** to the award.
- cover a large proportion of employees in lower skilled occupational groups in the hospitality, retailing and community service sectors.

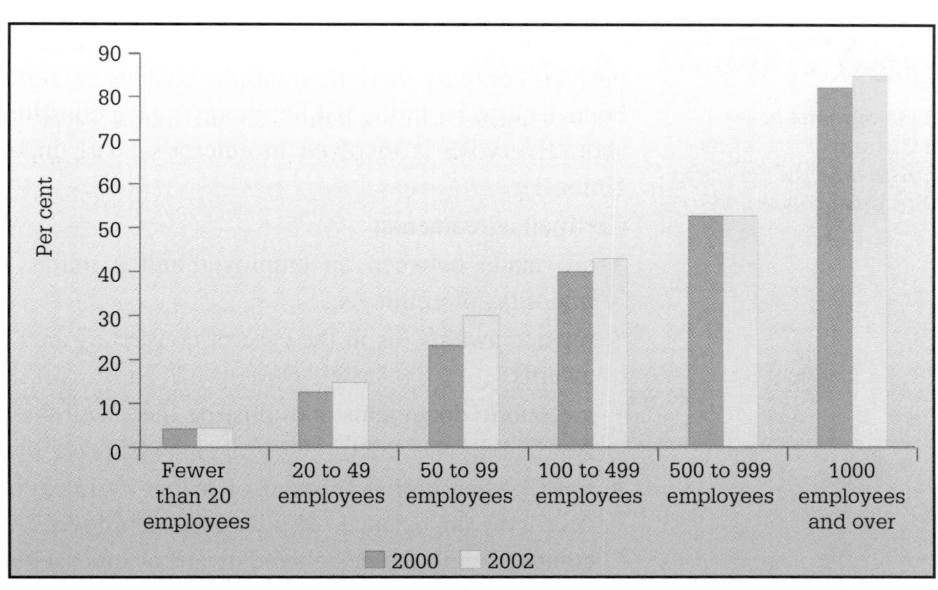

Figure 16.9 Collective agreement coverage by size of firm

- have been restructured and simplified in recent years to eliminate practices that restrict productivity, are discriminatory, and only cover a minimum number of allowable matters (20 in 2005). All additional issues such as clothing and study leave, may be negotiated in separate enterprise or over-award agreements.

Award breaches should be reported by employees to a union, as unions now may not enter a workplace to investigate a matter without giving notice.

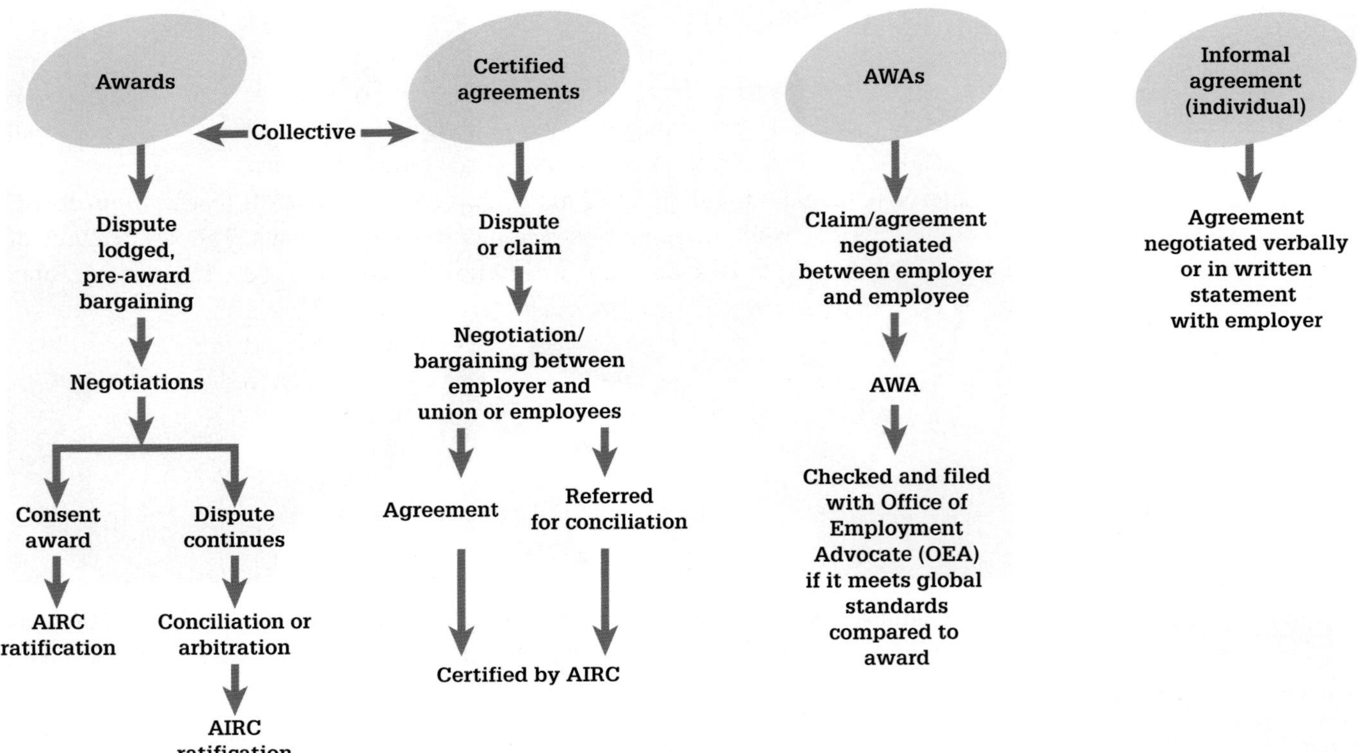

Figure 16.10 The agreement-making process

Agreements

Certified agreements

> **BiZ FaCT**
> *A union agreement is possible only if one of its members is in the business or enterprise concerned.*

Certified agreements are collective 'enterprise' agreements that may cover a single business or part thereof, multiple businesses (only if a full bench of the AIRC believes it to be in the public interest), or a constitutional corporation (see the Snapshot 'Everyone is involved in enterprise bargaining — even the Australian Rugby Union'!).

Certified agreements:

- are made between an employer and a union, or unions, or a group (a valid majority) of employees
- replace awards (as in the case of consent awards) or act as 'add on agreements' to awards
- are public documents and must be filed with the Australian Industrial Registry for approval by the AIRC. (This role may be taken over by the Employment Advocate.)
- must pass a global (instead of a line-by-line) 'no-disadvantage test' to ensure it does not, on balance, disadvantage employees wages and conditions overall, in comparison to the designated award or other legislation

- must have the genuine approval of the majority of employees covered by it. It must not contravene anti-discrimination laws.
- must also contain a dispute-settling mechanism and specify a nominal expiry date, no more than three years after the agreement commences.
- are replaced by a new agreement after their expiry date, terminated by both parties if agreed, or by the AIRC if one party requests that it be terminated in the public interest.

Awards and most agreements cover employees regardless of whether they are union members or not. Certified agreements must operate in line with other relevant state laws such as occupational health and safety laws.

During the negotiation of a new certified agreement for a single business, there is a period of two weeks during which the parties are protected if they wish to take industrial action, such as strikes by employees or lockouts by employers. Parties must first attempt to genuinely negotiate and obtain authorisation to take industrial action. Notice must be given of the intention to take action by either party.

Enterprise bargaining has allowed many employers to trade off restrictive or inefficient work practices for wage increases in industrial agreements. The key features of agreements negotiated include occupational health and safety, superannuation, hours of work, training, type of employment and termination matters.

Business profitability has improved significantly, as shown in figure 16.11 on page 364 (profit's share of GDP). Some workers are working longer and harder, but others appreciate the flexibility they have gained through new working arrangements.

Everyone is involved in enterprise bargaining — even the Australian Rugby Union!

The Australian Rugby Union (ARU) has signed a third collective bargaining agreement for the next four years with the Rugby Union Players Association (RUPA).

Key features include:

- rookie contracts for up to five players for each Super 12 Union
- a week's rest and regeneration period at the end of each season
- $2 million for training and career development, including study for a Certificate III in Sport
- an occupational health and safety committee to address player safety and welfare
- post-retirement medical assistance for players
- a minimum salary of $49 500, indexed from 2005
- a simple model to redistribute rugby revenue to all professional players.

RUPA chief Tony Dempsey says of the agreement:

> [It] ensures that as professional rugby continues to grow in Australia, the players who contribute to its growth will directly benefit . . . there are innovations in this agreement that address the critical issues of player burnout, welfare, and agent representation. They are going to be getting education in public speaking, computer training, business presentation, first aid.
>
> This is the most innovative collective bargaining agreement we have reached . . . It demonstrates the willingness of all parties involved to find solutions to pressing problems that face the modern professional game.

Sources: Rugby 365, 'New deal for Australian players', viewed 24 January 2005 http://www.rugby365.com/COUNTRY_BY_COUNTRY/Australia/Country_News/story_41120.shtml and Australian Broadcasting Corporation, 'ARU, players strike pay deal', viewed 24 January 2005 http://www.abc.net.au/sport/content/200501/s1287855.htm

SNaPSHoT Questions

1. Does the ARU believe this agreement is significant?
2. Select four of the features and explain:
   (a) what issues they address
   (b) how they benefit players.

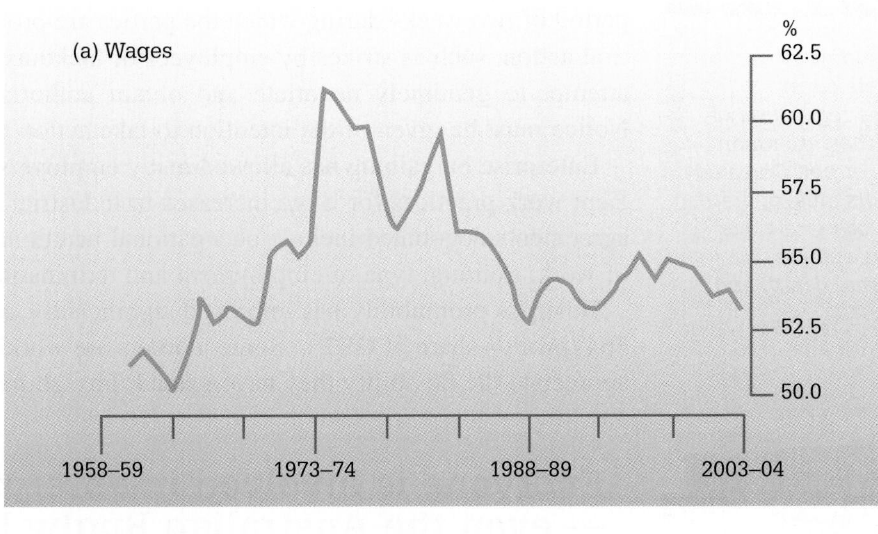

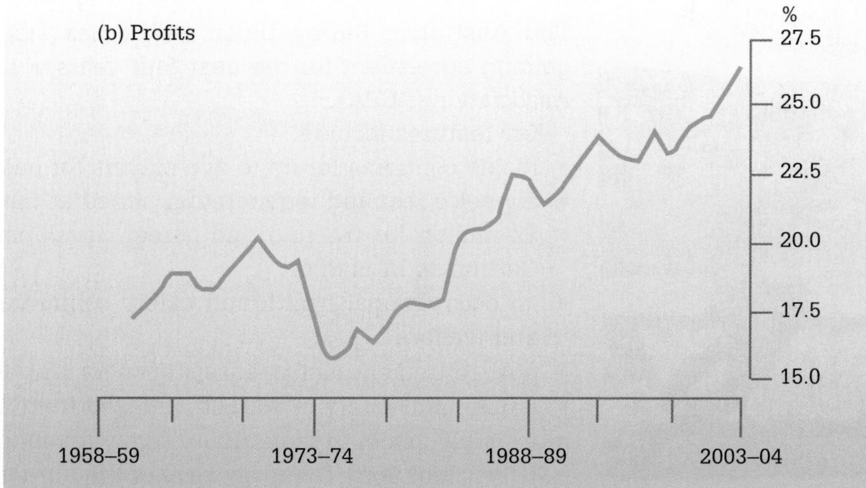

Figure 16.11 Wages (a) and profits share (b) of total factor income

AWAs and non-union collective agreements are more likely than union agreements to provide a daily span of hours of more than 12 hours.

Australian workplace agreements

Australian workplace agreements (AWAs) operate only at the federal level. AWAs are individual contracts, but they may be agreed collectively. They are, nevertheless, signed individually and are secret — that is, free from public scrutiny.

AWAs:

- cover incorporated businesses (constitutional corporations) and businesses in either of the territories
- exclude union involvement unless a union representative is invited to act as a bargaining agent
- must be lodged with the Employment Advocate (EA)
- would be able to run for up to five years

- must contain anti-discrimination and dispute resolution procedures
- must have been fully explained by the employer to the employee. The employee must genuinely agree to the AWA.
- can be terminated by either party on application and approval by the EA or the AIRC (if it is in the national interest and after the expiry date). Changes to AWAs need to be handled by the EA.
- prohibit industrial action by either employee or employer until the AWA expiry date has passed. Three days' notice must be given by either party of intended industrial action. An employer may not threaten an employee for taking industrial action in support of a proposed AWA after the AWA has expired.
- often undercut specific award minimum conditions by allowing employees to 'cash out' (or even 'cash under', that is, accept less) leave entitlements, including annual leave and sick leave. Some do not even stipulate weekly working hours.

Hours of work arrangements are the most common element of AWAs.

HOW INDIVIDUAL WORK CONTRACTS "SIMPLIFY THE EMPLOYMENT RELATION":
I'LL TAKE WHAT I CAN GET!
I'LL GET WHAT I CAN TAKE!

Figure 16.12 Awards versus individual workplace agreements

Figure 16.13 Provision for carers' leave in agreements is becoming increasingly important.

AWAs have not been taken up as rapidly as expected. Some larger businesses find it simpler to make collective agreements with their employees or to use 'common law' individual agreements, which offer employees much less protection.

***Individual contracts** exist when an employer and an individual employee negotiate a contract covering pay and conditions.*

Individual common law employment contracts

These **individual contracts** of service cover employees not on federal agreements or specific state agreements, and are growing at a much faster rate than AWAs.

Individual contracts are more common in the private sector, particularly in non-union enterprises, in partly or wholly owned foreign firms, in the wholesale trade, and property and business services. They are also more common at the professional and managerial level.

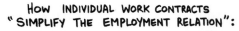

As the trend towards more individual contracts grows, employment relations managers will need to spend much more time focusing on the needs of the individual employee if they are to be retained.

Such contracts may be written or verbal. Many are informal (not ratified by an industrial tribunal) and offer much less protection than other agreements. Although around half vary significantly from their related awards, they are generally required to provide conditions that equate with minimum provisions of related awards; if they do not they are in breach of the law.

Around 42 per cent of Australia's employees are now covered by individual employment contracts, including AWAs. This reflects changing employment practices, facilitated by legislative change, and management preference in some industries. In the long term, if the trend to individualisation of agreements continues it is a threat to the survival of unions.

16.2 Types of employment contract

As the nature of work changes, greater variety is occurring in the types and features of employment contracts available.

Contracts for casual work

Casual *employees are in employment that is short term, irregular and uncertain; they are not entitled to paid holiday or sick leave.*

On-costs *are additional costs involved in hiring an employee, above the cost of their wages. These costs traditionally add around 25 per cent of the cost of the wage and include sick leave, holiday leave, leave loading, superannuation costs, retirement and redundancy payments, and other costs.*

Since 1990, **casual** employment has increased from 16 per cent of the workforce to 28 per cent in 2004.

Casual employees have contracts with employers for short term, irregular or seasonal work. Their work period may vary, they are paid by the hour or the day, and are not entitled to paid leave. Most casuals are female or young people, often students. Many employers prefer casual staff, as it reduces recruitment and dismissal costs and other **on-costs**. They often receive a 20 per cent loading (that is, extra pay) under awards, to compensate them for their lack of entitlements and job security. Where they are employed regularly or for a long period of time they may be eligible for some benefits such as superannuation and long-service leave.

Many casual employees find they miss out on training and promotion, experience fluctuating income, and have difficulty obtaining credit. They are also more likely to experience workplace accidents and are less committed to the organisations that employ them.

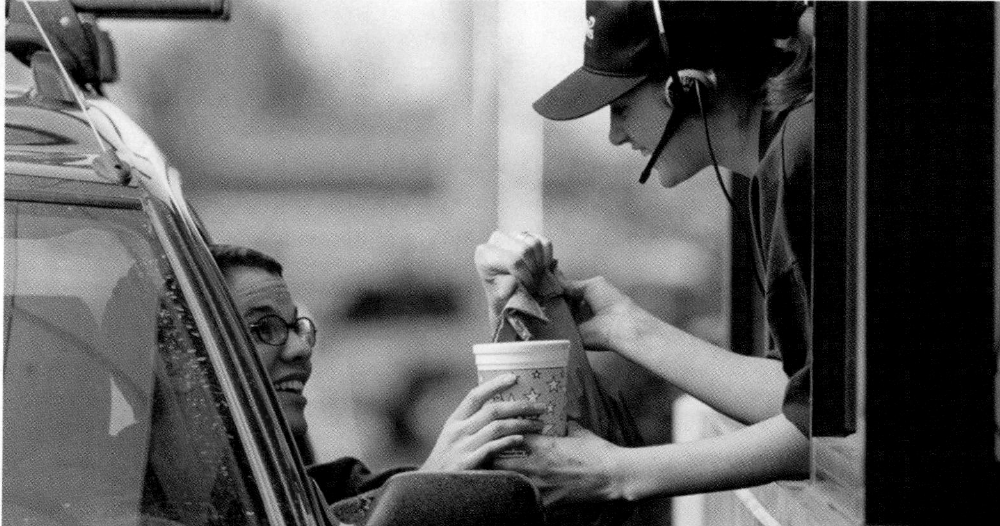

Figure 16.14 A high proportion of casual employees are young people.

Part-time contracts

As we saw in chapter 14, the trend towards part-time work is increasing in Australia. Part-time employees have a continuing employment contract, but work less than 35 hours per week. Unlike casual employees, they do have access to employment entitlements offered to full-time employees, but on a pro rata basis (in proportion to the percentage of time they work compared to a full-time employee).

Flexible employment conditions

As we saw in chapter 15, flexible working arrangements, particularly those related to working hours, are common in agreements and workplaces today.

Flexible working hours are a common feature of enterprise agreements and individual contracts, as they allow firms to operate shifts at more intensive levels during peak seasons. The benefits are passed on to employees all year round; for example, in the form of longer holidays in the quieter parts of the year.

Maxiflex allows employees to build up sufficient hours to take a day off. Employers are usually allowed to nominate the day off. *Flexitime* allows an employee to nominate starting and finishing times to suit their needs.

The flexibility offered by job sharing involves two employees voluntarily sharing one permanent full-time job. This arrangement has been very popular with women returning to the workforce after having children, but requires commitment and communication to be effective.

Permanent contracts

Regular or continuing employees

In August 2004, 75 per cent of employees were receiving holiday, long service and sick leave, and superannuation.

Regular or continuing employees can be full-time or part-time. They can expect that they have a continuing contract of employment and are required to work a specified number of hours per week. Permanent employees are entitled to a range of entitlements, depending on whether they are employed under state or federal awards or agreements. The main entitlements include long service leave, sick leave, annual leave, parental leave, termination rights, superannuation and public holidays.

Fixed-term employees

Only 7 per cent of Australians work between 9 am and 5 pm.

Fixed-term employees are employed on a contract for a specific period. They may be employed to replace staff absent for a period of time or on a project basis. Their employment ends when their contract period expires. If they are terminated prior to the expiry date, they may sue their employer for the wages due up to the expiry date.

Issues arising from the growth of part-time and casual work

The growth of part-time and casual work has provided many opportunities for women with families wanting limited working hours, and students needing financial support. Business has benefited from lower costs associated with increased flexibility in staffing, lower on-costs associated with casual staff, and the opportunities gained from being able to trade during extended hours. These benefits are reflected in the high level of casualisation, reported by the Australian Bureau of Statisics, in retailing for males and females, hospitality, health and community services for females, and manufacturing and property industries for males.

In 2004, 32 per cent of all female employees in Australia were employed on a casual basis, compared to 24 per cent of all males. A dramatic change occurring in the last decade has been the large increase in the number of casually employed males (up 151 per cent in the 15 years to 2003) compared to women (up 62 per cent).

The highest proportions of casual workers are in the 15- to 19-year-old age group (23.7 per cent), where many young workers are still students; however, these proportions remain high well into the 25- to 34-year-old age group, with 21.3 per cent still casual at this stage.

For many, casual employment reflects a lack of full-time employment, rather than a long-term preference for casual work. Casuals often find it difficult to access full-time or permanent jobs, particularly if they miss out on training and development opportunities available to full-time staff. Many exist on low or uncertain incomes, and are unable to obtain credit to purchase cars or homes.

EXERCISE 16.2 *Revision*

1. Draw a mind map to show all the different types of employment contract available today.
2. Amanda has just rung her employer association for advice on industrial agreements. Amanda is setting up a small business administrative support service. She will be employing 10 staff, eight on a full-time basis, two part-time. Write a script for her that is based on advice she receives about contracts and agreements she could use for her staff. Examine the agreements and contracts (e.g. fixed term), available under the Workplace Relations Act, as described in this chapter, for ideas. In your script include:
   (a) key features of each agreement
   (b) at least one advantage and one disadvantage of each type of agreement.
3. Match each of the following terms with a definition given below: Employment Advocate, award, certified agreement.
   (a) A collective agreement made directly between an employer and a union to last for a period up to three years.
   (b) This organisation vets and registers AWAs.
   (c) A collective agreement binding on all members of an employer association and a union, ratified by the AIRC.
4. Currently around 28 per cent of the workforce is casual. Read the following extract from a union journal on casualisation.

   'Unions are actively campaigning against casualisation. They want to build job security and wages protection into agreements, and believe they have significant community support. They believe that, with increasing casualisation of the workforce, a two-tiered labour market is developing, leaving those in casual work permanently disadvantaged, and the gap between the rich and poor growing wider.'

   (a) Research advantages and disadvantages of casual work on the Internet.
   (b) Discuss the disadvantages for workers locked into casual work for long periods.
   (c) Discuss the advantages and disadvantages for employers of a partly casualised workforce.

5. Prepare a summary of this chapter. A summary condenses the important issues and concepts presented in the chapter. Go to www.jaconline.com.au/businessstudies3e to compare your finished summary with the one provided for this textbook.

Extension

1. The Employment Advocate, which vets and registers AWAs, is required to have particular regard for the needs of disadvantaged workers, assisting workers to balance work and family responsibilities, and promotion of better work and management practices. Consider the trends in AWAs and assess the likelihood of achieving this goal.
2. Read the points listed in the box below, which describe some impacts of the decentralisation of the industrial relations system. Using all your resources, hold a class debate based on either statement (a) or (b).
   (a) 'Recent changes to the legal framework of employment relations will improve efficiency and reduce conflict in the workplace.'
   (b) 'Recent legislation has provided a framework for cooperative workplace relations that promotes the prosperity and welfare of the people of Australia.'

- Productivity and profits increased significantly in recent years fostering economic growth.
- There were far fewer disputes in the last decade than in the 1980s.
- This system has limited flow-ons of wage increases throughout the economy.
- Wage inequality increased significantly.
- Profit's share of income growth was at the expense of wages' share.
- There is not enough protection for workers in a weak bargaining position.
- The most common features of agreements suit the employer more than the employee.
- Family-friendly benefits are included in only a small percentage of agreements.
- The most common feature of agreements under the new system is trade-offs in flexibility of hours. Only 60 per cent of workers now work from just Monday to Friday.
- Much of the productivity gain is due to organisations operating with fewer staff (following extensive downsizing) working longer hours.
- There has been a loss of dispute-settling mechanisms.
- There is now more competition in the workplace and less cooperation.
- Some individual contracts and contracts for service allow employers to avoid their economic and social obligations to employees.

3. 'We don't believe that the system puts the employee in an inferior position in bargaining to the employer.' Evaluate this statement made by the Office of the Employment Advocate (OEA), responsible for supervising Australian workplace agreements. Discuss the advantages and disadvantages of using a template for AWAs designed by the OEA. To find out more about the workplace agreement template designed by the OEA, go to www.jaconline.com.au/businessstudies3e and click on the OEA weblink for this textbook.

CHAPTER

17 Industrial conflict

17.1 Definition and causes of industrial conflict

Conflict refers to disputes, disagreements or dissatisfaction between individuals and/or groups. A **dispute** is a disagreement. In industrial relations, a dispute officially exists when workers withdraw from work or place bans on work.

Conflict generally refers to **disputes**, disagreements or dissatisfaction between individuals and/or groups. The Australian Bureau of Statistics (ABS) defines an industrial dispute as a withdrawal from work by a group of employees, or refusal by an employer or number of employers to permit some or all of their members to work. Each withdrawal or refusal is made to enforce a demand, to resist a demand or to express a grievance.

The ABS publishes statistics on industrial disputation in Australia. These statistics are regularly available on the Internet and include the number of disputes, the number of working days lost (see table 17.1), the reported causes of the dispute (overt causes, as discussed on pages 371–2), the method used to resolve the dispute and other matters.

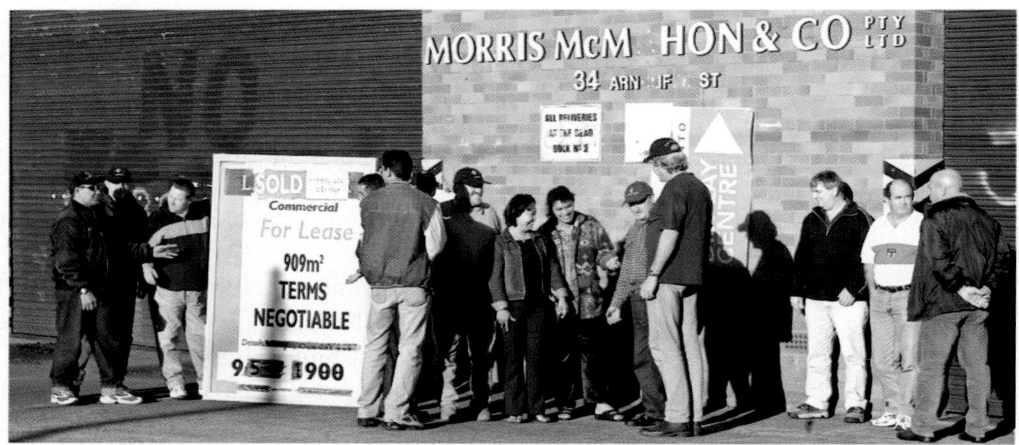

Figure 17.1 A picket line in the Morris McMahon dispute

TABLE 17.1 Industrial disputes in Australia, 1989–2002

Period	Number of disputes	Employees involved (in thousands)	Working days lost (in thousands)	Working days lost per thousand employees
1989	1402	698.6	1202.4	190
1990	1193	725.9	1376.5	217
1991	1036	1176.2	1610.6	265
1992	728	867.8	941.2	158

The number of disputes has been rising over the last six years; however, the size of each dispute in terms of the length of the dispute, or number of employees involved is decreasing.

The Australian Bureau of Statistics (ABS) classes the following as disputes (the types are discussed further on pages 375–8): general strikes; political or protest strikes; work stoppages initiated by employers, such as lockouts; unauthorised stop-work meetings; unofficial strikes; sympathy strikes (that is, in support of another group already on strike); and rotating or revolving strikes (when workers at different locations take turns to stop work). The ABS excludes from its dispute statistics any go-slows, bans (such as on overtime), sit-ins and work-to-rules.

This definition of conflict recognises overt (open) manifestations by groups but does not recognise covert (hidden) manifestations or types of conflict, which are mostly expressed individually and are much more common. When workers are dissatisfied or unhappy in the workplace, they may take time off (absenteeism), work slowly or resign from work. These expressions of conflict may be very costly to a business and are constantly 'benchmarked' by firms keen to achieve world's best practice.

Period	Number of disputes	Employees involved (in thousands)	Working days lost (in thousands)	Working days lost per thousand employees
1993	610	482.7	635.8	108
1994	560	262.1	501.0	76
1995	643	335.0	547.6	79
1996	543	575.9	928.5	131
1997	447	315.4	534.2	75
1998	518	348.3	526.2	72
1999	729	460.9	650.4	87
2000	698	325.4	469.1	61
2001	675	225.7	393.1	50
2002	766	159.7	259.0	32

Source: Based on Australian Bureau of Statistics, Cat. no. 6321.0.55.001 and 6322.0.

Managerial policy

Managerial policy is the single most common cause of disputes (see table 17.2). As a proportion of working days lost to disputes, managerial policy disputes decreased from 63 per cent of all days lost to disputes in 1997 to 38.1 per cent in 2003.

Disputes arising from managerial policy may be related to award restructuring, terms and conditions of employment, enterprise bargaining (a separate ABS classification since 2005), production limits or quotas, promotion, discipline, personal disagreements and changing work practices. As firms restructure, conflict often arises when managers handle retrenchments poorly and the workload of the remaining staff increases. This was a particular problem in the 1990s when the majority of businesses in Australia cut their workforces. In 2003, occupational health and safety matters accounted for nearly half of all disputes.

TABLE 17.2 Causes of industrial disputes as a percentage of total working days lost to industrial disputes in Australia, 2003

Major causes of disputes	1997	1998	1999	2003
Managerial policy	63.6%	62.0%	60.0%	38.1%
Wages	14.0%	6.0%	7.0%	13.5%
Physical working conditions	2.1%	7.9%	12.0%	13.5%
Other (includes situations other than the employer–employee relationship)	20.3%	26.3%	21.0%	34.9%

Source: Australian Bureau of Statistics, Cat. no. 6322.0, 6321.0.55.001 and *Year Book Australia* 1999.

Disputes are more common in large businesses where relationships and communication between employees and management tend to be more impersonal and the scope for mistrust and misunderstanding is greater.

Wage demands

Disputes over wages accounted for to 13.5 per cent of working days lost to industrial disputes in 2003. These figures are low, however, when compared with the levels of the early and late 1980s, when inflationary pressures were a major factor. In 1981, before the Accords were introduced (see chapter 16), disputes over wages accounted for 46.7 per cent of all disputes.

Working conditions

Working conditions are another major cause of disputes. Conditions can include leave, pensions, compensation, hours of work and physical working conditions. Disputes over physical working conditions include health and safety matters; for example, protective clothing and equipment, poor amenities, inadequate or unsafe equipment or production methods and the physical nature of the work itself. Disputes over physical working conditions increased to 13.5 per cent of industrial disputes in 2003.

Political goals and social issues

The category of 'other causes' can involve protests directed at persons or situations other than those relating to the employer–employee relationship. For example, disputes can be triggered when unionists feel strongly about social, economic or political issues. Examples include:

- the nationwide industrial action in 2005 in protest at the Howard government's proposed industrial relations reforms.
- action taken against French companies over French nuclear testing on Mururoa Atoll
- the refusal of construction unions to undertake work in certain areas for environmental or heritage reasons.

Figure 17.2 Emotions often run high in industrial disputes.

Trends in industrial conflict

Only disputes that amount to 10 or more working days lost are counted in ABS statistics.

In recent years, the number of working days lost to industrial disputes fell dramatically to levels last experienced in 1945. The number fell to 244 700 in 2002–03, but rose again to 552 200 in 2003–04. Some of the reasons put forward for the fall included:

- job insecurity, which reduces the incentive of employees to take action
- the provision in industrial agreements for 'no extra claims' until the agreement expires
- community distaste for damaging strike action, especially given high levels of household debt
- some unions working more closely with business, recognising that excessive claims lead to casualisation, downsizing or closure
- the decline in trade union membership.

An average of 67 working days were lost per thousand employees in 2003–04. Dispute levels remained high in the mining and construction industries.

There was a significant increase in the number of disputes — rather than the number of working days lost — after 1996 when the Workplace Relations Act was introduced and a new industrial relations climate prevailed. The restricting of legal industrial action to protected bargaining periods during negotiations over new agreements (see chapter 16) may be a factor in the simultaneous fall in working days lost and increase in disputes. For further information on the number of disputes and industry dispute levels go to www.jaconline.com.au/businessstudies3e and click on the ABS weblink for this textbook.

17.2 Perspectives on conflict

The unitary approach is increasingly popular in Australia.

The different stakeholders in employment relations view the relationship between employers and employees from a range of different perspectives. There is no right or wrong perspective. Three common perspectives influencing the nature of the employment relationship in specific workplaces are unitary, pluralist and radical.

Figure 17.3 Examples of three different approaches to employment relations reflecting perspectives on conflict

*A **unitary approach** to employment relations assumes stakeholders, such as employees and their employers, work 'hand in hand' to achieve shared goals.*

Unitary perspective

A **unitary approach** to employment relations assumes stakeholders, such as employees and their employers, work 'hand in hand' to achieve shared goals. It accepts that some differences occur occasionally in workplaces, but holds that appropriate managerial strategies and effective communications systems can create a positive working environment in which any conflict is temporary (rather than fundamental) or minimised.

*A **pluralist approach** recognises the active roles played by unions and employer associations and the framework developed by the government.*

Pluralist perspective

A **pluralist approach** recognises the active roles played by unions and employer associations and the framework developed by the government. This 'employment relations/industrial relations' approach sees conflict as a legitimate outlet for pressures and tensions between the stakeholders and their competing interests. In this approach, the focus is on limiting disputes through an industrial relations system. Governments (and tribunals) act as independent arbiters providing checks and balances to the power of the competing parties, thus protecting the weak and restraining the power of the strong. Unlike the radical view, the pluralist perspective recognises that some interests are shared and that decision making should be shared between the competing parties.

Some criticise the pluralist view for accepting that the bargaining power of each party is equal, and argue that management (and owners) have much more bargaining power than employees.

*The **radical (Marxist) approach** also recognises conflict as inevitable, and reflects the traditional view of an 'us versus them', conflict-based relationship between employer and employees.*

Radical perspective

The **radical (Marxist) approach** also recognises conflict as inevitable, and reflects the traditional view of an 'us versus them', conflict-based relationship between employer and employees. This relationship is just one aspect of class relations in a capitalist society, which sees the whole structure of society as based on those with wealth and power using their power to maintain their rewards and powerful position, and exploiting those who sell labour for wages. The government is not seen as acting in the 'public interest' to protect the weak. The radical view believes governments act in the 'national interest' to foster economic stability in order to protect private enterprise, profitability and investment.

The radical perspective was held by some members and supporters of the Maritime Union of Australia in the waterfront dispute in 1998 (see the Snapshot 'Waterfront dispute, 1998', pages 386–90).

Figure 17.4 A cartoon by Moir expressing a perspective on industrial conflict and the employment relationship

17.3 Types of industrial action

Industrial action is not necessarily experienced in every workplace. In more than two-thirds of Australian workplaces, workers have never taken industrial action.

There are many manifestations or types of industrial conflict. Some types of conflict are expressed collectively and may be highly visible (overt) to all parties (see the Snapshop 'Fuji Xerox industrial dispute 2004' on page 377). Strikes, for example, attract the most attention in the media and in the community. Other forms may be unofficial and more subtle, and taken by individuals rather than groups, but these covert forms of action could be even more damaging to a business in the long term (see figure 17.5).

Types of industrial conflict

Overt manifestations

By employees:
- Pickets
- Strikes
- Stop-work meetings
- Work bans and boycotts
- Work-to-rule

By management:
- Lockouts
- Stand-downs
- Dismissals, retrenchments

Covert manifestations

By employees:
- Absenteeism
- High labour turnover rates
- Theft and sabotage
- Higher defect rates
- Reduced productivity
- Lack of cooperation

By management:
- Discrimination
- Harassment
- Lack of cooperation
- Exclusion from decision making

Figure 17.5 Types of industrial conflict

Overt industrial action

Figure 17.6 A picket line is formed by striking workers to prevent vehicles and non-striking workers from entering the workplace.

Lockouts

A lockout occurs when employers close the entrance to a workplace and refuse admission to the workers. In some lockouts management has been brought in by helicopter to avoid the picket line of workers. Lockouts have been used frequently in long disputes in the manufacturing sector in recent years. They are often used to promote concession bargaining, and to push employees to sign individual agreements. They are also a common response to strike action.

Pickets

Pickets are protests that take place outside the workplace, generally associated with a strike. Unionists stop the delivery of goods and try to stop the entry of non-union labour into the workplace.

Strikes

Under the Workplace Relations Act, any party intending to take protected industrial action, such as a strike or lockout, must give three working days' written notice of the intention to take the industrial action. The party taking the industrial action must have genuinely tried to reach agreement with the other party and have complied with any orders from the Australian Industrial Relations Commission.

Strikes refer to situations in which workers withdraw their labour. They are the most overt form of industrial action and aim to attract publicity and support for the employees' case. Strike action is more common in public sector organisations and in the mining industries.

A range of different methods of strike action may be used, in combination if necessary, to achieve a solution to a dispute. Most strikes are tactical and are intended to last for a short period, sufficient to draw attention to the dispute. The types of strikes include the following:

- *Sympathy strikes* are those called in support of a group of workers already on strike. Under the Workplace Relations Act, sanctions have been reinstated against workers taking such action.
- *Rolling strikes* occur over a period of time, in between working periods. They tend to be short, sometimes of only a few hours duration, and are designed for their 'nuisance value', and to gain attention.
- *Rotating and revolving strikes* occur where workers at different locations take turns to strike.
- *Political strikes* involve employees taking strike action over political issues, against government policy or actions, such as the strike meetings held by the trade unions in 2005 against the Howard government's policy on industrial relations reform.
- *Wildcat strikes* are those that take place without union approval.
- *Lightning strikes* occur without an employer being notified.
- *General strikes* involve a large number of workers in different industries going on strike simultaneously.
- *Stop-work meetings* involve employees stopping work to hold a meeting on an industrial issue during work time. They may be held to communicate information concerning industrial action, to test support for industrial action or to pressure management into bargaining on an issue.

Figure 17.7 Stop-work meetings are held to register a protest or draw attention to an issue under dispute. The extent of support for industrial action can be tested by a 'show of hands'.

Work bans

A ban is a refusal to work overtime, handle a product, piece of equipment, process, or even a refusal to work with particular individuals. A green ban often refers to a refusal to carry out work that is considered harmful to the environment or natural resources such as forests.

Boycotts are a type of ban in which employees refuse to carry out part of their duties. A secondary boycott occurs when employees of Firm X place a ban on conducting business with another firm, Firm Z, in support of employees in Firm Z. The aim is to pressure the management of Firm Z to negotiate with its employees. This type of action has been illegal since the passing of the Workplace Relations Act, and has been important in limiting the spread of industrial action through the economy.

BiZ FaCT

If teachers refused to do bus supervision or mark homework, this would be a work-to-rule action.

Work-to-rule

In this action, workers refuse to perform any duties additional to the work they normally are required to perform. This is most common as a form of industrial action in community services.

Fuji Xerox industrial dispute 2004

CAUSE

- Bargaining for new certified agreement

CLAIMS

Fuji Xerox workers at their stop-work meeting

- Employees wanted a 4 per cent pay rise and guarantees about redundancy, including additional training resources for staff at risk of being made redundant.
- Fuji Xerox wanted to install global positioning devices in workers' cars to track their equipment via satellite, but staff felt the purpose was to track their movements at work.

ACTIONS TAKEN

- Stop-work meeting over new agreement in August 2004
- National dispute developed:
  - Strike commenced late August for one week, with 120 employees on strike in Victoria, supported by staff in other states and the Australian Services Union.
  - Picket line held outside head office in Sydney.
  - Fuji Xerox delivered DVDs with a personal message from the CEO asking the workers to return to work.
  - Fuji Xerox sent letters threatening striking staff with removal of their vehicles and mobile phones.
  - A strike-breaking force of 30 staff was imported from overseas under the guise of a training program in Australia to 'help minimise disruption' caused by industrial action.

(*continued*)

STRATEGIES USED TO RESOLVE DISPUTE

- Dispute referred to the AIRC by Australian Services Union for conciliation in mid October
- Agreement voted on by employees at the end of October
- Agreement certified by the AIRC

OUTCOMES OF DISPUTE

- New, three-year certified agreement
- Fuji Xerox agreed not to install technology without prior consultation with staff and not to monitor staff with technology.
- Base salary increased. Pay increases translated to 4–6 per cent increase.
- Bonus of $1000 for achievable performance improvements
- Increases to allowances including standby (20 per cent increase)
- Improved redundancy provisions, including extra $1000 for each year of service
- Fuji Xerox maintained its position as market leader on salaries.
- The AIRC denied some clauses as not pertaining to employment relationship

ADDITIONAL MATTERS CLARIFIED AND AGREED

- Grievance procedure/dispute resolution process
- Competency matrix to be used
- Mobile phone use

SNaPSHOT Questions

1. Describe the major external factors that would influence the way this business manages staff.
2. Describe the likely views of employees and the company at the beginning of the dispute.
3. Discuss the likely costs and benefits of this dispute for the parties involved.

Other types of overt industrial action

When work is not available or cannot be continued due to disruption of supplies, employers sometimes 'stand down' employees — that is, the workers are temporarily laid off work. Employers may also transfer employees to other locations, outsource tasks, casualise parts of the workforce or retrench employees. Termination of employees was used by Patrick Stevedores in 1994 and 1998, leading each time to an extended, disruptive and expensive waterfront dispute (see the Snapshot 'Waterfront dispute, 1998' on pages 386–91). A transfer of jobs to its London base in 2004 led to industrial action against Qantas by its staff, concerned about loss of jobs in Australia.

Absenteeism is higher in large workplaces than small workplaces, and is strongly influenced by the culture of the organisation. It is common where workers are unhappy with supervisors or co-workers and experience low job involvement and pay.

Covert industrial action

Absenteeism

High levels of absenteeism and/or lateness may indicate that workers are dissatisfied or that there is conflict within a workplace (see the Snapshot 'Sickies cost!' on page 379). Absenteeism tends now to be measured as the average rate of absenteeism of employees on an average day without sick leave or leave approved in advance.

Such unofficial expressions of conflict may be even more costly to firms (in terms of lost revenue) than official and overt forms of conflict. Revenue is lost as work is disrupted and can lead to lower productivity and higher labour costs, as firms need to have much higher staffing levels to cope with high absentee levels.

Sickies cost!

Jordan, a kitchen manufacturer, is overheard complaining to his mate Lloyd, owner of a recording studio.

Lloyd: When am I getting that kitchen delivered? The bands keep making a mess of my studio! I keep finding nuggets and dried out chips on my equipment!

Jordan: Mate, I'm doing my best. I've got up to seven of my 95 staff absent at the moment. It's been a real problem. They're such bludgers! I'm going to sack them! Good chance they'll leave anyway. Lots do.

Lloyd: Have you thought about your workplace practices?

Jordan: I haven't got the time for that fuzzy stuff. I'm flat out just trying to get people to make the stuff on time!

Lloyd: Does this happen a lot?

Jordan: Yeah, all the time. I've given them a hard time about it, but they just say nothing and take another day off, or eventually move on.

Lloyd: I wouldn't argue with someone of your size, knowing your boxing experience! You know, you should get some advice. I don't have a problem at all, but as you know I'm a good guy! My staff don't want to take time off because the work is great. I give them time off to look after their kids if they need it and get everyone to learn someone else's job, so they can take over when the others are off. I give them free CDs and concert tickets when they work hard, and they get to share the food we get catered for the big artists. Even Two Pac Diddy said he wouldn't mind working here when he came on a visit! What do you do for your staff?

Jordan: None of that. Work is work — not a play centre!

Lloyd: Well, it's costing you probably $1500 every time your staff have more than a week's sick leave a year. Multiply that by seven staff, add 30 per cent for lost productivity, and you get the idea! And that's not counting all the make-up work! When you lose full-time staff because you're a mean bean, you lose about $30 000 all up.

Jordan: Which is a major time waster. Geez! My hip pocket is hurting. What should I do? Who have you been talking to?

Lloyd: My wife! She's a human resources manager for a big record company. She reads all that stuff in her newsletters. Give your staff decent jobs. Chill out a bit about them taking time off and just get them to make it up later. Reward them with a few perks like a free trip to Byron for the lowest sick day count, and put in a child-care deal and promotions if they are really top-dollar employees. Find out why they take time off through meetings or a suggestion box.

Jordan: I can imagine the rude stuff I'd get in the box! And I don't want screamin' kids. You'll be telling me to take my staff to see hip hop next!

Lloyd: Try being a decent employer. Take a personal interest in, and listen to, your staff and then save money, mate!

SNaPSHOT Questions

1. Outline all the possible reasons for Jordan's high absenteeism and labour turnover levels.
2. List all of Lloyd's suggestions, and explain why each may be useful in resolving Jordan's problems.
3. Interview an adult about their opinions on absenteeism. Discuss these views with your class.

Sabotage

According to the Australasian InfoHRM Benchmarking program in 2003, voluntary labour turnover rates were 8.4 per cent and involuntary turnover rates 5.2 per cent. Employee-initiated turnover is higher for professionals (often moving to more attractive positions).

Sabotage/vandalism and internal theft are not uncommon, but are rarely discussed publicly by firms. They may involve employees taking action to harm or destroy the image of a firm; for example, by contaminating food or disrupting production.

High accident or defect rates indicate staff problems in an organisation. Recent public cases have involved staff whose employment was recently terminated.

Turnover

High voluntary labour turnover (resignation) rates are often linked with absenteeism rates as indicators of conflict and dissatisfaction in the workplace. Unskilled employees with mundane or repetitive jobs, low pay and little participation in decision making are more likely to resign.

High levels of labour turnover are of concern to firms because they involve large payout costs for entitlements, and high recruiting and training costs for new staff as a typical example shows below. Morale and productivity are also lower in firms with constantly changing staff.

Exit interviews		$794.89
Administration		$62.20
Lost productivity		$11 154.21
(a) Costs of separation of employee from company	=	$12 011.30
↓		
Prepare job descriptions, review resumes and interviewing		$1171.15
Recruitment agency and advertising		$15 760.00
Pre-employment tasks and orientation		$466.40
Lost productivity		$17 846.75
Training of new employees		$27 482.40
(b) Costs of replacement and training new employee	=	$62 726.70
↓		

Total turnover cost (a + b) = $74 738.00

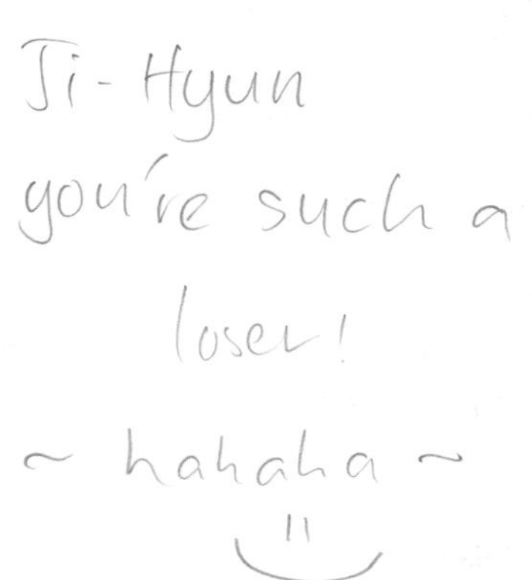

Figure 17.8 Typical total turnover costs for a middle manager in a large Australian business *Source:* Based on J. Abbott et al., 'Costing turnover' in *Asia Pacific Journal of Human Resources*, vol. 36, no. 1, 1998, p. 38.

Dismissal rates may indicate conflict but, since 1993, employees have been protected against unfair dismissal, making it much more difficult to dismiss staff. However, the recent changes to unfair dismissal laws will make it easier for employers to dismiss staff. The rate of dismissal is likely to be influenced by the degree of unionisation and the relationship between management and employees in the workplace.

Exclusion from decision making in business

Fines or complaints about problems such as sexual harassment or bullying may indicate a poor employment relations environment, which affects morale and efficiency.

Excluding groups or individuals from decision making indicates poor workplace relationships. Techniques used to exclude staff include not inviting them to attend meetings, making them a scapegoat when things go wrong, giving them irrelevant or unpleasant tasks, abusing them in meetings, and not offering them opportunities for training and development. This is common in environments in which employees complain or act as 'whistleblowers' against corrupt or unethical business practices. Such situations generally reduce workplace morale, develop into larger conflicts and the victims tend to leave the workplace — a waste of talented staff.

EXERCISE 17.1 Revision

1. Match each of the following types of industrial conflict with its appropriate description below: rolling strike, general strike, work-to-rule, green ban, secondary boycott, lockout, wildcat strike, tactical strike, sympathy strike, go-slow, stop-work meeting.
   (a) One group of workers goes on strike in support of other workers on strike.
   (b) Different groups of workers in an industry or enterprise take turns to go on strike.
   (c) This occurs when management refuses to allow employees to enter the workplace and carry out their normal duties.
   (d) Employees follow their duties exactly and do no overtime or extra duties.
   (e) Building workers refuse to demolish a building of historical value.
   (f) Workers deliberately reduce their speed of work to protest about an issue.
   (g) The Transport Workers' Union goes out in support of the striking Metalworkers' Union.
   (h) Workers hold a meeting to test the feelings of workers towards a strike proposal.
   (i) Workers are so upset about a management decision that they go on strike without the approval of union officials.
   (j) Widespread strike action is taken by many unions over government legislation to be introduced.
   (k) A brief stoppage is used to mount pressure on employers.
2. Research the topic of workplace absenteeism on the Internet. Go to www.jaconline.com.au/businessstudies3e and click on the Employment Practices weblink for this textbook.
   (a) Outline factors that appear to influence absenteeism.
   (b) Suggest strategies that firms can use to minimise this problem.
   (c) Suggest reasons for the following facts.
      (i) Public sector absenteeism is considerably higher than private sector absenteeism. The public sector, as estimated by the National Audit Office, loses 11.9 days per full-time employee, compared to 6.7 in the private sector.
      (ii) Absenteeism is higher in the following industries/sectors: mining, electricity, gas and water supply, transport and storage industries, communication services, government administration, and health and community services.
      (iii) Smaller workplaces are least likely to experience industrial action.
3. Suggest ways in which covert industrial action may be more costly than overt forms.

Extension

1. Is industrial conflict unavoidable? Debate the question.
2. Using newspapers or the Internet, find examples of industrial disputes and identify their causes according to the categories given on pages 370–1. Prepare a PowerPoint presentation and report to the class on two examples and give your ideas on how these disputes could be resolved or have been resolved.

17.4 Roles of stakeholders in resolving disputes

The key stakeholders involved in resolving disputes include employees, employers, governments, trade unions, employer associations and industrial tribunals (see figure 17.9).

Employers and managers

Use grievance procedures and negotiate agreements with employees to resolve disputes. Line managers are playing a much greater role today in resolving disputes.

Employees

Use grievance procedures and negotiate agreements with employers, with or without unions, on a collective or individual basis.

Employer associations

Provide information and support to employers, assist in negotiations with unions, represent employers in tribunals.

Trade unions

Represent employees in disputes from the shop floor to the national level, negotiate with management, employers and associations, represent employees in tribunals.

Governments

Provide the institutions, policy and legislative framework for the resolution of conflict. Investigate breaches of legislation.

Anti-discrimination boards (state)

Work closely with the Human Rights and Equal Opportunity Commission to ensure that disputes about discrimination on the basis of age, colour, sex, disability, criminal record, political opinion, race or religion in the workplace are resolved through provision of information, investigation and conciliation. Can refer cases to Administrative Review Tribunal for determination.

Human Rights Commission (federal)

Monitors and reviews how legislation relating to human rights is implemented. It can investigate and conciliate complaints about discrimination in employment opportunities or a person's treatment in the workplace. Refers complaints of sex discrimination in awards and agreements for determination to the Federal Court.

Industrial tribunals (AIRC)

Interpret legislation. Make and supervise awards and agreements. Provide conciliation and arbitration for the resolution of disputes and unfair dismissal claims.

Civil courts

Federal Court, state supreme courts. Enforce legislation. Handle common law actions.

Figure 17.9 Key stakeholders involved in resolving disputes

Recent changes in the roles of the stakeholders

Under the centralised system, a collectivist approach was used in resolving industrial matters. The parties depended on disputes being transferred to industrial tribunals, such as the Australian Industrial Relations Commission (AIRC), for conciliation and arbitration. After the introduction of enterprise bargaining, the focus moved to resolving conflict in the workplace, with employers now required to include dispute resolution procedures in all agreements.

Since the introduction of the Workplace Relations Act (discussed in chapter 16).

- the responsibility for resolving disputes has fallen even more upon employees and employers, but consultation is voluntary, not compulsory
- employers have powerful legal sanctions to use if disputes are not resolved
- courts are able to impose heavy fines on unions and employees for unlawful action, or action outside a 'protected bargaining period'
- unions have no involvement in any individual agreements unless invited as a bargaining agent
- the AIRC may conciliate on disputes involving awards or certified agreements; however, it may no longer arbitrate unless the matter is in the **public interest**.

The ***public interest test*** *requires the AIRC to consider the state of the economy and the likely effects (including employment and inflation) on the national economy of any award or order that the AIRC is considering, or proposing to make.*

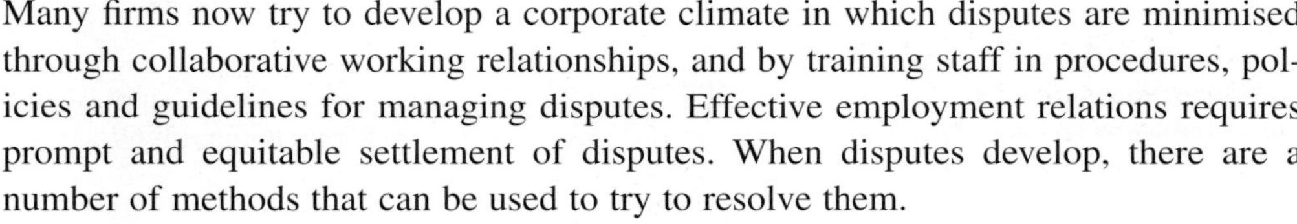

17.5 Dispute resolution procedures

Many firms now try to develop a corporate climate in which disputes are minimised through collaborative working relationships, and by training staff in procedures, policies and guidelines for managing disputes. Effective employment relations requires prompt and equitable settlement of disputes. When disputes develop, there are a number of methods that can be used to try to resolve them.

Options available to the parties involved may be determined by the nature of the industrial agreement covering employees (federal/state) and the goals of the parties.

In 2004, more than half of all Australian industrial disputes were resolved by resumption of work, without negotiation. Around 17 per cent were resolved by negotiation.

Grievance procedures

Grievance procedures are useful in reducing the risk of an issue rapidly becoming a serious dispute. Since the introduction of enterprise bargaining and the unfair dismissal legislation introduced in the *Industrial Relations Reform Act 1993* (Cwlth), most firms have established a formal process (now required in industrial agreements) by which issues can be handled (see figure 17.10). The most recent AWIRS survey found that 84 per cent of Australian workplaces (with over 20 employees) have formal written grievance procedures. Around 70 per cent of managers are involved in grievance handling, and cite the most common issues as personality conflicts, allowances/pay and discipline. Discipline is a greater issue in larger workplaces and personality conflicts are more common in smaller workplaces.

It is illegal for an employer to dismiss or threaten to dismiss any employee for engaging in protected industrial action.

Negotiation

Negotiation is a method of resolving disputes when discussions between the parties result in a compromise and a formal or informal agreement about a dispute. This process can benefit the parties involved by increasing their knowledge of company policy, organisational objectives, workers' concerns and issues involved in implementing change.

Negotiations may be held at the workplace, branch, industry, state or national level. The most common issues are wages and conditions, work practices, dismissals and retrenchments and award restructuring. The process of negotiating a new enterprise agreement is called enterprise bargaining.

In an interview with The Australian Financial Review *(14 August 2000) the former shadow federal treasurer Simon Crean commented: 'I learned very early from negotiations [during his time as a union representative] that you've got to try to produce a partnership ... the best outcome is when both sides come out thinking they've made advances.'*

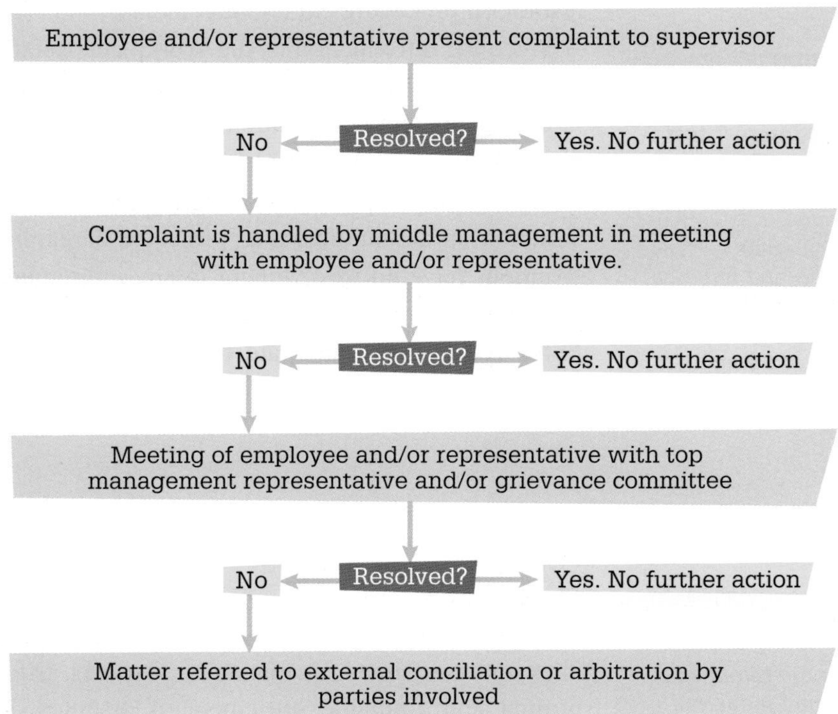

Figure 17.10 Steps in a typical grievance procedure. Complaints may be resolved at any of the stages indicated.

Conciliation

When a dispute cannot be resolved it may be referred to a third party, such as the AIRC. A conciliation commissioner is appointed to hear both sides of the dispute. The commissioner calls a compulsory conference and attempts to help both sides reach an agreement. The commissioner may require all parties to continue negotiations on some aspects, to reduce the ambit of the dispute, or to develop other strategies to resolve the dispute and then report back for another conference. The parties involved may object to a particular commissioner and ask that another be appointed (as occurred in the waterfront dispute in 1994).

***Orders** are decisions handed down by tribunals, such as the AIRC, which require employees or employers to carry out a direction from the tribunal. They may be inserted in awards or agreements. Orders may end a restrictive work practice or behaviour, such as a lockout, or require a secret ballot of union members if strike action is proposed. The tribunal may also order that staff be reinstated or that the parties return to the tribunal at a later date for further negotiations.*

Arbitration

If conciliation fails, the matter may be referred to arbitration, where a judge (such as an AIRC commissioner) or a panel of judges hears both arguments in a dispute in a more formal court-like setting. A judgement, for example, an **order**, is handed down based on the merits of the evidence that becomes legally binding on all parties. Appeals may be made 'in the public interest' and are heard by a full bench of the AIRC.

As the Workplace Relations Act clearly states under paragraph 89(a), the commission has a general function 'to prevent and settle industrial disputes:

- so far as possible by conciliation; and
- as a last resort and within the limits specified in this Act, by arbitration'.

Figure 17.11 Decision time. A case in progress at the Australian Industrial Relations Commission

Mediation

***Mediation** is the confidential discussion of issues in a non-threatening environment, in the presence of a neutral, objective third party. Many organisations now specify mediation as a first step in their dispute resolution or grievance procedures.*

Mediation is the confidential discussion of issues in a non-threatening environment, in the presence of a neutral, objective third party. The third party may be independent and agreed on by key parties in a dispute, or a representative from a business, tribunal or government agency, such as the Human Rights and Equal Opportunity Commission (HREOC) or the Anti-Discrimination Board (in New South Wales).

Mediation as an alternative dispute resolution technique is increasingly popular in Australia. It allows the parties to become empowered by resolving their own disputes and it reduces the risk of disputes escalating and leading to expensive legal costs or industrial action.

Common law action

Common law action is open to any party involved in or affected by industrial action. Parties may make direct claims for damages caused by the parties taking the action, or for breach of contract resulting from such action. An employer may ask a state or territory supreme court or the Federal Court for an injunction or stop order to prevent unlawful interference with the employer's trade or business; for example, where a nuisance is created by a picket line. This option is not available if the action is protected action during a bargaining period. Such action is costly and generally considered a 'last resort'. Common law action in civil courts is also available to those on individual employment contracts disputing matters not covered in legislation or relevant awards.

Business division/closure

Closure of a division or a business permanently or temporarily may also be a resolution or outcome of a dispute.

Some firms have outsourced some of the functions of the business, believing this will reduce industrial dispute levels, improve productivity and boost profits through lower costs.

Waterfront dispute, 1998

BACKGROUND TO THE DISPUTE

Efforts to reform the waterfront at Patrick Stevedoring Company led to two lengthy and expensive disputes, in 1994 and 1997–98.

The Sydney waterfront

These disputes remain significant in Australia's industrial relations history for their size and duration, national significance, the processes involved in their resolution and their wide ranging and long-term costs and benefits.

FACTORS INFLUENCING THE DISPUTE

Economic/financial: strong need for competitiveness

Stevedoring firms such as Patrick (Australian Stevedores) are in an extremely competitive market. They are under pressure to cut costs (especially labour costs), improve productivity and reduce their prices to attract shipowners.

Technology, productivity and the nature of container trade

The union believes measures of productivity on the waterfront fail to consider the impacts of obsolete technology or the nature of trade. Productivity comparisons with overseas ports cannot be made as there are major differences in technology, ship size, dockyard layout, cargo layout, patterns of ship arrivals, container yard congestion and the proportion of containers exchanged at each port.

Social: the ageing workforce

Older employees have been found to have safety problems and lower productivity (for example, due to poorer visual perception as they age). In 1990, 150 new recruits were employed, the first since 1974.

Government policy

The Workplace Relations Act introduced by the Howard government was perceived by the Maritime Union of Australia (MUA) and other unions to be focused on breaking their power.

VIEWS OF MAJOR STAKEHOLDERS IN THE DISPUTE

The union view in 1998

- The MUA wanted to retain full-time jobs and avoid casualisation of the workforce.
- Productivity, it believed, was low due to many other factors. A House of Representatives committee's report into the waterfront found that importers, exporters and transport companies failed to cooperate to boost efficiency.

- Waterfront reform and productivity improvement had already been significantly increased over the previous decade.
- The legislation enacted by the federal Liberal government appeared to the union to be aimed at breaking its power, introducing contractors and non-union labour on the waterfront, and undermining hard-won working conditions and real full-time jobs.

The view of Patrick

- Handling costs in Australia were higher and productivity lower than those of competitors overseas. Patrick needed to negotiate annualised salaries and changes to inefficient work practices and increase casualisation to improve cost-effectiveness.
- The union controlled employees and directed them where required, making it difficult for workers to develop links with their employer.

The federal Liberal government and National Farmers' Federation view

- The government saw the MUA (with 10 000 members and national income of $2.1 million) as holding a monopoly stranglehold over the waterfront through its union preference in employment rules.
- Union members were considered to be overpaid and fostering inefficient work practices which were making the Australian waterfront inefficient by international standards. Efforts of previous governments to reform the waterfront had failed.
- This MUA stranglehold had to be broken.

DEVELOPMENT OF THE DISPUTE

When Patrick merged with Australian Stevedores in 1994, the need for reform led to restructuring and retrenchments. The provocative retrenchment of active union delegates (from the Maritime Union of Australia) then culminated in a two-week national strike involving Patrick.

Ill-feeling persisted between management and the Patrick wharfies into 1997 and 1998, as Patrick and the union attempted unsuccessfully to negotiate a second enterprise agreement to change workplace practices on the waterfront. Patrick, meanwhile, modified its corporate structure so that its employees were subcontracted to four Patrick labour hire firms controlled by Patrick (internal outsourcing).

Industrial conflict, expressed by pickets, strikes and employer injunctions, developed in February 1998 when Patrick leased Webb Dock to P&C Stevedores, staffed by non-union workers. Strike action followed at Port Botany.

VIEWS OF MAJOR STAKEHOLDERS IN THE DISPUTE

The union view in 1998

- The MUA wanted to retain full-time jobs and avoid casualisation of the workforce.
- Productivity, it believed, was low due to many other factors. A House of Representatives committee's report into the waterfront found that importers, exporters and transport companies failed to cooperate to boost efficiency.

(*continued*)

Patrick announced its decision on the evening of 7 April 1998 to terminate the employment of its 1500 employees at ports. It then locked them out using hundreds of security guards and guard dogs. A picket line (technically called a community protest group) was established at the Patrick ports.

This photograph of security guards and dogs at Port Botany appeared in *The Sydney Morning Herald* on 8 April 1998.

The MUA sought and obtained an injunction to stop Patrick sacking its workforce on the grounds of discrimination on the basis of union membership. They were reinstated by the labour hire companies but were not back on their full pay for three months. This was the beginning of an expensive series of legal actions by Patrick and the MUA through the Federal and High Courts.

LEGAL ISSUES RAISED BY THE DISPUTE

There was no effective and efficient dispute-settling procedure available for the situation at Patrick. The power of the Australian Industrial Relations Commission (AIRC) to intervene in disputes had been recently eroded and Patrick would not refer the dispute for arbitration.

The federal government and Patrick believed corporate restructuring using the Corporations Law would override industrial law (the freedom of association clauses in the Workplace Relations Act) as a ground for terminating employees. The Federal Court, however, used its power to grant interim injunctions (as requested by the MUA) restraining the termination of employees for a number of reasons. The major reason was its belief that there had been a conspiracy to injure the Patrick employees by unlawful means. It found Patrick had restructured the companies so that unionised employees could be terminated and replaced by non-union labour.

In other circumstances, the AIRC would have brought the parties together before the dispute had escalated to this point. It would have heard the views of all parties involved and could have resolved the dispute either through conciliation or arbitration. However, the federal government did not invite the AIRC to intervene.

TERMS OF SETTLEMENT

All litigation (legal action) between Patrick and the MUA was to cease. Patrick was to:

- pay the MUA's legal costs
- pay $7.5 million into a fund to compensate small businesses for losses experienced in the dispute
- employ the employees directly at its seven ports
- make up the unpaid wages from the period of voluntary administration and pay the administrators
- outsource maintenance and security functions
- develop a new enterprise agreement with the MUA.

The MUA agreed to give Patrick control over manning levels and work allocation. It also agreed to a dispute-resolution procedure being incorporated in the settlement with the ACCC to avoid such a problem recurring.

A cartoon by Pryor that appeared in *The Sydney Morning Herald* on 5 May 1998

SOME COSTS OF THE DISPUTE

Financial

- Patrick had legal costs totalling over $20 million
- A $63.5 million loss was reported for Lang for the year
- Patrick lost market share to P&O and suffered damage to its reputation. Patrick also had to pay up to $7.5 million into a fund managed by the ACCC to compensate businesses harmed by the dispute.
- Security and repair of equipment damaged in the dispute was estimated at $3 million.
- Fees of $800 000 were paid to administrators.
- At Patrick, 400 employees lost jobs.
- MUA legal costs and the burden of supporting its workers in dispute were also high — estimated at $2–3 million.
- Cargo worth hundreds of millions of dollars was tied up on the docks, and many businesses suffered losses for at least one month due to the lack of stock.
- Three hundred and fifty-three P&C Stevedores workers had to be paid for three weeks without work, then later terminated (with a payout of $15 000–20 000 per contract) when Patrick employees returned to work.
- The National Farmers' Federation supported P&C Stevedores and incurred $500 000 in legal expenses.
- The federal government spent more than $500 000 on legal advice.
- P&O Ports had to remain competitive with Patrick, and so restructured its operations. Its redundancies and their entitlements were financed by the federal government's levy on imported cars and containers.
- Economic growth was affected as a result of lost profits by firms affected by the dispute.
- Unemployment was created by the dispute and redundancies at Patrick and P&C Stevedores.
- Australia's reputation may have been affected by extensive media coverage in surrounding countries where industrial action is illegal.

(*continued*)

Political

- The popularity of the federal government plummeted at the polls by 6.5 per cent after the dispute. The ACTU and unions came to view the federal Liberal government as 'anti-worker'.
- The existing civil law framework was shown to be inadequate for resolving disputes.

Social

- Some MUA members in Sydney felt let down by the union after redundancies were agreed to in settlement.
- Stress was caused to MUA families through having to defend the actions of the MUA at school, at work and in social situations.
- Workplace relationships with Patrick management were not improved.

Personal

- Management at Patrick had their lives turned upside down by the strength of the dispute and the animosity involved. Some managers at Patrick feared for their personal safety.
- Huge personal stress was suffered by workers and their families during the dispute. Security guards were harassed, with rocks and bottles thrown over picket lines. Workers were sprayed with mace.
- Employees now work 12-hour shifts at discretion, and shift starting times may be advanced or retarded by two hours on any day. Union fees are no longer deducted from an employee's pay, and subsidised canteens are no longer provided.

SOME BENEFITS OF THE DISPUTE

Financial

- For Patrick/Lang, the long-term share price and profitability has now risen. Inefficient practices, such as double-headers (8-hour consecutive shifts) and fixed manning numbers were removed, and the company controls rosters, training and allocation of duties.
- Employees are required to maintain health and fitness and can now be reclassified by the company or terminated for disciplinary or medical reasons.
- Productivity bonuses are now paid at a higher crane rate of 20.6 boxes per hour (previously 14).
- Redundancies have been funded by the government through a cargo levy.
- P&O gained a significant amount of Patrick contracts during the dispute. It was able to negotiate an agreement with the MUA that reduced staff, allowed outsourcing and changed work practices, without a major dispute.
- Higher base wages were achieved by employees in return for reductions in overtime.
- The air-freight business benefited from the re-routed transport of goods.
- Lawyers made more than $14 milllion in fees.

Political

- The MUA retained much of its power through effective strategies, including not resorting to illegal actions, mass picketing and mobilisation of international support.

Personal

- Employees saw the value of 'strength through unity'.

CURRENT SITUATION

Patrick and the MUA signed a new certified agreement in September 2004, without needing to resort to any industrial action. This agreement provided a 4 per cent wage increase over the following three-year agreement, and almost a complete phase-out of casuals in container terminals. These positions have largely changed to permanent positions, with CEO Chris Corrigan indicating that greater rostering flexibility in the new agreement made it viable to offer more permanent positions.

SNaPSHOT Questions

1. Identify all the parties involved in the dispute and state the perspective of each.
2. Draw up a table to show the actions taken by Patrick and the union during the dispute.
3. Identify and describe the key influences on the waterfront dispute. Label these 'internal' and 'external' influences.

17.6 Benefits and costs of industrial conflict

Conflict may provide benefits to a workplace; some researchers believe that a certain level of conflict may even be 'healthy' in a firm (see figure 17.13). Conflict may encourage employees and managers to share ideas and resolve problems that improve workplace practices and foster innovation. However, conflict is also costly. Not only the parties directly involved in industrial conflict suffer loss, but also many other stakeholders are indirectly affected.

Table 17.3 (on page 392) summarises the financial, personal, social, political and international benefits and costs of industrial conflict.

Figure 17.12 One of the benefits of industrial conflict is improved relationships

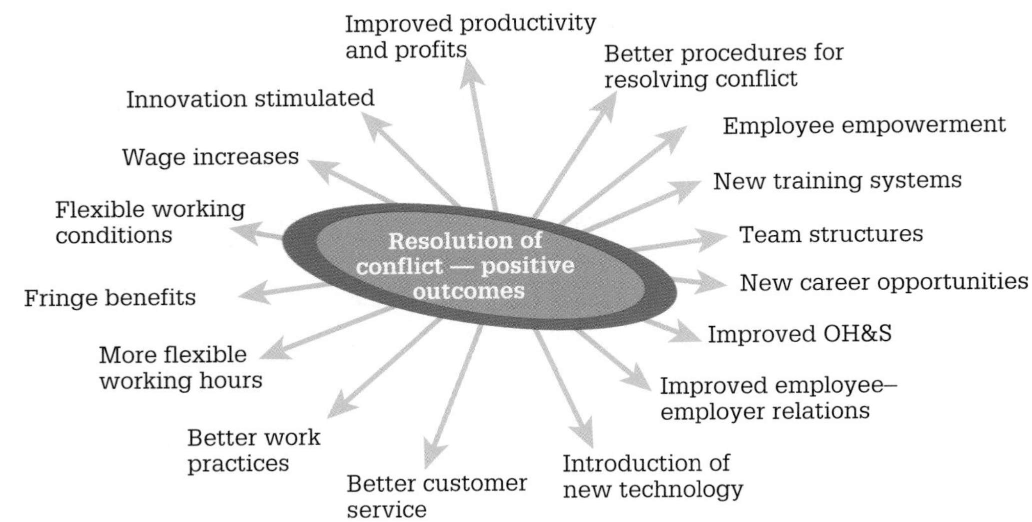

Figure 17.13 Benefits from agreements reached following conflict

Figure 17.14 Unionists clashing with police during a demonstration

TABLE 17.3	**Benefits and costs of industrial conflict**	
Types of benefit/cost	**Benefits of industrial conflict**	**Costs of industrial conflict**
Financial	Increases empowerment of all parties who 'own' an agreement. Empowerment can lead to increased productivity, fewer disputes and reduced absenteeism and labour turnover. Cost-cutting measures can lead to conflict but can ensure a firm's survival and competitiveness in the long term.	Lost production and sales adversely affect a firm's income and levels of debt, and reputation may be damaged. Some firms may close or relocate. Other businesses dependent on firms in dispute can be affected. Families can suffer significant loss of wages. Legal representation and fines imposed can be a financial burden on firms.

Types of benefit/cost	Benefits of industrial conflict	Costs of industrial conflict
Personal	Conflict helps workers to gain management's attention on major issues that may have caused dissatisfaction and stress for a long time. Better work relationships may result from a clearer understanding of work problems. Greater employee involvement and motivation may result from negotiated changes and improvements in training.	Stress can be created through intensification of work and changes due to restructuring of the workplace. Rumours or threats of downsizing cause fear, insecurity and lowering of staff morale. Absenteeism, accidents and defect rates can increase. Working relationships may suffer as a result of conflict or methods used to resolve it.
Social	Jobs can be saved in some cases. Employee and community welfare can be enhanced by changed work practices. Introduction of multiskilling, new training opportunities and career paths benefit individuals and society. Occupational health and safety problems may be reduced.	Community bitterness can be directed at unions, employees or employers in industries where disputes affect the general public. Verbal and physical abuse can occur. Demonstrations can disrupt communities, and violence and injuries may occur in extreme cases.
Political	Governments can change their policies in response to workplace conflict. Disputes draw public attention to the need to protect worker entitlements. Particular industries may be restructured to improve the economy.	Frequent and disruptive conflict has an impact on government or opposition policies, particularly at election times. Bitterness between unions and governments can lead to political conflict and large-scale civil unrest. Loss of national income in extended disputes can affect economic growth.
International	Changes to work practices following conflict can improve a business's international competitiveness. This may present opportunities for international expansion.	Loss of export income and markets can occur after periods of disruption. The nation's reputation for stability can be lost and overseas customers or investors may turn elsewhere.

EXERCISE 17.2 *Revision*

1. Briefly describe each of the methods available to resolve industrial disputes.
2. Identify the method used to describe the way these disputes have been resolved.
   (a) Garth Enterprises makes a two-year collective agreement with a majority of its employees, represented by the Australian Workers' Union.
   (b) Anna Baber is fed up with being asked to do unpaid overtime and leaves Fitzgerald's Garage forever.
   (c) Oktay Yimazturk threatens to shut his workshop tomorrow unless workers agree to productivity improvements in their agreement.
   (d) The commissioner orders Scalici Sofas to reinstate 12 workers sacked last month.

(e) Chow Machines finally reaches agreement with the CFMEU, after regular meetings with the commissioner and the union.
(f) Ramstine is fed up with his workmates playing practical jokes on him. He complains to Kevin Ly, his supervisor, who records the complaint and, as it is serious, takes it to the firm's group specially established to help deal with such problems.

3. Marie's employer tells her she will not be paid for the next week when her employer intends to lock out Marie and three other workmates during a bargaining period leading up to the negotiation of a new Australian workplace agreement (AWA). He states that, if she does not agree after the lockout to his new conditions, she will be dismissed. What are Marie's rights? What action can she take?
4. Prepare a summary of this chapter. A summary condenses the important issues and concepts presented in the chapter. Go to www.jaconline.com.au/businessstudies3e to compare your finished summary with the one provided for this textbook.

Extension

1. Research on the Internet (for example, the Maritime Union of Australia website) to find songs about industrial issues and write a summary of the issues raised in the song(s). An example is given in figure 17.15. Other examples include the Strawbs' 'You can't get me I'm part of the union' and Midnight Oil's 'Blue Sky Mining'.

We Belong to the Union (You Can't Break Me)

You can bruise my pride
Bust my face
Scatter my rights
All over the place
You can take the bread
From off my plate
But you can't break me!

Lock us out
Chain the gates
Put black shirts in
With dogs and mace
We'll hold the line
Won't step away
'Cause you can't break me!

Chorus:
I belong
You belong
We belong to the Union ...

Stocks rise up
On workers' backs
Profits soar
While you hand out the sack
And boardroom bellies
Growin' bloated and fat
But you can't break me!

Seen Australia sold
To mates offshore
Backroom deals
And shonky law
The day has come
To say no more!
'Cause you can't break me!

Chorus:
I belong
You belong
We belong to the Union ...

Don't count me out
When I'm on the floor
We'll win again
We've won before
The streets will ring
With a mighty roar
'Cause you can't break me!

We won't turn away
If you dare us to fight
I swear
I'll never lay down and die
I'm in the union mate
Got a right to belong
We'll be back
Millions strong
Women and men
United as one
'Cause you can't break me!

Figure 17.15 Excerpts from the lyrics for 'We Belong to the Union (You Can't Break Me)' by Tim O'Brien, 1998 (*Source:* CD produced by the ACTU, included on MUA website)

2. In groups and using newspapers and the Internet, research a range of industrial disputes. Report to the class on the costs of the disputes using a PowerPoint presentation or video clips.
3. In recent years, new legislation has forced employers and employees to increasingly resolve issues in the workplace, often on an individual basis. Discuss the advantages and disadvantages of this approach.
4. With reference to a case study, explain how an industrial dispute's benefits may outweigh its costs.

18 Ethical and legal aspects of employment relations issues

18.1 Ethical and responsible behaviour

Ethical business practices *are those practices that are socially responsible, morally right, honourable and fair.*

A wide range of employment relations issues arise in the workplace and, if they are not handled in an ethical, legal or socially responsible manner, they can lead to poor morale, low productivity, heavy costs and industrial disputes. **Ethical business practices** are those practices that are socially responsible, morally right, honourable and fair (see the Snapshot 'Management ethics matter' on pages 396–7).

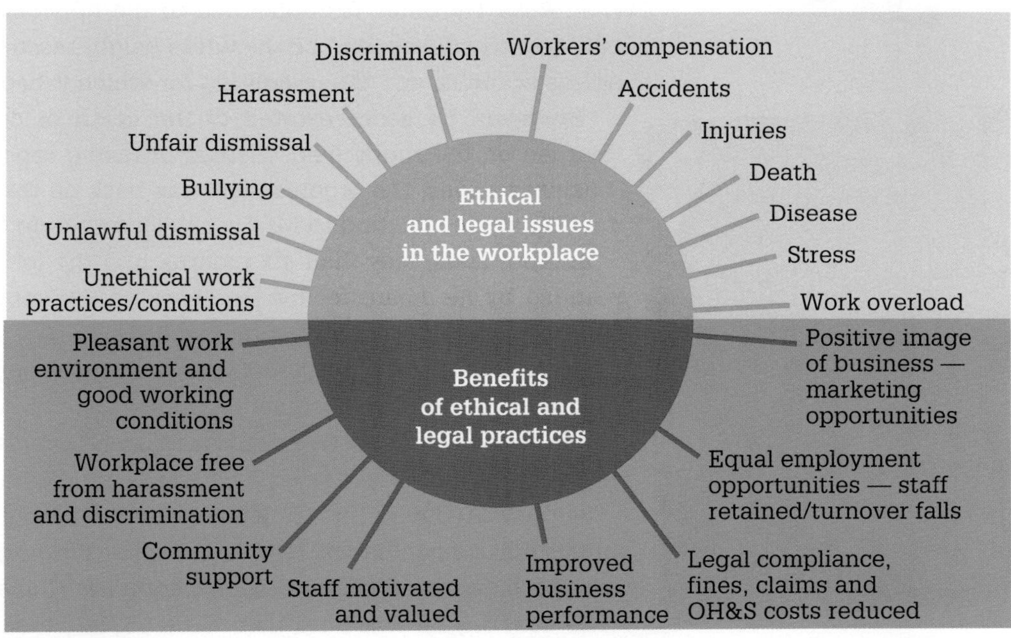

Figure 18.1 Some ethical and legal issues arising in the workplace and the benefits of dealing with them successfully

A socially responsible, ethical employer recognises that:

- a pleasant working environment and good working conditions are valuable in motivating and retaining staff
- performance and motivation are maximised when staff feel secure, confident in their work, recognised, safe, equally valued and rewarded for their efforts
- an effective workplace benefits from good working relationships and teamwork
- the business depends on community support, as a source of staff and as a source of business (that is, customers) and resources
- management should be committed to an ethical workplace culture
- customers eventually find out which businesses are acting responsibly and which are not.

Figure 18.2 Managers are important role models for ethical and responsible behaviour.

*A **code of conduct** is a statement of acceptable and unacceptable behaviours in a business.*

*A **code of ethics** is a statement of a firm's values and principles.*

***Best practice** refers to business practices that are regarded as the best or of the highest standard in the industry.*

An ethical framework must be developed for the workplace, in collaboration with the major stakeholders. This framework may include a **code of conduct** and a **code of ethics**. Key principles may include ensuring equity in workplace processes, legal compliance, and commitment to customers.

The benefits accruing from ethical practices are becoming increasingly evident from research and include the following:

- Staff retention and absenteeism rates improve as staff feel more valued and motivated.
- Business costs (such as recruitment and training) are reduced and business performance is enhanced.
- There are significant marketing and business opportunities — **best practice** employers enjoy regular publicity in the media, in journals and on the Internet.

Management ethics matter

MOTORING BODY'S WHITE KNIGHT FAILS IN RESCUE MISSION

When Ross Turnbull was appointed to the presidency of NRMA in October 2002, he was supposed to be the white knight rescuing the organisation from endless scandals and the in-fighting for which it had become infamous.

However, he soon resorted to the crash or crash through skills he'd learned on the rugby field. Instead of taking reports on the NRMA to the business pages, the organisation was back on the front page with embarrassing stories relating to Mr Turnbull's corporate excesses.

In April 2003, less than six months into the job, Mr Turnbull was reprimanded by his board for his expenses on the company credit card, which had been picked up in an internal audit.

In five months he'd put $90 000 on his card, a large portion of which was incurred at dining establishments around the city.

Soon dubbed Sir Lunchalot by the media, his Diners Club records, which have been seen by the *Herald*, reveal just what a prodigious diner Mr Turnbull was.

Take one 10-day period in January 2003. Turnbull started off on Monday January 13 by spending $219.20 on lunch at I'm Angus on the Park. He then spent $476 on dinner at the Golden Century in Chinatown.

The next day he was back there for a $525.20 lunch.

On Saturday he spent $149 at Dee Bees in Double Bay, then on Monday he spent $58.30 at Twenty-One in the same suburb. Later that day he spent $342 at Lucio's in Woollahra.

...

He rounded the week off at Corsetti spending a modest $83.

The total $90 000 bill was incurred from October to February. Turnbull had to repay $55 000 of it. However, his cheque for his first repayment bounced.

...

Also dogging Mr Turnbull's presidency were non payments of printer's fees for an election brochure for his team. Mr Turnbull was eventually sued.

Only a few months after his first public embarrassment over his credit card, Mr Turnbull was back in the news for his spending.

Alarmed at the president's expenditure, the NRMA had engaged external auditors to keep an eye on his expenses.

A leaked audit of the expenses revealed that his corporate expenses for just two months in 2003 totalled more than $34 000. He also spent $11 000 on limousine hire over four months.

...

The most damaging moment of his presidency came mid-way through last year when management turned against him over his meddling in the bitter dispute with the NRMA's patrolmen.

The board and management had agreed on a tough course of action with the patrol crew, only to discover that Mr Turnbull was trying to broker his own deal with the union.

The CEO, Tony Stuart, threatened to resign over Mr Turnbull's actions. In the end the board stood down Mr Turnbull for a month. It had been split about whether to reinstate him.

Some thought that the removal of his credit card and promises by Mr Turnbull that he would abide by a strict new code of corporate governance would see Mr Turnbull toe the line.

...

Note: On Friday 21 January 2005, the board had had enough, and voted unanimously to replace Mr Turnbull over his failure to follow agreed procedures over several months.

Source: 'Motoring body's white knight fails in rescue mission', *The Sydney Morning Herald*, 25 January 2005.

BiZ FaCT

As international awareness of the needs of individuals in the workplace has developed over the last few decades, a range of conventions have been developed by United Nations organisations, such as the International Labour Organization (ILO), to protect the health, safety and welfare of employees. Australian governments have enacted social justice legislation that is both an outcome of governments' experience of industrial issues and its constitutional (external affairs) power to make treaties (and implement ILO conventions).

SNaPSHOT Questions

1. Describe some of the unethical practices allegedly used by Mr Turnbull.
2. Why did the board vote him out? Analyse the reasons for their decision.
3. Describe some of the likely outcomes of their decision.
4. Why is management commitment to ethical practices so important for employment relations?

18.2 Working conditions

An ethical employer can be expected to achieve safe and fair working conditions that improve the welfare of employees. This is achieved through:

- compliance with social justice and industrial legislation covering areas of occupational health and safety, anti-discrimination and equity in all aspects of the employment relationship (see chapter 16)
- providing a safe and healthy working environment, safe working practices and equipment, appropriate supervision and training in safety and health, without which, workplace incidents may occur (see the Snapshot 'Pizza with the works?' on page 398)

- creating challenging, interesting and meaningful work or job design to stimulate intrinsic rewards for staff
- improving communication, and fostering teamwork and empowerment of staff (discussed in chapter 15)
- providing study leave and training opportunities to reduce skills obsolescence and improve access to management positions
- offering equitable and open rewards and benefits subject to clear criteria which value each employee's contribution
- offering flexible working hours and conditions that promote a balance between work and life (see chapter 15)
- a strategic plan supported by management that incorporates ethical responsibility in major organisational strategies
- implementing change through collaboration with staff
- establishing a **code of practice** to show to customers, employees and suppliers the organisation's commitment to equity and ethical business practice
- evaluating and benchmarking its performance in these areas in order to ensure it is operating at best practice.

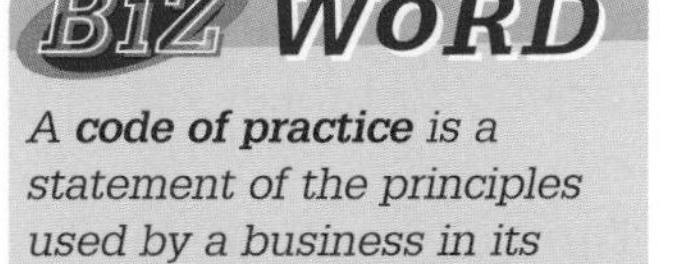

A ***code of practice*** *is a statement of the principles used by a business in its operations. It generally refers to practices that are seen as ethical or socially responsible.*

Pizza with the works?

A case was brought to a local court in Sydney in which a 19-year-old pizza delivery boy charged his employer with assault. The pizza store manager allegedly:

- locked him in the freezer for almost half an hour, ignoring his pleas to be released because of his asthma
- tied the boy to the bonnet of his car while he drove it back and forwards
- sprayed a fire extinguisher under the door of a toilet cubicle where the boy was hiding
- hit the boy in the head, jammed his ankle in a door and cut his face with a wristwatch during a scuffle.

In court, the 27-year-old manager defended his actions, claiming they were part of the teenager's 'initiation' into the company. The manager was found guilty on four counts of criminal assault. He was fined $650 and placed on a 12-month $500 good behaviour bond.

SNaPSHOT Question

Identify the ethical and legal issues arising from the treatment of the pizza delivery boy.

18.3 Occupational health and safety (OH&S)

Growing community and worker awareness of safety and environmental issues, along with ballooning compensation costs in recent decades, have prompted both federal and state

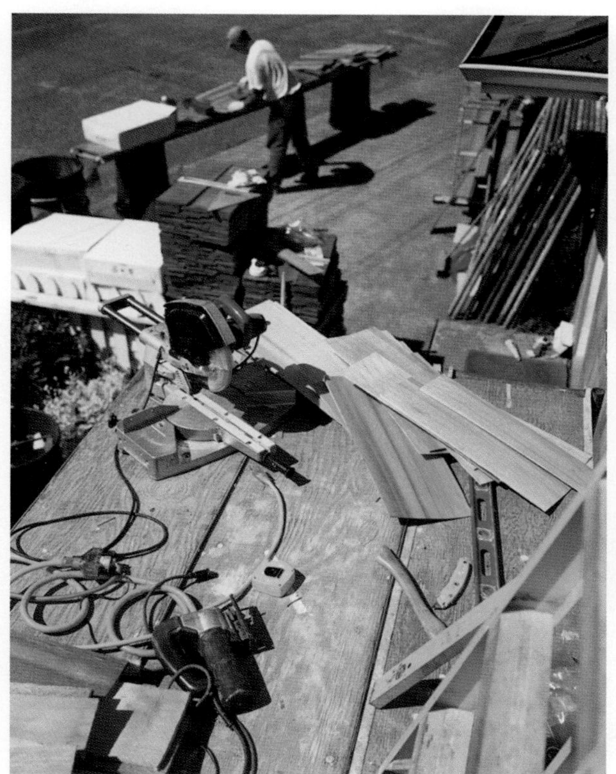

Figure 18.3 Workplace accidents are most common in construction, manufacturing and retailing industries.

governments to improve workplace occupational health and safety (OH&S). In 1985, the Commonwealth government, concerned at the high levels of injury, accidents and disease in the workplace, introduced the *National Occupational Health and Safety Commission Act 1985*. Worksafe Australia, the National Occupational Health and Safety Commission, was established to develop and implement a national health and safety strategy. It conducts research and develops national standards, codes of practice and common approaches to occupational health and safety (OH&S) legislation, which are endorsed by state governments. However, due to constitutional limitations, the ability to enact and enforce OH&S legislation has passed to the states. Common law supports laws developed by the states; for example, by requiring that employers provide competent staff and a reasonably safe system of work as undertaken at General Motors (see the Snapshot 'Occupational health and safety at Holden Australia' on pages 400–1).

Legislation on occupational health and safety covers employees, employers and the self-employed. In New South Wales, under the *Occupational Health and Safety Act 1983* (amended in 1990 and 2000), the following are required:

- Employers must ensure the health, safety and welfare at work of all employees by providing a safe system of work; ensuring that plant and substances are used, handled, stored and transported safely; giving employees the necessary information about the plant and substances, and training and supervision in their work; maintaining the site in a safe condition; and ensuring that the goods they design, make, supply, install or repair will not injure or damage the health of others.
- All employers must take out workers' compensation insurance, or face imprisonment or a $55 000 fine.
- Employers must take steps to ensure that people on-site who are not employees are not exposed to risks arising from work being undertaken.
- Employees are required to take reasonable care for the health and safety of others, to cooperate with employers and comply with OH&S requirements.
- Employees who engage in bullying, skylarking or interfering with machinery or any other behaviour that puts other employees at risk are breaching their duties and could be fined.
- Health and Safety committees must be established at workplaces with more than 20 employees if requested by a majority of employees or if directed by WorkCover (see the Biz Fact on the left).
- WorkCover inspectors may inspect the workplace, collect information, and issue improvement and prohibition notices under the *Factories, Shops and Industries Act 1962* (NSW). This may, in some cases, mean that work ceases.
- WorkCover must be notified of any deaths or serious injuries in the workplace, and any plans to carry out dangerous work.
- Corporations may be fined up to $550 000, $825 000 if repeat offenders, (in New South Wales) and individuals, $10 000 for breaches.

WorkCover recommends employers use a six-step approach to occupational health and safety to prevent accidents, disease, injuries and work-related ill health (see figure 18.4).

BiZ FaCT

More than 500 people are killed each year at work in Australia; two thousand two hundred die from work-related injury or illness and 5 million work days are lost per year. Australia's work injury bill in recent years has been over $30 billion per annum.

Q: Who is responsible for occupational health and safety?

- *Employers*
- *Manufacturers, designers and suppliers*
- *People in control of workplaces*
- *People who erect and install plant and equipment*
- *Employees*

A: Everyone.

It is an offence to dismiss an employee or alter an employee's job to his or her detriment because the employee has pursued an occupational health and safety matter. Managers must visibly and actively support supervisors in solving OH&S issues.

1. Develop an OH&S *policy* and related programs
2. Set up a *consultation* mechanism with employees, through meetings, workshops, suggestion boxes, surveys and noticeboards. Ensure input is gained from all staff.
3. Establish a *training* strategy for new and existing staff at all levels. This may include emergency procedure training, or specific hazard training.
4. Establish a *hazard* identification and workplace assessment process. This should aim to identify hazards through regular safety audits, workplace inspections, accident investigations, injury and illness record assessment, complaints handling observation and staff input.
5. Develop and implement *risk control*. This will involve minimising, rectifying, eliminating and reviewing workplace risks.
6. Promote, maintain and improve these strategies. Key to successful programs is regular *feedback* and advice from staff, and evaluation of records.

Figure 18.4 A six-step approach to OH&S

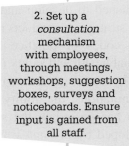

Australia's safety record does not rate well against that of other countries, with 84 work-related deaths each year per million workers, compared with 37 for the United States, 24 for the United Kingdom and 22 for Sweden.

Advertisements by WorkCover NSW state: 'The workplace kills more people than die on the roads.' WorkCover encourages workers to 'think for a moment about the hazards in your workplace — machines, noise, chemicals, dust. Works tasks which involve lifting and carrying can also be hazardous. Accidents are preventable.'

Work can be a health hazard!

The following statistics reveal a serious workplace health and safety problem in Australia.

- Around 97 per cent of work-related deaths can be prevented.
- Around 93 per cent of work-related deaths are males.
- The average male worker under 25 years of age has a one in 12 chance of being injured at work each year, compared with one in 18 for older workers. Often the legacy is a lifelong disability.

The workplace continues to be even more dangerous than the roads. Inadequate training, lack of appreciation of the seriousness of health and safety issues, and an attitude of 'she'll be right' all contribute to carelessness. They are the three principal causes of workplace injuries and illnesses. For this reason, all businesses need to adopt a systematic, legally compliant approach to managing occupational health and safety.

Occupational health and safety at Holden Australia

Holden Australia is a subsidiary of General Motors, which is currently establishing a common global health and safety management system structured around the ISO 9000-2000 Quality Management System. This framework encompasses its safety program and procedures, including best health and safety practices, ergonomics, safety through design, contractor safety, employee wellbeing and employee assistance programs.

Its view of safety is 'there will be no compromise of an individual's wellbeing in anything we do … the company will comply with all applicable health and safety laws and regulations. It is a leadership responsibility. Continuing improvement and support of this effort is the responsibility of everyone'.

Specific strategies implemented to promote high health and safety standards include:

- a health and safety centre of excellence providing advice and support at all levels
- ongoing benchmarking and auditing of safety matters and reports
- a safety council reporting to management on corporate governance of health and safety
- a diversity program addressing gender, race, age, disability and family responsibilities, designed to eliminate discrimination, hostility, harassment and bullying
- a work–life strategy to promote work–life balance and to provide family support; for example, through relocating assistance, flexitime and counselling and flexible working arrangements
- regular monitoring of employee satisfaction through an independently conducted General Motors global employee census
- initiatives to promote employee health such as a recent Holden-subsidised quit smoking plant-wide program for 300 staff, which operated in conjunction with the Cancer Council.

Source: information from Holden website, viewed 1 June 2005, http://www.holden.com.au.

Direct costs
(medical bills, compensation and insurance)

Indirect costs
(wages and time lost, contamination, wastage, production delays, repairs, fines, lower morale)

Figure 18.5 Financial costs of accidents and injuries in the workplace — the 'iceberg effect'

SNaPSHOT Questions

1. Explain why four of the strategies listed to promote high standards of occupational health and safety would be considered essential.
2. Outline the role you would play as a senior manager at Holden in promoting a safe workplace.

Management examines accident statistics for information on the type of occupation involved in injuries, types of accident, frequency rate (hours of lost time to accidents per number of employee hours worked during the period) and the severity rate (number of days lost as a result of accidents per million employee hours worked).

Unions also play an active role in OH&S. The Australian Council of Trade Unions (ACTU) conducts its own surveys; for example, a recent study of around 10 000 employees about employment security and working hours found that 49 per cent of employees suffered health problems because of their working arrangements, including stress (76 per cent) and continual fatigue (72 per cent), and 25 per cent experienced accidents or near misses.

Best practice organisations have regular safety audits and comprehensive safety programs. (Policy statements, safety signs and reminders are visible and there is regular ongoing training for staff who are aware of safety rules and prepared for emergencies.) When considering changes in the workplace employers consult employees and health and safety personnel on the implications of the change. Such firms save on compensation claims, absenteeism, lost work time, replacement costs for damaged equipment and loss of morale in the workplace. Customers appreciate the effort businesses make in producing a safer product or service; therefore, such businesses also improve their image to their customers.

18.4 Workers' compensation

Workers' compensation *provides a range of benefits to an employee suffering from an injury or disease related to their work. It is also provided to families of injured employees when the injury/disease was caused by, or related to, their work.*

State legislation covers employees for **workers' compensation** matters, unless they are Commonwealth government employees.

All employers must:

- take out a policy with a licensed insurer. There has been a strong focus under recent legislation on getting injured employees back to work as soon as possible.
- keep time and wages records, a register of injuries, and complete accident and internal investigation forms, or face a penalty of $55 000, or six months' jail.
- notify insurers of significant injuries within 48 hours
- establish, in consultation with the insurer and the employee's doctor, an injury management plan and a return-to-work plan for all injured workers, when fit for 'suitable duties'. Failure to display and comply with the plan (which may include employing a rehabilitation coordinator) may result in increased premiums for the employer, or loss of benefits for the employee (if they don't comply).
- pass on compensation monies to the person entitled as soon as possible. Premiums are closely linked to the number, frequency and size of claims, so it is in the employers interest to focus on achieving high standards for OH&S.

Employees must notify their employer as soon as possible of an injury or work-related illness. Compensation is provided to employees (and/or their dependants) suffering injuries or illnesses (including psychological illnesses) substantially developed from their work. Workers temporarily absent from work or injured on a journey to or from work are also covered by the Act.

In New South Wales an employer may be breaking the law if an injured employee is dismissed within six months of being injured or their position offered to a replacement employee within two years of the date of injury without the employee being first advised that she or he might not be reinstated. Full-time injured employees unfit for work receive their award wage for 26 weeks and then a fixed rate until they are fit for some work. The casual employees' benefit is based on the average hours previously worked per week. Partially incapacitated workers being retrained or without suitable work receive benefits for up to one year, after which the insurer assesses their earning capacity and pays the difference between this amount and the pre-injury wage.

An injured employee may claim compensation, a lump sum payment or sue for common law damages for negligence. Compensation today is subject to thresholds and caps on claims. It is paid for:

- loss of wages for time off work
- medical and rehabilitation expenses, and the cost of associated travel and modifications to the home or vehicle
- permanent impairment or loss of use of a part of the body
- pain and suffering if the damage is assessed as being over $10 000.

Benefits are payable if employees experience total or partial incapacity to perform work; there is a need for medical, hospital or rehabilitation treatment; or if there is permanent or partial loss of use of parts of the body. This includes facial disfigurement and damage to body organs, including bowel injuries. A lump sum payment and weekly payment to dependants are payable if a worker dies as a result of the injury.

Benefits may not be payable if employees have deliberately injured themselves, or are solely responsible for the injury through their wilful misbehaviour or misconduct. Permanent disablement or death in these circumstances does, however, allow the payment of benefits. If an employee on a journey to or from work substantially increases the risk by deviating from or interrupting the journey, benefits may not be payable.

Since 2000, legislative amendments have been successively introduced in response to a massive blow-out in the value of compensation awarded. For most employees, 'provisional liability payments' are made for up to 12 weeks after an injury, and claims for medical expenses compensation up to $5000 are accepted generally on the basis of verbal or written notification. Formal claims are generally made for matters extending beyond this period or for medical costs greater than $5000, and should be

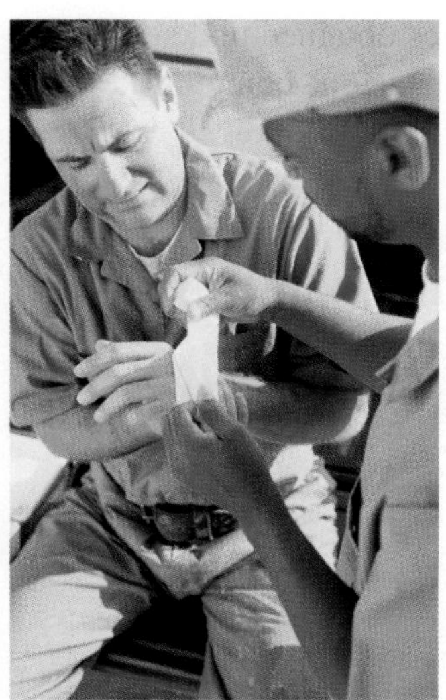
Figure 18.6 Compensation rules have changed.

made within six months of the date of injury or accident, unless the claim relates to serious or permanent injury, death or disablement. In such cases the time limit is extended.

Eligibility for lump sum payments and the calculation of these payments under statutory law is now based on the principle of thresholds for degree of body 'permanent impairment' (loss of use, rather than disability), and is capped at $250 000, plus weekly income support and medical costs for life. Pain and suffering compensation is only paid for a degree of permanent impairment greater than 10 per cent. For employees with less than the 'lump sum' threshold impairment (around 15 per cent), normal wages and medical costs are payable.

The maximum penalty for a false claim under the NSW Workers Compensation Act is $5500 or 12 months' imprisonment, and for insurers who delay commencing payments penalties up to $50 000 apply.

For further information about workers' compensation go to www.jaconline.com.au/businessstudies3e and click on the WorkCover and Workers Compensation and Injury Management weblinks for this textbook.

State and/or federal agencies

The Workers Compensation Commission is a free service and conducts face-to-face conferences or teleconferences to resolve issues.

The WorkCover Authority of New South Wales is responsible for administering the laws relating to occupational health and safety, rehabilitation and workers' compensation. It appoints licensed insurers to administer workers' compensation insurance policies, in accordance with the NSW Compensation Act 1987 and the NSW Workplace Injury Management and Workers Compensation Act 1998.

In the case of disputed claims, there is a two-tiered dispute resolution process:

1 WorkCover screens disputes in the first instance.
2 Compulsory conciliation or arbitration is then undertaken by the Workers Compensation Commission. It deals with disputes related to weekly compensation, workplace injury management, medical and related expenses, permanent impairment and pain and suffering, and worker deaths.

Common law redress

Employees may take action against an employer when the employer or another employee has been negligent or breached their duty, if the employee has a permanent body impairment of more than 15 per cent and if the injury occurred at least six months prior to the claim. Common law action has been taken for serious diseases such as those caused by asbestos (see the Snapshot 'Compensation for asbestos victims — James Hardie Industries' on page 404). Such claims are heard in the district or supreme courts, and once an employee has successfully achieved a settlement, there are no further payments. If employees are unsuccessful in their actions, they will continue to receive workers' compensation as required under statutory law.

Common law action has been taken for serious diseases, such as those caused by asbestos.

Some legislation, such as the Factories, Shops and Industries Act, may provide additional provisions, which employees may claim have been breached. Any worker making such a claim would need to prove that there were reasonable ways in which the employer could have avoided the risk, could have reasonably foreseen the injury or did not take reasonable care for the safety of the employee. If a claim is proven, damages will be awarded in a lump sum. Contributory negligence on the employee's part reduces the damages awarded.

Legal advice must be considered before seeking damages obtained under common law redress. Employees injured may not claim both damages at common law and lump sum compensation for permanent impairment under statutory law.

Compensation for asbestos victims — James Hardie Industries

The James Hardie Industries asbestos case has been called Australia's largest corporate scandal. The ACTU secretary Greg Combet commented on ABC's *Lateline* program on James Hardie's efforts to avoid paying compensation to its asbestos victims: 'This is one of the largest exercises to avoid moral and legal obligations in Australia's corporate history and we are going to fight very hard to bring them to justice.'

The James Hardie asbestos compensation issue has been controversial.

Hardie has been Australia's largest asbestos manufacturer. Asbestos is a building material present in one-third of homes and buildings built before 1970. Asbestos-related diseases such as mesothelioma and other asbestos-related lung diseases are expected to affect 30 000 Australians in the future. Seven thousand, five hundred Australians have already died from mesothelioma.

Two members of Hardie's senior management resigned in 2004, including its CEO, under pressure from a commission of inquiry, which found it had not fully told the truth to the New South Wales Supreme Court, and its management had been less than honest with the Australian Stock Exchange and the community on the issue of asbestos. It had not put enough money into a compensation fund to compensate future claims, and its chief financial officer was prepared to be deceitful where asbestos was concerned. Claims alleged that Hardie management had deliberately restructured operations to a Netherlands base to avoid their obligations for compensation of victims of asbestos. The two members of senior management who resigned are alleged to have received executive payouts totalling $10 million.

Under pressure from victims' lawyers, the ACTU and other groups, James Hardie signed a landmark agreement in December 2004, providing asbestos sufferers with compensation valued at over $4 billion, over a 40-year period.

James Hardie's current CEO, Meredith Hellicar, hailed the agreement as a 'compassionate' outcome, which is 'fair and equitable for all parties' and she hoped it 'convinces the Australian community that we are seriously committed to that responsibility'. The company is capping payments into a special purpose fund for current and future victims, at 35 per cent of its free cash flow. A key feature of the agreement is recognition by all parties that ongoing James Hardie viability is essential to long-term benefits for its victims.

SNaPSHOT Questions

1. Explain why management may have behaved in such an unethical manner for so long.
2. Do you think the Hardie executives who resigned as a result of the commission of inquiry into their management practices should have been paid $10 million? Justify your response.
3. What are the reasons for the capping of annual payments at 35 per cent of the company's free cash flow?

EXERCISE 18.1 *Revision*

1. Look at the photograph (figure 18.3, page 399) and list some safety concerns associated with the work. Identify the likely occupational health and safety risks faced by people in the following jobs: auto mechanic, teacher, ship refueller, scientist, process worker in a textile factory, hairdresser, miner, bank officer, police officer, truck driver, airline pilot.
2. Investigate and discuss the most common factors contributing to accidents at work.
3. Draw a table listing employer and employee responsibilities for workplace safety.
4. Management may use a range of strategies to evaluate the effectiveness of occupational health and safety programs; for example, safety tours of a plant, reviewing specific aspects on a random basis, risk assessments for changes in the workplace and specific job safety analysis. Suggest some additional strategies you would use.
5. Which age group and gender group face the greatest risk of workplace death or injury?
6. Suggest reasons for the high number of accidents within these two groups.
7. Substance abuse is becoming a problem in many workplaces in which employees experience stress. Should employers have the right to drug test employees? Give reasons for your answer.

Extension

1. A high-volume, Internet-based financial services business operates 24 hours a day. Some of its 100 staff work a rotating night shift, while others take turns to be 'on call'. The majority of staff operate from 7.30 am until 6–7.00 pm, although official working hours are 9 am to 5 pm.
   (a) Identify the factors leading to high levels of stress in such a business.
   (b) Discuss the possible outcomes of high levels of staff stress in this business.
   (c) Explain why substance abuse could be a problem in this business. Outline some points you would include in a policy to deal with substance abuse in this business and give reasons.
2. Investigate recent issues and updates related to workers' compensation matters by going to www.jaconline.com.au/businessstudies3e and clicking on the WorkCover weblink for this textbook.

18.5 Anti-discrimination

Discrimination occurs when a policy or a practice disadvantages a person or a group of people because of a personal characteristic that is irrelevant to the performance of the work.

Discrimination occurs when a policy or a practice disadvantages a person or a group because of a personal characteristic that is irrelevant to the performance of the work. It includes harassment (offending behaviour or intimidation) and vilification (a public act which is discriminatory and incites hatred).

Anti-discrimination legislation has been enacted to protect employees from direct and indirect discrimination (see figure 18.7) in recruitment, selection, training, promotion, remuneration, termination, and opportunities to access any other employment benefits or practices. To prevent discrimination and to avoid large fines, employers need to:

- comply with legislation
- audit all policies and practices to ensure they do not discriminate.

Employers and managers working in employment relations need to be familiar with the following legislation:

- *Human Rights and Equal Opportunity Commission Act 1986* (Cwlth)
- *Affirmative Action (Equal Employment Opportunity for Women) Act 1986* (Cwlth)
- *Sex Discrimination Act 1984* (Cwlth) and the *Anti-Discrimination Act 1977* (NSW).

The agencies available to support the legislation are the Human Rights and Equal Opportunity Commission (HREOC), the Equal Opportunity for Women Agency and the Anti-Discrimination Board (NSW).

Under discrimination laws it is illegal to discriminate on the grounds of a person's:

- sex, colour or age
- physical or mental disability
- religious faith or political opinion
- social origin
- marital status and family responsibilities
- pregnancy or potential pregnancy.

It may, however, be acceptable to discriminate in particular circumstances; for example, in employing only males to clean male toilets. Employers may apply for exemptions.

Further protection exists under the Workplace Relations Act. It allows freedom of association for members or non-members of a union and protection against termination for employees taking action against employers for alleged violation of laws or regulations, or for refusing to negotiate an Australian workplace agreement.

People who suffer discrimination may take a range of actions internally, formally or informally (see figure 18.8).

Strategies used increasingly by businesses to eliminate discrimination include:

- committing to a workplace free from discrimination
- writing and communicating policies to prevent discrimination and harassment, including a code of conduct
- making sure all policies and procedures are clearly documented and accessible to employees, and offer informal and formal options, and guarantee timely responses, confidentiality and objectivity

Direct discrimination
Treating a group less favourably than another person or group in similar circumstances

Indirect discrimination
Treatment which seems fair but which has an unequal or unfair impact on one person or a group compared with others

Figure 18.7 Direct and indirect discrimination

Australia's workforce is one of the most multicultural in the world, with nearly 25 per cent of the workforce born overseas.

Typical outcomes from a complaint may include:
- *a formal apology*
- *counselling*
- *official warnings*
- *mediation or conciliation*
- *disciplinary action.*

Outcomes will be influenced by the evidence, previous incidents, the wishes of the person experiencing discrimination, and the severity and frequency of the discrimination or harassment.

An employer may be held liable if any of the following discriminates against or harasses an employee: an employee or a group of employees, agents, contract worker, partner, director, supervisor, manager, or trade union representative.

- training managers and staff in cultural diversity issues and ways to prevent or deal with discrimination and harassment, primarily using face-to-face and interactive training programs
- appointing a grievance officer and specifying grievance procedures involving issues such as sexual/racial harassment
- regularly evaluating record keeping, implementation and effectiveness of policies, workplace culture and action taken to resolve complaints.

All employers are required to take reasonable steps to eliminate discrimination. Whether reasonable steps have been taken is considered on a case-by-case basis, as a large corporation is clearly capable of a different level of action than a small business. Employer associations and anti-discrimination agencies can help businesses develop a strategy that ensures consistency and fairness in handling of complaints.

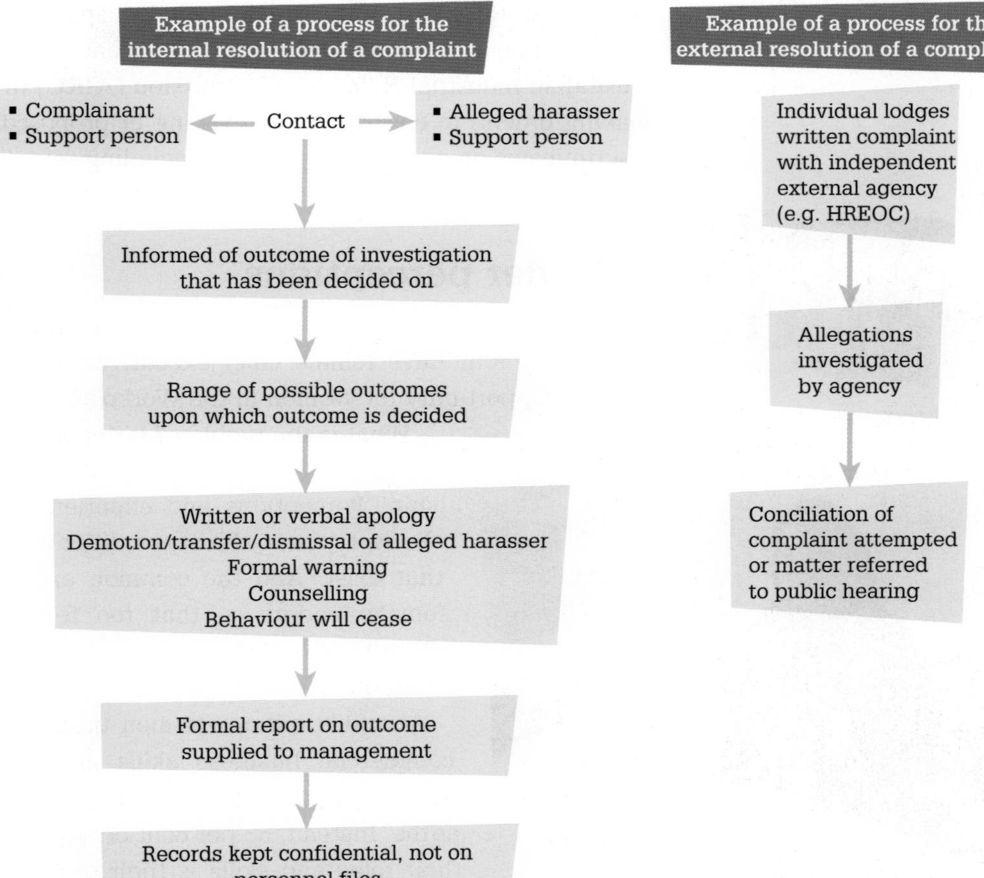

Figure 18.8 Options available in resolving a complaint of discrimination

18.6 Equal employment opportunities

Organisations that have met ongoing compliance criteria may apply for a waiver period of up to three years

Equal employment opportunities (EEO) refer to equitable policies and practices in recruitment, selection, training and promotion. They ensure that the best person for the job is chosen, the organisation gains the person with skills and abilities most appropriate to its needs, and a more positive work environment is promoted.

The level of equity in an organisation is reflected in the extent to which women and minority groups have access to different occupations and positions within the organisation. It is also reflected in the grievances expressed or legal action undertaken on the grounds of discrimination or sex-based harassment.

Affirmative action refers to measures taken to eliminate direct and indirect discrimination, and for implementing positive steps to overcome the current and historical causes of lack of equal employment opportunity for women.

Private sector employers with more than 100 employees are obliged to develop an **affirmative action** program in consultation with employees, and to provide a progress report to the Equal Opportunity for Women in the Workplace Agency. The report must:

- establish the workplace profile and analyse the issues in the specific workplace
- report on the actions taken by the employer to address priority issues
- describe the action plans for the following period and evaluate the strategies used.

Firms are then assessed as complying or not complying with requirements.

The aim of the program is to remove discriminatory employment barriers and take action to promote equal opportunity for women in the workplace.

Businesses also need to comply with the sex discrimination provisions in the Workplace Relations Act, which includes specific provisions relating to equal remuneration (including over-award payments) for work of equal value. The Australian Industrial Relations Commission (AIRC) must now take action (including making orders) to ensure that no existing or proposed award or certified agreement discriminates on a variety of grounds, including sex.

Gender perceptions

Of the top 200 public companies in Australia, only two are chaired by women and only four have female chief executives, according to a report by the Equal Opportunity for Women in the Workplace Agency.

What is the problem? It depends whether you ask a man or a woman. According to a British survey, 'Women and leadership: Perceptions and experience of female progression in the workplace', the sexes differ in their view of the obstacles that exist. And the common explanation for the paucity of female leaders — that too few have high-level financial experience — is given a new twist in the survey released in October.

Almost a quarter of men think the lack of management or commercial business skills is the biggest obstacle to the advancement of female leaders, but only 6 per cent of women agree. Instead, 55 per cent of women think the stereotyping of their roles and skills is their biggest obstacle; 37 per cent of men agree. And although 28 per cent of men cited lack of support for family commitments, only 19 per cent of women think this is the main reason they have failed to advance.

Source: G. McColl, 'Gender perceptions', *Business Review Weekly*, 21–7 October 2004, p. 78.

BiZ FaCT

Firms failing to lodge a report or submitting a report that does not comply with the Act may be publicly named in a report tabled in parliament that also receives significant media publicity. They are also excluded from government contracts and industry assistance grants.

SNaPSHOT Questions

1. How different are male and female views about the lack of women in management?
2. Who do you think is right?

BiZ FaCT

Most gender discrimination happens in the recruitment stage, according to the Equal Opportunity for Women in the Workplace Agency (EOWA).

Affirmative action for women arose from the *Affirmative Action (Equal Employment Opportunity for Women) Act 1986* (Cwlth). It is not about discrimination to favour women but about achieving selection and promotion on the basis of merit and ensuring that women have equal access to opportunities that are available at work. Women occupy 44.5 per cent of the workforce, but only 10.2 per cent of senior executive positions (see the Snapshot 'Gender perceptions' on page 408). Most with children under 12 take employment breaks due to childbirth, child care or the need to care for another person.

The Equal Opportunity for Women in the Workplace Agency recommends that businesses focus on six areas to improve equity within their organisation: recruitment, promotion and separation; access to all occupations and areas; equitable total remuneration; training and career development; work and life balance; sexual harassment (see the Snapshot 'Sexual harassment behaviour') and working relationships.

Some specific strategies firms can use to improve equity include the following.

- establishing a strategic plan that incorporates the business objectives, strategies and targets
- developing a policy statement and informing all staff that an affirmative action program has been initiated. Goals should be established and staff consulted about the program.
- developing a code of practice to communicate to customers and suppliers the organisation's commitment to equity
- implementing a system to gather, monitor and evaluate statistics on employment
- evaluating all current work policies, practices and industrial agreements for equity/discrimination
- training all recruitment staff and interview panels in EEO awareness
- making awareness of EEO a criterion in performance appraisal and promotion
- keeping all staff, including those on leave, informed of vacancies or other opportunities within the organisation
- conducting exit interviews to ascertain reasons for employee resignations
- benchmarking to analyse the effectiveness of the organisation's strategies on EEO.

BiZ FaCT

Women earn, on average, 15 per cent less than men.

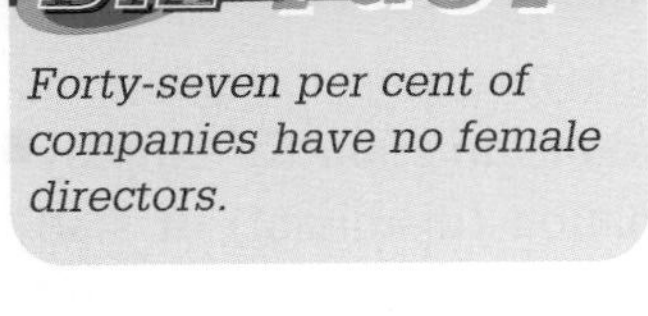

BiZ FaCT

Forty-seven per cent of companies have no female directors.

Sexual harassment behaviour

What types of behaviour could be either harassment or sexual harassment? Depending on the circumstances, each of the following kinds of behaviour may be harassment:

- material that is racist, sexist, sexually explicit, homophobic (anti-homosexual) and so on that is displayed in the workplace, circulated, or put in someone's workspace or belongings, or on a computer or fax machine or on the Internet
- verbal abuse or comments that put down or stereotype people because of their sex, age, pregnancy, race, homosexuality, disability, marital status, transgender (transsexuality) or age
- jokes based on gender, pregnancy, race, marital status, homosexuality, disability, transgender (transsexuality) or age

(continued)

- offensive gestures based on race, sex and so on
- ignoring, isolating or segregating a person or group because of their sex, homosexuality, race, transgender (transsexuality) and so on
- staring or leering in a sexual manner
- sexual or physical contact, such as slapping, kissing or touching
- intrusive questions about sexual activity
- sexual assault
- unwelcome wolf-whistling
- repeated sexual invitations when the person invited has refused similar invitations before
- initiation ceremonies that involve unwelcome sexual, sexist, racist and so on behaviour such as 'greasing' or 'grazing'.

Source: Information from the NSW Anti-Discrimination Board website http://www.lawlink.nsw.gov.au, viewed 5 June 2005

SNaPSHOT Question

Interview an adult and ask them what they think are the negative impacts of sexual harassment on staff. Discuss your results with the class.

18.7 Unfair dismissal

Figure 18.9 A cartoon by Tandberg on the impact of downsizing

An employment contract is legally binding, so employers must terminate the contract in a legally compliant manner. An important function for employment relations managers, therefore, is the termination (dismissal) of staff. Businesses in recent years have struggled to reduce costs and improve productivity through reducing staff numbers, flattening management structures and making greater use of technology. Widespread restructuring and managerial policies are major factors contributing to industrial disputes and unfair dismissal claims.

Selecting staff for dismissal can be risky and requires awareness of legislation and industrial agreements to avoid litigation and industrial action. Employees must be given proper notice and employers must comply with procedures established in law, including the unfair dismissal laws in the Workplace Relations Act. To avoid misunderstandings written warnings and/or notice is preferable. Written confirmation of resignation is also preferred to verbal statements made in the 'heat of the moment'.

BiZ WoRD

***Retrenchment** and **redundancy** refer to employees losing their jobs because they are no longer needed by an organisation for commercial reasons.*

There are three ways in which an employee may be dismissed or their employment terminated:

1. Summary dismissal occurs when there is a serious breach of the employment contract, such as serious misconduct, which would cover theft from an employer, fraud, intoxication (to the point of being unfit to perform), or assault of an 'employer'. This is instant and given without notice.
2. A dismissal 'on notice' is based on poor performance in a position.
3. Dismissal due to the employer no longer needing the employee for economic or commercial reasons is known as **retrenchment** or **redundancy**.

Severance pay *is money paid out after the termination of the employment contract to cover entitlements built up by the employee for each year of service; for example, four years' service typically entitles an employee to eight weeks' pay on termination, plus other entitlements.*

Protection from unfair dismissal has been incorporated in legislation and test cases (see pages 412–13), and in the Workplace Relations Act, giving access to a cheap, simple and fair process of appeal. However, this form of protection for employees is likely to be removed under proposed reforms.

In addition, most awards and agreements have common provisions relating to termination, change and redundancy that cover matters including the procedures for retrenchment, amount of notice to be given or pay in lieu of notice and **severance pay**. These supplement and override legislation if conditions are more favourable.

Until 2005, all employees under federal agreements were protected against unfair dismissal. It is proposed that under new legislation, only employees in firms with more than 100 employees, or those covered by state agreements, are protected by unfair dismissal legislation.

For employees wishing to appeal a dismissal, there are two types of termination commonly handled by industrial tribunals such as the AIRC:

- harsh, unjust or unreasonable termination
- unlawful termination.

Industrial tribunals, in dealing with a dismissal claimed to be harsh, unjust or unreasonable, have generally considered whether:

- there was a valid reason for the termination related to the capacity or conduct of the person
- the employee was notified of the reason, including unsatisfactory performance
- the employee was given a chance to respond to the reason given (see the Snapshots 'AIRC backs for "the finger"' on page 412 and 'Office romance not a sacking offence' on pages 412–13).

If conciliation fails then a tribunal may arbitrate, making orders for remedies such as reinstatement, or compensation for lost remuneration.

More companies are recognising that managers need to be trained specifically to handle dismissals in a way that:

- *takes account of the legal and financial implications*
- *minimises the trauma for both parties*
- *does not have adverse effects on the morale of the remaining staff.*

Employees may feel they have no option but to resign as their work contract has changed (due, for example to a move to a new location, an increase in duties or sexual harassment that has not been stopped) at the initiative of the employer. This constitutes a *'constructive dismissal'* and the employees are still entitled to the same conditions as if they had been dismissed.

Businesses can be badly hit by such claims. Many have found the need for a lengthy procedural approach frustrating, particularly the need to give employees time to improve their performance after a warning has been given.

In unfair dismissal cases in which the employee is successful, payments of up to six months' pay for award employees and a maximum of $45 200 (indexed) for non-award employees may be awarded.

Of 7049 applications for unfair dismissal filed in 2004 half were decided in favour of the employee and around 75 per cent were settled by conciliation.

Many firms have preferred to avoid the risk by hiring casuals and contractors. Other firms have tightened up their contracts of employment (often called 'corporate pre-nuptial agreements') and included job descriptions, probation periods and measurable targets, to allow for dismissal of staff if required. They are keen to avoid unfair dismissal claims, which create adverse publicity for the business internally and externally, with the potential to lose customers. For many it has been regarded as cheaper and less time consuming (no court appearances) to settle the claim, regardless of whether or not it is valid. Many have needed to consult specialists in the area of termination to avoid these problems.

In response to these issues, the Howard government has proposed exempting all businesses with fewer than 100 employees from this legislation. As most Australian businesses employ fewer than 100 employees, most employees will no longer be protected, unless they take expensive common law action.

AIRC backs sacking for 'the finger'

An airline flight attendant who publicly raised her middle finger at her manager was justifiably dismissed, the Australian Industrial Relations Commission has found.

On the day in question, the attendant, who had worked for National Jet Systems for about seven years, was scheduled for two flights: Perth to Kalgoorlie return and Perth to Paraburdoo return. While she was walking from the terminal to the aircraft for the return leg of the first flight, the airport manager signalled her to hurry. The attendant muttered, within earshot of another employee, 'I'm not frigging running — it's 40 degrees' and, with one hand on the aircraft door, she showed the manager her middle finger.

The flight attendant was asked to fly to Adelaide the next day to discuss the incident, and given a letter asking her to respond to allegations. She provided a written explanation, but was dismissed the next day by faxed letter. Dismissal was said to be for unprofessional conduct, namely the offensive language and gesture. Her performance record was also mentioned; she had received several warnings and was on a final warning.

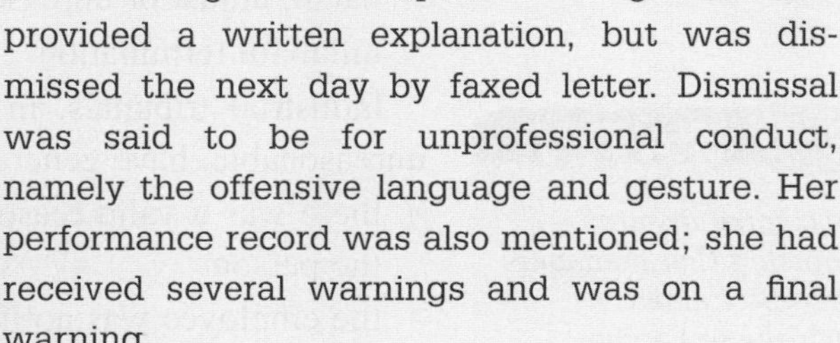

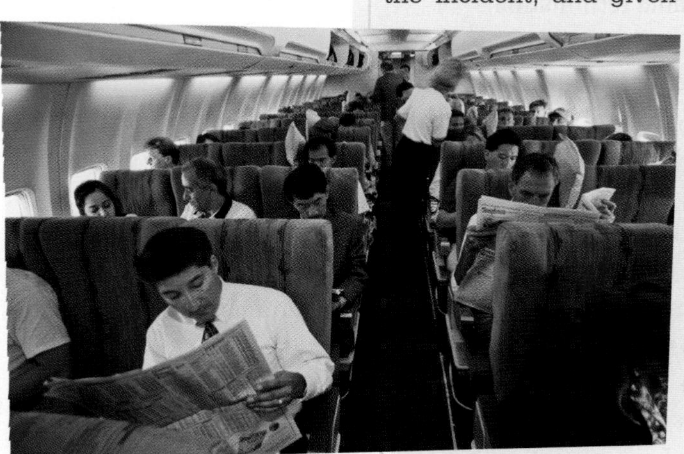

The commission said the attendant understood the conduct standards detailed in the employer's flight attendant service.

Source: C. Louw, 'AIRC backs sacking for "the finger"', *HR Monthly*, September 2004, p. 18.

SNAPSHOT *Questions*

1. Why was this employee sacked?
2. For what reasons may an employee be dismissed?
3. Outline the reasons why a dismissal may be considered unfair.
4. Do you agree with the decision of the commission? Why?

Office romance not a sacking offence

An employer was not entitled to dismiss an employee because she started a personal relationship with a member of the organisation's sales team, the Queensland Industrial Relations Commission has found.

The employee had worked as a personal assistant for about five months when she was summoned to a meeting and told her employment would be terminated if her relationship with the sales representative continued. No performance issues were raised. The employee refused to choose between her job and the relationship, and assured her employer that no breach of confidentiality would arise from the relationship.

Two days later, she was sacked on a week's notice because of the relationship and because she socialised with sales representatives and telemarketers outside of the office. She was offered contract positions in sales or telemarketing, but declined them.

At the hearing, performance issues were raised for the first time. A co-employee who had written two letters relating to performance admitted to writing them at the employer's request after court proceedings were initiated. She said her employers told her 'the little bitch is taking us to court'. Another purported letter of complaint tendered at the hearing turned out to have been prepared by the employer for the purposes of the hearing.

The commission found that the only reason for termination was the employee's personal relationship and the fact that she had socialised with sales staff after hours. If disclosure of personal information was ever of concern to the employer, it had to put that clearly to the employee and allow her an opportunity to respond. Since this was not done, termination was unjustified.

Source: C. Louw, 'Office romance not a sacking offence', *HR Monthly*, November 2004, p. 18.

SNAPSHOT Questions

1. Why was this claim of unfair dismissal accepted by the commission?
2. What would need to be shown before someone could be terminated for having personal relationships within an organisation?
3. How would this situation be managed without protection against unfair dismissal?
4. What are the benefits of having the claim heard in an industrial relations tribunal?

EXERCISE 18.2 Revision

1. Complete these paragraphs.
   (a) Common ethical and legal issues arising in the workplace include disputes over working conditions, _____, and unfair and unlawful dismissals.
   (b) Through its membership of international organisations, such as the _____, Australia has signed conventions that have obliged it to introduce legislation which protects the _____ safety and _____ of employees.
   (c) Legislation protecting workers' health and safety has been introduced by _____ governments due to constitutional limitations. In New South Wales the body responsible for supervising occupational health and safety and _____ is WorkCover NSW. All employers are required to provide a safe system of work and to carry _____ insurance.
   (d) Legislation protecting employees from discrimination has been passed at the _____ and _____ level, and prohibits direct or indirect discrimination in employment practices on the basis of a person's _____, _____, _____, physical or mental disability, religion, political opinion, trade union membership, marital status, family responsibilities or pregnancy.
   (e) Assistance is available with discrimination complaints from _____ or state agencies.
   (f) Businesses that do not comply with industrial legislation or do not behave in an ethical manner are likely to experience _____, and industrial disputes.

2. The proportion of female to male average weekly earnings for full-time adult employees is 85 per cent. There are a number of reasons for the differences. Discuss with your class all the possible reasons why this may occur.
3. Rachel is a human resource consultant. Complete the letters she is writing to four of her clients.

Dear Rachel
I manage a clothing store in a major shopping mall. I am having a lot of trouble getting staff for positions in this area. It doesn't help that this is an expensive area to live in, which makes it hard for young people to find accommodation. Please help!

Ivy Wharry

Dear Ivy
Have you thought about using some of the older people in this area? Although they may not have the energy for full-time work . . .

Dear Rachel
I am a single dad who works full-time and I am a member of the MMM Union. I have two kids aged 5 and 8, who attend after-school care. My supervisor at Meen Machines insists we work 9 am to 5 pm, and I am finding it hard to make the starting times each day after dropping my kids off in the morning. I have been unable to get before-school care. Sometimes he also expects me to stay back, but gives no warning. This is a real problem as care ends at 5.15 pm. Please help, as I don't want to lose my job, which will happen if I refuse.

Joe Parr

Dear Joe
You should be aware that the Workplace Relations Act 1996 was designed to protect people with issues associated with balancing their work and life responsibilities. My suggestions are that you first contact . . .

Dear Rachel
I recently hired four staff in a hurry. One person has left already, one is fitting in well but the other two are not working out at all. These two do not get on with the other staff, who themselves also never got on all that well. Racial comments have been flying around the office. Unfortunately, I am now going through the process of dismissing two of them for poor performance, and I estimate it will cost me $70 000 to dismiss them and hire new staff. What advice can you give to help me avoid such mistakes in future?

Way Set Do

Dear Way Set
Are you aware of anti-discrimination legislation? Did you undertake careful human resources planning before hiring?

Let's start with the first question. To have a workplace in which everyone respects each other requires . . .

Dear Rachel
I recently worked for a games store for five weeks as a part timer. I got the job 'on trial', and was paid $50 per week for five nights' work after I worked one week for free. When I asked for more money after the second week, the boss said I'd get more when I was fully trained. He then told me that I was too young and that my job was over. I'm 17! I never got any more money. Have I been ripped off?

Nat Tinkin

Dear Nat
You certainly have. First of all, employers must pay you for work done at the rate in your award. Secondly, discrimination on the basis of age is illegal. You should contact ...

4. Prepare a summary of this chapter. A summary condenses the important issues and concepts presented in the chapter. Go to www.jaconline.com.au/businessstudies3e to compare your finished summary with the one provided for this textbook.

Extension

1. Referring to current examples, discuss how businesses' recruiting and selection processes will be affected by anti-discrimination legislation.
2. 'The aim of EEO legislation is to abolish discrimination against women in the workplace by giving them unfair advantages over others. This is not fair or sustainable.' Do you agree or disagree with this statement? Give reasons for your answer.

Topic 5

Global business

To examine the implications of globalisation on business structure, functions and management.

Students should be able to:

- explain the impact of the global business environment on the role and structure of businesses
- critically analyse the role of businesses in Australia
- describe and analyse business functions and operations and their impact on business success
- evaluate processes and operations in global business
- evaluate the effectiveness of management in the organisation and operations of businesses and their responsiveness to change
- analyse the impact of management decision making on stakeholders
- critically analyse the social and ethical responsibilities of management
- evaluate management strategies in response to internal and external factors
- select, organise and evaluate information and sources for usefulness and reliability
- plan and conduct an investigation into businesses to present the findings in an appropriate business format
- communicate business information, ideas and issues using relevant business terminology and concepts in appropriate forms.

Mind map showing the specific aspects examined for the 'Global business' topic

Going global — SOTA Limited

SOTA (State Of The Art) Limited was established in 1968. The business expanded to become one of Australia's most successful electrical engineering organisations, with production facilities in 18 different locations across the country. What initially began as a medium-sized, family-owned business became a large, profitable, publicly owned operation employing 4185 people, with a turnover of $628 million. Earnings before interest and tax (EBIT) were 13 per cent.

SOTA's core business is the manufacture of specialised electronic components used in a wide range of information technology and communications equipment. The business's main strengths are:

- its ability to identify new niche markets
- its reputation as a high-quality, price-competitive operator
- the depth of experience and talent of its employees
- a well-developed customer base
- its ability to respond quickly to changes within the marketplace.

Nevertheless, the business faced two major obstacles. First, SOTA's future expansion within Australia was severely restricted as it already had a 65 per cent share of the domestic market. Trying to increase the existing domestic customer base would be extremely difficult due to the specialised nature of the product. Also, the marketing department's research showed that the Australian market was expected to increase by only 1.5 to 2 per cent a year over the next five years. The second obstacle was the reduction in government protection measures, especially the tariff rate. This had resulted in the price of foreign-made competitors' products falling. SOTA lost some of its price advantage to cheaper imports.

SOTA now had two options. It could continue trading as previously and hope the business survived, possibly on a reduced scale. Alternatively, it could consider tapping into overseas markets by exporting its products. The board of directors was initially reluctant to consider selling to global markets. They were daunted by the possibility of currency fluctuations, cultural differences, possible language barriers, different legal systems, insurance requirements, methods of payment and transportation arrangements.

However, the prospect of seeing the business stagnate forced them to act. They decided to undertake a feasibility study of the possibility of exporting, with the intention of modifying their existing business plan if the study was favourable.

The strategic business unit made contact with Austrade, a federal government department established to assist with export opportunities for Australian businesses. With a network of offices in over 100 countries, Austrade could introduce SOTA to established contacts and provide a wealth of global business intelligence.

SOTA, like many other Australian businesses, was now attempting to decide if its future success relied on selling overseas — that is, going global.

CHAPTER

19 Globalisation

19.1 Introduction to the global economy

We live in a global world, rather than a world limited by national borders. Consider the news and entertainment we receive from around the world, the clothing and footwear brands being sold worldwide, the rapid telecommunications access to all parts of the globe, and the large number of products Australia sells on the world market. Australia now supplies an extraordinary array of products to the world, including tourism, raw materials, genetic technology, cultural products, education and foodstuffs.

> **BIZ WORD**
>
> *The **global economy** is the world economy and refers to the economic activity going on in the world. It includes the flow of all trade, finance, technology, labour and investment. Consequently, it is the total economic activity within and between countries.*

The **global economy** is the world economy and refers to the economic activity going on in the world. It includes the flow of all trade, finance, technology, labour and investment. Consequently, it is the total economic activity within and between countries.

Australia is part of the global economy and, since the mid 1980s, global influences have been instrumental in bringing about revolutionary change in the Australian business environment. Some of these global influences include:

- *Increasing globalisation and a changing international business environment*. Increasing trade between nations has created vast opportunities for business expansion. However, businesses also face considerable uncertainty as competition has increased. Australia's business practices and operations are undergoing fundamental change to accommodate changes in the external environment.
- *Changes in protection policies*. Until the 1980s, Australian businesses operated in a protected and regulated environment. Since then government industry reforms and free trade agreements have promoted policies that increasingly expose businesses to foreign competition. Australia is now a much more open trading nation.
- *An increasing trend by Australian businesses towards the establishment of overseas operations*. This trend of global expansion will have wider implications for Australia, affecting employment, economic growth and national income. The world is becoming a very small place!

'Yeah, the T-shirts look great. We had them screen printed by prison labour in Kazakhstan and shipped under Liberian flag to a Russian distributor in L.A. who's registered in Antarctica for tax reasons.'

Figure 19.1 We live in a global world.

19.2 Nature and trends of globalisation

__Globalisation__ is the movement across nations of trade, investment, technology, finance and labour.

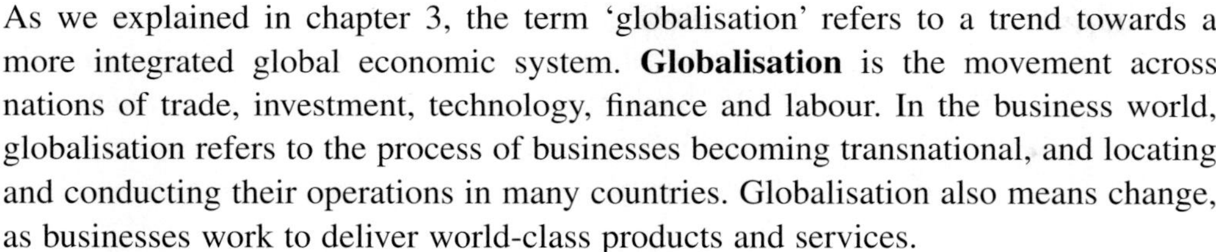

As we explained in chapter 3, the term 'globalisation' refers to a trend towards a more integrated global economic system. **Globalisation** is the movement across nations of trade, investment, technology, finance and labour. In the business world, globalisation refers to the process of businesses becoming transnational, and locating and conducting their operations in many countries. Globalisation also means change, as businesses work to deliver world-class products and services.

The process of globalisation, assisted by the technological revolution in communications and computers, is radically altering the shape of world markets, as well as the nature of business and everyday life (see the Snapshot below giving one view on 'What is globalisation?').

What is globalisation?

Globalisation is what happens when you lose your job in Brunswick, Bankstown or Elizabeth because the company for which you work has been bought out by the Australian subsidiary of a Dallas-based transnational company that has decided to relocate its production of T-shirts to Mexico because of cheaper wage costs and lower health and safety standards. It is what happens when you finally get a new job in Brisbane under a new employment contract that lowers your wages and conditions and your boss explains that this is essential to compete with Mexican, or Indonesian, or Chinese, workers. It is what happens when your sister is sacked from her hospital job because of budget cuts by a state government that defends its actions by saying it must meet the demands of international credit-rating agencies for balanced budgets and lower taxes. And it is what happens when you get skin cancer because of the hole in the ozone layer created by chemicals released by refrigerators and aerosol cans all over the world.

But globalisation is also what happens when you use the computer at your local library to connect to the Internet and find pages of information from unions and community organisations in England, Mexico or Indonesia, which are trying to link up with workers around the world to stop the driving down of wages and the repression of trade-union activists. Globalisation is what happens when young London musicians of English, Caribbean and Indian descent begin to create new cross-rhythms of black reggae, white trance and Hindi rap. Globalisation describes the moment when thousands of women from all over the world come together in Beijing to affirm the solidarity of the women's movement. And globalisation is also what happens when a child sees photographs of this planet taken from space and realises that the Earth is indeed finite.

Source: Extract from J. Wiseman, *Global nation? Australia and the politics of globalisation*, Cambridge University Press, Melbourne, 1998, pp. 13–14.

Globalisation has not been welcomed by everyone. Critics of the process point to:

- *exploitation of workers, especially in developing countries*
- *loss of jobs in developed countries due to industrial rationalisation*
- *loss of national economic control to an external money market*
- *fragmentation of towns and cities into districts of success and failure*
- *an increasing economic divide between globalisation's 'winners' (skilled and educated people) and 'losers' (unskilled and poorly educated people)*
- *industrial restructuring and its social impacts*
- *the winding back of the public sector.*

SNAPSHOT Question

Assume you have been selected for a debating team that must debate the topic 'globalisation is good for all'. Present arguments for both sides.

Globalisation is not a new process. Trade, exploration and movement of people and ideas around the world has been occurring for centuries. However, it is only since the 1950s and, in particular, the last 20 years, that the world has experienced such rapid and widespread globalisation. The current process of globalisation is remarkable for its phenomenal speed and reach, especially in relation to flows of finance and information.

We have moved away from a world in which national economies are relatively isolated from each other. Now, national economies are merging into one huge, interdependent global economic system at an ever-accelerating rate.

Globalisation of markets and production

In the world of business, globalisation has two main components: the globalisation of markets and the globalisation of production.

The **globalisation of markets** (finance/capital, labour and consumers) refers to the combining of once separate and distinct national markets into one huge global marketplace. **Globalisation of production** refers to the practice of many businesses to purchase their inputs from around the globe as well as the tendency to manufacture components in low-cost locations (see figure 19.2).

BiZ WoRD

*The **globalisation of markets** refers to the combining of once separate and distinct national markets into one huge global marketplace.*

***Globalisation of production** refers to the way many businesses purchase their inputs from around the globe and tend to manufacture components in low-cost locations.*

Figure 19.2 Globalisation of production — Vietnamese factory workers stitching shoes for Nike in Ho Chi Minh City

19.3 Growth of the global economy

As globalisation continues, flows of finance, labour and consumer products between countries will increase (see figure 19.3) as these markets undergo structural change.

Figuratively speaking, the globe is shrinking in many ways, with nations more closely linked than ever before. Many businesses must become global players just to survive, let alone prosper. Australian companies are now forced to compete with foreign suppliers as well as attempting to sell their products overseas. The Australian company Paperlinx Limited, the world's leading global fine paper distributor and manufacturer of the Reflex brand, is an example of how one business has responded to these influences. Paperlinx has operations spanning five continents and 31 countries, offering a wide variety of packaging and communication papers. Paperlinx is now truly 'global' in the distribution of its operations, and derives approximately 76 per cent of its sales revenue from foreign transactions.

The expansion of the global economy is occurring at a rapid pace.

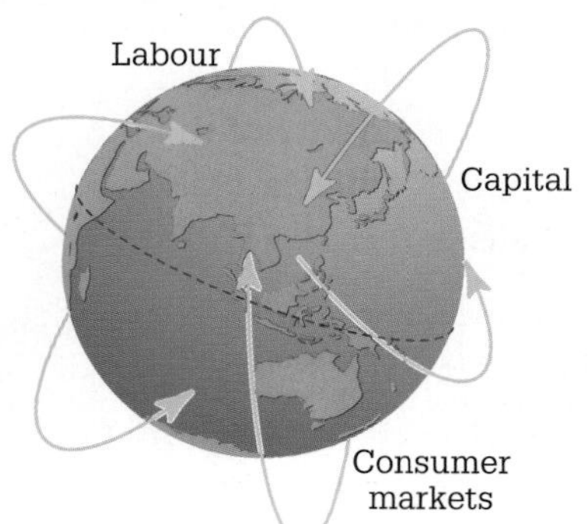

Figure 19.3 The flow of finance, labour and consumer products between countries

EXERCISE 19.1 Revision

1. Identify the main global influences affecting the Australian business environment.
2. What is meant by the terms 'globalisation', 'globalisation of markets' and 'globalisation of production'?
3. List 10 different products you regularly use, such as your computer, stereo, DVD player, shoes, drink or clothes. Once you have written your list, answer the following questions for each product:
   (a) What is the brand name of the product?
   (b) What business made the product?
   (c) In which country is the business based?
   (d) In which country is the product made?
   (e) Why do you think the product was made there?
   Compare your list with other class members, noting similarities and differences.
4. Demonstrate the impact of global business upon your daily life.
5. Examine figure 19.3 on page 420. What does it suggest about the flow of finance/capital, labour and consumer products?

Extension

1. In 2005, Australia and the United States signed a free-trade agreement.
   (a) What is a free-trade agreement?
   (b) Discuss the impact of the free-trade agreement on Australian businesses.
2. 'Whether we like it or not, we are part of an international community that is becoming increasingly global . . . But whether people fear globalisation or not they cannot escape it.' Discuss.
3. Three interrelated forces are leading international businesses to the globalisation of production and marketing. These are:
   (a) advances in computer and communications technology
   (b) the reduction of barriers to investment and trade by most governments
   (c) the establishment of trading blocs.
   Examine the role of each of these forces in the process of globalisation.

19.4 Changes in markets

Changes in financial/capital markets

Finance (capital) is now more mobile and flows relatively easily between countries, especially since the 1970s, when many countries phased out their controls on foreign exchange trading. As a result, international financial flows have expanded rapidly over the last two decades. In 1980, global foreign exchange trading was 10 times the value of world trade. In 2005 total world foreign exchange trading was estimated by the Bank of International Settlement (BIS), to be 85 times the value of world trade and growing. Consequently, the world capital market is now more integrated than ever before.

The following stock market index measurements have become familiar segments in our news programs, a reflection of the free flow of capital. The Japanese Nikkei Index, Hong Kong Hang Seng Index, English FTSE (Financial Times Stock Exchange) Index and United States NASDAQ (National Association of Securities Dealers Automated Quotation System).

Capital flows to those countries where the investment opportunities and returns are favourable. It is now much easier for individuals and businesses to access overseas share markets and purchase equity in foreign companies (see figure 19.4).

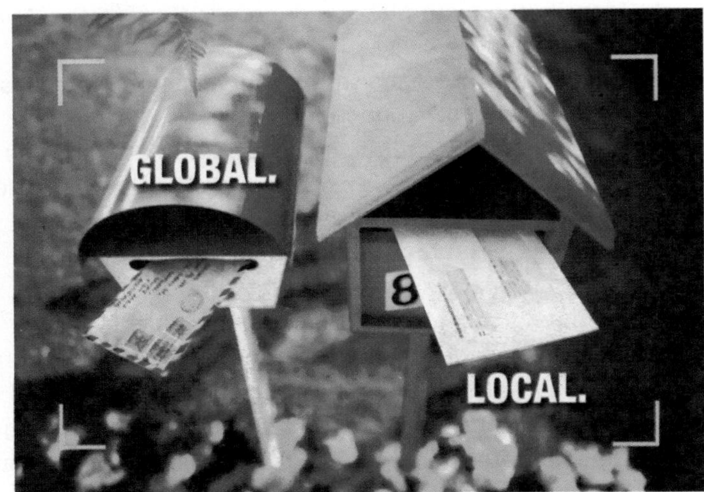

GLOBAL.
8
LOCAL.
A BANK THAT GETS YOU THINKING ABOUT INVESTING. WHICH BANK?
Australia accounts for just 1.5% of the world's equity markets.* If you're a local investor, you could be missing out on opportunities that lie abroad. Our Financial Planners can present new possibilities by helping you invest with a diversified portfolio that spans the entire globe. Plus, they can give you a fresh perspective on superannuation, retirement and other types of investments.
See the world in new ways. Make a no-obligation appointment now to see a Financial Planner or ask about a free seminar.
Commonwealth
Financial Planning
A member of the Commonwealth Bank Group

Figure 19.4 Many Australian financial institutions provide assistance regarding international investments.

Changes in labour markets

The labour market has not been 'freed up' to the same degree as other markets. If anything, the labour market has become less global in the last 60 years. Due to political barriers, the flow of people between countries is now more restricted than it was from 1850 to 1900, when waves of migration occurred. This trend seems likely to continue, especially the restrictions placed on the movement of low or unskilled labour. For example, even within the European Union, which gives citizens of any member nation the right to work and live in any other member nation, only a small proportion of workers travel across national borders.

However, two trends in the labour market have resulted in the movement of workers. First, the movement of large numbers of temporary migrant workers has been very important in Europe and Asia. For example, large numbers of unskilled Turkish and Filipino workers work in numerous countries. Second, the growing demand for highly trained employees means that such people are increasingly mobile.

Changes in consumer markets

There has been phenomenal growth in the amount and value of world trade, especially since the end of World War II. For example, from 1995 to 2005, global trade in goods and services increased by approximately 150 per cent. Countries are achieving cost savings by specialising in products they can produce efficiently. This results in cheaper prices on the world market and, in turn, generates increased sales in existing markets. New consumer markets also emerge, particularly in developing countries.

Improved technologies and communications have also changed consumer markets. With the advent of the Internet, innovative, visionary Australian businesses may reach much larger markets and take advantage of economies of scale. Consumers around the world will just as readily browse an Internet shopping site as examine a catalogue delivered to their private letterboxes.

19.5 Trends in global trade since World War II

Perhaps no area has changed more dramatically in recent years than that of global trade. As figure 19.5 reveals, the last 50 years have seen unprecedented growth in merchandise exports. **Merchandise exports** are domestically made products sold to customers in another country.

BiZ WoRD

***Merchandise exports** are domestically made products sold to customers in another country.*

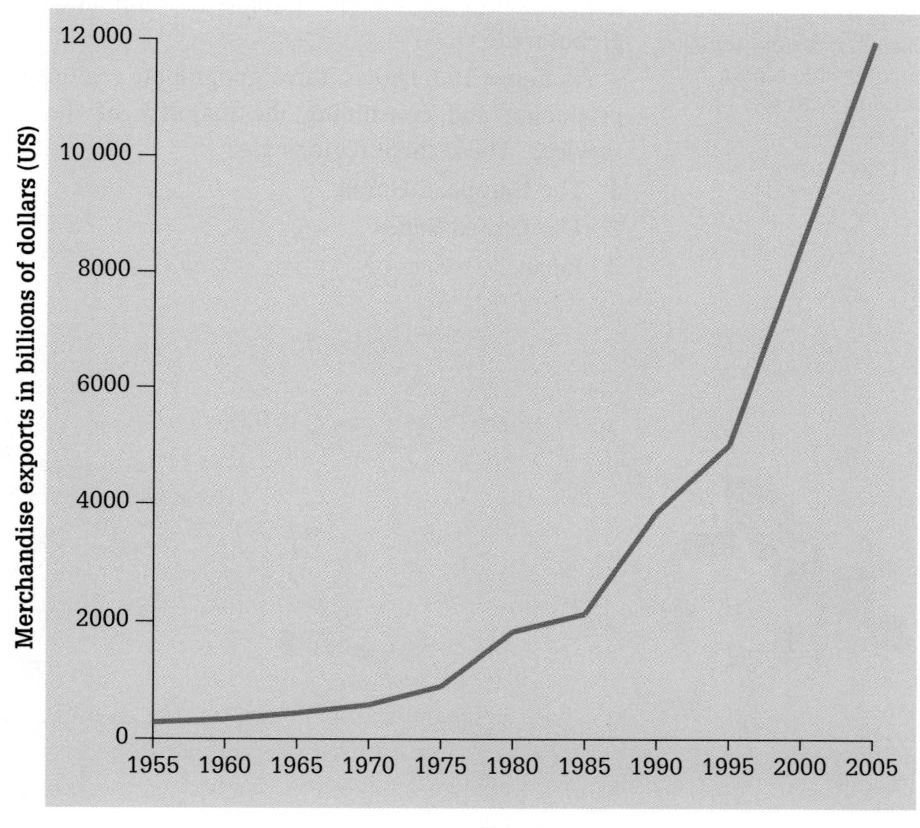

Figure 19.5 The growth in merchandise exports since 1955

1945 to 1960 — United States domination of global trade

The United States exports 21 per cent of the world's total exports compared with 15 per cent for Japan, 13 per cent for Germany and 2 per cent for Australia.

At the end of World War II, only the United States (US) had an economy able to produce goods on a large scale. The industrial regions of Europe and Japan suffered enormous damage, which left them virtually in rubble. Consequently, US businesses faced little competition at home or overseas. US corporations were the main suppliers of inputs for the rest of the world's manufacturers. US brand names and consumer products became recognised around the world. As a result, US transnational corporations dominated global business.

1960 to 1980 — Japan and Europe re-emerge

By the end of the 1950s Europe and Japan had largely rebuilt their industries. They were now ready to recommence selling to the rest of the world. Products carrying brand names such as Nestlé, Philips and Unilever (from Europe) and National Panasonic, Toyota, Hitachi and Sony (from Japan) started to appear on the world market. However, up until the mid 1970s United States businesses still dominated the world economy and, in 1975, 64 of the world's 100 largest firms were US-based companies.

The Coca-Cola trademark is recognised by 94 per cent of the Earth's population and 'Coca-Cola' is the second most universally understood phrase after 'OK'.

During this period some Australian manufacturing businesses began to adopt more of an export-oriented business philosophy. Nevertheless, apart from the traditional commodities such as wool and wheat, which Australia had been exporting for more than 150 years, many Australian firms were still reluctant to undertake an export program.

Today United States trade across the Pacific is already 60 per cent higher than across the Atlantic. The United States is increasingly trading with the Asia–Pacific region rather than with the European Union.

1980 to the present — the global marketplace

As previously outlined, the process of globalisation accelerated from the early 1980s. Integration of the world's markets has dramatically altered the nature and pattern of global trade.

As figure 19.6 shows, three geographic regions now dominate the world economy, producing and consuming the majority of the world's production of goods and services. These three regions are:

1 The European Union
2 The United States
3 Japan.

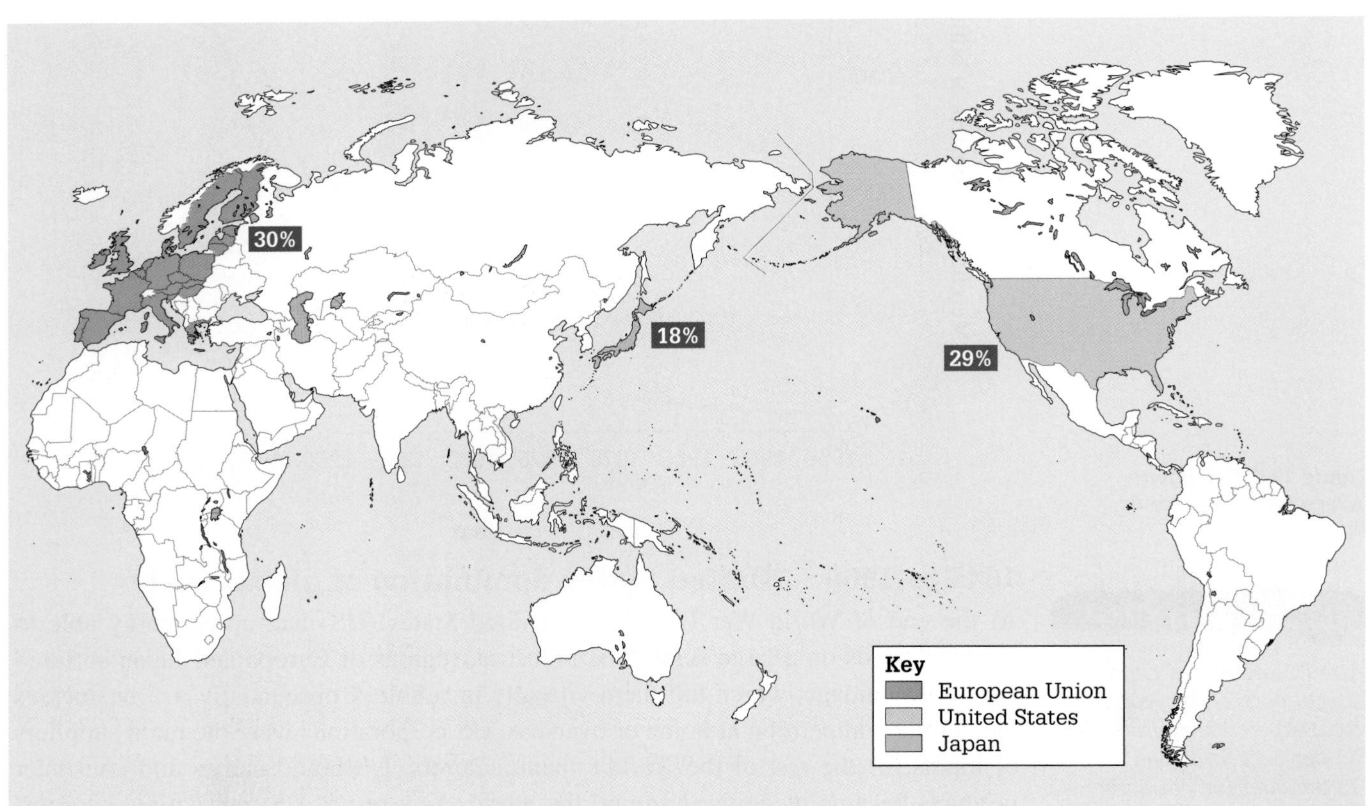

Figure 19.6 Shares of the world's GDP

EXERCISE 19.2 Revision

1. Why does finance flow more easily between countries today than 20 years ago?
2. Identify the two major movements of labour between countries.
3. Predict the impact of the Internet on consumer markets.
4. What is meant by the term 'merchandise exports'?
5. Trace the changes to global trade through the periods 1945–1960, 1960–1980 and 1980 to the present. Present the information as a point summary.

Extension

1. 'Adopting a global export-oriented philosophy is only suitable for large businesses, not small to medium-sized enterprises.' Critically evaluate this statement.
2. According to many trade analysts, China is set to become the next economic superpower by 2030. Discuss the possible implications such a development will have on Australia's trading pattern and performance.

19.6 Drivers of globalisation

Five interrelated forces are leading businesses to the globalisation of their production and marketing (see figure 19.7).

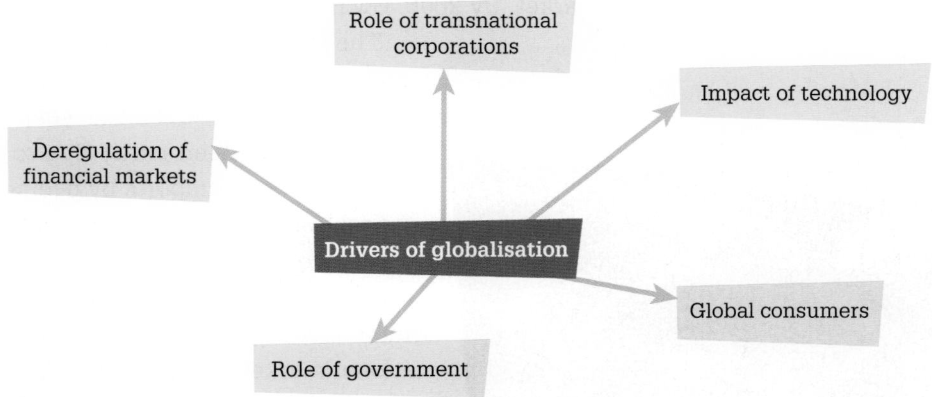

Figure 19.7 The drivers of globalisation

BIZ WORD

*A **transnational corporation** (TNC) is any business that has productive activities in two or more countries and that operates on a worldwide scale.*

Role of transnational corporations

A **transnational corporation** (TNC) is any business that has productive activities in two or more countries and that operates on a worldwide scale.

A TNC attempts to combine the benefits of economies of scale with the benefits of responding to local conditions. The TNC also represents the highest level of involvement in global business, where national borders do not represent barriers to trade but are seen merely as lines drawn on a map. TNCs often conduct a large percentage of their business outside their home country.

South Korea's rapid economic transformation over the last 25 years has been largely due to the success of its transnational corporations. This diversified business group, known as the chaebol, *includes Samsung, Hyundai and LG (formerly Lucky Goldstar).*

TNCs come in many different forms. Mitsubishi Heavy Industries, NEC, McDonald's, BP, Unilever, Ford, BHP, Boral and CSR are just a few of the well-known foreign and Australian TNCs. However, all TNCs have a number of features in common. In a fully developed TNC, finance, assets, technology, information, employees, patents, goods and services all flow freely from one country and one subsidiary to another. These resources may be shared within the corporation. For example, information may be pooled through corporation-wide databases, and patents and technologies may be utilised on a global scale.

The desire to maximise returns for shareholders' funds has spurred the world's TNCs to globalise, acting as one of the main driving forces of the process.

Global consumers

Another driver of globalisation is the increasing uniformity of consumers around the world. For example, the same television commercials are shown across the globe. Internationally, millions of people want to purchase a particular brand of soft drink, jeans, sunglasses, computer, DVD player or car (see the Snapshot 'The Monaro goes Pontiac!'). Today's consumers have access to the World Wide Web and pay TV, and are more likely to want to purchase foreign-made goods.

The Monaro goes Pontiac!

On the streets of Los Angeles, the Australian-made Pontiac GTO is in high demand. These vehicles are based on the legendary Holden Monaro, with a few modifications for the US market. In 2003, General Motors Holden (GMH) had orders for 20 000 Pontiacs, yet could produce only 18 000 for the export market. By 2005, GMH plans to be exporting 50 000 vehicles.

The success of Australian car makers such as GMH, Toyota and Ford has contributed billions of dollars to Australia's balance of trade over the years and created thousands of jobs. This has been partly due to a global reduction in tariffs (taxes placed on imports by overseas countries to protect local goods), but Australian car makers have also been highly innovative.

According to GMH, on average, around 2500 Holden Commodores and Statesman models leave Adelaide for international markets every month. They are destined for a variety of world markets, including the Middle East, South America, Africa and New Zealand.

Commodore and Statesman models are also sold to Middle Eastern police fleets. These vehicles are fitted to order at the Elizabeth plant with extras like bull bars, flashing warning lights, internal screens, handcuff restraints and extra wiring, then shipped as finished products. Furthermore, the models are engineered to suit Middle Eastern requirements, being adjusted to cope with extremely high temperatures and humidity. Holden's Elizabeth plant is one of the most flexible automotive operations in the world — which is essential to serve markets with different needs.

SNaPSHOT Questions

1. What two factors have led to a growth in export sales of Australian produced cars?
2. List the countries GMH exports to.
3. Outline the benefits to the Australian economy of this export program by Australian car makers.

As the world has evolved into a global marketplace, the world's consumers have become global in their buying behaviour. For example, consumers with access to the Internet can purchase products from any country in the world.

Impact of technology

The world grew smaller in the nineteenth century, due to improvements in transport and communications, and this accelerated in the twentieth century. The introduction of jet aircraft, as well as satellites able to handle thousands of telephone calls simultaneously, completely revitalised transport and communications. Most recently, the computer and the microchip have revolutionised information processing and communications. With each successive technological development, the globe shrinks in size (see figure 19.8).

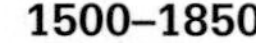

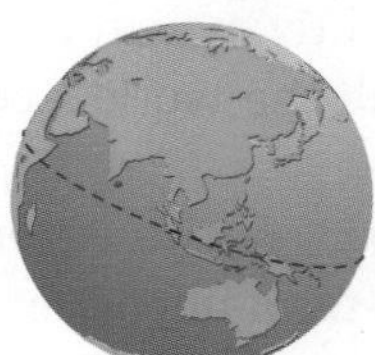

Figure 19.8 The shrinking globe — average speeds of transport and communications have increased dramatically.

Moore's Law predicts that every 18 months the power of microprocessor technology doubles and its cost of production halves.

Information technology (IT) is at the heart of modern organisations and is a driving force for global change. Advances in IT allow an increased flow of ideas and information across borders, so customers learn about overseas-made goods. Global communications systems make it possible for businesses to coordinate design, production and distribution worldwide. The cost of global communications is decreasing and the tools of information technology are becoming easier to use. The Internet, mobile phones, interactive video and electronic funds transfer are helping to open up the global marketplace at an unprecedented rate.

EXERCISE 19.3 *Revision*

1. Identify the five drivers of globalisation.
2. What is meant by the term 'transnational corporation' (TNC)?

3. Explain how the business practices of TNCs have acted as a catalyst for globalisation.
4. Outline how the development of global consumers encourages the process of globalisation.
5. Illustrate, by using an example, how technology has hastened the speed of globalisation.
6. Many of the TNCs referred to in this chapter publish their global activities on the World Wide Web. Go to www.jaconline.com.au/businessstudies3e and click on the weblinks for the following companies.
   - Ford
   - Procter & Gamble
   - Boral
   - CSR
   - The Body Shop
   - BHP Billiton

   Prepare a brief report on one business's global activities.

Extension

1. 'A country whose GDP is smaller than the sales revenue of a TNC is in no position to enforce its wishes on the local subsidiary of that business.' Do you agree or disagree with this proposition? Provide reasons for your answer.
2. 'Although forces in the global marketplace are the same as those in the domestic environment, they operate differently.' Explain why this is so.
3. In its desire to globalise, Shell has recently moved into many new markets. These markets serve approximately half the world's consumers. The company has hired 450 000 extra employees.
   (a) Why do you think that Shell has been able to enter so many new markets?
   (b) What do you think will be the long-term impact of Shell's prosperity and growth on people living in the regions where Shell is developing production capacity?

Role of government

Over the last 40 years, governments have progressively reduced the barriers to trade and investment, expanding growth opportunities for global businesses. Governments have negotiated reductions in **tariffs**, taxes placed on imported goods, as well as other protective measures.

*A **tariff** is a tax placed on imported goods.*

*A **free-trade agreement** is an agreement between two or more countries that results in reductions in barriers to trade such as tariffs, import quotas and government restrictions on foreign ownership.*

Over the last two decades, Australian governments have been active in trade liberalisation talks, especially through regional negotiations. In 1983, the Australian government entered into a **free-trade agreement** with New Zealand, titled the Closer Economic Relationship (CER). More recently, free trade agreements have come into effect, including the:

- Australia–United States Free Trade Agreement (AUSFTA)
- Thailand–Australia Free Trade Agreement (TAFTA)
- Singapore–Australia Free Trade Agreement (SAFTA).

In 2005, negotiations commenced on two free-trade agreements: between the Association of South-East Asian Nations (ASEAN), and Australia and New Zealand (ASEAN-CER-FTA); and between China and Australia (CAFTA).

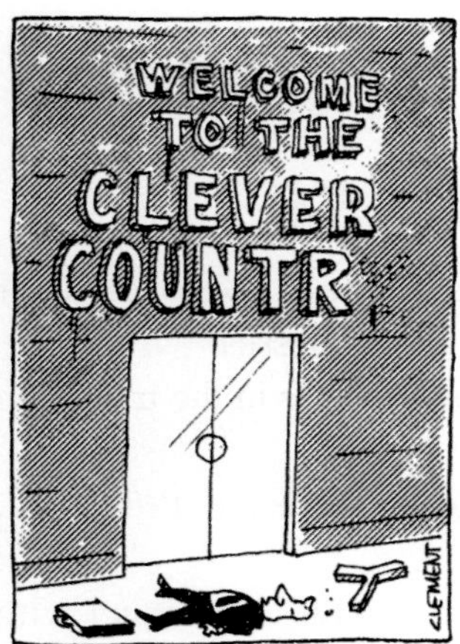

Figure 19.9 A cartoon by Clement commenting on the idea of the clever country

Foreign direct investment (FDI) *is investment made for the purpose of actively controlling companies, assets or property outside a business's home country.*

In a desire to transform Australia into a 'clever country', exporting a wide range of elaborately transformed manufactured products to new and expanding overseas markets within the Asian region, Australian government policy has encouraged Australian businesses to become more globally focused.

Governments around the world support integration of the world's markets as a way of delivering future economic growth.

Deregulation of financial markets

Paralleling the trade liberalisation process is the deregulation of financial markets. Deregulation is the process of removing government regulation from industry in order to achieve efficiency through greater competition. In many countries, industries that were once protected are now being deregulated, especially the world's financial markets. This has seen the barriers to foreign direct investment (FDI) progressively eased.

Foreign direct investment (FDI) is investment made for the purpose of actively controlling companies, assets or property outside a business's home country. Deregulating financial markets created more foreign direct investment opportunities, supporting the process of globalisation.

Money is now more mobile and flows relatively easily between countries due to the globalisation of equity (share) markets. This has come about because financial services companies such as Deutsche Bank, Citibank, Goldman Sachs and Nomura Securities have expanded into many countries. These businesses are keen to arrange finance deals and provide advice for customers anywhere around the world.

Figure 19.10 Stock exchanges, such as the New York Stock Exchange (NYSE), have facilitated the flow of equity finance.

19.7 Interaction between global business and Australian domestic business

From the early 1990s, there was a heightened sense of awareness of the need for domestic businesses to increase their interactions with global businesses.

Australian businesses and managers have three specific advantages in the transition phase:

1 Many of the TNCs that operate in Australia have done so since the 1960s and, therefore, networks and relationships are well established.
2 The multicultural make-up of the Australian workplace provides personnel with language skills and people who understand and appreciate cultural differences.
3 Governments and numerous consultants provide advice, financial assistance and contacts to encourage export-oriented businesses.

As the process of globalisation continues, Australian businesses face increased competition as well as increased opportunities. Australian companies that have successfully gone global include those in the areas of building materials, recycling processes, banking, wine, tourism, education, bioengineering and a host of small to medium-sized enterprises (SMEs) across a wide range of products and services (see the Snapshot 'Espresso Supremo').

Espresso supremo

In 2002–03 James Fitzgerald's company, Foodco Group Pty Ltd earned 21 per cent of its estimated $120 million revenue from exporting, due to the success of the company's fast-growing retail food concepts, Muffin Break and Jamaica Blue. Both of these have achieved upward export growth in markets including New Zealand, the UK, the Middle East and, recently, the US.

The key to each brand's international success, it could be said, lies somewhere between a flexible market strategy based on a highly effective franchising format, and Fitzgerald's conviction that, notwithstanding the quality of a product, location is everything. 'Retail is as much a property story as it is a conceptual or operational one', he explains. 'You have to have access to good real estate — it's fundamental.'

. . .

With both Muffin Break and Jamaica Blue stores now located in over 190 and 40 sites respectively across Australia and New Zealand, Fitzgerald is flying solo, having bought out his business partner four years ago. His sights, it is fair to say, are firmly set on driving the company towards further overseas expansion.

Already, Jamaica Blue is up and running in the Middle East, with eight shops following Foodco's decision two years ago to grant a licence for the coffee bar to a Kuwaiti retail property company. In addition to operational support and design assistance from Foodco, the company receives supplies of Jamaica Blue coffee. Plans to open a Muffin Break pilot store in Dubai under a similar agreement are slated for sometime in the mid-year.

Fitzgerald calls Muffin Break's concept 'a specialist bakery/ coffee shop'.

Meanwhile, in the US and UK, Foodco is directly exporting Muffin Break and Jamaica Blue in their original franchise format. In the short term, says Fitzgerald, plans are afoot for Foodco to open another 12 to 15 Muffin Break shops in the UK to complement the eight sites already established. While in California, a Jamaica Blue pilot store and second Muffin Break store, additional to the one already operating in the western US state, are slated for later in the year.

...

The small size of the local retail food market is why Foodco initially opted to expand into its overseas locations. According to Fitzgerald, the bakery and coffee bar niches occupied by Muffin Break and Jamaica Blue in Australia are now 'overheated' with so many participants the market has become 'ferociously competitive'. 'For instance, we only opened 15 new shops in Australia last year despite having the infrastructure and capacity to open 30 to 35 new locations', he says.

...

However, Fitzgerald cautions businesses to remain mindful that exporting is not an overnight sensation, but rather a long-term project involving just as many risks as surprises. 'People have to be prepared to hold their breath', he says. 'For example, while Muffin Break will more than likely break even in the UK by the middle of this year after two years in the market, I would say that it will take longer than that before we stop feeding our operations in the US.'

...

Source: K. Clifford, 'Espresso Supremo', *Export*, May 2004, pp. 18–22.

SNaPSHOT Questions

1. What is the key to each brand's international success?
2. List the countries in which Foodco is operating.
3. Identify the main reason Foodco decided to expand overseas.
4. Why does James Fitzgerald regard exporting as a long-term project?

EXERCISE 19.4 Revision

1. What is meant by the term 'tariff'?
2. Explain how tariffs act as a barrier to world trade.
3. What do the acronyms 'AUSFTA', 'TAFTA' and 'SAFTA' stand for?
4. Why do you think governments want to establish free-trade agreements?
5. What is meant by the terms 'deregulation' and 'foreign direct investment'?
6. Explain the relationship between the deregulation of financial markets and foreign direct investment.
7. Identify three characteristics of the Australian economy that will assist businesses as they undertake the process of globalisation.
8. Refer to the topic opener story about SOTA Limited on page 417 and then answer the following questions:
   (a) Identify the influences on SOTA that forced it to consider undertaking global expansion.

(b) List the main obstacles to exporting as identified by the board of directors.
(c) Imagine you have been asked by the board of SOTA Limited to advise them on going global. From what you have learned in this chapter what advice would you give the board of directors?

9. Prepare a summary of this chapter. A summary condenses the important issues and concepts presented in the chapter. Go to www.jaconline.com.au/businessstudies3e to compare your finished summary with the one provided for this textbook.

Extension

1. In past years Australia has used tariffs and import quotas to protect domestic firms. Research the arguments for and against trade protection.
2. Trade liberalisation and the resultant globalisation of business is severely criticised by many people across the globe. They argue that the bulk of trade is not 'global' but between a small number of 'developed' economies in the northern hemisphere. Research the validity of their argument. Should Australian business managers be concerned with such arguments? Provide reasons for your answers.
3. Go to www.jaconline.com.au/businessstudies3e and click on the World Trade Organization weblink for this textbook. Research the role this organisation plays in encouraging globalisation.
4. 'The growing integration of national economies is said to have changed the way the world works.' Critically analyse the validity of this statement.
5. Go to www.jaconline.com.au/businessstudies3e and click on the Department of Foreign Affairs and Trade weblink for this textbook. Research the economic growth rates of Australia's major trading partners. Predict the impact the different growth rates will have upon Australian exporting businesses.

20 Global business strategy

20.1 Introduction

Each year more Australian businesses are choosing to conduct business in the global marketplace, with exports growing steadily over the last decade. This growing trend to export can be linked to changes within the external business environment, especially:

- government encouragement and incentives giving rise to new business opportunities
- the adoption within the Australian business community of a more global outlook.

A business needs to answer two simple, but important, questions when expanding internationally: what *method* will the business use and what are the *reasons* for wanting to expand?

20.2 Methods of international expansion

In recognition of the importance of global business to the Australian economy, the federal government, through Austrade, AusIndustry and the Department of Foreign Affairs and Trade (DFAT) provides invaluable assistance to exporters. Other institutions, such as banks and industry exporting groups, offer a comprehensive range of export services and information.

When a business decides to expand from being a domestic business to a global operation it can do so in several ways (see figure 20.1).

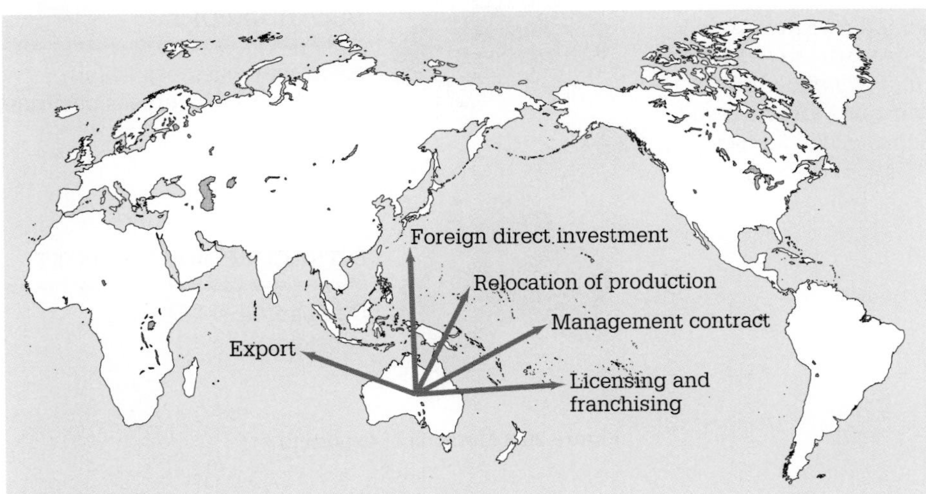

Figure 20.1 Five methods of global expansion

These different strategies require varying degrees of involvement in global business. Normally, a firm commences its global operations at the simplest level; for example, exporting its products and services to a foreign country. Then, depending upon its long-term goals and the success of its previous ventures, it may progress to a more complex level of involvement, such as foreign direct investment.

Export

Exporting occurs when a business manufactures its products in its home country and then sells them in foreign markets.

Indirect exporting is the most basic level of exporting where a business sells its products to a domestic customer, who then exports the product.

Direct exporting involves the exporting business selling its products to an agent, intermediary or final consumers in another country.

A **trading company** is a business that buys and sells products in many countries.

Exporting occurs when a business manufactures its products in its home country and then sells them in foreign markets. Increased sales and profits are normally the main incentives for exporting.

Exporting can be a relatively low-risk method of entering overseas markets. Although large businesses dominate the world of exporting, there are many opportunities for small and medium-sized firms (see the Snapshot 'Pregnant with opportunity' on page 435).

There are three different methods of exporting (see figure 20.2). Each method requires a different level of involvement for the exporting business.

- **Indirect exporting** is the most basic level. A business sells its products to a domestic customer, who then exports the product. The domestic customer then assumes all the risks of distribution, ownership, sales and transportation.
- **Direct exporting** happens when the exporting business sells its products to an agent, intermediary or final consumers in another country. Often the intermediary is a **trading company**, a business that buys and sells products in many countries.

Austrade research reveals that approximately one-third of all initial direct export sales are the result of an unsolicited order.

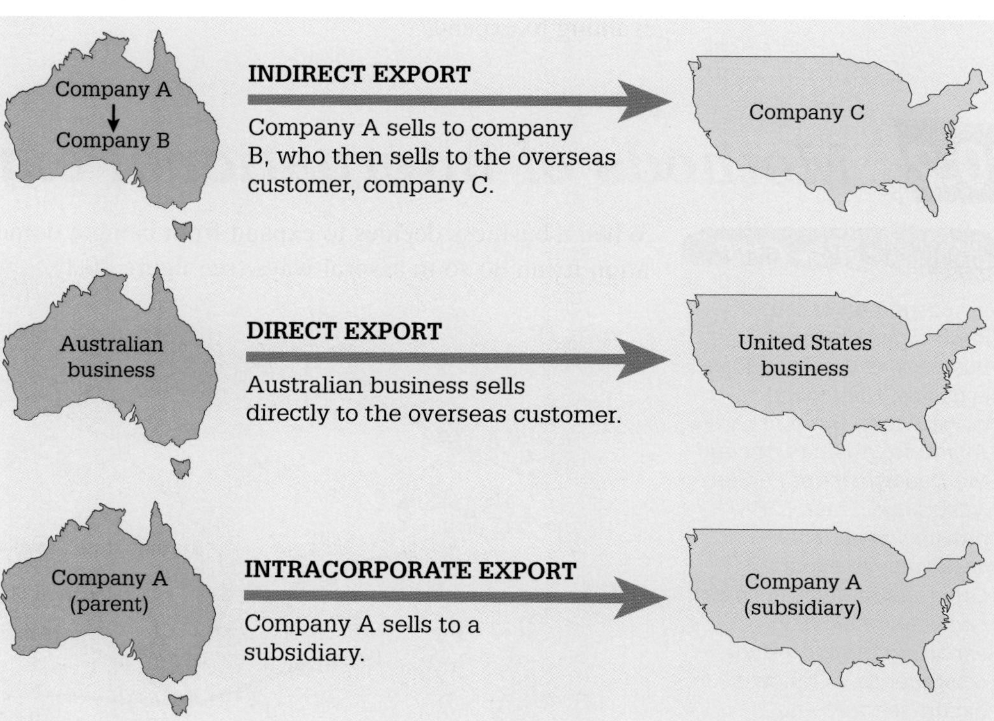

Figure 20.2 Methods of exporting

Intracorporate exporting (transfer) is the selling of a product by a firm in one country to a subsidiary firm in another.

- **Intracorporate exporting** (also known as **transfer**) is the selling of a product by a firm in one country to a subsidiary firm in another. As transnational corporations (TNCs) have increased in size, this form of exporting has become much more important. For example, if Ford (US) ships body panels and engine parts from its manufacturing plant in Australia to its Mexican subsidiary, the transaction is recorded as an Australian export, but all the money for the transaction stays within Ford.

Pregnant with opportunity

In the 1990s, a common fantasy of every pregnant woman, after sifting furiously through racks of pink frilly dresses decorated with chocolate-box bows, was to run off and start their own maternity clothes business.

So it was with young, fashion-conscious interior designer Lisa Balakas, who had her first baby at 20. By the time she was 27 and a mother of three, she was so fed up with the clothes on offer, she decided to turn her fantasy into reality.

Balakas joined up with a friend, Kate Beaconsfield, also 27, and their Melbourne business, Ripe Maternity Wear, now has revenue of almost $10 million. 'It's lucky we were naive. There are so many negative things written about how Australian products cannot survive that we wouldn't have dared.'

. . .

Export was not on their agenda. 'We thought the different cultures would affect what people would buy and worried about the difference between the Northern and Southern Hemispheres. We thought the red tape would be difficult and we could not get the clothes there in time.'

In 2000, Beaconsfield bumped into an acquaintance visiting from the United Arab Emirates (UAE) who invited them to export there. 'We thought it was a joke but on her return she opened a shop and we began exporting to her.'

A year later they began exporting to Hong Kong, after an approach by somebody who saw the clothes in the UAE. 'By then we were confident enough to tackle the US. Red tape looks far more scary than it is', she says.

The pair sent catalogues to maternity stores and were contacted by a Texan agent who was so enthusiastic about the label that he introduced the company to other agents, including one in Canada. 'We launched in the US with our basic range but customers thought it was not different enough and we nearly lost our opportunity with the agents. We should have launched with our most exciting stuff', Beaconsfield says.

. . .

Predicted difficulties such as the fashion time lag did not eventuate. 'We make clothes for Australia first and then sell to the Northern Hemisphere. The clothes are still in fashion and we have ironed out small errors by then.'

Thanks to a new custom-built warehouse, the company carries stock. 'Our customers like that because it decreases their risk. We can do it because we manufacture locally.' Orders are filled quickly and then airfreighted to the export destination. 'We pay duties, airfreight prices and sell in their currency so we are easy to deal with.' But watch the errors made by Customs. 'We go through all bills with a fine-tooth comb', she says.

About 45 per cent of Ripe Maternity's revenue comes from exports to 15 countries. Its revenue is heading towards $10 million and it has 18 staff.

Source: A. Gome, 'Pregnant with opportunity', *Business Review Weekly*, 2–8 December 2004, p. 40.

SNaPSHOT Questions

1. List the countries Ripe Maternity Wear exports to.
2. Describe the strategies Ripe Maternity Wear used to gain sales in overseas markets.

The main advantages of exporting as a method of overseas entry are as follows:

- It is relatively inexpensive, especially compared to establishing production facilities overseas.
- It provides an opportunity to gain valuable experience, although this would depend upon the exporting method selected.

The main disadvantages are as follows:

- Overseas countries may use a number of barriers to trade, which could result in an increase in the price of the exported products.
- High transport costs may make exporting uneconomical, especially if air transport is involved.
- Overseas agents or intermediaries may not do as good a job as the business itself.
- It could be uneconomical, especially if there are more favourable low-cost locations for manufacturing overseas.

BiZ FaCT

According to General Motors Holden (GMH), on average, around 2500 Holden Commodore and Statesman models leave Adelaide for international markets every month.

EXERCISE 20.1 Revision

1. Identify the five methods of global expansion.
2. What is meant by the term 'exporting'?
3. Using examples, distinguish between indirect, direct and intracorporate exporting.
4. Briefly outline the main advantages and disadvantages of exporting as a method of global expansion.
5. A friend has decided she wants her jewellery business to expand by entering an overseas market. Which method of exporting would you recommend? Give reasons for your answer.

Extension

1. Under what conditions might a business prefer a joint venture to a wholly owned subsidiary when engaging in foreign investment?
2. Go to www.jaconline.com.au/businessstudies3e and click on Austrade's Export Capability Tool weblink for this textbook. Outline the preparation Austrade recommends a business should carry out prior to exporting.

Foreign direct investment (FDI)

As was outlined in chapter 19, foreign direct investment (FDI) occurs when a business from one country owns property, assets or business interests in another country. For example, the Australian building and construction company, Boral Limited, owns production facilities in over 11 overseas countries.

There are three methods of foreign direct investment:

- The **greenfield strategy** involves commencing a new business venture from scratch. The business purchases land (the 'green field'), constructs new facilities and commences production.

Greenfield strategy *involves commencing a new business venture from scratch.*

An **acquisition strategy** occurs when one business acquires, through a takeover or merger, an existing business already operating in a foreign country.

A **joint venture** means two or more businesses agree to work together and form a jointly owned but separate business.

- The **acquisition strategy** is appropriate for any business that wishes to move quickly into an overseas market. It involves a business acquiring, through a take-over or merger, an existing business already operating in the foreign country.
- A **joint venture** means two or more businesses agree to work together and form a jointly owned but separate business. In a typical joint venture, the two partners each hold 50 per cent ownership. For example, Simsmetal (Australia) Limited, a global metals recycling company, is in a joint venture with Birmingham Steel to operate the largest scrap processing operation in Canada.

The main advantages of foreign direct investment include the following:

- It provides the parent business with direct control over the foreign facilities.
- As the products are being produced in the overseas country there is a subsequent reduction in transport costs.
- Transfer of technology, people, products and intellectual property becomes easier.
- The parent business is in a better position to be able to monitor and adapt to changes in the foreign country's business environment.

The main disadvantages include the following:

- Increased financial risk is likely, especially when investing in a business that is located in a politically unstable country.
- The parent business is exposed to the economic uncertainties of the foreign country.
- Adverse currency fluctuations may wipe out any cost efficiencies.
- Legal, social, cultural and language barriers may create problems.
- Joint venture profits must be shared between all the parties involved.

In some countries, government regulations make joint ventures the only way to gain a foothold in the market.

Relocation of production

As was outlined in the previous section, a greenfield strategy is an accepted method of entering a foreign market. **Relocation of production** takes this strategy one step further. It involves closing down the domestic production facilities, which are then set up in a foreign country. This is sometimes referred to as relocating offshore.

Relocation of production occurs when the domestic production facility is closed down and then set up in a foreign country.

The motivation behind this strategy is cost reduction. Increased global competition is forcing businesses to increase efficiency and reduce costs of production. In the last two decades there have been increased closures of some businesses in developed economies as production facilities have been relocated, usually to a low-cost, developing country (see figure 20.3).

The main advantages of this strategy include the following:

- Moving to a low-cost labour country should help decrease costs of production.
- Decreased production costs may result in increased profits.
- More modern, up-to-date facilities can be constructed, adding to other cost efficiencies.
- Some governments provide financial assistance to cover relocation expenses.

The main disadvantages include the following:

- The parent business may be faced with social, cultural and language barriers in the overseas country.
- The possibility of a consumer backlash if exploitative work practices are used.
- The business needs to recruit a local workforce and train it to meet its standards. This could be time consuming and expensive.
- The business may be perceived as foreign and no longer a local business, which may result in some consumers being reluctant to purchase the products.

Figure 20.3 Workers inspect shoes at a Reebok shoe factory in Zhongsham, China.

Management contract

*The **management contract** is an arrangement under which a global business provides managerial assistance and technical expertise to a second or host business for a fee.*

The **management contract** is an arrangement under which a global business provides managerial assistance and technical expertise to a second or host business for a fee. This method of entry allows the global business to operate in many foreign countries without the expense of production facilities. For example, Hilton Hotels provides management expertise for hotels that use the Hilton name but that are not company-owned. The business that provides the expertise is guaranteed a fee, while at the same time the host business gains operational assistance.

The advantages of this strategy include the following:

- The global partner has greater control over production standards in a joint venture operation.
- The fees paid by the subsidiary are a business expense and, therefore, a tax deduction.
- The global business is able to earn extra revenue.

The main disadvantages include the following:

- The host business does not gain any managerial training.
- The global business may face political pressures from the host business's government, especially with regard to foreign exchange restrictions.

Licensing and franchising

***Licensing** is an agreement in which one business (licensor) permits another (licensee) to produce and market its product.*

At a fairly basic level of global business is licensing. **Licensing** is an agreement in which one business (licensor) permits another (licensee) to produce and market its product, brand name, trademark, copyright and technology, and other intellectual properties in return for a royalty fee (see figure 20.4). You may have seen the words 'made under licence' on some products. This refers to the licence to use the intellectual property of a business.

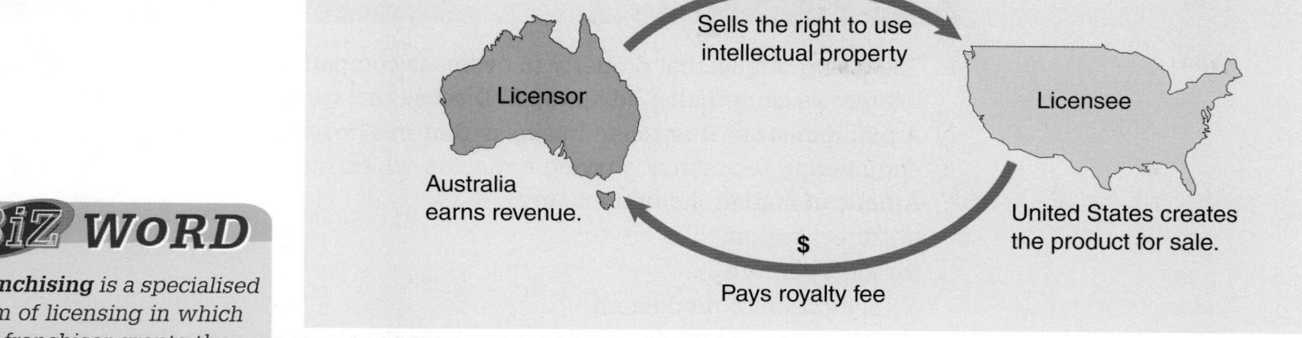

Figure 20.4 An example of the licensing process

BiZ WORD

***Franchising** is a specialised form of licensing in which the franchisor grants the franchisee the right to use a company's trademark and distribute its product.*

Franchising is a specialised form of licensing in which the franchisor grants the franchisee the right to use a company's trademark and distribute its product. The franchisor will often assist the franchisee to establish and run the business, but also insists that the franchisee agree to abide by strict operating rules.

Franchising is more common in the United States (US) than in other countries. Therefore, across the globe there are more US franchise operations than those from any other country.

BiZ FaCT

Examples of franchise chains in Australia include McDonald's, Wendy's, KFC, Avis, Benetton and Dunkin' Donuts.

Australian businesses that have successfully used the franchising strategy to expand overseas include Cash Converters, Bob Jane T-Mart, and Jim's Mowing.

The main advantages of licensing and franchising include the following:

- There is little financial risk for the licensor/franchisor.
- It is a useful option for firms lacking the capital to develop an overseas operation.
- The licensor/franchisor is able to develop a global presence relatively quickly.

The main disadvantages include the following:

- There is a risk of losing intellectual property rights to the licensee/franchisee.
- It is difficult to maintain quality control over a wide range of locations.
- International franchising is more complex than domestic franchising, often requiring the need for extensive legal advice.
- The profits are shared between the two parties.

EXERCISE 20.2 Revision

1. Distinguish between the terms 'greenfield strategy', 'acquisition strategy' and 'joint venture'.
2. If a business wants to directly invest in a foreign market in as short a time as possible, which method would be most suitable? Give reasons for your answer.
3. One major advantage of a joint venture is that the risks are shared between the two parties. Outline two possible disadvantages of this method of international expansion.
4. Contrast the strategies of relocating production offshore and exporting.
5. Summarise the benefits of a management contract to both the host and donor business.
6. Why might a business decide to bypass direct exporting and use a licensing/ franchising strategy?
7. Refer back to the topic opener story about SOTA Limited on page 417. Which method of international expansion would you recommend for SOTA? Give reasons for your answer.

Extension

1. 'Licensing intellectual property to overseas competitors is the best way to lose a business's competitive advantage.' Discuss the accuracy of this statement.
2. A medium-sized Australian business that has developed a new genetic engineering technique is trying to decide which method is best for entering the American market. Its options are:
   (a) direct export
   (b) joint venture
   (c) relocation of production.
   Which option would you advise it to choose? Give reasons for your answer.
3. Research the number and nature of Australian businesses that are franchising in Asia. Select one particular business and describe and analyse the reasons for its international expansion.

20.3 Reasons for expansion

Global businesses enter foreign markets for a number of reasons (see figure 20.5), all of which are ultimately linked to the desire to increase sales and profits.

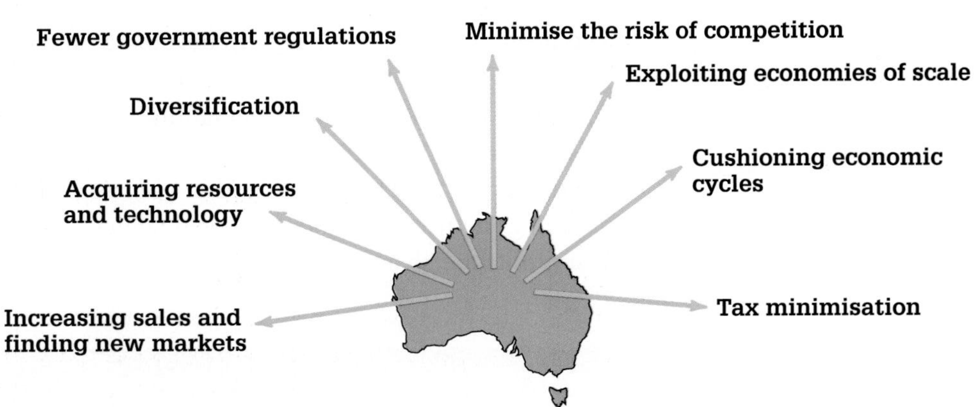

Figure 20.5 Reasons for expansion

Some businesses are initially reluctant to expand internationally because of the difficulties they believe they will face. However, once a business learns of the opportunities presented by such expansion, they may regard it as an exciting strategy that offers numerous advantages.

QBE's founding company was established in North Queensland in 1886 and has grown into an international insurance and reinsurance group operating from over 200 offices in 30 countries worldwide. It has just entered the Vietnamese market as part of its global growth strategy.

Increasing sales and finding new markets

Businesses are always under pressure to increase sales revenue and profits. This can become difficult if the domestic market:

- becomes saturated
- has stopped expanding due to a low population growth rate
- is dominated by a competitor
- is experiencing an economic downturn
- is being flooded by foreign-made products.

Such conditions often result in a search for new markets outside the home country. Many markets around the world are growing as countries experience economic growth. As a result, domestic businesses may see profit-making opportunities opening up in new markets. Opportunities have been created in China as this economy is opened up. India is starting to ease restriction on imports into its economy. The result is that approximately 2.5 billion people are becoming part of the global marketplace, bringing enormous potential profits.

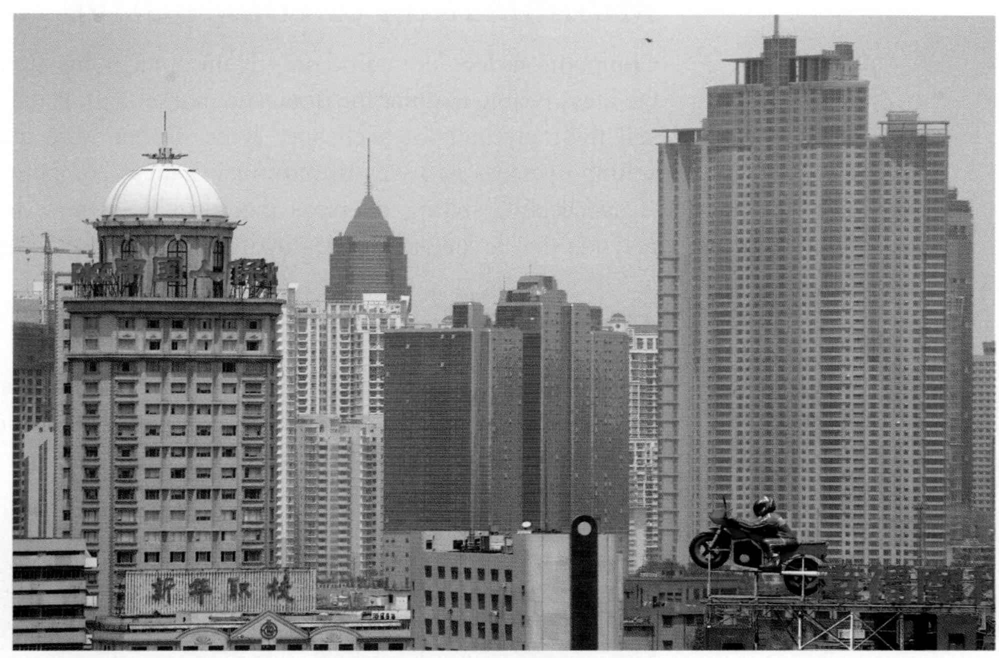

Figure 20.6 China, currently Australia's second largest merchandise export market, is set to become one of the economic superpowers of the world.

Acquiring resources and technology

Few countries, even developed ones, possess sufficient domestic supplies of raw materials. As well, no one country is technologically self-sufficient. To guarantee a continuous supply of raw materials, many businesses (especially in industrialised countries) are directly investing in developing countries. Developing a number of raw material sources spreads the risk, so that if one source of supply is restricted there is another to rely on. Also, if the resources can be obtained more cheaply, the business's costs of production decrease.

Businesses sometimes experience a shortage of technological or management expertise. To gain access to the latest technology, a business may choose either to enter into a joint venture or operate under a licence or management contract.

Diversification

Diversification is a process of spreading the risks encountered by a business.

Diversification is a process of spreading the risks encountered by a business. This strategy is based on the principle of 'not putting all your eggs in one basket'.

In terms of global business, diversification can occur at a number of different levels. These are:

- *geographic diversification* (i.e. operating in foreign locations). Having a number of markets across the world helps minimise the risk of business failure should one market suffer a decrease in sales.

- *product diversification.* A business may decide to enter a foreign market as a way of increasing the range of products sold. Should sales decrease for one product the business can fall back on its other products.
- *supplier diversification.* As outlined previously, businesses prefer to have a number of suppliers of raw materials. For a business to be solely reliant on one supplier puts it at a distinct disadvantage.

Minimisation of competitive risk

Competition does not come only from other domestic producers. Often, an overseas business is able to enter the domestic market and, if they are more efficient producers, sell their products at a cheaper price. Either way, a domestic producer may view selling overseas as a way of minimising these competitive pressures. This is because, if successful, selling overseas can provide a new market and another source of revenue that reduces the risks involved from these competitive pressures.

Exploiting economies of scale

***Economies of scale** refers to the reduction in costs of production that arise from increasing the size or scale of the production facility and spreading overhead (fixed) costs over a larger output.*

Economies of scale refers to the reduction in costs of production caused by increasing the size or scale of the production facility and spreading overhead (fixed) costs over a larger output (see figure 20.7).

Figure 20.7 The Holden car plant at Elizabeth, South Australia — economies of scale due to mass production

Increasing sales by exporting lowers the cost of production, and research and development costs, and reduces raw material purchases due to bulk buying. As well, a business can further reduce the cost of each item produced by operating on long production runs and having one factory supply one product globally.

Cushioning economic cycles

The level of economic activity fluctuates between a boom and a recession. When the domestic economy is booming, sales are rising and production may be close to or at full capacity. In this situation, a domestic business may not be motivated to sell overseas. However, boom periods do not last indefinitely. Eventually, the domestic economy will begin to contract, leaving the business with a reduction in sales and excess capacity. Then, the business may decide to expand overseas to cushion the impact of a reduction in local demand.

However, due to the globalisation of the world's markets, booms and recessions tend to be worldwide, especially if there is a simultaneous downturn in the economies of the industrialised countries. Consequently, a business needs to be aware of the economic conditions both domestically and internationally. A downturn in one economy may require attempts to find new markets.

Responding to regulatory differences

***Regulations** are restrictions placed by governments on the activities of either individuals or businesses.*

Regulations are restrictions placed by governments on the activities of either individuals or businesses. Over the last two decades, the number and type of regulation imposed by governments of industrialised nations has dramatically increased. Regulations covering environmental protection, minimum working and health standards for employees, improved labelling of products and more stringent taxation requirements have been the focus of various governments. Conforming to such regulations may add to the cost of production and encourage businesses from industrialised nations to relocate production facilities to developing nations. They may be attracted by a lack of business regulations, particularly laws protecting employees and the environment from exploitation. This practice raises numerous ethical questions which will be explored in more detail in chapter 23.

Critics of globalisation liken the current process to a driverless machine. The invisible driver is, they argue, the urge to maximise profits by searching out the cheapest labour it can find, usually in developing countries.

Tax minimisation

Of particular interest to many businesses is the company tax imposed by a country's government. Industrialised countries tend to have higher rates of company tax compared to developing countries. The high tax rate could act as a disincentive to a domestic producer, encouraging them to move to a location with lower tax rates.

To attract transnational corporations, the Malaysian government established the International Offshore Financial Centre of Labaun. This small island operates as a free port where no sales tax, import or export duties are charged.

Figure 20.8 Malaysia offers taxation incentives, hoping to attract overseas businesses. This photograph shows the skyline of the Malaysian capital, Kuala Lumpur.

*A **tax holiday** occurs when no tax is paid for a certain period of time.*

*A **tax haven** is a country that imposes little or no taxes on business income.*

Some developing countries offer taxation incentives such as tax holidays and tax havens to businesses and their managers if they invest in their country. A **tax holiday** is a scheme in which no company or personal tax is paid for a certain period of time. A **tax haven** is a country that has low or no taxes on business income.

These practices raise a number of ethical issues and will be examined in more detail in chapter 23 .

EXERCISE 20.3 Revision

1. Why do some businesses not rely solely on the domestic market?
2. Outline the advantages to a business of a resource acquisition strategy.
3. 'Diversification means playing it safe.' Explain the meaning of this statement.
4. What is meant by the term 'economies of scale'?
5. In groups of two or three, research and identify some economies of scale that operate in your school. Present an oral report to the rest of the class.
6. Contrast the economic conditions that occur during a boom with those of a recession.
7. Outline how expanding overseas may cushion the impact of fluctuations in the economic cycle.
8. Illustrate, using examples, how government regulations can act either as an incentive or disincentive for a business to relocate its production facilities.
9. What are some of the motives behind a business relocating to a country with less rigid regulations?
10. Distinguish between a tax holiday and a tax haven.
11. Prepare a summary of this chapter. A summary condenses the important issues and concepts presented in the chapter. Go to www.jaconline.com.au/businessstudies3e to compare your finished summary with the one provided for this textbook.

Extension

1. Collect from magazines or newspapers five articles dealing with Australian businesses that are planning to expand overseas.
   (a) Select one article and prepare an executive summary of it.
   (b) For each article, identify the overseas expansion strategy the business is planning to use and the reasons for the expansion.
   (c) Present your findings as an oral presentation to the rest of the class.
2. Go to www.jaconline.com.au/businessstudies3e and click on the Paperlinx and CSR weblinks for this textbook. Investigate each company in terms of:
   - global strategies
   - geographic locations
   - products marketed at each location.

   What do the two companies have in common in terms of their global strategies?
3. In pairs, arrange an interview with the manager of a local business that sells its products overseas. Discuss the reasons for the business deciding to expand overseas. Outline the strategies the business used to expand globally. Present your interview to the rest of the class.

21 Specific influences on global business

21.1 Introduction

A business that operates globally has to deal with a more complex set of factors compared to a business that operates only in a domestic market, including:

- *difficulty of assessment*. It is often difficult to assess changes within a foreign country, especially to legal and political structures.
- *different value systems*. Individual value systems often differ widely and may sometimes be in opposition (see the Biz Fact on the left).
- *decision making is more complex*. Managers must take into account the specific influences in each country in which the business operates. Consider the difficulty facing a manager in the head office who must make decisions affecting subsidiaries in 15 different countries.
- *cultural differences*. Perhaps the single most important cause for the added complexity of global business is managers' unfamiliarity with other cultures. Managers will sometimes try to transfer their own cultural preferences to a foreign work site. This only makes matters worse.

What may in one country be regarded as an act of bribery or corruption may be viewed as an essential business gift in another.

Each country is unique. Any business that wishes to sell in the global marketplace must be aware of the unique differences and specific influences that exist in foreign countries (see the Snapshot 'Doing business in China — a check list of specific influences').

Doing business in China — a checklist of specific influences

MAJOR DIFFICULTIES

- Regulations vary between regions.
- Quality of production is not always a high priority.
- The political environment is uncertain and based largely on personal contacts.
- The legal system is underdeveloped, but this is improving.
- A high degree of corruption may be encountered.
- The rigid bureaucracy causes inefficiencies.
- Copyright and patent laws have been developed and are being applied more frequently, but not heavily.

ADVANTAGES

- China's economy is growing rapidly.
- The wealthy, urban population is growing.

(*continued*)

- The government allows private sector businesses access to foreign capital, technology and tariff-free intermediate imports.
- Taxation levels are low.
- There is plentiful supply of relatively cheap labour.
- Foreign investors are allowed to have more than 50 per cent share ownership of any business.
- Foreign investors are given a fair degree of freedom.
- The population of 1.4 billion people is highly concentrated in 622 cities.

CULTURAL ISSUES

- Local staff need to be trained and encouraged to show initiative.
- Rapid delivery time is crucial.
- As a sign of respect, when hosting a meal it is important to arrange for as many courses as practical.
- People prefer the 'cash and wrap' method for household purchases.

SOLVING DIFFICULTIES

- It is important to build personal relationships.
- Recognise that assertive individualism is a Western characteristic not popular within an Eastern culture.
- Be very patient and take time to establish relationships. Do not expect instant returns.
- It is important to undertake extensive market research.
- Learn social skills to avoid causing loss of face.

FINANCIAL REQUIREMENTS

- Equity joint venture partners must contribute at least 25 per cent of the capital.
- The currency, renminbi, is not convertible into foreign currency, unless foreign exchange certificates are submitted.
- Foreign exchange certificates must be used to transfer profits overseas.
- Joint or non-joint venture operations that have an office or place of business in China must pay a tax of 33 per cent on profits before income tax.
- A tax also applies to the production of industrial and agricultural goods, as well as commercial retailing, services, transport and communications activities, at a rate ranging from 5 to 10 per cent.

SNAPSHOT Question

Why do you think potential exporters should research the specific influences that exist in the country(ies) they intend to trade with?

Global businesses are exposed to four main influences (see figure 21.1). These are discussed in the following section. The success of the business's international expansion activities is determined largely by the specific business strategies put in place to effectively manage these influences.

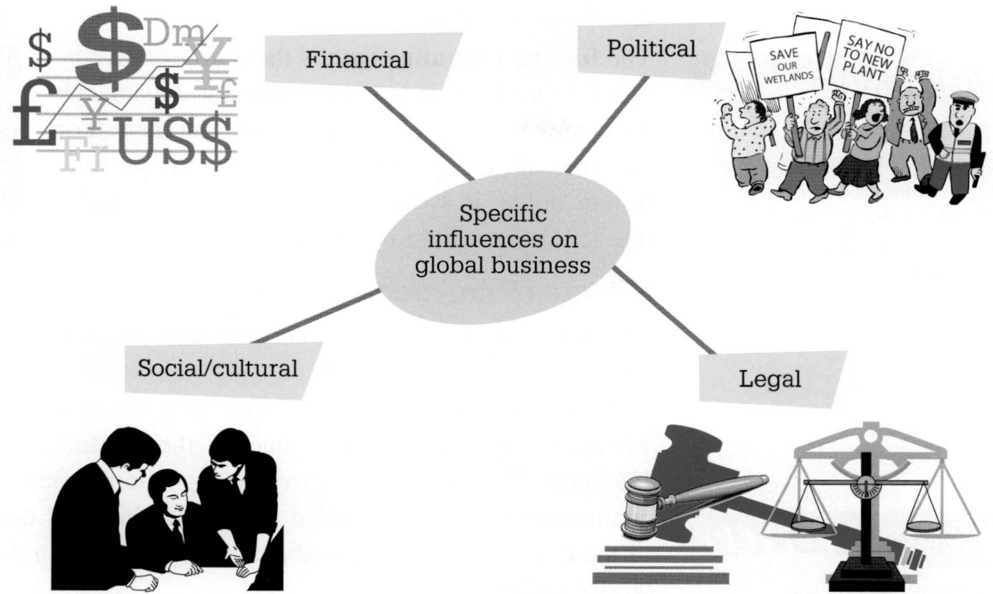

Figure 21.1 The four main specific influences on global business

21.2 Financial influences

Financial risks associated with global expansion are greater than those encountered domestically, but such risk taking is necessary for the business strategy to be implemented.

Largely 'uncontrollable' financial influences include currency fluctuations, interest rates and overseas borrowing. 'Uncontrollable' means that these influences are part of the external business environment and may not be significantly controlled by the business. However, a business can put in place appropriate financial management strategies to minimise their negative effects.

*The **foreign exchange (forex** or **fx) market** determines the price of one currency relative to another.*

One of the most difficult financial influences to manage is currency (exchange rate) fluctuations.

Currency fluctuations

The European Monetary Union established a single currency, the euro, to encourage free trade between members.

Countries have their own currency, which they use for domestic purposes. This means that when transactions are conducted on a global scale, one currency must be converted to another. For example, if an Australian business (importer) purchases machinery from Japan, the Japanese firm (exporter) will want to be paid in Japanese yen not Australian dollars. Similarly, if a Japanese tourist visits Australia, he or she will pay for accommodation, restaurant meals and other products in Australian dollars, not yen. Therefore, in all global transactions it is necessary to convert one currency into another. This transaction is performed through the **foreign exchange market**, commonly abbreviated to **forex** or **fx**, which determines the price of one currency relative to another.

Foreign exchange dealers around the world are constantly buying and selling each other's currency. In this way the price or value of each country's currency is established. This value or price is called the exchange rate.

*The **foreign exchange rate** is the ratio of one currency to another; it tells how much a unit of one currency is worth in terms of another.*

Exchange rates

The **foreign exchange rate** is the ratio of one currency to another; it tells how much a unit of one currency is worth in terms of another. For example, if A$1 = US$0.70, that means one Australian dollar is worth 70 US cents. Conversely, one US dollar would be worth A$1.43.

Figure 21.2 Foreign exchange market dealing room — setting the exchange rate

Effects of currency fluctuations

Exchange rates fluctuate over time due to variations in demand and supply.

Such fluctuations in the exchange rate create further risk for global business. For example, suppose that the value of the Australian dollar falls from US$0.70 to US$0.60. This downward movement of the Australian dollar (or another currency) against the US dollar is called a **depreciation**. (Of course, this means that the value of the US dollar has increased against the Australian dollar, with one US dollar being worth A$1.66.)

*A **depreciation** is a downward movement of the Australian dollar (or any other currency) against another currency.*

The impact of this currency fluctuation is twofold:

1 A currency depreciation lowers the value of the Australian dollar in terms of foreign currencies. This means that each unit of foreign currency buys more Australian dollars. However, one Australian dollar buys less foreign currency. Therefore, a depreciation makes our exports cheaper on international markets but prices for imports will rise.

The result of the depreciation, therefore, improves the international competitiveness of Australian exporting businesses.

2 A currency appreciation has the opposite impact. An appreciation raises the price of Australian dollars in terms of foreign currencies. Therefore, each unit of foreign currency buys fewer Australian dollars. The result is that our exports become more expensive and the price of imports falls.

An appreciation, therefore, reduces the international competitiveness of Australian exporting businesses.

Currency fluctuations, therefore, will impact on the revenue profitability and production costs.

In 1983, Australia floated the Australian dollar. This meant that the market forces of demand and supply set the value of the Australian dollar. Prior to 1983, the exchange rate for the Australian dollar was set by the government.

The worldwide volume of foreign exchange trading is estimated at $US1.5 trillion per day — that is, $US1 500 000 000 000!

Figure 21.3 Currency fluctuations

Currency fluctuations create risks for businesses when they sell to overseas markets. However, as will be explained in chapter 22, financial managers have strategies for dealing with this type of risk.

Interest rates

In the mid 1980s, when Australia's interest rates were high, some Australian banks were encouraging customers to borrow offshore. A number of loans were arranged in Swiss francs. Most of these borrowers were badly hurt when the Australian dollar depreciated against the Swiss franc, causing a rapid rise in the total repayments. Subsequently, the banks were sued for damages but, after a long and complex court case, most of the borrowers lost heavily.

A business that plans to either relocate offshore or expand domestic production facilities to increase direct exporting will normally need to raise finance to undertake these activities. Traditionally, Australian interest rates tend to be above those of other countries, especially the United States and Japan. Thus, Australian businesses could be tempted to borrow the necessary finance from an overseas source to gain the advantage of lower interest rates.

However, the real risk here is exchange rate movements. Any adverse currency fluctuation could see the advantage of cheaper overseas interest rates quickly eliminated. In the long term the 'cheap' interest rates may end up costing more (see the Biz Fact on the left).

Overseas borrowing

Businesses operating at the global level can borrow money from a diverse range of sources within the international capital market. This market consists of businesses, financial institutions, individuals and governments that lend and borrow worldwide. A business that cannot raise finance from domestic sources can use the services of international financial institutions such as Citibank, Bank of China, GE Finance and Goldman Sachs.

There are two main sources of international finance:

1 *International equity (share) market.* This involves selling shares of ownership to new or existing owners worldwide. Businesses will use the international market if there is a shortage of funds in domestic markets. This was the case with Rupert Murdoch's News Corporation when, in 2004, it relocated from Australia to the United States. Listing on the US stock market provided News Corporation with a larger pool of finance to draw from.

2 *International bond market.* A **bond** is an IOU from one business to another and requires the borrower to repay a certain amount, plus interest, by a specified date. A bond, therefore, is like a loan certificate indicating that its issuer has borrowed a sum of money from the bondholder. A business that wants to take advantage of lower interest rates or access a larger pool of funds will issue an international bond.

*A **bond** is an IOU from one business to another and requires the borrower to repay a certain amount, plus interest, by a specified date.*

As we have just outlined, the temptation to borrow offshore due to relatively lower interest rates needs to be considered carefully. This is because it exposes the business to the risks of fluctuating exchange rates on the forex market. For example, assume an Australian business borrows US$6 million for one year at an exchange rate of A$1 = US$0.60. The total repayment will be A$10 million plus interest (US$1 = A$1.66). However, if the value of the Australian dollar depreciates to US$0.50 during the year, then the business must repay A$12 million plus interest (US$1 = A$2).

There are two types of international bonds: foreign bonds and Eurobonds. Eurobonds are the most common and, unlike foreign bonds, are issued in the borrower's own currency.

The depreciation could easily destroy any advantage of a cheaper overseas interest rate. To help avoid such risks the exporter can use a process called hedging, which will be outlined more fully in chapter 22.

EXERCISE 21.1 Revision

1. Identify four factors that make operating globally more complex than operating only in a domestic market.
2. Why are financial influences often classified as 'uncontrollable'?
3. Outline the role played by the foreign exchange market.
4. What is meant by the term 'exchange rate'?
5. Write each of the following exchange rates as a sentence:
   (a) A$1 = US$0.85
   (b) A$1 = US$0.70
   (c) A$1 = US$0.63
   (d) A$1 = US$0.52
   Do the rates (a) to (d), when taken sequentially, show the Australian dollar depreciating or appreciating?
6. Calculate the value of one US dollar for each of the rates in the previous question.
7. What effect do (a) depreciation and (b) appreciation have upon the prices of exports and imports?
8. Explain the possible impact of currency fluctuations upon a domestic business.
9. Distinguish between the international equity market and the international bond market.
10. Predict what would happen if a domestic firm borrowed US$5 million offshore just before a massive depreciation of the Australian dollar compared to the US dollar.

Extension

1. Your business enters into a contract to pay a certain amount of foreign currency to someone in six months. Who bears the risk of currency fluctuation? Explain.
2. FX rates can be found in the business sections of most daily newspapers. Access this information and record the value of the Australian dollar against five other currencies over a three-week period. Comment on the trend.
3. Research the role of the European Union (EU). What is the euro? Outline how these two developments assist free trade between the countries involved in the union.

21.3 Political influences

There are political risks whenever a business sells to an overseas market. As with the financial influences, the political risks need to be carefully assessed and managed. A **political risk** is defined as any political event that results in a drastic change to the country's business environment, and that ultimately has a negative impact on business operations and profit.

*A **political risk** is any political event that results in a drastic change to the country's business environment and that ultimately has a negative impact upon business operations and profit.*

Political risks tend to be greater in countries experiencing social and economic unrest, particularly terrorism, war or other violent conflict. In such situations, businesses may have to find means to directly influence politically powerful people in order to obtain permission to operate in the country.

Of course some political influences could act as incentives, encouraging businesses to relocate. For example, although most governments own businesses, they are privatising them in increasing numbers, even in former communist countries. The process of privatisation offers opportunities for businesses to expand quickly into new markets.

Tension between protectionism and free trade

Protectionism *is the practice of creating artificial barriers to free trade in order to protect domestic industries and jobs.*

The main forms of trade protection measures include:

- *tariffs*
- *import quotas*
- *embargoes*
- *foreign exchange control.*

In 1766, Adam Smith, the founder of modern-day economics, argued that free trade should be the system of international trade adopted by the whole world. Over 230 years later, the debate Smith initiated is hotter than ever. At the centre of this debate is the concept of **protectionism**, creating artificial barriers to free trade, in order to protect domestic industries and jobs.

As outlined in chapter 19, free trade policies are one of the major driving forces for globalisation. At the same time, many people are urging that trade restrictions should be reintroduced or tightened. Politicians, economists, workers and consumers are still debating which policy is correct — free trade or protectionism — with both sides presenting convincing arguments (see figure 21.4).

Protectionism (Trade restrictions)	
Arguments for	**Arguments against**
1. To protect weak domestic industries from foreign 'attackers'	1. Causes higher prices for consumer and producer products
2. To protect domestic jobs	2. Restricts consumer choice (less variety)
3. To protect national security by restricting sale of certain technology	3. Loss of jobs from export-oriented businesses
4. To protect the health of citizens by banning products that do not meet specified health and safety standards	4. Props up inefficient businesses, which is a waste of scarce resources
5. To retaliate against another country's trade restrictions	5. Leads to lower economic growth rates

Figure 21.4 Arguments for and against protectionism

The policy on free trade adopted by a country's government affects business operations. For example, free-trade policies could encourage domestic businesses to expand internationally as previously closed markets open up.

Figure 21.5 US Trade Representative, Robert Zoellick (left), and Australian Minister for Trade, Mark Vaille, announce the conclusion of the Australia–United States Free Trade Agreement (AUSFTA) in 2004.

Free-trade policies could also lead to cheaper foreign-made products entering the domestic market. This would be welcomed by consumers but not by domestic producers, who would face increased competition. However, although protectionism provides a degree of safety for a business in its domestic market, it may restrict domestic businesses from expanding overseas due to similar barriers erected by other countries. This is an ongoing debate.

International organisations and treaties (World Trade Organization)

Since the end of World War II, countries have joined to form a number of international organisations. Any international business manager who plans global expansion must be aware of the existence and functions of these organisations. The actions and decisions of such organisations have an enormous impact upon global businesses. They may provide finance or regulate procedures. They may even initiate policies that result in business opportunities.

The main international organisations are:

- *World Bank (WB).* Businesses supply products to borrowers in bank-financed projects. The lending activities of the World Bank result in billions of dollars being spent each year. Another important function of the World Bank in terms of world trade is that it acts as a centre for resolving difficulties experienced by businesses in overseas countries.
- *International Monetary Fund (IMF).* This organisation's main role is to foster orderly foreign exchange arrangements and a workable international monetary system.
- *Bank for International Settlement (BIS).* This is one of the most discreet financial institutions in the world. Ten times each year, in Switzerland, the central bankers of the main industrialised countries meet to discuss and monitor the global financial system. Their main objective is to provide certainty and stability to the world's financial system.
- ***World Trade Organization (WTO)***. Previously the General Agreement on Tariffs and Trade (GATT), the WTO has become the major international organisation responsible for managing world trade and investment activities, with special reference to international trade laws. Its main goal is to reduce or eliminate tariffs and other barriers to global trade. The WTO has taken central stage over the last decade, promoting its policies of trade liberalisation. It also undertakes a regular review of the trade policies of member nations, presently numbering 134, through a continual process of revising the rules of international trade.

The IMF plays a crucial role in bringing a degree of order and stability to the world's financial system.

World Trade Organization (WTO) *was founded in 1995 to manage world trade and investment activities.*

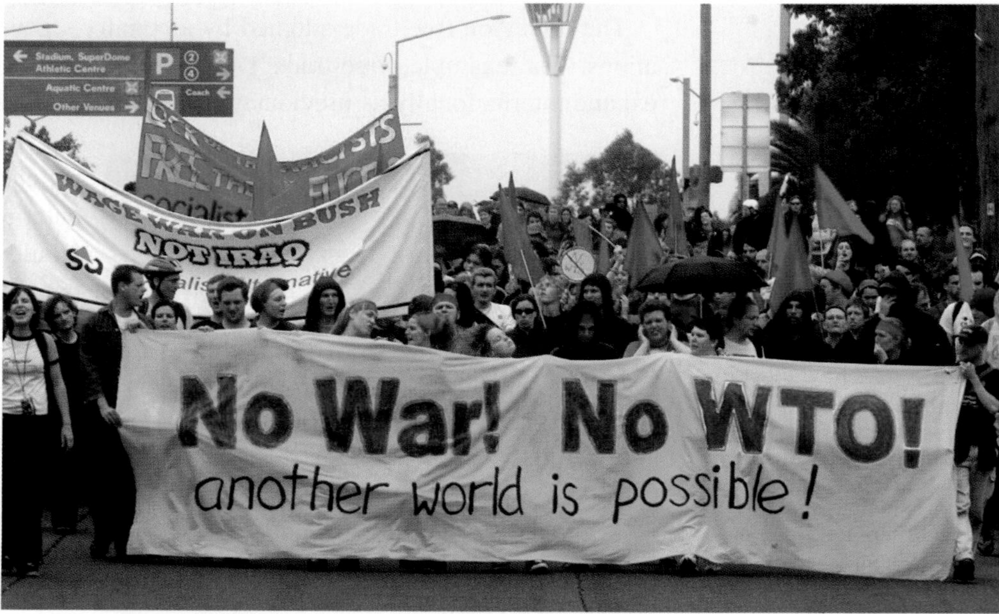

Figure 21.6 Demonstrators use WTO meetings to campaign against what they believe to be the consequences of the WTO agenda — exploitation of foreign labour, loss of national sovereignty and the perpetuation of inequalities in wealth.

Trade agreements and regionalism

A **trade agreement** is a negotiated relationship between countries that regulates trade between them.

An **economic community**, or **trading bloc**, is an organisation of nations formed to promote free trade (the free movement of resources and products) among its members and to create common economic policies.

Regional economic integration or **regionalism** means that there is a focus on securing trade agreements between groups of countries in a geographic region.

The main aim of the WTO is to remove barriers to international trade. On a smaller scale, many nations have joined together in **trade agreements**, which are negotiated relationships that regulate trade between member countries.

Countries that participate in a trade agreement form economic communities. An **economic community**, or **trading bloc**, is an organisation of nations formed to promote free trade (the free movement of resources and products) among its members and to create common economic policies. Trade agreements have fostered the development of regional economic integration; this is effectively globalisation, but on a smaller scale. **Regional economic integration** or **regionalism** means that there is a focus on securing trade agreements between groups of countries in a geographic region.

Various trading blocs and regional trade agreements now exist, with the main ones being:

- *European Union (EU)*. Formed in 1957, this is the oldest regional trading bloc. Today the EU is closer than ever to removing barriers to trade within Europe, having established its own parliament, commission, court and currency (the euro).

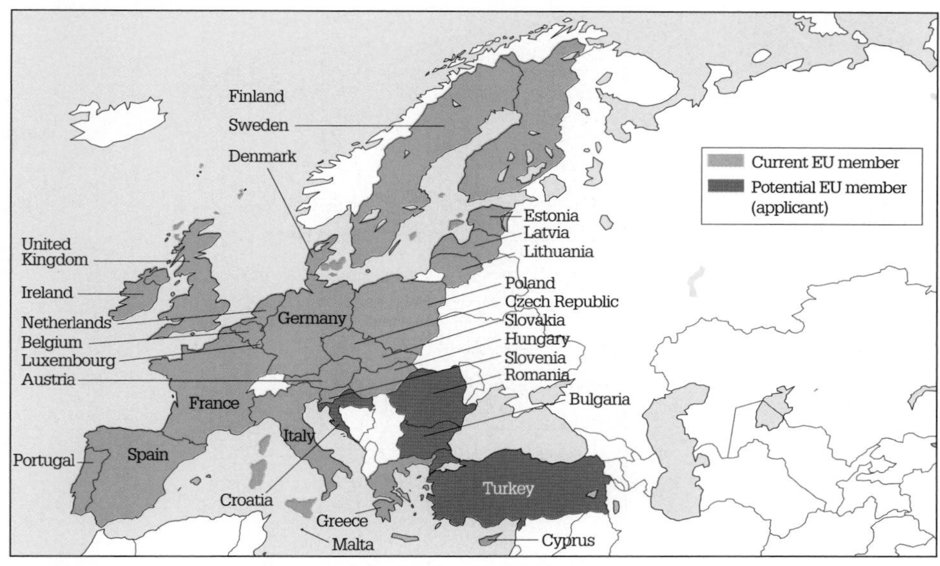

Figure 21.7 Current members of the European Union and nations that have applied for membership

- *North American Free Trade Agreement (NAFTA)*. In 1994, the free-trade zone incorporating Canada, the United States and Mexico was officially established. Over 15 years the economies of these three countries will be integrated, with successive reductions in tariffs.
- *Association of South-East Asian Nations (ASEAN)*. The ASEAN Free Trade Area (AFTA) was formed in 1993, with the aim of creating a common market by the year 2008. Today, approximately 420 million people live in the ASEAN economies, which gives them great potential for future growth.
- *Asia–Pacific Economic Cooperation (APEC)*. At the suggestion of Australia, APEC was established in 1990 in response to the growing interdependence between the economies of the Asia–Pacific region. APEC currently has 21 member states, which currently account for approximately 50 per cent of the world's GDP and 47 per cent of world trade.

The Asia–Pacific region is of utmost importance to Australian businesses. If APEC's goals are achieved, this region will become the world's largest free-trade area, presenting many opportunities to Australian businesses.

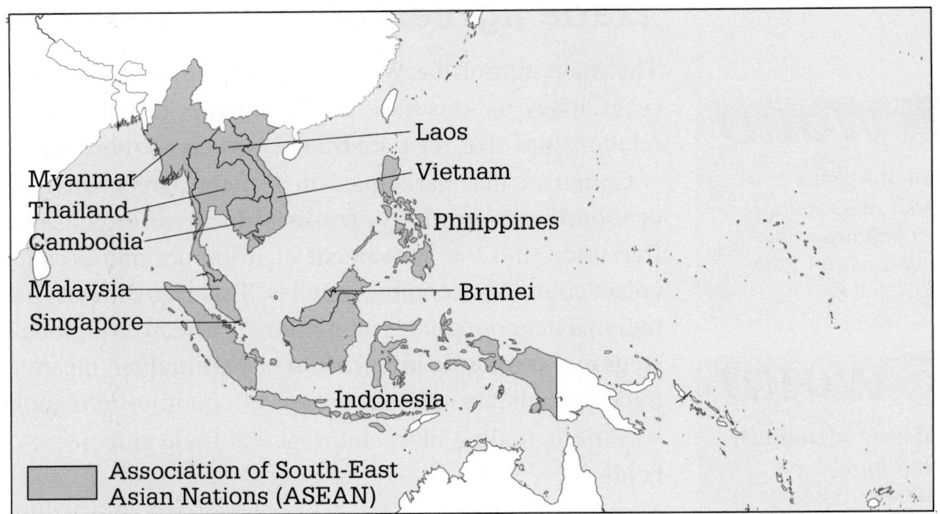

Figure 21.8 ASEAN (AFTA) member countries

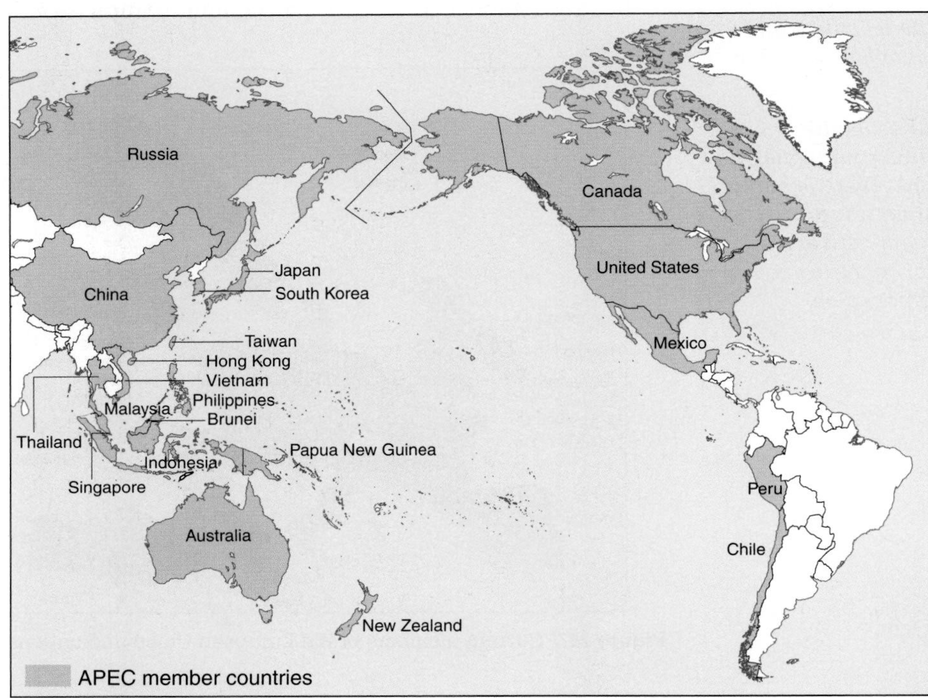

Figure 21.9 Asia–Pacific Economic Cooperation (APEC) member countries

Ultimately, APEC has the potential of creating new market opportunities for businesses in its member nations.

War and civil unrest

As outlined earlier in this chapter, social unrest, that escalates into prolonged civil disturbances or war can have devastating consequences for any international business conducting trade with that country, especially if the business owns production facilities there. In such situations, the safety of personnel needs to be constantly monitored. Should war break out, production facilities may be either destroyed, or taken over by military.

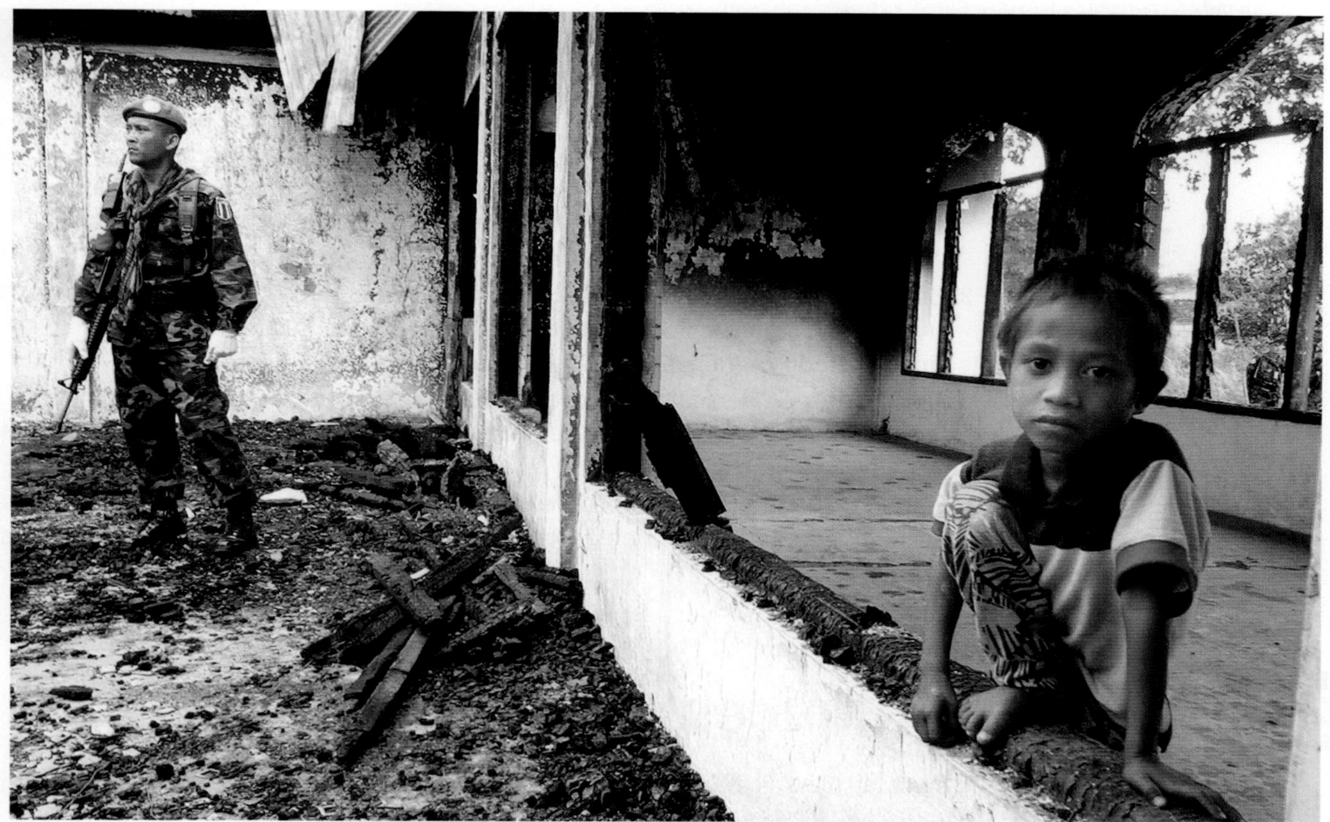

Figure 21.10 War destabilises a country's economy, discouraging foreign investment and creating great financial hardship for its population

Many countries experience periods of severe instability. All international businesses should constantly monitor the level of political risk and instability in the countries in which they do business. Within Australia, the Department of Foreign Affairs and Trade (DFAT) and Austrade provide up-to-date information about the level of political risk for each country of the world.

EXERCISE 21.2 *Revision*

1. What is meant by the term 'political risk'?
2. Illustrate, using examples, how a political influence could act as an incentive to international businesses.
3. Explain the difference between 'free trade' and 'protectionism'.
4. Examine figure 21.4 on page 451. Which of the two sets of arguments do you support? Give reasons for your choice.
5. Why should international business managers be familiar with the roles of some of the world's main international organisations?
6. What is the role of the WTO?
7. Distinguish between a trade agreement and a trading bloc.
8. Identify the reasons for countries forming regional trading blocs.
9. Predict the possible consequences for an Australian electrical engineering business that wishes to expand overseas as a result of the Australia–United States Free Trade Agreement.

Extension

1. You are managing director of a business that has to choose between making a $150 million investment in either Malaysia or Indonesia. The return on the investment is the same for both markets. Assess the risks for both countries. Which country would you choose? Why? In your answer, consider financial, political, legal and social factors.
2. List and describe four of the most common trade barriers used by countries wishing to stop the flow of imports. Illustrate, using examples, the possible impact trade barriers will have on international businesses.
3. Analyse APEC's success in encouraging trade and investment between the member nations. Investigate the reasons for APEC not wanting to establish itself as a free-trade bloc.
4. 'The creation of the World Trade Organization has been a failure. International businesses are still restricted from entering an overseas market on equal terms.' Discuss.

21.4 Legal influences

*The **legal system** of a country refers to the laws, or rules, that regulate behaviour and the procedures used to enforce the laws.*

Global business is affected by many thousands of laws and regulations, because each country has its own unique set of laws, and **legal systems** vary dramatically between countries.

Any global business must be aware of the legal system of the host countries in which their business is conducted. International businesses should rely on the knowledge and expertise of local lawyers in each country in which they operate. In particular, they should be aware of three important issues that can affect the conduct of their operations. These are laws relating to:

- contracts
- dispute resolution
- intellectual property.

Contracts

*A **contract** is a legally enforceable agreement.*

A **contract** is a legally enforceable agreement. It outlines the details of the agreement and the rights and obligations of each of the parties involved. If one of the parties believes that an obligation in the contract has not been fulfilled they will normally resort to contract law.

Contract law, as well as methods for enforcing contracts, varies significantly among countries. Therefore, different types of contract will be used. This is the result of differences in legal traditions over time.

***Civil law** is the world's most common legal system. It is based on a detailed set of laws and is organised into codes that list what is permissible and what is not.*

There are two main legal systems in the world today: common law and **civil law**.

A country's legal system greatly influences the nature of a contract. For example, under a common law system, contracts tend to be very detailed, with all possible eventualities covered. This is because common law is relatively less detailed than civil law. In civil law systems, contracts tend to be shorter and less specific because many of the issues that could arise are already covered in a civil code.

A contract with South Korean businesspeople will not spell out all the details. They regard a written contract as a typically legal document that changes as conditions do.

The Australian wine industry was criticised for many years by French winemakers for intellectual property rights infringement by using French place names, such as Burgundy, Champagne and Beaujolais, in the names of wines. Now the Australian wine industry uses the names of specific grape varieties, such as cabernet, chardonnay and sauvignon blanc, to designate different wine styles. A bottle of 'bubbly' in Australia is no longer sold as 'champagne' but as 'sparkling wine'.

***Intellectual property** refers to property that is created by an individual's intellect.*

*A **patent** is a government grant that gives the inventor exclusive right to make, use or sell, as well as license others to make or sell, a newly invented product or process.*

***Copyright** is the exclusive right of an author, artist, musician or publisher to publish, perform, copy or sell an original work.*

Of course, a country's legal system must be considered in the context of its cultural traditions. For example, a handshake in some cultures is more binding than any legal contract. Contracts in some countries, such as Greece, signal the start of negotiations rather than the end.

Dispute resolutions

As in domestic business, international business may experience conflict. Due to the expense sometimes incurred during a court case, businesses avoid resorting to the legal system. Instead, many international businesses attempt to resolve disputes using less expensive methods, such as negotiation, mediation or arbitration.

If these three methods of dispute resolution fail, then the legal system is the only remaining alternative.

Court solution

When an international business resorts to the courts, it needs to answer three important questions:

1. Which country's legal system applies?
2. In which country should the dispute be settled?
3. How will the final decision be enforced?

As a safety precaution many international business contracts specify answers to these questions. This reduces the uncertainty and cost should a dispute arise. However, if a lengthy court case is necessary then a business may incur high legal fees.

The courts of most major trading nations respect and enforce the conditions of such contracts.

Intellectual property

Intellectual property refers to property, such as a brand name, a new drug formula, a computer program or an artistic work, that is created by an individual's intellect.

It is possible to establish ownership rights over intellectual property through intellectual property rights, including patents, trademarks and copyright. Weak protection of intellectual property rights can cost international businesses a great deal of money. For example, in China the pirating of films, music and computer software is estimated to cost the United States alone approximately $US3 billion each year. Many of the Chinese factories producing the pirated copies are owned by the government.

Intellectual property rights protection in many developing countries is weak.

Patents, trademarks and copyrights

A **patent** gives the inventor exclusive right to make, use or sell, as well as license others to make or sell, a newly invented product or process. A trademark is a brand name or design that is officially registered; for example, McDonald's, Levi's, Sony and Stussy. **Copyright** is the exclusive right of an author, artist, musician or publisher to publish, perform, copy or sell an original work.

There are presently several international treaties that give some protection of intellectual property rights. These include:

- International Convention for the Protection of Industrial Property, often referred to as the Paris Convention
- Berne Convention for the Protection of Literary and Artistic Works
- Universal Copyright Convention.

Treaties such as these provide some protection, although not all countries have signed the treaties. Further, enforcing any infringements is quite difficult because some signatories have adopted a lax attitude.

Figure 21.11 Examples of trademarks

21.5 Social and cultural influences

International business is conducted on the world stage. This results in people working in societies and cultures that differ from their own. Almost every aspect of a business's international dealings (including contract negotiation, marketing decisions, human resource management policies and production and finance) may be affected by differences in culture.

__Social and cultural characteristics__ are the values, beliefs, rules, techniques and customs that are shared among a society's people.

Social and cultural characteristics (also called sociocultural characteristics) are the values, beliefs, rules, techniques and customs that are shared among a society's people. It is imperative that international businesspeople fully understand and appreciate the unique characteristics of the countries they deal with. Failing to do so may result in either embarrassment or lost business opportunities.

Sunbeam Corporation released a mist-producing hair curling wand called 'Mist-Stick' onto the German market. After an expensive advertising campaign Sunbeam discovered that mist means 'excrement' in German.

Languages

Spoken languages

The most obvious sociocultural difference is the means of communication, especially the spoken language. Not being able to understand a foreign language may prevent a person from fully understanding a country's culture. Language can be a difficult barrier to overcome.

Because English is a second language for many people, it is becoming the language of international business. However, most people prefer to converse in their own language, and being able to speak the local language helps establish a better relationship and build the rapport essential for any business deal.

International businesses may make use of translators, although misunderstandings may still occur (see the Biz Fact on the left) and cause embarrassment.

__Non-verbal communication__ refers to the messages we convey through body movements, facial expressions and the physical distance between individuals.

Non-verbal language

While differences in the spoken language may be addressed by a business, it may be more difficult to understand the unspoken or non-verbal language of manners and customs. **Non-verbal communication** refers to the messages we convey through body movements, facial expressions and the physical distance between individuals.

Extreme care should be taken with non-verbal communication, because gestures can have different meanings in different cultures. For example, making a circle with the thumb and the forefinger is a friendly gesture in Australia, but it means 'you are worth nothing' in France and acts as a vulgar sexual invitation in Greece and Turkey. Failing to understand non-verbal gestures can lead to difficult situations.

Figure 21.12 Non-verbal language includes such gestures as bowing politely.

Tastes

Sociocultural differences between countries are also reflected by people's tastes. Tastes refer to a particular liking for something, such as foods, clothes and music. Differences in tastes will have practical implications for product marketing, especially product design, packaging and advertising. International businesses need to be aware of how local tastes influence the demand for their products, adapting the products to suit local preferences.

In response to Japanese tastes, the Australian Ricegrowers' Cooperative Limited has recently begun exporting a newly developed rice to Japan. Called the Opus rice variety, it was aimed specifically at the Japanese market. Opus features softness after cooking, a characteristic valued by Japanese customers.

Religion

Awareness of a business colleague's religious traditions is essential for building a lasting relationship. Those traditions may influence what a person can and cannot eat, as well as particular holy days and schedules that are very important to any devout follower. Being insensitive or unsympathetic to religious traditions could cause lasting damage to a business relationship.

Religious holidays and rituals may affect the times at which business meetings can be arranged. When members of different religious groups work together there may be some tension within the group. International managers need to respect the religious beliefs of others and adapt business practices to the religious constraints of other cultures.

Figure 21.13 Religious differences must be accepted.

Varying business practices and ethics

Business practices vary the world over. International managers must research the acceptable business practices and ethics of the countries with which they wish to conduct business so as to avoid awkward situations, embarrassments and insults. There are no rights or wrongs when it comes to these practices, only cross-cultural differences.

The Department of Foreign Affairs and Trade offers free advice to Australian business managers who want to learn about the local customs and standards of behaviour for countries with which they trade.

An international business manager has to adapt to his or her host's way of doing things to ensure business success (see the Snapshot 'Customs and traditions — some useful information for the global businessperson').

Customs and traditions — some useful information for the global businessperson

- Don't pass documents with the left hand in Saudi Arabia. The left hand is considered unclean.
- It is best not to discuss business over dinner in France.
- In Spain, business meetings are very formal affairs and business is not discussed until after dinner.
- Saudi Arabians greet each other with kisses on the face and forehead and walk hand-in-hand.
- New Zealand businesspeople talking in a group will stand about 50 centimetres apart.
- In Saudi Arabia the normal conversational distance is 25 to 30 centimetres.
- Australians tend to dislike silence during meetings. In Japan it may indicate that a person is thinking and further conversation would be inappropriate.
- Indonesians place less emphasis on time; what cannot be done today can be done tomorrow.
- Exposing the soles of your shoes is taboo in Muslim countries.

- Businesspeople in Great Britain place a lot of importance on proper etiquette and protocol.
- Placing your hand on someone's head in Singapore or Thailand is highly offensive as the head is considered sacred.
- Gift giving in many Asian countries is considered very important.
- When having a meal in Egypt it is considered very impolite not to leave some food on your plate.
- It is considered rude to leave any food on your plate when eating in Malaysia or Singapore.
- In many Asian countries, touching someone is considered an invasion of privacy but in some European countries it is taken as a gesture of friendship and warmth.
- Japanese businesspeople like to take their time over negotiations. Australians prefer to come to the point straight away, which may cause offence.

The following are some Japanese customs.

- Do not point at another person. This is considered very rude and hostile.
- Avoid direct eye contact. It can be perceived as an intrusion into the other person's space.
- Shake hands or bow, depending which gesture is offered by the person you are greeting.
- Present a business card after being introduced.
- Personal relationships are more important than written contracts.
- Japanese cover their face with their hands when they are embarrassed.

SNaPSHOT *Question*

Why do you think it is important to learn as much as possible about potential clients' customs and traditions.

Gifts

One area of business practice that can cause real difficulties is that of gifts. The 'language' or etiquette of gift giving varies among cultures and a businessperson should understand the etiquette involved. For example, in Japan gifts are always wrapped and presented in a humble manner. The recipient is not expected to open the gift in front of the giver. Japanese gifts should never contain four of anything because the word for 'four' is similar to the word meaning 'death'.

Gift giving can be tricky but if a business relationship is to last it must be conducted according to local etiquette.

Bribes

Should an international business pay bribes to government officials to gain market access, a favour, a large order or protection? This is one of the most sensitive ethical issues faced when conducting business in some countries. Many Australians believe that bribery is corrupt. However, in many countries payments to government officials are a way of life. There is often a very small distinction between someone requesting a 'gift' and demanding a 'bribe'.

EXERCISE 21.3 *Revision*

1. What is meant by the term 'legal system'?
2. Briefly outline the purpose of a contract.
3. What can a business do to reduce the uncertainty and costs should a dispute about a contract arise?
4. Explain the difference between 'intellectual property' and 'intellectual property rights'.
5. Assume you are a composer and your latest song is being pirated by a business operating out of an overseas country. What type of intellectual property right protects your artistic work? List the international treaties that could provide you with some protection.
6. Use the following words in a sentence to explain their meaning.
   (a) social and cultural
   (b) non-verbal communication
7. Why is it important for an international businessperson to understand the meaning of non-verbal gestures of the society in which the business operates?
8. An Australian exporting business recently introduced a set of four kitchen utensils packaged in a white and black container to sell in some Asian countries. The product failed because it was associated with death. How could this mistake have been avoided?
9. Where could an international manager access information about the business etiquette practices of a particular country?
10. Prepare a summary of this chapter. A summary condenses the important issues and concepts presented in the chapter. Go to www.jaconline.com.au/businessstudies3e to compare your finished summary with the one provided for this textbook.

Extension

1. The World Trade Organization provides information regarding the protection of intellectual property. Provide a brief description of the two main types of intellectual property right. Go to www.jaconline.com.au/businessstudies3e and click on the WTO weblink for this textbook.
2. 'Culture is pervasive in all international business activities.' Discuss.
3. Assume your export consultancy firm has been asked to prepare a cultural analysis for a potential market. Your client wants to direct export dried Australian mangoes. In groups of three or four, select a country to act as the potential market and prepare the analysis. In particular you will need to report on the following areas:
   - language
   - tastes and preferences
   - religion
   - business practices and etiquette.
4. Discuss some reasons why it is probably best to seek an out-of-court settlement in international business legal disputes rather than to sue.
5. Justify the existence of intellectual property rights. Who gains and who loses from enforcement of these laws? Discuss the advantages and disadvantages to the international businessperson arising from the existence of the international agreements on patents, copyrights and trademarks.

22 Managing global business

22.1 Introduction

There are a number of both private and government organisations to which a business manager may turn for assistance with a particular aspect of managing a global business. The Australian government operates an important organisation to encourage international trade and investment. This organisation is called Austrade (the Australian Trade Commission).

Managing a global business is a challenge, but can also be a rewarding experience.

Austrade's main purpose is to help Australian exporters 'take their products to the world'. Austrade also provides a comprehensive range of information and advice about exporting and foreign investment, and provides a number of specialised services to encourage and assist Australian exporters. Of prime importance is Austrade's ability to offer assistance on financial, marketing and operational management issues (see figure 22.1).

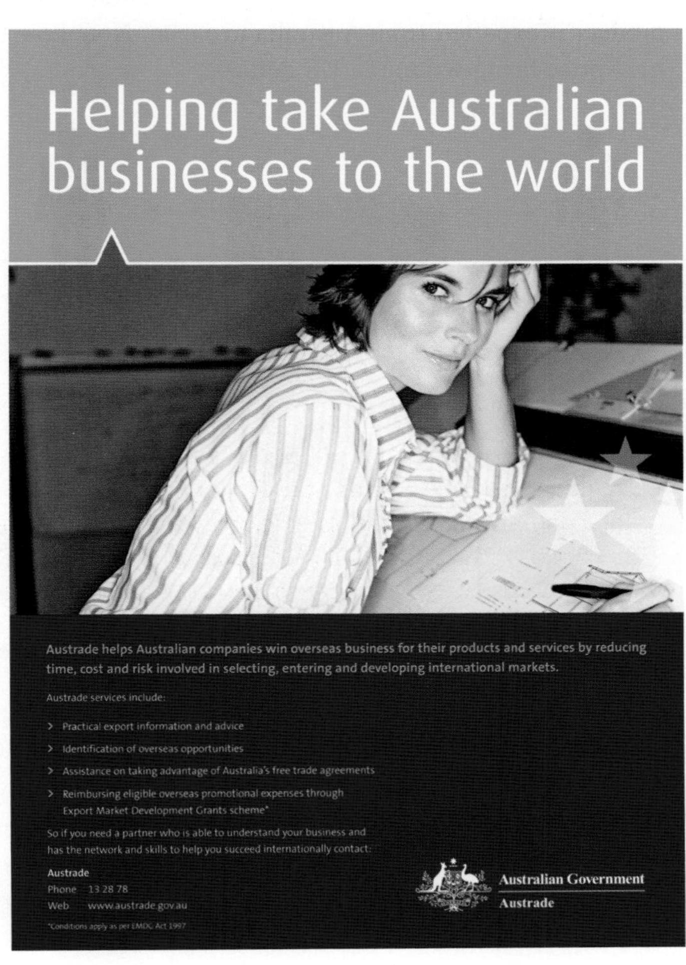

Figure 22.1 Austrade offers assistance on financial, marketing and operational management issues as well as assessing a business's export readiness.

22.2 Financial management

A number of larger financial institutions offer a range of services to facilitate the financial management of global business.

Global business brings extra concerns for financial managers — in particular, currency exchange fluctuations, methods of payment, credit risks and insurance. In addition, financial managers must consider the financing of their operations.

Method of payment and credit risks

One of the most crucial aspects of financial management is to select an appropriate method of payment. Payment is complicated by the fact that the business may be dealing with someone they have never seen, who speaks another language, uses a different monetary system, who abides by a different legal system and/or who may prove difficult to deal with if problems occur later on. One major worry for the exporter is that if the products are shipped before payment is received, there may be no guarantee that the importer will pay.

On the other hand, the buyer is faced with a similar situation. The importer may worry that if payment is sent before the products are received, there is similarly no guarantee that the exporter will send the products. This dilemma is as old as global business itself. Neither party completely trusts the other.

To solve this problem, a method of payment using a third party, whom both parties trust, is required. This third party is normally a bank, which acts in an intermediary role. Figure 22.2 provides a simple explanation of the payment procedures when a product is exported from Australia to Japan. Note how both parties agree to the contract price being written in US dollars.

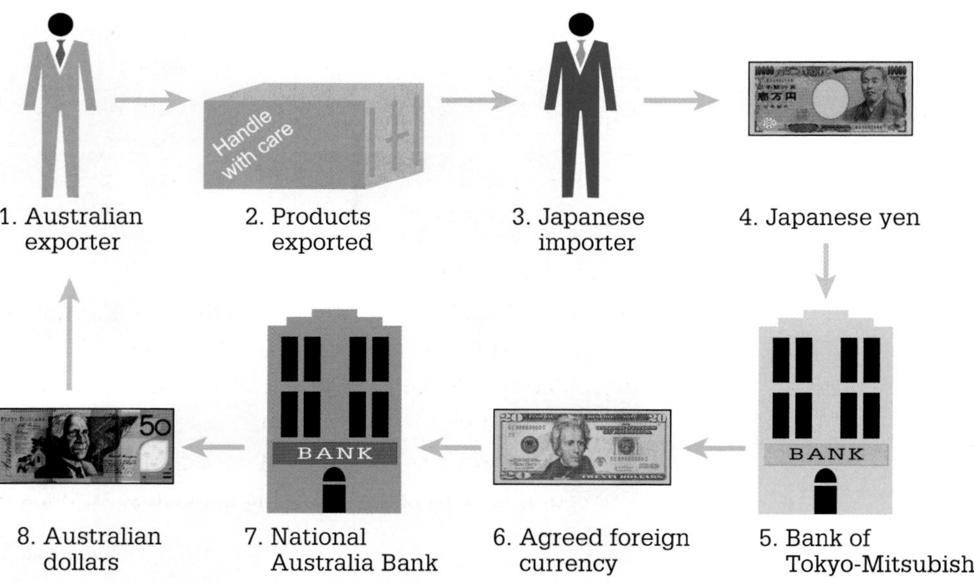

Figure 22.2 Simple international payment system showing the intermediary role of banks

There are five basic methods of payment a business can select:

- payment in advance
- letter of credit
- clean payment
- bill of exchange
- open account.

The option selected will largely depend on the business's assessment of the importer's ability to pay — that is, the importer's creditworthiness. Of course, as with all financial transactions, each method carries varying degrees of risk, especially when credit payments are involved (see figure 22.3).

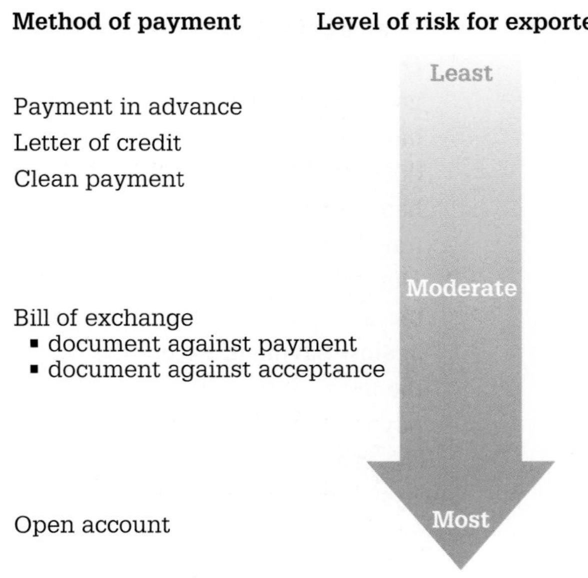

Figure 22.3 Degree of credit risk for different methods of payment

The following section discusses the different methods of payment in order of increasing risk to the exporter.

Payment in advance

*The **payment in advance** method allows the exporter to receive payment and then arrange for the goods to be sent.*

*A **letter of credit** is a commitment by the importer's bank, which promises to pay the exporter a specified amount when the documents proving shipment of the goods are presented.*

***Clean payment (remittance)** occurs when the payment is sent to, but not received by, the exporter before the goods are transported.*

The **payment in advance** method allows the exporter to receive payment and then arrange for the goods to be sent. This method exposes the exporter to virtually no risk and is often used if the other party is a subsidiary or when the credit worthiness of the buyer is uncertain. However, very few importers will agree to these terms because it exposes them to the most risk. Furthermore, they have no guarantee that they will receive what they ordered.

Letter of credit

A **letter of credit** is a commitment by the importer's bank, which promises to pay the exporter a specified amount when the documents proving shipment of the goods are presented. In all but exceptional circumstances, once the bank has made such a commitment it cannot be withdrawn.

Only payment in advance offers less risk and, for this reason, a letter of credit is very popular with exporters. This is because it relies on the overseas bank rather than the importer.

Clean payment (clean remittance)

This is the easiest and quickest method of settling an international transaction. **Clean payment** (remittance) occurs when the payment is sent to, but not received by, the exporter before the goods are transported. Such an arrangement requires complete trust between both parties.

Clearly in this method the risk to the exporter is minimal, but unfortunately it is not a method of payment favoured by importers.

Bills of exchange

*A **bill of exchange** is a document drawn up by the exporter demanding payment from the importer at a specified time.*

A **bill of exchange** is a document drawn up by the exporter demanding payment from the importer at a specified time. This method of payment is one of the most widely used and allows the exporter to maintain control over the goods until payment is either made or guaranteed.

There are two types of bill of exchange:

1. *Document (bill) against payment*. Using this method, the importer can collect the goods only *after* paying for them. The exporter draws up a bill of exchange with his or her Australian bank and sends it to the importer's bank along with a set of documents that will allow the importer to collect the goods. The importer's bank hands over the documents only after payment is made. The importer's bank then transfers the funds to the exporter's bank.
2. *Document (bill) against acceptance*. Using this method, the importer may collect the goods *before* paying for them. The same process applies as with documents against payment, except the importer must sign only acceptance of the goods and the terms of the bill of exchange to receive the documents that allow him or her to pay for the goods at a later date.

The risk of non-payment or payment delays when using a bill of exchange is always greater than for a letter of credit. However, documents against acceptance expose the exporter to much greater risk than documents against payment. The risk with documents against payment is that the importer may not collect the documents nor pay for the goods. With documents against acceptance there is the risk the importer may delay payment or not pay at all.

Open credit (account)

***Open credit** allows the importer access to the goods, with a promise to repay at a later date.*

This method of payment does not involve any letters of credit or bills of exchange. It operates in exactly the same way as a credit sale within the domestic market. **Open credit** allows the importer access to the goods, with a promise to repay at a later date. This method of exposes the exporter to the greatest amount of risk as the exporter is totally reliant on the importer's ability and willingness to pay.

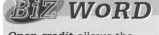

Countertrade is becoming more popular as a trading or payment system, similar to bartering.

Figure 22.4 Selling overseas carries certain risks.

Hedging

*The **spot exchange rate** is the value of one currency in another currency on a particular day.*

***Hedging** is the process of minimising the risk of currency fluctuations.*

When two parties agree to exchange currency and finalise a deal immediately, the transaction is referred to as a spot exchange. Exchange rates determining such 'on-the-spot' transactions are referred to as spot exchange rates. The **spot exchange rate** is the value of one currency in another currency on a particular day. Therefore, when an Australian tourist in Tokyo goes to a bank to convert her dollars into yen, the exchange rate is the spot rate for the day.

Although there are situations when it is necessary to use a spot rate, it may not be the most favourable rate. As was explained in the preceding chapter, exchange rates can change constantly. Such currency fluctuations can be a cause of real concern for an exporter. However, it is possible for businesses to minimise the risk of currency fluctuations. This process is referred to as **hedging**.

Hedging helps reduce the level of uncertainty involved with international financial transactions.

Natural hedging

A business may adopt a number of strategies to eliminate or minimise the risk of foreign exchange exposure. In this way the business provides itself with a natural hedge. For example, the range of natural hedges adopted by Kohler BioGenetics Limited includes:

- establishing offshore subsidiaries
- arranging for import payments and export receipts denominated in the same foreign currency. Therefore, any losses from a movement in the exchange rate will be offset by gains from the other.
- implementing marketing strategies that attempt to reduce the price sensitivity of the exported products
- insisting on both import and export contracts denominated in Australian dollars. This effectively transfers the risk to the buyer (importer).

Financial instrument hedging

Apart from such natural hedges there are a growing number of financial products available, called derivatives, that can be used to minimise or spread the risk of exchange rate fluctuations.

Derivatives

To minimise the financial risks involved with exporting, financial institutions are continually developing new types of products, collectively referred to as derivatives. Derivatives are simple financial instruments that may be used to lessen the exporting risks associated with currency fluctuations.

Derivatives, if used unwisely, can be as dangerous as the risks against which they are supposed to protect. For example, in 2000 the Australian business Energex Technologies Pty Ltd came close to collapse as a result of having inappropriately used derivatives to hedge itself against changes in oil prices.

The three main derivatives available for exporters include:

- forward exchange contracts
- option contracts
- swap contracts.

Forward exchange contract

A **forward exchange contract** is a contract to exchange one currency for another currency at an agreed exchange rate on a future date, usually after a period of 30, 90 or 180 days. This means that the bank guarantees the exporter, within the set time period, a fixed rate of exchange for the money generated from the sale of the exported goods.

Options contract

Foreign currency options provide another strategy for risk management. An **option** gives the buyer (option holder) the right, but not the obligation, to buy or sell foreign currency at some time in the future.

Option holders are protected from unfavourable exchange rate fluctuations, yet maintain the opportunity for gain should exchange rate movements be favourable.

Swap contract

Since its introduction in the 1980s, swaps have become a very popular financial instrument for businesses wanting to hedge. A **currency swap** is an agreement to exchange currency in the spot market with an agreement to reverse the transaction in the future. It involves a spot sale of one currency together with a forward repurchase of the currency at a specified date in the future. For example, swapping $50 million Australian dollars for US dollars now and an agreement to reverse the swap within three months.

Businesses also use currency swaps when they need to raise finance in a currency issued by a country in which they are not well known and are, therefore, forced to pay a higher interest rate than would be available to a better-known borrower or a local business.

For example, a medium-sized Australian business may need Japanese yen, but even though it is a reputable business and has a good credit rating, it may not be well known in Japan. If it can find, or if a broker or bank can team it with, a Japanese business that wants Australian dollars, the swap would work as follows. The Australian business would borrow Australian dollars in Australia, where it is well known and can arrange a loan at cheaper interest rates; the Japanese business would borrow yen in Japan for the same reason. They would then agree to swap the currencies and repay each other's loan; that is, the Japanese business would repay the Australian dollar loan, while the Australian business would repay the Japanese yen loan.

The main advantage of a swap contract is that it allows the business to alter its exposure to exchange fluctuations without discarding the original transaction.

*A **forward exchange contract** is a contract to exchange one currency for another currency at an agreed exchange rate on a future date, usually after a period of 30, 90 or 180 days.*

*An **option** gives the buyer (option holder) the right, but not the obligation, to buy or sell foreign currency at some time in the future.*

*A **currency swap** is an agreement to exchange currency in the spot market with an agreement to reverse the transaction in the future.*

Market research shows that many small- to medium-sized exporters hesitate in taking on large deals because of exchange rate concerns. A large order can often put an exporter under great financial pressure, especially if they are unfamiliar with the process of hedging.

Cash flow is one of the biggest challenges facing small and growing exporters. In an ideal world, exporters would be able to build their turnover with the protection of pre-payment or letter of credit terms.

Insurance

As previously outlined, selling on the global market involves varying degrees of risk, especially when different payment methods are involved.

However, it is possible to insure against payment and financing risks by using the services of Export Finance and Insurance Corporation (EFIC), a federal government agency. EFIC's role is to use its insurance and finance products to help increase Australia's exports. It does this by providing Australian businesses with internationally competitive insurance and finance services, particularly for countries, businesses and contracts that the commercial insurance and financial markets may not be prepared to cover.

Other types of insurance available to exporters include the following:

- *marine insurance* — covering shipment by road, rail and air as well as sea
- *product liability insurance* — protecting the manufacturer and exporter from liability due to damage caused by the use of a product
- *currency risk insurance* — protecting the exporter from losses due to currency fluctuations. To cover this risk a business enters into a forward exchange contract with a bank.

Obtaining finance

Any businesses wanting to sell overseas, undertake foreign investment or relocate production facilities will probably require access to finance.

Australian businesses have a number of options in this regard. Finance may be arranged using the services of either domestic or international financial institutions.

Domestic capital market

The majority of Australian banks and non-bank financial institutions all have facilities for organising finance. For example, the National Australia Bank has its own international business specialists who provide advice, arrange finance, draw up letters of credit and undertake forex arrangements.

International capital market

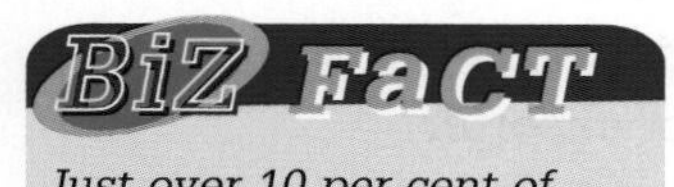

Just over 10 per cent of enterprises with a turnover of less than $20 million have had to forgo a large export order because they could not get access to the working capital required.

If a business decides to borrow overseas rather than domestically, it will need to use the services of financial institutions that make up the international capital market. These financial institutions play a specialised role in accessing finance from a wide range of sources. Also, they are accustomed to dealing with businesses wishing to expand globally.

International banks are important to the functioning of the forex markets. They also provide:

- finance for exporting and importing
- working capital loans
- cash management services
- finance for mergers and joint ventures between foreign and domestic businesses.

Because of their extensive global network these international banks can access and transfer large amounts of money around the globe whenever it is required. Some of the larger international banks include: Bank of America, Bankers Trust, Banque Nationale de Paris, Chase Manhattan, HSBC, Bank of Tokyo-Mitsubishi and Deutsche Bank.

Eurocurrency market

*A **eurocurrency** is the currency of one country that is placed in a bank in another country.*

A **eurocurrency** is the currency of one country that is placed in a bank in another country. The four main eurocurrencies are the United States dollar, the German deutschmark, the British pound and the Japanese yen. As these are the currencies of the major economies of the world, one of them is usually nominated as the currency of choice when undertaking a eurocurrency arrangement. The eurocurrency makes offshore borrowing easier because it allows businesses to access foreign currency from within their own country.

EXERCISE 22.1 *Revision*

1. Examine figure 22.1 on page 463. Identify four ways that Austrade can assist Australian exporting businesses.
2. Go to www.jaconline.com.au/businessstudies3e and click on Westpac's ImpExTrade Banking Online weblink for this textbook. Explain how this service can facilitate the financial management of Australian businesses selling globally.
3. Go to www.jaconline.com.au/businessstudies3e and click on the Austrade weblink for this textbook and answer the following questions:
   (a) What is Austrade?
   (b) What is Austrade's mission statement?
   (c) Briefly outline how Austrade assists Australian businesses.
   (d) What is the EMDG scheme?
4. List some of the main financial risks associated with exporting overseas.
5. Explain how a lack of mutual trust between the exporter and importer may be overcome.
6. Copy the following table into your notebook. Show the five basic methods of payment for exports and how each method works. The first one has been completed for you.

Method of payment	How it works
1. Payment in advance	▪ Exporter receives payment and then sends goods ▪ No risk for exporter ▪ Few importers use this method
2. Letter of credit	
3. Clean payment	
4. Bill of exchange (a) against payment (b) against acceptance	
5. Open credit	

7. What is meant by the terms 'spot exchange rate' and 'hedging'?
8. Identify three natural hedge strategies a business could implement.
9. What is meant by the term 'derivatives'?
10. Compare and contrast forward exchange contracts and options contracts.
11. What is the main advantage of a swap contract?
12. An Australian business manager would like to export electronic scanners. However, she is concerned about currency fluctuations. Explain how this risk could be reduced.
13. An Australian business hopes to establish two new operating plants in Malaysia and Thailand, but it is experiencing some difficulties in raising the necessary finance for the projects. Outline the range of domestic and international sources of finance the business could use.
14. What is a 'eurocurrency'? List the four main currencies nominated when undertaking a eurocurrency arrangement.

Extension

1. Compare the advantages and disadvantages of bills of exchange, letters of credit and open account.
2. Go to www.jaconline.com.au/businessstudies3e and click on the EFIC weblink for this textbook and prepare a two-page pamphlet outlining:
   (a) EFIC's mission
   (b) EFIC's role
   (c) two payment risk products
   (d) two financing risk products
   (e) a market grade for a country.
3. Futures and options are two other types of derivatives. Research how these two financial instruments help reduce the risk of exporting.

22.3 Marketing

A business's marketing plan — the strategies it uses to achieve its marketing objectives — must be modified and adapted to suit overseas markets. Within each foreign market, the business will be faced with a marketing environment and target markets that differ from the domestic scene. Product, pricing, promotion and distribution need to be adapted accordingly.

Many transnational corporations (TNCs) adopt a global marketing approach that involves developing marketing strategies as if the entire globe were one large market (see figure 22.5). Alternatively, some businesses believe the marketing mix should be customised to take into account differences among countries' cultures, religion and tastes.

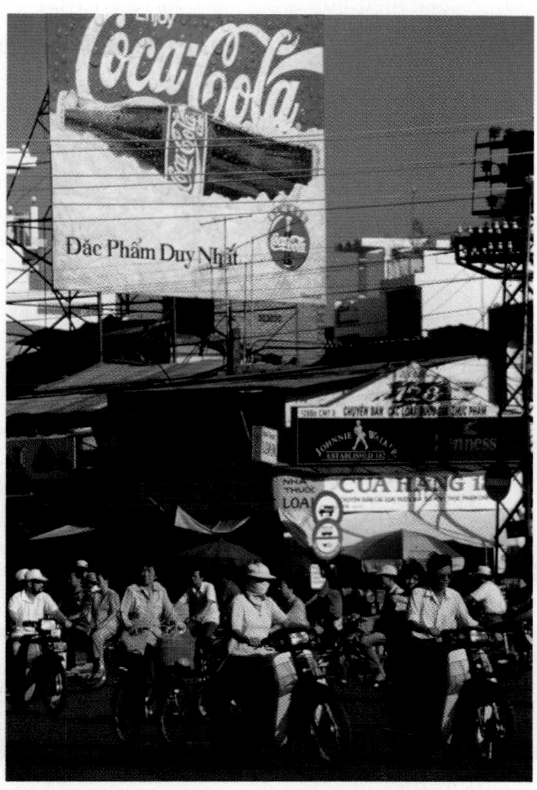

Figure 22.5 Coca-Cola — a global marketing approach

Irrespective of which approach is adopted, all businesses marketing on a global scale need to rely on market research so that they may understand the complexities of the international marketing environment before they design the marketing mix.

General Electric once had a shipment of electrical goods refused entrance to Saudi Arabia because the electrical cords were six feet long instead of the required two metres (6 feet 6 inches).

Research of market

What should a business know before it decides to engage in international marketing? First, it needs information to make specific marketing decisions, such as the price to charge, the type of packaging necessary, the distribution channel to use and any product characteristics needing modification. Second, information about the country's economic, political, social and cultural features should be gathered.

PepsiCo makes local soft drinks such as Shani, a currant-and-blackberry soda popular in the Middle East during Ramadan, the Muslim holy month.

Gathering secondary data should be the first step in analysing a foreign market. Sources of information include government publications, international organisations, such as the United Nations and the World Trade Organization, specialist trade magazines, banks, international chambers of commerce and private consulting firms.

Marketing managers may also need primary data. Although this is more time consuming to collect, its main advantage is that it may be modified to meet the needs of a specific country. This market research data can provide valuable insights into a specific market's cultural and economic features. After gathering and analysing secondary and primary data, marketing managers should plan a marketing strategy.

BiZ WORD

***Global branding** is the worldwide use of a name, term, symbol or logo to identify products of one seller and differentiate them from those of the competitor.*

Global branding

We are surrounded by global products all carrying global brand names. **Global branding** is the worldwide use of a name, term, symbol or logo to identify products of one seller and differentiate them from those of competitors.

Businesses are increasingly using global branding for a number of reasons:

- It can be cost effective because one advertisement can be used in a number of locations.
- It provides a uniform worldwide image.
- The successful brand name can be linked to new products being introduced into the market.

Figure 22.6 An example of global branding

A successful brand is one of the most valuable resources a company has. For example, the value of Kodak, Sony, McDonald's, Coca-Cola, Mercedes-Benz, Kellogg's and Nike is indisputable. Global branding equates to global recognition, irrespective of the language barrier (see figure 22.6).

Once a business has established its name, it usually attempts to market the brand globally. Even if the business has to modify the product to suit local conditions, such as when Fuji Xerox changes the language keys on the control panel of its photocopiers or when Ford modifies the steering wheel from left- to right-hand drive, the companies will not alter the brand name on their products.

Standardisation and differentiation

*A **standardised approach** is an international marketing strategy that assumes the way the product is used and the needs it satisfies are the same the world over.*

As global marketing increases, businesses are faced with a difficulty: should they use a standardised or differentiated marketing strategy or a combination?

A **standardised approach** is an international marketing strategy that assumes the way the product is used and the needs it satisfies are the same the world over. Therefore, the marketing mix will be the same in all markets — that is, globalised. It is a case of 'one marketing plan fits all'. Examples of standardised products are electrical equipment, videotapes, soft drink, rock music, cosmetics, movies and fast foods.

This strategy offers obvious cost savings to businesses: production runs may be larger, thereby achieving economies of scale; research and development costs are reduced; spare parts and after-sales service are simplified; promotion strategies may be standardised; and any evaluation and modification of the plan is a much simpler task.

In spite of these advantages, many businesses find it necessary either to modify the existing marketing mix or develop a new one when entering an overseas market. In doing so they are adopting a differentiated approach. A **differentiated approach** (also called a **local approach**) is an international marketing strategy that assumes the way the product is used and the needs it satisfies are different between countries.

*A **local** or **differentiated approach** is an international marketing strategy that assumes the way the product is used and the needs it satisfies are different between countries.*

Adopting this philosophy requires customising the marketing plan to fit the economic, political and sociocultural characteristics of the target country.

Of course, it is possible for a business to adopt a middle path — that is, a combination of the two approaches. One company to do this successfully is McDonald's. Although it has standardised its name, logo, production methods and much of its menu, there are local variations. For example, McDonald's serves beer in France and Germany, sake in Japan and noodles in the Philippines.

Over the last decade it has become apparent that the standardised approach is being used more frequently than the differentiated approach.

22.4 Operations

As the number of businesses entering global markets increases, global competition increases. To remain competitive, businesses are forced to find ways to reduce costs of production and improve their products. One solution is to examine different sourcing methods.

Sourcing

Global businesses face **sourcing decisions**; these are decisions about whether they should make or buy the resources that are needed to create their products.

***Sourcing decisions** are made about whether a business should make or buy the resources that are needed to create its own products.*

***Outsourcing production** occurs when a business buys component parts from either a domestic or overseas supplier.*

***Vertical integration** refers to the expansion of a business's production in different but related areas.*

When **outsourcing production**, a business will buy component parts from either a domestic or overseas supplier in order to obtain:

- lower prices
- higher quality and better designed components
- more advanced technology.

In the manufacture of sports shoes, industry outsourcing has been taken to extremes. Companies such as Reebok and Nike do not manufacture any of their shoes — all production has been outsourced, mainly to factories based in countries where there is cheap labour.

However, if a business decides to make the component parts itself, it must determine the extent to which it will vertically integrate production. **Vertical integration** refers to the expansion of a business's production in different but related areas. This happens, for example, when a computer assembly factory takes over a silicon chip manufacturing plant and a plastics factory.

The aim of such a strategy is to cut costs, gain economies of scale and raise profitability. Businesses constantly face 'make or buy decisions', especially when the product being produced is highly complex. For example, the typical car contains about 11 000 components. Because of this, most car manufacturers produce some components and outsource the rest.

Global web (components produced in different countries)

As we mentioned in the previous section, businesses are facing increasing competition, and are being forced to adopt strategies that reduce the costs of production. One popular strategy is for firms to create a **global web** of production sites located around the world. Each site specialises in the part of the production process that it can most efficiently perform (see figure 22.7). The result is a network of cost-effective locations all contributing to the final product.

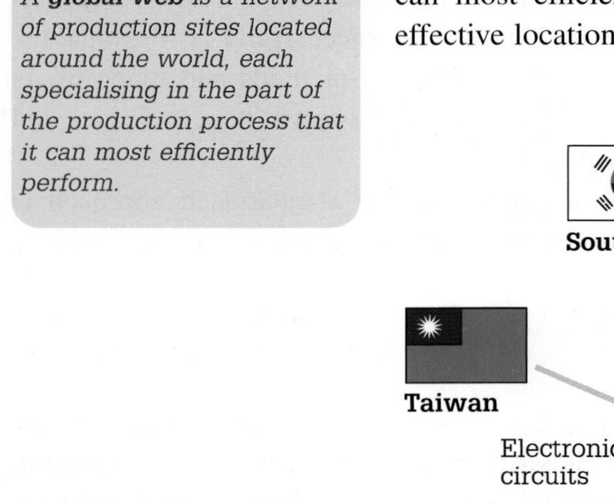

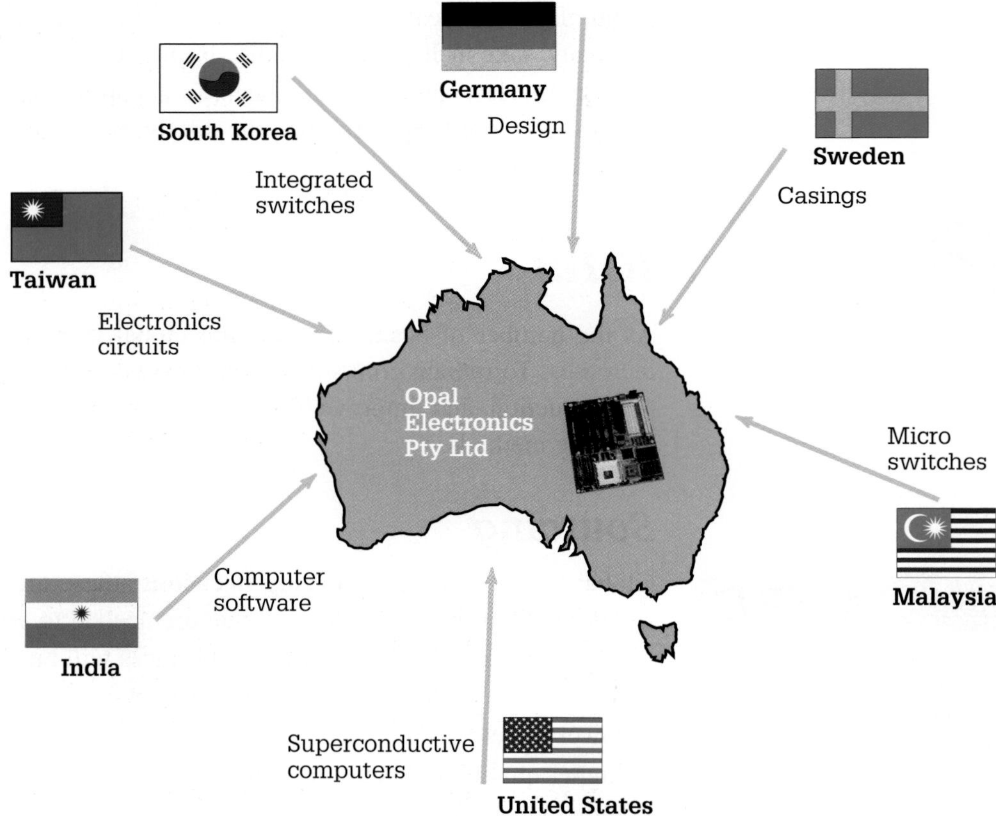

Figure 22.7 Global manufacturing: the component network for Opal Electronics switchgear

EXERCISE 22.2 *Revision*

1. Briefly outline the purpose of market research.
2. Why is it important to conduct research of an overseas market?
3. List a number of secondary data sources, and outline why a company would access information from these sources.

4. Although collecting primary data is a complex and time-consuming procedure, it has one major advantage. Give details of this advantage and how a business can use the information effectively.
5. What is meant by the term 'global branding'? Elaborate on the three main reasons why businesses use a global branding strategy.
6. Illustrate, using examples, the difference between a standardised and differentiated global marketing strategy.
7. Provide reasons why McDonald's would use a combination of a standardised and a differentiated marketing strategy.
8. What are the two sourcing decisions facing a business?
9. Illustrate, using an example, how a business could use a global web to produce a product.

Extension

1. 'Standardisation of production is of greater benefit to the producer than the consumer. It allows transnational conglomerates to treat the world as one single market, irrespective of social and cultural differences.' Do you agree with this statement? Give reasons for your answer.
2. Procter & Gamble (P & G) is a large United States consumer products company that markets more than 80 brands worldwide. Its main products include cleaning products, detergents and personal care products. Go to www.jaconline.com.au/businessstudies3e and click on the Procter & Gamble weblink for this textbook. Research the range of products and the worldwide brands it sells in each of its market regions.
3. Identify and research the difficulties a global business may face when it decides to outsource the majority of its production to an overseas firm.
4. A business must decide whether to establish a factory to make a component or to contract the manufacturing to an independent supplier. What are the advantages and disadvantages of each option? Which would you recommend? Give reasons for your answer.

22.5 Employment relations

The most important asset of any business is its employees. At the most basic level, all businesses, from the smallest corner store to the largest TNC, are nothing more than a collection of employees performing a wide range of tasks. Therefore, the business's success is very much determined by the abilities and performance levels of its employees.

The quality, quantity and composition of the available labour force are important considerations for any business as it undergoes global expansion, as well as establishing and maintaining effective employment relations.

Organisational structure

Businesses develop an organisational structure to achieve specific objectives. The structure eventually chosen by a business will depend on a number of factors, including the extent of its global operations and whether it makes or buys components. As the business expands globally and modifies its objectives, it must also adapt its organisational structure.

Global structure

The shift to a global structure means a change in the way decisions are made. Although the board of directors in the parent company may still have control over long-term decisions, more decisions will be made at a local level as power is decentralised. Where once the global business may have had only a marketing department in an overseas country, it may now develop a structure that integrates the regional divisions (see figure 22.8).

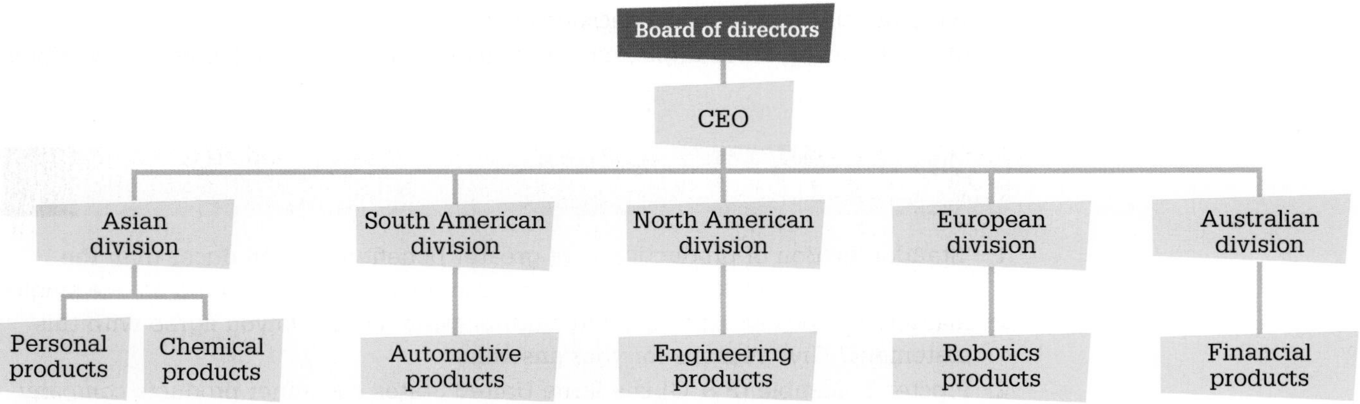

Figure 22.8 A simplified global organisational structure

Staffing

Staffing *involves the recruiting and selecting of qualified people to ensure the success of the business.*

The function of **staffing** is to recruit and select qualified people to ensure the success of the business. In a global business, finding the right people can be extremely difficult, especially for management positions. These positions require people who are preferably bicultural, able to appreciate and understand the business practices and customs in the host country, and who can speak the languages of both home and host country.

Businesses may adopt one of three methods to staff an overseas operation, as shown in figure 22.9.

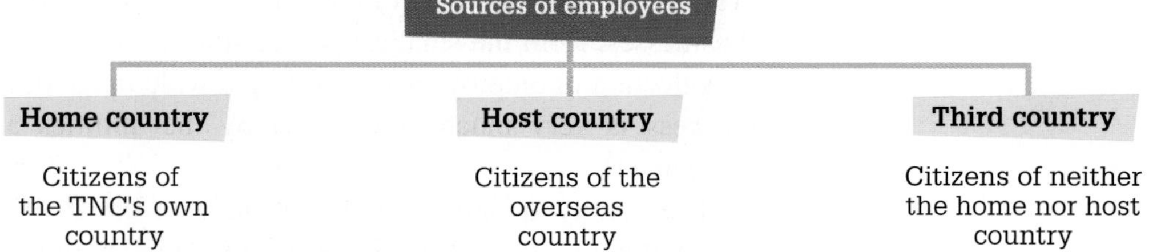

Figure 22.9 Sources of employees for a global business

There is one other aspect of global staffing that all businesses must heed: do not disregard the effect of the local culture when selecting employees. For example, in many cultures, tribal and family relationships are more important than technical qualifications when hiring employees. Therefore, a local manager may hire a relative or tribal member in preference to someone with more appropriate qualifications. Although such a practice may be unfamiliar to an employer with Western attitudes and values, disregarding it could possibly lead to staffing difficulties and a loss of productivity in the long term.

Shortage of skilled labour

As we mentioned previously, a global business may sometimes have difficulty finding suitable host country employees for management positions. This shortage of skilled labour is normally overcome by the global business transferring citizens of the home country, **expatriates**, to manage the operation until local people can be found and trained. Sometimes it may be necessary for the global business to send a team of specialists to remedy a particular problem. Teams may be sent to assist in the establishment of a production facility, staying until local personnel are trained to run and maintain the new facilities.

*An **expatriate** is a citizen of one country working in another country.*

Labour law variations

Virtually every country has a set of laws regulating working conditions and wages for its labour force. Often governments place restrictions on the use of foreign labour, as well as requiring the employment of local people. Table 22.1 provides examples of labour regulations imposed by various countries.

TABLE 22.1 Selected labour laws

Country	Labour law regulations
Philippines	▪ Voluntary labour–management committees negotiate productivity wage agreements. ▪ Employees who are paid on a piecework basis must not be paid less than the legal eight-hour minimum wage.
Taiwan	▪ Mines and factories provide employees with either a fixed-term or a non-fixed-term contract. ▪ Hours of work are seven hours a day for arduous work, eight hours for industrial and transport work and nine hours for commercial and other types of work.
Vietnam	▪ All workers receive work diaries to record their own working hours.
Korea	▪ Employers contribute to a wages claim fund, which pays workers who lose wages due to a business bankruptcy. ▪ Minimum terms and conditions of employment are set by law.
Indonesia	▪ Employment of foreign nationals is allowed when locally qualified people are not available. ▪ Minimum terms and conditions of employment are set by law.

Source: Adapted from the International Labour Organization (ILO).

*A **staffing system** is concerned with the selection of employees for particular jobs.*

Staffing systems

A **staffing system** is concerned with the selection of employees for particular jobs.

When operating in another country, a business may adopt one of three approaches to staffing: the ethnocentric approach, the polycentric approach and the geocentric approach (see figure 22.10).

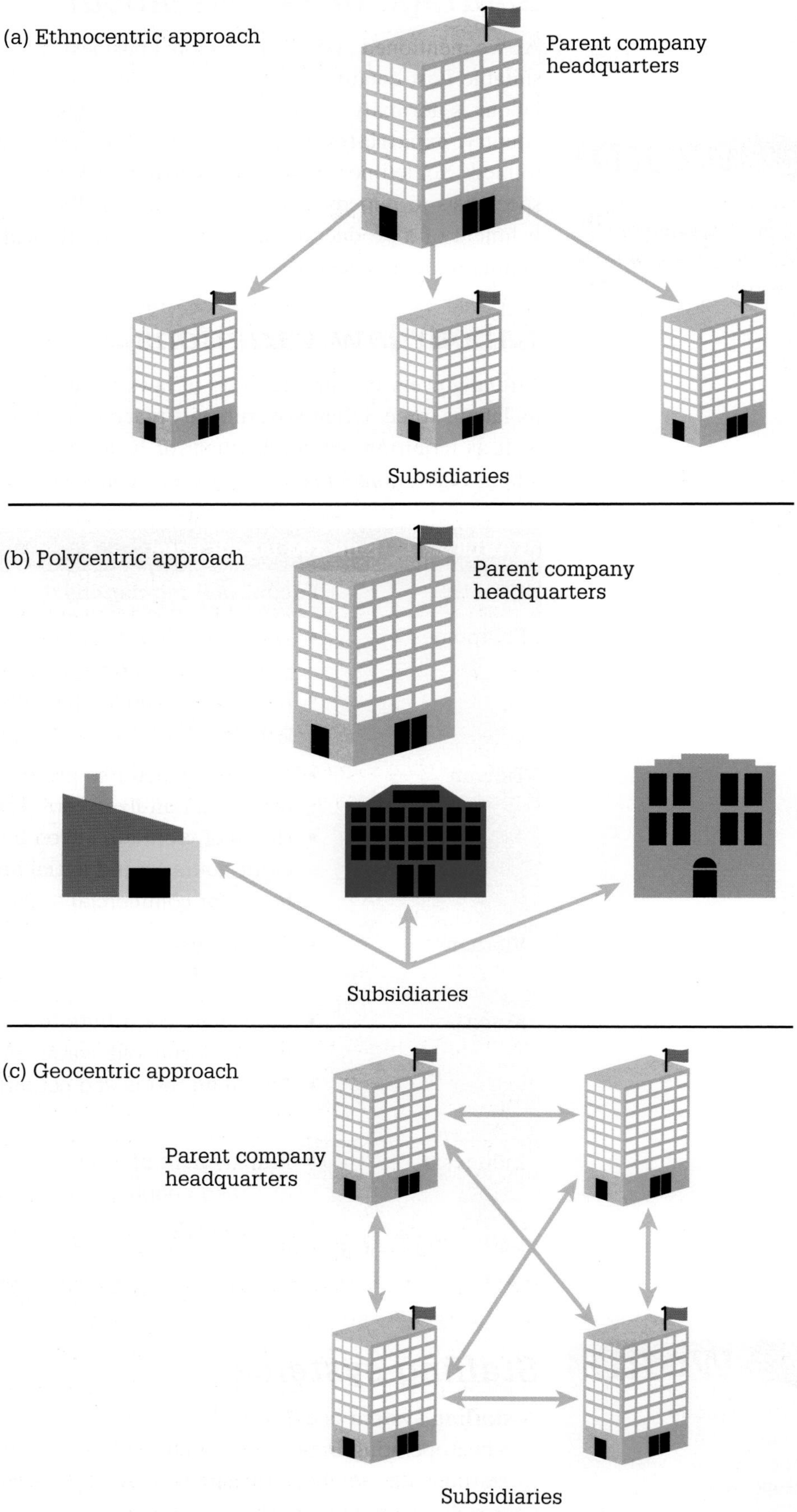

(a) Ethnocentric approach

Parent company headquarters

Subsidiaries

(b) Polycentric approach

Parent company headquarters

Subsidiaries

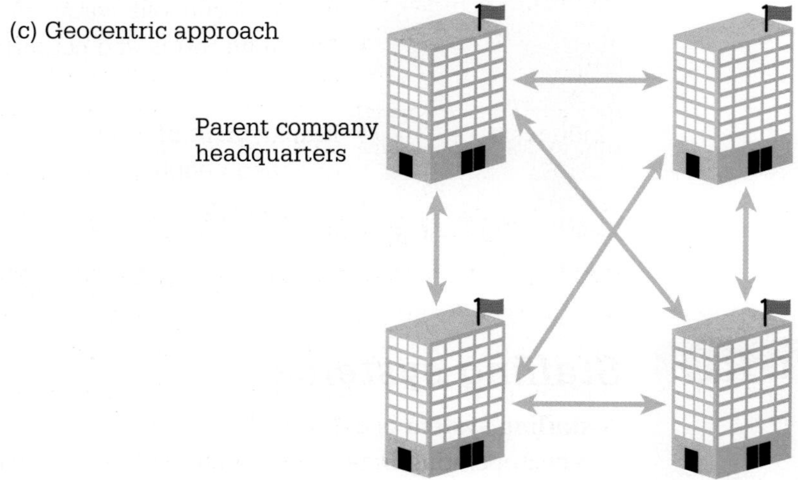

Figure 22.10 Staffing systems. In an ethnocentric approach (a), managers are posted to subsidiaries from within the parent company. In a polycentric approach (b), subsidiaries recruit managers from their geographic base. In a geocentric approach (c), managers are recruited from throughout the organisation

*An **ethnocentric approach** to staffing is one in which all key management positions at all company locations are filled by parent company personnel.*

*A **polycentric approach** to staffing is one in which personnel from the host country manage the subsidiaries, while the parent company personnel fill the key roles at company headquarters.*

*A **geocentric approach** to staffing means seeking the best people for key jobs throughout the entire organisation, irrespective of nationality.*

Ethnocentric approach to staffing

In an **ethnocentric approach** to staffing, all key management positions at all company locations are filled by parent company personnel. Although it may still be practised when a business undertakes its first overseas expansion, ethnocentric staffing is now less popular among established TNCs.

Polycentric approach to staffing

A **polycentric approach** to staffing is one in which personnel from the host country manage the subsidiaries, while the parent company personnel fill the key roles at company headquarters.

While host countries prefer this system compared to the ethnocentric approach, it may still cause a degree of resentment among local employees within the subsidiary. This is because the host country management have limited opportunities to work outside their own country, thus limiting their experience.

Geocentric approach to staffing

Today's businesses with a global outlook have realised that they must consider the world, rather than simply one country, as their 'home'. These companies adopt a **geocentric approach** to staffing, seeking the best people for key jobs throughout the entire organisation, irrespective of nationality.

These businesses adapt their recruitment and selection practices to different cultures while maintaining their worldwide policies and identity. The parent company trains and develops managers at all levels from a worldwide pool of talent. Companies such as IBM, Ford, General Electric, Dow Chemicals and Procter & Gamble often bring their managers from around the world to meetings and workshops with the intention of broadening everyone's appreciation and understanding of the global environment. Businesses that have operations across many regions tend to implement geocentric strategies.

22.6 Evaluation — strategies with reference to a particular global market

So far in this topic we have been examining the larger environment in which a business competes and the way it manages particular business functions. We now focus on the business's evaluation of the strategies it used to enter and operate in a global market. This is a crucial step for any business because it influences the future direction and success of the organisation.

Evaluating the strategies

Once the global business strategy is implemented, managers must evaluate the results. Evaluating involves the comparison of planned performance against actual performance. Management must constantly ask the following questions:

- What does the business want the strategic plan to achieve; that is, what are the business's objectives?
- Are those objectives being achieved?

By considering these questions regularly, management may clearly assess the degree of success of a particular strategy.

Evaluating global strategies is a complex process due to the impact of financial, political, legal and sociocultural influences. Generally though, businesses that have operated successfully in the global market have adopted specific strategies in response to changes in that market (see the Snapshot 'Global evaluation strategies implemented by Opal Electronics Pty Ltd').

Global evaluation strategies implemented by Opal Electronics Pty Ltd

Opal Electronics operates in the global market exporting electrical switchgear to 28 countries in Europe, North America and South-East Asia. Its administrative headquarters and main manufacturing plant is located in Australia, with production facilities in five overseas countries. Two of these production facilities are operated as joint ventures, while the other three are directly owned.

Each year, Opal Electronics undertakes extensive evaluation of its business plan. It divides its export markets into three distinct regions with each regional manager being responsible for the evaluation process. The results are then compared within the region over time and between regions. Any major modifications to the existing business plan will only be initiated after consultation with the senior management for each region, the chief executive officer and a working party of four members of the board of directors.

The evaluation is divided into four separate sections: production, marketing, staffing and finance. Each region has to measure its performance in these four areas against predetermined performance standards. For example, Opal's last evaluation contained a performance standard for all its production facilities. This was to increase productivity by 5 per cent over the following 18 months and to reduce lost time due to workplace injury by 10 per cent within 12 months. A marketing performance standard for the European region was to improve sales revenue per salesperson by 10 per cent over the following 12 months.

Due to recent economic growth in a number of Asian economies, Opal Electronics was forced to significantly re-evaluate its business operations in the Asian region. In 2004 its sales to this region were up by 56 per cent. In response, the company decided to expand production by 25 per cent at both its Australian and Malaysian plants. At the same time, it decided to increase the productive capacity of its European and North American facilities as these economies were growing quite rapidly. Marketing strategies were modified in order to concentrate more on the European and Asian markets. This approach has proved successful as the financial improvements in these two major markets increased by a combined 28 per cent during 2004 to 2005. Research undertaken by Opal suggests that its main Asian markets will continue to expand during the next decade. Consequently, Opal is presently evaluating the option of a joint venture production facility with a partner in Guangzhou, China.

By constantly evaluating its business plan, Opal is able to be proactive and is, therefore, in a better position to withstand changes within the external business environment.

SNAPSHOT Questions

1. List the regions Opal Electronics Pty Ltd exports to.
2. Outline how Opal Electronics Pty Ltd evaluates its global business operations.

22.7 Modification of strategies according to changes in global markets

Global markets, just like domestic markets, constantly change. Therefore, a business should be constantly scanning the environment for changes that might affect it. Also, as we explained in the last section, a business needs to constantly evaluate its present strategies. With the combined information gathered from the environmental scan and the evaluation process, a business is in a strong position to respond to the changes by modifying its existing strategies. One company that has displayed remarkable skill in constantly modifying its global strategies is McDonald's (see the Snapshot 'Even McDonald's must modify its strategies').

Even McDonald's must modify its strategies

However global and dominant it may be, McDonald's must still modify its business strategies in response to changes in the global market. For example:

1. PROBLEM OF DOMESTIC MARKET SATURATION IN THE 1980S

In response to a domestic slowdown in sales, McDonald's rapidly increased its expansion into overseas markets. In 1980, 28 per cent of the chain's new restaurant openings were overseas; by 2002 this figure had grown to approximately 73 per cent. The markets of Mexico, South America and Central America have been targeted for expansion over the next few years.

2. STAFFING AND STAFFING SYSTEM

Whereas McDonald's adopted a largely ethnocentric staffing policy in the 1950s, the 2000s has seen the company move to a geocentric approach.

3. RESPONDING TO LOCAL TASTES

McDonald's is seen by many as selling a standardised product. In reality it does modify aspects of its operations, most importantly its marketing mix between countries. The menu is varied in response to local tastes. Recently, salads, low-fat chicken wraps and fruit were added to the traditional menu in response to the community's concern about the increase in obesity. McDonald's also modifies its distribution strategy from country to country. In the United States most restaurants are located within easy access by car, but in densely populated Japan, choice of location is determined by walking distance.

(*continued*)

McDonald's has expanded into 116 countries around the world, but it still tailors its business strategies to suit different parts of its market.

4. SUPPLIER DIFFICULTIES

When McDonald's opened its first restaurant in Moscow it discovered that the quality of locally supplied foodstuffs was below its minimum standard. In response, McDonald's decided to vertically integrate backwards and supply its own raw materials. This was a major modification to its global strategy of outsourcing its requirements.

5. DIFFERENT WORKPLACE CULTURES

McDonald's prides itself on producing a standardised product across the globe. However, it has proved more difficult to transfer its workplace culture to all countries around the world. To assist in this task, McDonald's has modified its global strategy and established joint ventures with local businesses. The role of the local business is to train local workers in McDonald's values and work practices.

6. CUSTOMISED 'GLOBAL' IMAGE

McDonald's implements a number of strategies to provide a globally branded product that must satisfy predetermined standards. However, even within the homogeneous United States market the company retains 78 different advertising agencies to customise its promotion for local markets.

7. ECOLOGICAL SUSTAINABILITY

Consumers around the world have become more conscious of the need to protect the environment. Some governments have passed laws banning plastic packaging. In response to these changes in attitudes, McDonald's modified its packaging systems to include more recycled materials.

8. PRODUCT LIFE CYCLE

From the mid 1990s McDonald's sales in industrialised countries began to plateau. (Sales in developing countries, however, continue to increase.) Research undertaken by McDonald's highlighted a change in the cultural and social attitudes of consumers, especially those in the United States, European and Australian markets. Changing demographics had increased supermarket sales of home meal replacements. In response, McDonald's is investigating the introduction of 'meal solutions' products, a major strategic modification.

SNaPSHOT Question

Construct a mind map to show how McDonald's modified its global strategy in response to changes in the market.

EXERCISE 22.3 *Revision*

1. Examine figure 22.8 on page 476. What are the advantages to the business of adopting this type of organisational structure?
2. Examine figure 22.9 on page 476. Briefly explain the three sources of employees for a global business.

3. You have been appointed human resource manager for a global business. The manager of a new production facility in a developing country is having difficulty finding suitably qualified staff. What strategy could you implement to overcome this staff shortage?
4. What is meant by the term 'expatriate'? Why should a global business be aware of the labour laws of a country in which it operates?
5. Explain the difference between an ethnocentric, polycentric and geocentric staffing system. When is each strategy appropriate?
6. What is the underlying purpose of evaluating specific business strategies?
7. Prepare a summary of this chapter. A summary condenses the important issues and concepts presented in the chapter. Go to www.jaconline.com.au/businessstudies3e to compare your finished summary with the one provided for this textbook.

Extension

1. When staffing overseas operations, what are some advantages and disadvantages of hiring host country employees?
2. Human resource management (HRM) incorporates all the activities involved in acquiring, developing, maintaining and motivating a business's human resources. In what ways does domestic HRM differ from global HRM? Present your report to the rest of the class.
3. If you were being posted to an overseas position as production manager, what training would you request from your employer?
4. 'Every business, no matter how large, must constantly evaluate and modify its global business strategies.' Discuss.

CHAPTER

23 Management responsibility in a global environment

23.1 Introduction

In 1984 the Indian town of Bhopal experienced the largest industrial disaster in history when a cloud of toxic gas leaked from a storage tank at a Union Carbide pesticide plant. This disaster killed 2500 people and seriously affected another 300 000. The ramifications of this accident are still being felt. It also raised a number of serious ethical issues, many of which are still being discussed.

As we discovered in chapter 19, the rise of global companies, which are becoming more numerous and influential, can exert enormous pressure on national governments. Some global businesses have abused their market power and engaged in highly questionable business practices. Because of their strength within the marketplace, these businesses were able to override local government attempts to regulate their behaviour. In addition, over the last few decades some large transnational corporations (TNCs) have come under worldwide criticism for their potentially harmful operating procedures in developing countries (see the Biz Fact on the left).

As businesses become more global in their operations, the managers of many of these organisations recognise the importance and necessity of pursuing global business goals with a consciousness of social and ethical responsibilities. Global businesses that take seriously their social and ethical responsibilities are often 'rewarded' with improved business performance. For example, according to research undertaken by Global Business Responsibility Centre, companies that implemented a policy of caring for the 'triple bottom line' — economic, environmental and social performance — outperformed other companies in the stock market.

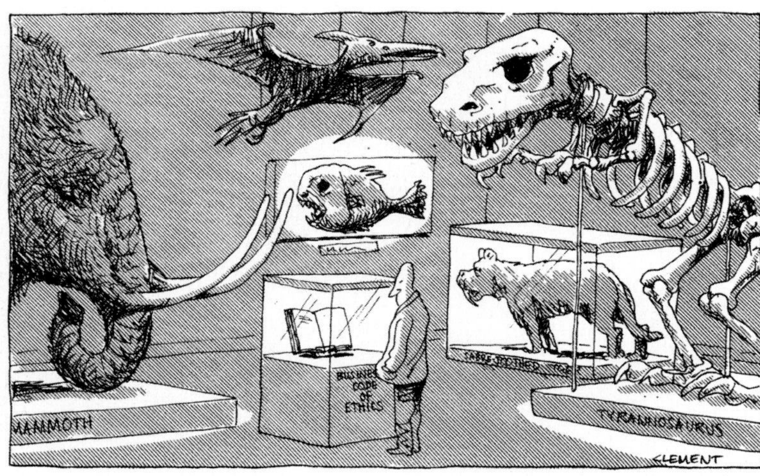

Figure 23.1 Business ethics — an extinct 'species'?

23.2 Ethically responsible corporate strategy

Conducting global business presents many challenges to businesses and their managers. There is no 'quick-fix' solution to solving these dilemmas. Perhaps understanding why social and ethical issues arise is the first step in seeking a solution.

However, managers can plan for such challenges by designing a global corporate social strategy that matches the business's economic strategy.

Designing a corporate social strategy helps managers achieve triple bottom line results. The following questions are a good place to start when designing a social strategy:

- Are we being socially responsible in all that we do?
- Do we conduct our business in ways that respect the values, customs and religions of each culture, recognising that there may be times when conflict may arise?
- Do we respect and obey the host government's legislation and policies?
- Are we responsive to all of the stakeholders in each country where we do business?
- Are we responsive to the emerging social and ethical issues within the countries and societies where we operate?
- Are all our employees aware of, and following, the business's social corporate strategy?

One company that has actively pursued the implementation of a global corporate social strategy is Billabong International Limited, the Australian manufacturer of surf and extreme sports apparel and accessories (see the Snapshot 'Billabong's supplier policy and corporate social responsibility (CSR)').

Levi Strauss and Co., the United States clothing manufacturer, is another global business that takes its ethical and social responsibilities seriously. In 1991, Levi Strauss was the first TNC to establish guidelines designed to evaluate the operations of its global suppliers. The program has been instrumental in bringing about improvements to the working conditions of many employees, especially in developing countries.

Billabong's supplier policy and corporate social responsibility (CSR)

Billabong has a global quality assurance program in place based on QAL4 global standards that covers Factory Inspection reports (general), Factory Inspection reports (human rights), Factory Inspection reports (environmental issues) and Lab Tests standards. Suppliers are required to abide by a comprehensive Quality Assurance Procedures Manual and to operate their factory in compliance with all legal and moral obligations that may apply to their operations. Suppliers and their factories are evaluated using Billabong's quality control processes before Billabong will consider engaging a supplier. Re-evaluation of a supplier's factory occurs annually. A factory evaluation involves an inspection of the factory and detailed discussions with management and employees. The evaluation process looks at physical facilities, quality performance (pre-production, production and quality assurance policies and procedures) and a compliance audit (employment ethics, working hours and wages, environment, health and safety, fire prevention and illegal transhipment).

Source: Billabong Corporate, 'Frequently asked questions', viewed 1 June 2005 http://www.billabongcorporate.com/

SNaPSHOT Questions

1. What does Billabong's global quality assurance program cover?
2. Outline the purpose of the quality assurance program.
3. How does the quality assurance program assist Billabong to fulfil its corporate social responsibility?

Tax havens and transfer pricing

Like many businesses operating within Australia, global companies attempt to minimise their taxation liability so as to maximise their after-tax profit.

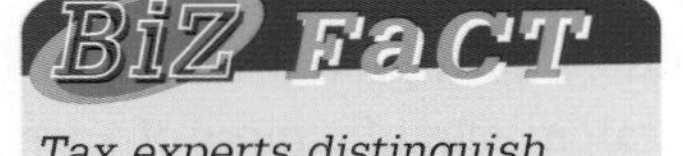

Tax experts distinguish between tax minimisation, where a business uses legal methods to reduce its tax obligation, and tax evasion, where a business uses illegal activities to decrease its tax payments.

Two tax minimisation strategies widely used by global businesses are tax havens and transfer pricing. These two strategies are perfectly legal and considered to be good business practices by many. Others, however, question the morality of such practices. For example, tax minimisation schemes save a TNC millions of dollars, which benefits shareholders. However, such practices decrease the tax revenue available to the TNC's home country to help solve such social problems as unemployment and poverty. Others argue that as long as the TNC is only engaging in tax minimisation measures, and not undertaking tax evasion (see the Biz Fact on the left), then this is an ethical business practice.

Tax havens

To reduce its tax liability a business can locate its activities in a tax haven. Tax havens are countries that impose little or no company income tax. There are three different types of tax haven arrangement, as shown in figure 23.2.

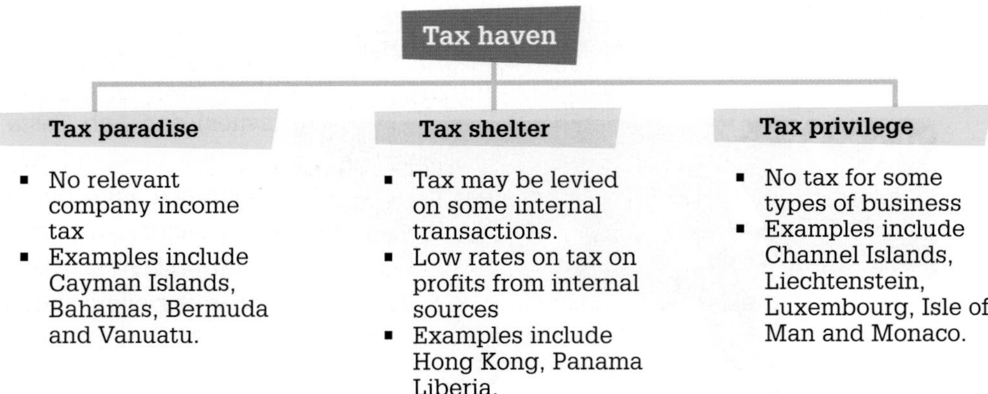

Tax haven
Tax paradise
Tax shelter
Tax privilege
▪ No relevant company income tax
▪ Examples include Cayman Islands, Bahamas, Bermuda and Vanuatu.
▪ Tax may be levied on some internal transactions.
▪ Low rates on tax on profits from internal sources
▪ Examples include Hong Kong, Panama Liberia.
▪ No tax for some types of business
▪ Examples include Channel Islands, Liechtenstein, Luxembourg, Isle of Man and Monaco.

Figure 23.2 The three different types of tax haven

The main role of a tax haven is obviously to provide a business with the means to avoid taxes. It does this by allowing a business to transfer income from subsidiaries in high-tax countries to the subsidiary operating in the tax haven.

Transfer pricing

A special type of exporting called intracorporate sales, or transfer pricing, is becoming increasingly common among the subsidiaries of TNCs. In an effort to achieve economies of scale, a TNC may require a subsidiary to specialise in the manufacture of a particular product, which will then be exported to other subsidiaries within the group. For example, car engines may be made in one country and transported to another to

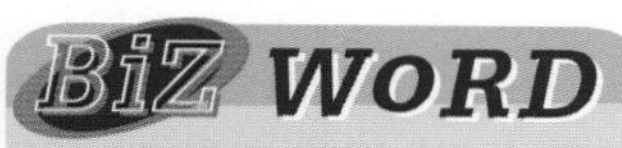

***Transfer pricing** refers to the prices one subsidiary of a company charges a second subsidiary for goods and services.*

be mounted into car bodies. Such actions often involve **transfer pricing**, where one subsidiary of a company charges a second subsidiary for goods and services.

Transfer pricing provides the opportunity for the business as a whole to gain while both the buying and selling subsidiaries 'lose'. This is because the subsidiaries receive a lower price for their product than if the transaction took place on the open market. This effectively hides any profit (see figure 23.3).

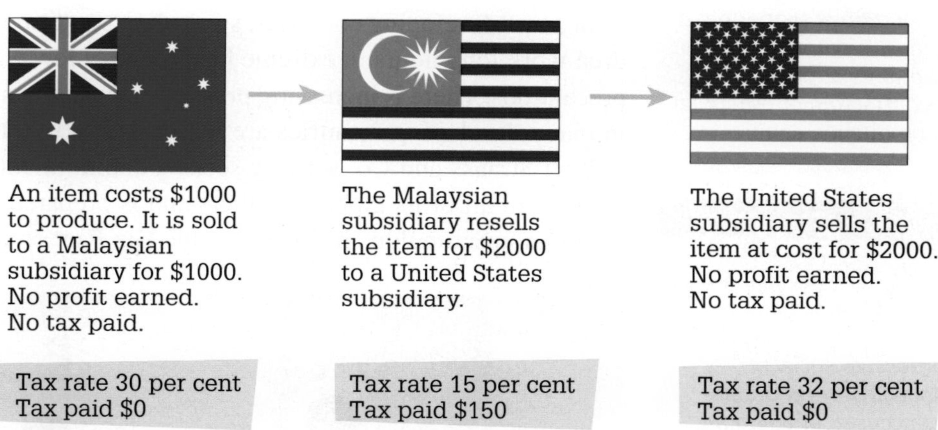

An item costs $1000 to produce. It is sold to a Malaysian subsidiary for $1000. No profit earned. No tax paid.
The Malaysian subsidiary resells the item for $2000 to a United States subsidiary.
The United States subsidiary sells the item at cost for $2000. No profit earned. No tax paid.
Tax rate 30 per cent Tax paid $0
Tax rate 15 per cent Tax paid $150
Tax rate 32 per cent Tax paid $0

Figure 23.3 Hiding profits with transfer pricing

The TNC, therefore, obtains a profit from both the seller and the buyer. Not only is any profit hidden, but also the manipulation of the transfer price also reduces customs duties and import tariffs.

EXERCISE 23.1 Revision

1. What is meant by the term 'triple bottom line'?
2. Briefly outline the findings of the Global Business Responsibility Centre's research concerning corporate responsibility and economic performance.
3. Describe the benefits of developing a corporate social strategy.
4. Briefly explain the difference between tax avoidance and tax minimisation.
5. List the arguments for and against tax minimisation practices.
6. What is a tax haven? Refer to figure 23.2 on page 486 and explain the difference between a tax paradise, tax shelter and tax privilege.
7. Describe, using an example, how transfer pricing can be used to minimise the tax obligations of a business.

Extension

1. Debate the following topic: 'It is ethical to use tax havens to reduce a company's taxes.'
2. The Global Business Responsibility Resource Centre provides information about the social and ethical responsibilities of business. Go to www.jaconline.com.au/businessstudies3e and click on the Business for Social Responsibility weblink for this textbook. Undertake a search of the 'Global News' database. Select one item which interests you, then research the article and outline the ethical and social issues involved.
3. Examine why professional codes of ethics are difficult to develop and implement globally.

Minimum standards of labour

As outlined in chapter 22, each country has specific labour laws that outline the minimum wage and non-wage conditions for employees. Obviously, there are regional or cultural differences in labour standards. **Labour standards** refer to those conditions that affect a business's employees, or those of its suppliers, subcontractors or others in the production chain.

In some developing countries, sweatshop conditions exist in which women and children work long hours in extreme heat for very low wages and with virtually no safety precautions. There is increasing pressure to ensure employees who work for low wages in many developing countries are not exploited by unscrupulous businesses.

Levi Strauss and Co. actively seeks a commitment to socially responsible employment from all of its global suppliers and is prepared to take action against those who act in an unscrupulous manner (see the Biz Fact on the left).

Labour standards refer to the conditions that affect a business's employees, or those of its suppliers, subcontractors or others in the production chain.

In 1991, Levi Strauss & Co., a United States business that has a reputation for progressive social responsibility programs, was accused of using an unethical contractor in Saipan. The contractor was accused of keeping some workers as virtual slaves. Wages were below the island's legal minimum, and conditions were wretched and unsafe. Levi Strauss & Co. fired the contractor and formed a committee of senior managers to review procedures for hiring contractors.

In 1992, the company implemented a wide-ranging set of guidelines for its contractors. The guidelines cover:

- *the treatment of workers*
- *the environmental impact of production.*

Levi Strauss & Co. now sends inspectors to conduct audits of work and safety conditions at the factories of all its contractors. Deficiencies must be corrected promptly or Levi Strauss & Co. will cancel the contract.

Figure 23.4 Increasingly, consumers are showing concern about unethical business practices, such as poor working conditions and wages in the sweatshops of the textile and clothing industry.

One area of special concern is the use of child labour in developing countries. According to studies undertaken by the International Labour Organization, there are up to 500 million child workers around the world. This represents half the children in the developing world aged from 5 to 14. Often, children work and live in dangerous and filthy conditions for extremely low wages or no payment at all. Sometimes these children are involved in the manufacture of products for well-known TNCs that outsource production to countries that offer low-cost labour.

To counter such conditions, some global businesses have adopted specific programs to eliminate child labour. One such business is Reebok International, the sports goods manufacturer. Through its human rights program it targeted the elimination of child labour in the manufacture of soccer balls.

Human rights codes of conduct

A human rights code of conduct is one method of attempting to conduct business in a socially responsible way. Once a code of conduct has been established, the organisation may insist that all its suppliers conform to it. Reebok, for instance, has regularly taken action against suppliers who do not live up to its code of conduct requirements (see the Snapshot 'Our business practices').

Our business practices

> We believe that the incorporation of internationally recognized human rights standards into our business practice improves worker morale and results in a higher quality working environment and higher quality products.
>
> — Reebok Human Rights Production Standards

As a responsible corporation, we account for something bigger than our core business. For over a decade, we have integrated human rights principles into our business practices.

Our commitment to human rights extends to the thousands of workers worldwide who make our products. Like most global companies in our industry, we do not own the factories that make our products. Yet, we promote the fair treatment of the workers who do make them. We know that to be proud of the products we put our name on, we cannot be indifferent to the conditions in which they are made. That is why, in 1992, we were the first in our industry to adopt *production standards*, calling for decent conditions for workers in factories making our products.

Turning a code of conduct into reality is a complex process, and our compliance staff plays a critical role in *improving conditions*, such as our initiatives to help ensure *no child labor* is used in the production of our soccer balls. We also develop sustainable mechanisms, through innovative worker participation programs, for improving conditions for factory workers over time.

No brand can guarantee that every factory complies with every regulation all the time. Compliance is an ongoing process, and we recognize that there is much more to be done. We are committed to making a difference in workers' lives. We will continue to use our influence with the factories that make our products to respect the rights of workers.

Source: Reebok, 'Our business practices', viewed 14 March 2005 http://www.reebok.com/Static/global/initiatives/rights/text-only/business/

SNaPSHOT Question

Prepare an oral report on the value of such a document. Present your report to the rest of the class.

Reebok actively encourages other global businesses to publicly promote human rights in the countries in which they operate. Some businesspeople doub*t whether such individual company codes can stop labour abuses in other countries, in part because other competitors may not abide by similar standards.

Dumping illegal products

Over the last 30 years, industrialised countries have developed stringent health and safety laws relating to a wide range of products. The aim of such laws is to protect the consumer from harmful products. However, such government regulations in developing countries are often non-existent or very weak. This has tempted a number of TNCs to use these vulnerable markets as a means of disposing of harmful or illegal products that cannot be sold in other markets. Products such as harmful chemicals, poorly designed machinery and inappropriate foodstuffs have been dumped onto the markets of developing countries in recent years.

Figure 23.5 The imbalances of market power

Of particular concern is the dumping of hazardous materials, including nuclear waste, in developing countries. Countries are often coerced into taking such materials; they may receive financial or other incentives, and extra revenue may be used to repay staggering foreign debts. Often the environmental laws of the host country are so lax that this hazardous material is not properly treated or stored. As a result, contamination of dumping sites may be extremely high. Improper storage of these products would be illegal in developed countries, where communities increasingly oppose the building of disposal sites.

Since there are few laws prohibiting the disposal of hazardous products in many developing countries, such actions of TNCs are not technically illegal, but they are highly unethical. Of course, TNCs have little fear of any retaliatory actions from individual citizens of developing countries.

Figure 23.6 Environmental protection responsibilities

Ecological sustainability

As outlined in chapter 3, there is growing pressure for businesses to adopt ecologically sustainable operating practices. This is in response to concerns about climate change and the destruction of the natural environment. Concern for our environment operates at both the local level as well as on a global scale.

Over the last two decades, the global business community has undertaken many initiatives to put the principle of sustainable development into practice. For example, the jeans manufacturer Levi Strauss and Co. has developed its own environmental philosophy and guiding principles. Levi Strauss will conduct business only with partners who share its commitment to the environment.

Businesses that have been successful in their environmental management have learned that new processes, procedures and strategies are often needed. For example, one particular organisational element that many proactive 'green' companies share is the development and implementation of an environmental policy.

Through communication and training, responsible businesses can ensure that all employees and contractors are environmentally aware.

Arguments for and against corporate social and ethical responsibility

Corporate social and ethical responsibility is a contentious area. The main arguments for and against global businesses assuming such responsibility are discussed in this section.

Those who argue for greater corporate responsibility perceive a business to be more than simply a profit machine. They argue that:

- a better society means a better environment for doing business. By adopting a philosophy of enlightened self-interest, a business can turn today's problems into future profits.
- businesses are unavoidably involved in social issues. Therefore, they have certain social rights and responsibilities.
- businesses have the resources to help solve complex social problems. With their base of financial, technical and human resources businesses can play a positive role.
- corporate social action will prevent government regulation. It is better to self-regulate than have governments force companies to comply with certain standards.

The opponents of corporate social responsibility believe that:

- a business is essentially an economic organisation which, therefore, lacks the ability to pursue social goals. Economic inefficiencies could result if managers are forced to undertake an extra role.
- maximising profits ensures that society's resources are used efficiently. Providing the best quality products at the lowest price should be the goal of all businesses because this benefits society.
- business managers are appointed, not elected. Therefore, they are not accountable to society.

These arguments are based on the assumption that businesses should stick to what they do best: pursuing profits by producing products that satisfy the wants and needs of consumers.

EXERCISE 23.2 Revision

1. What is meant by the term 'labour standards'?
2. Assess the value of the actions by Levi Strauss, the International Labour Organization and Reebok in bringing about improvements to working conditions in developing countries.

3. Explain why some businesses have developed human rights codes of conduct.
4. Go to www.jaconline.com.au/businessstudies3e and click on the Reebok Human Rights and Environment weblinks for this textbook.
   (a) What is the role of the Reebok Human Rights Foundation?
   (b) Outline Reebok's commitment to the environment.
5. In groups of three or four, prepare a list of reasons why the dumping of illegal products should be banned. Compare your list with other class groups.
6. Examine figure 23.5 on page 490. What message do you think the cartoonist is attempting to present?
7. 'Many believe that voluntary actions by businesses cannot solve environmental problems. What is required is tough legislation to force businesses to accept their responsibilities.' Do you agree or disagree with this statement? Provide reasons for your answer.
8. Read the arguments for and against corporate social and ethical responsibility. Which set of arguments do you support? Why? Provide reasons for your answer.
9. Prepare a summary of this chapter. A summary condenses the important issues and concepts presented in the chapter. Go to www.jaconline.com.au/businessstudies3e to compare your finished summary with the one provided for this textbook.

Extension

1. 'There are those who believe that human rights codes of conduct and environmental policies are only clever marketing strategies by many transnational corporations. In reality, profit maximisation will win out over any social responsibility in decision making.' Assess the validity of this statement.
2. Levi Strauss places a great deal of importance on its corporate social responsibilities. This company has taken action against overseas suppliers based on its human rights and environmental codes of conduct. Go to www.jaconline.com.au/businessstudies3e and click on the Levi Strauss & Co. weblink for this textbook. Research its commitment to its social obligations with reference to global sourcing. Prepare either an oral or a written report and present it to the rest of the class.
3. Research a social or ethical issue confronting a global business. Write a short report, addressing the following:
   (a) Outline the issue.
   (b) How has the global business reacted to the situation?
   (c) What indicators would you use to determine the success or failure of the business's response to the situation?
4. The term 'environmental racism' has been used to describe the deliberate siting of hazardous waste sites in many poor countries of the world. If you were the manager of a waste management company, what factors would you take into consideration in selecting a new facility site?

24 CASE STUDY LEND LEASE

Figure 24.1 Development of Melbourne's Docklands — a major Lend Lease project

Lend Lease: overview

Lend Lease Corporation Limited is a parent company, an Australian public company and a major, global commercial property developer. Lend Lease:

- is also one of the largest real estate investment managers in the world, with more than $19.6 billion in assets under management
- has 400.2 million shares on issue to over 63 000 shareholders, with a market capitalisation of $4.1 billion
- was ranked by *Business Review Weekly* as 18th out of the top 1000 companies in Australia in 2004 (it was ranked 9th in 2000), based on its revenue of $9725.5 million
- has operations spanning approximately 40 countries
- incorporates Bovis Lend Lease, a leading worldwide construction and project manager; Actus Lend Lease, a developer and manager of US military housing; Delfin Lend Lease, one of Australia's largest residential/urban community developers; and Lend Lease Real Estate Investments in the Asia–Pacific region, which manages both retail and wholesale property trusts on behalf of investors; and its retail group, which manages the retail assets of these funds.

Development of the company

Lend Lease began as Civil and Civic in 1951. Later, managing director Dick Dusseldorp floated Lend Lease to allow it to sponsor its own development projects by developing a financial arm to provide the funds for construction and leasing of investments. It went on to acquire other businesses such as Bovis, now one of the top 10 global construction management companies.

Today Lend Lease's subsidiaries and businesses are geographically (as shown in table 24.1) and functionally diversified, providing excellent opportunities for it to gain synergies from its businesses to service its ongoing business relationships.

TABLE 24.1 Lend Lease — geographic locations

Location	Revenue 2004 $m	Revenue 2001 $m	Profit 2001 $m	Profit as % revenue 2001	Assets 2001 $m
Americas	4513.2	6032	82.6	1.4	4497
Europe	2157.2	2859	80.1	2.8	2437
Australia and Pacific	1797.8	2041	31.8	1.6	1754
Asia	391.4	406	5.4	1.3	437
Group treasury	—	114	(33.8)	(29.5)	—
Group finance and hedging costs	—	44.5	(48)	(108.1)	—

Sources: Lend Lease, *Annual Report* 2004; IBISWorld Pty Ltd, *Report*, 2001.

Topic 1: business management and change

Nature of management

Recently appointed Lend Lease CEO Greg Clarke reports to the board of directors, which is chaired by David Crawford. To achieve the business's goals, Greg and the management team need to coordinate all aspects of the business effectively and:

- use *interpersonal*, *decisional* and *informational management roles* and management *skills* including people skills and high ethical standards
- use a range of management skills in negotiating and *reconciling the different interests and issues of its stakeholders*. Lend Lease stakeholders include shareholders, clients (primarily multinationals and local and overseas governments), different business units, 9060 employees around the world, and the communities in which Lend Lease operates.
- ensure they and their staff behave ethically and *demonstrate high personal standards*. At Lend Lease, staff are encouraged to promote the following core values:
  - respect for others: their culture, views, health and safety, and knowledge
  - integrity: no compromising the individual's or company's integrity
  - innovation: thinking outside the box, daring to do things differently and being creative
  - collaboration: a company culture that involves sharing knowledge and sharing insights through teamwork
  - striving for excellence: in all activities, from design, to construction and safety.

Management theories

Political approaches are important in developing *strategic alliances*, *joint ventures* and *network structures* with other firms. These allow Lend Lease to expand beyond the small Australian market to increase its international competitiveness, market power and scale of operations, and to benefit from market knowledge, and industry and political contacts overseas. Lend Lease applies *systems* theory in its focus on developing a responsive business culture and *behavioural* approaches in ensuring its staff are well trained and operate in an injury-free workplace. *Political theory* is reflected in the performance-based rewards and retention payments for 'achievers'.

Managing change: external influences

Market influences

Lend Lease's major competitors are Mirvac, Meriton Apartments, Australand, Grocon, Leighton Holdings, AW Baulderstone, Multiplex and Barclay Mowlem, which have a similar market share of the industry. The market value of industry turnover is $4.42 billion for residential construction and $8 billion for commercial construction. These activities allow Lend Lease to profit from vertical integration.

Demand is strong from governments and multinational clients for firms such as Lend Lease when they can:

- provide strong international organisational capabilities and a good track record in managing projects in either the private or public sector and public–private partnerships
- provide multidisciplinary approaches combining technical inputs with non-technical skills
- quickly form network structures, alliances or consortia to meet client needs
- evolve as the market changes and meet demand for new services, such as environmentally sustainable communities.

Economic and political influences

Economic factors, including government spending on infrastructure, defence and health, and *political* factors, including the regulatory framework and increasing demands placed on developers for additional features or services, are major influences on this industry. Economic factors such as economic stability are important influences on investment decisions. The United States (US) market is a major market for Australian real estate investors, who are attracted by the stability of the real estate market (especially when the $US depreciates) and availability of a large range of investment assets.

Technological influences

Adoption of *e-commerce* is critical to business success today. Lend Lease strives to implement technology to support its business culture and enhance the capabilities and productivity of its staff. Recent e-commerce strategies include:

- installation of M-tech Information Technology's Identity Management Solution to streamline help-desk call volumes and the work of staff supporting over 9000 employees
- use of advanced software to monitor budgets, schedules and plans for each project
- online interaction with suppliers to maximise supply chain efficiency and online tendering
- Internet-based market research tools
- use of multi-channel marketing, which combines media and website publicity.

Managing change: internal influences

A strategic review and structural response to change

During 2004–05 Lend Lease was involved in a bid for General Property Trust (GPT), for which it has management rights. Lend Lease's bid was a result of a strategic review in which it had three options: break up the company and sell all divisions; continue as normal with growth through acquisitions and capital (funds) management; or join its operations to those of GPT, which it had floated in the past. Lend Lease's bid was not successful, but it is keen to establish a property trust that will fund its future development, providing 'third party capital'. It has not yet given up offering a better deal for GPT than its competitor, Stockland.

Managing the change process

Lend Lease's decision to withdraw from the US Real Estate Investments (REI) operations in 2003 and its restructuring of its European REI business reflects a change in strategy, based on analysis of external and internal issues and recent business performance.

Under its new management, Lend Lease's new *objectives* are to:

- value-add the core businesses — where the group can maximise the benefits from third party capital
- exit activities not clearly delivering synergies or returns. In businesses such as the US REI operation, Lend Lease lacked effective distribution channels, the market was complex, financial returns were poor and fee income was low.
- restore profitability after declining revenues and returns
- develop a business model that allows it to gain a sustainable income stream and reduce its dependence on irregular fees from project work. Its lack of success in this area is partly reflected in the fall of its share price from $21 in 2000 to $11 in 2005; however, it should be noted that Lend Lease sold MLC to National Australia Bank in 2000, and returned $1.8 billion of capital to shareholders.

Figure 24.2 A forcefield model of change issues for Lend Lease

Driving forces
Strong global economic growth — strong basis for global construction industry
Small market in Australia
Growth opportunities in Japan and other Asian markets
Opportunities to gain from vertical integration, economics of scale, political and business contacts in overseas markets
Urban renewal opportunities overseas
Opportunities from ageing population — growth in single accommodation, urban communities, expansion of healthcare
Resisting forces
Economic influences — sluggish growth in US and UK commercial sectors
Losses experienced in UK and US markets — shareholders concerned about new risks, ongoing risk profile of Lend Lease's existing structure

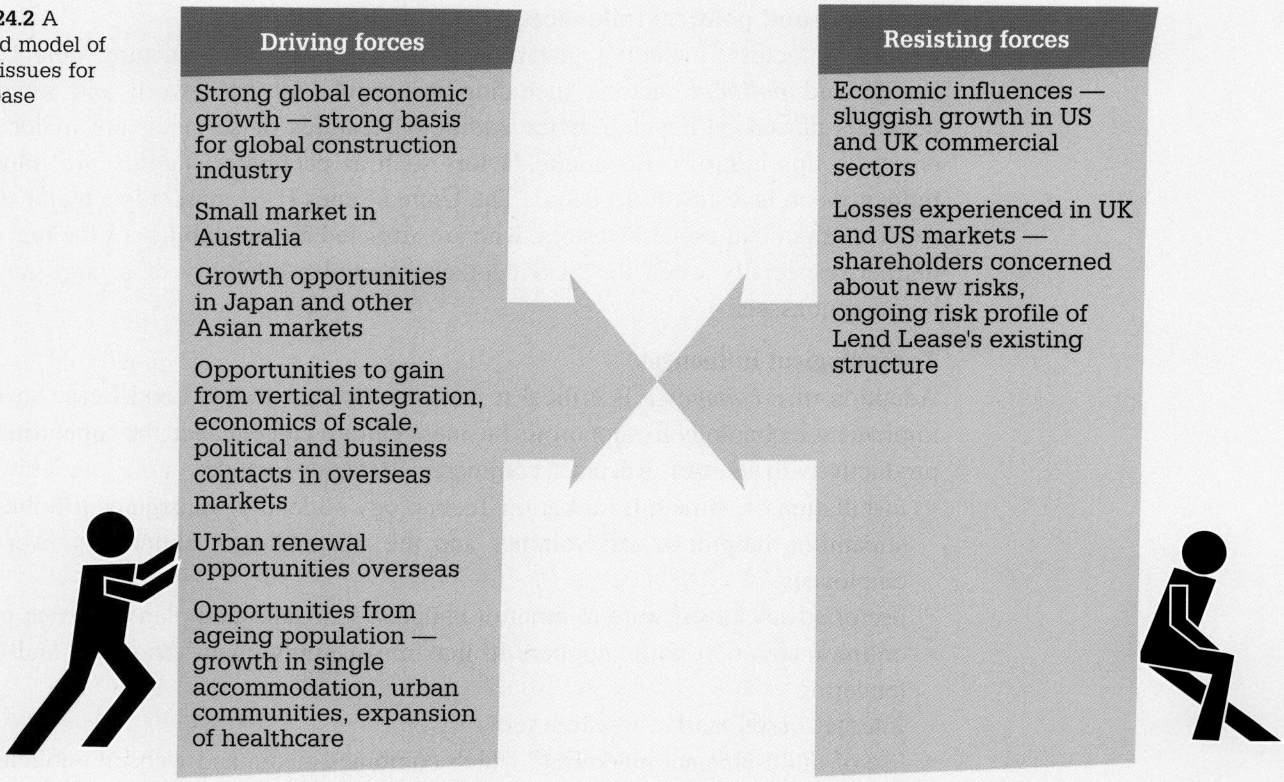

The change management process

Because a significant number of senior executive staff and key directors on the board left during the period of the failed REI operation, *resistance* to this change strategy does not appear to be strong. To implement this new strategy, Lend Lease has continued to use multiskilled teams as change agents in addition to senior management. These teams are used to:

- develop people who can then move between *teams* as needed, thus fostering innovation and adaptability to change. When staff manage change effectively, they are rewarded through performance-based rewards related to organisational goals and targets.
- develop and reinforce its *business culture* and to drive the new strategy. This approach is based on the vision that 'the quality inside the organisation wins the market outside'.

Change and social responsibility

Lend Lease's rating on the Australian Corporate Responsibility Index (the Index) is 69 per cent. Specific aspects of Lend Lease's business practices reveals that in terms of:

- *corporate governance.* Some of its board members do not fulfil the independence criteria for the Index and it has no specific commitment to human rights instruments, despite operating in more than 40 countries.
- *workplace relations.* Its record is positive. It promotes equal employment opportunity (EEO) and family-friendly flexibility, and indicates it will not tolerate discrimination or harassment.
- *political patronage.* Lend Lease does not make cash donations to any political parties, politicians or people standing for public office.
- *social responsibility.* It provides little public reporting on its social or environmental performance or that of its contractors, except in terms of occupational health and safety.
- *community relationships.* It is well known for its Community Day activities; however, it is criticised for relying too heavily on its employees for contributions, rather than investing directly. Lend Lease has often been praised for its work with indigenous communities affected by its operations.
- *environmental management.* In Europe, the Middle East and Africa, Lend Lease maintains its ISO 14001 certified environmental management system. It has been criticised in Australia for achieving less in terms of its environmental impacts and environmentally sustainable designs than its stated commitment. Lend Lease does not agree with this view, and is proud of its achievements. Its most recent achievement is the use of energy-efficient glass in an apartment building at Melbourne's Docklands, which has taken the building from being a 2.5-star rated building under the Australian Building Greenhouse Rating system to a 5-star rated building. Lend Lease claims to deliver ecologically sustainable development by establishing ecologically sustainable development (ESD) performance targets, policies and strategies after stakeholder consultation. It states that it uses technical modelling and life cycle assessment to confirm performance and documents design solutions, supporting these through technical support for each project. Lend Lease is keen to develop more credentials in this area, and to ensure there is a balance between economics, the environment and the needs of the community.

Lend Lease has a dedicated sustainability unit, although it has been criticised for not embedding ESD principles throughout its processes rather than through a specific unit. Lend Lease's new headquarters in Sydney is, nevertheless, the first commercial building to achieve five stars under the Australian Building Greenhouse Rating.

Recent strategies have included a focus on reducing the environmental impact of buildings; better planning for transport and community hubs; reducing water consumption; improving internal environmental quality aspects (acoustic, air quality, light quality); and modifying materials consumption to focus on products with reduced environmental impacts.

Topic 2: financial planning and management

Key financial management issues that have recently affected Lend Lease's achievement of the *financial objectives* of liquidity, profitability, solvency, efficiency and growth are:

- *variable income flows.* These are managed through such strategies as staggered lease expiry dates for assets under management. Fortunately, cash flows in the commercial property management industry tend to be more stable than for many other sectors, particularly as contracts are signed for one year's duration. Lend Lease is working on a business model and strategy to better manage this issue, perhaps through a listed property trust, which can deliver stable returns. Trends in Lend Lease's financial performance are illustrated in figure 24.3.
- *management of risk and losses.* Following recent losses on projects in the United States and Australia, a strategic review found evidence of poor adherence to existing risk-management principles. These are being addressed by management, and a return to profitability is expected from 2005.
- *credit risk.* There is always a risk of parties involved in projects failing to pay (defaulting) or delaying payment.
- *a need to eliminate loss-making operations.* Today, the selling off of REI operations in the United States has been completed and other operations are closely monitored for performance.
- *cost control and supply chain inefficiencies.* Lend Lease is continuing its focus on cost reductions, especially corporate overheads, already reduced by $67 million before tax in 2003–04, to restore profitability and boost shareholder confidence.

Financial objective	Lend Lease 2004	Lend Lease 2001	Industry averages 2000
Profitability			
Revenue $ million	9726 .0	11 454.0	—
ROE (Return on owners' equity)%	11.4	66.79	–2.32
PAT (Profit after tax) $ million	237.0	151.0	—
Operating profit after tax %	8.3	4.1	—
Earnings per share	57.4	33.5	—
Solvency			
Gearing (Debt to equity)	30.4	25.0	41.5
Liquidity			
Current ratio	1.04	1.20	1.28
Efficiency			
Acc R T/O ratio (Accounts receivable turnover) (days)	—	42.61	31.08
Revenue/employee $ '000 (thousands)	1080.6	1092.5	3931.5

Figure 24.3 Overview: financial performance for Lend Lease

Sources: Data derived from IBISWorld 2000; Lend Lease, *Annual Report*, 2004; Commsec report on Lend Lease Corporation Ltd, 2005.

The four-year trend analysis shown in figure 24.4 shows the downturn in revenue experienced by Lend Lease since 2001 and its relatively low net profit margins, which are slowly improving following the change in Lend Lease's strategy.

Year	2004	2003	2002	2001
Revenue $ million	9726.0	10 114.0	12 478.0	11 454.0
PAT (excluding abnormals)	237.0	230.0	226.0	151.0
ROE% (before amortisation)	9.0	8.0	8.0	6.0
Net profit margin %	2.7	2.3	1.9	1.4
Return on equity	8.4	7.7	6.0	4.2

Figure 24.4 four-year trend analysis — profitability of Lend Lease group

Note: Lend Lease PAT reported (after sale of asset) in 2004: 333.5 million.

Source: Lend Lease, *Annual Report*, 2004.

Figure 24.5 shows Lend Lease's performance in comparison to some of its major competitors.

Company	Revenue 2004 $ million	NPAT 2004 $ million	ROE	Gearing (Total Liability: Assets)	Employees (% change on 2003)
Lend Lease	9726	333.5	11.8	60.2	9060 (–9.3)
Westfield America Trust	2321	596.8	9.3	55.9	NA
Westfield Trust	1915.3	564.1	7.7	42.2	NA
Westfield Holdings	1253.5	(196.3)	(14.6)	55.4	4352 (5.4)
Stockland	1371.0	574.1	11.4	30.2	1 161 (18)
Mirvac Group	1385.6	252.7	11.3	48.0	2702 (–5.8)

Figure 24.5 Competitor performance — Property and business services

Note: Westfield companies merged in June 2004 to form the Westfield Group.

Note: NPAT = net profit after tax.

Source: IBISWorld Business Information as reported in *Business Review Weekly* 2004, 'Australia's biggest enterprises', *BRW 1000*, Nov 11–Dec 15.

Strategic financial planning

Strategic financial planning underpins Lend Lease's long-term allocation of funds and return requirements (financial objectives) that form its investment framework. Lend Lease's businesses operate within individual frameworks. They address their current business performance, identify opportunities and evaluate risks, and prioritise opportunities to deliver results in line with the business objectives.

Key financial strategies used to achieve these objectives include:

- diversification of earnings sources geographically and by type over the longer term
- management of risk through quarterly reviews of framework and forecasts, a strong balance sheet, a strong asset base in property ($10 billion), and interest rate and currency risk management through strategies including hedging

- identification of strategies to maximise returns and raise investment capital
- a focus on achievement of an 'A' credit rating from the international credit rating agencies Moody's and Standard & Poor's
- maintenance of funding flexibility to maximise opportunities, including a dividend reinvestment program to raise regular capital.

Global strategies

In 2003, following the failure of its REI business in the United States, Lend Lease recognised that its global business strategy, with its universal approach to all markets had failed. One critic commented: '[The company] would know all about unjustified global aspirations. The company poured much of its wealth into becoming one of the largest real estate managers in the world and promptly lost over a billion dollars.'

This saw a sharp drop in the company's share price from a peak of $23 in 2000. Lend Lease's new strategy today retains its presence in the same markets, but uses a new business model, based on lower cost, differentiated services in sectors and markets suited to its capabilities.

Topic 3: marketing

Market research

Lend Lease undertakes ongoing market research into market opportunities in each region in which it operates to ensure its marketing efforts are directed most effectively towards achieving business goals. The sources of this research are shown in figure 24.6.

Primary sources

- Client interviews
- Past client interviews
- Shopper surveys
- Analysis of sales trends, by territory, products/service, staff and financial reports
- Staff feedback
- Visitor feedback — display homes

Secondary sources

- Industry association research
- Economic reports — supply and demand, employment, business services growth trends
- Marketing research
- ABS data and surveys (e.g. housing affordability, demographic trends)
- Government reports
- Annual reports, business reports
- Magazines and journal reports

Figure 24.6 Before Lend Lease develops a leisure resort it undertakes extensive market research to clearly identify customers' needs.

Lend Lease assesses the attractiveness of each market, carefully considering:

- the level of economic growth of the market
- the history of the market and industry. Commercial property development issues considered include trends in vacancy rates, market rents and construction starts.
- political, economic, social, cultural, geographic, legal and institutional influences and trends. In the case of Delfin's plans for urban communities, key trends are the growth of smaller households, the need for affordable housing, higher numbers of

single-person and aged households, increased numbers of people working from home and time-poor households. To meet pressure for environmental sustainability, Lend Lease researches the latest building materials, water systems and designs to improve energy efficiency, and incorporates such elements in its new designs.

- market growth and profitability potential, current servicing levels by other operators and opportunities that may arise
- the attractiveness of the customer profile
- the suitability of potential projects to Lend Lease expertise
- accessibility of markets via existing marketing or distribution networks, joint ventures, acquisitions and contacts, using regional advantages if required
- potential client needs. In designing a hospital in Anchorage, Alaska, Bovis Lend Lease needed to incorporate geographic influences, such as a high risk of significant seismic activity and temperatures so extreme that footpaths are heated to melt snow.

The attractiveness of the major markets targeted by Lend Lease is shown in figure 24.7.

Business	Asia–Pacific region	US	UK/Europe	Key operational benefits
▪ Real estate funds management ▪ Asset management and ownership	▪ General Property Trust (GPT) ▪ Australian Prime Property Fund ▪ Real Estate Partners ▪ Real Estate Securities	▪ King of Prussia Shopping Mall	▪ UK Retail Partnership ▪ Overgate Partnership ▪ Bluewater Shopping Mall	▪ Access to assets outside Australia ▪ Access to broader business relationships ▪ Ability to grow wholesale funds management business faster
▪ Retail asset development	▪ Retail property management ▪ Retail development	▪ Urban communities*	▪ Retail property management ▪ Retail development	▪ Delivers economies of scale to expand business ▪ Creates options to pursue direct ownership as well as third party capital model in UK and Singapore ▪ Secures access to earnings from all parts of the value chain
▪ Urban community development	▪ Delfin Lend Lease ▪ Lend Lease Development ▪ Senior Living	▪ Actus Lend Lease ▪ Urban communities*	▪ Greenwich Peninsula ▪ Urban communities*	▪ Provides economies of scale to accelerate growth opportunities in all three regions ▪ Enhances capacity to derive integrated earnings (i.e. retail asset ownership within major communities)

(*continued*)

Business	Asia–Pacific region	US	UK/Europe	Key operational benefits
▪ Project and construction management (includes global markets)	▪ Bovis Lend Lease	▪ Bovis Lend Lease	▪ Bovis Lend Lease	▪ Increases economies of scale and enhances capacity to raise finance through bonds ▪ Reduces risks by investment asset creation and redevelopment ▪ Underpins competitive advantage to win major contracts

Figure 24.7 Lend Lease businesses and global activities

Note: * = planned

Source: Lend Lease, 'JP Morgan Australasian investment conference, Edinburgh, October 2004', viewed 16 June 2005, http://www.lendlease.com.au/llweb/llc/main.nsf/images/pdf_jpmorgan_conference.pdf/$file/pdf_jpmorgan_conference.pdf

Market segmentation

Lend Lease segments its markets so it can direct its marketing strategies to specific groups of customers rather than the total market. This allows Lend Lease to better satisfy the wants and needs of a targeted group.

Lend Lease segments its markets primarily using geographical, product and customer variables. Its primary geographic markets lie in the United States, United Kingdom and Australia and the Asia–Pacific region. It is also prepared to follow its long-time customers into new markets. In each market Lend Lease targets market needs suited to its business capabilities, such as health care, defence, education, commercial, industrial and government projects. The ability to choose the correct target market is an important marketing function because it will influence Lend Lease's marketing mix.

Delfin Lend Lease focuses on the growth segment of urban communities and, in Australia, has gained considerable expertise in this area.

Lend Lease Development targets high-value niche sites in major population centres characterised by medium and high-density mixed-use integrated developments. Lend Lease Development generates construction and project management work for Bovis, which then increases revenue for Lend Lease's operations in Australia overall, and reduces the delivery risk associated with more complex developments.

Global Markets is a part of Bovis Lend Lease that concentrates on multinational corporations and focuses on long-term client relationships. It works with companies such as Nokia, BP and Merck to provide specialist design and engineering, technical knowledge and systems for multi-location systems, such as in telecommunications infrastructure networks.

Figure 24.8 shows a SWOT analysis of Lend Lease, which forms an important basis for its segmentation, positioning and marketing. Understanding its SWOT is critical for Lend Lease's short- and long-term competitive strategy and planning.

Strengths	Weaknesses
▪ Highly qualified, culturally diverse and experienced workforce, with strong technical and management skills ▪ Reputation for professionalism ▪ Strong performance in buildings and structures, and infrastructure sectors ▪ Strong business and government networks ▪ Vertically integrated and provides full range of services to clients ▪ Focus on high-quality, large-scale building sites in high growth markets is yielding good results. ▪ Long-term contracts with US military (seven for 50 years) provide long-term earning streams.	▪ Strategy still needs further development — investors and commentators believe Lend Lease needs to acquire a listed property trust to maximise its opportunities ▪ Lack of reliable profitability and stable cash flow in property development area — increases risk profile of business ▪ Shareholder sentiment neutral to negative due to recent losses in United States, uncertainty over GPT plan and other strategies implemented by new CEO and board ▪ Operating costs — room for further improvement
Opportunities	**Threats**
▪ Acquisition of listed property trust to finance and fully integrate Lend Lease activities and strategies ▪ Diversification into new regions, sectors or services, particularly in areas recently entered, including Central Asia, the Gulf region and Africa. ▪ Strong market prospects in Eastern Europe, Latin America, Western Europe, North America ▪ Financial sponsorship of specific projects increasing, particularly public–private partnerships ▪ Rent growth opportunities in all markets ▪ Non-residential construction is experiencing best conditions in Australia at the moment ▪ Macro factors — improving economies in Asia–Pacific region, increasing transparency levels, falling regulatory barriers and the increasing globalisation of the commercial property market providing opportunities in that market ▪ Growth anticipated in integrated property development in health care, defence and retail (Lend Lease is already active in this area both in Australia and overseas.) ▪ Wholesale funds management businesses to benefit from retirement savings into property over the next few years ▪ UK market opportunities strong — government has made commitment to 10-year investment plan for health care, with 100 hospitals to be rebuilt	▪ Competition from growing size of international project development and construction firms as merger activity increases ▪ Political, financial and economic risks associated with operations in developing nations. Current geo-political unrest and risk of terrorism a major reason for large corporate decisions to reduce priority of projects in South-East Asia, and to refocus on China. ▪ The Asian financial crisis of the 1990s highlighted concerns regarding the risks associated with operations in developing nations ▪ Corruption poses a risk to tendering and project management in developing nations ▪ Increasing taxation in Australia on the construction industry by all levels of government ▪ Australian Reserve Bank action to reduce the level of growth in real estate prices ▪ A shortage of skilled labour in Australia, which is leading to increased construction costs in Australia. Hard to cope with penalties and additional costs inflicted by clients when projects delayed. Industry poor at managing risk. ▪ Credit risks — with large projects risk of default can have serious impacts ▪ Liquidity is more of an issue for a firm still over-dependent on large projects

Figure 24.8 SWOT analysis for Lend Lease

Lend Lease's *sustainable competitive advantage* lies in making the most of opportunities arising from its international performance and ongoing relationships with large multinational clients and governments, its economies of scale, vertical integration and organisational capabilities. These capabilities are founded on its highly skilled and professional workforce and leadership talent, developed through its unique business culture. In order to maximise its opportunities in attracting its target markets, Lend Lease uses the following marketing mix.

The marketing mix

Product

The Lend Lease product is totally responsive to client needs. For clients requiring a shopping centre, such as Bluewater in the United Kingdom, the focus of planning is on convenience; range and variety; consistency in the quality of retailers; comfort; services; environment; entertainment; the centre as a meeting place; and a good tenancy mix. For shopping centres managed by Lend Lease, much attention is given to ongoing market research into these features through shopper surveys and monitoring of competitor offerings.

Figure 24.9 Bluewater shopping centre, United Kingdom

All projects are *positioned* against other developments. Issues such as building quality, image, design, lighting, the incorporation of cutting-edge technology and environmental features are key positioning elements.

Major Australian projects in recent years include the urban renewal of Melbourne's Docklands, the international airports in Sydney and Brisbane, and the Sydney Olympic village.

Delfin Lend Lease's success originates from its mega display home centres, which show innovative living home designs that have flair and flexibility. Lend Lease uses its market research to compete more effectively by designing for changing market needs. In the housing market, Lend Lease has responded to increased demand for SOHOs (solo out of a home offices), coastal beach homes, warehouses, traditional homes and master-planned communities for specific market niches.

Figure 24.10 Lend Lease prides itself on design innovation. This photo shows the Sydney Olympic Village, built for the 2000 Olympic Games.

Promotion

Lend Lease uses the full range of promotion strategies to raise awareness of its products and services.

Advertising that combined newspaper and Internet reports recently extended the reach and targeting of apartment purchasers in Victoria Harbour in Melbourne. This strategy successfully tapped into the professional, time-poor, high-income users, and produced four times the normal rate of enquiry. It provided a good mix of visibility and content, and involved organising targeted property features in the press, and placing electronic advertisements on the website of a metropolitan newspaper.

Magazine and news coverage of its new developments allows Lend Lease's work to sell itself. Mass mailings of fact sheets on new properties and fliers in major magazines supplement these strategies.

Publicity material such as brochures, banners and online marketing is designed to reinforce the brand, to catch the eye and build customer trust. Launch parties and strikingly decorated display units build awareness and excitement, and allow clients to complete purchases in property developments. Lend Lease frequently wins, and publicises, awards for its designs in industry journals such as *Property Australia*. Recent awards have included the Australian Property Institute award for excellence in property, and other awards for energy efficiency, heritage and property development.

Public displays emphasise Lend Lease's excellent safety record. One example is the iconic 'Hello Darling' illuminated sign on Lend Lease's Darling Park project. This projects an image of workers arriving home safe and sound, a key priority in

Lend Lease's employment relations strategy, while promoting evidence of corporate social responsibility.

Lend Lease's website, and those of its businesses, provide excellent opportunities to showcase its scale of operations and performance through illustrated case studies of its major projects in each market.

Lend Lease's newsletter builds internal marketing skills and reinforces the company's culture.

Price

Lend Lease's pricing methods are competitive. It uses a combination of cost-plus and market-based pricing related to the nature of the product or service supplied. For large commercial and government projects, Lend Lease submits tenders (bids) and clients select projects on the basis of a range of factors, including price competitiveness and the ability to deliver ongoing maintenance and/or management of facilities. Delfin prices its housing in relation to the quality sought by the client, but clearly is attempting to attract clients who want affordable housing.

Place

Lend Lease bids for projects around the world in markets it considers attractive, and in which it believes it can take advantage of existing networks and capabilities. Much of its work originates in Australia, the United Kingdom, the United States and the Asia–Pacific region. It has a strong presence in these markets, both in terms of offices and/or strategic alliances with key firms.

People

Highly skilled staff that produce quality products and services are what 'sells' the business.

Relationship marketing and *networking* is critical to firms seeking large government and multinational projects and investments. Sponsorship of community events and staff attending industry functions, making presentations and writing articles are strategies used by Lend Lease to build its reputation and valuable contacts in government and business.

Managing stakeholder conflict is a critical management skill for projects such as Bluewater, the United Kingdom's and Europe's largest retail centre, which Lend Lease developed and now manages. Lend Lease manages 20 shopping centres around Australia, which require specific marketing strategies, including special promotions and regular liaison with retailers and community organisations. Lend Lease is increasingly involved in public–private partnerships with government (for example, South Australia's Golden Grove Development) and interpersonal skills are critical in negotiation and ongoing management.

Legal issues affecting the marketing of Lend Lease's products and services

As consumer and government expectations grow, increasing regulation is a significant influence on developers. Regulation of trading hours, tenancy protection, building depreciation and planning regulation are major influences on business activities, particularly of the businesses Lend Lease manages, such as GPT. The Property Council has been a strong advocate in Australia for less regulation of the property development industry, particularly regarding taxes such as the GST and stamp duty on commercial property deals.

Figure 24.11 Lend Lease employees work on projects in over 80 countries.

Topic 4: employment relations

Lend Lease staff are predominantly located in Australia and the Pacific, the United Kingdom and United States, with smaller numbers in Asian markets.

The following employment relations strategies provide insight into how Lend Lease's professional development operates to create its renowned *corporate culture*. Commentators suggest leaders from companies such as Lend Lease are in high demand, particularly because they are given ongoing responsibilities. If something goes wrong the culture encourages staff to find out why. Lend Lease people, therefore, adapt well to changing situations in organisations as they are used to building *teams*, delegating, and working to tight deadlines with fixed targets.

Human resources planning

Lend Lease has always carefully planned for its workforce needs, aware of the external legal, social and economic influences, such as the domestic skills shortage, and global opportunities to take advantage of its high-quality technical and professional skills base. Today, it is also focused on developing a management team that complies with risk and control features that may arise in the future.

Recruitment and selection

Lend Lease's excellent reputation as a leadership 'university' and employer of choice enhances its ability to recruit high-quality staff for its global businesses. Through its links to universities it is able to attract top students, and maintain a multicultural workforce.

Training and development

Following induction of new staff, Lend Lease's training and development program focuses less on narrow individual competencies and more on the core competency of being able to absorb, adapt, apply and improve within team-based systems. Old skills are of less importance to Lend Lease; coaching, communicating, facilitating, integrating, information sharing, managing change and projects, and system evaluation are the key skills needed by employees today.

Lend Lease's training and development program supports this by:

- developing coaching and leadership skills for emerging leaders
- initiating employee focus workshops, in which ideas on an issue are sought from a small group
- developing multiskilled, multifunctional teams and job rotation within teams
- supporting mentoring partnerships and networks developed within the organisation.

Lend Lease uses a leadership capability framework for succession planning and for employees demonstrating high potential. This approach:

- uses *performance appraisal* strategies to focus on the leadership qualities needed by Lend Lease — leadership, management and technical capabilities. All employees are rated on the same criteria, and the results are discussed with the employee's supervisor.
- tracks employee performance indicators over time to determine trends and modify plans for both individual and general professional development

- has given Lend Lease a reputation as one of the top 'leader factories' in Australia — its staff are often headhunted by other companies. The success of these strategies is also evident in recent awards received by Lend Lease, including WorkCover's 2004 Safe Work Awards for best training program, which was won by Bovis Lend Lease.

For senior management, Global CEO meetings, annual business Top 100 meetings, regional conferences, coaching interventions, CEO coffee talks and other learning opportunities help to build leadership potential.

All employees can apply to participate in Springboard conferences, which are held annually in different locations around the world where Lend Lease operates. In its most recent format, this program is designed to help employees realise and continuously reach their individual potential in their professional and personal lives.

Managing conflict and industrial relations

Lend Lease fosters a high quality of work through supportive relationships with staff. Its training and development programs, *team structures*, *effective internal communications* systems, and adherence to *legal compliance* in all areas of employment law provide a strong foundation for these relationships.

Lend Lease believes *enterprise agreements* should be the result of workplace reform, rather than the 'vehicle to bring it about'. Lend Lease wants its enterprise agreements to provide opportunities for 'concept productivity', allowing it to learn faster and deliver innovation faster than its competitors.

Rewards and motivation

Lend Lease has a flexible approach to rewards. Staff are offered options including a cash-only package or a cash-plus benefits package including car lease, in-house child care, laptops, salary sacrificed superannuation payments, access to financial planning, and a company share acquisition program. This flexibility allows employees to select a mix of benefits that meets their needs at each stage of their career or family life cycle.

Lend Lease's rewards are regularly reviewed and *benchmarked* against other firms through networking, use of industry data and employee feedback. Internal focus groups help determine what staff see as popular packages. Changes to *legislation* are carefully evaluated for significant impacts on benefits. Rewards strategies are always analysed carefully for their cost effectiveness and competitiveness. But for Lend Lease, attractive and relevant packages and its high-quality corporate culture are significant motivators and key factors in the retention of staff. Compensation is largely based on market conditions and personal performance, which is based on financial, corporate and personal targets, and includes cash and shares, or awards under share plans.

To appraise team leaders and managers Lend Lease uses the 360-degree feedback method. This provides anonymous feedback to the job holder from the employees who interact with him or her and is an important way of identifying the qualities needed for leadership. When an employee is regarded as an outstanding performer, retention awards may also be applied.

Equal employment opportunity

Lend Lease has always been a pacesetter in relation to benefits, being one of the first companies to ever offer in-house corporate child care for staff and the same benefits for all employees regardless of position; for example, child care benefits are the same for staff regardless of the location in which they work. To assist mothers in returning to work, Lend Lease has introduced a range of initiatives including breastfeeding rooms in some of its workplaces, a company nurse specialising in parenting issues, and access to part-time and home-based work (through its child-care centres) following parental leave. Bovis Lend Lease's gender initiatives include a project control group, which obtains and analyses organisational data on salary, bonus levels and separation rates, and that sponsors internal debate on gender diversity and prioritisation of possible initiatives. Bovis Lend Lease's aim is to ensure it retains the talent that reflects the businesses and communities with which it interacts.

Occupational health and safety

Lend Lease is committed to operating incident and injury-free, and to working proactively with all its stakeholders — employees, clients, designers and contractors — to achieve this goal through a safety culture. It has agreed to pioneer a national program, the 'Environmental Health and Safety Management System' with the Housing Industry Authority on Delfin Lend Lease's 20 projects, ensuring that anyone on these projects is trained to the highest level in environmental and workplace safety standards.

Reviews are regularly undertaken of occupational health and safety (OH&S) to protect the employees, stakeholders and communities with which Lend Lease interacts. Lend Lease has focused extensively on improving OH&S and has achieved an excellent safety record. At this level it is more challenging to improve performance further, so workshops are regularly undertaken to ensure staff remain focused and that records are shared across the organisation. Internal awards programs reinforce this approach to OH&S.

Lend Lease also offers all staff members a free and confidential counselling service. To provide anonymity for its employees, this service is provided by an external company.

Code of conduct

Lend Lease has a code of conduct which includes the following specific standards. Staff must:

- be aware of conflicts of interest
- not participate in insider trading or make unauthorised gains or payments (i.e. bribes), particularly where they are involved in a tender. This contravenes Australian anti-bribery laws and laws in many other jurisdictions.
- use company assets only as authorised, including brands, computer systems, passwords and corporate charge cards
- avoid disclosing confidential information (for example, about its customers or suppliers) and take care not to make any unauthorised public statements
- ensure all staff have equal opportunities and act with integrity and professionalism
- compete fairly in all markets, and refuse to associate with illegal market practices such as price-fixing schemes
- consider all environmental, health and safety impacts before making any business decision
- not make any unauthorised political donations on behalf of Lend Lease
- be familiar with the business unit policies and procedures related to the workplace
- be prepared to help colleagues and work collaboratively.

Topic 5: global business

Lend Lease enters global markets through a *range of methods*, including tendering for international contracts, often through joint ventures or consortia based on its regional offices.

Lend Lease carefully *researches markets* for opportunities where it has a competitive advantage, and assesses whether potential partners are aligned with its organisational culture and business plan. In global markets, firms such as Lend Lease use their political and business networks to deal with the complex legal, taxation, financial and regulatory environments. Lend Lease's objective is to implement a strategy, such as a merger, to provide it with a more efficient capital structure for expansion, while benefiting from a reliable earnings base from the portfolio of a property trust. In *managing* its global business, Lend Lease recognises that by focusing on *business practices* delivering high standards — in terms of design and construction quality and environmental health and safety — it is building the foundations for future ongoing relationships with governments and multinational clients in overseas markets.

In managing *cultural* and *political influences*, it has found connections to be essential in China, an important long-term market for Lend Lease. Advantages exist for firms willing to engage in technology transfer and involvement of Chinese design institutes is important.

Partnerships or consortia offer advantages including access to a physical site, comprehensive market knowledge, distribution networks, access to raw materials, and political and commercial connections. Critical issues include visiting the market regularly, and participation in trade shows.

In managing staffing issues, Lend Lease builds *cultural awareness* and *business and management skills* through teams that consult local communities and work with local partners out of its many global offices, and by fostering *staff mobility* between these offices.

In the United Kingdom, opportunities exist for firms that are price competitive, innovative, design environmentally smart buildings and use technology that has well-designed fixtures. There are strong market opportunities arising from government privatisation initiatives, United Kingdom and European Union legislation, social trends and the preference for wealthy people to live in the south-east of England. *Legal and cultural similarities*, particularly those affecting business practices and ethics, make investment in the United States and United Kingdom attractive to firms such as Lend Lease.

In managing *financial influences*, Lend Lease complies with Australian Accounting Standards, and is moving through the planning stage towards full compliance with International Financial Reporting Standards. This phase has involved assessment of the impacts on the business and its key processes, analysis of training requirements and preparation of conversion plans for policies, business processes, reporting systems and staff training. It operates a comprehensive risk-management program, including hedging using derivatives to manage currency risk. It recognises the translation risk of changes in foreign exchange rates on its consolidated financial statements as a separate component of equity, and also in the statement of consolidated financial performance.

EXERCISE 24.1 *Revision*

1. List all the businesses that operate as part of the Lend Lease group, and identify their functions.
2. Analyse the advantages of vertical integration for Lend Lease.
3. Explain why success in overseas markets is often difficult.
4. Outline the financial management lessons learned by Lend Lease from recent experience.
5. Develop a list of strategies that are essential to successful operations in global markets.
6. Discuss the chances of success of Lend Lease's new strategy.
7. Imagine you are planning to enter a new market for Lend Lease. You fly to the country and undertake market research for the company on this new market. Draw a table listing the type of research you would undertake and the sources and methods used for your research.
8. Imagine you are setting up an office in this new market for Lend Lease. You have followed one major client into this market. Outline the strategies you would use to develop local demand for your services in this market.
9. You attend a government function run by the foreign affairs department in the new overseas market. Explain how you might use this function to build your business.
10. One of your staff members has caused offence (not sexual or criminal) to a senior official at a meeting. Using the Internet, find out what is considered to be appropriate professional behaviour in the country you have selected. Outline five forms of offence that may affect your business dealings.
11. Examine the code of conduct on page 509. Complete the table to demonstrate your understanding of the importance of a code of conduct by selecting four of the items listed. Reduce each one to keywords in the table under item.

Item	Possible reason for inclusion in code	Likely impacts

12. Explain why Lend Lease staff are regularly headhunted by other firms.
13. Read about Lend Lease's approach to enterprise bargaining (page 508). What are your opinions of this approach?
14. What strategies does Lend Lease follow in order to build relationships with its overseas customers?
15. Identify the advantages for Lend Lease of a partnership or consortia.
16. What is involved in Lend Lease's risk-management program?

HSC PRACTICE QUESTIONS

Topic 1
Business management and change

Multiple-choice questions

For each question, choose the best alternative.

1 Maria has recently purchased a business from Tamara. The business has been losing sales for the past 12 months. It has been suggested that mismanagement is the cause. Maria should
(a) adopt better training practices for staff.
(b) restructure the administration staff.
(c) hire new managers.
(d) review the strategic plan and set new organisational objectives.

2 Flattening the organisational structure in a business would
(a) change the management structure.
(b) eliminate the board of directors.
(c) increase the number of middle managers.
(d) all of the above.

3 For the past 10 years, Tessa has been the managing director of Worldwide Express, an international business employing 3680 employees. Tessa expects all employees to carry out the decisions made by management. The power basis for her leadership is most likely to be
(a) legitimate. (b) expert.
(c) referent. (d) coercive.

4 In implementing strategic plans, organising involves
(a) improving staff employment strategies.
(b) determining and delegating work tasks.
(c) involving staff in decisions about changes in practices.
(d) reviewing use of technology in business.

5 Comparing the following two organisational charts, which of the following is true?
(a) Business A has a taller structure with a narrower span of control than business B.
(b) Business A has a flatter structure with a narrower span of control than business B.
(c) Business B has a taller structure with a narrower span of control than business A.
(d) Business B has a flatter structure with a narrower span of control than business A.

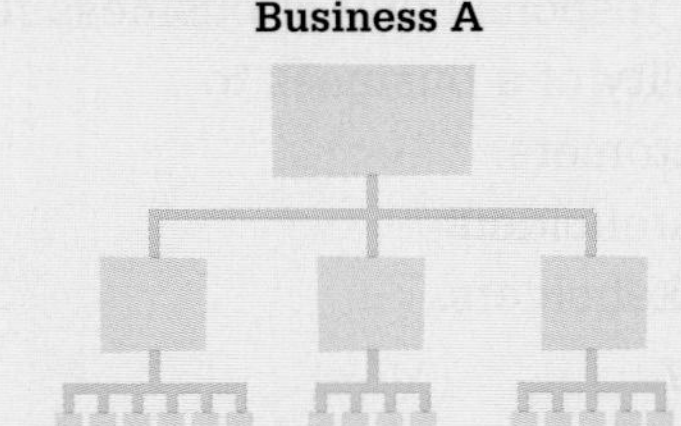

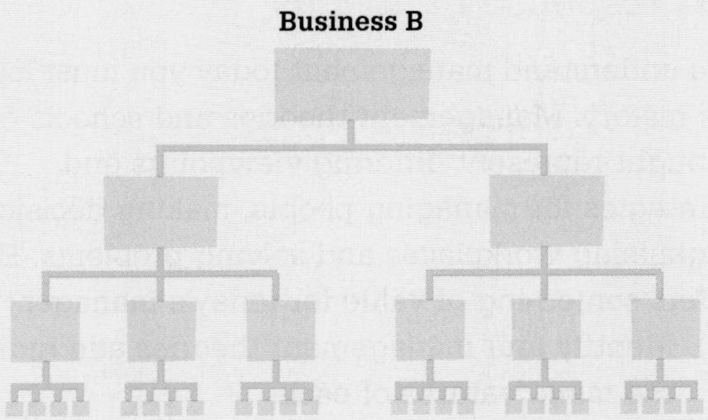

6 Planning for change that is proactive involves
(a) responding quickly to internal and external influences.
(b) adopting only strategies that match past trends.
(c) anticipating future trends and implementing strategies in advance.
(d) none of the above.

7 Lewin advocated that change agents must
(a) change and then refreeze the organisation.
(b) change, unfreeze and then refreeze the organisation.
(c) unfreeze and then refreeze the organisation.
(d) unfreeze, change and then refreeze the organisation.

8 The contingency approach to management refers to
(a) seeking continuous improvement in employee performance and productivity levels.
(b) the need for flexibility and adaptation of management practices and ideas to suit changing circumstances.
(c) setting predetermined goals and formulating strategies to generate possible solutions.
(d) a situation where the main emphasis of management is to improve interpersonal skills within the management teams.

9 Resistance to change in management and employees is common. This is most likely to be due to
(a) perceived fear of financial loss.
(b) inertia of managers and business owners.
(c) fear of job losses.
(d) all of the above.

10 The social responsibility of business refers to the responsibility of a business to
(a) its customers.
(b) its shareholders.
(c) its stakeholders.
(d) society.

Short response questions

1 'To understand management today you must look at its history. Management theories and schools of thought represent differing viewpoints and strategies for managing people, making decisions, organising workplaces and solving problems. Each offers something of value for today's manager.'
(a) Identify four management theories and indicate the main features of each.
(b) Explain how these theories could influence contemporary management practices.
(c) Outline the relationship between management theory and the types of organisational structure that a business could adopt.

2 (a) What is a management 'role'?
(b) Distinguish between interpersonal, informational and decision-making management roles.
(c) Suggest why effective management requires the adoption of all three roles.

3 (a) Define the term 'stakeholders'.
(b) Identify and describe two possible conflicts that could arise between various stakeholders.
(c) Suggest possible strategies managers could adopt to reconcile any possible conflicts of interest.

4 For each of the following situations, identify and explain the management skills and strategies that could be used.

Case 1. A dispute has arisen between the computer section and the accounting section of a business regarding the introduction of a new computer invoice system. The accountant wants the new system introduced by the beginning of the new financial year, but the computer manager believes that the staff will not be sufficiently trained by then to handle it successfully. You are the human resource manager in charge of this project and must negotiate agreement without further delay.

Case 2. As the human resource manager you are trying to convince senior management that the staff training and development budget is presently inadequate and needs increasing by 35 per cent over the next two years. This is a great opportunity for you to show your skills as a negotiator.

5 (a) Define the term 'social responsibility'.
(b) Describe the main advantages of a business acting in a socially responsible manner. Are there any possible disadvantages?
(c) Suggest reasons why the improvement of business ethics is ultimately an individual response.

Extended response questions

1 'Over the last 10 to 15 years, the process of globalisation has been instrumental in bringing about revolutionary change in the Australian business environment.' Elaborate. In your answer refer to a business you have studied.

2 Compare and contrast the classical–scientific, behavioural, political and contingency management theories. From a business you have studied, outline how management theory has influenced the business's structure.

3 'The only constant in business is change. The pace of change is accelerating, with change coming from both internal and external sources. How a business responds to these changes will ultimately determine the organisation's future.' Critically examine the strategies used to manage change effectively in a business you have studied.

4 Your school has decided to determine your final results for this course on team tests as opposed to individual tests as presently conducted. Propose and justify the strategies your school will need to implement to 'unfreeze' or prepare students who are not familiar with this approach.

5 'Inevitable resistance to change must be overcome if the organisation is to succeed. Employees and managers resist change for many reasons.' Analyse the nature and sources of change in business. Illustrate, with reference to a business you have studied, the main reasons for resistance to change.

HSC PRACTiCE QUESTiONS

Topic 2
Financial planning and management

Multiple-choice questions

For each question, choose the best alternative.

1 Equity financing requires
(a) selling shares to investors.
(b) distributing profits among the owners.
(c) raising finance through borrowing from a financial institution.
(d) increasing sales through more advertising.

2 For most small businesses, which of the following sources of finance should make up the highest percentage?
(a) Leasing
(b) Owners' equity
(c) Bank loans
(d) Commercial bills

3 Short-term borrowing is provided by
(a) bank overdrafts.
(b) bridging finance.
(c) commercial bills.
(d) all of the above.

4 Working capital is best described as
(a) plant and equipment.
(b) current assets less current liabilities.
(c) cash available for use in the business.
(d) contributions of the owners to the business.

5 Which of the following ratios assists to evaluate a firm's liquidity?
(a) Gross profit ratio
(b) Current ratio
(c) Accounts receivable ratio
(d) Debt to equity ratio

6 The rate of return on assets is a
(a) liquidity ratio.
(b) profitability ratio.
(c) gearing ratio.
(d) leverage ratio.

7 An immediate increase in cash flow will result from
(a) giving credit to a valued customer.
(b) upgrading technology in the factory.
(c) obtaining a loan from the bank.
(d) selling a non-income producing part of the firm.

8 A business sells its accounts receivable. Identify the external source of finance.
(a) Leasing
(b) Factoring
(c) Leverage
(d) Cash management

9 An example of a fixed cost in a business is
(a) materials used in production.
(b) commission on sales.
(c) advertising.
(d) building insurance on factory.

10 An example of a variable cost in a business is
(a) depreciation on factory equipment.
(b) rent.
(c) auditor's fees.
(d) freight outwards.

Short response questions

1 Debra and Ian are considering setting up a business offering catering services to the corporate sector. In the short term they will work from home and, where possible, use local suppliers.
(a) Explain to Debra and Ian the advantages and disadvantages of a cash-only business.
(b) Explain, with examples, internal and external sources of funds available to Debra and Ian.
(c) Compare financial risk factors in long-term external finance for Debra and Ian.

2 CCD Enterprises has been successfully producing and selling a range of sporting goods in the Australian market. It has decided that there is potential in the Asian market.
(a) Explain two financial objectives that CCD Enterprises might be considering.
(b) Compare two strategies that CCD Enterprises might consider to ensure that there is sufficient cash flow for the expansion.
(c) Evaluate the costs and benefits of CCD Enterprises' expansion plans.

3 The management of Jaico Tools wishes to expand the business. It must decide whether to increase the mortgage over the current property or use reserves to raise finance.

(a) Compare two costs and two benefits of the options being considered.

(b) Explain the concept of leverage (gearing) to Jaico Tools.

(c) Explain how level leverage (gearing) will affect the business.

4 Refer to the following balance sheet.

	$	$
Current Assets		
Cash	7 000	
Receivables	6 000	
Inventories	2 000	15 000
Non-current Assets		
Property, plant and equipment		18 000
Total Assets		33 000
Current Liabilities		
Creditors		14 000
Net Assets		19 000
Owners' Equity		
Capital	16 500	
Net Profit	2 500	19 000

(a) Calculate the working capital of this business.

(b) Explain two strategies that could be used to manage its working capital.

(c) Explain how a bank overdraft of $2000 would affect working capital.

5 DRE's debt to equity ratio stands at a low 16 per cent, a level that leaves many company analysts impatient for acquisition.

(a) Explain what is meant by debt to equity ratio.

(b) What strategies could DRE put in place to change the debt to equity ratio?

(c) If the parent company injected $450 million equity by offering options, explain how this injection would affect the company.

Extended response questions

1 Discuss how the strategies for effective financial planning can assist successful management of change.

2 Discuss the ethical responsibilities of management in making financial decisions relating to their interactions with global markets.

3 A high debt to equity ratio financed by both short-term and long-term borrowing has led to a decision by a firm to downsize its operations. Discuss the effects of such a decision on stakeholders in the business.

4 The following have been identified by management:

- difficulties in matching cash inflows with outflows
- declining liquidity
- declining accounts receivable turnover and expense ratios.

Management is considering a wider use of technology in its interactions with markets. Write a report to management suggesting a range of strategies to improve the position of the business.

5 Brixton Jams & Pickles have decided to take advantage of the strong demand for its Australian products by developing markets in Japan, Korea and the United States. This decision will require finance from a range of sources. Write a report to management analysing the financial aspects that need to be considered in making this decision.

HSC PRACTICE QUESTIONS

Topic 3 Marketing

Multiple-choice questions

For each question, choose the best alternative.

1 Which of the following statements most completely defines the term 'marketing'?

(a) Marketing is the distribution of goods and services from the wholesaler to the retailer so that they are available when the customer wants them.
(b) Marketing is a total system of interacting activities designed to plan, price, promote and distribute goods and services to present and potential customers.
(c) Marketing includes all those activities involved in the production and promotion of goods and services to the end customer.
(d) Marketing is any set of activities undertaken to produce and promote a range of goods and services to satisfy customers' needs.

2 Which of the following statements is true?

(a) A business that supports socially responsible practices and individuals who act ethically will have a positive impact on society.
(b) If a social responsibility issue is widely discussed within a business then the chances of reaching an acceptable solution are increased.
(c) Marketing ethics and social responsibility work together.
(d) All of the above.

Question 3 refers to the following diagram.

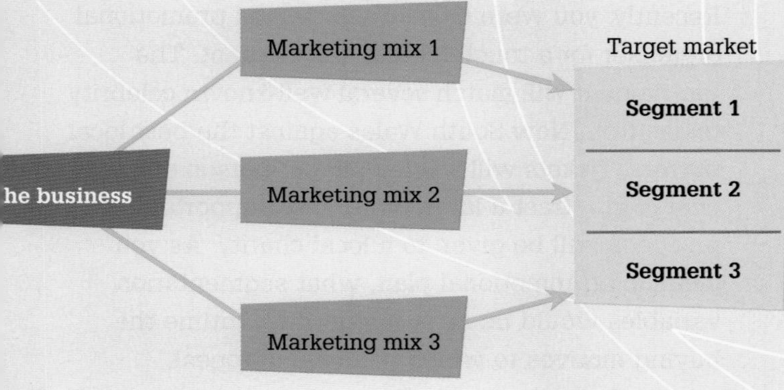

3 The type of market segmentation illustrated in the diagram

(a) is effective when customers' needs are diverse.
(b) is effective when customers' needs are homogeneous.
(c) is effective when it is difficult to differentiate a good or service.
(d) is effective only for the marketing of food items.

4 Marketing managers are concerned with consumer behaviour because

(a) consumers always behave in a rational and predictable manner.
(b) the way consumers behave is easily controlled by marketing strategies.
(c) the way consumers behave is always unpredictable.
(d) the way consumers respond to a business's marketing strategies has a large impact on the business's success.

5 The resellers market consists mainly of

(a) consumers.
(b) manufacturers.
(c) wholesalers and retailers.
(d) industrial users.

6 Market research can collect data

(a) only from primary sources.
(b) only from secondary sources.
(c) from both primary and secondary sources.
(d) any of the above.

7 Question 7 refers to the following information.

Techtronics Limited is a producer of computers and consumer electronics. Updating technology is the main business strategy at Techtronics with most employees having an engineering orientation. Management spends a great deal of time on design and manufacturing processes rather than on researching customers' needs.

Which of the following statements is true?

(a) Techtronics is practising the marketing approach.
(b) Techtronics is not practising the marketing approach.
(c) Techtronics is practising the selling approach.
(d) Techtronics is not practising the production approach.

8 Exclusive distribution is the form of distribution used primarily for
   (a) convenience products that are bought frequently.
   (b) infrequently bought products.
   (c) products that have a high replacement value.
   (d) both (b) and (c).

9 Penetration pricing occurs when a business
   (a) charges the lowest price possible so as to achieve a large market share.
   (b) charges a high price to provide a certain image.
   (c) charges a price above that of its competitors.
   (d) is forced to charge a high price to cover the costs of distribution.

10 A market niche
   (a) is a broadly selected target market segment.
   (b) involves a business directing its marketing efforts to two or more target market segments.
   (c) is a narrowly selected target market segment.
   (d) involves a business directing its marketing efforts to an international target market.

Short response questions

1 (a) What is marketing?
   (b) Explain why marketing needs to be an evolutionary process.
   (c) In your opinion, is marketing manipulative or informative?

2 Managing the marketing effort correctly is essential for the long-term survival of the business. However, with approximately 70 per cent of all new products failing within the first two years, marketing plans are not always successful. With reference to a marketing process you have studied, answer the following.
   (a) Outline the strategies used by the business to monitor its marketing plan.
   (b) Describe the modifications the business has made to its marketing plan in response to changes within the marketing environment.
   (c) In your opinion, how successful has the business been in managing the marketing plan?

3 (a) What is meant by the 'social responsibility of marketing'?
   (b) Should a marketing manager take into account any social consequences of a marketing campaign? Give reasons for your answer.
   (c) How would a marketing plan reflect a business's socially responsible philosophy?

4 With reference to a business you have studied:
   (a) describe the elements of the marketing mix
   (b) evaluate the effectiveness of the marketing mix in increasing market share
   (c) suggest changes to the marketing mix to improve market share.

5 (a) What is marketing?
   (b) Describe the main elements of the marketing plan.
   (c) Explain how developing a marketing plan helps in achieving the business's goals.

Extended response questions

1 You have recently been promoted to the position of marketing manager for Omega Computer Software Ltd. The business has been losing market share over the last few years. It has developed a number of excellent products, especially software designed to help businesses keep a more accurate record of stock. As a result, the board wants you to develop a marketing plan specifically for the computerised inventory software. Omega has a reputation of designing excellent programs, with well-trained backup staff. Its main problem has been in the positioning of its products and being able to utilise the correct promotional methods. The board wants the marketing plan to include a breakdown of the forecast expenditures and revenue for the first year.

2 With reference to a business you have studied, analyse and evaluate the marketing strategies used for a product or service.

3 'Through knowledge of consumer behaviour, marketing managers can learn to manipulate the consumer to buy their products.' Critically evaluate this statement.

4 Recently, you were elected to serve as promotional organiser for a touch football tournament. The tournament will match several well-known celebrity teams from New South Wales against the best local players. Tickets will sell for $30 per person and your goal is to attract a large number of supporters. All proceeds will be given to a local charity. As you develop a promotional plan, what segmentation variables would be most important? Outline the buying motives to which you would appeal.

HSC PRACTiCE QUESTiONS

Topic 4
Employment relations

Multiple-choice questions

For each question, choose the best alternative.

1 An employer, for legal purposes
(a) exercises control over employees.
(b) determines the leave entitlements of employees.
(c) must follow federal occupational health and safety legislation.
(d) must ensure employees are covered by a federal award or agreement.

2 A current trend affecting employees is
(a) the growth in manufacturing employment.
(b) lower wage outcomes for those on enterprise agreements.
(c) higher wage outcomes for those on awards.
(d) pressure to trade off working hours and conditions for higher wages.

3 A strategic approach to employment relations
(a) is commonplace in Australian businesses.
(b) focuses on eliminating conflict.
(c) is effective when changes in employment practices are management driven.
(d) considers the best way to manage the employment relationship in the longer term.

4 Key practices in effective employment relations are
(a) human resources planning, compliance with employment legislation, cost control.
(b) human resources planning, outsourcing, providing opportunities for collaboration.
(c) managing occupational health and safety, developing a culture of trust, simplifying contracts.
(d) compliance with employment legislation, human resources planning, managing complaints.

5 Employment relations in the workplace is governed by
(a) common law, statute law, awards and agreements.
(b) statute law, awards and agreements.
(c) the employment contract, common law, awards and agreements.
(d) awards and agreements, constitutional law.

6 Australia's Constitution gave the federal government power to make laws about
(a) terms and conditions of employment.
(b) occupational health and safety.
(c) workers' compensation.
(d) the settlement of interstate industrial disputes.

7 A social influence on employment relations is
(a) the cost of workers' compensation.
(b) downsizing.
(c) feminisation of the workforce.
(d) declining union membership.

8 Two strategies to resolve disputes are:
(a) award simplification, conciliation.
(b) mediation, business closure.
(c) arbitration, benchmarking.
(d) grievance procedures, deregulation.

9 An unethical employer
(a) is more likely to be legally compliant.
(b) aims to develop jobs with intrinsic rewards.
(c) is committed to equity in employment.
(d) is more likely to experience high labour turnover.

10 The employment relations function aims to
(a) develop competent, productive employees.
(b) minimise industrial conflict.
(c) recruit and select suitably qualified staff.
(d) all of the above.

Short response questions

1 Recent surveys found that Australian firms show clear weaknesses in managing staff, known as 'people skills'.
(a) Identify one area in which management of employees needs to improve.
(b) Outline two impacts on business if a manager has poor 'people skills'.
(c) Describe two ways in which improvements in the people skills of Australian managers could be achieved.

2 (a) Identify a current trend in union membership.
(b) Give three reasons for the trend.

(c) Describe one strategy unions are using to attract new members.

3 (a) Define recruitment.
(b) Define selection.
(c) Discuss three ways in which the recruitment and selection process can be evaluated.

4 (a) Identify two causes of conflict in the workplace.
(b) Describe one benefit of conflict.
(c) Discuss two ways in which conflict may be resolved in the workplace.

5 (a) Describe two forms of discrimination in employment.
(b) Describe one formal action an employee may take if he or she suffers from racial discrimination in a workplace.
(c) Identify one institution that can assist employees suffering racial discrimination.
(d) Discuss one strategy an employer may use to eliminate sex discrimination in the workplace.

Extended response questions

1 (a) Outline the function of employment relations.
(b) Describe the roles of employers and governments in employment relations.
(c) Evaluate the impact of economic influences on the roles played by employers and federal governments in employment relations.

2 With reference to a business you have studied:
(a) explain how social influences and organisational behavioural influences affect employment relations strategies
(b) evaluate the role played by the employer in responding to these changes
(c) describe the costs of failing to respond to these changes.

3 (a) Outline the role of the line manager and specialist in employment relations today.
(b) Explain why their roles have changed in recent years.
(c) Evaluate the importance of effective management of employment relations in a rapidly changing global market.

4 (a) Explain how economic and social factors have influenced unions in the last few decades.
(b) Evaluate the importance of unions and employer associations in employment relations today.
(c) Evaluate the costs and benefits of organisational change on employees over the last decade.

5 Jayla Roberts has worked independently as a sales manager at Brito Automotives for seven years. Six months ago she was promoted to a more senior managerial position. Her new manager, Tarek, is not consulting her in this new role. Three months ago she discovered that he holds meetings with other employees about issues related to her function. She confronted Tarek, who said the matters were not related to her role. He then continued the same pattern of meetings. Recently, in another meeting, he undermined her authority over a key decision she had made and stated that she had made poor decisions without his approval. He even denied receiving key information she had provided on the decision.

When she confronted him about the situation he told her she worked in isolation, had no evidence of work, made bad decisions and was not achieving her goals. He commented that this would be reflected in the performance review he gave her shortly.

A concerned Jayla then took her grievance to the Human Resources Manager, indicating that this was the first time in her role that she'd been told there was a problem with her work.

Jayla received her completed review by email a few days later. It stated she should attend a meeting with the manager the next day. In the meeting with the manager she was told that she was being dismissed for poor performance.

(a) Evaluate the effectiveness of employment relations practices at Brito Automotives.
(b) Identify the actions Jayla could take in relation to her dismissal, and the possible outcomes of such actions.

6 Explain how alternative employment relations strategies may have prevented this dismissal.

HSC PRACTICE QUESTIONS

Topic 5
Global business

Multiple-choice questions

For each question, choose the best alternative.

1 Which of the following distinguishes global business from domestic business?
(a) The use of money as a medium of exchange
(b) The existence of different currencies
(c) The absence of a highly mobile workforce
(d) Consumer demand determines the nature and level of production

2 Refer to the table below to answer the questions that follow.

Year	A$	US$
1	1.00	0.654
2	1.00	0.547

Other things being equal, the movement in the value of the Australian dollar against the United States dollar over the two years shown will mean that
(a) our exports are cheaper and our imports are dearer.
(b) our exports are dearer and our imports are cheaper.
(c) both our exports and our imports are cheaper.
(d) both our exports and our imports are dearer.

3 One of the main aims of the World Trade Organization (WTO) is to
(a) promote the growth of trading blocs.
(b) eliminate agricultural trade.
(c) encourage free trade.
(d) encourage non-tariff trade barriers.

4 Arguments presented against the location of transnational subsidiaries in a host country include
(a) the parent businesses are exporting jobs to their subsidiaries overseas.
(b) transfer pricing.
(c) the profits of transnationals are not passed on to parent countries' domestic markets as cheaper prices.
(d) weakening of investing countries' markets and production capabilities.

5 The main driver(s) of globalisation are
(a) the expanding role of transnational corporations.
(b) the impact of technology.
(c) the deregulation of financial markets.
(d) all of the above.

6 Refer to the graph below to answer the questions that follow.

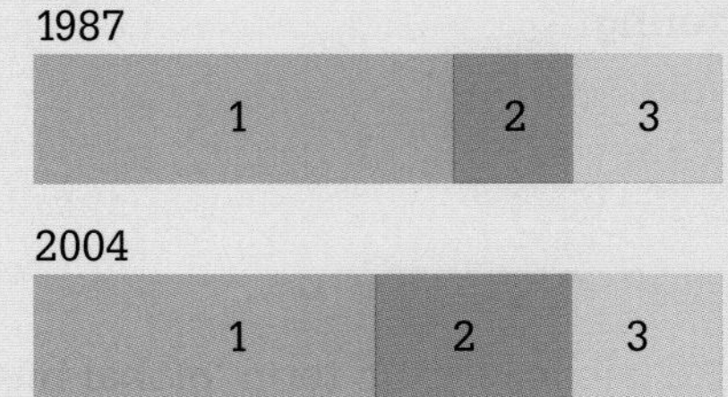

Composition of Australia's exports 1987 and 2004

Between 1987 and 2004
(a) Australia became more dependent on commodity exports.
(b) Australia became less dependent on manufactured exports.
(c) Australia became less dependent on service exports.
(d) Australia became less dependent on commodity exports.

7 Global branding is the worldwide use of a name, term or symbol to
(a) identify products of one seller and to differentiate them from those of competitors.
(b) identify products of one buyer and to differentiate them from those of other buyers.
(c) identify non-specific goods and services across a global market.
(d) identify the difference between domestically and globally produced goods and services.

8 The most basic level of exporting is
(a) redemption exporting.
(b) differentiated exporting.
(c) intracorporate transfer.
(d) direct exporting.

9 The main benefits of outsourcing production include
(a) lower prices.
(b) access to higher quality and better designed components.
(c) access to more advanced technology.
(d) all of the above.

10 The process by which it is possible for a business to minimise the risk of currency fluctuations is referred to as
(a) hedging.
(b) factoring.
(c) devaluing.
(d) indexing.

Short response questions

1 (a) What is meant by the term 'global business'?
(b) Compare and contrast global and domestic business.
(c) Outline the reasons why Australian firms engage in global business.

2 'The managing director of Sonica Limited, Jonathan Burge, realised that the future success of the company was dependent upon developing and implementing strategies to trade globally.'
(a) Suggest two reasons for Jonathan's desire to trade globally.
(b) Identify and explain two legal and two political influences on Sonica's global operations and explain the influence they may have.

3 Consider the following headline:
'New joint venture announced between Goldstar Electronics and PC Integrated Systems Limited.'
(a) What is meant by the term 'joint venture'?
(b) Identify two advantages and two disadvantages of a joint venture operation for the host country.
(c) Suggest two ways in which the businesses could minimise the risks associated with a joint venture.

4 'Australian business managers are adopting a new attitude to exporting. As the process of globalisation accelerates, due mainly to the revolution in technology, Australian managers are becoming more globally focused. However, they must realise that global business entails a certain number of risks.'
(a) Outline two advantages and two disadvantages of a business expanding globally.
(b) Suggest two reasons why a business would relocate part of its production facilities to another country.
(c) Identify and describe the main activities of two federal government departments that provide assistance to Australian businesses wishing to engage in global trade.

5 'The Australian dollar has fallen to a yearly low of 58.6 US cents. Only six months ago it was trading at 69.8 US cents.'
(a) Outline one main risk to an Australian exporting business of excessive fluctuations in exchange rates.
(b) Identify and describe two strategies a business can implement to help minimise the risk of exchange rate fluctuations.

Extended response questions

1 'As a business expands operations abroad, the organisational structure typically evolves from the addition of a position responsible for marketing, to the creation of an international division, to the development of a global structure.'

With reference to a business you have studied, describe the impact of the global business environment on the business's role and structure. In your answer refer to specific strategies designed to manage changing global activities.

2 'Managing a global business is more complex than managing a domestic business. There are a number of unique factors a manager must take into account when conducting international business, with the main ones being:
- methods of payment
- employment relations, especially the staffing system selected.'

Distinguish between domestic and global business. Critically examine the management strategies a business can implement to deal effectively with the methods of payment and employment relations.

3 'It has recently been revealed that a number of well-known transnational corporations have been exploiting the labour and natural resources of their developing host countries.' Critically analyse the social and ethical responsibilities of management

when conducting business operations in a developing country. Clarify the steps you would take as a manager to prevent your employees from making questionable payments while they are conducting international business activities on behalf of the company.

4 Explain why the effective management of a transnational corporation would be more difficult than managing an organisation with domestic operations only. Outline the strategies adopted by a business you have studied to manage its global business activities.

5 'Global competition is mounting. The huge increase in import penetration, plus the massive amounts of overseas investment, mean that firms of all sizes face competition from everywhere in the world. This increasing globalisation of business is requiring managers to have a global business perspective.'

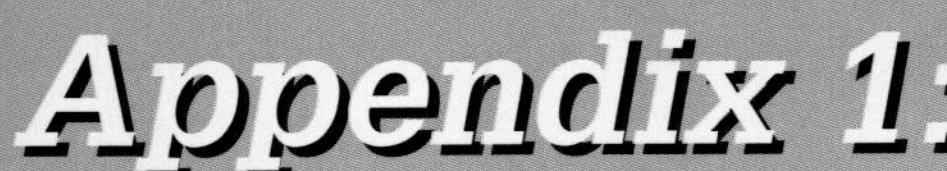

Appendix 1:

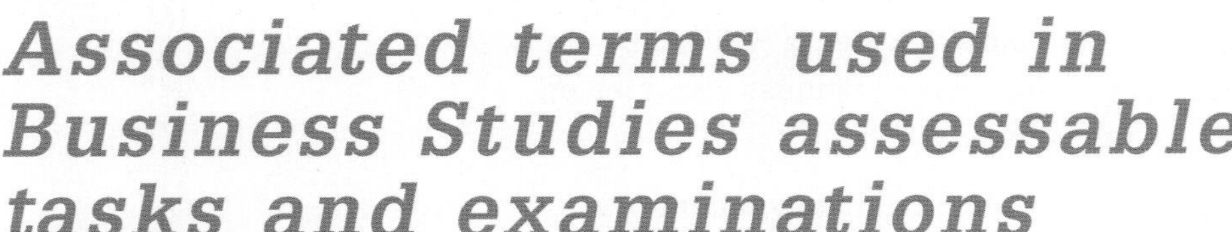

Associated terms used in Business Studies assessable tasks and examinations

It is important to understand the meaning of the terms used in assessable tasks and the short and extended response questions of the examination.

The terms listed below are the most frequently used.

Account	Account for: state reasons for, report on. Give an account of: narrate a series of events or transactions
Analyse	Identify components and the relationship between them; draw out and relate implications
Apply	Use, utilise, employ in a particular situation
Appreciate	Make a judgement about the value of
Assess	Make a judgement of value, quality, outcomes, results or size
Calculate	Ascertain/determine from given facts, figures or information
Clarify	Make clear or plain
Classify	Arrange or include in classes/categories
Compare	Show how things are similar or different
Construct	Make; build; put together items or arguments
Contrast	Show how things are different or opposite
Critically (analyse/ evaluate)	Add a degree or level of accuracy, depth, knowledge and understanding, logic, questioning, reflection and quality to (analysis/evaluation)
Deduce	Draw conclusions
Define	State meaning and identify essential qualities
Demonstrate	Show by example
Describe	Provide characteristics and features
Discuss	Identify issues and provide points for and/or against
Distinguish	Recognise or note/indicate as being distinct or different from; to note differences between
Evaluate	Make a judgement based on criteria; determine the value of
Examine	Enquire into
Explain	Relate cause and effect; make the relationships between things evident; provide why and/or how
Extract	Choose relevant and/or appropriate details
Extrapolate	Infer from what is known
Identify	Recognise and name
Interpret	Draw meaning from
Investigate	Plan, enquire into and draw conclusions about

Justify	Support an argument or conclusion
Outline	Sketch in general terms; indicate the main features of
Predict	Suggest what may happen based on available information
Propose	Put forward (for example, a point of view, idea, argument, suggestion) for consideration or action
Recall	Present remembered ideas, facts or experiences
Recommend	Provide reasons in favour
Recount	Retell a series of events
Summarise	Express, concisely, the relevant details
Synthesise	Put together various elements to make a whole

Appendix 2:

Answering HSC examination questions

The HSC examination in Business Studies has four sections:

I. Multiple-choice questions
II. Short response questions
III. Extended response questions — business report format; integrated topic areas
IV. Extended response questions — case study/studies; integrated topic areas.

Section I — Multiple-choice questions

Section I of the HSC examination consists of 20 compulsory multiple-choice questions. They may include interpretation of stimulus material, calculations and definitions. Therefore, it is important that you become familiar with answering this type of question. For each question choose the best of the four alternatives given.

Section II — Short-response questions

Section II consists of five short-response questions examining all the five topic areas. It is essential to recognise the key directive words that are listed in Appendix 1. Be guided by the number of lines and marks awarded as to how much needs to be written.

Section III — Extended-response questions: business report

In Section III of the HSC you are required to write a business report. This section contains a single extended-response question based on stimulus material (see the questions on page 527). The question integrates a number of the HSC topics.

A business report format style of writing will require you to disregard much of what you have previously been taught when writing traditional essay-style answers. Business report answers use:

- an executive summary (a brief paragraph that outlines the purpose of the report)
- headings and subheadings
- bullet points followed with explanations when appropriate
- short paragraphs
- diagrams, tables and graphs
- underlining for emphasis
- condensed conclusions and/or recommendations when required.

Newspaper articles adopt a report writing style. Each paragraph is brief and to the point, and short sentences are used. It is important that you become familiar with answering this style of question.

Your answer in Section III will be assessed on how well you:

- use your knowledge and the information provided
- communicate using relevant business terminology and concepts
- present a logical, well-structured answer to the question in the form of a business report.

Section IV — Extended-response questions: case study/studies

In Section IV, you are required to answer one out of two extended-response questions, which also integrate a number of HSC topic areas that were not the focus of Section III. In your answer, you must refer to a relevant business case study/studies.

Your answer in Section IV will be assessed on how well you:

- use your knowledge and relevant business case study/studies
- communicate using relevant business terminology and concepts
- present a logical, well-structured answer to the question.

Sample business report questions

1. An Australian electrical engineering company is investigating the possibility of expanding into an overseas market by entering into a joint venture arrangement with a Chinese company. The board of directors is aware of the increasing competition within the domestic market and wishes to achieve lower costs of production through improved economies of scale. As adopting a global perspective represents a major change in attitude within the business, resistance is expected from some managers.

   Write a business report to the CEO of the company that describes and analyses the reasons for international expansion and the management strategies needed to overcome any resistance to the change.

2. A computer business established in 1997 has experienced rapid growth over the last five years. As a consequence, the company has experienced the following 'growth difficulties': establishing a workable organisational structure that is responsive to change a shortage of venture capital ineffective cash flow management an inappropriate marketing plan that has not been modified in response to technological changes.

   Write a business report to the owners of the business that explains the importance of effective financial planning and outline how the business functions and operations will need to be modified to overcome the present difficulties.

3. You have been appointed Human Resources Manager of Quantro Chemicals Limited, a large Australian business with operations in all states and employing 2670 staff. Your main task is to negotiate a new enterprise agreement with eight different unions operating at the five facilities. In the past, wage negotiations have been marked by protracted and costly industrial disputation. The company is considering the possibility of moving production offshore if a successful wage settlement cannot be gained within a three-month period.

   Write a business report to the group general manager that outlines how conflict and change can be managed in the business and analyse the impact of management decision making on the stakeholders.

Glossary

accounting equation: equation that forms the basis of the accounting process and shows the relationship between assets, liabilities and owners' equity

accounting framework: the raw data that is processed, stored and then summarised in a meaningful and accepted form

acquisition strategy: when one business acquires, through a takeover or merger, an existing business in a foreign country

advertising: a paid, non-personal message communicated through a mass medium

advertising media: the many forms of communication used to reach an audience

affirmative action: measures taken to eliminate direct and indirect discrimination, and overcome the current and historical causes of lack of equal employment opportunity for women

analysis: involves working the financial information into significant and acceptable forms that make it more meaningful and highlight relationships between different aspects of an organisation

assets: the property and other items and effects of a business, such as business premises, machinery, vehicles and cash (tangible assets) and patents, trademarks and goodwill (intangible assets)

attitude: a person's overall feeling about an object or activity

audit: an independent check of the accuracy of financial records and accounting procedures

autocratic leadership style: a leadership style in which the manager tends to make all the decisions, dictating work methods, limiting worker knowledge about what needs to be done to the next step to be performed, and sometimes giving feedback that is punitive

award simplification: the process of reducing the number of 'allowable matters' in each award to 20, and eliminating inefficient work practices

awards: legally enforceable, formal agreements made collectively between employers and employees and their representatives at the industry level. They are determined by an industrial court or tribunal and set out minimum wages and conditions of employees.

bait and switch advertising: when a few products are advertised at reduced and, therefore, enticing prices to attract customers

balance sheet: a document that provides information on an organisation's assets and liabilities at a particular point in time, expressed in money terms, and represents the net worth of the business

bank overdraft: as a means of helping a business or individual to overcome temporary cash shortfalls, the bank allows an account to be overdrawn up to an agreed limit and for a specified time

behavioural approach: an approach to management that stresses that people (employees) should be the main focus of the way in which the business is organised

below-the-line promotions: promotional activities for which the business does not make use of an advertising agency

best practice: those business practices that are regarded as the best or of the highest standard in the industry

bill of exchange: a document drawn up by the exporter demanding payment from the importer at a specified time

bond: an IOU from one business to another that requires the borrower to repay a certain amount, plus interest, by a specified date

brand: a name, term, symbol, design or any combination of these that identifies a specific product and distinguishes it from its competition

brand name: the part of the brand that can be spoken

brand symbol: a graphic representation that identifies a business or product; also known as a logo

budgets: information in quantitative terms (facts and figures) about requirements to achieve a particular purpose

bureaucracy: the rules and regulations that control a business

business culture: a set of mostly unwritten or informal rules that spell out how people are to behave most of the time

business market: market that consists of all those businesses that purchase goods and services for further processing or for use in their production process

buyer: the individual or group who purchases the product

buyer behaviour: the decisions and actions of people involved in buying and using products

capital expenditure: the amount spent on an organisation's non-current or fixed assets

cash flow: the movement of cash in and out of a business over a period of time

cash flow budget: a record of the expected receipts of cash (cash inflows) and expected payments of cash (cash outflows) over a period of time

casual: employment that is short term, irregular and uncertain. Casual employees are not entitled to paid holiday or sick leave.

centralised industrial relations system: a system that uses a third party, such as a tribunal like the AIRC, to resolve disputes and determine wages

chain of command: a system that determines responsibility, supervision and accountability of members of the organisation

change: any alteration in the business and work environment

change agent: a person, or group of people, who acts as a catalyst, assuming responsibility for managing a change process

channel: any method used for conveying a message

channels of distribution: the routes taken to get the product from the factory to the customer; also known as marketing channels

civil law: the world's most common legal system; it is based on a detailed set of laws and is organised into codes that list what is permissible and what is not.

classical: a perspective on management that emphasises how to manage and organise work more efficiently so as to improve productivity

clean payment (remittance): this occurs when payment is sent to, but not received by, the exporter before the goods are transported

coalition: two or more people who combine their power to push or gain support for their ideas

code of conduct: a statement of acceptable and unacceptable behaviours in a business

code of ethics: a statement of a business's values and principles

code of practice: a statement of the principles used by a business in its operations; it generally refers to practices that are seen as ethical or socially responsible.

collective agreement: an agreement made between a group of employees or one or more unions representing employees, and an employer or group of employers

common law: legal system developed by courts and tribunals. Under common law, judges make decisions based on the facts of a case, guided by precedent (decisions made in the past).

communication: the exchange of information between people; the sending and receiving of messages

concentrated market approach: an approach to marketing that requires the business to direct its marketing mix towards one selected segment of the total market

conflict: disputes, disagreements or dissatisfaction between individuals or groups

consumer markets: markets that consist of individuals (that is, members of a household) who plan to use or consume the products they buy

consumerism: the act of buying goods and services

contingency theory: a theory that stresses the need for flexibility and adaptation of management practices and ideas to suit changing circumstances

contract: a legally enforceable agreement

control process: involves establishing standards in line with the objectives of the organisation, measuring the performance of the organisation against those standards or benchmarks and making changes where necessary to ensure that the objectives of the organisation have been met

controlling: the comparison of planned performance against actual performance and taking corrective action to ensure the objectives are achieved

copyright: the exclusive right of an author, artist, musician or publisher to publish, perform, copy or sell an original work

corporate governance: the way that companies are directed and controlled

cost centres: particular areas, departments or sections of a business to which costs can be directly attributed

cultural diversity: the multitude of individual differences that exist among people

currency swap: an agreement to exchange currency in the spot market with an agreement to reverse the transaction in the future

current assets: assets that a business can expect to convert into cash within the current accounting period; they usually include cash, accounts receivable, inventories and short-term investments.

customer orientation: a business's tendency to base its marketing decisions and practices on its customers' wants

customer service: responding to the needs and problems of the customer

debenture: a certificate acknowledging a debt issued by a company for a fixed rate of interest and for a fixed period of time

debt finance: the short-term and long-term borrowing from external sources by an organisation

decentralised industrial relations system: a system in which wages and conditions and other employment matters are largely determined through the interaction of employers and employees in the workplace

decision making: the process of identifying the options available and then choosing a specific course of action to solve a specific problem

decision-making role: a role that involves solving problems and making choices

delegation: the handing over of certain tasks or responsibilities to an employee who is suitably capable and qualified to carry them out

demography: the study of particular features of a population — its size, age, gender, income, cultural background and family size

depreciation: a downward movement of the Australian dollar (or any other currency) against another currency

deregulation: the removal of government regulation from industry, with the aim of increasing efficiency and improving competition

derivatives: financial instruments used to hedge against risk by businesses that have to deal with uncertain prices of their own products or their purchases

de-skilling: when employees are no longer required to perform skilled tasks due to changes in work methods, usually resulting from new technology

differentiated approach: an international marketing strategy that assumes the way the product is used and the needs it satisfies are different between countries; also known as a local approach

direct exporting: when an exporting business sells its products to an agent, intermediary or final consumers in another country

discretionary income: disposable income that is available for spending and saving after an individual has purchased the basic necessities of food, clothing and shelter

discrimination: when a policy or practice disadvantages a person or a group of people because of a personal characteristic that is irrelevant to the performance of the work

dispute: a disagreement. In industrial relations, a dispute officially exists when workers withdraw from work or place bans on work.

disturbance-handler role: a role that requires the manager to make decisions necessary to keep the business operating under extraordinary circumstances

diversification: a process of spreading the risks encountered by a business

division or specialisation of labour: the degree to which tasks are subdivided into separate jobs

downsizing: workplace staff reductions, with the elimination of jobs

driving forces: those forces that initiate, foster, encourage and support a change

economic community: an organisation of nations formed to promote free trade (the free movement of resources and products) among its members and to create common economic policies; also known as a trading bloc

economies of scale: the reduction in the costs of production that arise from increasing the size or scale of the production facility and spreading overhead (fixed) costs over a larger output

effectiveness: measures the degree to which a goal has been achieved

efficiency: the ability of a firm to use its resources effectively in ensuring financial stability and profitability of the business

electronic commerce (e-commerce): the use of electronic communications to do business

employee: a worker under an employer's control. Control may involve the location of the workplace, the way in which the work is performed and the degree of supervision involved. These criteria are critical in determining legal disputes over the employment contract.

employee selection: a process that involves gathering information about each applicant and using that information to choose the most appropriate applicant

employer: a person or organisation that exercises control over employees, has responsibility for payment of wages and holds the power to dismiss employees

employer associations: organisations that represent and assist employer groups

employment contract: a legally binding, formal agreement between employer and employee

employment relations: the total relationship between an employer and employee

enterprise agreement: agreement about wages and conditions made at the enterprise level between an employer and a union or a majority of employees in the workplace; known as a certified agreement at the federal level

equitable reward: a reward that is seen as fair or deserved by employees. Equity may be seen from an internal (inside the business) or extended (in comparison with other businesses) viewpoint.

equity: in the workplace, this refers to the provision of equal opportunities for all employees to gain access to jobs, training and career paths

equity finance: the internal sources of finance in the organisation

ethical behaviour: behaviour that is consistent with society's standards about what is morally acceptable and conforms to society's judgements about what constitutes right and wrong actions

ethical business practices: business practices that are socially responsible, morally right, honourable and fair

ethics: personal moral principles and values. Laws are society's values and standards, which may be protected by the courts.

ethnocentric approach: an approach to staffing in which all key management positions at all company locations are filled by parent company personnel

eurocurrency: the currency of one country that is placed in a bank in another country

exchange traded markets: those traded on an authorised exchange, such as the Australian Stock Exchange (ASX) and Sydney Futures Exchange (SFE)

expatriate: a citizen of one country working in another country

exporting: when a business manufactures its products in its home country and then sells them in foreign markets

external business environment: the factors and characteristics that are largely outside the direct control of owners, directors and managers

external data: published data from outside the business

external finance: the funds provided by sources outside the business, including banks, other financial institutions, government, suppliers or financial intermediaries

extrinsic rewards: rewards given or provided outside the job itself. They may be monetary, for example, incentive payments, or non-monetary, for example, flexible work schedules.

factoring: the selling of accounts receivable for a discounted price to a finance or factoring company

financial budgets: budgets that relate to financial data and include the budgeted revenue statement, balance sheet and cash flows

financial controls: the policies and procedures that ensure that the plans of an organisation are achieved in the most efficient way

financial decision making: decision making that requires relevant information to be identified, collected and analysed to determine an appopirate course of action

financial intermediaries: people or organisations who receive money from people with excess funds and provide finance to those wishing to borrow money

financial management: the planning and monitoring of an organisation's financial resources to enable it to achieve its financial goals

financial markets: markets made up of the individuals, institutions and systems supplying excess funds to those people or organisations who require them. The term 'financial' relates to money and 'market' indicates trading activity.

financial resources: those resources in a business that have a monetary or money value

financial risk: the risk to the business of being unable to cover its financial obligations

financial statements: documents that summarise the activities of an organisation over a period of time

fitness of purpose: the product is suitable for the purpose for which it is being sold; that is, it will perform as the instructions or advertisement implies

fixed costs: costs that are not dependent on the level of operating activity in a business

flatter organisational structures: structures that evolved due to a 'de-layering' of management structures, resulting in the elimination of one or more management levels

force-field analysis: analysis that identifes, analyses and balances the driving and restraining forces

foreign direct investment (FDI): investment made for the purpose of actively controlling companies, assets or property outside a business's home country

foreign exchange (forex or **fx) market:** this market determines the price of one currency relative to another

foreign exchange rate: the ratio of one currency to another; it tells how much a unit of one currency is worth in terms of another.

formal organisation: the formal lines of communication and chain of command. The organisational structure determines how work is allocated, the levels of authority and communication patterns.

forward exchange contract: a contract to exchange one currency for another currency at an agreed exchange rate on a future date, usually after a period of 30, 90 or 180 days

franchising: a specialised form of licensing in which the franchisor grants the franchisee the right to use a company's trademark and distribute its product

free trade: a policy of reducing or abolishing barriers to imports

free-trade agreement: an agreement between two or more countries that results in reductions in barriers to trade such as tariffs, import quotas and government restrictions on foreign ownership

generic brand: product with no brand name

geocentric approach: an approach to staffing that involves seeking the best people for key jobs throughout the entire organisation, irrespective of nationality

geographical representation: the presence of a business and the range of its products across a suburb, town, city, state or country

global branding: the worldwide use of a name, term, symbol or logo to identify products of one seller and differentiate them from those of the competitor

global economy: the world economy. It refers to the economic activity going on in the world and includes the flow of all trade, finance, technology, labour and investment. It is the total economic activity within and between countries.

global web: a network of production sites located around the world, each specialising in the part of the production process that it can most efficiently perform

globalisation: the movement across nations of trade, investment, technology, finance and labour

globalisation of markets: the combining of once separate and distinct national markets into one huge global marketplace

globalisation of production: the practice of purchasing inputs from around the globe as well as the tendency to manufacture components in low-cost locations

goods and services tax (GST): a broad-based tax of 10 per cent on the supply of most goods and services consumed in Australia

greenfield strategy: commencing a new business venture from scratch

green marketing: the development, pricing, promotion and distribution of products that either do not harm or have minimal impact on the environment

growth: the ability of the organisation to increase its size in the longer term

hedging: the process of minimising the risk of currency fluctuations

historical cost accounting: a method of accounting in which values are stated at the cost incurred at the time of purchase or acquisition

household spending: the combined purchases of individuals living together; also known as family spending

human resources: the employees of a business; generally its most important asset

implementation: the process of putting the marketing strategies into operation

implied conditions: the unspoken and unwritten terms of a contract

indirect exporting: the most basic level of exporting, in which a business sells its products to a domestic customer, which then exports the product

individual contract: an agreement between an employer and an individual employee covering pay and conditions

industrial market: a market that includes industries and business organisations that purchase products to use in the production of other products or in their daily operations

inertia of management: an unenthusiastic response from management to proposed changes

informal organisation: the informal communication network that develops between employees throughout an organisation

information resources: the knowledge and data required by the business, such as market research, sales reports, economic forecasts, technical material and legal advice

informational role: a role in which the manager gathers and disseminates information within the business, also providing it to the outside world

institutional customers: schools, hospitals, clubs, churches and other non-profit organisations

intangible assets: those assets that have value for a business, but their value is difficult to measure, such as licences, patents, trademarks, brand names, intellectual property and goodwill

intellectual property: property that is created by an individual's intellect

intermediate market: a market that consists of wholesalers and retailers who purchase finished products and resell them to make a profit

internal business environment: the factors and characteristics that are within the direct control of owners, directors and managers

internal data: information that has already been collected from inside the business

internal finance: the funds provided by the owners of the business (capital) or from the outcomes of business activities (retained earnings)

interpersonal role: a role in which the manager deals with people

interpretation: making judgements and decisions using the data gathered from analysis

intracorporate exporting (transfer): the selling of a product by a firm in one country to a subsidiary firm in another

intrinsic rewards: rewards that the individual derives from the task or job itself, such as a sense of achievement

inventory control: a system that maintains quantities and varieties of products appropriate for the target market

job enlargement: increasing the breadth of tasks in a job

job enrichment: increasing the responsibilities of a staff member

job rotation: moving staff from one task to another over a period of time

job sharing: when two employees voluntarily share one permanent full-time job

joint venture: when two or more businesses agree to work together and form a jointly owned but separate business

judicial power: the power of the courts to interpret and apply laws

labour standards: the conditions that affect a business's employees, or those of its suppliers, subcontractors or others in the production chain

leading: having a vision of where a business should be in the long and short term, and being able to direct and motivate the human resources in an organisation to achieve its objectives

learning organisation: an organisation that monitors and interprets its environment, seeking to improve its understanding of the interrelationship between its actions and the business environment. All of its employees are involved in developing knowledge and insights that allow the organisation to continuously grow and improve.

leasing: a long-term source of borrowing for businesses. It involves the payment of money for the use of equipment that is owned by another party.

legal system: the laws, or rules, that regulate behaviour and the procedures used to enforce the laws

letter of credit: a commitment by an importer's bank that promises to pay the exporter a specified amount when the documents proving shipment of the goods are presented

leverage: the proportion of debt (external finance) and the proportion of equity (internal finance) that is used to finance the activities of a firm

licensing: an agreement in which one business (licensor) permits another (licensee) to produce and market its product

line manager: person responsible for the management of staff contributing to the prime function of the business; for example, a production manager, service manager or sales manager

liquidity: the extent to which a business can meet its financial commitments in the short term

log of claims: a list of demands made by workers (often through their union) against their employers. These demands cover specific wages and conditions. Employers may also serve a counter-log of claims on the union.

loss leader: when a business deliberately sells a product below its cost price to attract customers

management: the process of working with and through other people to achieve business goals in a changing environment. Crucial to this process is the effective and efficient use of limited resources.

management contract: an arrangement under which a global business provides managerial assistance and technical expertise to a second or host business for a fee

management hierarchy: the arrangement that provides increasing authority at higher levels of management

manager: the person who coordinates the business's limited resources in order to achieve specific goals

manufacturer's brand: brands owned by a manufacturer; also known as national brands

market: a group of individuals, organisations or both who need or want a product, have the money (purchasing power) to purchase the product, are willing to spend their money to obtain the product, and are socially and legally authorised to purchase the product

market coverage: the number of outlets a business chooses for its product

market research: the process of systematically collecting, recording and analysing information concerning a specific marketing problem

market segmentation: when the total market is subdivided into groups of people who share one or more common characteristics

market share: the business's share of the total industry sales for a particular market

marketing: the process of planning and executing the conception, pricing, promotion and distribution of ideas, goods and services to create exchanges that satisfy individual and organisational objectives. It can also be defined as a total system of interacting activities designed to plan, price, promote and distribute products to present and potential customers.

marketing concept: a business philosophy that states that all sections of the business are involved in satisfying a customer's needs and wants while achieving the business's goals

marketing data: the information, usually expressed as facts and figures, relevant to the defined marketing problem

marketing management: the process of monitoring and modifying the marketing plan

marketing mix: the combination of the four elements of marketing, the four Ps, that make up the marketing strategy: product, price, promotion and place

marketing objective: a statement of what is to be achieved through the marketing activities

marketing profitability analysis: a method in which the business breaks down the total marketing costs into specific marketing activities

marketing strategies: plans that outline how a business will use its resources to achieve its marketing objectives

mass market: a market to which the seller mass-produces, mass-distributes and mass-promotes one product to all buyers

mass marketing: an approach that seeks a large range of customers. Products that can be marketed using the mass marketing approach include basic food items, water, gas and electricity; also called a total marketing approach

materialism: an individual's desire to constantly acquire possessions

mediation: the confidential discussion of issues in a non-threatening environment, in the presence of a neutral, objective third party

merchandise exports: domestically made products that are sold to customers in another country

merchantable quality: the product is of a standard a reasonable person would expect for the price

model: a simplified version of reality

monitoring: checking and observing the actual progress of the marketing plan

monopolistic power: occurs when only one business operates in a market and, therefore, controls prices in that market

mortgage: a loan secured by the property of the borrower (business)

motivation: the individual, internal process that energises, directs and sustains an individual's behaviour

motive: the reason that makes an individual do something

negotiating: a decision-making process among people with different expectations; also known as bargaining

negotiating role: a role that requires the manager to arrange for, or bring about through discussions, the settlement of an issue

net working capital: the difference between current assets and current liabilities. It represents those funds that are needed for the day-to-day operations of an organisation to produce profits and provide cash for short-term liquidity.

network structure: a structure that exists solely to provide administrative control of another business or set of businesses that performs all the functions needed to produce and sell the product

niche market: a market that is created when the mass market is finely divided into smaller markets consisting of buyers who have specific needs or lifestyles; also known as a concentrated or micro market

noise: any interference or distraction that affects any or all stages in the communication process

non-store retailing: retailing activity conducted away from the traditional store

non-verbal communication: the messages we convey through body movements, facial expressions and the physical distance between individuals

on-costs: additional costs involved in hiring an employee, above the costs of their wages; these include holiday leave, sick leave, superannuation and so on.

open credit: allows the importer access to the goods, with a promise to repay at a later date

operating budgets: budgets that relate to the main activities of an organisation and may include budgets relating to sales, production, raw materials, direct labour, expenses and cost of goods sold

operational planning: planning that provides specific details of the way in which the firm will operate in the short term

opinion leader: a person who influences others

option: gives the buyer (option holder) the right, but not the obligation, to buy or sell foreign currency at some time in the future

orders: decisions handed down by tribunals such as the AIRC, which require employees or employers to carry out a direction from the tribunal. They may be inserted in awards or agreements.

organisational objectives: goals that break the business operations into achievable and managable outcomes that can be measured and evaluated

organisational politics: the often unwritten rules of work life. They involve the pursuit of self-interest through informal methods of gaining power or advantage.

organisation process: the range of activities that translate the objectives of a business into reality

organising: the structuring of the organisation to translate plans and the business's objectives into action

outsourcing: the contracting out of some business operations to outside suppliers

outsourcing production: when a business buys component parts from either a domestic or overseas supplier

over-the-counter (OTC) markets: markets in which transactions take place via telephone and other means of communication rather than on an exchange

owners' equity: the funds contributed by owners or partners to establish and build the business

packaging: development of a container and the graphic design for a product

participation rate: the proportion of women aged 15 to 69 employed or actively looking for work

participative or democratic leadership style: a leadership style whereby the manager consults with employees to ask for their suggestions and seriously considers those suggestions when making decisions

patent: a government grant that gives an inventor the exclusive right to make, use or sell, as well as license others to make or sell, a newly invented product or process

payment in advance: this method of payment allows the exporter to receive payment and then arrange for the goods to be sent

people skills: the skills needed to work and communicate with other people and to understand their needs; also referred to as interpersonal/human skills

perception: the process through which people select, organise, and interpret information to create meaning

performance appraisals: strategies used by management to evaluate the performance of employees. In some cases, employees evaluate the performance of managers too.

performance standard: a forecast level of performance against which actual performance can be compared

personal selling: the activities of a sales representative directed to a customer in an attempt to make a sale

personal spending: consumer purchases by individuals

personality: the collection of all the behaviours and characteristics that make up a person

physical distribution: the activities concerned with the efficient movement of the products from the producer to the consumer

physical resources: resources that include equipment, machinery, buildings and raw materials

placement: locating an employee in a position that best meets the needs of the organisation and best uses the skills of the employee

planned obsolescence: the built-in, predetermined life of a product that will, therefore, require it to be replaced

planning: the preparation of a predetermined course of action for a business

planning processes: the setting of goals and objectives, determining the strategies to achieve those goals and objectives, identifying and evaluating alternative courses of action and choosing the best alternative for the organisation

plant layout: the physical arrangement of people and machinery within a business

pluralist approach: an approach to industrial relations that recognises the active roles played by unions and employer associations and the framework developed by the government. This approach sees conflict as a legitimate outlet for pressures and tensions between the stakeholders and their competing interests.

political risk: any political event that results in a drastic change to a country's business environment, and that ulitmately has a negative impact on business operations and profit

politics: in business, the use of methods, sometimes unstated and/or unethical, to obtain power or advancement within an organisation

polycentric approach: an approach to staffing in which personnel from the host country manage the subsidiaries, while the parent company personnel fill the key roles at company headquarters

power: the ability to gather together resources to get something done

prestige pricing: when a high price is charged to give the product an aura of quality and status

price: the amount of money a customer is prepared to offer in exchange for a product

price discrimination: the setting of different prices for a product in separate markets

price lining: when a limited number of prices, or price points, are set for selected lines or groups of merchandise

price penetration: when a business charges the lowest price possible for a product or service so as to achieve a large market share

price skimming: charging the highest price possible for innovative products

primary data: the facts and figures collected from original sources for the purpose of the specific research problem

primary markets: financial markets that deal with new issues of debt instruments by the borrower of funds.

primary target market: the market segment at which most of the marketing resources are directed

private brand: a brand that is owned by the retailer or wholesaler; also known as a house brand

privatisation: the process of transferring the ownership of a government business to the private sector

proactive: a management style that incorporates dynamic action and forward planning to achieve particular objectives

problem solving: a broad set of activities involved in searching for, identifying and then implementing a course of action to correct an unworkable situation

product: a good, service or idea, or any combination of the three that can be offered in an exchange

product deletion: the elimination of some lines of products

product differentiation: the process of developing and promoting differences between the business's products and those of its competitors

product mix: the total range of products offered by a business

product placement: the inclusion of advertising into entertainment

product positioning: the development of a product image as compared with the image of competing products

productivity sharing: the practice of rewarding employees for productivity levels above specific targets

profit and loss statement: document that provides information for a particular period of time regarding sales, operating profit before and after tax and extraordinary items, as well as dividends to be paid and retained earnings

profit sharing: the practice of calculating an employee's portion of a monthly profit pool

profitability: the ability of an organisation to maximise its profits

project budgets: budgets that relate to capital expenditure and research and development

promotion: the methods used by a business to inform, persuade and remind a target market about its products

promotion mix: the various promotion methods a business uses in its promotional campagin. Methods include personal selling, advertising, below-the-line promotions, and publicity and public relations

protectionism: the practice of creating artificial barriers to free trade in order to protect domestic industries and jobs

psychological factors: influences within an individual that affect his or her buying behaviour

public interest test: a test that requires the AIRC to consider the state of the economy and the likely effects (including employment and inflation) on the national economy of any award or order that the AIRC is considering, or proposing to make

public relations: those activities aimed at creating and maintaining favourable relations between a business and its customers

publicity: any free news story about a business's products

radical (Marxist) approach: this approach to industrial relations recognises conflict as inevitable and reflects the traditional view of an 'us versus them', conflict-based relationship between employer and employees

record systems: the mechanisms employed by an organisation to ensure that data is recorded and the information is accurate, reliable, efficient and accessible

recruitment: the process of locating and attracting the right quantity and quality of staff to apply for employment vacancies or anticipated vacancies at the right cost

redundant: when an employee's skills are no longer required by the business

reference group: a group of people with whom a person closely identifies, adopting their attitudes, values and beliefs; also called peer group

regional economic integration: a focus on securing trade agreements between groups of countries in a geographic region; also known as regionalism

regulations: restrictions placed by governments on the activities of either individuals or businesses

relationship marketing: the development of long-term and cost-effective relationships with individual customers

relocation of production: when the domestic production facility is closed down and then set up in a foreign country

resale price maintenance: when the manufacturer or supplier insists that a retailer sell a product at a certain price

resource-allocator role: a role that requires the manager to share out or allocate the limited resources of the business

resource market: a market that consists of those individuals or groups who are engaged in all forms of primary production, including mining, agriculture, forestry and fishing

respondents: in relation to an award, respondents are all the union parties and employers registered as included in the award at the federal level

restraining forces: those forces that work against a change, creating resistance

restrictive covenants: conditions that set down what a borrower can or cannot do for the period of a loan

retrenchment: when employees lose their jobs because they are no longer needed by an organisation for commercial reasons; also known as redundancy

return on capital: the amount of profit returned to owners or shareholders as a percentage of their capital contribution

revenue statement: document that shows the operating results for a period. It shows the revenue earned and expenses incurred over the accounting period with the resultant profit or loss.

role: a part that a person plays

safety net increases: increases in wages awarded by the AIRC to all employees on awards who are not covered by enterprise agreements to ensure that they do not miss out on the economic gains achieved, or fall too far behind

sale and lease-back: the selling of an owned asset to a lessor and leasing the asset back through fixed payments for a specified number of years

sales analysis: comparing actual sales with forecast sales to determine the effectiveness of the marketing strategy

scientific management: an approach that studies a job in great detail to discover the best way to perform it

secondary data: information that has already been collected by another person or organisation

secondary markets: financial markets that deal with the purchase and sale of existing securities.

secondary target market: usually refers to a smaller and less important market segment than the primary target market

self-managing: adopting techniques that allow people to manage their own behaviour so that less outside control is necessary

severance pay: money paid to an employee after termination of the employment contract; it should cover entitlements built up by the employee for each year of service.

situational analysis: investigation of marketing opportunities and potential problems

SME: small to medium-sized enterprise. Whether a business is an SME is determined by turnover, number of employees and asset value.

social and cultural characteristics: the values, beliefs, rules, techniques and customs that are shared among a society's people

social justice: businesses being responsible or behaving in a fair and ethical manner towards their employees, customers and the broader community

social responsibility: a business's management of the social, environmental and human consequences of its actions

social wage: improvements in social benefits, such as better health care, education, welfare and taxation reform, that act like a wage increase

sociocultural influences: forces exerted by other people and groups that affect customer behaviour

solvency: the extent to which a business can meets its financial commitments in the longer term. Solvency is measured using leverage or gearing ratios.

sourcing decisions: decisions about whether a business should make or buy the resources that are needed to create its own products

spot exchange rate: the value of one currency in another currency on a particular day

staffing: the recruiting and selecting of qualified people to ensure the success of the business

staffing system: the selection of employees for particular jobs

stakeholder audit: involves identifying all the parties that could be affected by the business's performance and decisions

stakeholders: groups and individuals who interact with the business and thus have a vested interest in its activities

standardised approach: an international marketing strategy that assumes the way the product is used and the needs it satisfies are the same the world over

statement of cash flows: a financial statement that indicates the movement of cash receipts and cash payments resulting from transactions over a period of time

statistical interpretation analysis: the process of focusing on the data that represents average, typical or deviations from typical patterns

statutes: laws made by federal and state parliaments; for example, laws relating to employment conditions, wage and salary determinations and dispute resolution

strategic alliance: occurs when two or more businesses join together and pool their resources

strategic marketing planning: the process of developing and implementing marketing strategies to achieve marketing objectives

strategic plan: a plan that encompasses the strategies that an organisation will use to achieve its goals.

strategic planning: long-term planning to determine where in the market the firm wants to be and what the firm wants to achieve in relation to its competitors. It involves setting mission statements and determining organisational objectives.

strategic thinking: a style of thinking that allows the manager to see the business as a whole — as a complex of parts that depend on and interact with each other, like the gears in a machine

strategy: the major tool adopted by an organisation to achieve its goals.

structural change: changes in how the business is organised, that is, the organisational structure

sugging: stands for 'selling under the guise of a survey', a sales technique disguised as market research

survey: gathering data by asking or interviewing people

synergy: combined action that makes the whole greater than the sum of its parts

system: a set of interrelated parts that operate as a whole in order to achieve a common goal

systems management approach: this approach views organisations as an integrated process in which all the individual parts contribute to the whole

tactical planning: flexible, adaptable, short-term planning, usually over one to two years, that will assist in implementing the strategic plan

target market: the group of customers to which the business intends to sell its products

tariff: a tax placed on imported goods

tax haven: a country that imposes little or no taxes on business income

tax holiday: a scheme in which no company or personal tax is paid for a certain period of time

teamwork: involves people who interact regularly and coordinate their work towards a common goal

tendering: a process whereby firms submit quotes to supply a good or service. The lowest bid that meets the specifications is usually accepted.

trade agreement: a negotiated relationship between countries that regulates trade between them

trade unions: organisations formed by employees in an industry, trade or occupation to represent them in efforts to improve wages and the working conditions of their members

trademark: signifies the brand name or symbol is registered and the business has exclusive right of use

trading company: a business that buys and sells products in many countries

traditional definition of management: the process of coordinating a business's resources to achieve its goals

training and development: changing employees' attitudes and behaviours; this may involve teaching them specific skills.

transfer pricing: when one subsidiary of a company charges a second subsidiary for goods and services

translating plans into reality: using the strategic, tactical and operational plans to achieve a business's objectives

transnational corporation (TNC): any business that has productive activities in two or more countries and that operates on a worldwide scale

triple bottom line: the economic, environmental and social performance of a business

unitary approach: in employment relations, this assumes stakeholders, such as employees and their employers, work hand in hand to achieve shared goals

user: the individual or group who actually uses the product being purchased

variable costs: costs that change proportionately with the level of operating activity in a business

variance reports: reports that show the difference between budgeted and actual performance

venture capital: funds supplied by private investors or specialist investment organisations, either to new businesses (sometimes referred to as 'seed capital') or to established businesses ready to grow or diversify

vertical integration: the expansion of a business's production in different but related areas

vision: the clear, shared sense of direction that allows people to attain a common goal

warehousing: a set of activities involved in receiving, storing and dispatching goods

warranty: a promise by the business to repair or replace faulty products.

word-of-mouth communication: when people influence each other during conversations

workers' compensation: benefits provided to an employee suffering an injury or disease related to their work

working capital: the funds available for the short-term financial commitments of an organisation

working capital management: determining the best mix of current assets and current liabilities needed to achieve the objectives of the organisation

World Trade Organization (WTO): an organisation founded in 1995 to manage world trade and investment activities

Index

absenteeism 378–9
accounting equation 153–4
accounting framework 149–54
accounts receivable turnover ratio 163, 165
achievable goals 88
acquiring resources and technology 441
acquisition strategy 437
advertising 269–70
  deceptive and misleading 285–6
advertising media 270
affirmative action 408–9
Affirmative Action (Equal Employment Opportunity for Women) Act 1986 (Cwlth) 406, 409
analysis 157
anti-discrimination 406–7
Anti-Discrimination Act 1977 (NSW) 406
Anti-Discrimination Board 306, 385, 406
arbitration 384
ASEAN Free Trade Area (AFTA) 453, 454
Asia–Pacific Economic Cooperation (APEC) 453, 454
asset stripping 196
assets 153
attitudes
  changes in the workforce 311
  of customers 254
audit 194
audited accounts 194–5
Austrade 463
Australian Competition and Investments Commission (ACCC) 70, 71
Australian Council of Trade Unions (ACTU) 296, 299, 401
Australian Industrial Relations Commission (AIRC) 303–4, 348, 349, 360–1, 383, 384, 408, 412
Australian Securities and Investments Commission (ASIC) 70, 71, 196
Australian Stock Exchange (ASX) 118, 125–6, 194
Australian workplace agreements (AWAs) 297–8, 305, 360, 364–5
autocratic leadership style 40–1
award simplification 303
awards 303, 347, 360–6
bait and switch advertising 286
balance sheet 151–3
bank bills 136
Bank for International Settlement (BIS) 452
bank overdraft 136
banks 119–21
bargaining 55
Beau's Floral Studio, marketing plan 230–7
behavioural management approaches 42–51, 62
  flat organisational structure 48–9
  management as communicating 46–8
  management as leading 43–4
  management as motivating 45–6
  Mayo's Hawthorne studies 42–3
  participative or democratic leadership style 50–1
  strengths and weaknesses 57–8
  work teams 49–50
below-the-line promotions 271
benchmarking 37
best practice 396
bills of exchange 466
bonds 449
boom 255
boycotts 37
brand 264
brand name 264
brand symbol 264
branding 264–5
  global 472
Branson, Richard 77
bribes 461
budget development 108–9
budgeted financial reports 112
bureaucracy 33
Business Council of Australia 300–1
business culture 76–7
business customers 249
business cycle, phases of 68
business division/closure 385
business market 249
business plan, financial elements of 106–7
business practices and ethics, overseas countries 460–1
business-to-business e-commerce 75
business-to-consumer e-commerce 75
buyer behaviour 247
buyers 252
buying process 251–2
capital expenditure 105
capital markets, changes in 421–2
career prospects, loss of 85
case study, Lend Lease 493–510
cash 177
cash and securities markets 118, 119
cash flow 183–4
cash flow budget 110
cash flow crisis, avoiding 113–14
cash flow management 183–8
  strategies 186–8
cash flow statements 184–6
casual work, growth of 367–8
casual work contracts 366
centralised industrial relations system 311, 349
certified agreements 303, 360, 362–4
chain of command 39
change 65–6
  and social responsibility 91–5
  external influences 67–72
  identifying need for 88
  internal influences 67, 74–7
  nature and sources of 66–80
  resistance to 81–5
  structural responses to 78–80
change agents 89
change management 26, 87–91
  creating a culture of change 88–9
  setting achievable goals 88
change models 89–91
changing nature of markets 68
changing work patterns 309–10
channel choice 273–4
channels 271
channels of distribution 273
children as customers 248–9
China, doing business in 446–7
civil unrest 454–5
classical perspective on management 33
classical–scientific approaches 34–41, 62
  autocratic leadership style 40–1
  hierarchical organisational structure 38–9
  management as organising 36–7
  management as planning 35–6
  strengths and weaknesses 57
clean payment 465
coalitions 55–6
Coca-Cola
  marketing plan 200–1
  marketing techniques 276–7

code of ethics 396
codes of conduct 396, 488–9
codes of practice 27, 398
coercive power 54
collective agreements 360
commodity markets 118
common law 456
  in employment relations 345–6
common law action
  for workers' compensation 403–4
  over industrial action 385
common law employment contracts 365–6
communication
  in employment relations 323–5
  in management 46–8
  non-verbal 459
  oral 458
communication process (promotion) 271–3
comparative ratio analysis 168–9
competition-based pricing 266
competitive risk, minimisation 442
competitors, impact on employment relations 315
complex problem-solving and decision-making skills 21–2
concentrated market approach 260–1
conciliation 384
conflict *see* industrial conflict
conflict resolution 321, 383–91
conflicts of interest, reconciling 27–8
consumer laws 284–5
  and specific marketing practices 285–8
consumer markets 204
consumerism 27
contemporary definition of management 5–6
contingency theory 61, 63
continuing employees contracts 367
contraction 255
contracts 456–7
control process 37
controlling 37, 226
  comparing actual and planned results 227–8
  establishing performance standards 226–7
copyright 457
corporate citizenship 24–5
corporate governance 194
corporate raiders 196
corporate social responsibility 24–5, 91–5, 484–7
  arguments for/against 491
Corporations Act 2001 (Cwlth) 194, 196, 305
cost centres 190
cost control 189–90
cost estimate 227
cost plus margin pricing 266
courts 303–4, 305, 457
covert industrial action 378–81
credit risks, global business 464–6
cultural diversity 94–5
cultural influences, on global business 458–61
culture 254
culture clash 83–4
currency fluctuations 447–8
currency swap 468
current assets 174
  control of 177–8
current liabilities, control of 179–80
current ratio 158, 164
customer behaviour 247
customer choice
  economic influences 255–6
  government influences 256
  psychological influences 252–4
  sociocultural influences 254–5
customer database 210
customer-oriented approach 208, 209
customer relationship marketing (CRM) 209–10
customer service 219–20
customers, types of 247–50
customs and traditions, overseas countries 460–1

data analysis and interpretation 245–6
data collection 241–5
debentures 137
debt finance 134–8, 143–4, 145
debt to equity ratio 159–60, 164
decentralised industrial relations system 311, 349
deceptive and misleading advertising 285–6
decision making 21–2
  exclusion from 381
decisional roles 12
delegation 43
demography 69
depreciation 448
deregulation 70, 429
derivatives 128, 467–8
derivatives markets 118
de-skilling 84–5
development programs 331
differentiated approach to international marketing 473
differentiation of product and services 261
direct discrimination 406
direct exporting 434
discretionary income 207
dismissal of employees 410
dispute resolution, international business 457
disputes *see* industrial disputes
distribution 224, 229, 273–5
  local government regulation 276
  technology effects 275–6
distribution channels 273
disturbance handler 12
diversification 441–2
division of labour 38
domestic business, interaction with global business 430–1
domestic capital market 469
domestic market influences 127
downsizing 68
driving forces 90
dumping illegal products 489–90

e-commerce 75, 95
early retirement 311
ecological sustainability 26–7, 92, 490–1
economic communities 453
economic cycles 312–13, 442–3
economic influences
  on business 68–9
  on customer choice 255–6
  on employment relations 312–15
economies of scale 442
effective financial planning 183–92
effective management 31
  importance of 7–8
effective people, habits of 20
effectiveness 6
efficiency 103, 162–3
employee selection 320–1
employees 292, 294–5
  and shareholders 28–9
  sources of, overseas operations 476
  unfair dismissal 410–13
employer associations 300–1
employers 292, 294
employment, legal framework 344–68
Employment Advocate 305
employment contract 344–66
  awards 360–6
  common law 345–6, 366–7
  statutes 347–59
  types of 366–8

employment relations
communication role in 323–5
economic influences 312–15
ethical and responsible behaviour 395–7
global business 475–9
influences on 308–15
legal influences 311, 322, 348–9, 350
managing 306–7, 319–22
measures of effectiveness 337–40
nature of 292–3
new organisational behavioural influences 312
qualitative evaluation of effectiveness 340
quantitative measures of effectiveness 338–40
role of 318–22
social influences 309–11
stakeholders in 293–306
employment relations audit 337
employment relations managers 306–7
enterprise agreements 303, 360
total wage payment 332–3
enterprise bargaining 297
entrepreneurs 12
environmentally responsible products 281–2
Equal Employment Agency 306
equal employment opportunities (EEO) 407–9
Equal Opportunity for Women in the Workplace Agency 406, 408, 409
equitable rewards 328
equity finance 133–4, 144–5
equity policies 345
ethical aspects
of financial management 193–6
of marketing 279–84
ethical behaviour 22–3
in employment relations 395–7
ethically responsible corporate strategy in global environment 484–7
arguments for/against 491
ethics
of product placement 280–1
of sponsorship deals 280
ethnocentric approach to staffing 478, 479
eurocurrency market 469
Europe, global trade 1960–80 424
European Union (EU) 453
exchange rates 448
exchange traded markets 118
exclusive distribution 274
existing markets, expanding 219
expansion 256
see also international expansion
expatriates 477
expense ratio 162–3, 165
experiments 244
expert power 54
Export Finance and Insurance Corporation (EFIC) 468–9
exporting 434–5
external audits 194–5
external business environment 67–72
changing nature of markets 68
economic influences 68–9
financial markets 69
geographical influences 69
legal influences 70
political influences 70–2
social influences 69–70
technological developments 72
external data 245
external finance 134–9
extrinsic rewards 326, 327

Factories, Shops and Industries Act 1962 (NSW) 399, 403
factoring 138–9, 181
Fair Pay Commission 361
families, and buying behaviour 254
family-friendly programs 310, 336–7
Fayol, Henri 9, 33
federal awards 361
Federal Court 305
finance
debt 134–8, 143–4, 145
equity 133–4, 144–5
external 134–9
for global business 469
internal 133–4
matching source with purpose 141–2
finance companies 121
financial budgets 109
financial controls 112–13
financial costs, and resistance to change 82–3
financial decision making 133
financial forecasts 227
financial influences, on global business 447–9
financial instrument hedging 467
financial intermediaries 118
financial leases 137–8
financial management 101
ethical and legal aspects 193–6
global business 464–9
objectives 102–4
financial markets 69, 118–19
Australian Stock Exchange 125–6
changes in 421–2
domestic market influences 127
major participants 119–24
overseas market influences 128–30
trends 131
types of 118
financial planning
effective 183–92
strategic role 100–1
financial planning cycle 105–15
financial ratios 157–65
financial reports 111
limitations 169–71
see also financial statements
financial resources 4
managing 101
financial risk, minimising 114–15
financial stability 157–8
financial statements 149–53
financing activities (cash flows) 185
financing business activities, factors to consider 142
fitness of purpose 287
fixed costs 189–90
fixed-term employees contracts 367
flatter organisational structure 48–9, 79–80, 312
flexibility and adaptability to change skills 19
flexible employment conditions 332–7, 367
flexible remuneration agreements 332–5
flexible working hours 335
flexitime 367
focus groups 242
force-field analysis 89–90
Ford, Henry 34
foreign direct investment (FDI) 429, 436–7
foreign exchange markets 118, 447
foreign exchange rates 448
formal organisation 56
forward exchange contract 468
four Ps of marketing 212, 223–4
franchising 439
free-trade agreements 428, 453–4
free-trade policies 72, 451
Fuji Xerox, industrial dispute 377–8
funds 133–40
external sources 134–9
internal sources 133–4
matching source with purpose 141–2
venture capital 140
see also finance

gearing 145
gender perceptions 408
generic brands 265
geocentric approach to staffing 478, 479
geographic diversification 441
geographical influences 69
geographical representation 219
gifts 461
global branding 472
global business
  employment relations 475–9
  ethically responsible corporate strategy 484–7
  financial influences 447–9
  financial management 464–9
  influences on 445–61
  interaction with Australian domestic business 430–1
  legal influences 456–8
  managing 463–82
  marketing 471–3
  operations 473–4
  political influences 450–5
  social and cultural influences 458–61
  strategies 433–44
global consumers 426–7
global economy 418
  growth of 420
global environment, management responsibility in 484–91
global expansion, methods of 433–9
global market
  evaluation of strategies 479–80
  modification of strategies 481–2
global organisational structure 475–6
global trade, trends since WWII 423–4
global web 474
globalisation 68, 94, 314–15, 418–31
  definition 419
  drivers of 425–9
  of markets 420
  trends 419–20
goods and services tax (GST) 72
goodwill 171
government customers 250
government influences on customer choice 256
government organisations, role in employment relations 301–6
government regulators 70–1
governments
  role in employment relations 301–6
  role in trade liberalisation 428–9
  role in workplace relations 348
grants 140
green marketing 282
greenfield strategy 436
grievance procedures 323, 383
gross profit ratio 161, 164
growth 103

Hawthorne studies 42–3
hedging 467
hierarchical organisational structure 38–9
hire purchase 182
historical cost accounting 170
Holden Australia, occupational health and safety 400–1
house brands 265
household spending 248
Howard government industrial relations reform 351–6
human resource planning 320
human resources 4
Human Rights and Equal Opportunity Commission 306, 385, 406
Human Rights and Equal Opportunity Commission Act 1986 (Cwlth) 406
human rights codes of conduct 488–9

illegal products, dumping 489–90
implementing the marketing plan 225–6
implied conditions 287
increasing sales 440
indirect discrimination 406
indirect exporting 434
individual contracts 365–6
individual customers 248
induction 329–31
industrial action 375
  covert 378–81
  overt 375–8
industrial agreements 297–8, 303, 305, 322, 360, 362–5
industrial conflict
  benefits and costs of 391–3
  pluralist perspective 374
  radical perspective 374
  trends 373
  unitary perspective 374
industrial disputes
  causes of 371–2
  definition 370
  Fuji Xerox 377–8
  in Australia 371–2
  resolution procedures 321, 383–91
  stakeholders role in resolving 382–3
  waterfront dispute, 1988 386–91
industrial market 203–4
industrial relations
  changes 1983–2005 351
  decentralisation under Workplace Relations Act 350–1
  dual system 347–9
  evolution from centralised to more decentralised system 311, 349–50
  federal legislation 348–9
  fourth term Howard Liberal government reform 351–6
  impact of reforms on stakeholders 354–6
  legal framework in NSW 356–7
  New South Wales legislation 350
  statutory framework in Australia 347–56
  see also employment relations
Industrial Relations Commission (NSW) 356–7
industrial tribunals and courts 303–4
inertia of management 83
informal organisation 56
information needs, determining 241
information resources 4
informational roles 12
institutional customers 249
insurance 468–9
insurance companies 121–2
intangible assets 170–1
integrated marketing plan 215
intellectual property 457–8
intensive distribution 273–4
interactive technology 275
interest rates 449
intermediate market 204
internal audits 194
internal business environment 67, 74–7
  e-commerce 75
  effects of accelerating technological change 74
  new business culture 76–7
  new systems and procedures 75–6
internal data 245
internal finance 133–4
international bond market 449
international capital market 469
international equity (share) market 449
international expansion
  methods of 433–9
  reasons for 440–4
international financial reporting standards (IFRS) 194–5

international marketing 471
  differentiated approach 473
  global branding 472
  research 471–2
  standardised approach 472–3
  see also global market
International Monetary Fund (IMF) 452
international organisations 452
Internet marketing 275
interpersonal roles 12
interpretation 157
interviews 242
intracorporate exporting 434
intrinsic rewards 326, 327
inventions, marketing strategy 128–30
inventories 177–8
inventory control 275
investing activities (cash flows) 185
investment banks 122–3

James Hardie Industries, compensation for asbestos victims 404
Japan, global trade 1960–80 424
job enlargement 312
job enrichment 312
job rotation 312
job sharing 335
joint consultative committees 324–5
joint venture 437
judicial power 305

labour law
  overseas countries 477
  see also employment relations; industrial relations
labour markets, changes in 422
labour standards 488–9
labour turnover 380
laissez-faire leadership style 40
language
  non-verbal 458–9
  spoken 458
leaders, good characteristics 43–4
leadership styles 39–40
  autocratic 40–1
  laissez-faire 40
  participative/democratic 40, 50–1
leading 43–4
learning new skills 85
learning organisation 330
leases 137–8, 181–2
leasing 137–8, 181
legal aspects
  of financial management 193–6
  of marketing 279, 283–8
legal framework of employment 344–68
  New South Wales 356–7
legal influences
  on business 27, 70
  on employment relations 311, 322, 348–9, 350
  on global business 456–8
legal systems 456
legitimate power 54
Lend Lease Corporation, case study 493–511
letter of credit 465
leverage 145
Lewin's change models 89–91
liabilities 153
licensing 438–9
life insurance companies 122
limitations of financial reports 169–71
line managers 306
liquidity 102, 157–8
  management 174–82
loans 179–80, 182
local government regulation 276
lockouts 375
logo 264
logs of claims 300
long-term borrowing 135, 136–7
long-term planning 36, 105
loss leader 267

management
  as communicating 46–8
  as controlling 37
  as leading 43–4
  as motivating 45–6
  as negotiating and bargaining 55
  as organising 36–7
  as planning 35–6
  contemporary definition 5–6
  responsibilities to stakeholders 24–9
  traditional definition 4, 5
  within the business 6–7
management audits 194
management contract 438
management hierarchy 38
management roles 9–14
  Fayol's view 9
  Mintzberg's view 10–11
management skills 15–23
management theories 32
  behavioural 42–51
  classical and scientific 33–41
  contingency 61
  political 52–7
  strengths/weaknesses of classical, behavioural and political approaches 57–8
  summary and comparison 62–3
  system management 60
managerial policy, and industrial disputes 371
managers 5
manager's job, myths and realities 13–14
managing change 65–95
manufacturer's brand 264–5
market coverage 273
market pricing 266
market research 240
market research process 241
  data analysis and interpretation 245–6
  data collection 241–5
  determining information needs 241
market segmentation 222, 259–61
market share 218
market share analysis/ratios 228
marketing 200–1
  approaches to 206–8
  as evolutionary process 213
  definition 201
  global business 471–3
  production approach (1820s to 1910s) 207
  role in business and in society 201–2
  sales approach (1920s to 1960s) 207
marketing approach (1960s to present) 207–8
marketing channels 273
marketing concept 208–9
marketing data 241–5
marketing management 212–13
marketing mix 212, 223–4, 259
  changes in 229
marketing objectives 211–12
  establishing 217–20
marketing plan 212–13, 215
  elements of 215–30
  for Beau's Floral Studio 230–7
  for Coca-Cola 200–1
  identifying target markets 222
  implementing 225–6
  marketing objectives 217–20
  marketing strategies 223–4
  monitoring and controlling 226–9
  situational analysis 211, 215–16
marketing planning process 211–13
marketing profitability analysis 228

marketing strategies 212, 223–4
  developing 258–76
  revision 228–9
marketing techniques, used by Coca-Cola 276–7
markets
  changes in 421–3
  definition 203
  globalisation of 420
  types of 203–5
mass market 205
mass marketing 260
materialism 283–4
maxiflex 367
Mayo, Elton 42–3
mediation 385
medium-term planning 36
merchandise exports 423
merchant banks 122–3
merchantable quality 287
mergers and takeovers, cultural incompatibility 83–4
minimum standards of labour 488–9
Mintzberg, Henry
  managerial 'facts of life' 13–14
  managerial roles 10–11
misleading advertising 286
monitoring 226
mortgage 137
motivation 45–6
motives 253
mutual funds 123

national brand 264
National Occupational Health and Safety Commission 306, 399
National Occupational Health and Safety Commission Act 1985 306, 399
natural hedging 467
negotiating 12, 55
negotiation 283–4
net profit ratio 161, 164
net working capital 174
network structure 80
new business culture 76–7
new equipment purchase 82
new product development 229
new systems and procedures 75–6
niche markets 205, 260–1
noise 272
non-store retailing 275
non-verbal communication 458–9
North American Free Trade Agreement (NAFTA) 453
new markets, search for 441

observation (data collection) 244
Occupational Health and Safety Act 1983 (NSW) 399
occupational health and safety (OH&S) 306, 322, 398–401
  at Holden Australia 400–1
  six-step approach to 400
  unions' role 401
on-costs 366
open credit (account) 466
operating activities (cash flows) 185
operating budgets 108
operating leases 137
operational (short-term) planning 36
operations of global business 473–4
opinion leaders 272
options contract 468
organisation process 36–7
organisational behaviour influences on employment relations 312
organisational goals and objectives 100
organisational 'iceberg' 56
organisational politics 53
organisational structure
  flatter 48–9, 79–80, 312
  global 475–6
  hierarchical 38–9
organising 36
outsourcing 78–9
  production 473
over-the-counter markets 118
overdrafts 180
overseas borrowing 449
overseas market influences 128–30
overt industrial action 375–8
owners' equity 133–4, 153, 154

packaging 265–6
part-time contracts 367
part-time work 335–6
  growth 367–8
participation rate 310
participative/democratic leadership style 40, 50–1
patents 457
payables 179
payment in advance 465
payment methods, global business 464–6
peer groups 254
people skills 17
perception 252–3
performance appraisals 330
performance standard 226–7
permanent contracts 367
personal selling 268–9
personal spending 248

personal standards and ethics 22–3
personalised communication 210
personalised service 210
personality 254
physical distribution 274–5
physical resources 4
pickets 375
place (distribution) 224, 229, 273–5
placement (staffing) 320
planned obsolescence 27
planning 36
  levels of 36
planning cycle 105–15
planning processes 106
plant layout, reorganising 83
pluralist perspective on conflict 374
political goals, and industrial disputes 372
political influences
  on business 70–2
  on global business 450–5
political management approaches 52–3, 63
  management as negotiating and bargaining 55
  stakeholder view 56–7
  strengths and weaknesses 58
  structures as coalitions 55–6
  uses of power and influence 53–5
political risk 450
politics 52–3
polycentric approach to staffing 478, 479
population shifts 310–11
positioning 263
power 53
  abuse of 54
  and influence 53–4
  matching to situations 54–5
  sources of 54
present financial position 106
price 224, 229, 266
  and quality interaction 267
price discrimination 287
price lining 267
price penetration 266
price skimming 266
pricing methods 266
pricing policy 191
pricing strategies 266–7
primary data 242–4
primary market 125
primary target market 260
private brand 265
private companies 123
privatisation 70
proactive approach 19
problem solving 21

product 224, 229, 262–3
  branding 264–5
  packaging 265–6
  positioning 263
product deletion 229
product differentiation 261
product diversification 442
product life cycle 216–17
product mix 218–19
product placement, ethics 280–1
product positioning 263
product range 218
production, globalisation of 420
production approach to marketing (1820s to 1910s) 207
production-oriented approach 207
productivity sharing 332
profit sharing 332
profitability 102, 160–2
profitability management 189–92
project budgets 108
promotion 224, 229, 268–73
promotion mix 268–71
promotional opportunities, loss of 85
protectionism 451
psychological influences on customer choice 252–4
public companies 123
public interest 383
public relations 271
publicity 271
purchasing new equipment 82
pyramid-shaped organisational structure 38, 39

qualitative evaluation, employment relations effectiveness 338–40
quality and price interaction 267
quality circles 325
quality of working life 93
quantitative evaluation, employment relations effectiveness 338–40
questionnaires 242

radical (Marxist) perspective on industrial conflict 374
receivables 177
recession 256
record systems 112
recruitment 320–1
redundancy 410
redundancy payments 82
reference groups 254
referent power 54
regional economic integration 453
regional trade agreements 453–4
regionalism 453
regular employees contracts 367
regulations 276, 443
relationship marketing 209–10
religion 459
relocation of production 437
resale price maintenance 288
resellers 204
Reserve Bank of Australia (RBA) 123–4
resistance to change 81–2
  cultural incompatibility in mergers and takeovers 83–4
  financial costs 82–3
  inertia of managers and owners 83
  staffing considerations 84–5
  strategies for reducing 87–8
resource allocator 12
resource market 203
respondent 361
restraining forces 90
restrictive covenants 144
retail developments, impact of 284
retained profits 134
retraining the workforce 83
retrenchment 410
return on capital 103
return on owners' equity ratio 162, 164
revenue controls 190–1
revenue estimate 227
revenue statement 150–1
reward power 54
rewards management 321, 326–8

sabotage 380
safety net increases 303
sale and lease-back 181
sales analysis 227–8
sales approach to marketing (1920s to 1960s) 207
sales mix 190, 191–2
sales objectives 190
sales-oriented approach 207
Sarbanes–Oxley Act 2002 (USA) 194
scientific management 33–4
  see also classical–scientific approach
secondary data 244–5
secondary market 125
secondary target market 260
selective distribution 274
self-managing skills 19–20
self-managing work teams 325
semi-autonomous teams 325
separation 322
service 262
severance pay 411
Sex Discrimination Act 1984 (Cwlth) 406
sexual harassment behaviour 409–10
shareholders
  society and future generations 28
  versus employees 28–9
short-term borrowing 135, 136
short-term planning 36
situational analysis 211, 215–16
skilled labour shortage 477
social class 254
social influences
  on business 69–70
  on employment relations 309–11
  on global business 458–61
social issues, and industrial disputes 372
social justice 26, 311, 322
social responsibility 91–5
social wage 296
socially responsible companies 24–5, 91–2, 484–7
sociocultural influences
  on customer choice 254–5
  on global business 458–61
solvency 159–60
sourcing decisions 473–4
specialisation of labour 38
specialist managers 306–7
spoken languages 458
sponsorship deals, ethics 280
spot exchange rate 467
staffing
  and change 84–5
  overseas operations 476
staffing systems, global business 477–9
stakeholder audit 57
stakeholders 24, 57–8
  impact of Howard government industrial relations forms on 354–6
  in employment relations process 293–306
  responsibilities of management to 24–9
  role in resolving industrial disputes 382–3
standardised approach to international marketing 472–3
state awards 361
statement of cash flows 184–6
statement of financial performance 150–1
statement of financial position 151–3
statistical interpretation analysis 245
statutes 347–59
statutory framework in Australia on industrial relations 347–56

strategic alliances 80
strategic marketing planning 211–13
strategic planning 36
strategic plans 100, 101
strategic role of financial planning 100–1
strategic thinking skills 17–18
strikes 376
structural change 78–80, 312–13
subcultures 254
sugging 284
superannuation funds 123
supplier diversification 442
surveys 242–3
swap contract 468
SWOT analysis 216
Sydney Futures Exchange (SFE) 118
synergy 7
system management approach 60, 63
systems 60

tactical planning 36
target markets 212, 222
tariffs 428
tastes 459
tax havens 444, 486
tax holidays 444
tax minimisation 443–4
Taylor, Frederick W., scientific management 33–4
team briefings 325
team structures 312
teams 49–50
teamwork 49, 88–9
teamwork skills 20–1
technological developments 72
  accelerating rate of 74
  and social responsibility 94
  effect on distribution 275–6
  impact on employment relations 315
  impact on globalisation 427
telemarketing 275
tendering 250
termination 322
  see also unfair dismissal
total market, segmentation of 259
total marketing 260
total product concept 262
total quality management (TQM) 37
trade agreements 453–4
trade credit 139
trade practices 285
Trade Practices Act 1974 (Cwlth) 70, 71, 285
trade unions 295–8, 299, 401
  development 295
  membership decline 296, 297
trademarks 265, 457, 458
trading blocs 453
trading companies 434
traditional definition of management 4, 5
training and development 83, 321, 328–31
training programs 329–31
transfer pricing 486–7
transnational corporations (TNCs) 425–6
transport 274
triple bottom line 28, 484
turnover 380

unfair dismissal 410–13
unfreeze/change/refreeze model 90–1
unions *see* trade unions
unit trusts 123
unitary perspective on conflict 374
United States, domination of global trade 1945–60 423–4
users 252

variable costs 189, 190
variance reports 114
venture capital 140
vertical integration 473
vision skills 18–19
wage demands, and industrial disputes 372
war 454–5
warehousing 275
warranties 287–8
waterfront dispute, 1988 386–91
Weber, Max 33
Wesfarmers Limited, community obligations 25
Winnie-the-Pooh on management 15–16
word-of-mouth communication 273
work bans 377
work–life balance 333–5
work pattern changes 309–10
work teams 49–50
work-to-rule 377–8
WorkCover NSW 399, 400, 40
worker participation 324–5
workers' compensation 402–4
  common law redress 403–4
  state and/or federal agencies 404
working capital 174
working capital cycle 174
working capital management 174–82
  control of current assets 177–8
  control of current liabilities 179–80
  strategies 180–2
working capital ratio 158, 175–6
working conditions 397–8
  and industrial disputes 372
Workplace Australia 306
workplace health hazards 400
workplace relations *see* employment relations; industrial relations
Workplace Relations Act 1996 (Cwlth) 304, 350–1, 383, 384, 406, 408, 410
World Bank 452
World Trade Organization (WTO) 452